The Constitutional Convention of 1787

The Constitutional Convention of 1787

A COMPREHENSIVE ENCYCLOPEDIA OF AMERICA'S FOUNDING

Volume One: A–M

John R. Vile

Foreword by Jack N. Rakove

ABC●CLIO

SANTA BARBARA, CALIFORNIA   DENVER, COLORADO   OXFORD, ENGLAND

Cataloging-in-Publication data is available from the Library of Congress.

ISBN 1-85109-669-8 (hardback : alk. paper)
ISBN 1-85109-674-4 (e-book)

Design by Jane Raese
Text set in Berthold Garamond

05   06   07   08   10   9   8   7   6   5   4   3   2   1

This book is also available on the World Wide Web as an eBook.
Visit abc-clio.com for details.

ABC-CLIO, Inc.
130 Cremona Drive, P.O. Box 1911
Santa Barbara, California 93116-1911
This book is printed on acid-free paper.

Manufactured in the United States of America

03053   7060

Dedicated to

The delegates, and the families of the delegates, to the Constitutional Convention, who sacrificed the summer of 1787 in Philadelphia in the belief that it was possible to construct a government that would better secure liberty under law.

May the heirs of the Framers honor their predecessors by continuing to share their thirst for liberty, their love for truth, and their sacrificial spirit on behalf of justice and the common good.

Contents

Entries, A to Z

List of Entries, A to Z

⋐ Volume One ⋑

Volume Two

List of Sidebars

Topical Table of Contents

Foreword

AMERICANS RARELY READ the entire Constitution under which they have been governed since 1789. When they have occasion to consult it, their purpose is almost always to consider some particular question about the meaning of one or more of its numerous clauses. Students are rarely if ever encouraged to memorize the Preamble, the way they might sometimes be asked to learn the opening paragraphs of the Declaration of Independence or the concise marvel of Abraham Lincoln's Gettysburg Address of 1863. Year in and year out, countless works of scholarship are devoted to the analysis of the Constitution, but the vast preponderance of these writings address very specific matters of constitutional interpretation.

Of course, the whole of the Constitution is far more than the sum of its parts. From its separate articles, clauses, and sections, we can distill an entire philosophy and program of republican government. That philosophy begins with the opening phrase of the Preamble, "We the people of the United States." These seven words tell us not only that this is a government founded on a theory of popular consent and popular sovereignty, but also that it recognizes that Americans will always live in separate states that retain essential powers and functions of self-government.

The Preamble then states the first of the purposes for which the Constitution has been drafted: "to form a more perfect Union." To a modern ear this language often sounds quaint,

even strange. Something is either perfect or it is not, in the same way that something is either unique or it is not. More perfect does not make any sense. But in the eighteenth century, which had a deep sense of the idea of human progress, *perfect* was used more as a verb than an adjective. To perfect something was to pursue its development and refinement, the way an engineer, for example, might seek to make a device or mechanism more efficient or accurate, less subject to wear-and-tear or malfunction. By saying they were seeking to form a more perfect union, the Framers of the Constitution were thus recognizing a fundamental truth about constitutional government: It is always, and necessarily, a work in progress.

The institutions a constitution creates—the institutions this Constitution created—can never be static. They evolve over time, as each develops its own rules and ways of proceedings, as each explores its relations with other branches, and as the entire government responds to the political concerns and passions that swirl through the larger society. The Framers of the federal Constitution did not want these institutions to be too malleable. They worried, with good reason, that future events might make the American union less perfect than they hoped it would become. Even so, they understood that constitutions had to be written on parchment and paper, not carved in stone. Their own work was the culmination of a decade of constitutional experimentation that had begun in 1776, when the Americans first began writing new instruments of government to replace the colonial charters whose authority had already lapsed.

Once past the Preamble, and into the body of the Constitution's main articles, we encounter the actual government of the United States. There are rules for electing or appointing the members of each department, and sometimes for removing them as well; lists of powers to be exercised, or whose exercise is to be restricted; rules for reaching decisions, or discouraging decisions from being reached; and other commitments that must be kept if the Union is to be perfected. The Constitution is in fact a mass of detail. By modern standards, it is still a remarkably concise, even economical, document. Most of the constitutions that other nations have adopted since, and most of the constitutions of the states of the American Union, are far longer and much more specific. But anyone who truly wants to understand the Constitution has to be prepared to approach it in its detail.

The structure of our government depends upon these individual provisions, and most of these provisions have a history of their own. Some, like the clause limiting the suspension of "the great writ" of *habeas corpus,* reached centuries-deep into the constitutional history of England. Others, like the two-year terms given to members of the House of Representatives, reflected modifications of the republican principles Americans had long embraced. A few, like the provisions for the elec-

tion of the president, or the establishment of the curious office of the vice presidency, were efforts to solve problems for which the Framers of the Constitution had no useful precedents. Yet whatever their origins, virtually all of these clauses have contributed something significant to the constitutional development of the United States since 1789. And from time to time, Americans learn that clauses that have long seemed moribund can suddenly leap back into constitutional life, as the impeachment clause did in 1974 and again in 1998.

These aspects of the Constitution and its continuous history make the approach adopted in this encyclopedia especially rewarding. But so does one other key fact that this volume also recognizes. The clauses that collectively comprise the Constitution were something more than the accrued debris of English and American history. They were rather the result of a remarkable exercise in collective deliberation: the nearly four months of concentrated debate that took place in the Pennsylvania Statehouse (Independence Hall) from the late spring through the late summer of 1787. Reflecting on the various constitutions that had been drafted a decade earlier, the delegates to the Constitutional Convention enjoyed–and seized–a remarkable opportunity to perfect the experiments in self-government that began with the decision for independence. This encyclopedia recognizes their achievement.

Jack N. Rakove

Preface

IT IS EXCITING to be able to write an encyclopedia on the United States Constitutional Convention of 1787. Although I do not endorse all the elements of his accompanying theory, I believe that Bruce Ackerman (1991, 58) is correct to identify the Constitutional Convention as an important "constitutional moment." Like Ackerman, I consider this Convention, and the events preceding and surrounding it, to be one of the pivotal events in American history, an event that has affected just about everything of political consequence that has followed it.

I have sometimes read introductions to books wondering whether the authors were being completely candid about the "joys" of writing, particularly when the work is, like this one, a fairly long reference volume or volumes that include hundreds of entries that might for the most part be considered to have involved fairly menial labor. I can nonetheless say with complete candor that few of the scholarly projects I have worked on have provided greater satisfaction than this. My wife, two daughters, colleagues, acquaintances, and anyone else who has fearfully watched the ever-growing and -shifting stacks of books and papers in my office can testify to my virtual obsession with this project over a period of time that has tested the endurance of even my closest friends. During this period, the project grew from one volume to two. In other projects my interest has waned as the project proceeded, but I can

truly say that I became increasingly excited about this project the longer it continued.

I take some comfort in the fact that my obsession is apparently not unique. I have observed that many individuals who have written on the Constitutional Convention have returned to the topic time and time again. Toward the end of this project, I purchased a volume on the Constitutional Convention that had been reissued at the time of the Constitutional Bicentennial. It had been suitably inscribed and signed by the editor (the son of the original author), who then dated his signature 1787! There were many days when I certainly felt more pressed by the issues of 1787 than I did by the events of the passing hours.

As a professor who specializes in U.S. constitutional law, I have long been fascinated by the Constitution and the Convention that birthed it. Indeed, I made my very first scholarly presentation some 25 years ago on James Madison. It was not, however, until relatively recently (and with a good nudge from my editors) that I recognized that there might be both a need and a demand for a pair of volumes that would serve as a ready reference to the Convention. There are, to be sure, many fine narratives of the Constitutional Convention as well as many specialized works that deal with one or another aspect of the Convention's work (I have included many of these in the essay "Motives of the Founding Fathers"). Moreover, there are a number of volumes that present encyclopedic treatment of the interpretations of the various provisions of the U.S. Constitution. At a time when encyclopedias and reference works are proliferating, there is, however, no other work like this that provides comprehensive information about the Convention and its product in a single readily accessible work. That is the purpose of these volumes.

If the sidebar essays are included, this book has more than 400 entries. Because the topics are so varied, the book includes both an alphabetical and a topical table of contents as well as an extensive index. Because of these resources, I will not describe all the entries in the following paragraphs, but most fall into several broad categories.

People

There are, first of all, entries on people. If all the individuals who participated in the ratification of the Constitution were included, there would literally be a cast of thousands. Somewhat less ambitiously, this volume contains essays on each of the individuals who attended the Convention as well as contemporary Americans, like John Adams and Thomas Jefferson, or foreigners, like John Locke, David Hume, and Louis Montesquieu, who influenced the ideas behind the document. Fortunately, there are a number of very helpful reference books that already catalog the lives of most of the Framers and (especially) the signers of the Constitution. I have relied fairly heavily on two sources: M. E. Bradford's *Founding Fathers* (1981) and David C. Whitney's *Founders of Freedom in America* (1964) for basic biographical information on most of the Founders and have followed up with essays from the *American National Biography* (1999). In contrast to some volumes that largely focus on the personal lives of the delegates, I have tried to concentrate primarily on what each delegate said or did at the Constitutional Convention, drawing chiefly from notes of the Convention. Not every delegate commented on every issue (indeed, some did not speak at all), but in the cases of those who participated actively in debates, I have generally organized their comments for comparative purposes

into separate treatments of the legislative, executive, and judicial branches of government, noting, where possible, the manner in which they might have altered their positions during convention debates. Readers can, to be sure, garner such information by reading the records of the Convention (for which there can be no real substitute), but I hope that the information I present here will be far more accessible to both the layperson and scholar alike, especially those who need help finding the answer to a short-term problem.

Constitutional Provisions

The largest set of entries in this book consists of entries on individual constitutional provisions that emerged from the Convention. I am aware that there are a number of scholarly studies on almost all of these, but, in contrast to most of these works, I have attempted to keep the primary focus on what we know from records of debates at the Convention itself rather than from subsequent developments in constitutional interpretation. Although I began my work with several months of extensive and meticulous note-taking from Convention records, as collected by Max Farrand from the records of James Madison and other delegates, I found Philip B. Kurland and Ralph Lerner's *The Founders' Constitution* (1987), as well as numerous other secondary sources, to be particularly useful in checking and supplementing my own findings as to the content and progress of such debates at the Convention.

States and Nations

I have included entries on each of the 13 states then in existence as well as the states of Vermont, Kentucky, Tennessee, and Maine, which were already in the process of being born. In each case, I have attempted to provide some background on the constitution and governmental institutions within each state. I have also introduced the delegates who represented each state and included information on how ratification of the Constitution proceeded within each. One of the impetuses for the U.S. Constitution was the perceived threat from foreign nations, so I have also included essays on other major powers of the day and on previous leagues or governments that served as sources of information or inspiration for the delegates.

Events

I have included accounts of events, like the American Revolution, Shays's Rebellion, the Mount Vernon Conference, the Annapolis Convention, and other contemporary events that appear to have directly influenced the calling and/or deliberations of the Convention. Where such information was available, I have also recorded the reactions of members of the Convention to such events.

Committees

Knowing about the use of comparable institutions in Congress and other such bodies, I should not have been surprised, but one aspect of the Constitutional Convention that has impressed me is how much work the delegates did in committee and how little is written about, and how little we generally know about, these committees. I have accordingly identified 12 regular committees (as well as the Committee of the Whole) at the Convention and included an essay on each identifying the individuals who served on it, the issues the delegates entrusted to each, and the decisions at which the committee arrived. I have also included a summary essay on this topic.

Documents

As Donald Lutz has so convincingly demonstrated (1998), there are literally hundreds of predecessors to the U.S. Constitution. These include colonial charters, the Mayflower Compact, state constitutions, prior proposals for continental union, the Articles of Confederation, and the Virginia Declaration of Rights. In addition to entries

on such predecessors, I have included some generic entries that treat such documents collectively.

Plans and Forms of Government

This book includes essays on at least five plans that were prepared for the Convention. These include the Virginia, New Jersey, and Hamilton Plans, which were actually discussed as well as the Pinckney and Dickinson Plans, which were not.

The Framers were classically educated, and they were aware that governments fell into certain generic forms, especially those related to whether governments were governed by the one, the few, or the many and those related to whether, and how, powers were divided between central and regional authorities. I have included entries on the forms of government with which the Framers were most familiar. I have generally used modern terminology but have tried to indicate where such terminology has changed. Thus, I have an entry on unitary government but explain that the Framers would have called this either a "national" or a "consolidated" government. Readers should also be able to trace how the term "federal" changed from a designation for a government like that under the Articles of Confederation, which scholars today designate as a "confederal" government, to a government like that which the Constitution created.

Ideological Influences

One of the difficulties in interpreting the Constitution is that of ascertaining the primary political philosophy that motivated its Framers. Historians and political scientists have divided in recent years into those who believe the Framers were primarily motivated by the natural rights philosophy of social contract theorists like John Locke (a view often associated with historian Louis Hartz [1955]) and those who believe their work was founded on republican Whig ideology—sometimes identified with the English "Country" Party (as delineated by historians Bernard Bailyn [1967] and Gordon Wood [1969]). Scholars have clouded the picture still further by citing the Framers' reliance on classical history, emphasizing how contemporary events shaped the thoughts of the Founders, or highlighting the role of Scottish Enlightenment thinkers or Protestantism.

A reference book is certainly not the place to settle the controversy over respective influences. My own considered judgment is that each delegate represented a somewhat different mix of influences and that some were more clearly "republican," "liberal," or "Protestant Christian" than others. I have accordingly included essays on all these movements and have tried to include enough secondary reference materials for individuals who are so inclined to follow various lines of influence and weigh the relationships among them. For the most part, however, I have let delegates speak for themselves by trying to stay faithful to the arguments that they advanced within the Convention.

Ideas

We associate the Constitution with a number of ideas and principles that are not specifically stated there. Neither "checks and balances" nor "separation of powers," for example, is listed there, but scholars generally consider both terms to be important. Similarly, delegates to the Convention frequently discussed the ideas of corruption and virtue (albeit not always with meanings that we would attribute to them today), and they listed the idea of promoting justice in the Preamble. In part because such terms, and others like them, do not always appear in the index to the records of the Convention, and because there is no concordance to them, such terms are easy to miss. I have included essays on key terms that I have been able to identify.

Ratification

It is difficult to separate the process of constitutional construction from that of constitutional ratification. Although I deal in these volumes primarily with the former, I have included some entries that relate to the latter. These include some discussion, under each state, of ratification debates that occurred there. I have also included essays on Federalists, Antifederalists, the Bill of Rights, and other issues that delegates fleshed out during this debate.

Miscellaneous

Because of its pivotal role in U.S. history, there are books and articles on all kinds of topics related to the Constitutional Convention. I have accordingly provided entries on the weather, the city of Philadelphia, the Pennsylvania State House, and other topics that help illuminate the context of this extraordinary event. At my editor's suggestion, I have included some information that I thought would give further context to the proceedings in sidebar essays.

Other Helps

It is common practice to include a copy of the U.S. Constitution in books that discuss the Constitutional Convention. I have followed this practice but have also included other documents that appear to have influenced the fundamental law. The documents selected are suggestive rather than exhaustive of the influences on this document. I have also included a table of contents, a bibliography, and an index.

There are few essays in this book that did not rely on the four-volume *Records of the Federal Convention* (1937), which historian Max Farrand compiled, as well as a subsequent fifth volume edited by James Hutson (1987). I have tried to indicate the sources that were most helpful in compiling each entry as well as compiling a bibliography for the volumes as a whole.

Audience for This Work

Every academic author probably dreams that his or her well-worn works will one day sit on every shelf beside a copy of the Bible and the works of Shakespeare. Although I do not have such a grandiose vision for these volumes, I have designed them to appeal to at least three distinct audiences. First, I have tried to appeal to high school and college students—and the reference librarians whom they so frequently ask to help them—who should find these volumes especially useful for writing term papers and reports on various aspects of the Constitution or in preparing for competitions testing their knowledge of this document. Although these volumes contain massive amounts of information, I have designed the A-to-Z format, the tables of contents, the extensive indexing, and the cross-references to make this material as accessible as it can be. Second, I have designed these volumes to be of value to fellow scholars, especially those in political science, history, and law who find that they need ready access to discrete information about events at the Constitutional Convention and constitutional provisions that emerged from it. Third, I have tried to make these volumes accessible to members of the general public who are genuinely interested in the development of the nation's founding document and who realize that the U.S. Constitution recognizes citizens rather than subjects. It is common to criticize Americans for their lack of knowledge about specific constitutional provisions, but I believe there is truth in Robert Goldwin's observation that "Americans may not have the text of the Constitution in their heads, but they have the meaning of it in their hearts and in their bones" (1990, 44). As a Protestant Christian, I believe that the idea of having a written Constitution, like the idea of a written Bible, is important because of the access to vital principles that it puts in the hands of ordinary citizens. I continue to respect the delegates to the Convention and believe that the Constitution that they formulated, as well as subsequent additions like the Bill of Rights and the provisions of the Fourteenth Amendment, have a continuing educative role to play.

My own training is in political science, and particularly political theory, and my primary teaching responsibility has been American constitutional law. The more I researched these volumes, the more apparent it became that I needed to draw not only from the writings of fellow political scientists but also from the works of historians and law professors. No one can fully master such a wide range of materials across such a wide range of disciplines, but I have made a conscientious effort to use indexes that would help me draw from all three disciplines as well as from others when they were relevant.

Acknowledgments

I am pleased once again to recognize the supportive environment that Middle Tennessee State University has provided for doing this project. I have been blessed to have increasing resources from the University library, which now includes access to Lexis-Nexis, to JSTOR, and to many other resources without which these volumes would not have been possible, and I have often made use of the competent and caring folks at the reference desk and interlibrary loan office of our library. I continue to have support from members of the Department of Political Science that I chair, and from members of the Department of History, with whom we share a hall. I owe special thanks to Dr. Mark Byrnes, Dr. Lynn Nelson, Dr. Jim Williams, Dr. Doug Heffington, and Dr. Fred Crawford for sharing their insights on topics covered in these volumes. I also owe thanks to Dr. John McDaniel, dean of our College of Liberal Arts, and to a host of others on campus. As in the past, I have enjoyed the support of Alicia Merritt, Michelle Trader, and others at ABC-CLIO.

My work as a department chair, mock-trial coach, and occasional tourist has enabled me to visit a number of other campuses where I was provided access to the libraries in doing research for this work. These include the library at Vanderbilt University (where I was privileged to teach a class in the fall of 2004) in Nashville, Tennessee; the library at Weber State University in Ogden, Utah; the library at the Cumberland School of Law at Samford University in Birmingham, Alabama; the library at Rhodes College in Memphis, Tennessee; the library at the Drake University School of Law in Des Moines, Iowa; the library of Eastern Kentucky University; the law libraries at the College of William and Mary and the University of Virginia; the library at the University of Tennessee in Knoxville; the library at Tarleton State University; and the library and archives at Independence National Historical Park in Philadelphia, Pennsylvania. In every case, librarians proved helpful.

I owe special thanks to Sheridan Harvey and Lynn Pedigo, both reference librarians at the Library of Congress, who responded to some e-mail requests by helping me to track down some obscure information. I also appreciate the help of Dr. James W. Mueller, chief historian at Independence National Historical Park, as well as archivist Karen D. Stevenson, on a similar task. I also extend thanks to Dr. Reuben Brooks at Tennessee State University.

I am thankful to many individuals whom I have met through eBay.com who have provided books and other resources at reasonable prices during the course of my research. I remain grateful to a kind and loving wife who has recognized my need to purchase many of these resources, who is a continuing source of encouragement, and who has been patient as I have turned our house into our own "Constitution Hall" of assorted prints from various commemorations of the Declaration of Independence and the U.S. Constitution.

Several students, or former students, at MTSU have helped in various stages of this project. They have included Brandi Snow Bozarth (now an attorney), who aided in compiling materials for research on this project, and Paul Lawrence, who helped locate additional information and helped with the appendices. I am also indebted to student aides James Arnold, Ashley Fuqua, and Jeremy Allen, who have helped me edit computer files. My secretary, Pam Davis, also provided valuable help with the ever-expanding and -multiplying computer files.

I am especially grateful to Professor Jack Rakove for writing the foreword to this volume. Although I have not had the honor of meeting him, I have become increasingly impressed by the manner in which he has provided so many studies on a variety of subjects that have been useful to political scientists, historians, and law professors.

I am truly humbled that he was willing to introduce these volumes.

I would like to thank a brother-in-law, Paul Christensen, for his work in photographing a number of the illustrations for this work.

Author's View

I suppose that every scholar hopes to be a pathbreaker who reinterprets familiar events in unfamiliar or novel ways that get the attention of fellow scholars and force major rethinking of an event or time period. If there has been a major disappointment that has emerged from my work on this project, it is that I have not in the process arrived at a unique interpretation of the Constitutional Convention or its work. Although somewhat disappointing, this realization is also comforting. Most people who approach a reference work like this are probably less interested in what the author thinks than in understanding what others who have dug deeply into the subject have thought; indeed, one might even express a certain warranted skepticism about an interpretation that did not emerge until more than 200 years after the event. In my case, I have achieved a good measure of contentment simply by deepening my own understanding of the Constitutional Convention and its relationship to the American Revolution and to the other events that preceded it and by attempting to share my findings with others. I will be quite happy if readers who turn to these volumes find that they help provide and explain the information they are seeking and guide them to other sources where they can find such topics discussed in even greater depth.

I began this study with the view that the delegates were extraordinary but flawed men who did their best to represent the interests of their own states and regions while at the same time keeping sight of larger principles and the common good, not only for themselves but also for posterity. After reading countless studies that suggest less noble, if not sinister, motivations (many centered on the economic interests of the delegates), I continue largely to hold to my original view. In reading accounts of the Convention, I have been especially impressed by the manner in which delegates felt it necessary to offer and record arguments for their proposals. I believe that the legacy of constitutional government that the Founders left is a worthy one that we need to appreciate, understand, and in some cases recover. As I have attempted to demonstrate in many of my other writings, the existence of an amending process within the Constitution indicates that the Founders recognized that their bequest was not perfect. I am among those who remain grateful that the promise of the Constitution has been extended so as more explicitly to include African Americans, women, and other minorities who were not initially as well protected as they are today. I am more inclined than some to give the Framers credit for the rights they were able to protect and advance than to criticize them on the basis of what they were unable to accomplish.

I realize that such a dedication is somewhat unusual, but I have chosen to dedicate this work to the men who attended the Constitutional Convention of 1787 and to their wives and families, who made their own sacrifices as their husbands and fathers were deliberating. I want especially to recognize the contributions of Virginia's James Madison, whom I have long admired and whose contributions to religious liberty I especially cherish.

Although the plan is for these volumes to appear on or before July 4, 2005, I have dated this introduction on the anniversary of the signing of the Constitution in 2004, the year I finished writing these volumes. This date is just three years away from the celebration of that document's two hundred twentieth anniversary. I hope that the Constitution and the government it established will continue to embody the ideals of human liberty and equality, which Mr. Jefferson articulated so eloquently in the Declaration of Independence.

John R. Vile
Middle Tennessee State University
September 17, 2004

REFERENCES

Ackerman, Bruce. 1991. *We the People: Foundations.* Cambridge, MA: Belknap Press of Harvard University Press.

Bailyn, Bernard. 1967. *The Ideological Origins of the American Revolution.* Cambridge, MA: The Belknap Press of Harvard University Press.

Bradford, M. E. 1981. *Founding Fathers: Brief Lives of the Framers of the United States Constitution.* 2nd ed. Lawrence: University Press of Kansas.

Farrand, Max, ed. 1937. *The Records of the Federal Convention.* 4 vols. New Haven, CT: Yale University Press.

Garraty, John A., and Mark C. Carnes, eds. 1999. *American National Biography.* 24 vols. New York: Oxford University Press.

Goldwin, Robert A. 1990. *Why Blacks, Women, and Jews Are Not Mentioned in the Constitution, and Other Unorthodox Views.* Washington, DC: AEI Press.

Hartz, Louis. 1955. *The Liberal Tradition in America: An Interpretation of American Political Thought since the Revolution.* New York: Harcourt, Brace and World.

Hutson, James H., ed. 1987. *Supplement to Max Farrand's* The Records of the Federal Convention of 1787. New Haven, CT: Yale University Press.

Kurland, Philip B., and Ralph Lerner. 1987. *The Founders' Constitution.* 5 vols. Chicago: University of Chicago Press.

Lutz, Donald S. 1998. *Colonial Origins of the American Constitution: A Documentary History.* Indianapolis, IN: Liberty Fund.

Whitney, David C. 1964. *Founders of Freedom in America: Lives of the Men Who Signed the Constitution of the United States and So Helped to Establish the United States of America.* Chicago: J. G. Ferguson Publishing Company.

Wood, Gordon S. 1969. *The Creation of the American Republic, 1776–1787.* Chapel Hill: University of North Carolina Press.

Introduction

I HAVE WRITTEN this encyclopedia in the twin convictions that the Constitutional Convention of 1787 is one of the pivotal events and that the Constitution it birthed is one of the most important documents in American history. The numerous individual entries in these volumes should provide ample evidence that a complete overview of the Convention and its work involves familiarity with a multitude of events, influences, people, compromises, constitutional provisions, and so forth; yet there are undoubtedly many readers who would like to survey the forest before they begin examining individual trees. Although no introduction can be a substitute for a book-length narrative, I have written this account to provide a starting point for those who want to know about the general history of the Convention and the circumstances that surrounded it.

A Long Intellectual and Historical Heritage

As with any pivotal event, there are many points at which one can begin telling the story because there are many cultures, historical events, and philosophers who influenced the Founding Fathers. The ancient Greeks left a legacy of democracy, and their philosophers provided means for future study by classifying and dividing governments into good and bad forms governed by the one, the few, or the many. The Romans further elaborated on the ideas of statesmanship, mixed

government, and the rule of law. Jews and early Christians bequeathed to the American Founders a deep ethical heritage and a realistic, if not pessimistic, conception of human nature. In the Magna Carta of 1215, English noblemen asserted rights against an obstinate king, rights that they continued to reassert and that gained increased meaning and widened application over time. The English further developed representative and legal institutions, most notably the Parliament and the common law and the system of courts. Protestant reformers emphasized individual responsibility and attempted to see that all of life's activities, including those in the secular world, gave glory to God.

Further influences found their way into the New World. English monarchs issued charters to intrepid explorers and settlers, which served as early constitutions. The Virginia House of Burgesses brought representative government to America when it began meeting in 1619. Pilgrims in Massachusetts signed what we today call the Mayflower Compact the next year. Lockean ideas of classical liberalism and the idea that government was a social compact were dispersed in both popular and scholarly circles of the New World as were ideas from the Scottish Enlightenment, from republican thinkers dating back to the Renaissance and beyond, and from Whig opposition thinkers within England.

The colonists refined their views in their dispute with Britain over the Parliament's power, or lack of power, to tax the colonists. The colonists committed themselves to liberty by fighting for their rights at Lexington and Concord, by writing the Declaration of Independence, and by creating new state constitutions. Some documents, like the Virginia Declaration of Rights (chiefly the brainchild of George Mason) and the Massachusetts Constitution of 1780 (largely written by John Adams) proved especially important. Although each influence was not equally significant, each contributed to the intellectual milieu of 1787 and to the writing of the U.S. Constitution.

Seeking more proximate causes, most who write accounts of the Convention begin with the years immediately preceding it. In words proclaiming that government is designed to protect the equal rights of all men and that it rests on the consent of the governed, Americans declared their independence from Great Britain in 1776. Colonies that were accustomed to dealing individually with the Crown recognized that there was security in union. At the time the second Continental Congress was making plans for the writing of the Declaration of Independence, its delegates were also preparing for foreign alliances in the war against Britain and for drawing up a continental plan of Union. The exigencies of waging war initially took priority over that of devising a formal union, but in 1777 the Congress recommended a plan of government, known as the Articles of Confederation, for state approval. Although it provided an informal blueprint for the interim period, the last state legislature did not ratify it, and it thus did not go fully into effect, until 1781.

The Articles of Confederation

John Dickinson, the "penman" of the Revolution who was at the time representing Pennsylvania (he later served at the Constitutional Convention as a delegate from Delaware where he had moved), drafted the Articles of Confederation, drawing in part on Benjamin Franklin's earlier Albany Plan of Union. During debates, Congress weakened the powers of the national government under the Articles of Confederation before sending it to states, which remained jealous of the in-

dependent sovereignty they had previously exercised vis-à-vis the British government. Just as current events and crises would be likely to serve as the primary influence on delegates who might serve in a contemporary convention to rewrite the existing Constitution, so too the primary influence on the delegates who attended the Constitutional Convention of 1787 was their experiences under the Articles of Confederation.

Consistent with its name, the Articles of Confederation represented what political scientists today identify as a confederal government. Like its federal successor, such a government divides power between a national authority and various components, which Americans call states. Unlike a federal government, a confederal structure further entrusts primary power in the component parts, with the central authority primarily confining its attention to matters of foreign policy (in this respect a confederation resembles a treaty). The central government had no authority to act directly on individual citizens but instead had to act on citizens through requests to the states. The key provision of the Articles of Confederation was thus Article II, which proclaimed: "Each state retains its sovereignty, freedom, and independence, and every Power, Jurisdiction and right, which is not by this confederation expressly delegated to the United States, in Congress assembled" (Solberg 1958, 42).

The government under the Articles of Confederation consisted of a unicameral Congress. Consistent with the treaty model, each state—represented in Congress by from two to seven delegates—had an equal vote. State legislatures selected delegates to one-year terms; they were subject to recall and could not serve in Congress for more than three out of any six years. Congress exercised a limited number of powers. Significantly, these did not include control over interstate commerce. Most matters relative to taxation and defense required nine of the 13 states to agree. This required majority was further complicated by the inability of some states to keep a quorum of their members (Delaware resorted for a time to recruiting out-of-state delegates to represent it) at the Congress and by occasional splits within delegations with equal numbers of representatives. With the exception of Canada, the admission of which the Articles of Confederation over-optimistically already agreed to, nine states had to consent to the admission of new states. Consistent with its confederal structure, Congress had to requisition the states both for tax revenues and for troops, and sometimes because they simply could not, and sometimes because they simply would not, states did not always meet such obligations. In order to change the Articles, Congress had to propose amendments and the states had to ratify them unanimously. On at least two occasions, twelve states agreed on the necessity for an amendment expanding national powers, only to be blocked by a single state.

Most states had written and adopted new constitutions on the eve of, or in the immediate aftermath of, the Declaration of Independence when Congress had encouraged them to do so. Although many formally adopted the model of separation of powers with which modern readers are familiar, in practice most states embodied the Whig principle of legislative sovereignty. State governors usually served for limited, often nonrenewable, terms and exercised relatively limited powers. In the Declaration of Independence, Jefferson had blamed Britain's George III for failing to ensure that judges were independent, but a number of states made the same error. In most states, constitution writers had considered popular democracy to be more important than checks and balances.

The Articles of Confederation were in place when the Americans won and negotiated the peace to end the Revolutionary War, and this government thus deserves some of the credit. However, George Washington, who commanded American forces, was among those who expressed constant exasperation during the war with Congress's inability to provide needed supplies. His recognition of the weakness of this government made his refusal to attempt to seize power by military force all the more extraordinary and commendable. One of the Articles' most remarkable achievements, the Northwest Ordinance of 1787, which provided for the eventual settlement of the Northwest Territory, was, in fact, adopted during the meeting of the Constitutional Convention.

Whatever its accomplishments, however, contemporary scholars, like earlier commentators, are more likely to cite the Articles of Confederation for their failures than for their achievements. One writer observed that "It has been usual with declamatory gentlemen in their praises of the present government, to paint the state of the country under the old Congress as if neither wood grew nor water ran in America before the happy adoption of the Constitution" (quoted in Corwin 1981, 171).

The Revolutionary War had disrupted traditional trading patterns, and, as they licked their wounds from defeat, the British were not inclined to aid in the economic recovery of the nation that had just bested them in war. The national government had little authority to enforce the treaty that ended the war with Great Britain, and the British were in turn disinclined to withdraw their remaining forces from the Northwest Territories. The state governments under the Articles of Confederation sometimes struggled valiantly to meet requisitions by the national government for cash, but they often found their citizens to be cash poor, and they faced the ever-present temptation (to which some of them succumbed) to abuse their right to coin money and allow, or even require, state debtors to repay loans in depreciated currency.

Most frighteningly, the government of Massachusetts showed itself to be surprisingly slow to respond to the domestic disturbance, known as Shays's Rebellion, in which groups of local citizens closed down courts that were collecting debts. Some observers circulated reports, as shocking as they were inaccurate, that the rebellious farmers were interested not only in postponing their own debts but in redistributing wealth. Congress limped along, barely able to muster a quorum in response.

The Mount Vernon and Annapolis Meetings

One of the difficulties under the Articles of Confederation was the absence of national control over interstate and foreign commerce. The result was that states that had fought together against

England to achieve liberty were working against one another's interest on matters of trade. New York and Pennsylvania both taxed trade from New Jersey, which contemporaries therefore likened to a cask with a tap on both ends. Observers likened states in similar situations to individuals bleeding from amputations of both sets of limbs.

Against this background, the states of Virginia and Maryland decided to hold a meeting to see if they could resolve problems connected to navigation on the Potomac River, which constituted the boundary between them. Because the state governors failed to inform all the state-appointed delegates of their selection, not all attended, but the meeting, which took place at George Washington's Mount Vernon in March 1785, resulted in significant progress. The meeting further served the interest of the increasing number of patriots who believed that a stronger government was necessary by providing an occasion for the state legislature of Virginia to call in January of 1786 for yet another meeting. It was to meet at Annapolis, Maryland to see if the states collectively might be able to come to an agreement similar to that which Virginia and Maryland had concluded with one another.

This meeting was held in September of 1786 and did not initially appear very promising. Only five states sent commissioners, or delegates, and these did not even include representatives from Maryland, where the meeting was held. Showing far more optimism than would appear to have been warranted, however, key delegates devised a way for this meeting to serve as legitimization for yet another meeting with expanded powers. Seizing on language found in the commissions of delegates from New Jersey, leaders at the Annapolis Convention, most notably James Madison and Alexander Hamilton, suggested that the next meeting should be widened to include not only matters of trade but "a correspondent adjustment of other parts of the Federal System" (Solberg, 58). Delegates proposed that this meeting should take place in Philadelphia the following May. They envisioned commissioning it:

> to take into consideration the situation of the United States, to devise such further provisions as shall appear to them necessary to render the constitution of the Foederal Government adequate to the exigencies of the Union: and to report such an Act for that purpose to the United States in Congress assembled, as when agreed to, by them, and afterwards confirmed by the Legislatures of every State, will effectually provide for the same. (Solberg, 59)

The anticipation of congressional and state approval, presumably to be consistent with the amending process under the Articles of Confederation, probably seemed relatively unthreatening. Still, those familiar with the history of the amending process under the Articles and with the spotty attendance at the Annapolis Convention may well have wondered how such unanimity would be achieved. Moreover, whatever problems it posed, the exercise of state sovereignty must have been a heady experience for states that had once had to wait upon, or anticipate, a veto of colonial legislation by a distant king.

In such an atmosphere, Shays's Rebellion, which transpired during the winter of 1786 to 1787, served as something of a wake-up call. Liberty would be illusive if state governments could not preserve their own existence, and if the national government could extend little help to them in times of crisis. They needed to do something. By February, Congress, which had previously formed a committee but had deferred any recommendation to this point, was ready to get on board. It passed a resolution, bound, like its predecessor at the Annapolis Convention, to the existing forms under the Articles of Confederation:

> Resolved that in the opinion of Congress it is expedient that on the second Monday in May next a Convention of delegates who shall have been appointed by the several states be held at Philadelphia for the sole and express purpose of revising the Articles of Confederation and reporting to Congress and the several legislatures such alterations and provisions therein as shall, when agreed to in Congress and confirmed by the states render the federal constitution adequate to the exigencies of Government and the preservation of the Union. (Solberg, 64)

The Response

Ultimately 12 of 13 states heeded the call to send delegates to Philadelphia. Rhode Island—which Convention delegates, who thought that its issues of depreciated currency and legislation requiring that it be accepted for debts were unjust, sometimes dismissively called Rogues Island—was the only state that chose not to send delegates, a fact for which some tradesmen wrote a letter of apology to the Convention. Given the requirement for unanimous approval of constitutional amendments under the Articles of Confederation, Rhode Island's absence served primarily to keep the problem of constitutional ratification in continual view. The problem was heightened by the fact that delegates did not arrive from the Convention from New Hampshire until late July (after delegates had already made the major decision on state representation in Congress), while the delegation of New York was continually split and would have only a single person present when it came time to sign the new document. The Convention generally created committees of one representative from each state, and no committee at the Convention (excluding the Committee of the Whole) ever had more than eleven members.

The Convention had been scheduled to begin on May 14, the second Monday in May, in Philadelphia. At the time, the city was the nation's largest and most cosmopolitan, second only behind London as the largest English-speaking city in the world. It was the city in which delegates to the Second Continental Congress had signed the Declaration of Independence. It took until May 25 before seven states had a majority of their members present. Consistent with requirements for a quorum with which delegates were familiar, the Convention did not begin until that time.

James Madison, the physically diminutive but intellectually powerful delegate from Virginia, who had spent almost a year reviewing the histories of previous confederacies prior to attending the Convention and who had actually written his findings in the form of essays, decided to make good use of the time. He met fairly regularly with fellow members of the Virginia delegation, a delegation that included the illustrious George Washington,

William and Mary law professor George Wythe, writer of the Virginia Declaration of Rights George Mason, and Governor Edmund Randolph, in addition to two lesser lights. The Virginia delegation was second in size only to Pennsylvania's eight-man delegation which included the illustrious Benjamin Franklin, the legal scholar James Wilson, the imposing Gouverneur Morris (who is recorded as speaking most frequently at the Convention), Robert Morris, the financier of the U.S. Revolution, and others. As days passed, Elbridge Gerry, Nathaniel Gorham, and Rufus King arrived from Massachusetts; Oliver Ellsworth, William Samuel Johnson, and Roger Sherman from Connecticut; Alexander Hamilton from New York; William Paterson from New Jersey; and John Dickinson from Delaware. Luther Martin from Maryland; Hugh Williamson from North Carolina; John Rutledge, Charles and Charles Cotesworth Pinckney, and Pierce Butler from South Carolina; Abraham Baldwin from Georgia; and other lesser-known delegates also attended. Together the 55 men who attended the Convention at one or another time during the summer gave the body a cosmopolitan outlook, which was still deeply rooted in individual state interests.

Thomas Jefferson, himself a genius who was then serving as a U.S. minister to France, exaggerated when he called the assembly an assembly of demigods (Farrand 1913, 39), but the Convention certainly included some of the best minds in the country. Many were veterans of the Revolutionary War. In contrast to some authors of constitutions in other countries, almost all the delegates were politically experienced either in state governments, in Congress (in which some were simultaneously serving as members), or in the writing of state constitutions. Those less intellectually, rhetorically, or politically gifted served an important role as a sounding board, or jury, for proposals by better-known and better-prepared delegates.

Motives of the Framers

What motivated the delegates to the Constitutional Convention? It seems clear from their letters and from the debates in which they engaged that many of the Framers thought the nation faced a genuine crisis. The Declaration of Independence had proclaimed that people instituted government to protect "life, liberty, and the pursuit of happiness," the last of which is often associated with rights to property. If threats to life were not yet widespread, there was a real chance that chaos would jeopardize both individual liberty and property. Public-spirited leaders needed to avoid catastrophe. In early American history, most writers thus saw a fairly seamless tie between those who had expressed their patriotism by opposing the British in 1776 and those who had expressed it by attempting to rescue the failing government in 1787, and many popular audiences share this sentiment today.

More suspicious of elite behavior, which they often associated with greed, and less enamored with the elaborate system of checks and balances, which they saw as obstacles to more direct forms of democracy, historians generally associated with the Progressive Era in the early twentieth century questioned this flattering portrait. They charged that the proponents of the Constitution had betrayed the lofty goals of liberty that the Declaration of Independence had announced and/or that had been chiefly motivated, like later "robber-barons," by financial considerations. Like contemporary elites, delegates at the Convention were wealthier than most citizens, but, as it turned out, so were their most articulate critics. Because they recognized that there is sometimes tension between democratic will and individual rights, proponents and critics of the Constitution both had reservations about direct democracy. In my judgment, although the warnings of Progressive historians serve as warnings about automatically taking anyone's professed motives at face value, the attempts to divide proponents and critics of the Constitution into aristocrats and democrats, or those with one form of property as opposed to another, have proven largely fruitless.

This does not mean that the Framers were completely dispassionate. The motives of such men were undoubtedly as diverse as they were, but the success of the Revolution had led many to understand that, even on the periphery in what once had been an empire in America, they could be players on the world stage. Douglass Adair has persuasively argued that many were especially motivated by the desire for fame, a desire for secular immortality that he believes is nobler than the more widespread desire for mere popularity, which is reflected in modern Andy Warhol culture, where everyone appears to grasp for ten minutes in the sun. By contrast, Adair has explained (in male-centered language that would have been familiar to the Founders) that "the love of fame encourages a man to make history, to leave the mark of his deeds and his ideals on the world; it incites a man to refuse to be the victim of events and to become an 'event-making' personality—a being never to be forgotten by those later generations that will be born into a world his actions helped to shape" (Adair 1974, 11). Gouverneur Morris was among the delegates to the Convention who observed that "The love of fame is the great spring to noble & illustrious actions" (Farrand 1937, II, 53). Charles Pinckney hoped to emulate the Romans in making "the temple of virtue the road to the temple of fame" (II, 490). In *Federalist* No. 72, Alexander Hamilton described the love of fame as "the ruling passion of the noblest minds" (Hamilton, Madison, and Jay 1961, 437).

Delegates to the Convention were well educated. They were at once children of Enlightenment reason and of gritty political experience. George Washington had optimistically proclaimed in 1783: "The foundation of our empire was not laid in the gloomy age of ignorance and superstition; but at an epoch when the rights of mankind were better understood and more clearly defined, than at any other period" (quoted in Corwin 1964, 1). But, at the Convention, John Dickinson added: "Experience must be our only guide. Reason may mislead us" (II, 278). In selling the work of the Convention in the *Federalist,* Alexander Hamilton proclaimed in *Federalist* essay No. 1 that the people were to decide "whether societies of men are really capable or not of establishing good government from reflection and choice, or whether they are forever destined to depend for their political constitutions on accident and force" (1961, 33).

Convention Preliminaries

The first item of Convention business was the selection of a president. Among the luminaries at the Convention, two men, George Washington and Benjamin Franklin, had not only continental but worldwide reputations. At 55, the former was arguably still near the height of his powers, while at 81, the latter was falling victim to the infirmities of old age, including gall stones and gout. Nonetheless, George Washington's nomination by Robert Morris of Pennsylvania (with whom he was lodging) represented goodwill on the part of the delegation that included Franklin. The states present unanimously accepted Washington's nomination. The Convention appointed a doorkeeper and a messenger, who may collectively have also served as sentinels, and chose Major William Jackson, a friend of Washington's, as Convention secretary. In light of Jackson's skimpy note-keeping, this turned out to be a regrettable decision that would have been of greater negative consequence had James Madison, who seems never to have missed more than a fraction of an hour in attendance, not taken his own careful notes of the Convention proceedings. Madison described his methods:

> I chose a seat in front of the presiding member, with the other members, on my right and left hand. In this favorable position of hearing all that passed, I noted in terms legible and in abbreviations and marks intelligible to myself what was read from the Chair or spoken by the members; and losing not a moment unnecessarily between the adjournment and reassembling of the Convention, I was enabled to write out my daily notes during the session or within a few finishing days after its close. (cited in Benton 1986, I, 3–4)

Delegates approached the Convention with a mixture of hopefulness and wariness. Washington had observed:

> It is possible that no plan we suggest will be adopted. Perhaps another dreadful conflict is to be sustained. If, to please the people, we offer what we ourselves disapprove, how can we afterwards defend our work? Let us raise a standard to which the wise and honest can repair; the event is in the hands of God. (Lee 1932, 25)

After the delegates elected him president of the Convention, he proceeded to the small raised platform in the first-floor East Room in the Pennsylvania State House, today's Independence Hall, and gave one of his only two recorded speeches at the Convention, expressing suitable humility but pressing the Convention to strive for what was necessary.

The Convention then appointed a three-person committee—the first of a dozen committees that it created during the subsequent months—to propose rules. It appropriately appointed Virginia's George Wythe, one of Thomas Jefferson's teachers and the first professor of law in the United States (the second, behind William Blackstone, in the English-speaking world), to chair it. Sadly, this was Wythe's only real contribution to the Convention as he was soon called home to take care of a dying wife and never returned.

The committee reported a set of rules designed to facilitate compromise and debate. As under the Articles of Confederation, each state delegation present had a single vote. Delegates could ask that votes be retaken as debates progressed. In order further to facilitate compromise, the secretary was instructed not to record votes under individual names. Individuals had to rise to address the president and were required to wait until he left the room at the end of each day's proceedings before they exited. Delegates were to keep the proceedings secret. James Madison was the last surviving member of the Convention, and his notes of the proceedings were not published until 1840, after his death.

The Virginia Plan

The agenda of a meeting can be set in the opening minutes. The Constitutional Convention was a longer meeting than most, but its agenda was also largely established on the opening day of business.

In the days between the scheduled beginning and the actual beginning of the Constitutional Convention, Madison had conferred with his fellow Virginia delegates (a number, including Washington, that he had recruited and persuaded to attend) to formulate a plan to present to the Convention. Because he was governor, and perhaps because he was considered to be a good speaker, the delegation tapped the winsome Edmund Randolph to present the rationale for such a plan as well as its particulars, but in substance it followed the critique that Madison had been making of the Articles as well as his suggested remedies.

Randolph pointed to a number of defects under the Articles of Confederation. It provided no security "against foreign invasion"; it was unable to deal with quarrels among the states or rebellions within them; it could not attain advantages that might be reaped from a uniform approach to commerce; it could not defend against state encroachments; and the existing government was not even clearly paramount to that of the states (Farrand, I, 18). Sensitive that some members of the Convention had once served in the Second Continental Congress and worked on the Articles of Confederation, Randolph observed that he had "a high respect for its authors, and considered them as having done all that patriots could do, in the then infancy of the science, of constitutions, & of confederacies" (I, 18), when subsequent problems had not yet manifested themselves.

Randolph then proposed a solution to the problems he had identified based on what he called "the republican principle" (I, 19). Introduced with the comforting resolution that the existing government "ought to be so corrected & enlarged as to accomplish the objects proposed by their institution" (I, 20), the plan was no mere correction or enlargement, but a bold move in the direction of the unitary government of Great Britain (without the hereditary elements) against which the former colonists had once fought. In analyzing the plan, it is difficult to decide whether to give primary emphasis to its elevation of the power of the large or most populous states, or to the increased powers it would invest in the national government.

To begin with the first aspect, the Virginia Plan proposed substituting a bicameral Congress in which states were represented proportionally by population in both branches for the unicameral Congress under the Articles of Confederation in which each state was represented equally. The people, rather than state legislators, were to elect members of the first branch. Members of this branch were in turn to choose members of the second branch from among nominees made by the state legislatures. Randolph proposed granting Congress the power to veto all state laws and, in a provision that Madison would shortly thereafter question, to use force against recalcitrant states. The Virginia Plan did not enumerate the powers of Congress, as the Articles of Confederation had done. Instead, the Virginia Plan proposed vesting Congress with the power "to legislate in all cases to which the separate States are incompetent."

Whereas Congress constituted the only branch of government under the Articles of Confederation, the Virginia Plan proposed a government of three branches. The plan designated Congress to select an executive who, with members of the national judiciary, would constitute a council of revision with power to veto acts of Congress and of the state legislatures. Congress would also choose members of the judicial branch who would serve during good behavior. Additional provisions covered the admission of new states, the necessity of providing a mechanism for constitutional amendments, the provision of a republican form of government for the states, and related matters.

Ideas incorporated in the Virginia Plan were most surely in the air before Randolph introduced it, but one wonders how the Convention might have fared if delegates had taken a stricter view of their commissions and had simply begun the proceedings by proposing one or more bandages for the most serious problems under the Articles of Confederation. There is also the question of what might have happened had the Convention begun with the plan that Charles Pinckney had apparently prepared. Despite occasional claims that Pinckney was the true author of the Constitution, Pinckney's own youth (which he exaggerated, claiming to be 25 rather than 29, in order to be thought the youngest) conspired against him; there is even the possibility that Pinckney largely patterned whatever plan he put together on ideas from discussions that were in the air relative to the anticipated Virginia Plan. Consistent with his exaggerations about his age, but possibly aided by a faulty memory, historians later proved that the outline of a plan he once claimed to have offered early in the proceedings in fact incorporated ideas that he did not at the time hold and that no delegates had yet formulated. In any event, the delegates did not discuss the Pinckney Plan on the floor, and the first two weeks of the Convention concentrated not on patching or repairing, but on completing reformulating and replacing the existing government.

For the following two weeks, the Convention began each day by constituting itself in a Committee of the Whole, with Oliver Ellsworth of Massachusetts (who had served as president of the Congress) taking the place in front of the assembly that George Washington would otherwise have occupied. Discussions proceeded on how members of both houses of Congress should be selected, on how long the president's term should be, on whether he should receive a salary (Franklin, who was otherwise sensitive to the interests of the common man, had introduced the novel idea that the president should be unpaid), on whether the presidency should be a unitary or plural office, on who should choose members of the judicial branch, on the length of congressional terms, and the like. Beneath the seeming attention to minor issues, discontent was growing, fueled by new delegates who were arriving from less populous states and by their concerns over the increased powers the large states would exercise in the proposed plan. Delegates from the small states were undoubtedly disheartened when the Convention virtually ignored a proposal that Connecticut's Roger Sherman introduced on June 11 for equal representation in at least one house of Congress—a proposal he had first introduced on May 29 (I, 52). By June 13, the Committee of the Whole had digested its work into a series of 19 resolutions, which it sent to the full Convention for consideration. The plan under consideration still differed radically from the Articles of Confederation; it continued to propose a national government of three branches, including a bicameral congress with increased powers.

The New Jersey Plan

By the next day, delegates with doubts about the direction of the Virginia Plan had rallied, and William Paterson of New Jersey stepped forward to ask for time to introduce a new plan. He presented it on the following day. In what others might regard as an embarrassing revelation, that same day, Madison recorded in his notes that John Dickinson had personally upbraided Madison for "pushing things too far" (Farrand, I, 242). Professing that fellow delegates from the small states favored a strengthened government with a Congress of two branches, Dickinson further told Madison that "we would sooner submit to a foreign power, than submit to be deprived of an equality of suffrage, in both branches of the legislature, and thereby be thrown under the domination of the large States" (I, 242).

Whereas the Virginia Plan emphasized the interests of the large states and of a much more powerful Congress, the New Jersey Plan emphasized the claims of the smaller states and was generally less generous in allocating new powers to Congress. It seems clear that the New Jersey Plan, as it came to be called, was more clearly aligned with the professed purposes of the Convention. Few delegates scoffed at the accuracy of the introductory resolution, as they had at a similar preface to the Virginia Plan, when Paterson proposed that "the articles of Confederation ought to be so revised, corrected & enlarged, as to render the federal Constitution adequate to the exigenc[i]es of Government, & the preservation of the Union."

In place of the broad grant of power proposed for Congress under the Virginia Plan, Paterson proposed essentially adding five related powers to the existing unicameral Congress in which states would remain equally represented. These included the power to raise revenue by imposing duties or levies, to make rules for such collections, to alter such provisions, to regulate interstate and foreign commerce, and to allow common law judges within the states to judge offenses under such rules (I, 243).

It is interesting to speculate as to what kind of plan Paterson might have introduced had he been the lead speaker on the opening day of the Convention. Perhaps his plan would largely have stopped with investing Congress (perhaps bicameral, perhaps not) with increased powers. Because his proposal followed two weeks of debate, however, his own plan incorporated a number of agreements at which the Convention had already arrived. He accepted the idea of an executive but lent his weight to those, like Edmund Randolph, who thought that it should be plural in nature. Perhaps as a way of avoiding legislative corruption, he further proposed that this executive, rather than Congress, should appoint members of the federal judiciary. In a provision that the Convention later revised and incorporated into the final document, he proposed that U.S. laws and treaties should be the supreme law of the land.

Scholars still vigorously debate the primary intent of the New Jersey Plan. Was it designed as a radical alternative to the Virginia Plan, or was it largely a stalking horse for those who insisted on keeping equal state representation in at least one house of the new Congress? The issue, which scholars will probably never fully resolve, is not new. The day after Paterson introduced the New Jersey Plan, Charles Pinckney of South Carolina somewhat cynically observed that if the delegates were to grant New Jersey "an equal vote . . . she will dismiss her scruples, and concur in the Natil. system" (I, 255).

One fascinating aspect of the New Jersey Plan is that, while its proponents argued that it had justice on its side, they tended not so much to stress the desirability of the plan in and of itself as to stress the compatibility of the plan with the task to which the Convention had been called. Paterson pointedly observed:

> I came here not to speak my own sentiments, but [the sentiments of] those who sent me. Our object is not such a Governmt. as may be the best in itself, but such a one as our Constituents have

authorized us to prepare, and as they will approve. (I, 251)

Because proceedings were secret, delegates could only guess at what the people outside the Convention might accept. Would the people toast the delegates as statesmen and praise them as heroes for rising to the challenges posed by the problems under the Articles of Confederation, or would the people condemn them for exceeding their commissions?

The Great Compromise

Paterson had slowed but not stopped the momentum of the Virginia Plan. By June 19, the Convention had voted to return to its discussion of the Virginia Plan, albeit now in full Convention rather than in a Committee of the Whole. The intervening days had been eventful.

On June 18 Alexander Hamilton took most of the day to advocate a form of government far stronger than that advanced in either the Virginia or the New Jersey Plan. He admitted to being enamored of the English system and was far more willing to suggest institutions, like a presidency for life and life terms for members of at least one house of Congress, which seemed closer to the unitary English system, in which there were no sovereign state governments, than to either the government under the Articles of Confederation or either plan on the table. Thus, Hamilton was far more dismissive of the states than either plan under consideration, believing that states should be kept only as "subordinate authorities" (I, 287). He accordingly proposed that the general government would appoint a governor or president of each state with the power to veto any laws that it passed. Not surprisingly, although delegates applauded the delivery of his speech, his plan appears to have had little consequence.

Some scholars have speculated that Hamilton intended for his plan to make the Virginia Plan seem more moderate and thus more acceptable by proposing a still stronger form of government. This may indeed have been the case, but the Convention voted for the Virginia Plan not after

Hamilton's speech but after what appears to have been a fairly formidable speech on its behalf on the next day by James Madison, its primary author. Reviewing the New Jersey Plan, Madison denied that it would either preserve the Union or remedy existing problems under the Articles of Confederation.

However consoling it must have been to Madison and members of the large state delegations, the vote of that day to continue with discussion of the Virginia Plan was not as authoritative as it first appeared. By June 20, Roger Sherman was again suggesting that the Constitution should apportion one house of Congress according to population and the other so as to represent each state equally. A week later, Maryland's more volatile Luther Martin delivered a long speech on the dangers that the Virginia Plan posed to states' rights. By June 28, the savvy Franklin found he was unable even to get the Convention to agree to follow in the footsteps of the Continental Congresses and begin each day with prayer!

Prayer would have helped. The next day, Connecticut's William Johnson renewed the suggestion to use one house of Congress to represent states as states and another to represent population. On June 30 Franklin reached into his bag of metaphors to argue for compromise:

> When a broad table is to be made, and the edges [of planks do not fit] the artist takes a little from both, and makes a good joint. In like manner here both sides must part with some of their demands, in order that they may join in some accommodating proposition. (I, 488)

This did not stop Delaware's Gunning Bedford from threatening that if the larger states dissolved the Confederation, the smaller ones "will find some foreign ally of more honor and good faith, who will take them by the hand and do them justice" (I, 492). Madison explained that Jonathan Dayton followed this by saying that "He did not mean by this to intimidate or alarm" (I, 492), but he omitted language noted by Robert Yates who recorded Bedford as bluntly stating, "*I do not, gentlemen, trust you*" (I, 500). By July 2, the Convention deadlocked in a 5-5-2 vote, an impasse that

led to the establishment of the first of three committees to deal with the subject.

The Convention created the first such committee, of eleven, that same day. Headed by Elbridge Gerry of Massachusetts, it proposed on July 5 that states would be represented in one house according to population and in the other equally, with only the House of Representatives having the power to originate money bills, a measure that Gerry had previously been unable to get the Convention to adopt. A Committee of Five, created on July 6, subsequently proposed on July 9 that the initial House of Representatives should be composed of 56 members. Yet a third committee revised this number to 65, and the Convention had to revisit how representation would be apportioned in those states with slaves.

On July 12, it voted to accept a formula previously adopted for other purposes, but never actually implemented under the Articles of Confederation, whereby five slaves would count as the equivalent of three whites, thus effectively relegating each slave to three-fifths of a person. In action that may have been at least somewhat related, the Congress meeting in New York voted the next day to adopt the Northwest Ordinance—an ordinance that forbade slavery in that territory, but which might, by implication, have accepted its spread into others. In a measure that may have been even more farsighted and consequential than the Northwest Ordinance, the Convention turned down a recurring attempt on the following day to limit representation in newly accepted states. Such a measure would almost surely have convinced western states that they were being treated as colonies, and in time it may well have led to disunion.

The big vote came on July 16, when the Convention voted 5-4-1 to accept representation according to population and three-fifths of the slaves in the House and to accept equal state representation in the Senate. Perhaps purposely, Paterson misinterpreted Randolph's suggestion on behalf of the large states for a temporary adjournment as a call for delegates to go home and take the sentiment of their constituents. Instead, delegates from the large states adjourned to lick their wounds, but ultimately agreed in a meeting the next morning, probably over breakfast, that they had to give in if the Convention were to proceed. Madison observed in his notes that the larger states had given in to a plan of government that they recognized to be "imperfect & exceptionable." He further observed:

> It is probable that the result of this consultation satisfied the smaller States that they had nothing to apprehend from a Union of the larger, in any plan whatever agst. the equality of votes in the 2d. branch.

James Madison had little time to recover from the disappointment. Although delegates voted the next day to continue to allow Congress to legislate in cases involving the interests of the entire Union and in cases "in which the harmony of the United States may be interrupted by the exercise of individual legislation" (II, 21), it rejected Madison's favored enforcement mechanism providing for a congressional veto on state laws. Madison was unable to review this measure, or his treasured Council of Revision, despite continuing attempts to do so, sometimes with the help of James Wilson, later in the Convention. As the Convention had progressed, the delegates had rearranged and redrawn the outlines of Madison's grand plan. It was less and less a Madison plan and more and more a collective product.

Federalism

It is often difficult to separate the discussion of state representation in Congress from the question of state power. In reconstituting Congress, to what extent did the Framers intend to alter the relationship between the nation and the states under the Articles of Confederation? Clearly, the Virginia Plan called for major departures from the government under the Articles of Confederation, and the new Constitution strengthened the hands of Congress over those of the states. Just as clearly, the delegates took no significant action on Hamilton's very nationalistic plan, did not abolish the states, and decided against adopting a number of nationalizing provisions in the original Virginia Plan, including a broad grant of congressional powers, the veto of state legislation, and the legislative veto.

Part of the problem in following what the delegates were doing is that they were effectively inventing a new form of government and using old terminology. They typically referred to what political scientists would today call a confederal government (where states are sovereign) as a federal government and to what political scientists would today call a unitary government (which has no permanent states) as a national, or consolidated, one. Picking up from terminology that delegates had employed to explain what they were doing during Convention debates, James Madison argued in *Federalist* No. 39 that the new government was neither "wholly national nor wholly federal" (1961, 246). A future civil war proved to be the most important indication that the Convention never fully resolved this issue (Madison's own stance in the Virginia Resolution of 1798, in which he had suggested state interposition against unconstitutional federal legislation, was another), and contemporary controversies over the Ninth and Tenth Amendments and over the scope of congressional powers under the commerce clause indicate that some issues still remain.

The Rest of the Story

The story of the Great Compromise was so consuming and so dramatic that it is more difficult to tell the story from its adoption by the Convention forward. Delegates had literally hundreds of minor issues to resolve, ranging from the terms of members of each department of government, to their qualifications, to their mode of selection or appointment, to the wording of specific provisions. The presidency posed special problems. Delegates remained at once fearful of the kind of executive power they had seen Britain's King George exercise and aware of the potential promise of the kind of responsibility and accountability that they had come to expect from the one-time commander-in-chief, who they were correctly expecting would initially assume such a role again in a civilian capacity. As the proceedings progressed, James Wilson of Pennsylvania was especially influential in shaping the presidency into a coequal branch of the national government.

One key to the power of the presidency was the decision to invest this power in a single individual. Another foundation of the institution was the series of compromises that led to the Electoral College. By establishing a mode of election largely independent of Congress, the Convention created a mechanism that allowed for the possibility of presidential re-eligibility for office without the likelihood of creating the "corruption" in Congress that republican theorists so feared. This mechanism largely emerged from the Committee on Postponed Matters, sometimes designated the Committee on Unfinished Parts, which the Convention created on August 31. This mechanism was also responsible for the birth of the vice presidency, which had not been anticipated in either the Virginia or New Jersey Plan. Almost as if to find something for the vice president to do, the Convention vested this officer with power to preside over the U.S. Senate.

Other committees also moved the process of debate forward. Most significant was the Convention decision of July 24 to create a five-man Committee of Detail, which was probably the most influential at the Convention. Headed by John Rutledge of South Carolina and meeting over a week's Convention recess, this committee presented a series of 23 resolutions to the Convention on August 6. This committee, which does appear to have drawn in part from ideas submitted by Charles Pinckney, arguably tilted the balance of the new Constitution further in the direction of states' rights. In a related vein, it substituted an enumeration of specific congressional powers in place of the broader congressional mandate that Madison and others had included in the original Virginia Plan.

The Convention was coming to recognize that it could solve some problems by leaving the status quo in place or by simply deferring decisions to the first Congress. On August 8, delegates decided that the voting qualifications of those who voted for members of the U.S. House of Representatives did not need to be uniform; the Convention simply provided that such qualifications would be the same as individual states used to select members of their state legislatures. The Convention further decided on August 25 to allow the national government to assume state debts without requiring that it do so. The delegates also decided to allow for Congress to institute lower courts without specifying how many there would be.

Divisions within the Convention

If the most obvious fissure at the Constitutional Convention was the division between states that were large and those that were small, there were many others. The nation was divided, like many states (which sometimes denied appropriate representation to the latter), into eastern and western sections. Some existing states, especially in the Northeast, were concerned about one day being outvoted by new states to the West. Southern states, which were often closely affiliated through commerce and migration patterns with areas in the West (Kentucky would be born from Virginia and Tennessee from North Carolina within a few years after the Convention), wished to protect commerce on the Mississippi River, which negotiations that John Jay had conducted with Spain had threatened. Southerners were fearful that Congress might tax their bountiful agricultural exports and, while succeeding in adopting a ban on congressional taxation of exports, were unsuccessful in attempts to require that Congress adopt all legislation related to navigation by a two-thirds vote. On other matters, the nation split rather neatly into Eastern (Northern), Middle, and Southern states, each with different climates and staple crops.

Although emotions on the subject were yet to rise to the fever pitch that they would achieve in the period before the Civil War, the most permanent division between states at the Convention was between those that were free and those that permitted chattel slavery. This division was reflected in the decision to count slaves as three-fifths of a person. The optimist looks at the resulting compromise and notes that it speaks of "persons" rather than of property; the pessimist wonders what it is like to be regarded as only "three-fifths" of a person.

At a time when educated Southerners were still more likely to regard slavery as a necessary evil than as the positive good that later Southern apologists would claim it to be, Northerners did not, however, have a monopoly on anti-slavery sentiment. Virginia's George Mason, who owned a substantial number of slaves, condemned slavery in language almost as harsh as that of Pennsylvania's Gouverneur Morris. Unfortunately, neither these nor any other delegates followed up on Morris's fleeting suggestion that the government should purchase the freedom of slaves when they came of age. Instead, the Convention debated whether to permit the continuation of the slave trade. It initially settled on a provision, proposed in committee, that allowed Congress to stop the trade in 1800, and later extended the deadline to 1808. Similarly, it adopted another provision providing that states were obligated to return fugitive slaves. As in the case of other such compromises, it studiously sought to minimize offense by specifically referring to the institution by name or specifying exactly who would be responsible for carrying out this unwelcome duty.

Scholars afflicted with "presentism" sometimes add concerns about the status of women to those of African Americans and Indians (whom the delegates effectively excluded from citizenship and almost uniformly referred to during debates as savages). Certainly, the new Constitution did not explicitly guarantee the rights of women. However, the only remotely sexist language in the Constitution is the occasional use of the male pronoun to designate individuals, like the president, who would hold office under the new government. Moreover, the constitutionally designated census that was to be the basis for state representation in the House of Representatives included men, women, and children equally, implying that all were persons. Because of delegates' decision to accept existing state voting qualifications rather than add new qualifications for federal offices, the Convention actually left in place women's suffrage in the single state, New Jersey, that then allowed it, at least for women (usually unmarried or widowed) with property in their own names. A more positive declaration forbidding states to discriminate against women would have to await the adoption of the Nineteenth Amendment in 1920.

Implementing the New Constitution

Calls for the Convention had been explicit. These calls had commissioned the Convention to consider proposals to revise and enlarge the Articles of Confederation, which it was to send for approval to Congress. Such proposals were only to become law when all the states ratified them. What were the chances of this? Rhode Island had never even appointed delegates to the Convention. Two of three delegates from New York had gone home, and the other, the precocious but frustrated Hamilton, was AWOL (absent without leave) for long periods of time. How likely were state legislators going to be to agree to a system under which their own powers would probably be reduced? These questions called for some creative statesmanship, and the delegates rose to the challenge by deciding to elevate democratic form and theory over previously specified practice.

In the time during which states had birthed their constitutions, citizens had increasingly recognized the role of conventions, which they regarded as embodiments of popular sovereignty, both to draw up and to ratify constitutions. The delegates to the Convention in Philadelphia recognized that no one had authorized them both to propose and ratify a Constitution—one reason they felt comfortable proposing more than they had been authorized to do was that their proposals would not be final unless ratified. Delegates recognized that a Constitution ratified by the people, via conventions, would have greater democratic legitimacy, and a greater chance of success, than would constitutions ratified by state legislatures. Similarly, it was not at all clear that Congress either wanted the responsibility of voting on the product of convention deliberations or that its consent was necessary. Ultimately, the delegates decided to report their work to Congress and let Congress report it on to the states, without necessarily commending it, for ratification by individual conventions. Requiring initial approval by all 13 states would have allowed a single state or set of states to thwart popular will. Despite provisions proclaiming that the Articles of Confederation were "perpetual," the Convention therefore decided that the new Constitution would go into effect when nine or more ratified.

Some modern scholars are scandalized by the fact that the proposal and ratification of the Constitution was not strictly "legal," and others have tried to construct grand theories of constitutional change out of what appear to be constitutional anomalies that surround the Convention. However, this scholar has little doubt that the proceedings that accompanied the writing and ratifying of the Constitution were "regular" enough in the context of the times to provide both the patina and the substance of legitimacy that the new government so desperately needed. By contrast, the Articles of Confederation had been proposed by an ad hoc Congress in the midst of war and ratified by state legislatures many of which had themselves been created by makeshift constitutions (for further discussion, see Rakove 1999).

Drawing heavily from the literary talents of Gouverneur Morris, the five-man Committee of Style and Arrangement, which the delegates appointed on September 8, incorporated these and other provisions in the document that it reported to its colleagues. With most of its other work done, the Convention finalized a constitutional amending process by which Americans could initiate future changes. It was to consist of a two-step process of proposal and ratification.

The Outline of the New Constitution

The document that the Convention proposed began with reference to "We the People of the United States" and articulated a list of noble purposes designed, among other things, "to secure a more perfect Union." It consisted of seven Articles. Consistent with the Framers' regard for the doctrine of separation of powers (a corollary to checks and balances), the first three of these outlined the three branches of the national government.

Article I described the legislative branch. It was the only branch of government under the Articles of Confederation, the one that had been the subject of the longest discussions, and the one that had engendered the greatest controversy at the Convention. It was to be bicameral. Voters were to choose members of the House of Representatives, with minimal age, residency, and citizenship requirements, for two-year renewable terms. Representatives were apportioned to the states according to population, with slaves ("such other persons") counted as three-fifths of a person. Each state was granted two senators. In a provision eventually changed in 1913 with the adoption of the Seventeenth Amendment, state legislators chose senators. They serve for six-year terms and have only slightly higher minimum requirements than members of the House. The Constitution granted the House of Representatives the power to impeach, or bring charges against, public officials for a limited set of specified offenses, and invested a two-thirds majority of the Senate with the power to convict them of such charges. The Constitution further vested the Senate with the power to give advice and consent to presidential appointments and vested a two-thirds majority of the Senate with the power to approve treaties.

To become law, both houses would have to pass identical bills, which would have to be either signed by the president or adopted by supermajorities of Congress over the president's veto. Article I, Section 8 enumerates the powers of Congress. They include the power to coin money, power over interstate and foreign commerce, and the power to declare war. In something of a prelude to the Bill of Rights, Article I, Section 9 listed limits on the powers of Congress, including prohibitions on bills of attainder, ex post facto laws, and the like. Article I, Section 10 followed with limitations on the states, adding a prohibition, born from bitter state experience under the Articles of Confederation, on state impairment of the obligations of contracts.

Article II outlined the executive branch. It was to consist of a single individual serving for a four-year renewable term, and elected through an elaborate electoral college mechanism. The Electoral College was built in part on the compromise between the large and small states—each state had a number of electors equal to its total number of U.S. senators and representatives. In a provision that the Twelfth Amendment later modified, each elector was to cast two votes, with the winner of the majority, if there was one, becoming president, and the runner-up becoming vice president. The Constitution designates the president as commander-in-chief of the nation's armed forces, and invests the president with the duty to enforce the laws. He is responsible for appointing ambassadors, heads of domestic offices, and judges and justices to office with the advice and consent of the Senate.

Article III provided only the broad outlines of the judicial branch to be headed by the Supreme Court. It specified the jurisdiction of federal courts, provided for jury trials in criminal cases, and narrowly defined treason and the circumstances under which individuals could be convicted for it. Curiously, it did not specify the critical power of judicial review, that is, the power of judges to declare acts of legislation arising in cases coming before them to be unconstitutional and therefore void, which such judges have subsequently exercised, sometimes rather enthusiastically.

Article IV dealt largely with relations among the states. It required states to give "full faith and credit" to the actions of their neighbors and guaranteed to citizens of neighboring states their full "privileges and immunities." It provided for the return of criminals and fugitive slaves. It made further provision for the admission of new states, for the governing of territories, for federal guarantees of a republican form of government to the states, and for protection against foreign invasion and domestic insurrections.

Article V outlined the amending process. Under this article, two-thirds of the states could request Congress to call a convention to proposed amendments to the Constitution, or two-thirds majorities of both houses of Congress could propose such amendments. Three-fourths of the state legislatures, or of special conventions called for this purpose, were required to ratify such amendments. In recognition of the importance of compromises related to slavery and state representa-

tion, Article V entrenched the compromise on slave importation and provided that no state's equal representation in the Senate could be altered except with its consent.

Article VI encompassed a number of other matters that did not fit conveniently in the previous ones. It left the status of debts where it was under the Articles of Confederation, proclaimed the U.S. Constitution and laws made under its authority to be the supreme law of the land, bound both state and federal officers by oath to uphold the new Constitution, but prohibited religious tests as a qualification for office. Article VII followed by providing that the new Constitution would go into effect when ratified by conventions in nine or more of the states.

What Kind of Government?

In this volume, I have included entries describing a number of forms of government with which delegates were familiar or which they discussed at the Constitutional Convention. Some terms, like "federal," "confederal," and "unitary" (discussed above), refer to the division of power between national and subnational authorities. Although they often disagree about precisely what this implies, most scholars agree that the government the Framers proposed was federal. The Framers employed other terms, like "monarchy," "aristocracy," and "democracy," to refer to whether power is exercised by one ruler, by a few rulers, or by the people, and still others, like mixed government, to describe combinations of such forms.

It is clearer that the Framers attempted to avoid the perceived perils of monarchical or aristocratical government than that they instituted a pure democracy. Although he had commended such a form, John Dickinson observed at the Convention that "A limited monarchy was out of the question. The spirit of the times—the state of our affairs, forbade the experiment, if it were desirable" (I, 87). Elbridge Gerry observed that "having no hereditary distinctions among us, we were destitute [sic] of the essential materials for such an innovation" (I, 215); professing, as he often did, to assess public opinion, he later argued that less than one in a thousand citizens favored any "approach toward Monarchy" (I, 425). Delegates to the Convention gave scant consideration to proposals, like Hamilton's for life terms for presidents or senators, and, although they agreed on such lengthy terms, they did not make the offices of judges hereditary. Tellingly, the only time that the delegates officially breached the rules of secrecy during their proceedings was to quiet public fears that they might be considering establishing such a monarchy. The Convention thus authorized a statement for publication on August 18 in the *Pennsylvania Herald* indicating that "'tho' we cannot, affirmatively, tell you what we are doing, we can, negatively, tell you what we are not doing–we never once thought of a king" (Van Doren 1948, 145).

What kind of government did the Framers propose? When Mrs. Elizabeth Powel, the wife of the former Philadelphia mayor and the owner of City Tavern, asked him this question, Benjamin Franklin reportedly responded, "A republic, if you can keep it" (III, 85). Republican terminology and republican theory were in the air. Similarly, the only such self-referential term that the Constitution itself employs is "republican," as in the provision in Article IV, Section 4 providing that the national government shall guarantee such a government to each of the states. The fact that all 13 existing governments apparently qualified as republican, however, indicates that this terminology probably covered some fairly diverse governments.

Largely in an effort to counter arguments that Antifederalists had borrowed from Montesquieu to question whether the proposed republican government was appropriate over an area the size of the United States, James Madison sought in his distinguished *Federalist* No. 10 essay to distinguish a republican from a purely democratic government. He argued that the primary distinction between a republican and a purely democratic government was that the former embodied a system of representation (through the election mechanism) in place of direct participation and could therefore cover a large land area. He further thought that a government spread over a large land area, by embracing a wider number of fac-

tions, would make it less likely that any such faction would dominate and be able to oppress others.

Some scholars prefer to call the government created by the Convention a "democratic republican" government, or simply "free government," to indicate its close ties to the people. Most observers agree that the government has been increasingly democratized throughout American history. Democratizing influences have included the rise of mass political parties; the expansion of the franchise and the recognition of the rights of African Americans, Native Americans, and women; the direct election of senators; and the development of primary and related mechanisms for selecting political candidates.

If the delegates to the Convention empowered the people and the government it created, the delegates, and those who later adopted the Bill of Rights and subsequent constitutional amendments, also limited them. It is therefore also appropriate to refer to the government that the Framers created as a limited, or constitutional, government. Many of the conflicts that emerge over the powers of the branches of government, and especially of the unelected members of the judicial branch, stem from conflicts over the appropriate balance between deference to popular will and adherence to, or judicial interpretation and expansion of, constitutional restraints (Murphy et al. 2003, 43–78).

The Signing of the Constitution

What must it have been like to have stayed through an entire summer at the Convention, to have worked six days a week (sometimes serving on committees when the Convention itself was not in session), and to have decided either not to sign, or to have been uncertain as to whether to sign, its work? On September 15, just two days before the document would be signed, three delegates expressed serious reservations. Virginia's George Mason began by expressing concern over the fact that the new Constitution granted a bare majority of Congress to adopt navigation acts (II, 631). Fellow Virginian Edmund Randolph (who, as he told fellow delegates that he might, eventually decided to support the new Constitution at the Virginia ratifying convention) suggested that state conventions should be permitted to propose amendments, which would then be accepted or rejected by yet another Convention. Fearing that the new constitution "would end either in monarchy, or a tyrannical aristocracy," Mason, who would later print a more extensive set of objections in pamphlet form (see II, 637–640), observed that the Convention had drafted the Constitution without the knowledge of the people and lauded the idea of a second convention as being better than the Convention's "take this or nothing" approach (II, 632). Although he would soon confess to "the painful feelings of his situation, and the embarrassment" of making objections (II, 646), Elbridge Gerry presented his own laundry list on the Convention floor objecting to "the duration and re-eligibility of the Senate," House control over its journals, congressional control over the places of election and over its own salary, the representation allocated to his home state of Massachusetts, the three-fifths clause, the possibility that monopolies might be established under the new government, and the vice president's role as head of the Senate (II, 632–33).

South Carolina's Charles Pinckney observed that such objections gave "a peculiar solemnity to the present moment" (II, 632). After months of debates, the pressure on the dissenters must have been intense, something like the pressures a lone juror must feel when all the juror's colleagues are ready to convict. As in a jury, the more delegates who agreed that the new document was an improvement, the greater would be the pressure on those who were unconvinced. Seemingly cognizant of such feelings, Benjamin Franklin sagely proposed that the Convention attest to the fact that the Constitution was ratified unanimously by the states present. Delegates who wanted could simply say that they were attesting to the vote rather than to its wisdom.

The proposal, which seems actually to have originated with Gouverneur Morris, was a bit too clever, but there may be no speech in American history that better embodies the spirit of democratic humility than the one that Benjamin Franklin offered on September 17. In this speech, he urged those like Mason, Randolph, and Gerry with reservations about the Constitution to consider the possibility that, however distasteful sections of the Constitution might be, it might simply be the best product that such a collective entity could formulate. Benjamin Franklin observed:

> I agree to this Constitution with all its faults, if they are such; because I think a general Government necessary for us, and there is no form of Government but what may be a blessing to the people if well administered . . . I doubt too whether any other Convention we can obtain may be able to make a better Constitution. For when you assemble a number of men to have the advantage of their joint wisdom, you inevitably assemble with those men, all their prejudices, their passions, their errors of opinion, their local interests, and their selfish views. . . . It therefore astonishes me, Sir, to find this system approaching so near to perfect as it does. (II, 642)

Maryland's James McHenry, who decided to sign, may have reflected the sentiments of others when he observed that he signed despite his opposition "to many parts of the system" (II, 649). He explained:

> I distrust my own judgement, especially as it is opposite to the opinion of a majority of gentlemen whose abilities and patriotism are of the first case; and as I have had already frequent occasions to be convinced that I have not always judged right. (II, 649)

He further observed that the document provided for a means of amendment, and ended with a comparison of costs and benefits:

> Comparing the inconveniences and the evils which we labor under and may experience from the present confederation, and the little good we can expect from it—with the possible evils and the probable benefits and advantages promised us by the new system, I am clear that I ought to give it all the support in my power. (II, 649–50)

In the end, Mason, Randolph, and Gerry remained unconvinced and refused to sign. Thirty-eight remaining delegates (Delaware's Read signing not only for himself but also carrying a proxy vote for John Dickinson) advanced to the raised platform where Washington was sitting, dipped a quill into a silver inkwell, and signed the document, signatures to which Secretary William Jackson attested. Looking at the back of the Chippendale chair where Washington had been seated during most of the Convention proceedings, Franklin professed that the sun painted there was rising on a new day rather than setting on an old one. Delegates dispersed to a local tavern for dinner and headed to Congress, to state legislatures, or to their homes.

Ratification Debates

The controversy at the Convention between the majority who signed and the minority who refused to sign was a pale reflection of the clamor that awaited the document once the delegates published it to a waiting world. The press, which had widely publicized the defects of the Articles of Confederation, had been surprisingly complicit in the secrecy of the Convention, and most newspapers joined in calls for prompt constitutional ratification. Writers pointed to the presence of George Washington and Benjamin Franklin at the Convention as a sure sign of its wisdom and public spiritedness.

Although few critics chose to impugn the characters of Washington and Franklin, some remained unconvinced that the new document should be ratified. Luther Martin soon published a highly critical account of the Convention in his home state of Maryland. New York's John Lansing and Robert Yates opposed the Constitution in New York. Patrick Henry, who had refused to attend the Convention because he had "smelt a rat," joined Richard Henry Lee and James Monroe in opposing it in Virginia. Others, whom Federalist supporters of the Constitution soon labeled as Antifederalists, began to raise a hue and cry about the new document. They offered a variety of critiques, which varied from one speaker

and one part of the country to another. According to such critics, the Constitution leaned toward monarchy, toward aristocracy, or toward both. It vested too much unaccountable power in the judiciary. It perpetuated slavery. It did not adequately provide for slave interests. Republican government was inappropriate over an area the size of the United States. The Constitution created a Congress with too many powers, or with powers that were too indefinite. The Constitution did not adequately protect rights. Its proponents were trying to railroad the people into ratifying. Yet another Convention should meet to reexamine the proposal and suggest amendments. If states ratified the Constitution, they should do so only conditionally.

Federalists, especially those who had attended the Convention, had the advantage of generally knowing the document better and of being better organized than their Antifederalist opponents. They were also advocating a positive remedy at a time when most citizens recognized that there were definite problems with the Articles of Confederation. In a culture in which people were ever vigilant for their liberties and almost always suspicious of governmental power, Federalist proponents of the new document nonetheless had their hands full. With Delaware taking the lead on December 7, 1787 by a unanimous vote of 30 to 0, a few states, mostly small ones, stepped readily into line, and at least one large one (Pennsylvania) ratified but only after the use of questionable political tactics that served an immediate purpose but tended to bring the Federalist movement into disrepute. The battle was most clearly drawn in the large states like Massachusetts, Virginia, and New York, without whose participation the new government could probably not have succeeded, no matter how many other states had agreed to join. Citizens could now examine and debate the document about which they could only speculate while the Convention had been in session.

Debate was widespread. Alexander Hamilton, James Madison, and John Jay wrote essays under the pen name Publius and the title *The Federalist* in New York that are now generally acknowledged as the most thoughtful and comprehensive set of writings to emerge from this debate. However,

Herbert Storing has collected numerous thoughtful essays that also demonstrate that many Antifederalists were giving the document careful scrutiny. Federalists were especially concerned about heading off the possibility of yet another Convention that might undo much of the work of the first.

The highly contested ratification in Massachusetts ultimately represented something of a breakthrough. The state convention ratifying the new Constitution on February 6, 1788 proposed a series of amendments, but presented them as being recommendatory rather than as conditions for ratification. Federalists, who had previously opposed a bill of rights as unnecessary or even dangerous, could accept this. Although debate continued to be strong, Virginia and New York respectively ratified the Constitution, with similar recommendations, on June 25 and July 26. Consistent with the provision that nine or more states could ratify the document, the Constitution actually went into effect before North Carolina and Rhode Island approved it.

James Madison had come to recognize that concerns about the absence of a bill of rights could be turned to positive good if proponents of the Constitution could persuade opponents to ratify the Constitution with the promise that such a bill would follow. Much more clearly the father of the Bill of Rights than of the Constitution that is so often attributed to him, Madison recognized that for the new government to be effective, both Federalists and Antifederalists would have to accept it. He was the primary sponsor of the Bill of Rights in the first Congress and insisted on action at a time when many congressmen thought other issues were more pressing. He saw that the amendments that Congress recommended primarily focused on protecting individual liberties rather than on redrawing lines among the three branches of government or between the national government and the states (the Tenth Amendment recognized the existence of powers reserved to the states but did not specify what they were). At the time Madison thought that smaller states posed a more significant threat to liberty than did the larger national government. Thus, Madison's central disappointment in shepherding the Bill of Rights

through the first Congress was that he failed to win approval of a provision that would have initially limited the states as well as the national government. The Supreme Court eventually accomplished this task via provisions of the Fourteenth Amendment, adopted in 1868, by which the Court "incorporated" specific prohibitions within the Bill of Rights into those guarantees.

The early adoption of the Bill of Rights had the intended consequence of gaining legitimacy for the new Constitution and the government it created. Within a very short period of time, and through much of the late eighteenth and early nineteenth centuries, former Federalists and Antifederalists lauded the new Constitution as a sacred charter of government, and its authors as the truest of patriots. Such praise did not keep partisans from disagreeing over its meaning. Thus, although Alexander Hamilton and James Madison had united in defending the new Constitution in *The Federalist,* during the Washington administration they soon found themselves on opposite sides of the divide between the emerging Federalist and Democratic-Republican Parties that began with Hamilton's plan to institute a national bank, despite the lack of explicit constitutional authority for doing so.

Lessons to Be Learned

The only continually operating written constitution that is older than the U.S. Constitution is that of the state of Massachusetts, which served as one of its models. Formally amended only 27 times, the U.S. Constitution remains both an instrument of government and a symbol of national aspirations. Citizens continue to debate fundamental issues of public policy in constitutional terms.

In these volumes, I have provided a lot of information about the Constitutional Convention. In the process of writing these entries and composing this introduction, I hope that I have clarified and refined a number of issues that the Convention discussed, but I cannot claim that this book sheds substantial new light on the constitutional text. What if it did? If I had discovered and conclusively proved through an examination of the records of Convention debates and other documents that the Framers intended to institute three presidents rather than one, should we go back and revise our understanding accordingly? What if I had discovered that two-year terms for members of the House of Representatives had been an error in transcription, and that delegates had actually intended for them to serve for three years? To address more controversial contemporary issues, what if I could prove that the delegates to the Convention had definitely intended for fetuses to be considered or not considered as human beings, or, conversely, that states should approve, or disapprove, gay marriages?

As fascinating as such discoveries would be, and as much as I respect appeals to original intent, I doubt that such belated discoveries should prove conclusive in matters of constitutional interpretation. One might, however, hope that any such discoveries about such original intent would be accompanied by discoveries of forgotten arguments, and that such arguments, like the less earth-shattering results recorded in this and other books about the Constitutional Convention, would lead contemporaries to the same kind of reflections and debates in which the Framers engaged.

I think that knowledge is valuable in its own right, so I will be pleased if many students and scholars simply use these volumes as a way of understanding what the Framers did at the Convention and what reasons they offered for doing so. I think the more important role of any study of these proceedings, however, is that of engaging us in the fundamental questions with which they grappled. The Framers left us with a priceless legacy, but the fact that they included an amending process is an indication that they recognized both the variability of time and their own fallibility.

Someone, perhaps Justice Oliver Wendell Holmes, Jr., once said that there is no sillier reason for doing something than that it was done that way in the reign of some obscure king. Silliness gives way to tragedy, however, when nations abandon established ways of doing things not because they have proven unworkable or undesirable but simply because those who practice them

have lost sight of the reasons they were instituted. In an age when commentators "debate" one another on television by shouting, hurling accusations, and calling names, it is refreshing to see a group of men assemble privately and offer reasons and arguments in place of assertion and invective. Unlike some modern pundits, these were not the men of whom the Irish poet William Butler Yeats (1865–1939) wrote in "The Second Coming":

> The best lack all conviction, while the worst
> Are full of passionate intensity. (Abrams 1968, II, 1582)

However unfortunate and short of perfect some of the resulting compromises of the Constitutional Convention might have been, I believe the debates still offer a positive example of debate, deliberation, and compromise from which we can learn more than 200 years later. The fact that the Framers decided on a given structure commends it, but by no means insulates it from criticism. I would trust, however, that we would not tamper with a unitary presidency, a bicameral Congress, the veto or impeachment powers, or with basic liberties, until we understood why the Framers instituted and/or sought to protect them.

Although his voice was probably not the most influential, I am ultimately convinced that the wisest voice at the Convention was that of Benjamin Franklin. As one advances in age, it pays to advance in humility. One should certainly hold to one's convictions, but conviction is not equivalent to certainty. For all we know, we could be wrong about our most passionately held beliefs. Even when we are right, what we most want may not be achievable in practice. From such a perspective, the work of a Convention that wrote a Constitution that refined and secured a system of liberty under law that had endured for over 200 years looks like quite a remarkable achievement indeed!

American scholars can approach the Convention, or the Constitution that it produced, as an instrument or symbol, as an assembly worthy of study or as the creators of a work that should be celebrated (Corwin 1964). My hope is that, with some suitable caveats, readers will find its work to be worthy of both. Certainly, it is high time that someone devoted an encyclopedia to this pivotal event!

FOR FURTHER READING

Abrams, M. H., ed. 1968. *The Norton Anthology of English Literature*. Rev. ed. 2 vols. New York: W. W. Norton.

Adair, Douglass. 1974. "Fame and the Founding Fathers." In Trevor Colbourn, ed. *Fame and the Founding Fathers: Essays*. New York: W. W. Norton, 3–26.

Bernstein, Richard B., with Kym S. Rice. 1987. *Are We to Be a Nation? The Making of the Constitution*. Cambridge, MA: Harvard University Press.

Benton, Wilbourne E., ed. 1986. *1787: Drafting the U.S. Constitution*. 2 vols. College Station: Texas A and M University Press.

Bowen, Catherine Drinker. 1966. *Miracle at Philadelphia: The Story of the Constitutional Convention, May to September 1787*. Boston: Little, Brown.

Collier, Christopher, and James Lincoln Collier. 1986. *Decision in Philadelphia: The Constitutional Convention of 1787*. New York: Random House.

Corwin, Edward S. 1981. "The Constitution as Instrument and as Symbol." *Corwin on the Constitution*, vol. 1. Ed. Richard Loss. Ithaca, NY: Cornell University Press.

———. 1964. "The Progress of Constitutional Theory between the Declaration of Independence and the Meeting of the Philadelphia Convention." *American Constitutional History: Essays by Edward S. Corwin*. Ed. Alpheus T. Mason and Gerald Garvey. New York: Harper and Row.

Farrand, Max. 1913. *The Framing of the Constitution of the United States*. New Haven, CT: Yale University Press.

———, ed. 1937. *The Records of the Federal Convention*. 4 vols. New Haven, CT: Yale University Press.

Goldwin, Robert A. 1997. *From Parchment to Power: How James Madison Used the Bill of Rights to Save the Constitution*. Washington, DC: The AEI Press.

Hamilton, Alexander, James Madison, and John Jay. 1961. *The Federalist Papers*. Ed. Clinton Rossiter. New York: New American Library.

Hutson, James H., ed. 1987. *Supplement to Max Farrand's* The Records of the Federal Convention of 1787. New Haven, CT: Yale University Press.

Lee, Howard B. 1932. *The Story of the Constitution*. Charlottesville, VA: Michie.

Murphy, Walter F., James E. Fleming, Sotirious A. Barber, and Stephen Macedo. 2003. *American Constitutional Interpretation*. 3rd ed. New York: Foundation Press.

Rakove, Jack N. 1996. *Original Meanings: Politics and Ideas in the Making of the Constitution*. New York: Alfred A. Knopf.

———. 1999. "The Super-Legality of the Constitution, or, a Federalist Critique of Bruce Ackerman's Neo-Federalism." *Yale Law Journal* 108 (June): 1931–1958.

Rossiter, Clinton. 1966. *1787: The Grand Convention*. New York: W. W. Norton.

Solberg, Winton U., ed. 1958. *The Federal Convention and the Formation of the Union of the American States*. New York: Liberal Arts Press.

Storing, Herbert J. 1981. *The Complete Anti-Federalist*. 7 vols. Chicago: University of Chicago Press.

Van Doren, Charles. 1948. *The Great Rehearsal: The Story of the Making and Ratifying of the Constitution of the United States*. New York: Viking Press.

Vile, John R. 2001. *A Companion to the United States Constitution and Its Amendments*. 3rd ed. Westport, CT: Praeger.

Wood, Gordon S. 1969. *The Creation of the American Republic, 1776–1787*. Chapel Hill: University of North Carolina Press.

Key Dates of the U.S. Founding and Its Background

1215   The English nobles force King John to sign the Magna Carta, ideas from which will later be incorporated in the U.S. Constitution and Bill of Rights.

1492   Attempting to sail west from Europe to India, Columbus discovers the New World.

1607   British settlers arrive in Jamestown, Virginia.

1619   Africans are first brought to Jamestown, Virginia, eventually resulting in the institution of slavery.

1619   The Virginia House of Burgesses is established.

1620   The Pilgrims sign the Mayflower Compact before disembarking from their ship.

1628   The English Petition of Right is signed.

1639   Fundamental Orders of Connecticut are drawn up.

1641   The Massachusetts Body of Liberties, which many scholars consider to be a precursor to the U.S. Bill of Rights, is written.

1643   The New England Confederation is formed.

1688   The English Bill of Rights is signed.

1689   John Locke's *Two Treatises of Government* is published for the first time.

1704   A Massachusetts postmaster starts the first newspaper in the colonies, the *Boston News-Letter*.

1706   Benjamin Franklin is born in Boston on January 17.

1732   George Washington is born on February 22 in Westmoreland County, Virginia.

1748   Montesquieu first publishes *The Spirit of the Laws*.

1754   The Albany Plan of Union is proposed.

1760   George III ascends the English throne.

1763   The French and Indian War ends; England decides to end its policy of "salutary neglect" toward the colonies. Canada becomes a British colony.

1763   The British attempt to limit trans-Appalachian settlement.

1764   The English enact the Revenue Act of 1764.

1765   The English enact the Quartering Act and the Stamp Act.

1765   The colonies convene the Stamp Act Congress in October.

1766   The British Parliament repeals the Stamp Act but continues to insist on its power to tax the colonies.

1767   The British enact legislation laying new duties and granting general search warrants, or writs of assistance.

1773   Disgruntled colonists, dressed as Indians, protest the Tea Act of 1773 by throwing tea into the Boston Harbor.

1774   The British Parliament orders closure of the Boston Harbor.

1774   The First Continental Congress meets in Philadelphia in September.

1775   Fighting between the Colonies and the

British begins at Lexington and Concord on April 19.

1775   The Second Continental Congress appoints George Washington as commander-in-chief of American forces on June 15.

1776   Thomas Paine publishes *Common Sense*, arguing against hereditary kingship and for independence.

1776   Thomas Jefferson writes and the Second Continental Congress revises and approves the Declaration of Independence on July 4.

1776   Adam Smith publishes his *Wealth of Nations*.

1776   States begin writing constitutions. Virginia's includes the historic Declaration of Rights, chiefly written by George Mason.

1777   Congress revises and approves the Articles of Confederation.

1778   The first compilation of U.S. state constitutions is published (in French) in Philadelphia.

1781   Maryland agrees to the Articles of Confederation, which now has the consent of all thirteen colonies.

1781   The British surrender at Yorktown.

1781   Twelve of the thirteen states required agree to a 5 percent congressional impost but Rhode Island refuses to approve.

1783   The Treaty of Paris formally brings an end to the Revolutionary War.

1783   Another proposal granting Congress power to enact imposts fails with the opposition of New York.

1783   On December 23, General Washington peacefully hands back his commission as commander-in-chief and returns to his home at Mount Vernon, Virginia.

1783   The British close the West Indies and Canada to U.S. trade.

1784   Spain closes the Mississippi River to U.S. trade.

1785   Representatives from Maryland and Virginia meet at Mount Vernon to discuss problems of navigation on the Potomac River.

1786   The Annapolis Convention meets and calls for a more comprehensive Constitutional Convention. Virginia adopts the Statute for Religious Freedom.

1786–87 Shays's Rebellion breaks out in Massachusetts, leading to widespread fears that the Articles of Confederation are crumbling.

1787   The Constitutional Convention meets in Philadelphia from May 25 through September 17.

1787   Debates begin between Federalist supporters and Antifederalist opponents of the new Constitution.

1787–88 Publication of *The Federalist*, written under the name of Publius by Alexander Hamilton, James Madison, and John Jay.

1788   The required number of nine states ratify the new Constitution.

1789   Electors unanimously select George Washington as the nation's first president.

1789   The new Congress begins meeting in New York where Washington is inaugurated as president.

1789   The first Congress proposes twelve amendments.

1789   The Judiciary Act is adopted, organizing lower federal courts.

1789   The French Revolution begins with the storming of the Bastille.

1790   The U.S. Supreme Court begins its first session in New York City.

1790   Rhode Island, the last of the original thirteen colonies, joins the Union.

1790   Philadelphia becomes the temporary capital of the United States.

1790   Benjamin Franklin dies on April 19.

1791   The required number of states ratify ten of the twelve amendments. These ten become known as the Bill of Rights.

1791   President Washington accepts Alexander Hamilton's proposal for establishing a national bank. This issue is a leading cause of the division of the nation into two parties. The Federalists favor broad interpretation of the powers of the new government. Democratic-Republicans favor stricter intepretation.

1791   Vermont is admitted as the fourteenth state.

1792   Kentucky is admitted as the fifteenth state.

1792   Publication of Mary Wollstonecraft's *Vindication of the Rights of Woman.*

1795   The Eleventh Amendment is ratified, reversing the Supreme Court's decision in *Chisholm v. Georgia* (1793) and thus limiting lawsuits against the states.

1795   After serving for two terms, George Washington announces that he will not run for reelection.

1796   John Adams is elected as the nation's second president.

1797   The XYZ Affair signals increased tension with France.

1798   The adoption of the Federalist-inspired Alien and Sedition Acts signals increased tension between America's two political parties.

1798   Adoption of the Alien and Sedition Acts leads James Madison and Thomas Jefferson to author the Virginia and Kentucky Resolutions, indicating that states have the right to "interpose" against what they consider to be acts of unconstitutional legislation.

1799   George Washington dies at Mount Vernon on December 14.

1800   The District of Columbia becomes the nation's permanent capital. The Adamses move into the White House.

1800   Democratic-Republican electors split their ballots between Thomas Jefferson and Aaron Burr producing a crisis that eventually results in the selection of Jefferson.

1801   Outgoing president John Adams appoints John Marshall as chief justice of the United States. Marshall's opinions about the meaning of the Constitution will be as important as many decisions that were made at the Constitutional Convention itself.

1803   John Marshall's decision in *Marbury v. Madison* establishes the power of federal courts to invalidate acts of Congress as unconstitutional.

1803   Initially seeking to ensure the right of navigation on the Mississippi River, the nation makes the Louisiana Purchase.

1804   The Twelfth Amendment is ratified so as to avoid repeats of the presidential election of 1800.

1804   The Lewis and Clark expedition, commissioned by President Jefferson, reaches the Pacific Ocean.

1808   James Madison, putative "father" of the U.S. Constitution, is elected president.

1812   War is renewed with Great Britain.

1814   British troops burn the U.S. capitol.

1815   The U.S. decisively wins the Battle of New Orleans. A peace treaty is signed with Great Britain.

1816   James Monroe, the last of the "Founding Fathers," is elected president.

1819   John Marshall gives judicial approval to the establishment of the national bank in *McCulloch v. Maryland.*

1819   John Marshall affirms the importance of contracts in *Dartmouth College v. Woodward.*

1820   The dispute surrounding the admission of Missouri (resulting in the Missouri Compromise that bans slavery in the northern portion of the Louisiana Purchase) signals the increasing tension between slave and free states that will eventually result in the Civil War (1861–65).

1823   The Monroe Doctrine, barring further European colonization in the New World, is proclaimed.

1824   Chief Justice John Marshall interprets federal commerce powers broadly in *Gibbons v. Ogden,* so as to preclude the exercise of conflicting state powers.

1824   A four-man race for president ends up in the House of Representatives where John Quincy Adams is selected over Andrew Jackson.

1826   John Adams and Thomas Jefferson both die on July 4, fifty years after the adoption of the Declaration of Independence.

1828   General Andrew Jackson is selected as president and serves for two terms.

1831   James Monroe, the last of the founding presidents, dies on July 4.

1832   South Carolina adopts the Ordinance of Nullification.

1833   Chief Justice John Marshall decides in

Barron v. Baltimore that the provisions in the Bill of Rights apply only to the national government and not to the states.

1833   Massachusetts becomes the last state to disestablish its official congregational church.

1835   Chief Justice John Marshall dies.

1836   James Madison, sole surviving delegate to the U.S. Constitutional Convention, dies at his home in Mount Pelier, Virginia.

1840   Madison's *Records of the Federal Convention* are first published.

1849   Dolley Madison, widow of James Madison, dies.

1854   Eliza Hamilton, widow of Alexander Hamilton, dies.

See Also   Timetable of the Constitutional Convention

FOR FURTHER READING

Linton, Calvin D., ed. 1975. *The Bicentennial Almanac.* Nashville, TN: Thomas Nelson Inc., Publishers.

Rakove, Jack N. 1998. *Declaring Rights: A Brief History with Documents.* Boston: Bedford Books.

Spaeth, Harold J., and Edward Conrad Smith. 1991. 13th ed. *The Constitution of the United States.* New York: HarperCollins.

Timetable of the Constitutional Convention

Below is a day-by-day report of some of the major events and votes of the Constitutional Convention. Because Convention rules permitted votes to be retaken on important matters, agreements made on one day were not always adhered to on later ones.

Monday, May 14, 1787
The Convention was scheduled to convene but did not have a quorum. Only Virginia and the host state, Pennsylvania, were represented. Between them, they had eight delegates.

Tuesday, May 15, 1787
Reconvened at 11:00 A.M. Edmund Randolph arrived from Virginia, but no new states were represented.

Wednesday, May 16, 1787
Virginia and Pennsylvania were still the only two states represented.

Thursday, May 17, 1787
John Rutledge and Charles Pinckney arrived from South Carolina. George Mason added to the Virginia delegation.

Friday, May 18, 1787
Representatives from New York appeared for the first time.

Saturday, May 19, 1787
No new state delegations arrived.

Sunday, May 20, 1787
Convention not in session.

Monday, May 21, 1787
Delegates from Delaware arrived.

Tuesday, May 22, 1787
Delegates from North Carolina arrived.

Wednesday, May 23, 1787
No new state delegations arrived, but delegates were reported to be present from Massachusetts, Georgia, Maryland and New Jersey.

Thursday, May 24, 1787
No new state delegations arrived.

Friday, May 25, 1787
Delegates from New Jersey arrived, making a quorum of seven states. Twenty-seven delegates were reported present. The Convention elected George Washington from Virginia as its president, and he gave a short speech. The Convention elected William Jackson (not a state delegate) as the official secretary. It also appointed a doorkeeper and a messenger and selected a three-person Rules Committee consisting of George Wythe, Alexander Hamilton, and Charles Pinckney and adjourned until Monday.

Saturday, May 26, 1787
Convention stood adjourned.

Sunday, May 27, 1787
Convention not in session.

Monday, May 28, 1787
Seven new delegates were seated, including enough to give representation to Connecticut and Massachusetts. George Wythe presented the report from the Rules Committee. The Convention adopted most of its recommendations and referred other suggested rules introduced on the floor for its consideration.

Tuesday, May 29, 1787
The Rules Committee reported a number of additional rules, to which the Convention agreed. Edmund Randolph presented the Virginia Plan, calling for a significantly expanded and reconfigured national government of three branches and a Congress of two houses. Charles Pinckney of South Carolina also submitted a plan.

Wednesday, May 30, 1787
The Convention decided to convene in a Committee of the Whole and selected Nathaniel Gorham of Massachusetts to preside over the committee. The committee decided on a different opening resolution for the Virginia Plan. The committee debated the method of representation in Congress.

Thursday, May 31, 1787
The arrival of Georgia delegates brought to ten the total number of states represented. The Committee of the Whole accepted popular election of members of the first branch of Congress but could not agree on the method of selecting the second.

Friday, June 1, 1787
The Committee of the Whole agreed to an executive with a seven-year term and with power to execute laws and appoint "all officers not otherwise provided for" (Farrand 1937, I, 70).

Saturday, June 2, 1787
The Committee of the Whole agreed to congressional selection of the president. Pennsylvania's Benjamin Franklin presented a speech proposing

that the president should not receive a salary. The committee decided that the president would be ineligible after his seven-year term and impeachable prior to this time.

Sunday, June 3, 1787
Convention not in session.

Monday, June 4, 1787
The Committee of the Whole voted that the presidency would be vested in a single person. He was invested with a veto, subject to override by two-thirds majorities in both houses of Congress. The committee also agreed to a national judiciary to consist of one supreme tribunal and such others as Congress should establish.

Tuesday, June 5, 1787
The Committee of the Whole struck out the provision in the Virginia Plan granting the legislature power to appoint members of the national judiciary. It also discussed the ratification of the new Constitution and affirmed the power of Congress to create lower courts.

Wednesday, June 6, 1787
The Committee of the Whole voted against allowing the state legislatures to select members of the first house of Congress. It voted against allying members of the judicial branch with the executive in a Council of Revision.

Thursday, June 7, 1787
The Committee of the Whole voted that state legislatures would choose members of the second house of Congress.

Friday, June 8, 1787
The Committee of the Whole discussed and rejected the idea introduced in the Virginia Plan of allowing for a congressional veto of all state laws.

Saturday, June 9, 1787
The Committee of the Whole rejected the idea of allowing state governors to choose the president. Paterson reintroduced the issue of state representation in the Senate.

Sunday, June 10, 1787
Convention not in session.

Monday, June 11, 1787
Connecticut's Roger Sherman proposed that states should be represented by population in the House of Representatives and equally in the Senate. The Committee of the Whole reaffirmed that representation in the first house of Congress should be based on an equitable ratio of representation, in which slaves would be counted as three-fifths of a person. It also voted to apportion representation in the second branch according to that in the first and to adopt a provision guaranteeing states a republican form of government.

Tuesday, June 12, 1787
The Committee of the Whole voted for a number of measures including a three-year term for House members and requiring that members of the second branch be 30 years of age or older and serve for seven-year terms.

Wednesday, June 13, 1787
The Committee of the Whole adopted a provision clarifying the scope of judicial jurisdiction and providing for Senate appointment of federal judges. The committee sent a series of 19 resolutions agreed upon to this point to the full Convention for consideration.

Thursday, June 14, 1787
William Paterson of New Jersey asked for further time to digest the report of the Committee of the Whole and to prepare a new "federal" form of government.

Friday, June 15, 1787
Paterson introduced a nine-point New Jersey Plan, essentially proposing to expand the power of the existing Congress under the Articles but also providing for a plural executive to be chosen by Congress and for a federal judiciary. Section 6 of the plan became the eventual basis for the supremacy clause. The plan was referred to the Committee of the Whole.

Saturday, June 16, 1787
The Committee of the Whole listened to arguments for and against the wisdom and the propriety of the New Jersey Plan.

Sunday, June 17, 1787
Convention not in session.

Monday, June 18, 1787
Alexander Hamilton of New York delivered an extended speech to the Committee of the Whole advocating a government far stronger than that proposed in either the Virginia or New Jersey Plan.

Tuesday, June 19, 1787
Madison gave an extended speech advocating the Virginia Plan, and the Committee of the Whole voted to re-report those parts and modifications of the plan that it had previously reported to the Convention.

Wednesday, June 20, 1787
The Convention agreed to drop the word "national" from its description of the new government. The Convention continued to debate the wisdom of a legislature consisting of two branches. Connecticut's Roger Sherman suggested the possibility of providing for two branches of Congress in which states would be proportionally represented in one house and equally represented in the other.

Thursday, June 21, 1787
The Convention continued to consider various resolutions proposed by the Committee of the Whole. It agreed, among other things, to the election of members of the House of Representatives by the people for two-year terms.

Friday, June 22, 1787
The Convention continued to consider various measures proposed by the Committee of the Whole. It agreed that members of Congress should receive "adequate compensation," and it agreed to a 25-year minimum age for members of the House of Representatives.

Saturday, June 23, 1787
The Convention continued to consider various proposals previously agreed to by the Committee of the Whole. Among other votes, it accepted a provision making members of Congress ineligible for other offices during their tenure in office but striking down a provision for continuing this ineligibility thereafter.

Sunday, June 24, 1787
Convention not in session.

Monday, June 25, 1787
Charles Pinckney of South Carolina delivered an extensive speech on the U.S. Senate after which the Convention voted to affirm that state legislatures would select senators who would be a minimum of 30 years of age. It was unable to agree on the length of senatorial terms.

Tuesday, June 26, 1787
The Convention continued to consider the various proposals of the Committee of the Whole, settling on a six-year term for senators and agreeing that both houses should be able to originate money bills.

Wednesday, June 27, 1787
The Convention began by considering proposals from the Committee of the Whole. Consideration of a proposal to vary suffrage in the House of Representatives from that under the Articles of Confederation led Maryland's Luther Martin to deliver a speech of more than three hours on the danger of national preemption of states' rights.

Thursday, June 28, 1787
A motion by John Lansing of New Hampshire and Jonathan Dayton of New Jersey to provide that representation in the House of Representatives would be like that under the Articles of Confederation led to heated discussion. Benjamin Franklin proposed that the Convention should begin each day with prayer, stirring debate but not leading to any concrete action.

Friday, June 29, 1787
Connecticut's William Johnson renewed the earlier suggestion of Roger Sherman that states be represented according to population in one house and equally in the other. The Convention voted to reaffirm that representation be according to population in the House of Representatives.

Saturday, June 30, 1787
The Convention continued to discuss representation in the Senate. Tempers rose as Delaware's Gunning Bedford suggested that if the large states dissolved the confederation rather than providing fair representation for the smaller states, the smaller states "will find some foreign ally or more honor and good faith, who will take them by the hand and do them justice" (I, 492).

Sunday, July 1, 1787
Convention not in session.

Monday, July 2, 1787
The Convention deadlocked in a 5-5-2 vote on whether states should be equally represented in the Senate. It appointed a committee of eleven delegates to consider this proposal.

Tuesday, July 3, 1787
Convention adjourned for Independence Day holiday. The Grand Committee met and chose Elbridge Gerry of Massachusetts as its chair. The committee formulated a plan whereby states would be represented according to population in the House of Representatives and equally in the Senate. Under this plan, only the House of Representatives would have power to originate money bills.

Wednesday, July 4, 1787
Convention adjourned for Independence Day holiday.

Thursday, July 5, 1787
Gerry presented the report of the Committee on Representation to the Convention. A number of delegates questioned the report. Delegates discussed it without coming to any final conclusions.

Friday, July 6, 1787
The Convention voted to create a special com-

mittee of five delegates to reconsider the ratio of representation for the House of Representatives previously proposed by the Grand Committee. The Convention voted to limit the origination of money bills to the House of Representatives.

Saturday, July 7, 1787
The Convention took a preliminary vote accepting the idea of giving states equal representation in the Senate.

Sunday, July 8, 1787
Convention not in session.

Monday, July 9, 1787
Gouverneur Morris of Pennsylvania reported on behalf of the committee of five and proposed an initial House of Representatives to be composed of 56 members, with states initially having from one (Rhode Island) to nine votes (Virginia). The report prompted extensive discussion as to how the committee had arrived at these numbers, and the Convention ended up appointing another eleven-person committee to reconsider this proposal.

Tuesday, July 10, 1787
Rufus King of Massachusetts reported from the new eleven-man committee, now proposing that the initial representation in the House of Representatives consist of 65 individuals. The Convention agreed to accept this suggestion. Robert Yates and John Lansing of New York left the Convention, leaving the state (which had three delegates) without a plurality for further votes.

Wednesday, July 11, 1787
The Convention discussed representation of slaves. It agreed that a census should be conducted at least every 15 years so that state representation could be periodically reapportioned in the House of Representatives.

Thursday, July 12, 1787
The Convention voted to apportion representation in the House of Representatives according to population, with slaves counting as three-fifths of a person. It decided that a census would be con-

ducted at least every ten years to adjust representation and taxation.

Friday, July 13, 1787
The Convention continued to discuss the issue of congressional representation. It voted to adjust representation in the future in cases where states divided or were enlarged by the addition of new territory. In a development that may have been related to the adoption of the Three-fifths Compromise, the Congress, meeting in New York City, adopted the Northwest Ordinance.

Saturday, July 14, 1787
The Convention rejected a proposal that would have kept new states from eventually obtaining more representatives than those of the existing states. Charles Pinckney proposed a plan whereby each state would be represented by one to five members in the House of Representatives, for a total of 36 members, but the Convention rejected it by a 6-4 vote.

Sunday, July 15, 1787
Convention not in session.

Monday, July 16, 1787
The Convention voted 5 to 4 to 1 to accept the report of the Committee on Representation, apportioning state votes in the House of Representatives according to population and apportioning these votes equally in the Senate. After no little wrangling, the Convention accepted the proposal of Virginia's Edmund Randolph to adjourn for the day so that "the large States might consider the steps proper to be taken in the present solemn crisis of the business and that the small States might also deliberate on the means of conciliation" (II, 18).

Tuesday, July 17, 1787
Delegates, mostly from the large states, met over breakfast and concluded that they should accept the compromise on representation in Congress. The Convention voted for a clause vesting Congress with power to legislate in cases involving the interests of the Union as a whole and in cases "in which the harmony of the United States may be in-

terrupted by the exercise of individual legislation" (II, 21). It voted against the congressional veto on state laws. The Convention unanimously agreed to the establishment of a single executive to be selected by Congress for a single seven-year term.

Wednesday, July 18, 1787
The Convention focused on the federal judiciary, agreeing to the establishment of a national judiciary whose members would serve during good behavior, and for the admission of new states. It also voted to provide that each state should be guaranteed a republican form of government and protected against foreign and domestic violence.

Thursday, July 19, 1787
The Convention voted for a plan whereby state legislatures would choose presidents for a six-year renewable term.

Friday, July 20, 1787
The Convention continued to discuss the presidency. It voted to forbid presidential electors from being members of Congress and provided that the president could be impeached and removed from office if convicted of "malpractice or neglect of duty" (II, 61). It further voted that the president should receive a fixed compensation to be drawn from the public treasury.

Saturday, July 21, 1787
The Convention continued to focus on the presidency. It defeated a proposal by Pennsylvania's James Wilson to ally key members of the judiciary with the presidency in exercising the veto power, but it did vote to vest this power in the president subject to an override by two-thirds majorities in both houses of Congress. The Convention reaffirmed the appointment of judges by the Senate.

Sunday, July 22, 1787
Convention not in session.

Monday, July 23, 1787
John Langdon and Nicholas Gillman arrived from New Hampshire, again putting representation at eleven states (New York no longer had a quorum,

and Rhode Island did not send delegates). The Convention voted to affirm the need for an amending provision and to bind members of the state and national governments by oath to support the Constitution. The Convention voted to submit its work to state constitutional conventions and to provide for per capita voting in the Senate, in which it agreed that each state would have two delegates. It voted for a committee of five members (known as the Committee of Detail) to draw up a Constitution consistent with resolutions previously agreed to.

Tuesday, July 24, 1787
The Convention voted that the president should be selected by state legislatures and discussed the length of presidential terms. It selected a five-person Committee of Detail to draw a draft of a Constitution for further consideration.

Wednesday, July 25, 1787
The Convention rejected a motion whereby state legislatures would select the president when he was re-eligible for election. It voted to give members of the Committee of Detail, but not members of the Convention generally, access to copies of the proceedings.

Thursday, July 26, 1787
The Convention voted to reinstate the provision whereby the president would serve for a single seven-year term. The Convention further voted to recommend a provision to the Committee of Detail whereby individuals in public office would have certain property qualifications. The Convention forwarded to the Committee of Detail not only its own resolutions but also the Pinckney Plan and the New Jersey Plan. It voted to adjourn until Monday, August 6.

Friday, July 27, 1787
Convention adjourned for the Committee of Detail to do its work.

Saturday, July 28, 1787
Convention adjourned for the Committee of Detail to do its work.

Sunday, July 29, 1787
Convention not in session.

Monday, July 30, 1787
Convention adjourned for the Committee of Detail to do its work.

Tuesday, July 31, 1787
Convention adjourned for the Committee of Detail to do its work.

Wednesday, August 1, 1787
Convention adjourned for the Committee of Detail to do its work.

Thursday, August 2, 1787
Convention adjourned for the Committee of Detail to do its work.

Friday, August 3, 1787
Convention adjourned for the Committee of Detail to do its work.

Saturday, August 4, 1787
Convention adjourned for the Committee of Detail to do its work.

Sunday, August 5, 1787
Convention not in session.

Monday, August 6, 1787
John Rutledge of South Carolina presented 23 resolutions to the Convention on behalf of the Committee of Detail. These resolutions are especially notable for enumerating the powers of Congress, much as had been done under the Articles of Confederation.

Tuesday, August 7, 1787
The Convention began to consider the proposals put forward by the Committee of Detail. It accepted the Preamble that the committee had proposed, agreed to designate the government as "the United States of America," voted against giving each branch of Congress a negative on the other, voted against changing the annual congressional meeting time from December to May, and voted against adding property qualifications for voters.

Wednesday, August 8, 1787
The Convention voted to keep the same voting qualifications for members of the House of Representatives as for members of the state legislature. It voted to require a seven-year citizenship and a one-year residency requirement for members of the House of Representatives. The Convention voted that there would be no more than one member of the House of Representatives for each 40,000 residents, provided that each state would have at least one representative in the House. The Convention struck out the provision requiring that all money bills originate in that body.

Thursday, August 9, 1787
The Convention voted to affirm that the House of Representatives would have the sole power of impeachment. It voted that senators should have been citizens for at least nine years. It also agreed to give Congress power to regulate the times and places of Senate elections.

Friday, August 10, 1787
The Convention voted against requiring property qualifications for members of Congress. It voted to require two-thirds of a vote by a house of Congress to expel a member.

Saturday, August 11, 1787
The Convention rejected measures that would have given Congress power to omit matters from its journals that it thought required secrecy. In conjunction with discussion of the provision related to congressional adjournment, delegates discussed possible locations for the national capital.

Sunday, August 12, 1787
Convention not in session.

Monday, August 13, 1787
The Convention engaged in extensive discussion as to how many years individuals should have to be U.S. citizens to qualify for election to public office. Randolph reintroduced the proposal for requiring all money bills to originate in the House of Representatives, but it failed after extensive debate.

Tuesday, August 14, 1787
The Convention engaged in extensive discussion as to whether members of Congress should be ineligible for other offices or whether they should simply have to vacate their position in order to accept them. The delegates rejected a proposal that had emerged from the Committee of Detail providing for state payment of members of Congress in favor of a provision whereby members of Congress would be paid out of the national treasury.

Wednesday, August 15, 1787
Madison reintroduced a motion for the executive and Supreme Court to have power to void laws subject to an override by a supermajority in Congress, but the delegates rejected this as well as proposals for an absolute executive veto. The Convention then voted to vest veto power in the president, subject to being overturned by three-fourths majorities of both houses of Congress.

Thursday, August 16, 1787
The Convention began to consider the list of enumerated powers that the Committee of Detail had provided and adopted a number of these, including the power to lay and collect taxes and the power to regulate interstate and foreign commerce. It postponed a decision on whether to prohibit export taxes. The Convention decided against giving Congress the power to "emit bills on the credit of the United States."

Friday, August 17, 1787
The delegates agreed to a number of additional congressional powers, but altered the provision granting Congress the power to "make" war so that it now vested Congress with the power to "declare" it.

Saturday, August 18, 1787
The Convention referred a number of newly proposed powers back to the Committee of Detail and appointed a committee of eleven to consider federal assumption of state debts. The delegates extensively discussed congressional regulation of state militia and also referred this issue to the newly created committee.

Sunday, August 19, 1787
Convention not in session.

Monday, August 20, 1787
The delegates referred a number of proposed new congressional powers, many apparently from Charles Pinckney, back to the Committee of Detail. The Convention adopted the "necessary and proper" clause and, after extensive discussion, agreed to the provision regarding the definition and punishment of treason.

Tuesday, August 21, 1787
New Jersey's William Livingston submitted a report on the assumption of U.S. debts and the governing of the militia from the committee that he chaired on the subject, but the Convention postponed consideration of these matters. It discussed the apportionment of direct taxes according to representation in the House of Representatives as well as congressional taxation of exports.

Wednesday, August 22, 1787
The Convention appointed a committee of eleven to look into congressional powers over trade and navigation. The Convention voted to prohibit Congress from adopting bills of attainder and ex post facto laws and provided that Congress should discharge the debts of the United States. The Convention adjourned early so that members could watch John Fitch demonstrate a primitive steamboat on the nearby Delaware River.

Thursday, August 23, 1787
The Convention reexamined regulations on the militia, voting to grant Congress power to organize, arm and discipline the militia while reserving the power to appoint their officers to the states. The delegates restricted the right of individuals holding public office under the U.S. from receiving gifts from foreign governments, reaffirmed the supremacy clause, and granted Congress power to "suppress insurrection and repel invasion." The Convention also discussed the power of the Senate to make treaties and appoint ambassadors and judges.

Friday, August 24, 1787

Livingston reported from the Committee on Slave Trade and Navigation recommending that the Convention agree to allow states to import slaves until the year 1800, keeping the provision apportioning capitation taxes according to the census, and dropping the provision requiring two-thirds of Congress to assent to navigation acts. The Convention voted to vest disputes between states regarding land claims in the courts. The delegates also decided that Congress would select the president through a joint ballot.

Saturday, August 25, 1787

The Convention agreed that debts against the U.S. would remain as valid under the new government as under the Articles of Confederation. It altered the suggestion from the Committee on Slave Trade and Navigation so as to permit slave importation until the year 1808. It created a Committee on Commercial Discrimination to consider the collection of duties and tariffs.

Sunday, August 26, 1787

Convention not in session.

Monday, August 27, 1787

After agreeing to the oath of the president, the Convention largely focused on the judiciary. It voted to vest U.S. courts with cases in law and equity, to create a U.S. Supreme Court and such other lower courts as Congress should authorize, and it discussed and agreed to some cases of judicial jurisdiction.

Tuesday, August 28, 1787

The Committee on Slave Trade and Navigation proposed that Congress should be prohibited from preferring one port over another. The Convention considered provisions related to the judicial branch of government, and adopted a number of provisions limiting the powers of the states. The Convention adopted the privileges and immunities clause and the provision related to extradition.

Wednesday, August 29, 1787

The Convention created a five-man Committee on Interstate Comity and Bankruptcy. The Convention voted to accept an earlier committee recommendation to strike out the requirement for two-thirds congressional majorities to pass navigation acts, and adopted the fugitive slave clause. It also struck a provision that would allow existing states to set conditions regarding the public debt in regard to new states and engaged in debate as to whether the consent of existing states should be required before the formation of new states within their territories.

Thursday, August 30, 1787

The Convention voted for the provision regarding the admission of new states and for the provision guaranteeing states against invasion and domestic insurrections. The Convention voted for the provision prohibiting religious tests and discussed how the Constitution should be ratified.

Friday, August 31, 1787

The Convention agreed that the new Constitution would go into effect when ratified by conventions in nine or more states. It also agreed that no commercial regulations should be made preferring one port over another or obliging vessels entering one state from paying duties in another. The Convention created a Committee of Postponed Matters to consist of eleven delegates.

Saturday, September 1, 1787

On behalf of the Committee of Postponed Matters, David Brearly offered provisions relative to eligibility of members of Congress for other offices and the full faith and credit clause, and the Convention adjourned.

Sunday, September 2, 1787

Convention not in session.

Monday, September 3, 1787

The Convention agreed to the full faith and credit clause and to the provision vesting Congress with authority to pass uniform laws related to bankruptcies. It also adopted the provision limiting the emoluments that members of Congress could accept while in office.

Tuesday, September 4, 1787

The Committee on Postponed Matters submitted a large number of recommendations to the Convention, one of the most important of which became the basis for the Electoral College. The Convention spent much of the day discussing the Electoral College provision.

Wednesday, September 5, 1787

Brearly offered further recommendations from the Committee on Postponed Matters, a number of which the Convention adopted. These included congressional power over the seat of government. The Convention continued to discuss the newly proposed Electoral College mechanism.

Thursday, September 6, 1787

The Convention continued to tinker with the Electoral College. It also decided to agree to a four-year term for the president.

Friday, September 7, 1787

The Convention agreed to a vice president with power to preside over the Senate. It agreed to vest appointment of ambassadors and judges in the president with the advice and consent of the Senate. The Convention rejected the establishment of a Council of State.

Saturday, September 8, 1787

The Convention vested ratification of treaties in two-thirds of the Senate and agreed to the mechanism for impeachment and trial. It also provided that all money bills would originate in the House of Representatives. The Convention appointed a five-person Committee of Style to add polish to the Constitution.

Sunday, September 9, 1787

Convention not in session.

Monday, September 10, 1787

The Convention questioned whether constitutional amendments should be formulated by conventions called at the request of two-thirds of the states and accepted a provision whereby three-fourths of the states would ratify constitutional amendments. It continued to discuss how the proposed Constitution should be ratified. Edmund Randolph expressed his reservations about a number of provisions to which the Convention had agreed.

Tuesday, September 11, 1787

The Convention met briefly and adjourned to await the report from the Committee of Style.

Wednesday, September 12, 1787

Although Gouverneur Morris of Pennsylvania is believed to have been the committee's most important draftsman, Connecticut's William Johnson delivered the report from the Committee of Style. The Convention substituted a two-thirds, rather than a three-fourths, majority of Congress to override a presidential veto. The Convention rejected a motion by Virginia's George Mason to prepare a Bill of Rights and discussed state inspection fees on exports.

Thursday, September 13, 1787

The Convention proposed a committee to consider sumptuary legislation and continued to approve various provisions in the plan submitted by the Committee of Style.

Friday, September 14, 1787

The Convention continued going through the proposals of the Committee of Style, focusing on restrictions on Congress. It decided not to add a provision specifically vesting Congress with the power to create corporations.

Saturday, September 15, 1787

The Convention continued examining the proposals of the Committee of Style. It settled on the current method for amending the Constitution, providing that no state could be deprived of its equal suffrage in the Senate without its consent. Randolph, Mason, and Gerry all expressed the reasons they intended not to sign the Constitution. The Convention ordered the Constitution to be engrossed.

Sunday, September 16, 1787

Convention not in session.

Monday, September 17, 1787

Benjamin Franklin delivered a speech urging delegates to accept the possibility that they might be mistaken on some matters and to agree to the Constitution. The Convention agreed to provide that state representation in the House should not exceed one representative for every 30,000 inhabitants, rather than the previously designated 40,000. As 39 of 42 remaining delegates signed the Constitution, Franklin professed to believe that the sun painted on the back of the president's chair was rising on a new day, and the Convention adjourned.

FOR FURTHER READING

"The Convention Timeline." www.usconstitution.net/consttime2.html. Accessed 5/20/03.

Historians of the Independence National Historical Park, National Park Service. 1987. *1787: The Day-to-Day Story of the Constitutional Convention.* New York: Exeter Books.

Ruane, Michael E., and Michael D. Schaffer. 1987. *1787: Inventing America: A Day-by-Day Account of the Constitutional Convention.* Philadelphia: Philadelphia Inquirer.

St. John, Jeffrey. 1987. *Constitutional Journal: A Correspondent's Report from the Convention of 1787.* Ottawa, IL: Jameson Books.

Warren, Charles. 1928. *The Making of the Constitution.* Boston: Little, Brown.

ACHAEAN LEAGUE

The Achaean League was "a confederacy of southern Greek city-states." It lasted from about 180 to 146 B.C., when the Romans dissolved it (Richard 1994, 109). John Adams mentioned this confederacy in his *Defense of the Constitution of Government of the United States* (1787), the first volume of which was published just before the Constitutional Convention. Members of the Convention cited this league, often in conjunction with references to the earlier Amphictyonic League (also from ancient Greece) or to modern European confederacies, to illustrate the weaknesses of the existing government under the Articles of Confederation, which were in effect at the time of the U.S. Constitutional Convention and which the delegates regarded as similar.

Pennsylvania's James Wilson cited both leagues during the Constitutional Convention on June 6 as examples of leagues that were dissolved "by the encroachments of the constituent members" (Farrand 1937, I, 143). Virginia's James Madison, who had studied this and other leagues and included an analysis of their weaknesses when he wrote his "Vices of the Political System," made an almost identical point on June 19 (I, 317), when he further connected the weakness of the Achaean League to its eventual dissolution by Rome (I, 319). Similarly, on June 20, Wilson cited the Achaean and Amphictyonic Leagues as examples of leagues "formed in the infancy of

political Science" that contained "radical defects" (I, 343).

A scholar of classical influences on the Framers has observed that the Framers had relatively little knowledge of the league. Nevertheless, it continued to serve as a point of reference during the ratification debates between the Federalists and Antifederalists (Richard, 110–112).

See Also Adams, John; Amphictyonic League; Articles of Confederation; Classical Allusions and Influences; Confederal Government; Madison, James, Jr.; Vices of the Political System of the United States

FOR FURTHER READING

Farrand, Max, ed. 1937. *The Records of the Federal Convention.* 4 vols. New Haven, CT: Yale University Press.
Larson, J. A. O. 1968. *Greek Federal States: Their Institutions and History.* Oxford, UK: Clarendon Press.
Richard, Carl J. 1994. *The Founders and the Classics: Greece, Rome, and the American Enlightenment.* Cambridge, MA: Harvard University Press.

ADAMS, JOHN (1735–1826)

John Adams was one of the most influential Founding Fathers who did *not* attend the Constitutional Convention of 1787. Born in Braintree, Massachusetts (now Quincy), outside Boston in 1735 (his boyhood home and the home where he and his wife lived are still open to the public), Adams attended Harvard, studied for the bar, rose relatively quickly in the legal profession, and became an ardent Patriot—which did not, however, stop him from defending the British officers involved in the Boston Massacre. Adams was among the first and most vocal members of the First and Second Continental Congresses who pushed for independence from Great Britain, and he placed George Washington's name in nomination as commander-in-chief of the colonial forces. One of Congress's most active committee members, Adams served on the five-man committee to draft the Declaration of Independence, but he left the primary work to Thomas Jefferson.

Adams began as a believer in the British Constitution but concluded that this balanced government was not balanced in regard to its treatment of its colonies in the New World. In 1776, Adams published his *Thoughts on Government*. At a time when states were beginning to write their own constitutions, it was designed to help establish—in words that Adams liked to quote from James Harrington's (1611–1677) *Commonwealth of Oceana* first published in 1656—"an Empire of Laws, and not of men" (Lint and Ryerson 1986, 26). *Thoughts on Government* advocated a bicameral legislature, with a representative assembly that was directly elected by the people, and a council. He believed the governor should have an absolute veto over the legislature and that judges should hold office during good behavior (for life). This model is believed to have directly influenced the constitutions of New Jersey, Virginia, and North Carolina and indirectly influenced a number of others. Adams believed these constitutions fell short, however, in not having been proposed by special conventions called for this purpose and then ratified by the people.

Adams was given a chance to improve on these models when he was asked by such a convention to write a constitution for his home state of Massachusetts in 1779. Adams did so, following some existing state constitutions by adding a bill of rights and by establishing three strong branches of

John Adams, primary author of the Massachusetts Constitution (Pixel That)

government, including a bicameral legislature. Adams was explicit about the fact that this government embodied separation of powers rather than legislative sovereignty. Adams's Massachusetts constitution went into effect in 1780 and remains the oldest such document in continuous operation. This document was one of the models that were familiar to the members of the Convention when they were considering a new Constitution for the United States. George W. Carey and James McClellan have accordingly observed that Adams was "in many respects the father of American constitutionalism" (2001, xxix, note 19).

Adams, who helped negotiate the Treaty of Paris that ended the Revolutionary War, was subsequently appointed as a minister to Great Britain, where he was serving at the time of the U.S. Constitutional Convention. The first volume of his three-volume defense of American state constitutions, entitled the *Defence of the Constitutions of the United States,* reached Philadelphia just before the Convention convened, but it appears to have served more as a justification of the separation of powers within existing state constitutions in the wake of challenges posed by Shays's Rebellion than as the source of new ideas (Lint and Ryerson, 30–31).

Delegates do not appear to have referred to Adams frequently at the Convention, but Robert Yates's notes for June 27 indicate that Maryland's Luther Martin observed that "even the celebrated Mr. Adams, who talks so much of checks and balances, does not suppose it [bicameralism] necessary in a confederacy" (Farrand 1937, I, 439). In addition, North Carolina's William Davie wrote to James Iredell on June 19 indicating that he thought Adams's book was of "particular merit." He described it as "one continued encomium on the British Constitution, and that unequaled balance and security produced by the admirable mixture of democracy, aristocracy, and monarchy in the Government" (quoted in Robinson 1957, 188).

Adams returned from Great Britain in time to be elected as the nation's first vice president. He was sometimes ridiculed for his attempts to set a "high tone" to this new government, as in his mode of address and in devising grandiose titles that Congress rejected for the president. Adams took the job presiding over the Senate seriously and often broke tie votes in favor of the Washington administration.

Although he was a strong Federalist, Adams often found himself at odds with Secretary of the Treasury Alexander Hamilton. Hamilton was unable to block Adams's election as the second president, but, in part because of Hamilton's maneuvers, a Democratic-Republican, Thomas Jefferson, was selected to serve as vice president. Adams succeeded in keeping the United States from war with France during his presidency but made the mistake of retaining cabinet members from the Washington administration (many of whom remained loyal to Alexander Hamilton) rather than appointing his own. His administration also marked the adoption of the Alien and Sedition Acts, which threatened civil liberties and prompted James Madison and Thomas Jefferson to pen the Virginia and Kentucky Resolutions in response. Adams left office embittered after being defeated in the election of 1800 by rival Thomas Jefferson.

One of Adams's most important contributions to the future interpretation and stability of the Constitution was his outgoing appointment of his secretary of state, John Marshall of Virginia, as chief justice of the United States. Marshall used this post to become the chief expositor of the new Constitution and a defender of a strong national government. Among his most important decisions were *Marbury v. Madison* (1803), establishing judicial review of congressional legislation, and *McCulloch v. Maryland* (1819), affirming the constitutionality of the national bank.

Later in life Adams and Jefferson, who had been friends during the Revolution, were reconciled and carried on an engaging correspondence (see Peterson 1976). Both died on July 4, 1826, the fiftieth anniversary of the adoption of the Declaration of Independence.

Although he was vain, ambitious, and desirous of distinction, Adams was also honest, hardworking, and devoted to his country. He was married to Abigail Smith Adams, the daughter of a clergyman, who was in many ways his intellectual equal and to whom he was extremely devoted. The Adamses' son, John Quincy Adams, was selected as the sixth president of the United States, the only such father-son pair to serve before the election of the two Bushes.

See Also Declaration of Independence; Federalist and Democratic-Republican Parties; Hamilton, Alexander; Jefferson, Thomas; Massachusetts; Massachusetts Constitution of 1780; Mixed Government; Paris, Treaty of; President, Title

FOR FURTHER READING

Appleby, Joyce. 1973. "The New Republican Synthesis and the Changing Political Ideas of John Adams." *American Quarterly* 25 (December): 578–595.

Carey, George W., and James McClellan. 2001. "Editor's Introduction." *The Federalist*. Alexander Hamilton, James Madison, and John Jay. Indianapolis, IN: Liberty Fund.

Ellis, Joseph J. 1993. Passionate Sage: *The Character and Legacy of John Adams*. New York: W. W. Norton.

Farrand, Max, ed. 1937. *The Records of the Federal Convention.* 4 vols. New Haven, CT: Yale University Press.

Lint, Gregg L., and Richard Alan Ryerson. 1986. "The Separation of Powers: John Adams' Influence on the Constitution." *this Constitution,* no. 11 (Summer): 25–31.

Pencak, William. 1999. "Adams, John." *American National Biography.* Ed. John A. Garraty and Mark C. Carnes. Vol. 1 of 24. New York: Oxford University Press, 100–106.

Peterson, Merrill D. 1976. *Adams and Jefferson: A Revolutionary Dialogue.* New York: Oxford University Press.

Robinson, Blackwell P. 1957. *William R. Davie.* Chapel Hill: University of North Carolina Press.

AFRICAN AMERICANS

At the time of the Constitutional Convention, most Africans in America had been brought there without their consent and were enslaved. Seventeen to 19 delegates to the Convention owned slaves. These delegates studiously avoided using the word "slavery" in the Constitution itself (slaves were most frequently referred to as "such other persons"), leading Abraham Lincoln later to observe that slavery "is hid away in the constitution, just as an afflicted man hides away a wen [cyst] or cancer which he dares not cut out at once, lest he bleed to death" (Kammen 1987, 102).

This precedent was not new. New Jersey's William Paterson observed at the Constitutional Convention that "the 8 art: of Confedn. had been ashamed to use the terms 'Slaves' & had substituted a description" (Farrand 1937, I, 561). Significantly, early proposals for specifically mentioning that voting would be apportioned according to the numbers of "white men" were also dropped from the document (II, 350), perhaps for the same reason that delegates found it useful not to refer directly to slavery.

Constitutional Provisions

Altogether, the delegates to the Convention adopted five provisions related to African American slaves. The three-fifths clause, found in Article I, Section 2 of the Constitution, provided that slaves, described as "such other persons," would be counted toward congressional representation as three-fifths of a person. A second provision, often linked by historians to the first although it was adopted independently, is found in the clause in Article I, Section 9 apportioning "direct" taxes by a similar formula. A third provision found in Article I, Section 9 limited taxation of slave importations for 20 years, replacing an earlier version that would have allowed for higher taxation in the year 1800. A fourth provision found in Article V entrenched the provisions related to slave taxation, representation, and importation so that they could not be amended. A fifth and final provision, found in Article IV, Section 2, and usually called the fugitive slave clause, required that "No Person held to Service of Labour in one State, under the Laws thereof, escaping into another, shall, in Consequence of any Law or Regulation therein, be discharged from such Service or Labour, but shall be delivered up on Claim of the Party to whom such Service of Labour may be due."

Other related clauses included a congressional obligation listed in Article I, Section 8, for suppressing insurrections; provisions in Article I, Sections 9 and 10, against taxing exports (which would have included staples produced by slave labor); indirect incorporation of the three-fifths clause in the formula for apportioning the Electoral College; and the provision in Article IV, Section 3, providing for the admission of future states. The requirements for supermajorities in the amending process and elsewhere in the Constitution arguably also provided a likely veto both to free- and slave-state combinations (for further elaboration, see Finkelman 1996, 3–6).

Modern sensibilities about the great injustices and inhumanity of chattel slavery, as well as the hindsight provided by the bloody Civil War (1861–1865) that later centered on this issue, led to the conclusion that the delegates' failure to deal decisively with the issue of slavery and the status of African Americans was arguably their greatest omission. Delegates at the Convention discussed the issue, but not as extensively as one might have expected given its later prominence. Moreover, although the strongest support for slav-

Death of Attucks, Boston Massacre by J. E. Taylor. A depiction of the death of Crispus Attucks, the first American killed by the British during the Boston Massacre. (Corbis)

ery came from the Southern states, delegates from the Middle states (including Virginia, where slavery was legal), including slaveholders, made some of the most impassioned declamations against this institution. Many undoubtedly shared the view of Virginia's Edmund Randolph, who, in referring to the three-fifths clause, "lamented that such a species of property existed. But as it did exist the holders of it would require this security" (I, 594).

One difficulty in interpreting Convention resolutions related to slavery is the temptation to read later discussions of slavery back into Convention debates and to assume that Northern opinion was strongly antislavery and that Southern opinion was strongly proslavery. There was, in fact, a nascent movement against the institution of slavery, and it was more prominent in the North than in the South. Notably, the Pennsylvania Society for the Abolition of Slavery had presented Benjamin Franklin with an address asking the Convention

to suppress the African slave trade, although Franklin had decided that he "had thought it advisable to let them lie over for the present" (Hutson 1987, 44). However, there is general agreement that the Convention preceded the time before widespread abolitionism had taken hold in the North or justifications of slavery as a "positive good" had taken hold in the South (on this subject, see Pease and Pease 1965). Delegates to the Convention discussed African Americans, who were usually referred to as "blacks," "Negroes," or "slaves," in a number of contexts.

Slave Revolts

Notes by New York's Alexander Hamilton for June 1 indicate that one of his fears of a plural executive was that "slaves might be easily enlisted" (Farrand I, 73), presumably by an Eastern (Northern) member attempting to leverage members of the Middle or Southern states. Virginia's James Madison later mentioned slavery in the context of "the internal tranquility of the States" and "the insurrections in Massts." (I, 318), an undoubted reference to the taxpayer revolt known as Shays's Rebellion. On a number of subsequent occasions, often in context of discussion of the provision whereby the national government was bound to suppress insurrections at the request of the states, members of Northern states referred to the burden of defending Southerners against slave revolts, while Southerners typically affirmed that, if necessary, they could defend themselves. Commenting on the continuing importation of slaves, Rufus King of Massachusetts observed that the new government was designed to protect against both external invasion and internal sedition and asked, "Shall all the States then be bound to defend each; & shall each be at liberty to introduce a weakness which will render defence more difficult?" (II, 220).

Slavery as a Source of Aristocracy

Plantation slavery, such as was common in the South, depended on keeping fellow human beings in bondage and on the pronounced distinction between master and slaves. It also produced great wealth for the white master class, increasing the economic distinctions among citizens. In Madison's discussion of insurrection cited in the previous paragraph of this entry, he observed that "where slavery exists, the Republican Theory becomes still more fallacious" (I, 318). As a reluctant slaveholder who was constantly emphasizing distinctions based on property at the Convention, and in his explication of this theme in *Federalist* No. 10, Madison was among those who recognized that slavery laid the basis for extreme inequality in those states where it existed.

Persons or Property?

Although others at the Convention emphasized the differences between the large states and the small ones, Madison argued that the greatest dis-

tinctions at the Convention were between the Northern and Southern states (I, 476). These distinctions, in turn, rested on what fellow Virginian George Mason called (in opposing giving equal representation to the slaves) "this peculiar source of property, over & above the other species of property common to all the States" (I, 581).

This description of slaves as property rankled some members of the Convention. In 1787, as in later conflicts over slavery, debate swirled around whether slaves were legally best characterized as human beings or as property. In part because of questions of representation and taxation, classifications did not always follow anticipated North-South divisions. Elbridge Gerry of Massachusetts wondered why "blacks, who were property in the South," should "be in the rule of representation more than the cattle & horses of the North" (I, 201). Without apparently giving it a second thought, Maryland's Luther Martin said that he would "not trust a government organized upon the reported plan [the revised Virginia Plan] for all the slaves of Carolina or the horses and oxen of Massachusetts" (I, 441). But New Jersey's William Paterson made a similar observation in opposing a proposal to represent states according to "numbers and wealth": "He could regard Negroes slaves in no light but as property. They are no free agents, have no personal liberty, no faculty of acquiring property, but on the contrary are themselves property, & like other property entirely at the will of the Master" (I, 561).

Gouverneur Morris of Pennsylvania did not directly compare slaves to property, but he did observe that if "blacks" were to be included in the census, "the people of Pena. would revolt at the idea of being put on a footing with slaves" (I, 583).

A State or National Concern?

In 1787, as today, the regulation of private property was typically understood to be an individual state concern. Especially for those who regarded slaves as property, one solution to the problem of slavery—which the Convention seems ultimately to have largely followed—was to regard the institution largely as a state domestic concern. Attempting to deflect discussions of the morality of slavery and of slave importation, Connecticut's Oliver Ellsworth argued that delegates should set moral considerations aside:

> Let every State import what it pleases. The morality or wisdom of slavery are considerations belonging to the States themselves—what enriches a part enriches the whole, and the States are the best judges of their particular interest. The old confederation had not meddled with this point, and he did not see any greater necessity for bringing it within the policy of the new one. (II, 364)

The Permanence or Impermanence of Slavery

Judgments of slavery were sometimes related to delegates' views as to the permanence or impermanence of the institution. Connecticut's Oliver Ellsworth thus observed:

> Let us not intermeddle. As population increases; poor laborers will be so plenty as to render slaves useless. Slavery in time will not be a speck in our Country. Provision is already made in Connecticut for abolishing it. And the abolition has already taken place in Massachusetts. (II, 371)

Similarly, Sherman observed that "the abolition of slavery seemed to be going on in the U.S. & that the good sense of the several States would probably by degrees compleat it" (II, 369–370).

Clearly, if this observation were true, there was little need for delegates to the Convention to stir the waters and risk opposition to the document they were proposing. This theme was in some tension, however, with a belief, frequently expressed at the Convention, that the Southern states—where slavery was flourishing—were growing, and would continue to grow, at a faster rate than the rest of the Union, entitling this region to ever more representation in Congress.

The Immorality of Slavery

To be sure, there were delegates at the Convention who condemned slavery as not only inconvenient

but immoral. Such delegates recognized the incongruity between the continuing existence of slavery and the lofty words of the Declaration of Independence (1776), which had proclaimed that "all men are created equal." In opposing the continuing importation of slaves, Maryland's Luther Martin noted that slavery "was inconsistent with the principles of the revolution" and that it was "dishonorable to the American character to have such a feature in the Constitution" (II, 364).

Gouverneur Morris made one of the most impassioned speeches in regard to slavery. He gave prominence to the immorality of slavery and, like other delegates, predicted that it would bring God's judgment. Madison summarized: "He never would concur in upholding domestic slavery. It was a nefarious institution—It was the curse of heaven on the States where it prevailed" (II, 221).

Morris's Speech and the Effect of Slavery on Manners

In words that must have been especially painful for Southern delegates to hear, Morris proceeded in a miniature travelogue to portray the effects of slavery on the states where it was countenanced:

> Compare the free regions of the Middle States, where a rich & noble cultivation marks the prosperity & happiness of the people, with the misery & poverty which overspread the barren wastes of Va. Maryd. & the other States having slaves. [Travel thro' ye whole Continent & you behold the prospect continually varying with the appearance & disappearance of slavery. The moment you leave ye E. Sts. & enter N. York, the effects of the institution become visible; Passing thro' the Jerseys and entering Pa—every criterion of superior improvement witnesses the change. Proceed Southwdly, & every step you take thro' ye great regions of slaves, presents a desert increasing with ye increasing proportion of these wretched beings.] (II, 221–222)

Morris went on to touch on some of the themes delineated above. What exactly was the status of slaves? "Are they men? Then make them Citizens & let them vote? Are they property?

Why then is no other property included?" Morris proceeded to question the morality of slavery and especially of the slave trade:

> The admission of slaves into Representation when fairly explained comes to this: that the inhabitant of Georgia and S.C. who goes to the Coast of Africa and in defiance of the most sacred laws of humanity tears away his fellow creatures from their dearest connections & dam[n]s them to the most cruel bondages, shall have more votes in a Govt. instituted for the protection of the rights of mankind, than the Citizen of Pa or N. Jersey who views with a laudable horror, so nefarious a practice. (II, 222)

Morris added, "The Houses in this City (Philada.) are worth more than all the wretched slaves which cover the rice swamps of South Carolina" (II, 222). Morris followed with another familiar observation: "The vassalage of the poor has ever been the favorite offspring of Aristocracy" (II, 222). He then asked whether the Northern states were "to bind themselves to march their militia for the defence of the S. States; for their defence agst those very slaves of whom they complain," commenting soon after that continuing slave importation increases "the danger of attack, and the difficulty of defence" (II, 222). Finally, Morris appealed to the interests of posterity and seemingly suggested a method for emancipation that no other delegate appears to have openly advocated: "He would sooner submit himself to a tax for paying for all the Negroes in the U. States. than saddle posterity with such a Constitution" (II, 223).

Mason's Speech and Reactions to It

As if not to be outdone by a Northern delegate, Virginia's George Mason repeated many of these themes in a speech that rivaled Morris's for its condemnation of slavery. Mason gave his speech on August 22 and repeated a charge against Great Britain that Thomas Jefferson had made in writing the Declaration of Independence: "The infernal traffic originated in the avarice of British Merchants. The British Govt. constantly checked the attempts of Virginia to put a stop to it" (II, 370). Agreeing with other critics, Mason observed that the presence of slaves had offered an opportunity to the British to stir up insurrection during the Revolutionary War and cited examples of such insurrections from classical history. Although Sherman had anticipated that slavery might expire on its own, Mason argued, in a position that seems to foreshadow the later position of Abraham Lincoln and the Republican Party, that if South Carolina and Georgia were permitted to continue slave importation, the institution would continue to spread in the West and will "fill that Country with slaves" (II, 370). Mason, himself a slave owner, now launched into his description of the evils of the institution, adding to some that had been mentioned earlier. As enlightened as his speech was, it reflected some racist assumptions in his comparisons of the value of blacks and whites:

> Slavery discourages arts & manufacturers. The poor despise labor when performed by slaves. They prevent the immigration of Whites, who really enrich & strengthen a Country. They produce the most pernicious effect on manners. Every master of slaves is born a petty tyrant. They bring the judgment of heaven on a Country. As nations can not be rewarded or punished in the next world they must be in this. By an inevitable chain of causes & effects providence punishes national sins, by national calamities. (II, 370)

Lest sharing the blame with the British might not be adequate, Mason proceeded to lament that "some of our Eastern brethren had from a lust of gain embarked in this nefarious traffic." He further "held it essential in very point of view, that the Genl. Govt. should have power to prevent the increase of slavery" (II, 370).

Mason's speech initiated renewed debate, but most of it touched on familiar themes. Connecticut's Oliver Ellsworth, who may well have resented Mason's deprecations against Northern merchants, fenced with his Southern colleague: "As he [Ellsworth] had never owned a slave [he] could not judge of the effects of slavery on character" (II, 370–371). Moreover, if Mason were to take the moral high ground, Ellsworth thought

A Petition against the Slave Trade

The Pennsylvania Society for the Abolition of Slavery presented Benjamin Franklin with an address asking the Convention to suppress the African slave trade. It relied heavily on religious terminology. After reviewing the history of the slave trade, the petition observed that American "Pretentions to a love of liberty or a regard for national Character" would be vain at the time the nation shared "in the profits of a Commerce that can only be conducted upon Rivers of human tears and Blood" (Hutson 1987, 44). The petition continued:

By all the Attributes, therefore, of the Deity which are offended by this inhuman traffic—by the Union of our whole species in a common Ancestor and by all the obligations which result from it—by the apprehensions and terror of the righteous Vengeance of God in national Judgments—by the certainty of the great and awful day of retribution—by the efficacy of the Prayers of good Men, which would only insult the Majesty of Heaven, if offered up in behalf of our Country while the Iniquity we deplore continues among us—by the sanctity of the Christian Name—by the Pleasures of domestic Connections and the pangs which attend these Dissolutions—by the Captivity and Sufferings of our *American* brethren in Algiers which seem to be intended by divine Providence to awaken us to a sense of the Injustice and Cruelty of dooming our *African* Bretheren to perpetual Slavery and Misery . . . and by every other consideration that religion Reason Policy and Humanity can suggest the Society implore the present Convention to make the Suppression of the African trade in the United States, a part of their important deliberations. (Quoted in Hutson, 45)

Although Franklin decided not to introduce the resolution at the Convention (and so informed the society on July 2, 1787) (Hutson, 44), many of the points made in the petition were introduced by delegates on the Convention floor.

FOR FURTHER READING

Hutson, James H., ed. 1987. *Supplement to Max Farrand's* The Records of the Federal Convention of 1787. New Haven, CT: Yale University Press.

---

that it was worth noting that the position of delegates from Virginia and Maryland reflected the fact that slaves multiplied rapidly enough in these states that they did not need further imports.

Such seemingly personal arguments aside, Ellsworth was convinced that slavery was not the business of the new government and that if left to itself the problem would vanish. Then, putting a most extraordinarily positive spin on the dangers of slave insurrections, Ellsworth observed that this danger "will become a motive to kind treatment of the slaves" (II, 371).

South Carolina's Charles Pinckney walked the line between countenancing and condemning slavery. On the one hand, the institution had been sanctioned throughout history: "In all ages one half of mankind have been slaves." On the other hand, he would himself favor discontinuation of slave importation, and he suggested that "if the S. States were let alone they will probably of themselves stop importations" (II, 371).

Pinckney's cousin, General Charles Cotesworth Pinckney, also from South Carolina, disagreed. He argued that South Carolina and Georgia "cannot do without slaves" and added to Ellsworth's analysis of the motives behind Mason's arguments by noting that by stopping slave importation, Virginians would increase the value of their own slaves. The general calculated the benefit of slavery by thinking about economics: "The more slaves, the more produce to employ the carrying trade; The more consumption also, and the more of this, the more of revenue for the common treasury" (I, 371).

Georgia's Abraham Baldwin reinforced the Pinckneys' attack on Virginia by arguing that his state had "hitherto supposed a Genl Governmt to be the pursuit of the Central States who wished to have a vortex for every thing" (II, 372). In an analogy that tended to suggest that slaves were not human, Baldwin referred to a sect (Madison's *Notes* do not record which one, although it may have been the Hindus) whose members "carried their ethics beyond the mere equality of men, extending their humanity to the claims of the whole animal creation" (II, 372).

Elbridge Gerry somewhat refined earlier arguments on the domestic rights of states by observing that although he "thought we had nothing to do with the conduct of the States as to Slaves," members of the Convention "ought to be careful not to give any sanction to it" (II, 372). Debate continued among a number of other delegates but largely along the lines of argument described above. Debates in state ratifying conventions further explored the status of free blacks.

Postscript

Prior to the Civil War, partisans on both sides of the slavery debate scoured the Constitution to find ammunition indicating that the Constitution was either chiefly a proslavery or an antislavery document. Radical abolitionists were among those who denounced the Constitution as "an agreement with hell, a covenant with death." In *Scott v. Sandford* (1857), Chief Justice Roger Taney effectively interpreted the Declaration of Independence and the Constitution to read "all white men are created equal," but his decision, denying citizenship to African Americans, did not avert the Civil War and was later overturned by the Fourteenth Amendment (1868).

Scholars continue to debate whether delegates to the Convention could have done more to undermine slavery than they did while still preserving the Union. The answer would seem to be that the delegates might at least have abolished the slave trade fairly quickly had they been willing to part with the three states south of Virginia. This could arguably have put both Virginia and the rest of the nation in a precarious position vis-à-vis

foreign governments and might or might not have resulted in the eventual abolition of slavery in those states joining the Union. Similarly, it is possible that an alliance giving still more direct support to slavery might have been made between the Southern and Middle states at the possible cost of some Northern ones. This too would have left open the possibility for eventual conflict between the two divisions.

Especially after Eli Whitney's invention of the cotton gin, which made the continuing production of cotton in the South economical, hopes for the gradual elimination of slavery proved chimerical, albeit in part because of the decision not to stop the importation of slaves for another 20 years. Although long since repealed by the Fourteenth Amendment, the three-fifths clause remains something of a constitutional embarrassment, and yet, despite its diminutive assessment of slaves, it referred to them as "persons" rather than as property. Compared to debates between the large states and small states over state representation in Congress, selection of the president, and the powers of Congress, slavery occupied relatively little debate at the Convention.

Although the delegates at the Convention effectively postponed ultimate resolution of this institution, the nation ultimately faced it with the Civil War and Amendments Thirteen through Fifteen, which were ratified from 1865 to 1870. The first of these amendments abolished chattel slavery; the second defined citizenship and guaranteed the rights of all persons; and the third, although initially quite ineffective, prohibited discrimination in voting on the basis of race. These amendments stand as testimony to the unfinished business that delegates left to future generations.

See Also Congress, House of Representatives, Representation in; Declaration of Independence; Fugitive Slave Clause; Slave Importation; Slavery; Three-fifths Clause

FOR FURTHER READING

Farrand, Max, ed. 1937. *The Records of the Federal Convention.* 4 vols. New Haven, CT: Yale University Press.
Finkelman, Paul. 1996. *Slavery and the Founders: Race*

and Liberty in the Age of Jefferson. Armond, NY: M. E. Sharpe.

Freehling, William W. 1972. "The Founding Fathers and Slavery." *American Historical Review* 77 (February): 81–93.

Horton, James Oliver. 1986. "Weevils in the Wheat: Free Blacks and the Constitution, 1787–1860." American Political Association, American Historical Association. *this Constitution: Our Enduring Legacy.* Washington, DC: Congressional Quarterly.

Kammen, Michael. 1987. *A Machine That Would Go of Itself: The Constitution in American Culture.* New York: Alfred A. Knopf.

Lively, Donald. E. 1992. *The Constitution and Race.* New York: Praeger.

Pease, William H., and Jane H. Pease. 1965. *The Antislavery Argument.* Indianapolis, IN: Bobbs-Merrill.

West, Thomas G. 1997. *Vindicating the Founders: Race, Sex, Class, and Justice in the Origins of America.* Lanham, MD: Rowman and Littlefield Publishers.

Wiencek, Henry. 2002. *An Imperfect God: George Washington, His Slaves, and the Creation of America.* New York: Farrar, Straus and Giroux.

AGES OF DELEGATES

The average age of the delegates to the Constitutional Convention was about 42. Gordon Lloyd and Jeff Sammon have prepared a most helpful chart of the ages of the delegates that shows that the ages ranged from a low of 26 for New Jersey's Jonathan Dayton to a high of 81 for Pennsylvania's Benjamin Franklin.

The chart indicates that there were four delegates, including Dayton, below the age of 30, 14 delegates who were in their thirties, 23 delegates who were in their forties, 8 delegates who were in their fifties, 5 who were in their sixties, none in their seventies, and only Franklin who was in his eighties. The ages of some of the better-known delegates were as follows: Charles Pinckney, 29; Alexander Hamilton, 30; Rufus King, 32; Edmund Randolph, 34; Gouverneur Morris, 35; James Madison, 36; Luther Martin, 39; Charles Cotesworthy Pinckney, 41; Oliver Ellsworth, 42; Pierce Butler, 43; Elbridge Gerry, 43; James Wilson, 45; Hugh Williamson, 52; John Dickinson, 55; George Washington, 55; George Mason, 62; and Roger Sherman, 66.

See Also Delegates, Collective Profile

FOR FURTHER READING

Lloyd, Gordon, and Jeff Sammon. "The Age of Framers in 1787." http://teachingamericanhistory. org/convention/delegates/age.html.

ALBANY PLAN OF UNION

Along with the New England Confederation (1643 to 1685), scholars often cite the Albany Plan of Union as one of the precursors of the Articles of Confederation, the weaknesses of which led to the Constitutional Convention of 1787. Benjamin Franklin, the primary author of the Albany Plan, used it as the basis of a proposed plan of government during the Second Continental Congress (a plan that was significantly modified in the writing of the Articles of Confederation), and, of course, he was one of Pennsylvania's delegates to the U.S. Constitutional Convention.

The Albany Plan, like the Articles that followed, was designed to provide for greater coordination among colonies that had previously rested on their individual resources. Just as the Articles of Confederation arose out of the need for united military action against the British, so, too, the Albany Plan arose out of the need to respond in concerted fashion against the alliance of French and Indians that would soon result in war.

Delegates from seven colonies met at the Albany Congress in 1754 under encouragement from the British Board of Trade (Foner and Garraty 1991, 24) and drew up a plan with a preamble and 23 sections. The preamble applied for an act of the British Parliament to form "one general government . . . in America, including all the said colonies, within and under which government each colony may retain its present constitution." This government would consist of a "President-General" appointed by the English crown and a

"Grand Council" appointed by state legislatures. Council members were to serve three-year terms, with states being represented by from two to seven delegates according to the "proportion of money arising out of each Colony to the general treasury." All acts of council would require the "assent of the "President-General" and, in a mechanism that resembles the modern legislative veto, all acts so adopted would remain in force if not subsequently disapproved by the English king in council within a three-year period.

The primary purposes of the Union related to defense and security. The plan would have given collective authority to the colonies to make war and peace, enter into treaties, purchase land from the Indians, govern new settlements, support the military, levy taxes, and the like. A quorum would require 25 members from a majority of the colonies. Provisions were made for replacing the president-general in case of his death and for allowing colonies to defend themselves in the case of sudden emergencies (the 1954 Albany Plan of Union).

It appears that, before the plan arrived for British inspection, the British government had already decided to pursue an alternate course and send regiments of Irish troops to defend the colonists. One historian observed that "apparently 1754 was a year in which English fear of an American revolt was enjoying one of its periodic revivals" (Olson 1960, 31). Although the colonies might have been more successful in offering collective resistance to the French and Indians under the Albany Plan, the English knew that the colonies might also resist them.

The provision for a Grand Council under the Albany Plan seems akin to the Congress under the Articles of Confederation. However, not only did the scheme of representation differ (being based on tax contributions) but the president-general appears more akin to the presidency established at the Constitutional Convention of 1787 than to the weak executives that operated under the Articles. The Albany Plan provided the basis for a plan of government introduced by Joseph Galloway of Pennsylvania in the First Continental Congress and rejected by a vote of 6-5.

See Also Articles of Confederation; Dominion of New England; Federalism; Franklin, Benjamin; Galloway Plan; New England Confederation

FOR FURTHER READING

Foner, Eric, and John A. Garraty, eds. 1991. *The Reader's Companion to American History.* Boston: Houghton Mifflin.

Isaacson, Walter. 2003. *Benjamin Franklin: An American Life.* New York: Simon and Schuster.

Matthews, L. L. 1914. "Benjamin Franklin's Plans for a Colonial Union, 1750–1775." *American Political Science Review* 8 (August): 393–412.

Olson, Alison Gilbert. 1960. "The British Government and Colonial Union, 1754." *William and Mary Quarterly,* 3rd ser. 17 (January): 22–34.

"The 1754 Albany Plan of Union." University of Oklahoma Law Center, http://www.law.ou.edu/hist/albplan.html.

AMENDING PROCESS

As the American colonists discovered in their conflict with Great Britain, a constitution that cannot bend or change is likely to break. Such change can take place formally, as in an amending process, or less formally, through the exercise of constitutional interpretation by institutions, especially the judiciary, entrusted with such powers.

Historical Background

The idea of a formal amending process grew in the New World setting, first appearing in some of the charters of William Penn as a complement to the idea of a constitutional covenant or compact, which eventually developed into constitutions. As they adopted their own constitutions, a number of states added formal amending provisions. Four states provided for amendments to be adopted through legislative action, three used the convention mechanism, and two had a council of censure that met periodically to revise their documents (Vile 1992, 25). In commenting on the Virginia state constitution and the Dutch confederacy on June 29 of the Constitutional Convention, Virginia's James Madison cited the inadequacy of state and confederal amending mechanisms as a reason not to load the document down with "inconsistent principles" (Farrand 1937, I, 475–476).

The Articles of Confederation followed the examples of several state constitutions by providing for an amending process, but their provision for legislative proposal and unanimous state consent proved to be too wooden, with one of the smallest states, Rhode Island, blocking a number of desired measures. As a result, the delegates to the Annapolis Convention called for a meeting of the states in Philadelphia. It was to be

> for the sole and express purpose of revising the Articles of Confederation and reporting to Congress and the several legislatures such alterations and provisions therein as shall, when agreed to in Congress, and confirmed by the states render the federal constitution adequate to the exigencies of Government and the preservation of the Union. (Solberg 1958, 64)

Today scholars routinely refer to the meeting in Philadelphia as the "Constitutional" Convention, implying that it was created for the purpose of drawing up a new constitution. In point of fact, contemporaries commonly referred to the Convention as a "Grand" or "Federal Convention." As one observer has noted, "The notion of a new 'constitution' would have scared away two-thirds of the members" (Bowen 1966, 4).

The Virginia and New Jersey Plans

When Edmund Randolph introduced the Virginia Plan on May 29, 1787, he went far beyond the congressional mandate. He essentially proposed a new form of government rather than attempting to patch the old. Defenders of the Convention's work later argued that the purpose for which the Convention had been called trumped their specific charge only to amend the document. Delegates could take further cover in the fact that their role was simply that of proposing the Constitution, while the people would ultimately have to approve or reject this document. As New York's Alexander Hamilton observed on June 18, "We can only propose and recommend—the power of ratifying or rejecting it is still in the states" (I, 295).

Randolph's proposal contained a vague provision for adopting amendments "whensoever it shall seem necessary" and, perhaps as a guard against the strengthened Congress that the plan proposed, added a stipulation that such amendment should not require congressional consent (I, 22). The first occasion that this provision was considered, South Carolina's Charles Pinckney openly doubted whether such a provision was necessary. Elbridge Gerry of Massachusetts responded that "the novelty & difficulty of the experiment requires periodic revision." He further observed both that "the prospect of such a revision will also give intermediate stability to the Govt." and that nothing in the experience of the states with such a mechanism suggested its "impropriety" (I, 122).

On June 11, there were still unspecified members who doubted the need for an amending process, but with a view to the situation that had brought the delegates to Philadelphia, Virginia's George Mason observed:

> The plan now to be formed will certainly be defective, as the Confederation has been found on trial to be. Amendments therefore will be necessary, and it will be better to provide for them, in an easy, regular and Constitutional way than to trust to chance and violence. (I, 203)

Commenting on the reservation contained in the Virginia Plan, Mason further observed:

> It would be improper to require the consent of the Natl. Legislature, because they may abuse their power, and refuse their consent on that very account. The opportunity for such an abuse, may be the fault of the Constitution calling for amendmt. (I, 203)

At that point, the delegates agreed to recommend an amending process but postponed the provision as to whether congressional consent should be required.

When William Paterson introduced the New Jersey Plan on June 15 (I, 242–245), he based his plan on revising, correcting, and enlarging, rather than on replacing, the Articles of Confederation. He did not specify an amending process, probably in anticipation of keeping the requirement for congressional proposal and unanimous state legislative approval in place.

July and August Discussions

Delegates reaffirmed their support for an amending process on July 23, but the provision was still inchoate (Farrand II, 87). In a fascinating detour, on this same day, members of the Convention discussed the desirability of oaths by governmental officials to support the Constitution. Pennsylvania's James Wilson expressed fear that such an oath could "too much trammel the Members of the Existing Govt in case future alterations should be necessary" (II, 87). Nathaniel Gorham of Massachusetts responded that "the oath could only require fidelity to the existing Constitution. A constitutional alteration of the Constitution, could never be regarded as a breach of the Constitution, or of any oath to support it" (II, 88).

Delegates appeared aware that the need for future amendments could be somewhat reduced by assuring that the Constitution was not too full of details. In notes taken from the Committee of Detail, Edmund Randolph thus observed that in writing the Constitution it was essential "to insert essential principles only, lest the operations of government should be clogged by rendering those provisions permanent and unalterable, which ought to be accommodated to times and events" (II, 137).

When, on August 8, Madison foresaw that guaranteeing one representative for every 40,000 U.S. residents could eventually "render the number of Representatives excessive," Nathaniel Gorham of Massachusetts doubted that the government would last this long. Connecticut's Oliver Ellsworth, in turn, observed that, if it did, "alterations may be made in the Constitution in the manner proposed in a subsequent article" (II, 221).

By August 30, the Convention had settled on a provision providing that "on the application of the Legislatures of two thirds of the States in the Union, for an amendment of this Constitution, the Legislature of the United States shall call a Convention for that purpose" (II, 467). The provision did not explain how amendments would be ratified. Although Gouverneur Morris of Pennsylvania suggested that Congress should be able to call such a convention whenever it pleased, the Convention simply approved the provision as it was.

The Final Week

The Convention reconsidered this provision seven days before its members signed the Constitution. Consistent with his increasing concern for states' rights, Elbridge Gerry of Massachusetts expressed concern that allowing two-thirds of the states to petition Congress for a convention might propose amendments "that may subvert the State-Constitutions altogether" (II, 557–558). Not surprisingly, the nationalistic Alexander Hamilton from New York had a different concern. Referring to the experience under the Articles of Confederation, he feared that the method under consideration was not easy enough. Specifically, he doubted that the state legislatures would apply for amendments "but with a view to increase their own powers." Moreover, Congress "will be the first to perceive and will be most sensible to the necessity of amendments, and ought also to be empowered, whenever two thirds of each branch should concur to call a Convention." Although no ratification mechanism was yet in place, Hamilton appeared to assume one because he further argued against the danger of allowing Congress to propose amendments by observing that "the people would finally decide the case" (II, 558).

Madison had practical concerns about the Convention mechanism. "How was a Convention to be formed? by what rule decide? what the force of its acts?" (II, 558).

In a motion seconded by Elbridge Gerry, Connecticut's Roger Sherman attempted to answer some of these questions by proposing that Congress should be able to propose amendments but that they would not become effective "until consented to by the several States" (II, 558). Undoubtedly remembering the effect of requiring state unanimity under the Articles of Confederation, Pennsylvania's James Wilson moved that amendments should require approval of two-thirds of the states. After this motion lost by a vote of 5-6, the Convention voted unanimously to allow three-fourths of the states to ratify (II, 559).

Still concerned over the Convention mechanism, Madison sought, in a motion seconded by Alexander Hamilton, to eliminate it. This motion proposed permitting two-thirds of both houses to propose amendments either on their own authority or upon application by two-thirds of the states, providing that such amendments would be ratified by either three-fourths of the state legislatures or by conventions in the same (II, 559).

After South Carolina's John Rutledge objected that he could never entrust such majorities to alter the provision permitting slave importation until 1808, Madison's amended motion was accepted by a vote of 9-1-1. Rutledge was not, however, the only delegate concerned about the interest of his own state and section. When debate on the resolution accordingly resumed on September 15, Connecticut's Roger Sherman expressed fears that the amending process might eventually undo the Great Compromise. He accordingly thought that the provision should be qualified so that "no State should be affected in its internal police, or deprived of its equality in the Senate" (II, 629). Perhaps remembering that the original Virginia Plan had proposed that congressional consent to amendments would be unnecessary, George Mason had yet another concern:

As the proposing of amendments is in both the modes to depend, in the first immediately, and in the second, ultimately, on Congress, no amendments of the proper kind would ever be obtained by the people, if the Government should become oppressive, as he verily believed would be the case. (II, 629)

Elbridge Gerry and Gouverneur Morris subsequently moved, as in an earlier proposal, to allow two-thirds of the states to apply for a convention. Madison did not think this provision was necessary, but his objection centered again on practical questions respecting "the form, the quorum &c" of the Convention mechanism.

If his sentiment is reported correctly, Roger Sherman then introduced a provision, which appeared to conflict with the concerns he had previously expressed about protecting state sovereignty. Indeed, if adopted, his provision–for allowing Congress to specify the majorities by which future amendments would be adopted–could arguably have led to legislative supremacy. Perhaps this is why his motion failed by a vote of 7-3-1. Similarly, Gerry's motion to strike the Convention mechanism for constitutional ratification failed by a vote of 10-1.

Sherman renewed his previous concern, moving that no state should "be affected in its internal police, or deprived of its equal suffrage in the Senate" (II, 630). Madison expressed concern over adding further reservations, and Sherman's motion failed by a vote of 8-3. The battle, however, was not over. Seconded by New Jersey's David Brearly, Sherman moved to strike the amending process altogether. Although this vote failed by a vote of 8-2-1, it was apparently sufficient to prompt Gouverneur Morris to move "that no State, without its consent shall be deprived of its equal suffrage in the Senate" (II, 631). Madison observed: "This motion being dictated by the circulating murmurs of the small States was agreed to without debate, no one opposing it, or on the question saying no" (II, 631).

Analysis

The amending mechanism, as incorporated in Article V of the Constitution, thus provided for two mechanisms for proposing amendments and two for ratifying them. Two-thirds majorities of

Jefferson and Madison on Constitutional Durability

Often designated as the "father" of the U.S. Constitution, in *Federalist* No. 43, James Madison defended the procedure for amending that document as "stamped with every mark of propriety" (Hamilton, Madison, and Jay 1961, 278). He observed that the process, which called for two-thirds of both houses of Congress to propose amendments, which would then be ratified by three-fourths of the states (or, in a still unused mechanism for two-thirds of the state legislatures to call a convention for amending the Constitution), guarded both "against that extreme facility, which would render the Constitution too mutable; and that extreme difficulty, which might perpetuate its discovered faults" (278).

Thomas Jefferson expressed one of his most fascinating ideas in a letter to his friend, fellow Virginian James Madison, dated September 6, 1789. In this letter, Jefferson articulated the idea "'that the earth belongs in usufruct to the living'; that the dead have neither powers nor rights over it" (quoted in Vile 1992). On the basis of this principle, which is arguably incorporated into modern "sunset" laws, Jefferson advanced the idea that neither one generation's debts nor its constitution should bind another; by this view each generation should review and potentially rewrite the constitution it had inherited.

In *Federalist* No. 43, Madison had opposed an idea raised by Jefferson in his *Notes on the State of Virginia*, whereby two-thirds of the members of any two branches of government could call for a constitutional convention. Madison was driven in part by his fear that frequent constitutional innovation would undermine the popular veneration that was useful in sustaining constitutional government. He had thus observed:

> As every appeal to the people would carry an implication of some defect in the government, frequent appeals would, in a great measure, deprive the government of that veneration which time bestows on every thing, and without which perhaps the wisest and freest government would not possess the requisite stability. (Hamilton, Madison, and Jay, 314)

Similarly, Madison poured cold water on Jefferson's idea, based largely on the doctrine that individuals who were born into society and decided to stay were giving their implied consent to that government (Vile, 64–65).

Despite the powerful arguments that Madison advanced in his correspondence, Jefferson continued to express greater tolerance for constitutional reform than did Madison. Most notably in a letter to Samuel Kerchival in 1816, Jefferson continued to point to the need for reform of the Virginia state government. Although his critique thus focused specifically on the state rather than

---

both houses can propose amendments, or two-thirds of the states can petition Congress to call a convention for this purpose. Amendments can, in turn, be ratified, at congressional specification, by three-fourths of the state legislatures or convention called therein. In two entrenchment clauses, the delegates specified that Article V would not interfere with slave importation prior to the year 1808 and would never deprive states of their equal representation in the Senate without their consent.

Article V should logically be considered in conjunction with the provision for constitutional ratification. Delegates sent their proposals to Congress, but they did not require, as the Annapolis Convention had specified, congressional consent. Moreover, they bypassed the requirement for unanimous consent of the existing state legislatures under the Articles of Confederation by specifying in Article VII of the document that the new Constitution would go into effect when ratified in conventions by nine of the states. If Rhode Island, which did not send delegates to the Convention, is excluded from the count, the nine-state ratification requirement was equivalent to the three-fourths requirement specified in the new amending process.

Although the proposed amending process con-

Jefferson and Madison on Constitutional Durability (continued)

on the national level, his words would have application to both kinds of constitutions:

> Some men look at constitutions with sanctimonious reverence, and deem them like the arc [sic] of the covenant, too sacred to be touched. They ascribe to the men of the preceding age a wisdom more than human, and suppose what they did to be beyond amendment. I knew that age well; I belonged to it, and labored with it. It deserved well of its country. It was very like the present, but without the experience of the present; and forty years of experience in government is worth a century of book-reading; and this they would say for themselves were they to rise from the dead. (Jefferson 1905, 12:10)

Jefferson went on to observe: "We might as well require a man to wear still the coat which fitted him when a boy, as civilized society to remain ever under the regimen of their barbarous ancestors" (12:12). As in his earlier correspondence with Madison, Jefferson again suggested that this should occur about once every generation, which he calculated at about 19 to 20 years.

The division is far too precise, but it is not inappropriate to suggest that Madison's view of cautious constitutional change has largely dominated at the national level while Jefferson's has been far more characteristic at the state level.

Whereas the U.S. Constitution has only been amended 27 times since its adoption, state constitutions have been amended and replaced far more frequently and, apart perhaps from that of Massachusetts, which was established in 1780, have not been as venerated. Madison seems to have worked on behalf of adoption of the Bill of Rights in part to prevent a second constitutional convention on the subject, and the mechanism in Article V of the Constitution for another national constitutional convention called by the states, although often threatened, has not yet been utilized.

FOR FURTHER READING

Hamilton, Alexander, James Madison, and John Jay. 1961. *The Federalist Papers.* Ed. Clinton Rossiter. New York: New American Library.

Jefferson, Thomas. 1905. *The Works of Thomas Jefferson.* Ed. Paul Leicester Ford. New York: G. P. Putnam's Sons, Knickerbocker Press.

Smith, Daniel Scott. 1999. "Population and Political Ethics: Thomas Jefferson's Demography of Generations." *William and Mary Quarterly,* 3rd ser. 56 (July): 591–612.

Vile, John R. 1992. *The Constitutional Amending Process in American Political Thought.* New York: Praeger.

---

tained a mechanism for the states to propose another convention, central proponents of the new document adamantly opposed taking such a route. On September 15, Edmund Randolph proposed that states might propose amendments as they ratified the Constitution. George Mason supplied a further argument:

> This Constitution had been formed without the knowledge or idea of the people. A second Convention will know more of the sense of the people, and be able to provide a system more consonant with it. It was improper to say to the people, take this or nothing. (II, 632)

South Carolina's Charles Pinckney appeared to reflect the majority viewpoint that "conventions are serious things, and ought not to be repeated" (II, 632).

The Amending Process and Constitutional Ratification

Pinckney and others thus argued that it would be better to secure the gains of the Convention and then push for additional amendments rather than take a chance that a second convention might undo the hard work of the first. Madison argued in the *Federalist Papers* that the amending mechanism guarded both "against that extreme facility, which would render the Constitution too mutable; and that extreme difficulty, which might perpetuate its discovered faults." He went on to argue against proposals, suggested by his friend Thomas Jefferson, for periodic constitutional revision. Having sought to replace one government he hoped to secure the next. He thus observed:

> As every appeal to the people would carry an implication of some defect in the government, frequent appeals would, in a great measure, deprive the government of that veneration which time bestows on every thing, and without which perhaps the wisest and freest governments would not possess the requisite stability. (quoted in Vile 1992, 36–37)

Although seemingly only mildly convinced that a bill of rights was necessary, Madison was its strongest advocate in the first Congress. He realized that until such a bill was adopted states would be tempted to call another convention that might undo the laborious work of the first. Although Madison hoped to intersperse new amendments within the existing constitutional text, Congress accepted the arguments of Roger Sherman for listing them separately at the end of the Constitution. Success in adopting the Bill of Rights is often cited as a reason for the success of the new document, thus vindicating a mechanism that, for better or worse, has proven more resistant to such adaptations throughout much of the rest of American history. Despite the introduction of thousands of amending proposals in Congress, most of them redundant, Congress has only proposed 33 by the necessary two-thirds majorities, and the states have successfully ratified only 26 of these.

See Also Articles of Confederation; Bill of Rights; Constitutional Convention Mechanism; Ratification, Convention Debates, and Constitutional Provision; Ratification in the States; Virginia Plan

FOR FURTHER READING

Bernstein, Richard B., with Jerome Agel. 1993. *Amending America: If We Love the Constitution So Much, Why Do We Keep Trying to Change It?* New York: Times Books.

Farrand, Max, ed. 1937. *The Records of the Federal Convention.* 4 vols. New Haven, CT: Yale University Press.

Kyvig, David E. 1996. *Explicit and Authentic Acts: Amending the U.S. Constitution, 1776–1995.* Lawrence: University Press of Kansas.

Vile, John R. 1992. *The Constitutional Amending Process in American Political Thought.* Westport, CT: Praeger.

———. 2003. *Encyclopedia of Constitutional Amendments, Proposed Amendments, and Amending Issues, 1789–2002.* 2nd ed. Santa Barbara, CA: ABC-CLIO.

Weber, Paul J., and Barbara A. Perry. 1989. *Unfounded Fears: Myths and Realities of a Constitutional Convention.* New York: Praeger.

AMPHICTYONIC LEAGUE

A scholar of classical influences on the Founding Fathers has described the Amphictyonic League as "a loose association of Greek city-states of the fifth and fourth centuries B.C." (Richard 1994, 104). Apparently a religious body without coercive power, Federalists used it as an example of an early confederal body that illustrated the weaknesses of systems similar to the Articles of Confederation. Antifederalists in turn cited it as an example of the power of small republics to triumph over larger foes, as the Greeks had prevailed over the Persians in the war they waged from 479 to 400 B.C.

Pennsylvania's James Wilson cited the Amphictyonic League, along with the Achaean League, in debates on June 6 as an example of "the encroachments of the constitutent members" (Farrand 1937, I, 143), and again on June 20 as among the examples of leagues "formed in the infancy of political science" and containing "radical defects" (I, 343). In his extended speech of June 18, New York's Alexander Hamilton further cited the league as an example of how threats of force against individual member states led to disunion and the rise of Philip of Macedon (I, 285). The following day, Virginia's James Madison cited the league as one among many examples illustrating the tendency in confederacies "of the parts to encroach on the authority of the whole" (I, 317; also see I, 320).

On June 27, Maryland's Luther Martin drew quite different conclusions from the league. He used the league to illustrate the dangers that occurred when larger members of the league excluded "some of the smaller states from a right to vote, in order that they might tyrannize over them" (I, 441). He repeated this argument the following day (I, 454). Madison answered by observing that "the contentions, not the coalitions of Sparta, Athens & Thebes, proved fatal to the smaller members of the Amphyctionic Confederacy" (I, 448). Opposing delay in changing the Articles, Madison added on June 29 that "the Defects of the Amphictionick League were acknowledged, but they never cd. be reformed" (I, 478).

A leading scholar of classical influences on the Founders observes that the debate over the Amphictyonic league continued into the ratification debates (Richard, 105–109). Although neither side appeared to be altogether accurately informed about this league, both used it as examples to validate their beliefs about the existing Confederation and its alternatives.

See Also Achaean League; Classical Allusions and Influences; Confederal Government

FOR FURTHER READING

Farrand, Max, ed. 1937. *The Records of the Federal Convention*. 4 vols. New Haven, CT: Yale University Press.

Richard, Carl. J. 1994. *The Founders and the Classics: Greece, Rome, and the American Enlightenment*. Cambridge, MA: Harvard University Press.

ANNAPOLIS CONVENTION

The Annapolis Convention, a predecessor to the Constitutional Convention of 1787, grew out of the Mount Vernon Conference which had dealt with common problems of navigation between the states of Maryland and Virginia under the Articles of Confederation. On January 21, 1786, with the support of James Madison, the Virginia legislature adopted a resolution appointing five delegates to meet with other state commissioners in Annapolis, Maryland

> to take into consideration the trade of the United States; to examine the relative situations and trade of the said States; to consider how far a uniform system in their commercial regulations may be necessary to their common interest and their permanent harmony; and to report to the several States such an act relative to this great object as, when unanimously ratified by them, will enable the United States in Congress effectually to provide for the same. (Jensen 1976, 180)

Edmund Randolph, the chair of the delegation, circulated a letter dated February 19, 1786, to state executives suggesting that they meet on the first Monday of September, and Governor Patrick Henry sent an accompanying or follow-up draft dated February 23, 1786.

Although nine states elected delegates, those from Massachusetts, New Hampshire, Rhode Island, and North Carolina failed to arrive in time. This left 12 delegates from five states, two of which (Pennsylvania and New York) did not have a quorum. Those in attendance were Alexander Hamilton and Egbert Benson from New York; Abraham Clark, William C. Houston, and James Schureman from New Jersey; Tench Coxe from Pennsylvania; George Read, John Dickinson, and Richard Bassett from Delaware; and Edmund Randolph, James Madison, Jr., and Saint George Tucker from Virginia. Significantly, eight of these delegates would be elected to and seven would attend the Constitutional Convention of 1787. They were Alexander Hamilton, William C. Houston, George Read, John Dickinson, Richard Bassett, James Madison, and Edmund Randolph.

Delegates stayed at George Mann's City Tavern and met in the old senate chamber at the State House (Chernow 2004, 223). The group convened on September 11, the second Monday of the month, rather than on the first Monday as originally planned. The delegates unanimously selected Delaware's John Dickinson (the "penman of the Revolution," who had authored the original plan for the Articles of Confederation) as chair and then appointed a committee to draft a report. The committee reported on September 13 and, on the next day, the delegates unanimously approved a document, largely devised by Alexander Hamilton. The report addressed not only the delegate's own respective state legislatures but also the legislatures of other states and the confederal Congress.

Many delegates would undoubtedly have regarded a meeting attended by a bare 30 percent of the states (which did not even include one of two states that had attended the Mount Vernon Conference) to be a failure, but those seeking remedies for the ills of the Confederation snatched victory from the jaws of defeat in what one historian has described as "one of the boldest and most momentous gambles in American political history" (Rakove 1986, 5). The convention report observed that the delegates from New Jersey had arrived at the convention with instructions not simply to consider matters of uniform commercial regulation but also "other important matters" that "might be necessary to the common interest and permanent harmony of the several States," and that these instructions were "an improvement on the original plan" (Jensen 1976, 183). As the convention report put it:

> The power of regulating trade is of such comprehensive extent, and will enter so far into the general System of the federal government, that to give it efficacy, and to obviate questions and doubts concerning its precise nature and limits may require a correspondent adjustment of other parts of the Foederal System. (184)

Responding to what appears to have been the suggestion of Abraham Clark of New Jersey (who was elected to but chose not to attend the Constitutional Convention), the Annapolis Convention report recommended

> the concurrence of the other States, in the appointment of Commissioners, to meet at Philadelphia on the second Monday in May next, to take into consideration the situation of the United States, to devise such further provisions as shall appear to them necessary to render the constitution of the Federal Government adequate to the exigencies of the Union; and to report such an Act for that purpose to the United States in Congress Assembled, as when agreed to, by them, and afterwards confirmed by the Legislatures of every State will effectually provide for the same. (Jensen, 184–85)

Initially somewhat diffident in its reaction to this report, Congress appointed a 10-member committee to examine it. The rise of unrest by farmers in a number of states that ultimately culminated in Shays's Rebellion in the winter of 1786–1787 led Congress to add two delegates to the committee on February 13, 1787. On February 19, by a one-vote majority, the committee endorsed the report of the Annapolis Convention. The full Congress, in turn, rejected a motion from New York that called upon Congress itself to call the convention, instead accepting a resolution from Massachusetts that has been said to have "implicitly acknowledged the call of the Annapolis Convention" (Jensen, 179). Closely following the language of this earlier call, the resolution, which Congress adopted on February 21, 1787, by a vote of 8–1 (each state present had one vote and Connecticut opposed it), specified that

> it is expedient that on the second Monday in May next a convention of delegates who shall have been appointed by the several states be held at Philadelphia for the sole and express purpose of revising the Articles of Confederation and reporting to Congress and the several legislatures such alterations and provisions therein as shall when agreed to in Congress and confirmed by the states render the federal constitution adequate to the exigencies of government and the preservation of the Union. (Jensen, 187)

Six states, many apparently responding to a circular letter that Virginia had sent, had already appointed delegates to the Constitutional Convention when Congress adopted this resolution. Six more subsequently followed suit. Congressional authorization clearly helped add legitimacy to the new proceedings, but, given the tide of events, it is not altogether clear whether or not it was critical to the success of the Constitutional Convention. Significantly, when the Constitutional Convention ultimately reported its plan to Congress, it did not specifically request, and did not specifically receive, its approval. Congress did, however, forward the document to the states for approval by conventions in nine or more states, thus again bypassing the amending mechanism of the Articles of Confederation, which called for unanimous state legislative approval of any amendments.

See Also Articles of Confederation; Congressional Call for Constitutional Convention; Dickinson, John; Hamilton, Alexander; Madison, James, Jr.; Mount Vernon Conference; Shays's Rebellion

FOR FURTHER READING

Chernow, Ron. 2004. *Alexander Hamilton.* New York: Penguin Books.

Jensen, Merrill, ed. 1976. *The Documentary History of the Ratification of the Constitution.* Vol. 1 of *Constitutional Documents and Records, 1776–1787.* Madison: State Historical Society of Wisconsin.

Rakove, Jack N. 1986. "The Gamble at Annapolis." *this Constitution,* no. 12 (Fall): 5–10.

ANTIFEDERALISTS

Even before the Convention met, there were some who were suspicious of its intentions—Virginia's Patrick Henry, for example, said he "smelt a rat." Once the Convention began, a number of delegates questioned whether the Convention had the authority to do anything other than revise and correct the Articles of Confederation, at least without additional authorization from their constituents. In addition to the three delegates who refused to sign the Constitution on September 17, 1787 (Elbridge Gerry of Massachusetts and Edmund Randolph and George Mason of Virginia), a number of others, including Maryland's

Luther Martin and John Lansing and Robert Yates of New York, had already left the Convention and returned to their home states to oppose the new Constitution.

Designation of Antifederalists

These opponents of the Constitution came in time to be known as Antifederalists, arguably a misnomer since one view of federalism (now generally called *confederalism* to reflect changes in contemporary usage) was that embodied within the existing Articles of Confederation. The importance of the Antifederalists is demonstrated by the vigorous debates that surrounded the Constitution in states like Virginia, Massachusetts, New York, and North Carolina. There is general agreement that, were it not for this debate, the first 10 amendments to the Constitution, known as the Bill of Rights, would not have been adopted.

Although there were many writings on behalf of the new Constitution (indeed, newspapers generally favored the new document), the Federalist position is sometimes easier to identify because of the publication of *The Federalist,* a work of 85 essays by Alexander Hamilton, James Madison, and John Jay written under the pen name of Publius, which so ably presents these views. Although many Antifederalist critiques were brilliant, they are not as easily identified with a single written work—fortunately, many have been collected, edited, and analyzed in a magisterial collection by Professor Herbert Storing (1981). Prominent Antifederalists included Samuel Adams of Massachusetts, George Clinton of New York, and Patrick Henry and Richard Henry Lee of Virginia.

Views of the Antifederalists

Antifederalists generally agreed that there were problems with the existing Articles of Confederation that demanded solution, but they were not as likely to attribute the problems to the existing governmental structure as to the consequences of emerging from under colonial domination. Moreover, they were generally warier of drastically entrusting the national government with significantly increased powers that might be abused. Many Antifederalists continued to believe that the existing government could simply be granted increased powers over taxation, commerce, and the like but that this government should remain fundamentally dependent upon the states. They were, by contrast, quite wary of constitutional provision granting Congress power to enact "necessary and proper" legislation or to tax and spend on behalf of the "general welfare."

Antifederalists were particularly focused on the argument that the French philosopher Charles Louis de Secondat de Montesquieu had advanced indicating that republican governments could not flourish over a large land area such as that which the Federalists anticipated would be under the control of the new government. Whereas Federalists generally anticipated that representatives would refine public opinion, the Antifederalists feared that they would create an aristocratic governing elite that would lose contact with its citizens. They feared that government over a large land area would have to substitute appeal to force rather than being able to rely upon the patriotic attachment of its citizens.

Although Antifederalists generally agreed that the national government needed somewhat greater powers to deal with other nations, they feared that national security might be purchased at the price of individual liberty. They tended to favor power in the states over that in a central authority. Consistent with republican ideology, they were especially concerned about the danger of standing armies and about the possibility that the national government might consider itself to be independent of the need for the support of state and local militias. Some also feared that the national capital might become an incubus of monarchy and of designs against the states.

Antifederalists often employed the language of republicanism. They have also been identified with the ideology of "Country" or opposition party in England (Hutson 1981). They especially feared those elements of the proposed government that they thought would have either monarchical or aristocratic tendencies. Many would have preferred a plural to a single executive. They

also feared both the U.S. Senate, with its relatively small size and longer terms of office, and the federal court system, with judges serving for life terms. One hope was to moderate the influence of the judicial branch of government through the widespread use of juries.

Although many Antifederalists favored separation of powers and checks and balances, some feared that the new government took these to extremes. They feared that the operation of such complex governmental machinery would have dire consequences, not all of which could be foreseen.

Antifederalists and the Bill of Rights

The expression of many of the Antifederalists' concerns led to deeper understanding of the new government, but their most important contribution was their insistence on a bill of rights that would serve both to enforce limits on the new government and to educate the public in regard to their rights. Antifederalists were especially concerned about protecting the right to trial by jury and freedom of the press and about reserving powers to the states. Once the Constitution was ratified, Antifederalists shifted their stance from that of opposing the Constitution to that of attempting to improve it through amendments.

Although Federalists initially resisted the call for a bill of rights, many eventually decided to promise to work for such a bill after the Constitution was adopted rather than to risk the possibility that Antifederalists would pursue a second constitutional convention that might risk undoing the work of the first. James Madison of Virginia took the lead in formulating the Bill of Rights in the first Congress and getting it adopted.

Contemporary Antifederalist Influences

Although former Federalists and Antifederalists soon rallied around the new Constitution, the philosophy of Antifederalism did not die with the creation of the new government (see Arthur

1989). Much of the rhetoric of Antifederalism was incorporated into the ideology of the Democratic-Republican Party, with its emphasis on limited governmental powers, states' rights, and agrarianism. Federalist and Antifederalist principles arguably still constitute the yin and yang of American ideology.

See Also Aristocracy; Armies, Standing; Bill of Rights; Federalist and Democratic-Republican Parties; *Federalist, The;* Federalists; Henry, Patrick; Montesquieu, Charles Louis de Secondat de; Ratification in the States; Republicanism

FOR FURTHER READING

Arthur, John. 1989. *The Unfinished Constitution: Philosophy and Constitutional Practice.* Belmont, CA: Wadsworth Publishing.

Bailyn, Bernard, ed. 1993. *The Debates on the Constitution: Federalist and Antifederalist Speeches, Articles, and Letters during the Struggle over Ratification.* 2 vols. New York: Library of America.

Boyd, Steven R. 1979. *The Politics of Opposition: Antifederalists and the Acceptance of the Constitution.* Millwood, NY: kto press.

Cornell, Saul. 1999. *The Other Founders: Anti-Federalism and the Dissenting Tradition in America, 1788–1828.* Chapel Hill: University of North Carolina Press.

——. 1990. "Aristocracy Assailed: The Ideology of Backcountry Anti-Federalism." *Journal of American History* 76 (March): 1148–1172.

——. 1990. "Symposium: Roads Not Taken: Undercurrents of Republican Thinking in Modern Constitutional Theory: The Changing Historical Fortunes of the Anti-Federalists." *Northwestern University Law Review* 85 (Fall): 39–73.

Hutson, James H. 1981. "Country, Court, and Constitution: Antifederalism and the Historians." *William and Mary Quarterly,* 3rd ser. 38 (July): 337–368.

Kenyon, Cecilia, ed. 1985. *The Antifederalists.* Boston: Northeastern University Press.

Main, Jackson T. 1961. *The Antifederalists: Critics of the Constitution, 1781–1788.* Chicago: Quadrangle Books.

Mason, Alpheus T., ed. 1972. *The States Rights Debate: Antifederalism and the Constitution.* 2nd ed. New York: Oxford University Press.

McWilliams, Wilson Carey. 1990. "Symposium: Roads Not Taken: Undercurrents of Republican Thinking

in Modern Constitutional Theory: The Anti-Federalists, Representation, and Party." *Northwestern University Law Review* 85 (Fall): 12–38.

Rutland, Robert A. 1966. *The Ordeal of the Constitution: The Antifederalists and the Ratification Struggle of 1787–1788.* Norman: University of Oklahoma Press.

Siemers, David J. 2003. *The Antifederalists: Men of Great Faith and Forbearance.* Lanham, MD: Rowman and Littlefield.

——2002. *Ratifying the Republic: Antifederalists and Federalists in Constitutional Time.* Palo Alto, CA: Stanford University Press.

Storing, Herbert J. 1981. *What the Anti-Federalists Were For.* Chicago: University of Chicago Press.

Storing, Herbert J., ed. 1981. *The Complete Anti-Federalist.* 7 vols. Chicago: University of Chicago Press.

Utley, Robert L., Jr., ed. 1989. *Principles of the Constitutional Order: The Ratification Debates.* Lanham, MD: University Press of America.

Wootton, David, ed. 2003. *The Essential Federalist and Anti-Federalist Papers.* Indianapolis, IN: Hackett Publishing.

APPOINTMENTS AND CONFIRMATIONS

Article II, Section 2, of the U.S. Constitution provides that the president shall appoint ambassadors, judges, and other U.S. offices with the advice and consent of the Senate. This important power was a compromise between those at the Convention who favored executive appointments and those who favored legislative appointments (Murphy, Pritchett, and Epstein 2002, 138).

Opening Discussions

The Virginia Plan that Edmund Randolph introduced at the Convention on May 29 proposed that Congress would choose members of the national judiciary. On June 1, Virginia's James Madison offered a motion, seconded by Pennsylvania's James Wilson, proposing to give the president power to appoint officers "not otherwise provided for," and the motion was adopted (Farrand 1937, I, 67).

When discussion of presidential appointment of the judiciary resumed on June 5, Wilson opposed such appointment by the Congress on the basis that such "numerous bodies" were subject to "intrigue, partiality, and concealment" and that such appointments would be better made "by a single, responsible person" (I, 119). John Rutledge of South Carolina not only wanted to limit the national judiciary to a single tribunal; he also argued that executive appointment would lean too much toward monarchy. Looking for alternatives to executive or legislative appointment, Pennsylvania's Benjamin Franklin quipped that in Scotland lawyers made the nominations and selected the best of their colleagues in order to get part of their practice!

Madison did not like the idea of judges being nominated by a numerous body, not only for the reasons that Wilson had articulated but also because he did not think that most members would be good "judges of the requisite qualifications." He thought the Senate might perform this task alone. Wilson seconded Madison's motion to strike the method of appointment and leave the decision for later, and this was adopted by a vote of 9-2. Charles Pinckney of South Carolina indicated that he planned to reintroduce the idea of legislative appointments.

Pinckney, supported by Connecticut's Roger Sherman, did so on June 13. Madison again questioned the competence of legislators to make such appointments. As before, he suggested that the Senate would be the appropriate body to make such appointments. Pinckney and Sherman withdrew their motion.

When William Paterson offered the New Jersey Plan on June 15, he proposed that the executive should appoint judges as well as "all federal officers not otherwise provided for" (II, 244). A plan that New York's Alexander Hamilton presented to the Convention on June 18 contained a provision for the president "to have the sole appointment of the heads or chief officers of the departments of Finance, War and Foreign Affairs" and the power to nominate ambassadors "subject to the approbation or rejection of the Senate." Hamil-ton did not specify how judges would be appointed (I, 292).

The Origin of the Current Mechanism

On July 17, the Convention unanimously reaffirmed that the president would make appointments to positions for which provision had not otherwise been made. The next day, it reconsidered the provision whereby the Senate (now configured so as to represent all states equally) would appoint judges and formulated for the first time the current mechanism for appointing judges. Nathaniel Gorham of Massachusetts indicated that it would be better for the Senate to appoint judges than for the entire Congress to do so, but he recommended presidential appointment and senatorial consent as a tested method that had worked in Massachusetts (Farrand II, 41). James Wilson, seconded by Gouverneur Morris, still thought that presidential appointments alone would be better, but he preferred Gorham's method to legislative appointment. By contrast, Luther Martin of Maryland thought the Senate would be better, since "being taken from all the States it wd. be best informed of characters & most capable of making a fit choice" (II, 41). Roger Sherman agreed, suggesting that delegates were being influenced in part by whether they represented large or small states.

Virginia's George Mason, however, had separate concerns. He observed that it would be inappropriate for the president to appoint judges if they were later to sit as courts of impeachment. He also feared that presidents would stay so long at the seat of government that they would become too attached to the interests of the state where the capital was located. Gorham responded that members of Congress were just as likely to develop such attachments as was the president. He further argued that senators would be indifferent to candidates other than those from their own states. Madison suggested that perhaps the president could appoint with the concurrence of one-third or two-fifths (he crossed the second number out and replaced it with the first) of the Senate, thus uniting "the advantage of responsibility in the Executive with the security afforded in the 2d. branch agst. any incautious or corrupt nomination by the Executive" (II, 42–43).

The debate continued. Sherman thought that the Senate would embody greater collective wisdom than would the president. Moreover, judicial candidates would find it more difficult to "intrigue" with them than with a single individual. Randolph indicated that, even after the Great Compromise, which gave greater powers than he wanted to the smaller states, he continued to favor Senate appointment. He suggested that the Convention might enhance Senate "responsibility" by requiring recorded votes on such matters. Delaware's Gunning Bedford opposed executive appointment and thought that the idea of executive responsibility was "chimerical" (II, 43). By contrast, Gorham thought that a single executive would be more accountable for appointments than would a collective body.

The Convention voted 6-2 against executive appointment. Gorham, again citing the Massachusetts precedent, then moved that the president should appoint judges with the advice and consent of the Senate. Gouverneur Morris seconded his motion, and the Convention split 4-4 on the matter. In a mechanism similar to the modern one-house legislative veto, which the U.S. Supreme Court has declared to be unconstitutional, Madison then proposed that the president should nominate judges who would take office if not disagreed to by two-thirds of the senators. The matter was postponed until the following day.

When discussion of his proposal resumed on July 21, Madison was ready with a speech in its defense. He thought that this mechanism combined executive responsibility with a guard against "any flagrant partiality or error" (II, 80). Portraying the president as "a national officer, acting for and equally sympathizing with every part of the U. States," he observed that there would be no guarantee that the Senate—whose members were representatives of individual states—would have such a national perspective (II, 80–81).

Charles Pinckney continued to favor senatorial appointment. Randolph thought that Gorham's proposal for presidential nomination and senatorial confirmation was the best. Oliver Ellsworth

suggested allowing the Senate to propose, the executive to be able to veto, and the Senate to be able to override this veto by a supermajority, but continued to favor appointment by the Senate alone. He feared that a single president would be more partial than a collective body.

Gouverneur Morris continued to support Madison's motion for presidential nomination subject to rejection by two-thirds of the Senate. He feared that states would frequently be self-interested in appointments of judges, that the Senate would be less informed about judges than would the president, and that, if the president could be trusted with commanding the military, then surely he could be trusted to appoint judges (II, 82). Gerry did not think that appointment by the president would give sufficient weight to state judgments; he commended the quality of congressional appointments under the Articles of Confederation. Madison indicated that he had no particular stake in what majority of the Senate would be able to reject a nomination and suggested one-half might serve as well as two-thirds. Mason feared that even this would vest too much authority in the president. The Convention rejected Madison's motion by a vote of 6-3 and cast a similar vote to allow for continued appointment of judges by the Senate. This provision, along with a similar provision for the appointment of ambassadors, made its way into the report that the Committee of Detail presented to the Convention on August 6; the president continued to have power to appoint officers not otherwise provided for (II, 183). On August 23, the Convention made a number of minor changes to provisions dealing with executive appointments.

Committee on Postponed Matters

On August 31, the Convention appointed an 11-man Committee on Postponed Matters, chaired by David Brearly of New Jersey. On September 4, this committee proposed that the president "shall nominate and by and with the advice and consent of the Senate shall appoint Ambassadors and other public Ministers, Judges of the supreme Court, and all other officers of the U.S. whose appointments are not otherwise herein provided for" (II, 495). Significantly, Gouverneur Morris and James Madison, both of whom had previously supported this mechanism, served on this committee.

The Convention discussed this mechanism on September 7. James Wilson objected that it blended legislative and executive powers and suggested the establishment of a Council of Advice like that advocated by George Mason. Charles Pinckney also opposed including the Senate in appointments, except in the case of ambassadors, whom he thought it was inappropriate for the president to appoint. Gouverneur Morris commended the committee's plan: "as the President was to nominate, there would be responsibility, and as the Senate was to concur, there would be security" (II, 539). Gerry thought the idea of presidential responsibility was "chimerical." After Rufus King of Massachusetts observed that a Council of Advice would be subject to many of the same problems as the Senate, the Convention unanimously voted to approve the provision. It subsequently voted to allow the president to appoint other U.S. officers and to fill vacancies that should arise during Senate recesses until the end of the next Senate session (II, 540). Commentators have observed that "though the Senate lost sole authority over the judges and ambassadors, it gained advice and consent powers for all appointments" (Wirls and Wirls 2004, 123).

On September 15, just two days before the delegates signed the Constitution, they added a provision stating that "the Congress may by law vest the appointment of such inferior Officers as they think proper, in the President alone, in the Courts of law, or in the heads of Departments." Tying on an initial vote (Madison and Morris had questioned its necessity), the Convention unanimously accepted it on a second vote. The Convention also added the phrase "and which shall be established by law" to the provision relating to other officers that the president could appoint.

Analysis

It seems clear that the current mechanism for appointing and confirming judges and ambassadors was a compromise between those who wanted to vest this power exclusively in the executive and those who wanted to vest it in one or both houses of Congress. The current mechanism appears to have been largely patterned after a mechanism in the Massachusetts Constitution.

Given the ferocity of recent confirmation battles, especially in the aftermath of President Ronald Reagan's unsuccessful attempt to get Robert Bork confirmed as a U.S. Supreme Court justice and the public allegations of sexual harassment surrounding the nomination of Clarence Thomas to this same body, it is interesting to contemplate the effect that the proposal for the president's nominees to take office unless rejected by the Senate within a particular time period would have had if it had been adopted. Because of the Senate's filibuster mechanism, which is not provided in the Constitution and which has been especially used during the George W. Bush administration, the Senate can block a nomination without a majority of its members being opposed. This would not have been possible had the alternate mechanism been adopted.

See Also Committee on Postponed Matters; New Jersey Plan; Virginia Plan

FOR FURTHER READING

Abraham, Henry J. 1999. *Justices, Presidents, and Senators: A History of the U.S. Supreme Court Appointments from Washington to Clinton.* Rev. ed. Lanham, MD: Rowman and Littlefield Publishers.

Farrand, Max, ed. 1937. *The Records of the Federal Convention.* 4 vols. New Haven, CT: Yale University Press.

Murphy, Walter F., C. Herman Pritchett, and Lee Epstein. 2002. *Courts, Judges, and Politics: An Introduction to the Judicial Process.* 5th ed. Boston: McGraw Hill.

Wirls, Daniel, and Stephen Wirls. 2004. *The Invention of the United States Senate.* Baltimore, MD: Johns Hopkins University Press.

ARISTOCRACY

Ancient political philosophers employed the term "aristocracy" to describe a government by a few men (women were not at the time permitted actively to participate in government) exercising leadership on behalf of the common good. By contrast, a government in which a small group of leaders served their selfish interests was frequently designated as an "oligarchy." Similarly, ancient philosophers classified government by one person as a "monarchy" or "tyranny," and by the people as either "democracy" or "mob rule."

The delegates to the Constitutional Convention, who were attempting to create a government representing "We the People," did not consider the terms "oligarchy" and "aristocracy" to be especially complimentary, but they did think that certain parts of the government (most notably the Senate and the federal judiciary) needed to embody some aristocratic features. Unlike the British, who had both a hereditary monarch and a hereditary House of Lords, the American Founders hoped that those aristocratic elements within the government they were creating would be chosen on the basis of talent and virtue (a "meritocracy") rather than on the basis of hereditary class distinctions. Many delegates would undoubtedly have agreed with South Carolina's Charles Pinckney that equality was "the leading feature of the U. States" (Farrand 1937, I, 400–401). By contrast, Americans of the period regularly associated the maldistribution of wealth that many had seen on trips they had taken to Europe with the presence of aristocrats who often used the forces of government to expropriate the labor of laborers for themselves (Hutson 1993, 1084).

Uses of the Term at the Convention

On June 30, Pennsylvania's James Wilson denied that the large states were likely to ally into either an aristocracy or monarchy (I, 483). On July 6, Virginia's George Mason, who was a particularly ardent adherent of republicanism, expressed the fear that if the senators had the power "of giving away the peoples money," as in the case of being able to originate money bills, "they might soon forget the Source from whence they received it. We might soon have an aristocracy" (I, 544). That same day, Pennsylvania's Gouverneur Morris said that he did not believe that there had ever been or ever could "be a civilized Society without an Aristocracy," but he immediately added that "his endeavor was to keep it as much as possible from doing mischief" (I, 545).

On August 7, delegates were debating whether there should be national voting qualifications, such as the possession of property. Connecticut's Oliver Ellsworth feared that if Congress could alter voting qualifications it could point the nation in the direction of an aristocracy (Farrand II, 207). At a time when voting was often done in public, Gouverneur Morris professed to fear that aristocracy could actually grow out of widespread franchise:

> The sound of Aristocracy . . . had no effect on him. It was the thing, not the name, to which he was opposed, and one of the principal objections to the Constitution as it is now before us, is that it threatens this Country with an Aristocracy. The aristocracy will grow out of the House of Representatives. Give the votes to people who have no property, and they will sell them to the rich who will be able to buy them. (II, 203)

Morris went on to assert that "the man who does not give his vote freely is not represented. It is the man who dictates the vote" (II, 203). Approaching the subject from a somewhat different vantage point, Virginia's James Madison observed that "the right of suffrage is certainly one of the fundamental articles of republican Government, and ought not to be left to be regulated by the Legislature. A graduate abridgment of this right has been the mode in which Aristocracies have been built on the ruins of popular forms" (II, 203).

The next day, in one of the Convention's most passionate speeches against slavery, Gouverneur Morris went on to associate this institution with aristocracy: "Domestic slavery is the most prominent feature in the aristocratic countenance of the proposed Constitution" (II, 222). Responding that same day to Morris's argument that the Senate should be able to originate money bills, George Mason again tied his fears of an aristocracy to the growth of the powers of the Senate:

His idea of an Aristocracy was that it was the governt. of the few over the many. An aristocratic body, like the screw in mechanics, working its way by slow degrees, and holding fast whatever it gains, should be ever suspected of an encroaching tendency–The purse strings should never be put in its hands. (II, 224)

Similarly, on August 11, Virginia's Edmund Randolph argued against allowing money bills to originate in the Senate by observing that omitting such a power "would make the plan more acceptable to the people, because they will consider the Senate as the more aristocratic body, and will expect that the usual guards agst its influence be provided according to the example in G. Britain" (II, 263). Delaware's John Dickinson reiterated this argument on August 13 when he observed that "when this plan goes forth, it will be attacked by the popular leaders. Aristocracy will be the watchword; the Shibboleth among its adversaries" (II, 278).

On August 14, Mason added another twist to usage when he ironically followed up a proposal by South Carolina's Charles Pinckney by suggesting that all limits be removed as to the offices that members of Congress could accept. He said that this would serve

as a more effectual expedient for encouraging that exotic corruption which might not otherwise thrive so well in the American Soil–for completing that Aristocracy which was probably in the contemplation of some among us, and for inviting into the Legislative service, those generous & benevolent characters who will do justice to each other's merit, by carving out offices & rewards for it. (II, 484).

Maryland's John Mercer then entered the fray with observations of his own. He stated:

It is a first principle in political science, that whenever the rights of the property are secured, an aristocracy will grow out of it. Elective Governments also necessarily become aristocratic, because the rulers being few can & will draw emoluments for themselves from the many. The Governments of America will become aristocracies. They are so already. The public measures are calculated for the benefit of the Governors, not of the people. (II, 284)

He used this argument on behalf of establishing an Executive Council consisting of members of both houses of Congress. Mercer observed: "Without such an influence, the war will be between the aristocracy & the people. He wished it to be between the Aristocracy & the Executive" (II, 285).

On September 5, Randolph feared granting the Senate, rather than the full Congress, power to choose the president in the case that no one got a majority of the Electoral College. He opined that granting the Senate such power would "convert that body into a real & dangerous Aristocracy" (II, 513). Mason exclaimed later in the day that "he would prefer the Government of Prussia to one which will put all power into the hands of seven or eight men, and fix an Aristocracy worse than absolute monarchy" (II, 515). The next day, Wilson also expressed concern that the electoral system had "a dangerous tendency to aristocracy" (II, 522; also see 524).

Ratification Debates

As had been predicted, one of the chief attacks on the new Constitution came from those who feared the aristocratic tendencies in the new government, especially as they thought these were manifested in the Senate and the federal judiciary. Backcountry Antifederalists challenged Federalist arguments that they should defer to the wise men who had written the Constitution and to the idea of a natural meritocracy (Cornell 1990). In response, the Federalists said that they had created a republican government in which the will of the people would still dominate. They argued that the power of judicial review would not elevate judges above the Constitution but would ensure that the Constitution served as fundamental law.

Concern over the evils of aristocracy continued into the first Congress. There the House beat back a proposal from the Senate that the president be addressed as "His Highness the President of the United States of America, and Protector of their Liberties," as members ridiculed Vice President John Adams for the attention that he gave to aristocratic titles (Bickford 1984, 31–33). Subsequent political movements have based opposition to the national bank (evident during Andrew Jackson's administration) and the desire to keep big businesses in check (a theme of the Populist movement, the Progressive Era, and the New Deal) on the desire to prevent special privileges or the concentration of power in a few hands, such as one finds in aristocracies.

See Also Antifederalists; Democracy; Forms of Government; Monarchy; Ratification in the States; Republicanism

FOR FURTHER READING

Bickford, Charlene N. 1984. "'Public Attention Is Very Much Fixed on the Proceedings of the New Congress': The First Federal Congress Begins Its Work." *this Constitution*, no. 5 (Winter): 26–33.

Cornell, Saul. 1990. "Aristocracy Assailed: The Ideology of Backcountry Anti-Federalism." *Journal of American History* 76 (March): 1148–1172.

Farrand, Max, ed. 1937. *The Records of the Federal Convention*. 4 vols. New Haven, CT: Yale University Press.

Hutson, James L. 1993. "The American Revolutionaries, the Political Economy of Aristocracy, and the American Concept of the Distribution of Wealth, 1765-1900." *American Historical Review* 98 (October): 1079–1105.

Sheehan, Colleen A. 1992. "The Politics of Public Opinion: James Madison's 'Notes on Government.'" *William and Mary Quarterly*, 3rd ser. 49 (October): 609–627.

ARMIES, STANDING

Among the principles of republicanism prominent at the time of the Constitutional Convention was a distrust of standing armies in times of peace. The fear was based on the prospect that a ruler could use such armies to subvert the liberties of the people. New York's Alexander Hamilton, who had served under George Washington during the Revolutionary War, has been credited as being among those founders who recognized that such armies, easily mobilized, might be necessary to deter attack (Walling 2003), but the fact that the Convention refused to prohibit such armies, just as the first Congress decided against prohibiting such armies in the Bill of Rights, indicates that he was not alone in recognizing that such defenses might often be necessary.

On August 18, during a discussion of regulation of the militia, Virginia's George Mason, who was a strong exponent of republicanism, indicated that "he hoped there would be no standing army in time of peace, unless it might be for a few garrisons" (Farrand 1937, II, 326). Elbridge Gerry of Massachusetts renewed this concern later in the day. Arguing, as he often did, from popular opinion, Gerry said that he did not think the people would favor allowing Congress to have such a power. However, he also indicated that he was opposed:

> He thought an army dangerous in time of peace & could never consent to a power to keep up an indefinite number. He proposed that there shall not be kept up in time of peace more than a thousand troops. His idea was that the blank should be filled with two or three thousand. (II, 329)

On August 20, Charles Pinckney of South Carolina further proposed a motion for consideration by the Committee of Detail that would have provided that "No troops shall be kept up in time of peace, but by consent of the Legislature" (II, 341). The Convention did not adopt this measure, and on September 5, Elbridge Gerry tied his objection to the possibility of two-year appropriations for the military with his earlier concern about standing armies:

it implied there was to be a standing army which he inveighed against as dangerous to liberty, as unnecessary even for so great an extent of Country as this, and if necessary, some restriction on the number & duration ought to be provided: Nor was this a proper time for such an innovation. The people would not bear it. (II, 509)

One of the problems with setting a limit on standing armies was choosing a number that would not prove precarious to the nation. When confronted with the suggestion that such an army should be limited to 3,000 people, George Washington was alleged to have responded that the Convention should adopt a countermotion that "no foreign enemy should invade the United States at any time, with more than three thousand troops" (Hutson 1987, 229). Similarly, although Mason had expressed concern about such armies, he acknowledged on September 24 that "an absolute prohibition of standing armies in time of peace might be unsafe" (II, 616). In a motion seconded by Edmund Randolph, Mason accordingly moved to preface the federal power to organize, arm, and discipline the state militia with the words "And that the liberties of the people may be better secured against the danger of standing armies in time of peace" (II, 617). Perhaps because this language was simply precatory, the Convention did not adopt it.

Significantly, of four individuals who stated a concern about limiting standing armies in one way or another, three (Gerry, Mason, and Randolph) refused to sign the Constitution. This indicates that the concern over such armies figured prominently in republican thought of the time.

The Second Amendment, which was ratified as part of the Bill of Rights, subsequently provided that "A well regulated Militia, being necessary to the security of a free State, the right of the people to keep and bear Arms, shall not be infringed." At the time, militias were not limited to select members of National Guard units, as at present, but consisted of all able-bodied men with arms (Rossum and Tarr 2003, 61). Even before ratification of this Amendment, James Madison had argued in *Federalist* No. 46 that any concerns about a standing army under the new Constitution would be mitigated by the fact that close to half a million militiamen could be mobilized for the protection of rights against even the largest standing army, which he estimated could consist of no more than 25,000 or 30,000 men (299).

See Also Bill of Rights; Congress, Militia Powers; Republicanism

FOR FURTHER READING

Farrand, Max, ed. 1937. *The Records of the Federal Convention.* 4 vols. New Haven, CT: Yale University Press.

Fields, William S., and David T. Hardy. 1992. "The Militia and the Constitution: A Legal History." *Military Law Review* 136 (Spring): 1–42.

Hamilton, Alexander, James Madison, and John Jay. 1961. *The Federalist Papers,* Rossiter ed. New York: New American Library.

Hutson, James H., ed. 1987. *Supplement to Max Farrand's* The Records of the Federal Convention of 1787. New Haven, CT: Yale University Press.

Rossum, Ralph A., and G. Alan Tarr. 2003. *The Bill of Rights and Subsequent Amendments.* 6th ed. Vol. 2 of *American Constitutional Law.* Belmont, CA: Wadsworth.

Walling, Karl-Friedrich. 2003. "Alexander Hamilton on the Strategy of American Free Government." *History of American Political Thought.* Ed. Bryan-Paul Frost and Jeffrey Sikkenga. Lanham, MD: Lexington Books, 167–191.

ARMIES AND NAVIES, RAISING AND SUPPORTING

Article I, Section 8, Clause 12 grants Congress the power "To raise and support Armies." It specifies that "no Appropriation of Money to that Use shall be for a longer Term than two Years." Article I, Section 8, Clause 13 further grants Congress the power "To provide and maintain a Navy."

The Articles of Confederation

Under the Articles of Confederation, Congress had the power "of determining on peace and war," of appointing officers in national services, and of building and equipping a navy. However, the states were empowered to raise troops, and the national government was expected to requisition such troops from the states when needed. In 1783, U.S. military forces numbered only 80 men (Edling 2003, 82)! In presenting the Virginia Plan, the first defect to which Edmund Randolph pointed in the Articles of Confederation was the fact that it "produced no security agai[nst] foreign invasion; congress not being permitted to prevent a war nor support it by th[eir] own authority" (Farrand 1937, I, 19).

Early Convention Plans

The Virginia Plan, which Randolph introduced on May 29, proposed granting Congress a general power "to legislate in all cases to which the separate States are incompetent, or in which the harmony of the United States may be interrupted by the exercise of individual Legislation" (I, 21) rather than enumerating the powers of Congress, like those to raise armies and navies. The New Jersey Plan, which William Paterson introduced on June 15, did not propose adding new powers to Congress in this area, although it did provide that the plural executive would "direct all military operations," albeit not by serving as field commanders (I, 244). The Pinckney Plan, which was eventually sent to the Committee of Detail, appears to have provided for Congress to "regulate the Militia thro' the U.S." (Farrand II, 136). It also designed the president as "Commander in chief of the Land Forces of U.S. and Admiral of their Navy" (II, 158).

Republican and Whig ideology was strongly suspicious of standing military forces (Cress 1979). In debates on June 29, James Madison observed:

> In time of actual war, great discretionary powers are constantly given to the Executive Magistrate. Constant apprehension of War, has the same tendency to render the head too large for the body. A standing military force, with an overgrown Executive will not long be safe companions to liberty. The means of defence agst. foreign danger,

have been always the instruments of tyranny at home. (I, 465)

Madison went on to observe that standing armies had been a problem in Rome but that England had been somewhat spared the need for such armies by its insular geography–a situation arguably relevant for a continent separated from Europe by an entire ocean. Americans seem especially concerned that standing armies bolstered the power of the executive branch (Edling, 81–82).

Committee of Detail

The Committee of Detail, which reported to the Convention on August 6, substituted an enumeration of congressional powers for a more generalized authority. Among the powers that this committee proposed vesting in Congress was the power "To make war; To raise armies; To build and equip fleets; and To call forth the aid of the militia" (II, 182). The Convention discussed the provision relative to raising armies on August 18. On the recommendation of Nathaniel Gorham of Massachusetts, it began by unanimously adding the words "and support" after "raise."

Elbridge Gerry, also from Massachusetts, then observed that the provision did not prohibit "standing armies in time of peace," and he considered this to be a major defect (II, 329). He wanted to limit the specific number of troops that might be kept during peacetime, suggesting that a limit of 2,000 or 3,000 might be appropriate–on one such occasion, Washington was said to have whispered to fellow delegates that this limitation would work only if Gerry could guarantee that no enemy would ever strike the U.S. with more than 3,000 troops (Fleming 1997, 365)! The Convention was more immediately concerned with altering the provision relative to navies to provide that Congress "provide & maintain a navy" (a decision that it made unanimously), and, without recorded dissent, it also added the power "to make rules for the Government and regulation of the land & naval forces" from the Articles of Confederation (II, 330).

Luther Martin of Maryland and Gerry now specifically moved to limit standing armies in peacetime to a specific undesignated number. General Charles Cotesworth Pinckney of South Carolina wondered whether the nation would have to wait until it was attacked to raise troops. Apparently contemplating that troops under the new government would, during peacetime, be under state authority, Gerry expressed fear that without a limit on standing armies, "a few States may establish a military Govt." (II, 330). North Carolina's Hugh Williamson thought that Congress could prevent this by limiting appropriations, while New Hampshire's John Langdon thought that Gerry was being overly distrustful of the people's representatives. After New Jersey's Jonathan Dayton observed that "preparations for war are generally made in peace, and a standing force of some sort may, for ought we know, become unavoidable" (II, 330), the states unanimously rejected Martin and Gerry's motion. The Convention proceeded to discuss the respective powers that the national and state governments should have over regulating the militia.

Committee on Postponed Matters

On behalf of the Committee on Postponed Matters, New Jersey's David Brearly submitted a resolution to the Convention on September 5 providing that the congressional power to raise and support armies be limited by the provision that "no appropriation of money to that use shall be for a longer term than two years" (II, 508). Gerry immediately expressed his concern; he could see no reason for a two-year appropriation, and he feared that the provision "implied there was to be a standing army which he inveighed against as dangerous to liberty." If such an army were needed, the Convention needed to limit its "number and duration," and, even then, Gerry doubted that the people would accept such an innovation (II, 509). Connecticut's Roger Sherman responded that the provision merely permitted, but did not require, a two-year appropriation and that Congress would be elected biennially and might not always find it convenient to adopt yearly appropriations. The Convention unanimously agreed to the provision.

On September 14, just three days before the delegates signed the Constitution, Virginia's George Mason moved to add the prefatory words "And that the liberties of the people may be better secured against the danger of standing armies in time of peace" to the congressional authorization to organize, arm, and discipline the militia (II, 617). Mason recognized that "an absolute prohibition of standing armies in time of peace might be unsafe," but thought it necessary to add some constitutional provision, and Edmund Randolph seconded him. Fellow Virginian James Madison could see no harm in the proposal:

It did not restrain Congress from establishing a military force in time of peace if found necessary; and as armies in time of peace are allowed on all hands to be an evil, it is well to discountenance them by the Constitution, as far as will consist with the essential power of the Govt. on that head. (II, 617)

Gouverneur Morris of Pennsylvania, however, thought that such a provision would denigrate the contributions of the military, and after Charles Pinckney and Delaware's Gunning Bedford joined in criticism, the Convention rejected the motion by a vote of 9-2, with Virginia and Georgia losing.

Analysis

Today it is difficult to conceive of not constantly having a national military force on call to prevent and respond to attacks, but even at the time of the Convention, in its zeal for liberty, republican ideology, which favored reliance on civilian soldiers, arguably clashed with national needs in the area of national defense. The Convention addressed this issue by limiting the duration of defense appropriations, but it did not take the more drastic, and arguably more dangerous, provision of prohibiting standing armies altogether. Significantly, the Second Amendment, adopted largely because of Antifederalist criticisms as part of the Bill of Rights, referred not to a national army but to "a well regulated Militia" as "being necessary to the security of a free State."

See Also Armies, Standing; Committee of Detail; Committee on Postponed Matters; Republicanism; Revolutionary War

FOR FURTHER READING

Cress, Lawrence Delbert. 1981. "Republican Liberty and National Security: American Military Policy as an Ideological Problem." *William and Mary Quarterly,* 3rd ser. 38 (January): 73–96.

———. 1979. "Radical Whiggery on the Role of the Military: Ideological Roots of the American Revolutionary Militia." *Journal of the History of Ideas* 40 (Jan.-Mar.): 43–60.

Edling, Max M. 2003. *A Revolution in Favor of Government: Origins of the U.S. Constitution and the Making of the American State.* New York: Oxford University Press.

Farrand, Max, ed. 1937. *The Records of the Federal Convention.* 4 vols. New Haven, CT: Yale University Press.

Fleming, Thomas. 1997. *Liberty! The American Revolution.* New York: Viking.

ARTICLES OF CONFEDERATION

When the delegates to the Constitutional Convention of 1787 met in Philadelphia, delegates were not without examples to follow. They knew, of course, about the British government, to which they made continual reference. They also had their own experiences with state constitutions, many of which dated back to 1776 and the years immediately following. They also were operating at the call of the Congress of the Articles of Confederation. Indeed, six of the delegates—Sherman, Dickinson, Carroll, Gerry, Gouverneur and Robert Morris—had all signed the previous document.

Background of the Articles

The Articles had been proposed in the Second Continental Congress in 1777, were ratified by the last state (Maryland) in 1781, and remained in effect until the government created in 1787 was inaugurated in 1789. The Constitution of 1787 referred at least indirectly to the Articles of Confederation in the Preamble when it stated the Framers' intentions of forming "a more perfect Union." Similarly, Article VI referred to "All Debts contracted and Engagements entered into, before the Adoption of this Constitution," as well as to the validity of "all Treaties made . . . under the Authority of the United States."

The Articles of Confederation grew out of the Second Continental Congress, meeting in Philadelphia, which adopted resolutions for securing foreign aid and for forming a confederation at the same time (June 7, 1776) it resolved to draw up the Declaration of Independence. On June 12, 1776, Congress appointed a committee consisting originally of 12 (a thirteenth was added on June 28) men—one from each state. These individuals were Josiah Bartlett of New Hampshire; Sam Adams of Massachusetts; Stephen Hopkins of Rhode Island; Roger Sherman of Connecticut; Robert R. Livingston of New York; John Dickinson, then representing Pennsylvania; Francis Hopkinson of New Jersey (the latecomer); Thomas McKean of Delaware; Thomas Stone of Maryland; Thomas Nelson of Virginia; Joseph Hewes of North Carolina; Edward Rutledge of South Carolina; and Button Gwinnet of Georgia.

Of these individuals, John Dickinson, the designated "penman of the Revolution" and a future delegate to the Constitutional Convention of 1787 from Delaware, was the most influential (Jensen 1966, 249). He presented his draft to Congress on July 12, 1776. Congress debated and altered these proposals on July 22 and on August 2, 6, 7, 8, and 20. Significantly, debates centered on a number of issues that would later become important at the Constitutional Convention. These included whether states should be represented equally or by wealth, numbers, or taxes; what authority Congress would have over Western land claims; how taxes would be apportioned; and, especially, how slaves would be counted in such apportionment (Jensen, 250).

Congress resumed debate over the Articles on April 8, 1777. Largely at the insistence of Thomas Burke of North Carolina, the Articles were altered so as to lessen the powers of the national government and to recognize state sovereignty. Congress appointed a committee to suggest further amendments to the Articles, and, as in the case of the U.S. Constitution, entrusted another committee with putting the document into final form (Jensen, 253). The Continental Congress did not send the Articles to the states for ratification until November 17, 1777. The last state, Maryland, which withheld ratification until states with large Western land claims agreed to give them up, did not ratify until March 1, 1781.

Provisions of the Articles

The Articles of Confederation contained 12 articles. The key article was Article II, which North Carolina's Thomas Burke had introduced. It specified that "Each state retains its sovereignty, freedom, and independence, and every Power, Jurisdiction and right, which is not by this confederation expressly delegated to the United States, in Congress assembled" (Solberg 1958, 42). The Confederation, as much a treaty as a national government, was designated in Article III as "a firm league of friendship" for "common defense, the security of their Liberties, and their mutual and general welfare" (Solberg, 42). Section IV of the Articles resembled Section IV of the future Constitution. It contained provisions for privileges and immunities for all free citizens, for the extradition of fugitives, and for full faith and credit for acts and judicial proceedings of other states.

In contrast to the government that would follow, Article V created a unicameral Congress. State legislatures appointed from two to seven delegates per state, but each state delegation had a single vote. Delegates could serve for no more than three years within a six-year span and were paid by and were subject to recall by the states. They were guaranteed freedom of speech within the body. Pointing to its reputation for weakness, at the Constitutional Convention, Pennsylvania's James Wilson observed that "the success of the Revolution was owing to other causes, than the Constitution of Congress" (Farrand 1937, I, 343).

Article VI imposed a number of limits on the states. These included limits on sending foreign ambassadors or forming foreign alliances, restraints on interstate compacts without congressional consent, limits on imposts or duties that might interfere with national treaties, restraints on keeping war vessels and provisions for state militia, and prohibition on wars without congressional consent. Article VII further allowed states to appoint militia officers, while Article VIII provided that defense expenditures on behalf of the Articles should be paid out of the general treasury.

Article IX enumerated the rights of Congress, giving it power over war and peace and diplomacy, allowing it to resolve boundary disputes between states, providing for the regulating of the value of coin, the fixing of weights and measures, the establishing of post offices, and appointing officers in the service of the United States. Dickinson had called for a Council of State that appears to have been designed to have provided for executive authority. By contrast, the finished Articles created "A Committee of the States" to sit during congressional recess, with relatively weak executive authority. Perhaps in deference to the large states who feared the result of equal state representation, this provision further specified that

> The United States in Congress assembled shall never engage in a war, nor grant letters of marque and reprisal in times of peace, nor enter into any treaties or alliances, nor coin money, nor regulate the value thereof, nor ascertain the sums and expences necessary for the defence and welfare of the united states, or any of them, nor emit bills, nor borrow money on the credit of the united states, nor appropriate money, nor agree upon the number of vessels of war, to be built or purchased, or the number of land or sea forces to be raised, nor appoint a commander in chief of the army or navy, unless nine states assent to the same.

This provision for supermajorities on key matters virtually crippled congressional authority under the Articles, effectively denying in practice the exercise of a number of powers that Article IX had appeared to grant.

Other articles made provision for the Committee of States to operate during congressional recesses, provided for the future admission of Canada, recognized existing congressional obligations, and provided for the perpetuity of the Confederation. Article XII, the final article, provided that future amendments would have to be agreed to in Congress and unanimously ratified by the states.

Forty-eight delegates signed the Articles of Confederation. Massachusetts had the largest number of signers, a total of six, with New Hampshire and New Jersey having the fewest, each with two. Six of the men who signed the Articles later signed the U.S. Constitution.

Accomplishments and Problems of the Articles

The Articles succeeding in bridging the gap between the dissolution of British rule and the new Constitution, and it enjoyed a number of successes. It witnessed the successful end of the Revolutionary War as well as the adoption of the Northwest Ordinance of 1787, which provided for the admission of Western states into the Union, thus avoiding treating the West as a huge empire. Congress also adopted the resolution calling for the Constitutional Convention of 1787 and subsequently forwarded the Convention's work on to the states for their approval.

Early nationalists portrayed the period of the Articles of Confederation as a "critical period" in American history when there was a relatively clear choice between continuing with an ineffective government and formulating a new one (Morris 1956). Similarly, most contemporary analysts focus on the failures of the Articles. As in other confederations, power remained in the individual states, which were often governed by majorities interested in little other than their own self-interests. Congress had no power to act directly on individuals, as in raising taxes or armed forces, but had to appeal to the states, which were not always forthcoming in meeting their obligations. Congress had no power over interstate commerce, and states began to tax goods coming from other states. Other congressional powers were severely limited by the requirement for the assent of nine or more states. The amending article was particularly unrealistic, the requirement for state unanimity serving as an obstacle to all proposals during the duration of the Articles. In 1781, Rhode Island cast the sole dissenting vote over an amendment granting Congress the power to level a 5 percent impost, and New York failed to consent to a similar revenue measure in 1783.

The weakness of the Articles led to economic problems at home, as state imposts impeded commerce, and to weakness abroad, as American diplomats found that Europeans were skeptical about the long-term survival of the new government and its ability to keep its promises. Stung by continuing state impositions on the lands of former Loyalists, the British refused to honor obligations under the Treaty of Paris ending the Revolutionary War to withdraw troops from the Northwest Territory. Nationalists were convinced that the Articles were doomed, and the failure of the national government to respond to Shays's Rebellion gave further resolution to those who read the call of the Annapolis Convention for a convention to meet in Philadelphia to consider commerce along with other problems of the Union. The Congress under the Articles of Confederation recommended that states send delegates to the Constitutional Convention for the purpose of revising the Articles. A number of delegates to the Constitutional Convention were serving simultaneously as members of the Confederal Congress, and there is evidence of at least some ongoing exchange between the two bodies.

Convention References to the Articles

The members of the Virginia Delegation made a bold move in the opening days of the Constitutional Convention when they effectively submitted a plan to replace rather than simply revise the Articles of Confederation. This plan called for three distinct branches of government and for a bicameral Congress with expanded powers in which states were to be represented by population. Perhaps by way of explanation, Virginia's Edmund Randolph, after identifying some of the defects of the Articles during the Convention's second day of business, observed that

> he professed a high respect for its authors, and considered them as having done all that patriots could do, in the then infancy of the science, of constitutions, & of confederations–when the inefficiency of requisitions was unknown–no commercial discord had arisen among any states–no rebellion had appeared as in Massts.–foreign debts had not become urgent–the havoc of paper money had not been foreseen–treaties had not been violated–and perhaps nothing better could be obtained from the jealousy of the states with regard to their sovereignty. (I, 18–19)

On June 4 of the Convention, Virginia delegate George Mason noted that "he could not but consider the federal system as in effect dissolved by the appointment of this Convention to devise a better one" (I, 101; but see Johnson 2003–2004). On June 19, James Madison, recounting several instances in which states had refused to heed federal requisitions, observed that under the law of nations "a breach of any one article, by any one party, leaves all the other parties at liberty, to consider the whole convention as dissolved, unless they choose rather to compel the delinquent party to repair the breach" (I, 315). On a number of occasions during convention debates, delegates noted that the plan for equal state representation under the Articles of Confederation had been adopted reluctantly and without due regard to democratic principles.

Initiation of the New Government

Had they followed the requirements for amending the Articles of Confederation, the delegates to the Constitutional Convention would have required the approval of the new document by Congress and by all the state legislatures. Although the delegates forwarded the plan to Congress for submission to the states, they did not specifically ask for congressional approval, and although Congress cooperated by sending the document to the states for approval, it did not specif-

ically give it. Moreover, convinced both that state legislatures would be reluctant to part with some of their existing powers and that popular approval would give the new Constitution a wider base, the delegates specified that the new document would be ratified by conventions called within each of the states. Finally, the delegates specified in Article VII that the new Constitution would go into effect when ratified by nine of the states (since Rhode Island had not even sent delegates, it seemed particularly unlikely that it would ratify the new document quickly); this number would likely have proved to be ineffective had large states like Virginia, New York, and Pennsylvania not given their assent.

It is important to realize that as the delegates to the Constitutional Convention were writing a new document, the Articles of Confederation remained in effect. Congress was then meeting in New York, and the physical separation was probably helpful in allowing the delegates at the Convention to think about the possibility of a new structure. Many of the Convention delegates had served in the Congress under the Articles of Confederation, and many undoubtedly gained a more continental vision from such service than had they remained as representatives within their own states. Calvin Johnson (2003–2004) has argued that greater attention needs to be paid to the continuity between the Articles of Confederation and the Constitution. He has sought justification for a number of contemporary practices on the basis that the new Constitution largely intended to maintain aspects of the Articles that it did not explicitly change.

See Also Albany Plan of Union; Annapolis Convention; Confederal Government; Critical Period; Dickinson, John; Northwest Ordinance of 1787; Revolutionary War; Shays's Rebellion

FOR FURTHER READING

Banning, Lance, "From Confederation to Constitution: The Revolutionary Context of the Great Convention." *this Constitution*, no. 6 (Spring 1985): 12–18.

Dougherty, Keith L. 2001. *Collective Action under the Ar-*

ticles of Confederation. Cambridge: Cambridge University Press.

Farrand, Max, ed. 1937. *The Records of the Federal Convention*. 4 vols. New Haven, CT: Yale University Press.

Hoffert, Robert W. 1992. *A Politics of Tensions: The Articles of Confederation and American Political Ideals*. Niwot: University Press of Colorado.

Jensen, Merrill. 1966. *The Articles of Confederation*. Madison: University of Wisconsin Press.

Johnson, Calvin H. 2003–2004. "Homage to Clio: The Historical Continuity from the Articles of Confederation into the Constitution." *Constitutional Commentary* 20 (Winter): 463–513.

McDonald, Forrest, and Ellen Shapiro McDonald, eds. 1968. *Confederation and Constitution, 1781–1789*. New York: Harper and Row, Publishers.

McLaughlin, Andrew C. 1962 [1905]. *The Confederation and the Constitution, 1783–1789*. New York: Collier Books.

Morris, Richard B. 1956. "The Confederation Period and the American Historian." *William and Mary Quarterly*, 3rd ser. 13 (April): 139–156.

Solberg, Winton, ed. 1958. *The Federal Convention and the Formation of the Union of the American States*. Indianapolis, IN: Bobbs-Merrill.

Wood, Gordon S. 1987. *The Making of the Constitution*. Waco, TX: Markham Press Fund.

Reproduction of Henry Hintermeister's
The Foundation of American Govenment, *ca. 1925*
(Libary of Congress)

ARTISTIC DEPICTIONS OF THE U.S. CONSTITUTIONAL CONVENTION

Historian Michael Kammen notes with relative surprise that depictions of the Constitutional Convention were relatively rare in the eighteenth and nineteenth centuries (1987, 92). There were two primary depictions of this event. One, painted by Junius Brutus Stearns in 1856, which graces the covers of this encyclopedia, was entitled *Washington Addressing the Constitutional Convention* or *Adoption of the Constitution* and was later tightly squeezed onto a three-cent stamp printed on the sesquicentennial of the Constitution. Another, painted by Thomas P. Rossiter in the 1860s, was entitled *Signing of the Constitution of the United States*. The preliminary version (the original has disappeared) of this painting was once displayed in Independence Hall.

As visitors assemble for visits to Independence Hall today, they are led to a room with a 1987 painting by Louis Glanzman of the signing of the Constitution, which features George Washington in the center of the picture and James Madison to his right. This painting, which is historically accurate according to what is now known about the room (including its current paint color, gray), features the signers. Because no previous portrait has been located of Delaware's Jacob Broom, Glanzman portrayed him as signing the document with his back toward the viewers.

Kammen acknowledges that painting collective portraits is not necessarily an artist's dream, but he notes that there were more such portraits of those who signed the Declaration of Independence. John Trumball's painting of the event, which was completed in the eighteenth century, although not accurate (unlike the Constitution, that document was not signed on a single day), particularly caught the public fancy (Wills 1978, 346–348). Moreover, Kammen cites a number of other paintings from the nineteenth century in both England and America of collective bodies.

It is possible that the medium of print was a more likely source to consult for early depictions of the Convention. There is at least one primitive woodcut on *The Grand Convention* from 1787 attributed to John Norman that appeared on the cover of *Weatherwise's Federal Almanack* of 1788. Another, more sophisticated woodcut, attributed to Elkanah Tistale and entitled *Convention in Philadelphia,* was engraved about 1823 and was published in Charles A. Goodrich's *A History of the United States of America* published that year (Bernstein with Rice 1987, 154–155).

By 1937, there were six known paintings of the Constitutional Convention, but none by particularly memorable artists (Marling 1987, 14). Representative Sol Bloom, the director of the Constitution's Sesquicentennial Commission, was influential in getting Howard Chandler Christy (the designer of the *Uncle Sam Wants You* recruiting poster during World War I) to design a poster entitled *We the People* that was later incorporated into a 20- by 30-foot painting in the Grand Stairway of the lower chamber of the Capitol Building. It allegorizes "We the People" as a winsome all-American girl (similar to other Christy girls of the time) with a garland on her head surrounded by other contemporary figures above a portrait of members of the Constitutional Convention (Marling 1987, 15).

A number of portraits have since been done, most in connection with the nation's bicentennial celebration of the U.S. Constitution, but, as in the nineteenth century, this celebration was clearly overshadowed by the bicentennial of the Declaration of Independence that preceded it. One of the most outstanding pieces from the bicentennial of the U.S. Constitution is a limited edition serigraph produced by Melanie Taylor Kent entitled *We the People.* Famous delegates to the Convention, and other statesmen including Abraham Lincoln, are featured in the foreground, some holding documents (like the Virginia Plan, the New Jersey Plan, and the Articles of Confederation) that made them famous. Independence Hall is in the background (the text of the Constitution is set against the sky) with participants of a parade, mimicking the Grand Federal Procession of 1787, celebrating the Convention in the middle. The print also features symbols of technological progress like an airplane, a train, a car, and even Albert Einstein.

More frequent than depictions of either the Second Continental Congress or the Constitutional Convention are reproductions of the documents themselves, often with border illustrations depicting notable Founding Fathers or the progress of the United States from the time that one or the other document was written until the time the document was published. Focusing on written constitutions as a specific literary genre, Robert Ferguson has observed that part of the ideological strength of the Constitution derives from "the visual importance of the Constitution as a painting or icon to be viewed in a certain way" (1987, 9). Significantly, America's most venerated ship, now docked in Boston Harbor, is appropriately designated the USS *Constitution.*

See Also Commemorations of the Constitutional Convention; Music

FOR FURTHER READING

Bernstein, Richard B., with Kym S. Rice. 1987. *Are We to Be a Nation? The Making of the Constitution.* Cambridge, MA: Harvard University Press.

Ferguson, Robert A. 1987. "1787: The Constitution in Perspective: 'We Do Ordain and Establish': The Constitution as Literary Text." *William and Mary Law Review* 19 (Fall): 3–25.

Kammen, Michael. 1987. *A Machine That Would Go of Itself: The Constitution in American Culture.* New York: Alfred A. Knopf.

Marling, Karal Ann. 1987. "A 'New Historical Whopper': Creating the Art of the Constitutional Sesquicentennial." *this Constitution,* no. 14 (Spring): 11–17.

Wills, Garry. 1978. *Inventing America: Jefferson's Declaration of Independence.* Garden City, NY: Doubleday.

ATTAINDER, BILLS OF

Article I, Section 9 of the U.S. Constitution, which limits Congress, and Article I, Section 10, which limits the states, both prohibit bills of attainder. Such bills are legislative punishments without benefit of a trial. Such punishments, which ignore due process, had been frequently abused in Great Britain, where Parliament had used them to punish ministers of the king. Pennsylvania's James Wilson also claimed that a number of states had adopted similar laws (see Farrand 1937, I, 172).

Elbridge Gerry of Massachusetts and James McHenry of Maryland moved to add a prohibition on congressional bills of attainder, and on ex post facto laws, on August 22. Gerry's reasoning for limiting Congress rather than the state legislatures was that since there would be fewer members of the former than the latter, they were more to be feared (Farrand II, 172). Pennsylvania's Gouverneur Morris agreed on the necessity of prohibiting bills of attainder (albeit not ex post facto laws), and as other opposition centered on whether or not to include ex post facto laws, the motion was divided, and the Convention unanimously agreed to the prohibition on bills of attainder.

On August 28, the Convention discussed limitations on the states, focusing on prohibiting them from impairing contracts or emitting bills of credit. In what almost appears to be an afterthought, South Carolina's John Rutledge proposed a motion to prohibit the states from passing bills of attainder or retrospective laws, and, although the ban on retrospective laws did not ultimately survive, the Convention voted to accept the motion by a vote of 7-3 (II, 440).

A scholar of the subject has associated the prohibition against bills of attainder with the desire for impartiality. This writer has further observed that bills of attainder have been adopted in four periods of U.S. history. These are the revolutionary and postrevolutionary period, when they were used against Loyalists; the Civil War, when both sides used them against their enemies; a time in the late nineteenth century when they were used against Mormons in Utah; and the period of the Cold War when they were enacted against Communists (Wormuth 1950, 58). The U.S. Supreme Court has used the constitutional provision against such bills to strike down a number of such laws.

See Also Congress, Limits on; States, Limits on

FOR FURTHER READING

Farrand, Max, ed. 1937. *The Records of the Federal Convention.* 4 vols. New Haven, CT: Yale University Press.
Wormuth, Francis D. 1950. "On Bills of Attainder: A Non-Communist Manifesto." *Western Political Quarterly* 3 (March): 52–65.

ATTENDANCE

One of the rules adopted early in the proceedings of the Constitutional Convention provided "that no member be absent from the House, so as to interrupt the representation of the State, without leave" (Farrand 1937, I, 17). This rule appears to have been largely honored in the breach. Clearly, such a rule could have little effect on those who arrived at the Convention late (travel conditions were considerably slower in the eighteenth century than they are today), and it does not appear to have been enforced against those who were there when the rule was adopted.

Seventy-four men were chosen to attend the Constitutional Convention, and 55 attended. Historian Clinton Rossiter has divided these 55 into three groups. Twenty-nine fall into the group of what he calls "full-timers." Of these, all but two (Johnson and Jenifer, who both arrived on June 2) appear to have been at the Convention by May 29 and to have attended every session, including the signing of the Constitution on September 17, 1787. These delegates include Elbridge Gerry, Nathaniel Gorham, and Rufus King of Massachusetts; William Johnson and Roger Sherman of Connecticut; David Brearly of New Jersey; George Clymer, Thomas Fitzsimons, Benjamin Franklin, Jared Ingersoll, Thomas Mifflin, Robert Morris, and James Wilson of Pennsylvania; Richard Bassett, Gunning Bedford, Jacob Broom, and George Read of Delaware; Daniel of St. Thomas Jenifer of Maryland; John Blair, James Madison, George Mason, Edmund Randolph, and George Washington of Virginia; Richard Spaight and Hugh Williamson of North Carolina; and Pierce Butler, Charles Pinckney, Charles Cotesworth Pinckney, and John Rutledge from South Carolina (Rossiter 1966, 164). Perhaps significantly, all but three of these individuals (Gerry, Mason, and Randolph) signed the document. Seven of the full-time delegates (the entire state delegation) were from Pennsylvania, meaning that they did not have far to travel to attend.

Rossiter classified 10 others as "full-timers except for a few missed weeks." They included Caleb Strong of Massachusetts, who began attending on May 28 and left on August 17; Oliver Ellsworth of Connecticut, who attended from May 28 to August 23; William Livingston of New Jersey, who began attending on June 5 and stayed to sign the document; Jonathan Dayton of New Jersey, who began attending on June 21; Gouverneur Morris of Pennsylvania, who went to New York during the Convention to do some business; John Dickinson of Delaware, who attended with some absences from May 29 to September 14; Luther Martin of Maryland, who attended from June 9 to September 3; Alexander Martin, who attended from May 25 to August 17; William Davie (May 23 to August 12) of North Carolina; and Abraham Baldwin (June 11 to September 17) of Georgia. Some missed because of family illnesses or losses; others to take care of other offices they held or business responsibilities; and still others left because they were bored by the proceedings or disagreed with the direction they were taking (Rossiter, 164–165).

Rossiter cited 12 members who "missed long and critical portions of the Convention." They included the following: Nicholas Gilman and John Langdon, the only two delegates from New Hampshire, neither of whom arrived until July 23; Alexander Hamilton, who left the Convention in midsession and returned toward the end to sign, as well as fellow New York delegates John Lansing and Robert Yates, who both left in disgust on July 10; William Paterson of New Jersey, who left on July 23; Daniel Carroll and James McHenry of Maryland, who both began attending on July 9; James McClurg of Virginia, who left on July 26; William Blount of North Carolina,

who did not arrive until June 20 and did not stay at the Convention the entire time; and William Few and William Houstoun of Georgia, the latter of whom attended from June 1 to July 26 (165).

Finally, Rossiter noted that four delegates missed so many of the sessions that they can also be classified with the absentees. They included William Houston of New Jersey, who left the Convention on June 5; John Mercer of Maryland, who attended from August 6 through August 17; George Wythe of Virginia, who left on June 4; and William Pierce of Georgia, who attended from May 31 to June 30. Of these, Wythe, who went home to comfort a dying wife, is known to have supported the Constitution (165–166).

Rhode Island did not send any delegates to the Convention. James M. Varnum carried a letter to the Convention from a group of Providence tradesmen and merchants asking the Convention to grant Congress increased powers, but the Convention apparently denied him a seat as an unofficial delegate (Kaminski 1989, 376).

In addition to the delegates, William Jackson, who was elected secretary, also stayed from May 25 through September 17, as presumably did the doorkeeper and messenger. States required the following quorums: New Hampshire 2, Massachusetts 3, Connecticut 1, New York 2, New Jersey 3, Pennsylvania 4, Delaware 3, Maryland 1, Virginia 3, North Carolina 3, South Carolina 2, and Georgia 2 (Anderson 1993, xi).

More specific dates of attendance for individual delegates may be found in specific notations within the text as well as in an appendix to Farrand's *Records of the Federal Convention* (Farrand, III, 486–490).

See Also Delegates Who Did Not Attend the Constitutional Convention; Rules of the Constitutional Convention

FOR FURTHER READING

Anderson, Thornton. 1993. *Creating the Constitution: The Convention of 1787 and the First Congress.* University Park: Pennsylvania State University Press, xi.

Farrand, Max, ed. 1937. *The Records of the Federal Convention.* 4 vols. New Haven, CT: Yale University Press.

Kaminski, John P. 1989. "RHODE ISLAND: Protecting State Interests." In Michael Allen Gillespie and Michael Lienesch, eds. *Ratifying the Constitution.* Lawrence: University Press of Kansas.

Rossiter, Clinton. 1966. *1787: The Grand Convention.* New York: W. W. Norton.

AUTHORSHIP OF THE CONSTITUTION

A total of 55 men from 12 states (all but Rhode Island) attended the Constitutional Convention of 1787. The Virginia Plan provided the original wording for much of the discussion of the Convention (James Madison, its putative author, is sometimes designated as the "father of the Constitution."), but a number of drafts of the Constitution also emerged from committee deliberations. Both the content and the style of the Constitution were therefore a collective product rather than the work of a single individual. Moreover, the document has been subsequently altered by 27 constitutional amendments, also composed by numerous individuals.

The individual most responsible for the final style of the Constitution of 1787, and particularly for the oft-quoted Preamble to the document—which begins with the words "We the People" and outlines the primary purposes of the document—was Pennsylvania's Gouverneur Morris. Morris was one of five delegates that the Convention elected to a Committee of Style on Wednesday, September 12, 1787. He and other delegates reported their document back to the Convention on Wednesday, September 12, and, with slight revisions, most of the remaining delegates signed the document on September 17, 1787.

In a letter to Timothy Pickering dated December 22, 1814, Morris indicated that the Constitution had been "written by the fingers, which write this letter." He further observed that he had attempted to write most of the document to be as clear as possible, while surrounding the judiciary with studied ambiguity:

> Having rejected redundant and equivocal terms, I believed it to be as clear as our language would permit; excepting, nevertheless, a part of what related to the judiciary. On that subject, conflicting opinions had been maintained with so much professional astuteness, that it became necessary to select phrases, which expressing my own notions would not alarm others, nor shock their selflove, and to the best of my recollection, this was the only part which passed without cavil. (III, 420)

See Also Committee of Style and Arrangement; Delegates, Collective Profile; Father of the Constitution; Morris, Gouverneur; Preamble; Signing of the Constitution; "We the People"

FOR FURTHER READING

Brookhiser, Richard. 2003. *Gentleman Revolutionary: Gouvernuer Morris—The Rake Who Wrote the Constitution.* New York: The Free Press.

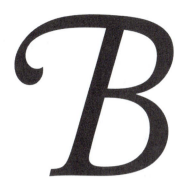

BALDWIN, ABRAHAM
(1754–1807)

Abraham Baldwin was born in Connecticut in 1754. His father was a blacksmith; a brother by his father's second marriage, Henry Baldwin, would later serve on the U.S. Supreme Court. Abraham entered Yale at an early age and stayed to tutor and study law, as he continued to study theology. He served with Joel Barlow, an American republican writer of some distinction, as a chaplain for Connecticut troops during the Revolutionary War. Barlow married Baldwin's sister, while Baldwin remained a lifelong bachelor.

Baldwin was admitted to the Georgia bar shortly after moving to Savannah in 1784. Within three months, he was elected to the state legislature, where he helped create Franklin College, which developed into the University of Georgia, where Baldwin served as president from 1786 to 1801, a time that included the period before the university actually offered classes. He also served from 1786 to the end of his life as a delegate from Georgia to the Continental Congress, to the Annapolis Convention, to the U.S. House of Representatives, and to the U.S. Senate. Baldwin did not speak extensively at the Convention, but his ties to Connecticut appear to have proven useful in forging compromises related both to representation in Congress and to slave importation.

Abraham Baldwin, delegate from Georgia
(Pixel That)

Baldwin was seated at the Constitutional Convention on June 11. His first recorded comments came on June 29 in reacting to a speech in which Oliver Ellsworth of Connecticut had proposed that small states be granted equal representation in the Senate. By contrast, Baldwin thought that the Senate should represent property. At this time, Baldwin also indicated that "he concurred with those who thought it wd. be impossible for the Genl. Legislature to extend its cares to the local matters of the States" (Farrand 1937, I, 470), a likely reference to opposition to the proposed congressional negative of state laws.

On July 2, Baldwin was appointed to the Committee of Eleven that proposed the Great Compromise between the large states and the small states regarding congressional representation. James Madison's notes indicate that earlier that day the Georgia delegation had been split on the matter, with Baldwin voting for equal representation in the Senate and Houston voting against it (I, 510). This resulted in a 5-5-1 vote that led to eventual compromise. Maryland's Luther Martin accused him of having done so not from conviction but from the fear that the delegates from the small states would otherwise leave and dissolve the Convention. Others have credited Baldwin for this conciliatory, and statesmanly, action (see Saye 1988, 85).

On August 13, the Convention was discussing qualifications for members of the U.S. House of Representatives. Some delegates thought it would be unfair to immigrants to require that, as a condition of election, they be citizens longer than required under the Articles of Confederation. Baldwin said he could see no difference between this qualification and the 25-year minimum age requirement (II, 272).

Although he had not lived very long in Georgia, Baldwin defended continuation of the slave trade, a position that appeared to coincide with his advocacy of states' rights. When the Convention was discussing the limitation of slave importation, Baldwin made it clear that he thought the delegates should distinguish between "national" and "local" matters. He also expressed concerns typical for someone from the southernmost state that put him at some odds with other Southerners (like those from Virginia) as well as with Northerners:

Georgia was decided on this point. That State has always hitherto supposed a Genl Governmt to be the pursuit of the central States who wished to have a vortex for every thing—that her distance would preclude her from equal advantage—& that she could not prudently purchase it by yielding national powers. From this it might be understood in what light she would view an attempt to abridge one of her favorite prerogatives. If left to herself, she may probably put a stop to the evil. (II, 372)

Although referring to the slave trade as an "evil" that Georgia might one day eliminate, Baldwin appears to have immediately questioned whether Georgia would in fact be inclined ever to end it. Thus, he offered as "one ground for this conjecture" the belief of a sect, presumably Hindus (see Bradford 1981, 205) "who carried their ethics beyond the mere equality of men, extending their humanity to the claims of the whole animal creation" (II, 372). If the people of Georgia were not altogether certain whether African Americans were equal, it hardly seemed likely that they would ever believe that the rest of the animal kingdom were so. Rather shockingly, Baldwin appeared, however indirectly, to be comparing claims for equality for African Americans to claims for the equality between men and beasts!

On August 18, Baldwin served on the Committee on State Debts and Militia. Four days later, he was appointed to the Committee on Slave Trade and Navigation, and on August 31, he was appointed to the Committee on Postponed Matters. Perhaps in part because of his service on the Committee on Slave Trade and Navigation, Baldwin altered a resolution on August 25 to provide that slave imports would be taxed according to the "common impost on articles not enumerated" (II, 416).

On September 3, Baldwin argued that the example of state eligibility to other offices was inapplicable to Congress. He reasoned that the state legislatures were "so numerous that an exclusion of their member would not leave proper men for offices. The case would be otherwise in the General Government" (II, 491). Baldwin's observation on September 14, indicating that the incompatibility clause would not apply to offices created by the Constitution itself, does not seem to have been followed up with any action on the part of the Convention delegates (II, 613–614).

During a discussion of the Electoral College on the following day, Baldwin indicated that he was warming to the plan. He observed that "the increasing intercourse among the people of the States" would diffuse knowledge about national characters and thus make it less and less likely that the Senate would have to resolve such matters (II, 501).

Life after the Convention

Baldwin signed the Constitution on September 17. In the first Congress, he served on the committee that helped draw up the Bill of Rights. Baldwin supported James Madison and gravitated toward the Democratic-Republican Party, being selected to the U.S. Senate in 1799. When he died in 1807, he was serving as president pro tempore of that body. Joel Barlow observed that Baldwin "lived without reproach, and has probably died without an enemy" (quoted in Johnson 1987, 139).

Baldwin is probably best remembered for his role in founding the University of Georgia as the capstone institution of learning in the state. Significantly, the university was to be a state-supported, secular institution. A provision forbidding the exclusion of anyone "on account of his, her or their speculative sentiments in religion" later became the basis by which women were admitted to the institution (Johnson, 143). Today there is a two-year residential institution called the Abraham Baldwin Agricultural College in Tifton, Georgia. It was established in 1908 and received its current name in 1933 when it became part of the University of Georgia system.

See Also Annapolis Convention; Bill of Rights; Committee of Compromise on Representation in Congress; Committee on Postponed Matters; Committee on Slave Trade and Navigation; Committee on State Debts and Militia; Connecticut; Connecticut Compromise; Georgia

FOR FURTHER READING

Bradford, M. M. 1981. *Founding Fathers: Brief Lives of the Framers of the United States Constitution.* 2nd ed. Lawrence: University Press of Kansas.

Farrand, Max, ed. 1937. *The Records of the Federal Convention.* 4 vols. New Haven, CT: Yale University Press.

Folden, April D. "Baldwin, Abraham." *American National Biography.* Ed. John A. Garraty and Mark C. Carnes. 24 vols. New York: Oxford University Press, Vol. 2: 43–44.

Johnson, Eldon L. 1987. "The 'Other Jeffersons' and the State University Idea." *Journal of Higher Education* 58 (March-April): 127–150.

Saye, Albert B. 1988. "Georgia: Security through Union." In Patrick T. Conley and John P. Kaminski, eds. *The Constitution and the States: The Role of the Original Thirteen in the Framing and Adoption of the Federal Constitution.* Madison, WI: Madison House.

BANKING

The Constitution does not specifically vest Congress with the power to establish a national bank, although the Convention did discuss this matter. After Benjamin Franklin of Pennsylvania proposed on September 14 that Congress be vested with the power to cut canals, Virginia's James Madison suggested widening this provision so as "to grant charters of incorporation where the interest of the U.S. might require & the legislative provisions of individual States may be incompetent" (Farrand 1937, II, 615). This grant was strikingly similar to the general grant of power that the Virginia Plan had proposed on May 29.

Rufus King of Massachusetts objected that Madison's provision was unnecessary. He further argued that it would divide cities like Philadelphia and New York, which had already been split under the Articles of Confederation over the desirability of establishing a national bank. Pennsylvania's James Wilson did not think that the issue of banks was likely to agitate the public, whereas Virginia's George Mason wanted only to authorize Congress to cut canals and, consistent with his republican ideology, was especially concerned about the possibility that Congress might create "monopolies" of any sort (II, 616). The Convention voted against Madison's motion.

This action was arguably inconclusive and later became a source of controversy when the consti-

Bank of the United States, Third Street in Philadelphia, 1800 (Corbis)

tutionality of a national bank was discussed during the Washington administration, when Alexander Hamilton, the former delegate to the Constitutional Convention from New York who was then serving as secretary of the treasury, was the bank's strongest proponent, whereas James Madison, then serving in Congress, opposed it. This controversy, which resulted in Hamilton's victory on the matter, led in part to the development of the Federalist and Democratic-Republican Parties, the first favoring, and the latter opposing, the bank. Chief Justice John Marshall later upheld the constitutionality of the national bank in *McCulloch v. Maryland* (1819), one of the seminal cases in establishing the doctrine of implied congressional powers. By that time, James Madison, who had initially opposed the bank but had helped re-establish such an institution during his presidency, had also concluded that the institution had been sanctioned by precedent.

See Also Corporations; Federalist and Democratic-Republican Parties; Hamilton, Alexander

FOR FURTHER READING

Clarke, M. St. Clair, and D. D. Hall. 1832. *Legislative and Documentary History of the Bank of the United States Including the Original Bank of North America.* Washington, DC: Gales and Seaton. Reprinted in 1967 in New York by Augustus M. Kelley.

Farrand, Max, ed. 1937. *The Records of the Federal Convention.* 4 vols. New Haven, CT: Yale University Press.

BANKRUPTCIES

Article I, Section 8 provides for Congress to establish "uniform Laws on the subject of Bankruptcies throughout the United States." This power is included in the same clause granting Congress the power to make uniform rules regarding naturalization. Charles Pinckney of South Carolina proposed the power over bankruptcy at the Convention as an amendment to the full faith and credit clause on August 29. Pinckney's version would also have extended power to deal with "the damages arising on the protest of foreign bills of exchange" (Farrand 1937, II, 447), but in time this latter part of the provision was dropped.

Pinckney's proposal was sent to a five-member committee on interstate comity and bankruptcy, headed by John Rutledge of South Carolina (other members included Connecticut's William Samuel Johnson, Nathaniel Gorham of Massachusetts, Pennsylvania's James Wilson, and Virginia's Edmund Randolph). On September 1, this committee recommended both that Congress be granted power "to establish uniform laws on the subject of Bankruptcies" and that the Convention adopt the full faith and credit clause.

The Convention considered the bankruptcy clause on September 3. Connecticut's Roger Sherman was concerned "that Bankruptcies were in some cases punishable with death by the laws of England—& He did not chuse to grant a power by which that might be done here" (II, 489). Although he recognized that "this was an extensive & delicate subject," Gouverneur Morris of Pennsylvania said that "He would agree to it because he saw no danger of abuse of the power by the Legislature of the U-S." (II, 489). The provision was adopted by a 9-1 vote, with only Sherman's Connecticut in dissent.

In an uncompleted preface to the debates at the Convention, Madison cited the lack of uniformity in bankruptcy cases as one of the defects of the Articles of Confederation (III, 542). In a speech to the U.S. House of Representatives on January 15, 1799, Georgia's Abraham Baldwin argued that states had power to legislate on the subject of bankruptcy until such time as Congress should act. The Supreme Court essentially concurred in this judgment in *Ogden v. Saunders* (1827), a time during which it would not have had Convention debates available. Congress did not adopt uniform laws on the subject until 1898 (Vile 2003, 37).

Prior to the adoption of the U.S. Constitution, it was common to imprison debtors. A number of states had systems in place where debtors petitioned the legislature for either an act of insolvency or bankruptcy, but other states did not always recognize such actions (Nadelmann 1957, 224–225). The bankruptcy clause thus gave Congress the power to establish uniformity in this area.

See Also Committee on Interstate Comity and Bankruptcy; Pinckney, Charles

FOR FURTHER READING

Farrand, Max, ed. 1937. *The Records of the Federal Convention.* 4 vols. New Haven, CT: Yale University Press.

Nadelmann, Kurt H. 1957. "On the Origin of the Bankruptcy Clause." *American Journal of Legal History* 1 (July): 215–228.

Vile, John R. 2003. *Encyclopedia of Constitutional Amendments, Proposed Amendments, and Amending Issues, 1789–2002* (Santa Barbara, CA: ABC-CLIO).

BASSETT, RICHARD (1745–1815)

Richard Bassett began attending the Constitutional Convention as a representative from Delaware on May 25, and he signed the Constitution on September 17. He is believed to have been one of the delegates who attended almost every session, and yet he was not recorded as making a single speech or motion. Records indicate that he voted on June 8 to oppose the proposed congressional veto of state laws, but they are otherwise silent as to Bassett's positions. He did not serve

Richard Bassett, delegate from Delaware
(Pixel That)

pears to have been one of the more evangelically minded delegates at the Constitutional Convention. He was a friend of Francis Asbury, the first U.S. Methodist bishop, served for a time as a Methodist lay minister, and helped construct a Methodist church in Dover. He allowed his property to be used for huge religious camp meetings.

Bassett served as a delegate to Maryland's Constitutional Convention, as a member of the state legislature, as a member of the state's Council of Safety, and as a delegate to the Annapolis Convention before being selected for the U.S. Constitutional Convention. In 1787, Bassett freed his slaves and introduced legislation in his state making it easier for others to do so.

In the U.S. Senate, Bassett helped draft the Judiciary Act of 1789, voted to move the nation's capital to the District of Columbia, and favored vesting the president with power to remove nonjudicial officials that he had appointed. He left his service in the U.S. Senate in 1793 to become chief justice of the Delaware Court of Common Pleas. After then serving as Delaware's governor, and as a presidential elector for John Adams, Adams appointed Bassett as a federal appellate judge, a position later abolished by the incoming Democratic-Republicans. Bassett died in 1815.

See Also Annapolis Convention; Delaware

FOR FURTHER READING

Saladino, Gaspare J. 1999. "Bassett, Richard." *American National Biography*. 24 vols. Ed. John A. Garraty and Mark C. Carnes. New York: Oxford University Press, Vol. 2, 43–44.

Whitney, David. 1974. *Founders of Freedom in America: Lives of the Men Who Signed the Constitution of the United States and So Helped to Establish the United States of America*. Chicago: J. J. Ferguson Publishing.

on any committees at the Convention. His political experience both prior to the Convention and afterward suggests that he was a man of great ability. Whether he was largely silent because his state was small, because he was intimidated by the reputations of other delegates, because he was preoccupied with other matters, or because he was in general agreement with the direction that the Convention took, it still seems a shame that he did not participate further.

Bassett was born in Cecil County, Maryland, the son of a tavern-keeper. After his father abandoned the family, his uncle, Peter Lawson, adopted him. A lawyer, Lawson trained Bassett in that profession and left him a huge Maryland estate. Bassett developed his law practice in Delaware, where he commanded a militia unit and was elected to the state legislature. He also took James Bayard under his wing. Bayard married his daughter and joined Bassett in the high ranks of Delaware politics. Bassett founded something of a Delaware political dynasty. He would become a U.S. senator from Delaware, as would Bayard, two of Bassett's grandsons, one of his great-grandsons, and one of his great-great-grandsons. Bassett ap-

BEARD, CHARLES (1874–1948)

Views of the Constitutional Convention and its works vary from one age to another. For much of

American history, the delegates to the Convention and the product they produced have been lionized (Kammen 1987). Abolitionists proved to be something of an early exception since they feared that the compromises with slavery had converted the document into "a Covenant with Death and an agreement with Hell" (quoted in Pease and Pease 1965, lx), but they took a much more positive attitude toward the Constitution once the Civil War resulted in the end of slavery.

One of the most influential and controversial interpretations of the Constitution was that first published by the prolific historian Charles Beard in 1913 under the title *An Economic Interpretation of the Constitution of the United States.* Beard, who had earned his Ph.D. in history at Columbia University, later withdrew from the university for what he considered its repressive policies during World War I and helped found the New School for Social Research, but he spent most of his life unaffiliated with any educational institution. Beard's central thesis in *An Economic Interpretation* was that much of the impetus for the individuals who planned, the delegates who wrote, and the men who ratified the Constitution had come from individuals with a vested financial stake in the outcome. He particularly believed the merchants, businessmen, and planters who lived in or near the urban coastal regions and had more personal property (money, private securities, manufacturing and shipping interests, and capital invested in western lands) than real property (landowning, especially small farms), had been far more likely to support the document than small farmers in the nation's interior or on the frontier. Beard believed that individuals who owned government securities or western lands were especially concerned with creating a government that would honor its financial commitments and provide stability that would increase their wealth. Beard furthered contended that the fight for constitutional ratification had not been nearly as democratic as it had often been portrayed (for Beard's conclusions, see 1949, 324–325).

Beard's work, which brought a barrage of criticism from established scholars, has thus been said to have "committed an act of desacralization" (Bendor, "Beard, Charles"). Beard further impacted the study of the U.S. Constitution by arguing that a majority of individuals who attended the Constitutional Convention intended to vest courts with the power, now known as judicial review, to declare laws to be unconstitutional.

Although Beard's critics often charged that his interpretation was Marxist in character, his work appears to have been more directly influenced by and made a greater contribution to the American Progressive movement. Scholars of this period often portrayed the Declaration of Independence as revolutionary but the Constitutional Convention as a reactionary development (see, for example, J. Allen Smith's *The Spirit of American Government,* first published in 1907). Adherents of progressivism were, at the time, attempting to democratize governmental institutions and to use government to control perceived excesses of businesses. Beard himself professed to have found support for his views that delegates were concerned about property in the words of the Framers themselves, and especially in *The Federalist.* He observed that James Madison had pointed out in *Federalist* No. 10 that the varying capacities of men and the resultant differences in the distribution of property were chief causes of faction, which the new government sought to cure.

Beard's views have been widely critiqued as focusing inordinately on property considerations, or as ignoring that individuals opposed to the Constitution were often motivated by economic considerations of their own. The most thorough critique is that of historian Forrest McDonald, who demonstrated that there were far more economic interests than Beard had considered and that these interests often interacted with other factors, including wider political views. McDonald concluded, "Economic interpretation renders intelligible many of the forces at work in the making of the Constitution. It is far from adequate to explain it in its entirety, however; this would require that countless noneconomic factors be taken into consideration" (1958, 415). Robert Brown, another critic, arrived at similar findings, which he summarized in two major conclusions: "the Constitution was adopted in a society which was fundamentally democratic, not undemocratic; and it was adopted by a people who were primarily middle-class property owners, especially owners who owned realty, not just by the owners of personalty" (1956, 200).

The overall effect of such critiques is not so much to have disproved that economic factors were at work at the Convention and in subsequent ratification debates but to show that these factors are considerably more complex than Beard recognized them to be and that they interacted with other factors at both the state and national levels. Thus, modern analysts of ratification of the Constitution within the states often use categories that Beard developed to explain the differences between those favoring and those opposed to the Constitution. A recent study of the Constitutional Convention and of the ratification of the Constitution, while reworking many of Beard's arguments, has sought to rehabilitate economic analysis as an important component in understanding the Founders' motives (McGuire 2003).

See Also Delegates, Collective Profile; *Federalist, The*; Judicial Review

FOR FURTHER READING

Beard, Charles A. 1949. *An Economic Interpretation of the Constitution of the United States*. New York: Macmillan.

Bendor, Thomas. "Beard, Charles Austin." American National Biography Online. http://www.anb.org/articles/14/14-00043-article.html.

Brown, Robert E. 1956. *Charles Beard and the Constitution: A Critical Analysis of "An Economic Interpretation of the Constitution."* Princeton, NJ: Princeton University Press.

Diggins, John Patrick. "Power and Authority in American History: The Case of Charles A. Beard and His Critics." *American Historical Review* 86 (October): 701–730.

Kammen, Michael. 1987. *A Machine That Would Go of Itself: The Constitution in American Culture*. New York: Alfred A. Knopf.

McDonald, Forrest. 1958. *We the People: The Economic Origins of the Constitution*. Chicago: University of Chicago Press.

McGuire, Robert A. 1988. "Constitution Making: A Rational Choice Model of the Federal Convention of 1787." *American Journal of Political Science* 32 (May): 483–522.

———. 2003. *To Form a More Perfect Union: A New Economic Interpretation of the United States Constitution*. New York: Oxford University Press.

Pease, William H., and Jane H. Pease, eds. 1965. *The Antislavery Argument*. Indianapolis, IN: Bobbs-Merrill.

Smith, J. Allen. 1965. *The Spirit of American Government*. Cambridge, MA: Belknap Press of Harvard University Press.

BECKLEY, JOHN (1757–1807)

Jonathan Williams Jr. wrote a letter from Richmond, Virginia, on April 9, 1787, to his cousin William Temple Franklin indicating that John Beckley, the clerk of the Virginia House of Delegates, was going with Governor Edmund Randolph to Philadelphia with the hope of being selected as clerk of the Convention (Hutson 1987, 1). If this were indeed Beckley's intent, he did not succeed in it. The records of the Convention indicate that William Temple Franklin and William Jackson were nominated for this position and that the latter was chosen. Curiously, Mathew Carey's *American Museum* listed Beckley as "esq. clerk to the house of delegates and delegate to the said convention," leading his biographers to speculate that "Beckley [who remained to explore the city and stayed until he had to leave for a meeting in Richmond on August 2] was so much in evidence, that spectators thought he had official status" (Berkeley and Berkeley 1973, 39).

Beckley would probably have been a better selection than William Jackson. An individual who had arrived in Virginia as an indentured servant, Beckley later achieved political prominence. He became the clerk of the U.S. House of Representatives and the first librarian of the Library of Congress, where he served from 1802 to 1807, during the administration of Thomas Jefferson. Beckley strongly supported Jefferson, for whom he had written campaign materials, including what is believed to have been the first campaign biography ("First Librarian").

See Also Jackson, William

FOR FURTHER READING

Beckley, John James. 1995. *Justifying Jefferson: The Political Writings of John James Beckley.* Ed. Gerald W. Gawalt. Washington, DC: U.S. Government Printing Office.

Berkeley, Edmund, and Dorothy Smith Berkeley. 1973. *John Beckley: Zealous Partisan in a Nation Divided.* Philadelphia, PA: American Philosophical Society.

"First Librarian of Congress, John James Beckley, Featured in New Book Published by Library of Congress." May 14, 1996. News from The Library of Congress. http://www.loc.gov/today/pr/1996/96-076.html.

Hutson, James H., ed. 1987. *Supplement to Max Farrand's* The Records of the Federal Convention of 1787. New Haven, CT: Yale University Press.

*Gunning Bedford, Jr., delegate from Delaware
(Pixel That)*

BEDFORD, GUNNING, JR. (1747–1812)

Gunning Bedford, Jr. was born in 1747 to the family of a Philadelphia architect who had served in the French and Indian War. Bedford attended the Philadelphia Academy and College of New Jersey (now Princeton University) and roomed with James Madison. After graduation Bedford studied law under Joseph Reed, moved to Delaware, and joined the bar. He served as Delaware's attorney general from 1784 to 1789 and was a delegate to the Continental Congress, where his attendance was sporadic. Delaware chose Bedford as a delegate to the Annapolis Convention, but he did not attend. Biographical information about Bedford can be confusing because he had an older cousin by the same name (generally, however, designated as Jr.) who was also active in governmental affairs, serving both as a state governor and, like his cousin, as a representative from Delaware to the Continental Congress.

Bedford began attending the Convention on May 28. He believed that the situation of the Union called for vesting increased powers in Congress. He is best known, however, for his passionate, arguably intemperate, defense of the small states and their equal representation in Congress and for suggesting that such states might seek foreign alliances if they were not treated fairly by the large states.

Congress

During discussion of the presidential veto, Bedford must have shocked some of his fellow delegates on June 4 when he said that he was opposed "to every check on the Legislative, including the Council of Revision first proposed" (Farrand 1937, I, 100). He continued:

> it would be sufficient to mark out in the Constitution the boundaries to the Legislative Authority, which would give all the requisite security to the rights of the other departments. (I, 100–101)
>
> . . .
>
> He did observe that he thought the fact that the Congress was divided into two houses would itself provide some security. (I, 101)

On July 17, Bedford supported a resolution that would have allowed Congress "to legislate in all cases for the general interests of the Union, and also in those to which the States are separately incompetent" (II, 26). Virginia's Edmund Randolph almost immediately objected that this power would be so broad that it would enable Congress to meddle in the police powers of the states, but Bedford argued that his resolution was not in fact very different from the one already under discussion (II, 27).

On September 14, Bedford opposed a constitutional provision that would have expressed concern over the presence of standing armies in time of peace. He presumably agreed with Pennsylvania's Gouverneur Morris in believing that this would set "a dishonorable mark of distinction on the military class of Citizens" (II, 617).

Presidency

Bedford was less firmly disposed to a strong presidency than to a strong Congress. When, on June 1, the delegates were discussing a seven-year term for the president, Bedford expressed strong opposition. He believed that this would be too long for someone who was discovered not to have the necessary abilities or for someone who once had them but lost them while in office, presumably because of physical or mental infirmity. He observed that impeachment would not be a solution since it "would reach misfeasance only, not incapacity" (I, 69). His own solution was to propose a three-year term, with presidents being ineligible after three terms (I, 69). The following day, Bedford seconded a motion by fellow delegate John Dickinson that would make the president removable by Congress at the request of a majority of the state legislatures (I, 85).

Judiciary

Bedford, who later served as a federal judge, favored selection of judges by the Senate rather than by the president. He feared that presidents would use such a power to curry favor with the larger states by appointing their citizens. Consistent with concerns expressed below, Bedford further indicated that "the responsibility of the Executive so much talked of was chimerical. He could not be punished for mistakes" (II, 43).

Federalism

Although Bedford had expressed willingness to give broad powers to Congress, he did not think that this power should include a negative over state laws. On June 8, Bedford raised the possibility that this power could be used to injure the small states. He figured that, under the Virginia Plan then being discussed, Delaware would have about one-ninetieth of the power in Congress, whereas Pennsylvania and Virginia would together have almost one-third of the power (I, 167; also see Hutson 1987, 61–62). He said that these ratios demonstrated "the impossibility of adopting such a system as that on the table, or any other founded on a change in the principle of representation" (I, 167). Having addressed the issue of fairness, Bedford went on to raise practical questions:

> How can it be thought that the proposed negative can be exercised? Are the laws of the States to be suspended in the most urgent cases until they can be sent seven or eight hundred miles, and undergo the deliberations of a body who may be incapable of Judging of them? Is the National Legislature too to sit continually in order to revise the laws of the States? (I, 168)

Bedford expanded on his views in a speech on June 30, which although criticized by fellow delegates as one of the most inflammatory at the Convention, probably had impact by reason of the fact that delegates realized that Bedford had only verbalized what other delegates may have been thinking. Bedford began by observing that "there was no middle way between a perfect consolidation and a mere confederacy of the States. The first is out of the question, and in the latter they must continue if not perfectly, yet equally sovereign" (I, 490). Bedford did not believe that the positions state delegates were taking could be understood apart from their interests, and he cut through what he considered to be the pretensions of states present to higher ideals. Identifying Georgia, South Carolina, North Carolina, Virginia, Maryland, Pennsylvania, and Massachusetts (most of whom had supported the Virginia Plan), Bedford argued that each had pursued either its present interest or its expectation of future interests, based on population growth. He further argued that Great Britain had not embodied equal representation, and it would be unwise to hold the United States to a higher standard. Interestingly, Robert Yates's notes, which contain a fuller account of this speech than Madison's, quote Bedford as saying, "*I do not, gentlemen, trust you.* If you possess the power, the abuse of it could not be checked; and what then would prevent you from exercising it to our destruction?" (I, 500).

Arguing that "we must like Solon [an ancient Greek lawgiver] make such a Governt. as the people will approve," Bedford did not think the smaller states would submit to "the proposed degradation of them" (I, 491). It was not that the people of the small states were unwilling to accept an increase in congressional powers but simply that they were unwilling to part with their own equality. Responding to delegates who had argued that this might be "the last moment for a fair trial in favor of a good Governmt," he said that "the Large States dare not dissolve the confederation" (I, 492). He continued with language that would stir apprehension in his fellow delegates: "If they do the small ones will find some foreign ally of more honor and good faith, who will take them by the hand and do them justice" (I, 492).

Almost as soon as he had spoken the words, he said that they were not intended "to intimidate or alarm" (I, 492). When Rufus King of Massachusetts objected to the "intemperance" of Bedford's remarks, Bedford attributed them to "passion" and indicated that he would not personally "court relief from a foreign power" (I, 493).

Bedford was still trying to defend his remarks on July 5. This time he attributed his remarks to "the habits of his profession in which warmth was natural & sometimes necessary" (I, 531). He argued that he had not been recommending that the small states seek outside intervention but only

pointing to the fact that "no man can foresee to what extremities the small States may be driven by oppression" (I, 531). Pointing to discussion of the executive veto, Bedford argued that it was just as important that the states be protected as that the president should be. Agreeing that the situation called for something to be done, Bedford said, "It will be better that a defective plan should be adopted, than that none should be recommended. He saw no reason why defects might not be supplied by meetings 10, 15, or 20 years hence" (I, 532).

Bedford, who served on the 11-man committee appointed on July 2 that formulated the Connecticut Compromise, apparently agreed to it, but as late as September 15, he was still trying to get an increase in the number of representatives allocated to his state and to Rhode Island (II, 624). Bedford was among the delegates who signed the Constitution on September 17.

Life after the Convention

Bedford returned to Delaware after signing the Constitution to urge its ratification. He served as a presidential elector for George Washington in 1789 and 1793. Washington subsequently appointed him as the first U.S. district judge for Delaware, a capacity in which he served from 1789 until his death in Wilmington in 1812. Prominent in the Masons, Bedford was president of the Wilmington Academy Board of Trustees and a member of the Delaware Society for Promoting the Abolition of Slavery.

See Also Committee of Compromise on Representation in Congress; Delaware

FOR FURTHER READING

Farrand, Max, ed. 1937. *The Records of the Federal Convention.* 4 vols. New Haven, CT: Yale University Press.

Hutson, James H., ed. 1987. *Supplement to Max Farrand's* The Records of the Federal Convention of 1787. New Haven, CT: Yale University Press.

Whitney, David C. 1974. *Founders of Freedom in Amer-*

ica: Lives of the Men Who Signed the Constitution of the United States and So Helped to Establish the United States of America. Chicago: J. J. Ferguson Publishing.

BELGIUM CONFEDERACY

See HOLLAND

BIBLICAL AND RELIGIOUS REFERENCES AT THE CONSTITUTIONAL CONVENTION

Taking the Founding era (the 1760s through 1805) as a whole, Professor Donald Lutz has observed that the book most frequently cited during this time period was the Book of Deuteronomy from the Old Testament (Lutz 1984, 192). He observes, however, that such references dropped off in the period from 1787 to 1788 when the Constitution was formulated and discussed, a trend he attributes to the fact that debate centered during this time "upon specific institutions about which the Bible had little to say" (194).

Delegates did, however, refer to the Bible, and to religious denominations, during the Constitutional Convention. Significantly, the delegates met in a city that had been founded by the English Quaker William Penn, who was a pioneer of religious tolerance. The bell, now designated as the Liberty Bell, in the "steeple" of the Pennsylvania State House (Independence Hall) where the Convention met, contained the inscription from Leviticus 25:10: "Proclaim liberty thro' all the land to all the inhabitants thereof" (Mires 2002). Scholars have shown that many sermons from the Revolutionary War and early national period were related to political topics (Sandoz 1991), and so it is perhaps not surprising that discussions of politics would in turn sometimes refer to religious topics.

Biblical References

At least in his speeches, of those who attended the Constitutional Convention, the worldly Franklin, who was a friend of the English evangelist George Whitfield, displayed the greatest knowledge of the Bible. In an early speech, he opposed monarchy by noting that "there is scarce a king in a hundrd who would not, if he could, follow the example of Pharoah, get first all the peoples money, then all their lands, and then make them and their children servants forever" (Farrand 1937, I, 83). When he later proposed that the Convention begin each day with prayer, he made at least three biblical references: he cited the words, attributed to Jesus, that a sparrow cannot fall to the ground without God's notice; he quoted a verse stating that "Except the Lord build the house they labour in vain that build it" (Psalm 127:1 [King James Version]); and he referred to the builders of the Tower of Babel (I, 451). He again cited Babel later in the Convention (II, 642), and referred to scripture in support of the proposition that rulers "should be men hating covetousness" (II, 249).

Gouverneur Morris of Pennsylvania cited the example of Rehoboam (whose haughty attitude toward his people and his threats to raise taxes led to the split between Judah and Israel) as an example of a ruler who did not follow in the footsteps of his predecessor, his father, King Solomon (I, 113). In discussing representation in Congress, Morris observed that "in Religion the Creature is apt to forget its Creator" (I, 512). At one point Morris observed (in a statement that could be interpreted either as an affirmation of a deistic God who did not interfere in public affairs or as a statement of humility) that "Reason tells us we are but men: and we are not to expect any particular interference of Heaven in our favor" (I, 512–513). He then referred to the need to bribe demagogues with "loaves & fishes" (I, 513), that is, with the expectation of higher offices in the U.S. Senate rather than in their own state legislatures. Still later in the Convention he referred to slavery as "the curse of heaven on the States where it prevailed" (II, 221).

Delaware's George Read used the biblical analogy of "putting new cloth on an old garment" (I,

137). Pennsylvania's James Wilson cited the story of Solomon in judging which of two mothers was a birth mother by saying that the large states had originally accepted unequal representation rather than accept the fatal loss of a limb (I, 348). Luther Martin referred to "the tenderness of the mother recorded by Solomon" in arguing that the smaller states (rather than the larger ones) had given up their claims to unappropriated lands (I, 441).

South Carolina's General Charles Cotesworth Pinckney, in arguing against restricting members of the general government from accepting state offices, referred, as Abraham Lincoln later would in a quite different context, to a kingdom divided against itself (I, 386). In a speech he prepared for the Convention but apparently never delivered, John Dickinson cited the "inspired Apostle" (Paul in I Cor. 6:12) as noting, in a somewhat shortened form, that "all things to thee are lawful but not convenient" (Hutson 1998, 137) and proceeded to record verses from the Book of Genesis about Reuben's talk with his brothers about selling Joseph into slavery (139). Later in the Convention, he said that aristocracy would be the "Shibboleth" of those opposed to the Constitution (II, 278), an analogy drawn from Judges 12:6.

Delaware's George Read observed that if Congress's power to produce paper money was not struck out, the words "would be as alarming as the mark of the Beast in Revelation" (II, 310). In defending state control over their militia, Elbridge Gerry of Massachusetts said that a provision giving this power to the national government would give the plan "as black a mark as was set on Cain" (II, 332), a reference to the curse that the Book of Genesis records being put on Cain for killing his brother Abel (and sometimes incorrectly associated with racial differences).

Religious References in Debates over Slavery

John Rutledge of South Carolina responded to criticism by Maryland's Luther Martin that slavery was inconsistent with the Revolution and dishonorable to the American character by observing that "Religion & Humanity had nothing to do with" the question of slave importation (II, 364).

By contrast, Virginia's Edmund Randolph noted that placating the Deep South states in regard to recognizing slaves as property "would revolt the Quakers, the Methodists, and many others" (II, 374). Similarly, Virginia's George Mason reflected contemporary notions of divine punishment by observing that slaves "bring the judgment of heaven on a Country." He explained, "As nations can not be rewarded or punished in the next world they must be in this. By an inevitable chain of causes & effects providence punishes national sins, by national calamities" (II, 370).

It is possible that religious terminology was even more pronounced in the debates at the Convention, and especially in debates over slavery, than James Madison's notes indicate. Although he may very well have included such references for rhetorical effect, in his report to the Maryland state legislature, Luther Martin, while confirming some of the arguments that Madison cited, thus couched his summary of the slavery debate at the Convention in much more explicit religious terminology:

It was said, that we had just assumed a place among independent nations, in consequence of our opposition to the attempts to Great Britain to enslave us; that this opposition was grounded upon the preservation of those rights to which God and nature had entitled us, not in particular, but in common with all the rest of mankind; that we had appealed to the Supreme Being for his assistance, as the God of freedom, who could not but approve our efforts to preserve the rights which he had thus imparted to his creatures; that now, when we scarcely had risen from our knees, from supplicating his aid and protection, in forming our government over a free people, a government formed pretendedly on the principles of liberty and for its preservation,—in that government, to have a provision not only putting it out of its power to restrain and prevent the slave-trade, but even encouraging that most infamous traffic, by giving the States power and influence in the Union, in proportion as they cruelly and wantonly sport with the rights of their fellow creatures, ought to be considered as a solemn mockery of, and insult to that God whose protection we had then implored, and could not fail to hold us up in detestation, and render us contemptible to every true friend of liberty in the world. It was said, it ought to be considered that national crimes can only be, and frequently are punished in this world, by national punishments; and that the continuance of the slave-trade, and thus giving it a national sanction and encouragement, ought to be considered as justly exposing us to the displeasure and vengeance of Him, who is equally Lord of all, and who views with equal eye the poor African slave and his American master. (III, 211, italics omitted)

Other Religious Terminology

In yet another wrinkle on religious terminology, Alexander Hamilton of New York referred to the gathering at Philadelphia as a "miracle." His argument, however, appeared to suggest that the "miracle" depended less on divine providence than on the remarkable confluence of events. Thus, he went on to argue that "it would be madness to trust to future miracles. A thousand causes must obstruct a reproduction of them" (I, 467).

Other References to Miracles or God's Providence

James Madison and George Washington of Virginia both repeated the idea that the work of the Convention represented a "miracle," and Catherine Drinker Bowen subsequently used this term in the title of her still popular narrative of the Convention (1966). She cited a letter from Washington to Lafayette on February 7, 1788, as indicating that it was "little short of a miracle, that the Delegates from so many different States (which States you know are also different from each other), in their manners, circumstances, and prejudices, should unite in forming a system of national Government, so little liable to well founded objections" (Bowen, xvii).

Focusing less on the Convention itself than on the nation, in essay No. 2 of The Federalist, New York's John Jay took pleasure in observing "that Providence has been pleased to give this one connected country to one united people" (38). Virginia's James Madison subsequently observed in Federalist No. 37 that "it is impossible for the man of pious reflection not to perceive in it a finger of that Almighty hand which has been so frequently and signally extended to our relief in the critical stages of the revolution" (231).

Analysis of Usages at the Convention

Members of the Convention appeared to resort to the Bible, much as they did to British, Greek, and Roman history, largely as illustrations. This does not necessarily indicate that either their religious beliefs or their biblical knowledge was shallow; the Convention included Methodist lay minister Richard Bassett of Delaware, a licensed Presbyterian minister, North Carolina's Hugh Williamson, and a former army chaplain, Georgia's Abraham Baldwin. Instead, it seems more likely to indicate that they may have been wary of using scriptural arguments in public debates.

Mentions of Religious Influences

Other references indicate that some delegates were concerned about religious divisiveness. Delaware's George Read opposed overshackling Congress lest "like Religious Creeds" they proved "embarrassing to those bound to conform to them & more likely to produce dissatisfaction and Scism, than harmony and union" (I, 582). James Madison observed that the division into religious sects could lead to factions and that "religion itself may become a motive to persecution & oppression" (I, 135).

By contrast, Benjamin Franklin commended the Quakers for giving their time in unpaid committee meetings to take care of matters that would otherwise go to court (I, 84). Similarly, Nathaniel Gorham of Massachusetts argued that an advantage of approving the new Constitution by state ratifying conventions rather than by state legislatures was that clergymen would not be excluded from the former as they sometimes were from the latter. Gorham observed that clergyman "are generally friends to good Government" and that "their services were found to be valuable in the formation & establishment of the Constitution of Massachts." (II, 90). Madison observed that the British Parliament sometimes excluded members to those "subservient to their own views, or to the views of political or Religious parties" (II, 250) and believed that this was at least one reason that the Convention did not heed Franklin's suggestion to begin each session with public prayer (Hutson, 531). The Convention adopted a provision against religious test oaths.

In proposing a national university, Virginia's James Madison and South Carolina's Charles Pinckney specified that "no preferences or distinctions should be allowed on account of religion" (II, 616). Finally, on the closing day of the Convention, Franklin observed that most religious sects thought themselves in full possession of the truth. He cited a book dedication in which an English author (Richard Steele) commented that "the only difference" between the English and Roman churches was that "the Church of Rome is infallible and the Church of England is never in the wrong" (II, 642).

References to Catholics

Most of the colonists were Protestants, and although there were two Catholic delegates at the Convention, there are a few indications at the Convention of criticism of the Roman Catholic Church. Remarking on "the tendency of abuses in every cases, to grow of themselves when once begun," Franklin observed that the system of providing for the apostles through charity had grown into "the establishment of the papal system" (I, 216). Although James Wilson cited the "steady" and "concerted" policy of the popes despite the advanced age of the pontiffs (II, 102), Gouverneur Morris had opposed selection of the president by Congress on the basis that "it will be like the election of a pope by a conclave of cardinals; real merit will rarely be the title to the appointment" (II, 29).

Other Influences

Long before the adoption of the establishment clause, the delegates recognized that religion could sometimes divide as well as heal, and their tendency to refer to the Bible as a source of illustration rather than of doctrine must be judged accordingly. Doctrinal views derived at least indirectly from the Bible might be evident in the Framers' statements about human nature, in their construction of a system of checks and balances, and in other ways that are not directly stated in the record. Some scholars believe that the very idea of a written constitution grew out of the biblical doctrine of covenants. William Trent has written an article suggesting that the U.S. Constitution and the constitutions adopted by various denominations had a reciprocal influence on one another and that the system adopted by a number of prominent denominations tying local, state, and national organizations together was a precursor to federalism (Trent 1889).

See Also Human Nature; Prayer at the Convention; Protestantism; Puritanism; Religious Affiliations of the Delegates

FOR FURTHER READING

Bowen, Catherine Drinker. 1966. *Miracle at Philadelphia: The Story of the Constitutional Convention May to September 1787.* Boston: Little, Brown.

Farrand, Max, ed. 1937. *The Records of the Federal Convention.* 4 vols. New Haven, CT: Yale University Press.

Hamilton, Alexander, James Madison, and John Jay. 1961. *The Federalist Papers.* New York: New American Library.

Hutson, James H. 1998. *Religion and the Founding of the American Republic.* Washington, DC: Library of Congress.

Lutz, Donald S. 1984. "The Relative Influence of European Writers on Late Eighteenth-Century American Political Thought." *American Political Science Review* 78 (March): 189–197.

Mires, Charlene. 2002. *Independence Hall in American Memory.* Philadelphia: University of Pennsylvania Press.

Reichley, James A. 1988. "Religion and the Constitution." *this Constitution*, no. 18 (Spring/Summer): 46–52.

Sandoz, Ellis, ed. 1991. *Political Sermons of the American Founding Era, 1730–1805*. Indianapolis, IN: Liberty Fund.

——. 1997. *Index to Political Sermons of the American Founding Era, 1730–1805*. Indianapolis, IN: Liberty Fund.

Trent, William P. 1889. "The Period of Constitution-Making in the American Churches." In *Essays in the Constitutional History of the United States in the Formative Period, 1776–1789*. Ed. J. Franklin Jameson. Boston: Houghton Mifflin.

BICAMERALISM

See CONGRESS, BICAMERALISM

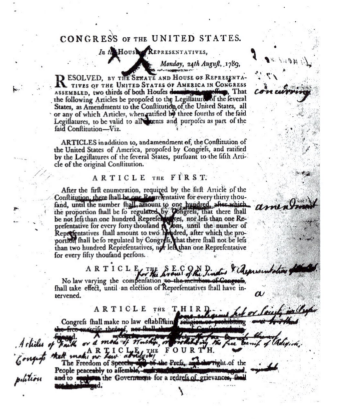

Copy of the Bill of Rights with handwritten amendment
(Pixel That)

BILL OF RIGHTS

One of the most striking omissions in the work of the Convention of 1787, and arguably one of the delegates' most strategic mistakes, was their failure to include a bill of rights. Not only had the English adopted such a bill of rights in 1689 (although this bill was arguably of limited utility since Parliament was considered to be sovereign, and such rights could not be enforced in court) but most American states had followed suit when they formulated their constitutions after they declared their independence from Britain.

In *Federalist* No. 84, Alexander Hamilton, who had attended the Convention as a delegate from New York, argued that "the Constitution is itself, in every rational sense, and to every useful purpose, a Bill of Rights," and to the degree that it delegated limited powers and attempted to control even these through separation of powers, elections, and other mechanisms, Hamilton was correct. Moreover, the document that the Convention produced has a number of guarantees and prohibitions that read much like those that would later be incorporated into the official Bill of Rights. Thus, Article I, Section 9 includes a number of specific limits—like prohibitions on ex post facto laws and bills of attainder—on congressional powers. Similarly, Article I, Section 10 includes a number of specific limits—like the limit on impairing contracts—on the exercise of state powers, and Article III guarantees the right of jury trials in criminal cases.

Discussions of a Bill of Rights at the Convention

On August 20, South Carolina's Charles Pinckney submitted a number of proposals for consideration by the Committee of Detail, including those that would today be associated with a bill of rights. These included a provision for the writ of habeas corpus (eventually incorporated into Article I, Section 9), a provision for liberty of the press (similar to that later included in the First Amendment), a prohibition against quartering troops in private houses without the owners' consent (similar to the provision of what would later become the Third Amendment), and a prohibition against religious oaths or tests (eventually incorporated in Article VI) (Farrand 1937, II, 340–341).

Discussion of a specific bill of rights emerged on September 12, just five days before the delegates signed the Constitution, in connection with a proposal by Hugh Williamson of North Carolina for juries in civil cases. Although Elbridge Gerry of Massachusetts supported this specific proposal, Nathaniel Gorham of Massachusetts and George Mason of Virginia both pointed to difficulties in operationalizing such a provision given the existing diversity within the states. Nonetheless, Mason used the opportunity to indicate that "a general principle laid down on this and some other points would be sufficient." Mason, the chief author of the Virginia Declaration of Rights of June 12, 1776 (Kurland and Lerner 1987, V, 3–4), went on to observe that "he wished the plan had been prefaced with a Bill of Rights, & would second a Motion if made for the purpose–It would give great quiet to the people; and with the aid of the State declarations, a bill might be prepared in a few hours" (II, 587–588).

Gerry made an actual motion to this effect, which Mason seconded. Connecticut's Roger Sherman said that he too favored securing the rights of the people, but he observed that the new Constitution would not repeal existing bills of rights and thought that legislatures could be trusted on the issue of jury trials in civil cases that had initiated the discussion. Mason correctly observed that "the Laws of the U.S. are to be paramount to State Bills of Rights" (II, 588).

On September 14, Pinckney and Gerry moved to add a provision to the Constitution, declaring "that the liberty of the Press should be inviolably observed" (II, 617). Sherman argued that the provision was "unnecessary" since "the power of Congress does not extend to the Press" (II, 618). The Convention then rejected the proposal by a vote of 7-4.

In printed remarks from September 15, Mason further observed that "there is no Declaration of Rights, and the laws of the general government being paramount to the laws and constitution of the several States, the Declaration of Rights in the separate States are no security" (II, 637). He further commented that "there is no declaration of any kind, for preserving the liberty of the press, or the trial by jury in civil causes [cases], nor against the danger of standing armies in time of peace" (II, 640). Still, the Convention rejected the idea of asking a committee to draft a bill.

Analysis of Convention Debates

Three aspects of the limited exchanges at the Convention regarding a Bill of Rights are particularly fascinating. First, this discussion occurred very late in Convention deliberations, almost as an afterthought, by delegates who already appeared to be leaning against approval of the document. George Mason, the primary advocate of a bill of rights, did not, like Madison on the opening days of the Convention, come with a text prepared but merely suggested it as part of a discussion involving jury trials. Second, George Mason seemed to indicate that a Bill of Rights would articulate broad general principles–he actually called for a "declaration" of rights–and, perhaps because he favored republicanism and himself feared a federal judiciary, did not make the strong case that he might have for the protections of individual rights that this would put into the hands of judges. Third, Mason justified such a bill as much for the soothing impact it would have on public opinion as for its intrinsic value. Cognizant that states already had bills of rights of their own, Convention delegates appear to have rejected the bill of rights not out of any unconcern for individual rights but simply out of a belief that such a bill would be unnecessary. Later arguments in the *Federalist Papers* that an enumeration of rights could actually prove dangerous on the theory that some might be left out seemed to contradict provisions for individual rights incorporated into the text of the Constitution.

Development of the Bill of Rights

The first 10 amendments to the U.S. Constitution, now known as the Bill of Rights, emerged from the debates between Federalists and Antifederalists over ratification of the Constitution. Although no state conditioned its ratification on the adoption of a bill of rights, a number of states accompanied their ratifications of the Constitution with proposals for specific amendments. Congress eventually proposed 12 amendments, 10 of which the states ratified in 1791 and another of which (relating to the timing of congressional pay raises) was belatedly ratified in 1992 as the Twenty-seventh Amendment. James Madison, the "father" of these amendments who shepherded them through the first Congress, clearly viewed them primarily as a way of calming public disquiet and of avoiding calling a second constitutional convention that might undo the work of the first, but he also appears to have been positively influenced by arguments that his friend Thomas Jefferson made on behalf of a bill of rights. The Amendments were ratified in 1791, seeming to vindicate the wisdom and workability of the constitutional amending process.

Content of the Bill of Rights

The First Amendment deals specifically with freedoms related to religion and political participation. Two clauses address religion. The first prohibits Congress from making laws "respecting an establishment of religion," and the second provides for its free exercise. The First Amendment made it clear that if religion were to flourish in America it would do so through private support. The First Amendment also provided guarantees for freedom of speech, freedom of the press, the right of peaceable assembly, and the right to petition government for redress of grievances. These clauses have been a frequent source for judicial decisionmaking.

The Second and Third Amendments have not received as much attention from the courts. The Second Amendment provides for the people's right "to keep and bear arms." There is continuing discussion as to whether this right is limited, as its preface–"A well regulated Militia, being necessary to the security of a free State"–suggests to some, to those serving in the military or whether it is de-

signed to articulate a personal right. Recent scholarly opinion appears to be shifting toward the latter interpretation. The Third Amendment, which grew out of British abuses that led to the Revolutionary War, limits the quartering of troops in private houses.

The Fourth Amendment protects the security of "persons, houses, papers, and effects, against unreasonable searches and seizures," again leading to numerous cases in which courts have had to decide whether searches were reasonable or not. The Fourth Amendment goes on to specify that when officers of the law seek search warrants, they must first establish "probable cause." The Amendment further outlaws "general warrants," like those by the British prior to the American Revolution, by providing that such warrants particularly describe "the place to be searched, and the persons or things to be seized." Courts have subsequently applied the exclusionary rule, which is not directly articulated within the Constitution, to limit evidence gathered by methods that violate this amendment.

The Fifth Amendment focuses on the rights of the criminally accused. It provides for grand jury indictments in capital cases, prohibits double jeopardy in such cases, protects individuals against compulsory self-incrimination, and prohibits the deprivation of "life, liberty, or property, without due process of law." Consistent with the Founding Fathers' regard for private property, this amendment further prohibits the governmental deprivation of private property without just compensation.

The Sixth and Seventh Amendments describe the rights of individuals who are on trial. The Sixth Amendment provides for speedy and public jury trials in criminal cases. It further requires the government to specify the charges against an individual, and it allows the individual to confront hostile witnesses, to have "compulsory process" for obtaining witnesses, and for the right to counsel. In the twentieth century, courts have widened the later right so that government must provide counsel to individuals who desire it but do not have the money to pay for it. The Seventh Amendment further extends the right to a jury trial to federal civil cases.

The Eighth Amendment prohibits excessive bail or fines. It also prohibits "cruel and unusual punishments." Courts have applied this provision to limit, but not as yet to outlaw, the application of the death penalty.

The Ninth Amendment was designed to address fears that Federalists had expressed during the debate with Antifederalists that a partial enumeration of rights would be interpreted so as to deny that the people had others. It accordingly specifies: "The enumeration in the Constitution of certain rights shall not be construed to deny or disparage others retained by the people." In similar fashion, the Tenth Amendment was designed to recognize that states had certain reserved rights, often referred to as "police powers." It thus specified: "The powers not delegated to the United States by the Constitution, nor prohibited by it to the States, are reserved to the States respectively, or to the people." Significantly, the Tenth Amendment ends where the Preamble began, with a reference to "the people." In part because of the work of James Madison in excluding the word "expressly" before the word "delegated," the Tenth Amendment did not, however, prevent the national government from exercising certain implied powers.

The Bill of Rights in American History

It should be evident that in formulating the Bill of Rights Madison focused chiefly on amendments that would guarantee individual rights rather than on amendments that would restructure the new government. The First Amendment specifically referenced congressional powers—"Congress shall make no law"—and Madison did not succeed in getting approval for a favored amendment that would limit state as opposed to federal powers. The Bill of Rights rarely served as the basis for litigation in the nation's early years, and in *Barron v. Baltimore* (1833), Chief Justice John Marshall examined the debates surrounding the birth of the Bill of Rights and sensibly concluded that it had been designed to limit the national government rather than the states.

When the Fourteenth Amendment was ratified in 1868 to limit state actions, some sponsors intended for it to serve in part as a way of overturning *Barron v. Baltimore* and applying the provisions of the Bill of Rights to the states, either through the privileges and immunities clause or the due process clause. Initially, the Supreme Court rejected this view and interpreted the amendment narrowly. In time, however, the Court began to "incorporate" fundamental guarantees of the Bill of Rights and apply them to the states. This trend, generally known as "selective incorporation," accelerated during the 1950s and 1960s (the time that Chief Justice Earl Warren presided over the Court), and today courts apply most, but not all, of the provisions in the Bill of Rights equally to state and national governments. The American people often express a dedication to the Bill of Rights equal to that of the Constitution itself. Periods commemorating the writing and adoption of the U.S. Constitution have frequently been extended to cover commemorations of the writing and ratification of the Bill of Rights as well.

See Also Amending Process; Antifederalists; Commemorations of the Constitutional Convention; Federalists; Jefferson, Thomas; Judicial Review; Madison, James, Jr.; Mason, George; Ratification in the States

FOR FURTHER READING

Amar, Akhil Reed. 1998. *The Bill of Rights: Creation and Reconstruction.* New Haven, CT: Yale University Press.

"Bicentennial Issue: The Bill of Rights." 1991. *Life* (Fall).

Cogan, Neil H., ed. 1997. *The Complete Bill of Rights: The Drafts, Debates, Sources, and Origins.* New York: Oxford University Press.

Conley, Patrick T., and John P. Kaminski. 1992. *The Bill of Rights and the States: The Colonial and Revolutionary Origins of American Liberties.* Madison, WI: Madison House.

Farrand, Max, ed. 1937. *The Records of the Federal Convention.* 4 vols. New Haven, CT: Yale University Press.

Goldwin, Robert A. 1997. *From Parchment to Power: How James Madison Used the Bill of Rights to Save the Constitution.* Washington, DC: AEI Press.

Kurland, Philip B., and Ralph Lerner. 1987. *The Founders' Constitution.* Volume 5 of 5: *Amendments I–XII.* Chicago: University of Chicago Press.

Rutland, Robert Allen. 1962. *The Birth of the Bill of Rights, 1776–1791.* New York: Collier Books.

Slonim, Shlomo. 2003. "The Federalist Papers and the Bill of Rights." *Constitutional Commentary* 20 (Spring): 151–161.

Vile, John R. 2003. *Encyclopedia of Constitutional Amendments, Proposed Amendments, and Amending Issues, 1789–2002.* 2nd ed. Santa Barbara, CA: ABC-CLIO.

BILLS OF ATTAINDER

See ATTAINDER, BILLS OF

BLACKS

See AFRICAN AMERICANS

John Blair, Jr., delegate from Virginia
(Pixel That)

BLAIR, JOHN, JR. (1732–1800)

Although Virginia sent seven delegates to the Constitutional Convention, two returned home before the Convention ended and two refused to sign, leaving only three state delegates who did so. Of these three, only James Madison spoke extensively at the Convention. By contrast, George Washington was recorded as delivering only two speeches, and John Blair is not recorded as having spoken once. Given Blair's previous political experience, it appears as though he might have had something substantial to say, especially regarding the organization of the judicial branch of the national government.

Blair was born in Williamsburg, Virginia, in 1732 to a wealthy family. His father, after whom he was named, was a merchant who also participated in Virginia politics. He had served as interim governor and in other positions that his son would later occupy. Not coincidentally, he also owned the Raleigh Tavern in Williamsburg, a gathering place for many of the early revolutionaries.

Blair attended the College of William and Mary before studying law at the Middle Temple of London and returning to Virginia with a new wife, Jean Blair (whom he had married in Edinburgh); he developed a profitable law practice. He was a delegate to the Virginia House of Burgesses from Williamsburg when it voted for independence, and he served to draw up the new state constitution and draft its Declaration of Rights. In 1778, he was appointed to the general court of Virginia. After becoming its chief justice, he became a judge of the state's high court of chancery and of its court of appeals, where he participated in the ruling in *The Commonwealth of Virginia v. Caton et al.* (1782), asserting the Court's right to strike legislation down that it considered to be unconstitutional. From his position on the judiciary, Blair was selected to serve at the Constitutional Convention.

William Blount, delegate from North Carolina
(Pixel That)

Washington appointed Blair as one of the original associate justices of the U.S. Supreme Court. He served in this position from 1789 to 1796, joining the majority in the case of *Chisholm v. Georgia* (1793), which was later overturned by the Eleventh Amendment. He resigned because of ill health. He died in the town of his birth in 1800 and is buried outside the Bruton Parish Church in that city.

See Also Judicial Review; Virginia; Virginia Declaration of Rights

FOR FURTHER READING

Cushman, Clare, ed. 1995. *The Supreme Court Justices, Illustrated Biographies, 1789–1995.* Washington, DC: Congressional Quarterly.
Farrand, Max, ed. 1937. *The Records of the Federal Convention.* 4 vols. New Haven, CT: Yale University Press.

About all that is known about Blair's contributions to the Constitution is that he signed the document and spoke in its favor at the Virginia state ratifying convention. Madison's notes of votes of various Virginia delegates further record that Blair, like Virginia's Governor Edmund Randolph, opposed the establishment of a unitary executive (Farrand 1937, I, 97), favored a congressional veto of state laws (I, 168), voted for a series of agreements about the president on July 26 (II, 121), opposed the requirement that money bills originate in the House of Representatives (II, 280), voted for requiring a two-thirds majority in Congress to enact export taxes rather than banning them altogether (II, 363), and opposed reducing the majority in Congress needed to override a presidential veto from three-fourths to two-thirds (II, 587). He is not recorded as having served on any of the Convention's committees.

After the Convention, Blair accompanied George Washington back to Virginia where, as noted above, Blair supported the Constitution as a delegate to the state's ratifying convention.

BLOUNT, WILLIAM (1749–1800)

A book on the Founding Fathers observed that William Blount "was more interested in what his country could do for him than in what he could do for his country" (Whitney 1974, 55). Born to a wealthy landholding family in Bertie County, North Carolina, in 1749, Blount gained an insatiable appetite for more land and for power. Elected in the early 1780s to the North Carolina legislature, and to the Continental Congress, Blount seems not to have taken his legislative responsibilities altogether seriously.

Blount was not seated at the Constitutional Convention until June 20, having been delayed by problems with "blind piles," or hemorrhoids, an ailment he referred to as "undoubtedly the most painful teasing Complaint that I have ever experienced" (Hutson 1987, 14). Once at the Convention, William Blount is not recorded as participating in a single discussion until it came time to sign the document. Then relying on a somewhat legalistic distinction, he indicated that while he had "declared that he would not sign so as to pledge himself in support of the plan," he was willing to sign, without committing himself, to "attest the fact that the plan was the unanimous act of the States in Convention" (Farrand 1937, II, 646).

Blount's fullest exposition of his thoughts on the Convention was contained in a letter of July 19 that probably violated the Convention's rule of secrecy. Posted from New York, indicating that Blount had left the Convention at least for some time, Blount referred to "H. W." (Hugh Williamson) as the head of the North Carolina delegation. He reported that North Carolina was following the lead of Virginia, primary leadership of which he attributed to James Madison. Further reporting that the Convention had settled on the main outlines of a new system, he reported that "I must confess not withstanding all I heard in favour of this System I am not in sentiment with my Colleagues for as I have before said I still think we shall ultimately end not many Years just be separate and distinct Governments perfectly independent of each other." Blount further noted that "the little States were much opposed to the Politicks of the larger they insisted that each State ought to have an equal vote as in the present Confederation" (Hutson 1987, 175).

After the Convention, George Washington appointed Blount as the superintendent of Indian affairs for territories south of the Ohio River. In this position, he engaged in extensive land speculation and in attempts to take land from the Indians. He eventually turned against the Federalist administration when it failed to support him in this endeavor.

Blount built an impressive house in Knoxville and helped organize the state of Tennessee. He served as president of its constitutional convention in 1796. Afterward elected as one of the state's two U.S. senators, he was the first and only such senator ever to be impeached after he was discovered to have conspired to stir up an Indian war against Spain. Although expelled from the Senate, he was not convicted on impeachment charges.

Still popular in the state he had helped to found, Blount resisted appeals to return to the nation's capital for his impeachment trial. He was, indeed, elected as speaker of the Tennessee state senate. Blount died in 1800.

See Also North Carolina; Tennessee

FOR FURTHER READING

Farrand, Max, ed. 1937. *The Records of the Federal Convention*. 4 vols. New Haven, CT: Yale University Press.

Hutson, James H., ed. 1987. *Supplement to Max Farrand's* The Records of the Federal Convention of 1787. New Haven, CT: Yale University Press.

Melton, Buckner F., Jr. 1998. *The First Impeachment: The Constitution's Framers and the Case of Senator William Blount*. Macon, GA: Mercer University Press.

Whitney, David D. 1974. *Founders of Freedom in America: Lives of the Men Who Signed the Constitution of the United States and So Helped to Establish the United States of America*. Chicago: J. J. Ferguson Publishing.

BORROWING POWER

Congress is recognized as having "the power of the purse." Consistent with this power, Article I, Section 8 vests Congress with authority "to borrow Money on the credit of the United States." Despite current disputes over federal budget deficits, this power received scant attention at the Constitutional Convention. Although such decisions required a two-thirds majority, under the Articles of Confederation Congress already had this power. Probably being guided by this document, in its report of August 6, the Committee of Detail proposed the power "To borrow Money, and emit Bills on the Credit of the United States" (Farrand 1937, II, 182).

The latter provision, which would specifically have allowed the government the right to issue paper money at a time when people were familiar with the phrase "worthless as a Continental" (a reference to the deflated currency issued by Congress during the Revolutionary War) and when delegates were constantly accusing Rhode Island of deflating its currency by issuing paper money, stirred the primary debate. Gouverneur Morris of Pennsylvania moved to strike the provision, and South Carolina's Pierce Butler seconded him. Morris observed, "If the United States had credit such bills would be unnecessary; if they had not unjust & useless" (II, 309). Madison proposed a compromise by which the Convention would simply prohibit making such bills "a tender" but apparently permitting promissory notes. Morris responded that striking the provision would still permit "notes of a responsible minister which will do all the good without the mischief" but claimed that the "Monied interests" would oppose the Constitution unless it prohibited "paper emissions" (II, 309).

Nathaniel Gorham of Massachusetts simply wanted to strike the words, but Virginia's George Mason was more torn on the subject. He did not believe Congress would have the power to issue such bills unless such a power was enumerated. Although he professed "a mortal hatred of paper money," because "he could not foresee all emergencies," he expressed his unwillingness "to tie the hands of the Legislature" (II, 309). He argued that the success of the Revolutionary War had depended on such issues.

Gorham said that Congress would have adequate power to accomplish its objectives through borrowing. Maryland's John Mercer was even more equivocal than Mason had been. He favored paper money, but not in the present temper of the country. He neither wanted to authorize the power nor prohibit it: "It will stamp suspicion on the Government to deny it a discretion on this point. It was impolitic also to excite the opposition of all those who were friends to paper money" (II, 309). Connecticut's Oliver Ellsworth thought that prohibiting paper money was likely to lead to further support for the Constitution. Virginia's Edmund Randolph worried that one should not strike out a power that might later be necessary. Pennsylvania's James Wilson thought it would "have a most salutary influence on the credit of the U. States to remove the possibility of paper money" (II, 310). Butler noted that no European powers resorted to paper money; Mason again expressed reservations about completely tying the hands of Congress on this matter; Delaware's George Read thought that the power would alarm the republic; New Hampshire's John Langdon said he would rather reject the whole document than retain the words; and the Convention voted 9-2 against including the phrase. It then unanimously affirmed Congress's power to borrow money.

Congress has freely used its borrowing power, especially in times of war and depression. Although its legal authority to do so has not been questioned, some critics believe this power has been abused. Recent years have witnessed increased attempts to enact a "balanced budget" amendment that would limit the size and/or growth of such deficits (Vile 2003, 32–35).

See Also Money, Congressional Coining

FOR FURTHER READING

Farrand, Max, ed. 1937. *The Records of the Federal Convention.* 4 vols. New Haven, CT: Yale University Press.

Savage, James D. 1988. *Balanced Budgets and American Politics.* Ithaca, NY: Cornell University Press.

Vile, John R. 2003. *Encyclopedia of Constitutional Amendments, Proposed Amendments, and Amending Issues, 1789–2002.* 2nd ed. Santa Barbara, CA: ABC-CLIO.

BREARLY, DAVID (1754–1790)

Born in 1745 in Spring Grove, New Jersey, Brearly studied law and became an ardent Patriot. He served during the Revolutionary War as a captain and a lieutenant colonel before being appointed as New Jersey's chief justice. In this position, he issued a decision in the case of *Holmes v. Walton* (1780) that helped establish the right of this court to strike down unconstitutional legislation.

Brearly was the first delegate to be selected to attend the Constitutional Convention. He was

David Brearly, delegate from New Jersey
(Pixel That)

present on May 25 for the opening day of business at the Convention, and he signed the document on September 17. The first record of Brearly's participation in debates was on June 9, when he seconded a motion by fellow New Jersey delegate William Paterson for a reconsideration of the Virginia Plan's proposal for apportioning suffrage in both houses of Congress according to population. Like Paterson, Brearly clearly supported the desire of the small states for equal representation. In his longest speech at the Convention, Brearly observed that this matter had already once been settled in creating the Articles of Confederation and argued that equal representation was essential to the preservation of the small states. He estimated that if representation were to be apportioned according to population, Virginia would have 16 votes to Georgia's 1. He further believed that the states of Virginia, Pennsylvania, and Massachusetts "will carry every thing before them" (Farrand 1937, I, 177). He observed that within his home state of New Jersey, large coun-

ties overwhelmed smaller ones when they were combined together.

Admitting that it did not seem fair to give the smallest states equal representation to the largest, Brearly made a radical proposal. He suggested spreading out a U.S. map and "that all the existing boundaries be erased, and that a new partition of the whole be made into 13 equal parts" (I, 177). Neither Brearly nor the Convention appears to have pursued this idea further, and it is probable that Brearly made the suggestion not so much because he favored it but because he hoped thereby to get the attention of the delegates from the larger states. In any event, Brearly continued to focus on a single theme at the Convention, namely the necessity of providing small states adequate representation so that they could protect their interests in the new government.

The Convention did not resolve the issue of state representation until it adopted the Great Compromise on July 16. In the meantime, Rhode Island, the smallest state, had refused to send delegates, and those from New Hampshire had not arrived. On June 30, Brearly accordingly moved that the president should write to the New Hampshire governor informing him "that the business depending before the Convention was of such a nature as to require the immediate attendance of the deputies of that State" (I, 481). The Convention rejected the request by a vote of 5-2. Madison observed that "it was well understood that the object was to add N. Hamshire to the no. of States opposed to the doctrine of proportional representation, which it was presumed from her relative size she must be adverse to" (I, 481).

Brearly is next recorded as speaking on August 24. Consistent with his earlier concerns about the small states, Brearly opposed the idea of electing the president by a "joint" ballot by both houses of Congress (II, 402). Brearly undoubtedly feared that, in such joint ballots, the more populous states would swallow up the votes of the smaller states. When the Convention voted to accept such a joint ballot, Brearly seconded a motion by New Jersey's Jonathan Dayton to grant each state a single vote (II, 403).

Brearly served on two committees at the Constitutional Convention—the 11-man committee to reconsider proportional representation that was appointed on July 9 and the Committee on Postponed Matters created on August 31. He chaired the latter committee, which proposed on September 1 that "the members of each House shall be ineligible to any civil office under the authority of the U.S. during the time for which they shall respectively be elected, and no person holding an office under the U.S. shall be a member of either House during his continuance in office" (II, 484).

On September 15, Brearly further seconded a motion introduced by Connecticut's Roger Sherman that would have eliminated the proposed constitutional amending process (II, 630). Sherman and Brearly appear to have been reacting, however, to the Convention's failure, to that point, to guarantee the provision for equal state suffrage within the Senate against further amendment. Although the motion to strike the amending process failed, it did result in a provision entrenching equal state representation in the Senate against such amendment (II, 631).

Brearly served as a presidential elector for George Washington, who appointed him as a federal district judge of New Jersey. He died at the age of 45 in 1790.

See Also Committee on Postponed Matters; Committee to Reconsider Representation in the House; New Jersey

FOR FURTHER READING

Farrand, Max, ed. 1937. *The Records of the Federal Convention.* 4 vols. New Haven, CT: Yale University Press.

Whitney, David. 1974. *Founders of Freedom in America: Lives of the Men Who Signed the Constitution of the United States and So Helped to Establish the United States of America.* Chicago: J. J. Ferguson Publishing.

BRITISH INFLUENCES ON THE CONSTITUTION

See GREAT BRITAIN

BROOM, JACOB (1752–1810)

Born in Wilmington Delaware in 1752 to a family that had acquired substantial parcels of land (Broom's father had started as a blacksmith), Broom was educated at the Wilmington Academy, after which he became a surveyor. He and his wife, Rachel Pierce, had three sons, two of whom were later elected to Congress, and five daughters. Prior to serving at the Constitutional Convention, Broom served as a burgess of the city of Wilmington for almost 10 years and as a member of the Delaware legislature for two years. He had been appointed to, but had not attended, the Annapolis Convention.

Broom was present for the opening day of Convention business on May 25, 1787, but he remained silent during the first month of business. Thereafter, he did not speak extensively. Indeed, he is more noted for seconding the proposals of others than for making his own or giving long speeches. However, he seems to have emerged as an individual willing to invest substantial power in the new government as long as the interests of Delaware and other small states were accommodated.

Congress

On June 26, Broom supported a motion to raise the term of senators from six years to nine years. He said that he favored service "during good behavior" but thought that nine years was the most he might realistically request. He observed that this number, like the number six, would allow for one-third of the members to rotate out in each election (Farrand 1937, I, 426).

On July 10, Broom agreed to setting the number of members of the U.S. House of Representatives at 65. He did so, however, with the understanding that his state should continue to have equal representation in the Senate (II, 570).

On August 14, Broom seconded a motion by Pennsylvania's Gouverneur Morris allowing members of Congress to vacate their seats in order to accept appointments in the army or navy (II, 290). On that same day, he supported a motion allowing members of Congress to set their own salaries. He observed, "The State Legislatures had this power, and no complaint had been made of it" (II, 291). He also favored a motion by which members of both congressional houses would be paid the same (II, 293).

On August 20, Broom seconded a motion by Rufus King of Massachusetts granting the Senate the "sole" power to declare punishments for treason (II, 348). Three days later, he seconded a far more important motion by South Carolina's Charles Pinckney that would have granted two-thirds of the members of both houses of Congress power to invalidate acts of state legislation that they thought conflicted "with the General interest and harmony of the Union" (II, 390). On August 25, however, Broom supported a motion by Pennsylvania's Gouverneur Morris to strike out a provision granting the president the right to correspond with state governors as being unnecessary and implying that, without such a provision, he would not have this power (II, 419).

President

On July 17, Broom supported reducing the presidential term from seven years. He tied this position to the Convention's decision to make the president re-eligible for election. Otherwise, he indicated that he would have supported a longer term (II, 33). Indeed, shortly thereafter, he supported a motion by Virginia's James McClurg to allow the president to serve "during good behavior" (II, 33). Two days later, Broom seconded a motion providing for selecting the president by state legislatures, allowing states to choose one to three electors depending on their size (II, 57). He later moved to postpone a somewhat different allocation of electors proposed by Elbridge Gerry of Massachusetts (II, 63–64; also see II, 103).

Continuation of the Convention

On July 16, the day on which the Convention agreed to the Connecticut Compromise, after Virginia's Edmund Randolph had suggested an adjournment, New Jersey's William Paterson had suggested that the secrecy rule should be suspended and that the delegates should adjourn and go home to receive instructions from their constituents. Broom was opposed to such a "sine die" adjournment. He thought this would be "fatal" to the Convention's work and said that "something must be done by the Convention tho' it should be by a bare majority" (II, 19).

Signing the Constitution

Broom is the only one of the signers of the Constitution for whom no portrait has been located. In the painting by Louis Glanzman, which was made in 1987 and displayed in the room at Independence Hall where visitors gather for orientation prior to going into the courtroom and the East Room, Broom is accordingly pictured as signing the document with his back to the viewers.

Life after the Convention

After signing the Constitution, Broom returned to Delaware and devoted himself chiefly to business affairs. He built a number of mills, served as a bank director, and helped establish the Chesapeake and Delaware Canal. He died in Philadelphia in 1810, bequeathing some of his wealth to the Female Benevolent Society and to a Wilmington group formed to educate African American children.

See Also Delaware

FOR FURTHER READING

Farrand, Max, ed. 1937. *The Records of the Federal Convention.* 4 vols. New Haven, CT: Yale University Press.

Whitney, David. 1974. *Founders of Freedom in America: Lives of the Men Who Signed the Constitution of the United States and So Helped to Establish the United States of America.* Chicago: J. J. Ferguson Publishing.

BUREAUCRACY

Today bureaucracy, although often decried, is generally recognized as being essential to modern governments. Bureaucratic structures combine hierarchy, a specialization of functions, and an emphasis on formalized rules to deliver predictable services. Such structures, although significantly more developed and complex, are not new. Michael Nelson has thus observed that many of the complaints about the British government that Jefferson articulated in the Declaration of Independence centered on King George III's abuses of administrative powers, as when Jefferson declared, "He has erected a multitude of new offices . . . and sent hither swarms of officers to harass our people and eat out their subsistence" (Nelson 1982, 750, quoting Declaration of Independence). Although the idea of bureaucracy fits in well with the idea of constitutionalism and the rule of law, bureaucracies that are unaccountable can conflict with ideas of democracy.

Under the Articles of Confederation, there was no independent executive. Congress initially attempted to administer the new government through committees. It then tried boards. In 1781 it created the Departments of Foreign Affairs, War, Marine, and Finance, the latter of which became the Treasury Department (Nelson, 751).

Alexander Hamilton proclaimed in *The Federalist,* especially *Federalist* No. 77, that the new government would enhance administration. He largely associated such enhanced administration with the creation of a singular executive. Article II, Section 1 vests the "executive power" in the president, and Article II, Section 3 entrusts the president with power to "take Care that the Laws be faithfully executed." Article II, Section 2 permitted the president to "require the Opinion, in writing, of the principal Officer in each of the executive Departments, upon any Subject relating to the Duties of their respective Offices," thus appearing to contemplate a continuation of the departments established under the Articles. Delegates at the Convention beat back a number of attempts to create a Council of Revision or a Privy Council that the president would be required to consult and/or through whom he might

exercise veto powers over state or national legislation, but it contemplated that he would be able to call upon department heads for advice.

The president was designated with the power to nominate all principal officers, with Congress granted the power to vest the appointment of inferior officers "in the President alone, in the Courts of Law, or in the Heads of Departments" (Article I, Section 2). Presidential appointments were subject to Senate confirmation.

The first Congress created the Departments of War, State, and the Treasury, as well as the Attorney General, as cabinet officers. Although the president appointed the heads of each, Congress appeared to regard the Treasury Department, with its ties to the power of the purse, as more of a legislative than an executive agency (Galloway 1958, 466).

Modern courts have recognized the power of the president to fire appointees, but the Constitution did not specify this power. Indeed, in *Federalist* No. 77, Alexander Hamilton, who was a proponent of strong presidential powers, nonetheless contemplated that a president would not be able to exercise such a power without Senate consent (Hamilton, Madison, and Jay 1961, 459).

Consistent with the doctrine of checks and balances, separation of powers permitted, and indeed encouraged, multiple checks on bureaucratic behavior. The president's power to appoint is checked by the Senate's power to confirm. Congress can exercise oversight through hearings and can exercise control through the power of the purse strings. Courts can further review administrative behavior through their powers of statutory interpretation (the power to construe laws) and judicial review (the power to invalidate unconstitutional laws or executive decisions).

The Convention's decision, incorporated in Article III, Section 1, to vest the judicial power "in one supreme Court, and in such inferior Courts as the Congress may from time to time ordain and establish," pointed the way to the current hierarchical system of courts that was outlined by the establishment of a three-tiered system of federal courts by the Judiciary Act of 1789 in the first Congress.

Early departments in the United States were

relatively small and were largely governed by elites. Andrew Jackson somewhat democratized this process with his "spoils system" (taken from the expression "to the victor belong the spoils") but opened up the possibility of promoting the kinds of corruption many of the Framers had feared. Partly in reaction, the Pendleton Act of 1883 created the Civil Service Commission and led to the development of a professionalized career civil service. The New Deal witnessed a significant expansion of the administrative state. John Rohr is among those who has attempted to defend independent regulatory agencies (whose members often have specified terms) against charges that they violate the principle of separation of powers as contemplated by the Founding Fathers (Rohr 1986). Michael W. Spicer has further argued that if bureaucracy is to be consistent with the Framers' view of human nature, public administrators should be able to exercise some discretion but should themselves be "checked by a system of administrative rules and procedures" (1995, 79).

See Also Appointments and Confirmations; Articles of Confederation; Checks and Balances; Council of Revision; Declaration of Independence; Judicial Organization and Protections; President, Council; President, Executive Power; President, Number of; Separation of Powers; Treasury, Secretary of the

FOR FURTHER READING

Beach, John C., et al. 1997. "State Administration and the Founding Fathers during the Critical Period." *Administration and Society* 28 (February): 23.

Galloway, George B. 1958. "Precedents Established in the First Congress." *Western Political Quarterly* 22 (September): 454–468.

Hamilton, Alexander, James Madison, and John Jay. 1961. *The Federalist Papers.* New York: New American Library.

Nelson, Michael. 1982. "A Short, Ironic History of American National Bureaucracy." *Journal of Politics* 44 (August): 747–778.

Patterson, C. Perry. 1949. "The President as Chief Administrator." *Journal of Politics* 11 (February): 218–235.

Rohr, John A. 1986. *To Run a Constitution: The Legitimacy of the Administrative State.* Lawrence: University Press of Kansas.

Rourke, Francis E. 1993. "Whose Bureaucracy Is This, Anyway? Congress, the President and Public Administration." *PS: Political Science and Politics* 26 (December): 687–692.

Spicer, Michael W. 1995. *The Founders, the Constitution, and Public Administration: A Conflict in World Views.* Washington, DC: Georgetown University Press.

BUTLER, PIERCE (1744–1822)

Pierce Butler was born to the family of an English baronet in County Carlow, Ireland, in 1744 and immigrated to South Carolina with a commission as a major in the English army that his family had purchased for him. He sold this commission after marrying the daughter of a wealthy plantation owner and was soon supporting the Patriot cause. He was chosen as a state legislator in 1778 and

Pierce Butler, delegate from South Carolina (Pixel That)

served there for about a decade, also being appointed the next year as the state's adjutant general. Unlike the other delegates from South Carolina, he had no formal legal training.

Pierce Butler was present for the first day of Convention business on May 25, 1787, having arrived with General Charles Cotesworth Pinckney on a ship the previous day. On May 28 Butler proposed that the Convention provide against having its business interrupted by preventing the absence of members and by presenting "licentious publications of their proceedings" (Farrand 1937, I, 13). The Convention did not, and probably could not, have adopted the first of these suggestions, but it did take secrecy very seriously.

Congress

Apportionment

On June 6, Butler indicated that he favored apportionment in the House of Representatives on the basis of wealth as well as population and that if his plan were adopted he was even willing to consider abolishing the state legislatures (I, 144). The next day, he was unwilling to give his view on the size of the Senate until he knew "the ratio of representation" (I, 151). On June 25, Butler further indicated that it would be better to settle on how representation would be allocated in the Senate before deciding on what powers to give that body (I, 407; also see II, 290).

On June 11, Butler joined fellow South Carolinian John Rutledge in proposing that suffrage in the House of Representatives should be apportioned according to states' tax contributions. He argued that "money was power; and that the States ought to have weight in the Govt.–in proportion to their wealth" (I, 196).

In time, the issue of House and Senate apportionment was tied in part to whether the Senate would be able to originate money bills. On June 13, Butler indicated that he saw no reason for limiting the origination of money bills to the House of Representatives. At a time when delegates were seeking to justify this limitation on the basis of British practice, Butler observed that "we were always following the British Constitution when the reason of it did not apply." He further observed that

> there was no analogy between the Ho[use] of Lords and the body proposed to be established. If the Senate should be degraded by any such discriminations, the best men would be apt to decline serving in it in favor of the other branch. And it will lead the latter into the practice of tacking other clauses to money bills. (I, 233)

On July 5, Butler reiterated his view that the privilege of originating money bills was inconsequential. At this time, he also indicated that he thought that states should be represented in the Senate according to their property (I, 529). It is not clear that Butler changed his mind on the wisdom of the provision related to the introduction of money bills, but on August 8 he indicated that he favored sticking with the existing compromise (II, 224).

When the Convention appointed a committee on July 6 to examine a proposal made by an earlier committee to grant states one representative for every 40,000 inhabitants, Butler indicated that he favored such reexamination. He continued to believe that population was an inadequate basis of representation. He cited the "changeableness" of this number as one reason, but he emphasized the role of government in supporting property, contending "that property was the only just measure of representation. This was the great object of Governt: the great cause of war, the great means of carrying it on" (I, 542). In this same speech, Butler indicated that he thought it was necessary to provide some "balance" between the existing states and any new Western states that might be admitted (I, 542). He reiterated his view that property should be factored into representation on July 9 (I, 562).

When a second committee appointed to deal with the subject proposed a House of Representatives consisting of 65 members, it initially apportioned five such representatives to Butler's South Carolina. Butler was among those who attempted to get adjustments for their own states, unsuccessfully proposing that his state should be granted six representatives instead (I, 568). He may not have been particularly bothered by his loss on this issue, as he later expressed the firm conviction that the movement of population growth in the nation was toward the South and West (I, 605).

Although Butler disfavored apportioning Congress on the basis of population, he proposed on July 11 that the three-fifths clause should be struck out in favor of a provision that would count blacks equally with whites (I, 580). Although such a formula would have obvious benefits for his state, Butler viewed counting blacks like others as a way of providing the representation for wealth that the Convention had otherwise rejected (I, 580). He thus observed that

> the labour of a slave in S. Carola. was as productive & valuable as that of a freeman in Massts., that as wealth was the great means of defence and utility to the Nation they were equally valuable to it with freemen; and that consequently an equal representation ought to be allowed for them in a Government which was instituted principally for the protection of property, and was itself to be supported by property. (I, 581; also see I, 592)

Selection and Compensation

On May 31, Butler indicated that he did not think that it would be practical for the people to elect members of the U.S. House of Representatives (I, 50); as under the Articles of Confederation, he thought state legislatures were "better calculated to make choice of such" (I, 58). Along with fellow South Carolinian John Rutledge, Butler proposed that members of the Senate should receive no compensation (I, 219), a motion undoubtedly prompted by the hope that the Senate would thereby become a more aristocratic body. When he later served as a U.S. senator, Butler proposed that senators should be paid $8 a day (it set that of representatives at $6 and that of senators at $7), arguing that "a member of the Senate should not only have a handsome income, but should spend it all" (Whitney 1974, 69).

Butler appears to have supported the idea that states should pay members of Congress (I, 374, where he seemed to push for a reconsideration after the Convention had voted otherwise). He thought this was particularly important in the case of senators, whose longer tenure and residence at the national capital might cause them to "lose sight of their Constituents unless dependent on them for their support" (II, 290).

Butler opposed a motion by Pennsylvania's Gouverneur Morris on August 7 that would have limited the right to vote for members of Congress to freeholders. Butler observed that "there is no right of which the people are more jealous than that of suffrage" (II, 202). He further associated the imposition of such qualifications with the establishment of aristocracy (II, 202).

Eligibility for Other Offices

Butler favored a measure limiting members of Congress from accepting offices during their term or for a year afterward. He viewed this as a way of preventing "corruption," which he believed had helped ruin the British government (I, 376). He thought a motion by Virginia's James Madison limiting this limitation to offices created or augmented during the terms of a member was too weak and could be too easily evaded (I, 386). He did not fear the consequences of disablement believing that "Characters fit for office Wd. never be unknown" (I, 389). On June 26, however, Butler favored striking a prohibition on the eligibility of members of the Senate to state offices (I, 428).

Qualifications of Members

On August 8, after two delegates had proposed a minimal residency requirement of one year for members of the House of Representatives, Butler joined John Rutledge in proposing that this be raised to three years (II, 218). The next day, Butler indicated that he did not favor allowing individuals to serve in Congress unless they had long resided in the country. This argument must have been especially effective coming from someone who was himself an immigrant. He observed that immigrants "bring with them, not only attachments to other Countries; but ideas of Govt. so distinct from ours that in every point of view they are dangerous." He further said that had he been admitted into government shortly after coming to the United States, "his foreign habits opinions & attachments would have rendered him an improper agent in public affairs" (II, 236). Again on August 13, Butler indicated that he "was strenuous agst. admitting foreigners into our public Councils" (II, 269).

Powers

On May 30, Butler introduced a motion, seconded by Virginia's Edmund Randolph, postponing a resolution that Randolph had introduced providing "that a national government ought to be established consisting of a supreme legislative, judiciary and executive" (I, 30). The Convention adopted this substitute motion, which took it far beyond its charge of revising, correcting, and enlarging the existing Articles of Confederation. Butler indicated that same day that he had been reluctant to grant further powers to a Congress constructed like that under the Articles of Confederation but that "the proposed distribution of the powers into different bodies changed the case, and would induce him to go great lengths" (I, 34). Apparently, Butler had previously asked Randolph to show how a strengthened national government was needed to preserve the states (I, 41). On June 1, Butler opposed a provision granting Congress the power to invalidate state laws, believing that it would be particularly detrimental to the "distant States" (I, 168).

On July 16, Butler questioned a provision that would have granted Congress power to "legislate in all cases to which the separate States are incompetent." He observed that "the vagueness of the terms rendered it impossible for any precise judgment to be formed" (II, 17).

On August 16, Butler seconded a motion by Gouverneur Morris to strike a provision granting Congress power to emit bills of credit (II, 309). The next day, he indicated that he thought it was preferable to vest war-making powers in the president rather than in the Senate (II, 318). If Congress were to be granted the power to declare war, he thought that it should also have the power to make peace (II, 319). On September 7, Butler seconded a motion by James Madison that would grant two-thirds of the Senate to enter into a treaty of peace without the president's consent (II, 540). Madison's concern, which Butler may or may not have shared, was that presidents, who would gain power during war, might otherwise seek to impede the establishment of peace (II, 540). On August 18, Butler indicated that he believed that since the national government had the responsibility of providing for the common defense, it should also have the power to govern all the state militias (II, 331).

On August 21, Butler supported a motion by Elbridge Gerry of Massachusetts that would have apportioned taxes prior to the first census according to apportionment in the House of Representatives. Arguing that it was "founded in reason and equity" (II, 358), perhaps Butler congratulated himself on the fact that the Convention had rejected his earlier proposal to grant his state an extra representative in that body.

Like many other delegates from the Deep South, Butler opposed allowing Congress to tax exports. On August 21, he argued that such a power would be "unjust and alarming to the staple States" (II, 360). The next day, he was even more emphatic: "he never would agree to the power of taxing exports" (II, 374).

When it was proposed on August 23 that Congress should assume state debts, Butler displayed a passion that would later show itself when this same issue was debated in the first Congress. He indicated that he feared that "it should compel payment as well to the Blood-suckers who had speculated on the distresses of others, as to those who had fought & bled for their country" (II, 392). He further indicated that he favored making distinctions between classes of bondholders. On August 25, however, Butler said that he intended "neither to increase nor diminish the security of the Creditors" (II, 413).

Butler was willing to accede to giving up the requirement that it take two-thirds majorities of

Congress to adopt regulations relating to commerce. He viewed this as an important concession. His explanation says much about the way that delegates from different sections of the country viewed one another. Butler thus observed that "he considered the interests of these and of the Eastern States, to be as different as the interests of Russia and Turkey" (II, 451).

Presidency

Rutledge joined fellow South Carolina delegate Charles Pinckney on June 2 in favoring a single executive. His arguments were practical but effective:

> If one man should be appointed he would be responsible to the whole, and would be impartial to its interests. If three or more should be taken from as many districts, there would be a constant struggle for local advantage. In Military matters this would be particularly mischievous. (I, 89)

Butler illustrated the problems of a plural executive in military affairs by citing examples from Holland. Butler qualified his views on June 4, however, by indicating that he would not have favored a single executive if he thought that this executive would be invested with an absolute veto over legislation. Noting that executive power had a tendency to increase, he feared that an absolute negative would allow "a Cataline [a Roman dictator] or a Cromwell [an English dictator]" to arise in the United States (I, 100). Butler proposed that the executive should only have the power to suspend legislation for a fixed period (I, 103).

On July 19, after a motion was rejected that would have granted presidents a seven-year term, Butler expressed concern that elections might become too frequent. Ever cognizant of his home state, he observed that Georgia and it were "too distant to send electors often" (II, 59).

On September 4, Butler indicated that he favored choosing the president through an Electoral College rather than by Congress. He feared that "cabal[,] faction & violence would be sure to prevail" if the decision were entrusted to the latter

body (II, 501). Butler later claimed to have originated the Electoral College (see Ulmer 1960, 364), and while this claim may have been exaggerated, he did serve on the Committee on Postponed Matters (as well as on an earlier committee on commercial discrimination) from which this mechanism emerged.

Judiciary

Consistent with his concern for federalism, Butler said that the people would not bear the establishment of lower federal courts and that "the States will revolt at such encroachments" (I, 125). His backup argument was perhaps more indicative of Butler's general view of the world. Observing that even if the delegates thought that such courts were desirable, they should not institute them, Butler noted that "we must follow the example of Solon who gave the Athenians not the best Govt. he could devise; but the best they wd. receive" (I, 125). On July 18, Butler reiterated his view that the establishment of lower federal tribunals would be unnecessary (I, 45).

Federalism

On May 31, Butler expressed his fears "that we were running into an extreme in taking away the powers of the States," and he asked Edmund Randolph to provide further explanation of the Virginia Plan (I, 53). On June 5, however, Butler indicated that the term "perpetual," which had been included in the language of the Articles of Confederation, "meant only the constant existence of our Union, and not the particular words which compose the Articles of the union" (I, 129). Moreover, on June 6, Butler said that if representation in the House of Representatives were to be apportioned not only by population but also by wealth, then he was willing to join Delaware's George Read in proposing to abolish the state legislatures and to institute "one Nation instead of a confedn. of Republics" (I, 144). On June 8, Butler expressed strong opposition to the congressional negative of state laws. He feared that it would cut off "all hope of equal justice to the distant States," and he was sure that they would oppose it (I, 168).

On August 29, Butler indicated that he thought that new states should not be formed within states without the consent of such states. He observed that otherwise demagogues would attempt to create new states any time that the people thought that taxes in existing states were unduly pressing on them (II, 455). On September 12, Butler seconded a motion by Delaware's John Dickinson designed to secure states against unjust taxes by their neighbors by requiring congressional consent to inspection duties (II, 589).

Slavery

As noted above, Butler favored counting slaves equally with free persons in the allocation of seats in the House of Representatives as giving a measure of representation to wealth in this body as well as to population. The Convention rejected this idea in favor of a provision counting blacks as three-fifths of a person. After Pennsylvania's Gouverneur Morris questioned even this representation, Butler went on the defensive, indicating that "the security of the Southn. States want is that their negroes may not be taken from them which some gentlemen within or without doors, have a very good mind to do" (I, 605).

On August 28, Butler introduced a motion that would "require fugitive slaves and servants to be delivered up like criminals" (II, 443). He withdrew the motion on this occasion with a view toward incorporating the provision in a more appropriate part of the Constitution. He successfully moved to do so the next day when the proposal was placed in what later became Article IV (II, 453–454).

Location of the Capital

Cognizant of his state's status near the periphery of the Union, Butler was among those who favored the establishment of the nation's capital in a central location (II, 128). Significantly, Butler had been influential in moving the capital in his own state from Charleston to Columbia (Whitney, 67).

Ratification of the Constitution

On August 30, Butler indicated that he favored allowing the new Constitution to go into effect when ratified by nine or more states. He thought it would be unreasonable to allow a single state or two to veto such a change (II, 469).

A scholar of Butler's role at the Convention observes that his efforts "were negative and defensive in nature" (Ulmer, 369). This scholar went on to say: "On the question of state power his concern was to maintain it; on the question of executive power his concern was how to control it; on the question of property his concern was how to protect it" (Ulmer, 369).

Life after the Convention

Butler attended a session of his state's legislature and urged its members to call a ratifying convention (Whitney, 69). Butler's letters seemed to reveal mixed feelings about the Constitution. In a letter he wrote to Englishman Weedon Butler on October 8, 1787, he said that "a Copy of the result of Our deliberations . . . is not worth the expence of postage, or I wou'd now enclose it to You" (quoted in Ulmer, 374). However, in a letter he wrote to Elbridge Gerry on March 3, 1788, Butler took a more positive tack:

> The Constitution, with all its imperfections is the only thing at this critical moment that can rescue the states from civil discord and foreign contempt–reflecting naturally our circumstances, on the too little disposition of most of the states to submit to any government. I preferred giving my consent to a trial of the Constitution in question with all its deficiencies, to what appeared to me the inevitable alternative–that there are parts of it I do not like you well know, but still I prefer a trial of it having within itself a power of amendment, to seeing the Gordian knot cut–the Knot of Union in my judgment Will be no more if this Constitution is rejected. (quoted in Ulmer, 374)

Similarly, in another letter to Weedon Butler dated May 5, 1788, Butler observed that the Convention saw I think justly, the Critical Situation of the United States. Slighted from abroad and tottering on the brink of Confusion at home; they therefore thought it wise to bring forward such a system as bid fairest for general approbation and adoption so as to be brought soon into operation. (quoted in Sikes 1979, 40)

In another interesting portal into Butler's thinking, he wrote a letter on July 18, 1788, to Weedon Butler, indicating that his support for slavery may have come from his belief that Southern states would not ratify the Constitution without it rather than because he favored the institution:

You may natural[l]y ask me why, with these sentiments, do You hold so many in Bondage. I answer You, that I would free every one of them tomorrow if I could do it, that is If the Legislature would permit it. I ardently wish I never had anything to do with such property. I daily beg of them to seek some Master that they think they would be happy with, that I may get done with them; but tho it is an Indulgence not unusual here they will not try for One. Nothing prevents my parting with them but the fear of their not bettering by the Change. (quoted in Sikes, 34)

After supporting the new Constitution in his home state, the legislature chose him as one of its first two senators. Initially leaning to the Federalists, he later gravitated to the Democratic-Republicans. He took a dim view of the adoption of the Bill of Rights and of the creation of lower federal courts under the Judiciary Act of 1789 and resigned from the Senate in 1796. He served for two more years beginning in 1802, during which time he supported the Louisiana Purchase but opposed the Twelfth Amendment, which he feared would limit the influence of the most populous states. He served as director of the second Bank of the United States from 1816 to 1819. Butler spent his last years in Philadelphia, where he died in 1822. Although he had no sons, Butler persuaded a son-in-law to name a child after him. When this namesake later married the English actress Fanny Kemble and took her to South Carolina, she was so horrified over slavery that she divorced him and published her *Journal of a Residence in America*.

See Also Committee on Commercial Discrimination; Committee on Postponed Matters; President, Selection; South Carolina

FOR FURTHER READING

Farrand, Max, ed. 1937. *The Records of the Federal Convention*. 4 vols. New Haven, CT: Yale University Press.

Sikes, Lewright B. 1979. *The Public Life of Pierce Butler, South Carolina Statesman*. Washington, DC: University Press of America.

Ulmer, S. Sidney. 1960. "The Role of Pierce Butler in the Constitutional Convention." *The Review of Politics* 72 (January): 361–374.

Whitney, David C. 1974. *Founders of Freedom in America: Lives of the Men Who Signed the Constitution of the United States and So Helped to Establish the United States of America*. Chicago: J. J. Ferguson Publishing.

CABINET

See PRESIDENT, COUNCIL

CALENDAR

When the Annapolis Convention issued a call for the Constitutional Convention, it proposed that it would begin meeting on the second Monday in May, which was May 14. However, delegates did not arrive from seven states (a quorum) until May 25. The official journal reports that "the Members present adjourned from day to day until Friday the 25th of the said month" (Farrand 1937, I, 1).

Once the Convention began, it met on Mondays through Saturdays from May 25 through September 17. It did not meet on Saturday, May 26, presumably to give time to the newly appointed Rules Committee to do its work. It recessed over July 3 and July 4 to allow the Committee of Five to deal with state representation and to celebrate Independence Day. The Convention recessed again from Friday, July 27, until Monday, August 6, to allow the Committee of Detail to compile the previous motions into a document.

The delegates signed the Constitution on September 17. Today, the week that contains this day is designated as Constitution Week.

Excluding the days, including May 14, that the members met and adjourned at the beginning of the Convention for lack of a quorum, delegates met from May 25 to September 17, 1787. The delegates thus met for a total of 88 days out of a total possible of 116.

See Also Annapolis Convention; September 17, 1787

FOR FURTHER READING

"The Debates in the Federal Convention of 1787 by James Madison." http://www.constitution.org/dfc/dfc_0000.htm.
Farrand, Max, ed. 1937. *The Records of the Federal Convention.* 4 vols. New Haven, CT: Yale University Press.

CALVIN, JOHN

See PROTESTANTISM

CANADA

One of the concerns that motivated the Framers of the U.S. Constitution was protection against foreign powers. Spain, which at the time owned

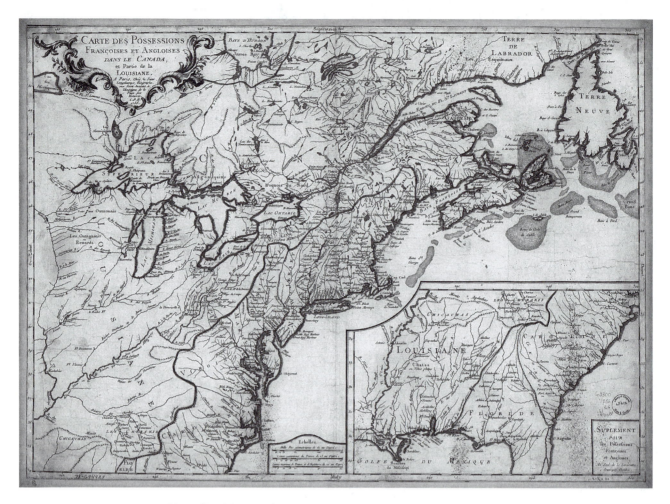

Map of Louisiana and other French possessions, 1756, by L. Thevenard
(Library of Congress)

the territory that the United States later bought from France in the Louisiana Purchase as well as present-day Florida, posed a potential threat to American navigation of the Mississippi and to westward development. As a colony of England, which it in turn had captured from the French, Canada posed a potential launching pad for attacks from the north.

Conflicts between the English and the 13 colonies on one side and the French and their Indian allies on the other had already led to one major war that affected the North American continent. British recognition in the Quebec Act of 1774 of the Catholic religion in Canada and of Canadian claims to land that the 13 states also claimed was among the causes that led to the distrust between the British and the 13 colonies, which were largely Protestant, prior to the Revolutionary War. Interestingly, Article XI of the Arti-

cles of Confederation had made provision for the entry of Canada into the union, but military expeditions to get Canada to join during the war had failed and no such union had materialized (Lawson 1952).

It is not surprising that Alexander Hamilton, a delegate from a state with Canada situated on its border, raised the issue of protection against Canada in his extensive speech of June 18. He linked defense against Canada with that of other continental military problems: "You have to protect your rights against Canada on the north, Spain on the south, and your western frontier against the savages" (Farrand 1937, I, 297). The U.S. Constitution, however, makes no mention of Canada and does not hold out the prospect, stated in the Articles of Confederation, that Canada might join the new union.

Canada remained under English sovereignty far

longer than the United States and eventually achieved its independence without a similar revolution. Fortunately, the United States and Canada have gone on to have a long history of amiable relations, and the long border between the United States and Canada is free of troop formations. It is interesting to speculate as to how union between the 13 colonies and Canada, at the time of the Constitutional Convention or at another time, might have affected the respective development of this area.

See Also Articles of Confederation; France; Great Britain; Spain

FOR FURTHER READING

Farrand, Max, ed. 1937. *The Records of the Federal Convention.* 4 vols. New Haven, CT: Yale University Press.
Lawson, Murray G. 1952. "Canada and the Articles of Confederation." *American Historical Review* 58 (October): 39–54.

Daniel Carroll, delegate from Maryland (Library of Congress)

CARROLL, DANIEL
(1730–1796)

Daniel Carroll was born in 1730 to Daniel and Eleanor Darnall Carroll in Upper Marlboro, Maryland. His father was a wealthy merchant and planter, and the family was Roman Catholic. A younger brother, John, was eventually selected as both the first Roman Catholic bishop and archbishop of the United States. Initially educated at home, Carroll received a Catholic education at St. Omer's College in French Flanders. Shortly after he returned home, his father died, leaving him in charge of his business and plantations, on which there were many slaves. Carroll married a distant relative, who brought him a handsome dowry, and became thereby connected to Charles Carroll of Carrolton, another wealthy merchant.

Carroll was elected to the Maryland Council of State, on which he served from 1777 to 1781, after which he was elected to the Continental Congress, where he signed the Articles of Confederation. He was subsequently elected to the Maryland state senate, where he served for a time as president, and he served on the commission for the Potomac Canal Company.

Carroll received notice in Annapolis of his appointment to the Constitutional Convention on May 24, 1787; Carroll had been appointed in place of a cousin, Charles Carroll, a signer of the Declaration of Independence who had declined his appointment but who had shared his ideas for a new government (many of which involved reform of the states rather than of the Articles of Confederation) with his cousin (Crowl 1941). Carroll wrote to a friend the next day saying that the appointment "was neither wished for, or expected by me," and indicating that it would be some time before he would be able to attend. He was, in point of fact, not seated until July 9, 1787, which means that, while he had missed much of the opening debates, he still had time to cast his vote on the Connecticut Compromise. He did not, however, express his views on the subject in recorded debates. Although he missed the initial two months of debate, Carroll took positions on many subsequent issues, rarely, however, giving long speeches.

Legislative Branch

Powers of Congress

Nine days after he arrived at the Convention, Carroll indicated that he thought it was essential to allow the national government to suppress rebellion within the states. He noted that the states should want such support, that it was not clear that they had it under the Articles of Confederation, and that the Convention should leave no doubt about the matter (Farrand 1937, II, 48).

On July 24, Carroll indicated his opposition to allowing Congress to enact direct taxes in proportion to representation prior to the first census (II, 106). Believing this to be a matter of fundamental fairness, he repeated this opinion on August 20 (II, 350).

Carroll's support of a ban on congressional imposition of ex post facto laws on August 22 is fascinating. Whereas Connecticut's Oliver Ellsworth had argued that such a prohibition was unnecessary because lawyers knew that such laws were in and of themselves void, Carroll responded that "experience overruled all other calculations" (II, 376). Such experience had demonstrated that, whatever lawyers thought, legislatures passed them, and they thereby needed to be prohibited.

Qualifications and Voting

On July 23, Carroll indicated that he did not necessarily oppose per capita voting in the Senate but that he did not think such a decision should be made in haste (II, 95)—on a number of occasions throughout the Convention, Carroll is on record as asking for postponements of votes (see, for example, II, 300; II, 468; II, 475). Three days later, Carroll opposed a provision that would have barred individuals from running for office who had unsettled accounts (II, 125). On August 13, Carroll unsuccessfully attempted to get the citizenship requirement for members of the House of Representatives lowered from seven years to five (II, 272).

On August 10, Carroll said that he did not think Congress should have the power to expel members from office without at least a two-thirds vote (II, 254), the majority that the Convention eventually settled on for this purpose. On this same day, Carroll unsuccessfully supported a motion that would require roll-call votes in the House on the application of one-fifth of the members but would have allowed any member of the Senate to record his dissent at any time (II, 255).

Carroll was displeased with the provision of the Connecticut Compromise that provided for the origination of money bills in the House of Representatives. He observed on August 13 that the attempt to decide which bills so qualified had been "a source of continual difficulty & squabble between the two houses" in his home state of Maryland (II, 280).

Carroll seconded one of the final motions at the Constitutional Convention in supporting a provision permitting one representative for each state in the House of Representatives for every 30,000 residents, in place of the previous provision of one for every 40,000 (II, 644). Significantly, this issue was the only one that prompted George Washington's verbal support in a speech at the Convention.

Carroll expressed concern about whether two-thirds of the Congress should be able to overturn a presidential veto. He observed that when this majority had been set the Convention had not agreed that a majority of each house would be sufficient to form a quorum, and he feared that if the two were combined together it might be necessary "to call for greater impediments to improper laws" (II, 300). On August 15, however, he favored postponing this matter until it was clear how the executive department was going to operate. The next day, he further suggested that, given the differing interests of the states in regard to duties, it might be wise to see a higher quorum for issues related to the imposition of duties (II, 305). He favored a blanket prohibition against taxation of exports (II, 308).

Carroll and fellow Marylander Luther Martin subsequently expressed fears that Congress might use its power over trade to favor ports in particular states, and they introduced a constitutional provision designed to prevent this from happening (II, 417–418). On August 31, Carroll reiterated that this issue "was a tender point in Maryland" (II, 481). However, on September 15, he indicated that he favored allowing states to lay duties for the purpose of "clearing harbours and erecting light-houses" (II, 625).

Location of the Capital

On August 11, Carroll expressed his fears that the capital would remain at New York (II, 262). This might have been tied to fears that this would give the North improper influence in the new government.

Pay

Carroll opposed a provision that would have allowed state legislatures to pay members of Congress. He feared that this mechanism, in combination with the fact that states could offer offices to members of Congress as inducements, made "the dependence of both houses on the States Legislatures" complete (II, 292). He observed that, if these provisions remained, "the new Govt. in this form was nothing more than a second edition of Congress in two volumes, instead of one, and perhaps with very few amendments" (II, 292). Carroll further argued that senators should represent the interests of the American people as a whole and not those of the individual states (II, 292).

Executive Branch

On July 24, Carroll seconded a motion by Pennsylvania's James Wilson favoring selection of the president by legislators chosen by lot to vote immediately (II, 105). This mechanism was presumably designed to avoid the likelihood that presidential candidates could corrupt the legislators. Carroll subsequently moved, with Wilson's second, to replace presidential selection by Congress with presidential selection by the people (II, 402). When this failed, Carroll seconded a motion by Pennsylvania's Gouverneur Morris providing for the people of the states to appoint electors who would elect the president (II, 404).

Federalism

Maryland had withheld its ratification of the Articles of Confederation until states with large land claims had ceded them to the United States. Carroll raised this issue on August 30 in opposing a provision that provided that states must give their consent to being divided. Madison recorded Carroll as saying "that it might be proper to provide that nothing in the Constitution should affect the Right of the U.S. to lands ceded by G. Britain in the Treaty of peace, and proposed a commitment to a member from each State" (II, 462). Carroll indicated that if this issue were not satisfactorily resolved some states could never agree to the document (II, 465–466). Carroll's willingness to allow Congress to suppress rebellions within states and his view that senators should represent all the people, and not simply those of their states, would indicate, however, that he was largely a nationalist.

Ratification of the Constitution

On August 30, when other delegates were suggesting that nine states might be sufficient to ratify the new Constitution, Carroll said that he did not think it would be possible to dissolve a confederation that had been created by unanimous consent without a similar vote (II, 469). He took the same position the next day (II, 477). When the Convention discussed ratifying the Constitution by convention, Carroll pointed out that his state provided only for one mode of ratification—presumably by state legislative approval (II, 475).

Two days before the Constitution was signed, Carroll indicated that he thought that the Convention should prepare an address to the people to accompany the Constitution. He said that "the people had been accustomed to such on great occasions, and would expect it on this," but his motion to create a committee to formulate such an address was defeated (II, 623). Carroll nonetheless signed the Constitution.

Life after the Convention

Carroll returned to Maryland to support the new Constitution and wrote essays supporting it under the designation of "A Friend of the Constitution." He served as one of the state's first members of the U.S. House of Representatives; in this capacity, he contributed to the wording of the First and Tenth Amendments. He is probably best known for his role as one of three commissioners responsible for laying out the new nation's capital at the District of Columbia, a position that put him into conflict with Major Pierre Charles L'Enfant. Carroll died in 1796 at Rock Creek, Maryland.

See Also Maryland

FOR FURTHER READING

Crowl, Philip A. 1941. "Charles Carroll's Plan of Government." *American Historical Review* 46 (April): 588–595.

Farrand, Max, ed. 1937. *The Records of the Federal Convention.* 4 vols. New Haven, CT: Yale University Press.

Whitney, David. 1974. *Founders of Freedom in America: Lives of the Men Who Signed the Constitution of the United States and So Helped to Establish the United States of America.* Chicago: J. J. Ferguson Publishing.

CELEBRATIONS OF THE CONSTITUTIONAL CONVENTION

See COMMEMORATIONS OF THE CONSTITUTIONAL CONVENTION

CENSUS

The provision in Article I, Section 2 of the Constitution for representing states according to population in the U.S. House of Representatives also specified that a census, or "Enumeration," would take place within three years of the first meeting of Congress and every 10 years thereafter. Such a census was to be "determined by adding to the whole Number of free Persons, including those bound to Service for a Term of Years, and excluding Indians not taxed, three-fifths of all other Persons," thus counting women, children, and slaves (or a proportion of them) even though not all could vote (Savage 1982, 195).

The need for a census was implicit in the proposal in the Virginia Plan to apportion Congress according to population and was suggested as early as June 11, when James Wilson of Pennsylvania and Charles Pinckney of South Carolina said that it would be appropriate to take such a census "every 5–7, or 10 years" (Farrand 1937, I, 201). Virginia's Edmund Randolph reintroduced this idea of a census on the same day, July 10, that the Committee of Eleven had proposed a House of Representatives consisting of 65 members. The earlier Committee of Five, of which Randolph had been a member, had proposed a House of 56 members to be apportioned so that there would be one representative for every 40,000 inhabitants (a provision that in turn grew out of the Grand Committee of Eleven that the Convention later altered to specify that there would be no more than one representative for every 30,000 inhabitants). Randolph moved to amend this report so as to require a census within a number of years still to be determined and to be repeated periodically "to ascertain the alterations in the population & wealth of the several States" (I, 570–571).

As uncontroversial as such a proposal might seem, Gouverneur Morris of Pennsylvania feared "such Shackles" on Congress (I, 571). His primary concern, however, was sectional. Like other delegates from the Middle and Eastern states, he feared that the population would gradually move westward and that reapportionment would shift the weight of the nation to new states there.

Discussion resumed on July 11. Connecticut's

Roger Sherman, who may also have feared western expansion, repeated Morris's argument against shackling Congress. Virginia's George Mason argued for the justice of apportioning the West like other states. Hugh Williamson of North Carolina made Randolph's resolution more explicit by specifying that in ascertaining population and wealth, the census "should be taken of the free white inhabitants and 3/5ths of those of other descriptions" (I, 579). Not unexpectedly, delegates who were earlier broken into defenders of the East and West now broke into defenders of the North and South, who wanted to exclude or include slaves, or some fraction thereof, in each census. By day's end, delegates had decided by a vote of 7-3 to conduct a census within a year of the first meeting of Congress and every 15 years thereafter (I, 588).

On July 12, Randolph proposed allowing Congress to take its first census within two years of its first meeting, a time changed, on a motion by General Pinckney of South Carolina, to six years. After rejecting a proposal to conduct a census every 20 years, by a vote of 8-2 the Convention accepted a proposal for conducting it every 10 years. On August 20, the Convention voted 9-2 to require a census within the first three, rather than within the first six, years.

The first U.S. census was conducted in 1790. The English followed with one the following year. The U.S. census is now "the oldest regularly performed national census" (Savage 1982, 196). Recent years have witnessed controversies as to how to deal with census "undercounts," which can affect not only state representation but also the distribution of federal aid to the states.

See Also Congress, House of Representatives, Representation in; Three-fifths Clause

FOR FURTHER READING

Anderson, Margo, and Stephen E. Fienberg. 1999. "To Sample or Not to Sample? The 2000 Census Controversy." *Journal of Interdisciplinary History* 30(1): 1–36.

Farrand, Max, ed. 1937. *The Records of the Federal Convention*. 4 vols. New Haven, CT: Yale University Press.

Savage, I. Richard. 1982. "Who Counts?" *The American Statistician* 36 (August): 195–200.

CHECKS AND BALANCES

Although the specific phrase is not used in the Constitution, scholars generally agree that the system of government created by the Constitution incorporates checks and balances. Such checks and balances are the logical outcome of a bicameral legislature, of a national government with three distinct branches (legislative, executive, and judicial), and of federalism, which balances power between the national government and the states.

Arguably, such checks were more important under the new Constitution than under the Articles of Confederation because the new government was assuming far greater functions. It seems clear that many of the delegates would have been unwilling to entrust such extensive powers to a government, like that of the Articles of Confederation, in which a unicameral legislature essentially dominated.

Notes that Virginia's James Madison compiled indicate that he delivered a fairly extended defense of the idea of governmental checks in a speech he made on June 26 during discussion of the terms of senators. At the time he appeared to favor a single nine-year term. In defending this view, Madison observed that governments were formed both "to protect the people agst. their rulers" and to protect them "agst. the transient impressions into which they themselves might be led" (Farrand 1937, I, 421). Aware that those entrusted with representing the public could betray their trust, Madison observed that "an obvious precaution agst. this danger wd. be to divide the trust between different bodies of men, who might watch & check each other" (I, 421). Madison went on to argue for longer terms for one branch as well as for a body small enough to resist the impetuousness of the larger lower house.

Madison further elaborated on the idea of checks and balances in *The Federalist*, where the doctrine was an important means of assuring

Antifederalists that the new Constitution would not take away their rights (see Hemberger 2001). Madison's most notable discussion occurs in *Federalist* No. 51. In discussing how to preserve separation of powers, Madison said that "the defect must be supplied, by so contriving the interior structure of the government as that its several constituent parts may, by their mutual relations, be the means of keeping each other in their proper places" (Hamilton, Madison, and Jay 1961, 320).

Although the view has been disputed (Robinson 1957), some have argued that the Framers' emphasis on checks and balances grew in part from the view of an orderly world fostered by the English scientist Sir Isaac Newton (1642–1727), as well as others who were making discoveries in the natural world (Striner 1995). In a related context, Delaware's John Dickinson observed at the Convention that the relation between the nation and the states (generally referred to as federalism) should resemble that of the "Solar System, in which the States were the planets, and ought to be left to move freely in their proper orbits" (I, 153).

One author thus observes: "It wasn't too hard for them to go from Newton's idea—of a universe governed by understandable laws and regulated with nature's checks and balances—to a constitution with clear laws and a government system kept orderly with its own checks and balances" (Hakim 2003, 165). Interestingly, some later critiques of the system of checks and balances in the U.S. Constitution focused on what was believed to be the outdated basis of this older worldview. Woodrow Wilson thus later argued that "the trouble with this theory is that government is not a machine, but a living thing. It falls, not under the theory of the universe, but under the theory of organic life. It is accountable to Darwin, not to Newton" (Wilson 1961, 56).

See Also Federalism; Madison, James, Jr.; Mixed Government; Separation of Powers

FOR FURTHER READING

Farrand, Max, ed. 1937. *The Records of the Federal Convention.* 4 vols. New Haven, CT: Yale University Press.

Hakim, Joy. 2003. *From Colonies to Country.* Book 3 of *A History of US.* New York: Oxford University Press.

Hamilton, Alexander, James Madison, and John Jay. 1961. *The Federalist Papers.* New York: New American Library.

Hemberger, Suzette. 2001. "What Did They Think They Were Doing When They Wrote the U.S. Constitution, and Why Should We Care?" Sotirios Barber and Robert P. George, eds. *Constitutional Politics: Essays on Constitution Making, Maintenance, and Change.* Princeton, NJ: Princeton University Press, 128–161.

Robinson, James A. 1957. "Newtonianism and the Constitution." *Midwest Journal of Political Science* 1 (November): 252–266.

Striner, Richard. 1995. "Political Newtonianism: The Cosmic Model of Politics in Europe and America." *William and Mary Quarterly,* 3rd ser. 52 (October): 583–608.

Wilson, Woodrow. 1961 (1908). *Constitutional Government in the United States.* New York: Columbia University Press.

CHIEF JUSTICE OF THE UNITED STATES

The only mention of the chief justice in the U.S. Constitution occurs in Article I, Section 3, which designates the chief justice as the presiding officer in the U.S. Senate in impeachment trials of the president (Vile 1994, 6). Although the Virginia Plan that Edmund Randolph introduced to the Convention on May 28 contained provisions for a "National Judiciary," to include "one or more supreme tribunals and inferior tribunals," it did not specifically mention a chief justice (Farrand 1937, I, 21). The plan did propose incorporating a select number of members of the judiciary, which presumably would have included a chief if one were to be so designated, in a Council of Revision with the power to invalidate state and congressional laws. Like the Virginia Plan, neither the New Jersey Plan nor the proposal offered by Alexander Hamilton mentioned a chief justice (I, 236–237, 292).

On August 18, Connecticut's Oliver Ellsworth advocated the establishment of a council to assist the president. He suggested that the chief justice should be one of the members of this council (II,

329). By contrast, Elbridge Gerry of Massachusetts opposed the idea of including either heads of department or the chief justice on such a council. He observed: "These men will also be so taken up with other matters as to neglect their own proper duties" (II, 329).

The Convention deferred additional discussion on August 18 but voted on August 20 to submit proposals by Pennsylvania's Gouverneur Morris and South Carolina's Charles Pinckney to the Committee of Detail, which included the idea of creating a Council of State consisting of the chief justice and other departmental secretaries. The Chief Justice was to be specifically entrusted with the responsibility of recommending from time to time "such alterations of and additions to the laws of the U.S. as may in his opinion be necessary to the due administration of Justice, and such as may promote useful learning and inculcate sound morality throughout the Union" (II, 342). This proposal also called for making the chief justice the president of the council when the president was absent.

When South Carolina's John Rutledge reported back to the Convention on behalf of the Committee of Detail, he did not entrust the chief justice with the extensive set of powers that had been recommended, but he did recommend that the chief justice should be a member of what he now designated as the Privy Council (II, 367). In discussing a provision for having the House of Representatives impeach a president who would then be tried before the Supreme Court, Gouverneur Morris observed that this would be especially improper were the "first judge" (presumably the chief justice) to be a member of the Privy Council (II, 427). Morris also suggested that the chief justice would be a more appropriate provisional successor to the president than would the president of the Senate (II, 427), who was then so designated, the Convention having not yet formulated the Electoral College and the accompanying institution of the vice president.

The Convention rejected the idea of the Privy Council. However, the Committee on Postponed Matters recommended to the Convention on September 4 that the chief justice would replace the vice president (designated as the president of the Senate) in cases where it was trying the president on impeachment charges (II, 498). The Convention accepted this provision on September 7.

Although the role is not specifically designated by the Constitution, chief justices typically take the lead in advocating legislation that they believe will smooth operations of the court system. By tradition, chiefs also preside over private court deliberations and make the assignment of those who will write decisions in cases in which they are in the majority.

See Also Council of Revision; Impeachment Clause; Judicial Organization and Protections; Supreme Court

FOR FURTHER READING

Farrand, Max, ed. 1937. *The Records of the Federal Convention.* 4 vols. New Haven, CT: Yale University Press.
The Office of Chief Justice. 1984. Charlottesville, VA: White Burkett Miller Center of Public Affairs.
Vile, John R. 1994. "The Selection and Tenure of Chief Justices." *Judicature* 78 (October): 96–100.

CHRISTIANITY

See PROTESTANTISM

CINCINNATI

See SOCIETY OF THE CINCINNATI

CITIZENSHIP

The delegates to the Constitutional Convention of 1787 did not include a definition of citizenship in the Constitution that they wrote, but they did discuss citizenship in at least three contexts. First, they specifically invested Congress with the power of naturalization, thus providing a measure of uniformity on this matter. Second, the delegates decided that individuals running for the presidency or for either house of Congress would have to be citizens. In the case of the former, such individuals had to be "natural-born." Finally, the Convention decided to allow new states in the West to enter the Union on a full basis with the existing states, thus ensuring that inhabitants of such states would not be considered "second-class" citizens.

The status of women under the Constitution was ambiguous. Most scholars agree that women were generally considered to be citizens, but without the same political rights as were exercised by men. Discrimination against women in voting rights was not outlawed at the national level until the adoption of the Nineteenth Amendment in 1920.

In *Scott v. Sandford* (1857), the U.S. Supreme Court decided that African Americans were not and could not be U.S. citizens. Ignoring the fact that some free blacks were citizens at the time the Constitution was adopted, Chief Justice Roger Taney said that the Framers had viewed blacks as inferior to whites and therefore could not have accepted them as citizens. Section 1 of the Fourteenth Amendment (1868) overturned this decision by declaring: "All persons born or naturalized in the United States and subject to the jurisdiction thereof, are citizens of the United States and of the State where they reside." This amendment, which subsequently became the basis through which the U.S. Supreme Court applied the Bill of Rights to the states, further extended the federal protection of rights to all persons in the United States.

See Also African Americans; Congress, House of Representatives, Qualifications of Members; Congress, Senate, Qualifications; Indians; Naturalization; President, Qualifications; States, Admission and Creation; Women

FOR FURTHER READING

Ferber, Linda K. 1998. *No Constitutional Right to Be Ladies: Women and the Obligations of Citizenship.* New York: Hill and Wang.

Scruggs, William L. 1886. "Ambiguous Citizenship." *Political Science Quarterly* 1 (June): 199–205.

CLASSES

Although the idea of analyzing the Constitutional Convention according to the financial interests of the delegates is usually attributed to historian Charles Beard, the delegates were themselves aware that they were responsible for writing a document that would apply to all classes of citizens. They also knew that there were significant differences among these interests and that all classes deserved some representation under the new government.

Mason Offers a Reason to Consider the Interests of All Classes

In one of the first statements related to this, Virginia's George Mason observed on May 31: "We ought to attend to the rights of every class of the people" (Farrand 1937, I, 49). In what could be regarded as an appeal to the enlightened self-interests of the delegates, many of whom can be assumed to have been individuals of relatively high social status, Mason went on to observe that one reason for doing so was that class lines were not fixed in America:

> He had often wondered at the indifference of the superior classes of society to this dictate of humanity & policy, considering that however affluent their circumstances, or elevated their situations, might be, the course of a few years, not only might but certainly would, distribute their posterity throughout the lowest classes of Society. Every selfish motive therefore, every family attachment, ought to recommend such a system of policy as would provide no less carefully for the rights—and happiness of the lowest than of the highest orders of Citizens. (I, 49).

Given this statement, it is interesting to hypothesize whether the delegates—all of whom

Upper-class neighborhood in Philadelphia, ca. 1800 (Pixel That)

were white—might have been less accommodating to slavery if they had thought that there was a chance that such bondage would apply to individuals on a basis other than color.

Madison on the Variety of Factions

In what appears to have been a warm-up to later arguments that he would make in *Federalist* No. 10, where he argued that a large republic would have the advantage of filtering interests through the medium of representatives and so multiplying factions that no single one would be likely to dominate, Virginia's James Madison disagreed with Connecticut's Roger Sherman in believing that the objects of the national government would be few. Madison indicated that an objec-

tive that Sherman had omitted was that of "providing more effectually for the security of private rights, and the steady dispensation of Justice" (I, 134). Madison offered a list of factions similar to that which he would later advance in *The Federalist:*

All civilized Societies would be divided into different Sects, Factions, & interests, as they happened to consist of rich & poor, debtors & creditors, the landed[,] the manufacturing, the commercial interests, the inhabitants of this district, or that district, the followers of this political leader or that political leader, the disciples of this religious sect or that religious sect. In all cases where a majority are united by a common interest or passion, the rights of the minority are in danger. (I, 135; also see I, 108)

Interestingly, this list includes not only factions formed around economic differences but also those formed by political and religious beliefs. Although he did not give slavery equal focus with the classes formed by economic differences, Madison did go on to observe: "We have seen the mere distinction of colour made in the most enlightened period of time, a ground of the most oppressive dominion ever exercised by man over man" (I, 135).

Madison offered similar remarks on the multiplicity of interests on June 26 when he was arguing for nine-year terms for members of the U.S. Senate: "In all civilized Countries the people fall into different classes havg. a real or supposed difference of interests. There will be creditors & debtors, farmers, merchts. & manufacturers. There will be particularly the distinction of rich and poor" (I, 422).

Madison was especially concerned that the increase of the lower classes could threaten the institution of property:

> An increase of population will of necessity increase the proportion of those who labour under all the hardships of life, & secretly sigh for a more equal distribution of its blessings. These may in time outnumber those who are placed above the feelings of indigence. According to the equal laws of suffrage, the power will slide into the hands of the former. (I, 422)

Consistent with some contemporary interpretations, Madison appeared to refer indirectly to Shays's Rebellion as one of the "symptoms of a leveling spirit" that "have sufficiently appeared in a certain quarters to give notice of the future danger" (I, 423).

Madison has been criticized for neglecting "the relation between economic and political power" (Belz, Hoffman, and Albert 1992, 60). Although Madison did often speak as though the control of factions chiefly consisted in the prevention of allowing any one faction to get a majority, he indicated on June 19 that some factions could wield greater power than their numbers might indicate. Indeed, he observed that this could happen in at least three different scenarios:

1. If the minority happen to include all such as possess the skill & habits of military life, with such as possess the great pecuniary resources, one third may conquer the remaining two thirds. 2. one third of those who participate in the choice of rulers may be rendered a majority by the accession of those whose poverty disqualifies them from a suffrage, & who for obvious reasons may be more ready to join the standard of sedition than that of the established Government. 3. Where slavery exists, the Republican Theory becomes still more fallacious. (I, 318)

Other Designations of Classes

On June 7, Elbridge Gerry of Massachusetts observed that the people were divided into two main interests, which he identified as "the landed interest, and the commercial including the stockholders" (I, 152). He believed that allowing the people to choose members of both houses of Congress would not provide for the latter, but he thought this could be provided for by state legislative selection of senators. New York's Alexander Hamilton made a similar argument in his long speech of June 18. Observing that the development of industry led to societal divisions "into the few & the many," that led to "separate interests," he elaborated: "There will be debtors & Creditors &c. Give all power to the many, they will oppress the few. Give all power to the few they will oppress the many. Both therefore ought to have power, that each may defend itself agst. the other" (I, 288).

On June 25, South Carolina's Charles Pinckney argued that the government "must be suited to the habits & genius of the People it is to govern" (I, 402). He proceeded to divide Americans into three classes. These were "*Professional men* who must from their particularly pursuits always have a considerable weight in the Government while it remains popular," "*Commercial men*, who may or may not have weight as a wise or injudicious commercial policy is pursued," and "the *landed interest*, the owners and cultivators of the soil, who are and ought ever to be the governing spring in the system" (I, 402). Having drawn such distinctions, Pinckney appeared to mute them by going on to

Almshouse in Philadelphia, 1799 (Pixel That)

claim that "these three classes, however distinct in their pursuits and individually equal in the political scale, and may be easily proved to have but one interest. The dependence of each on the other is mutual" (II, 402–403).

In later arguing that the requirement of a freehold for voting would not be fair to all, Madison would also divide citizens into "the landed[,] the commercial, & the manufacturing" (II, 124). He believed that the latter two interests were increasing and that the delegates also needed to attend to their interests.

In yet another take on the subject, Gouverneur Morris of Pennsylvania observed on July 24: "In all public bodies there are two parties. The Executive will necessarily be more connected with one than with the other" (II, 204).

Other Divisions

In addition to divisions based on economic and class interests, the delegates to the Convention clearly recognized that there were divisions between the large states and the small states and among different areas of the nation. Such differences were evident in disputes about whether new Western states would be treated equally to existing Eastern states. They were even more evident in the debates over slavery and related questions, where the most obvious divisions were between the North and the South, those areas where slavery was outlawed and dying, and those where it was still flourishing.

On occasion, delegates highlighted regional divisions as a way of minimizing divisions between the large and small states. Pointing to the three largest states, Madison observed on June 28 that "the Staple of Masts. was *fish*, of Pa. *flower* [flour], of Va. *Tobo*. Was a Combination to be apprehended from the mere circumstance of equality of size? Experience suggested no such danger" (I, 448).

In a passage that is curiously missing from Madison's own notes of the day, Robert Yates cites Madison as arguing on June 29 that

> the great danger to our general government is the great southern and northern interest of the continent, being opposed to each other. Look to the notes in congress, and most of them stand divided by the geography of the country, not according to the size of the states. (I, 476, italics omitted)

Spread out over 13 colonies that comprised a far larger land area than most European nations and anticipating still further western growth, the delegates appeared on occasion to be awed by the differences and their implications for continental government. Charles Pinckney, who had previously identified three classes of individual citizens, found even more divisions among the economic interests of the states, a diversity that he thought provided an argument for a two-thirds majority of Congress as a condition of regulating commerce. He explained on August 29:

> He remarked that there were five distinct commercial interests— 1. the fisheries & W. India trade, which belonged to the N. England States. 2. the interest of N. York lay in a free trade. 3. Wheat & flour the Staples of the two Middle States (N.J. & Penna.)—4. Tobo. the staple of Maryd. & Virginia [& partly of N. Carolina.] 5. Rice & Indigo, the staples of S. Carolina and Georgia.

Just as the division of Congress into two houses was intended in part to provide for some differences in representation among classes of citizens (not, as some had suggested, by providing property classifications for the latter and not the former, but by providing for longer terms that were thought to give the Senate greater independence in opposing popular measures from the House of Representatives), so too, federalism was one solution to the problem of state and regional differences.

See Also Beard, Charles; Federalism; Madison, James, Jr.; Parties, Factions, and Interests; Republicanism

FOR FURTHER READING

Belz, Herman, Ronald Hoffman, and Peter J. Albert. 1992. *To Form a More Perfect Union: The Critical Ideas of the Constitution.* Charlottesville: University Press of Virginia.

Farrand, Max, ed. 1937. *The Records of the Federal Convention.* 4 vols. New Haven, CT: Yale University Press.

Henretta, James A. 1987. "Society and Republicanism: America in 1787." *this Constitution,* no. 15 (Summer): 20–26.

Wiencek, Henry. 1993. *An Imperfect God: George Washington, His Slaves and the Creation of America.* New York: Farrar, Straus, and Giroux.

CLASSICAL ALLUSIONS AND INFLUENCES

Richard Gummere, a historian of the American colonial and revolutionary era, has observed that "in no field were Greek and Roman sources more often invoked; and at no time were they more frequently cited than during the preliminary discussions, the debates on the Constitution, the ratifying conventions, the *Federalist* papers and such publications as John Dickinson's *Fabius Letters*" (1962, 3). He further noted that many of the Founding Fathers had classical educations and read the classics from original Greek and Latin sources. Those that did not still looked to the ancients for inspiration. George Washington thus had Joseph Addison's *Cato: A Tragedy,* the play about the Roman statesman who opposed Caesar and committed suicide rather than submit to him, performed for his troops at Valley Forge (see

Lithograph of Great Seal of the United States, between 1850 and 1910 (Library of Congress)

Addison 2004). With the possible exception of their own experiences in the states and under the Articles and with the government and institutions of Great Britain, the delegates at the Constitutional Convention most frequently referred to individuals, institutions, and lessons from Greek and Roman history.

Individuals cited from classical history typically were statesmen or lawgivers, but sometimes they were tyrants. South Carolina's Pierce Butler thus feared the rise of "a Cataline or a Cromwell" (Farrand 1937, I, 100), one from Roman and the other from British history. Delaware's Gunning Bedford observed: "We must like Solon [a Greek lawgiver] make such a Governt. as the people will approve" (I, 491). On June 11, Butler recalled that, as a boy, he remembered reading a remark attributed to Rome's Julius Caesar declaring that if he had money he could purchase soldiers and other necessities to engage in war (I, 204). In notes he had prepared for a speech on June 30, Delaware's John Dickinson cited Caesar's desire for monarchy and Romulus's fratricide (Hutson 1987, 137).

Delegates were knowledgeable of classical institutions and were particularly interested in the Greek confederacies. Correctly or not, they read back into them the weaknesses they had experi-

enced under the Articles of Confederation. Virginia's James Madison, who had prepared for the Convention by reading through books sent by Thomas Jefferson from Paris and by writing an essay titled "Of Ancient and Modern Confederacies," in which he had taken notes on both the Lycian and the Amphictyonic Confederacies (Meyers 1973, 69–81), cited Greek and Rome as examples of internal class conflict and of oppression of their provinces (I, 135). Alexander Hamilton of New York later repeated this theme in a somewhat different context (I, 424). Madison cited the "intrigues" practiced by the Persian kings and by Philip of Macedon in the Amphictionic confederacy (I, 319). Madison further referred to the rivalry among Sparta, Athens, and Thebes and cited Plutarch's life of Themistocles as authority for how the "strongest cities corrupted & awed the weaker, and that Judgment went in favor of the more powerful party" (I, 448–449). Somewhat later, he observed that it was imprudent to leave governmental defects in place until a more propitious time, observing that "the Defects of the Amphictionick League were acknowledged, but they never cd. be reformed" (I, 478). He also used the Lycian confederacy as an example of a confederacy "in which the component members had votes proportioned to their importance" (I, 485).

Pennsylvania's Gouverneur Morris cited the "Grecian States" as among those that should have been united by a common language but were torn by factions among one another (I, 553). Morris later cited the Ephori at Sparta (II, 299), while South Carolina's Charles Pinckney attempted to use the examples of Greece and Rome to justify slavery (II, 371), a justification that John Dickinson questioned by noting that these empires had been "made unhappy by their slaves" (II, 372). Pennsylvania's James Wilson used the example of the Roman triumvirate and of Caesar and Augustus as an example of the dangers of a plural executive (I, 254). Arguing for a relatively small Senate, Madison observed that the Roman tribunes lost power as their numbers rose (I, 151–152) and that the Romans excited wars whenever they feared domestic insurrections (I, 465). Hamilton cited the election of the Roman emperors by the army (I, 290). Wilson used the example of Rome as among

Old Pine Street Church, Philadelphia, built in 1768 (Library of Congress)

those demonstrating the need for large governments to have subdivisions (I, 157; I, 323). Charles Pinckney argued against allowing noncitizens to be eligible for the Senate by observing that the Athenians made it a capital crime for a stranger to enter their legislative proceedings (II, 235).

Despite frequent classical allusions, the Framers of the Constitution, like earlier American revolutionaries, often tended to use classical examples as "window dressing" since, as Stanley Burstein has emphasized, they typically "provided precedents, not models for imitation." Burstein has observed that "the ancient republics . . . were primarily valuable as laboratory specimens to be analyzed and dissected in the best tradition of enlightenment historiography in order to determine the problems that had to be faced and overcome in establishing a federal republic" (1996, 36).

From time to time, delegates reminded their fellows that, as important as classical illustrations

could be, the situations were not identical. As observed above, Charles Pinckney and John Dickinson argued about the lessons of slavery in the classical world. Contending in a long speech that he delivered on June 15 that the Convention should be guided by the genius of the American people, Charles Pinckney observed:

The people of this country are not only very different from the inhabitants of any State we are acquainted with in the modern world; but I assert that their situation is distinct from either the people of Greece or Rome, or of any State we are acquainted with among the antients. —Can the orders introduced by the institution of Solon, can they be found in the United States? Can the military habits & manners of Sparta be resembled to our habits & manners? Are the distinctions of Patrician & Plebeian known among us. Can the Helvetic or Belgic . . . can they be said to possess either the same or a situation like ours? I apprehend not. –They are perfectly different, in their distinctions of rank, their Constitutions, their manners & their policy. (I, 402)

It would be almost absurd for a modern politician to point to such obvious differences. The fact that Pinckney felt it necessary to do so appears to confirm the importance that many delegates gave to their knowledge of the classics.

Gummere believes that Aristotle (on Aristotle's influence, see also Ketcham 1987, 578), Cicero, and Polybius especially influenced the American Framers (Gummere, 7) and that they consulted Plato "as a spiritual adviser rather than a political scientist" (Gummere, 8). Gummere observed that both Federalist supporters and Antifederalist opponents of the Constitution used classical illustrations in arguing for or against the Constitution. It is more difficult to trace specific institutions in the Constitution to classical influences although Gummere believes that the theme of "mixed government," particularly prominent in Polybius, was reflected in the American system of separation of powers and checks and balances. The designation of the "Senate" also paralleled the Roman use of the term (Gummere, 16).

As the new nation matured, references to their own history replaced allusions to the ancients. Classical references became less popular as the nation moved toward Jacksonian democracy (Miles 1974).

See Also Achaean League; Amphictyonic League; Biblical and Religious References at the Constitutional Convention; Education of Convention Delegates; Polybius

FOR FURTHER READING

Addison, Joseph. 2004. *Cato: A Tragedy and Selected Essays.* Ed. Christine Dunn Henderson and Mark E. Yellin. Indianapolis, IN: Liberty Fund.

Burstein, Stanley M. 1996. "The Classics and the American Republic." *History Teacher* 30 (November): 29–44.

Farrand, Max, ed. 1937. *The Records of the Federal Convention.* 4 vols. New Haven, CT: Yale University Press.

Gummere, Richard M. 1962. "The Classical Ancestry of the United States Constitution." *American Quarterly* 14 (Spring): 3–18.

Hutson, James H., ed. 1987. *Supplement to Max Farrand's* The Records of the Federal Convention of 1787. New Haven, CT: Yale University Press.

Ketcham, Ralph. 1987. "Publius: Sustaining the Republican Principle." *William and Mary Quarterly,* 3rd ser. 44 (July): 576–582.

Meyers, Marvin, ed. 1973. *The Mind of the Founder: Sources of the Political Thought of James Madison.* Indianapolis, IN: Bobbs-Merrill.

Miles, Edwin A. 1974. "The Young American Nation and the Classical World." *Journal of the History of Ideas* 35 (April-June): 259–274.

Richard, Carl J. 1994. *The Founders and the Classics: Greece, Rome, and the American Enlightenment.* Cambridge, MA: Harvard University Press.

Wiltshire, Susan Ford. 2001. "The Classical Vision." *Encyclopedia of American Cultural and Intellectual History.* Ed. Mary K. Cayton and Peter W. Williams. New York: Charles Scribner's Sons, 237–247.

———. 1992. *Greece, Rome, and the Bill of Rights.* Norman: University of Oklahoma Press.

CLYMER, GEORGE
(1739–1813)

George Clymer was born in Philadelphia in 1739 to the family of a sea captain. After his parents died a year later, a maternal aunt and her husband, a merchant and a leader of the Proprietary Party, raised him. Clymer inherited a large sum of money from his uncle, formed a merchant partnership, and also became active in the Proprietary Party. Clymer was one of the delegates to the Continental Congress who signed the Declaration of Independence. After serving in a number of positions that aligned him with the patriots, Clymer had again represented Pennsylvania in Congress from 1780 to 1782 and then served in the Pennsylvania state legislature. Serving simultaneously in this body and as a delegate to the Constitutional Convention, Clymer apparently devoted most of his attention to his former responsibilities and was a relatively silent delegate at the Conven-

George Clymer, delegate from Pennsylvania
(Pixel That)

tion in a state delegation known for its brilliance and for its participation in debates.

Positions Taken at the Convention

Although seated at the Constitutional Convention on May 28, Clymer does not appear to have spoken until August 21. Three days earlier he had been appointed to his first committee at the Convention, an 11-man committee on state debts and militia. On August 22, he was appointed to a similar committee on slave trade and navigation, the only other such committee on which he would serve.

On August 21, the Convention was discussing whether state or national governments should be permitted to tax exports. Virginia's George Mason had indicated that the South was particularly concerned about the possibility that the other states might tax its tobacco. Clymer responded that other states had their own concerns. Middle states like Pennsylvania had just as much cause to be concerned about their "wheat flour, provisions, &c. and with more reason, as these articles were exposed to a competition in foreign markets not incident to Tobo. rice &c." (Farrand 1937, II, 363). He further observed that these Middle states had as much cause to fear a combination of the Eastern and Southern states as the Southern states had to fear from a combination of the Eastern and Middle ones. Clymer then introduced a motion, rejected by a vote of 7-3, that would have qualified the prohibition of taxing exports by limiting the prohibition to those enacted "for the purpose of revenue" (II, 363).

Clymer became involved in another North-South conflict on August 25 when he concurred with a motion by Connecticut's Roger Sherman not to mention the word *slavery* in the Constitution. His apparent motivation was to avoid sectional offense (II, 415).

Although he had thus attempted to reconcile the North and South, Clymer, who had served in 1777 as a member of a congressionally appointed commission investigating conditions on the frontier, was among those who feared the future development of the American West. On August 28, after Pennsylvania's Gouverneur Morris indicated that the coastal states might use the taxing power to prevent access to the Mississippi River by the Western states, Clymer indicated that he "thought the encouragement of the Western Country was suicide on the old States" (II, 442). He observed that "If the States have such different interests that they can not be left to regulate their own manufactures without encountering the interests of other States, it is a proof that they are not fit to compose one nation" (II, 442).

The next day, the Convention was discussing whether two-thirds majorities should be required in Congress for regulating matters of commerce. Clymer opposed this provision, again pointing to the diversity of interests within the United States: "The diversity of commercial interests, of necessity creates difficulties, which ought not to be increased by unnecessary restrictions. The Northern & Middle States will be ruined, if not enabled to defend themselves against foreign regulations" (II, 450).

On August 31, Clymer supported a motion by Virginia's James Madison to allow the new constitution to go in effect when ratified by a majority of people in a majority of the states (II, 476). Clymer later opposed a proposal by Alexander Hamilton of New York referring the Constitution to Congress for its approval on the basis that it might "embarrass" that body (II, 563). On September 6, Clymer further indicated that he thought an earlier plan whereby the Senate would appoint public officials was too "aristocratic" (II, 524).

Life after the Convention

After signing the Constitution, Clymer used his influence in the Pennsylvania legislature to call a convention to ratify the new document, even approving mob action in bringing opponents into the legislature to provide a quorum for action. Although he was not elected to the state ratifying convention, Pennsylvania chose Clymer to represent it in the first House of Representatives. There he supported the fiscal program advocated by Alexander Hamilton and helped secure the temporary establishment of the nation's capital in Philadelphia. He later was a tax collector in his state during the volatile period leading to the Whiskey Rebellion, which tested the power of the new national government.

Washington appointed Clymer in 1795 to negotiate a peace treaty with the Creek tribe in Georgia. He devoted much of the rest of his life to philanthropy and served as a trustee of the University of Pennsylvania and as president of the Pennsylvania Academy of Fine Arts. Clymer died in 1813.

See Also Pennsylvania

FOR FURTHER READING

Farrand, Max, ed. 1937. *The Records of the Federal Convention.* 4 vols. New Haven, CT: Yale University Press.

Grundfest, Jerry. 1982. *George Clymer: Philadelphia Revolutionary, 1739–1813.* New York: Arno Press.

Whitney, David. 1974. *Founders of Freedom in America: Lives of the Men Who Signed the Constitution of the United States and So Helped to Establish the United States of America.* Chicago: J. J. Ferguson Publishing.

COALITIONS

In legislative and other collective bodies, it is common for delegates to form coalitions, or alliances, around matters of ideology and interest. Delegates might vote together on the basis of geographical similarities, race, gender, perceived economic interests, party affiliation, conservative or liberal leanings, and so on.

The delegates at the Constitutional Convention were similar in this respect. Since all were white males, and national political parties had not yet developed, their voting patterns cannot be analyzed on the basis of race, gender, or party. There are, however, many other dimensions of agreement and disagreement, many of which they would have been aware.

The New York delegation, in which John Lansing and Robert Yates almost always took different sides than did Alexander Hamilton, shows that state delegates were not always in agreement, but more often than not one would expect delegates from the same states to vote similarly—delegates from the same state had an additional incentive to vote together because if a state tied on a vote, it carried no weight. Delegates also reflected differences among the East (North), the Middle states, and the South. There were additional differences within regions. Although slavery existed in all the Southern states, there were fewer slaves in North Carolina than in neighboring states, and the Deep South states were more interested in the continuing importation of slaves than were the other Southern states. The Virginia and New Jersey Plans pitted proponents of the larger more populous states against smaller less populous states. There were additional differences among those who thought that the nation's problems simply required vesting additional powers in Congress and those who thought that more drastic changes were needed.

Modern social scientific methodologies enable coalitions to be measured in ways that were not possible in the first century or so of the nation's history. One of the most interesting findings of modern research is that coalitions were not necessarily stable throughout the Convention. One such study indicates that it might be possible to reconcile explanations of the Convention that are primarily based on interests, particularly economic in nature, and those based on principles. It suggests that the Convention alternated between periods of higher lawmaking and disputes about interests (Jillson and Eubanks 1984). This theory provides interesting parallels to Bruce Ackerman's more recent hypothesis that the normal phases of American politics have from time to time been punctuated by "constitutional moments" involving more fundamental changes (Ackerman 1998).

Another such study has identified three different pairs of coalitions, or voting blocs, at the Convention. First was the conflict roughly from the beginning of the Convention on May 25 through the adoption of the Connecticut Compromise on July 16, pitting the three largest states (Massachusetts, Pennsylvania, and Virginia) and their allies (North Carolina, South Carolina, and Georgia) against the remaining smaller states (Jillson 1981, 606). This conflict resulted in the Connecticut Compromise.

A second set of coalitions appears to have taken place when New Hampshire and Massachusetts in the Northeast joined the Carolinas and Georgia in the South in opposition to the Middle states. Chief issues during this time period, roughly from July 17 to August 28, centered on "the composition and powers of the executive branch . . . the nature of and possible restrictions on citizenship, citizen participation, office holding and the very divisive regional issues of slavery and commerce" (Jillson, 607). The primary lines of alignment "centered on the stance that the new nation would take toward its current citizens, future immigrants, and its compound parts, particularly the new states then rising in the West" (Jillson, 607).

Yet a third set of issues dominated the Convention after the report of the Committee on Postponed Matters and lasted roughly from August 29 to September 3, involving renewed conflicts between the large and small states. This, in turn, gave way to yet another set of coalitions from September 7 through September 17 in which a bloc of mostly small Northern states consisting of New Hampshire, Connecticut, New Jersey, Delaware, and Maryland were joined by Massachusetts and Georgia to moderate the powers of the new national government and secure the smaller states by obtaining greater power for the Senate, where they were represented equally.

If these descriptions are accurate, or roughly so, the Convention can be viewed as moving in stages, with differing alignments being influential at different times (see Jillson and Eubanks 1984).

See Also Compromise; Connecticut Compromise; Parties, Factions, and Interests

FOR FURTHER READING

Ackerman, Bruce. 1998. *We the People: Transformations.* Cambridge, MA: Belknap Press of Harvard University Press.

Hutson, James H. 1987. "Riddles of the Federal Constitutional Convention." *William and Mary Quarterly* 44, 3rd ser. (July): 411–423.

Jillson, Calvin C. 1981. "Constitution-Making: Alignment and Realignment in the Federal Convention of 1787." *American Political Science Review* 75 (September): 598–612.

Jillson, Calvin, and Thornton Anderson. 1977. "Realignments in the Convention of 1787: The Slave Trade Compromise." *Journal of Politics* 38 (August): 712–729.

———. 1978. "Voting Bloc Analysis in the Constitutional Convention: Implications for an Interpretation of the Connecticut Compromise." *Western Political Quarterly* 31 (December): 535–547.

Jillson, Calvin C., and Cecil L. Eubanks. 1984. "The Political Structure of Constitution Making: The Federal Convention of 1787." *American Journal of Political Science* 28 (August): 435–458.

Ulmer, S. Sidney. 1966. "Sub-group Formation in the Constitutional Convention." *Midwest Journal of Political Science* 10: 288–303.

COLLEGES AND UNIVERSITIES

See EDUCATION OF CONVENTION DELEGATES

COLONIAL PRECEDENTS

The American constitutionalism that came to full flower in the Constitutional Convention of 1787 had its roots not only in the Magna Carta and the common law of Great Britain but also in developments within the 13 colonies prior to independence.

From Britain, the colonists had absorbed notions of "limited government, consent, and local control" (Greene 1994, 33). These ideas were furthered by royal charters and by early covenants like the Mayflower Compact and the Massachusetts Body of Liberties and by the development of colonial representative assemblies. Significantly, however, even after English monarchs revoked colonial charters, as they had done in all but five of the American colonies by 1750, colonists, like their English forebears, relied upon what Jack Greene has called "unwritten customary constitutions" (34). Just as the British Parliament had reigned in the prerogative power of the monarchs within Britain, so, too, the colonists thought that their own assemblies had wrested power from a distant government to achieve autonomy in local affairs. Colonists believed that their constitutional orders were "at once local, consensual, participatory, lay-directed, and customary" (Greene, 38). Long before the American Founders invented the idea of federalism, they had come to view their relation with Britain as a type of federal arrangement in which the king and Parliament exercised primary responsibility for matters involving the empire and colonial legislatures were understood to have primary authority over local affairs, including the all-important power of taxation.

When the British authorities refused to recognize the legitimacy of these colonial claims, the colonies in turn proclaimed their independence and sought to secure traditional rights through the device of written constitutions. In relatively short order, the former colonists further tied the formulations of such constitutions to special conventions, the work of which was ideally then subject, as in the case of the Massachusetts Constitution of 1780, to popular approval.

In writing the new Constitution, a sufficient number of delegates remembered the indignities they had suffered under British rule to prevent the imposition of similar restrictions on Western territories. James Wilson was among those who had argued on July 13 for liberal treatment of the Western states. In addition to reasoning from democratic theory, he clearly attempted to draw lessons from British mistakes:

> The majority of people wherever found ought in all questions to govern the minority. If the interior Country should acquire this majority they will; not only have the right, but will avail themselves of it whether we will or no. This jealousy misled the policy of G. Britain with regard to America. The fatal maxims espoused by her were that the Colonies were growing too fast, and that their growth must be stunted in time. What were the consequences? first. enmity on our part, then actual separation. Like consequences will result on the part of the interior settlements, if like jealousy & policy be pursued on ours. (Farrand 1937, I, 605).

Had the delegates not so provided for the admission of new states on an equal basis with the old, the continent might eventually have split into rival confederacies.

See Also Common Law; Constitutional Convention Mechanism; Constitutionalism; Federalism; Great Britain; Magna Carta; Massachusetts Body of Liberties; Massachusetts Constitution of 1780; Mayflower Compact; State Constitutions; States, Admission and Creation

FOR FURTHER READING

Farrand, Max, ed. 1937. *The Records of the Federal Convention.* 4 vols. New Haven, CT: Yale University Press.

Greene, Jack P. 1994. *Negotiated Authorities: Essays in Colonial Political and Constitutional History.* Charlottesville: University Press of Virginia.

Lutz, Donald S. 1998. *Colonial Origins of the American Constitution: A Documentary History.* Indianapolis, IN: Liberty Fund.

——. 1980. "From Covenant to Constitution in American Political Thought." *Publius* 10 (Fall): 101–134.

COMMEMORATIONS OF THE CONSTITUTIONAL CONVENTION

The U.S. Constitution, and the Convention that framed it, have from time to time been objects of commemoration, although many such commemorations have been overshadowed by those of the Declaration of Independence. The Declaration received an early boost as the national commemoration of choice when on July 4, 1826, fifty years to the day after it was adopted, both Thomas Jefferson (its primary author) and John Adams (a member of the five-man committee commissioned to write it) died on the same day. James Monroe, the last of the founding presidents, died on the same day five years later.

Initial Celebrations

The ratification of the Constitution was followed by parades and speeches called "Federal Processions" in a number of seaport towns. The most notable was the celebration in Philadelphia on July 4, 1788. It featured a massive three-hour parade of craftsmen designed to show the new Constitution to be what has been described as a "well constructed 'fabric,' 'frame,' and 'edifice'" and was tied to a song composed by Francis Hopkinson titled "The Raising: A Song for Federal Mechanics" (Rigal 1996, 253, 261–262). As the date for the parade suggests, early celebrations often tied the nation's independence and its Constitution together.

Fifty-Year Anniversary of U.S. Constitution

The 50-year anniversary of the U.S. Constitution appears to have passed relatively quietly. John Quincy Adams delivered his "Discourse on the Constitution" in 1839 in conjunction with the celebration of George Washington's inauguration, but that address was tedious and fairly lackluster (Kammen 1987, 90).

1876 and 1887

The year 1876 witnessed an exposition in Philadelphia that was designed to highlight the progress of the nation in the hundred years since independence—it had, in turn, followed a somewhat ill-planned commemoration of the beginning of the Revolution a year before (Little 1974). Plans for commemorating the Constitution also encountered difficulties. These stemmed in part from the fact that some individuals thought the most appropriate time to celebrate was on June 21 of 1888, the centennial of the ratification by New Hampshire, the critical ninth state, while others wanted to focus on the inauguration of George Washington or the beginning of the first Congress. John A. Kasson, an Iowa congressman, was appointed to head a centennial commission, but he was appointed relatively late, and many of the preparations for celebration were not finalized until the last minute. Ultimately, the city of Philadelphia came to the rescue, appropriating money for the occasion and encouraging participation by local businesses. A huge outdoor mass was held in Philadelphia to commemorate the event. A parade held on September 16, 1887, had 30,000 participants; scholars believed that about half a million people observed it (Kammen, 139). President Grover Cleveland and Justice Samuel Miller delivered addresses in Independence Square the next day.

In 1889, New York subsequently hosted celebrations of Washington's inauguration. That same year the nation's capital commemorated the convening of the first Congress. Still another celebration was held on February 4, 1890, in New York City to mark the establishment of the U.S. Supreme Court. Hampton Carson, the secretary of the centennial commission, published a massive two-volume set of books on the event, with the first volume largely featuring information about the Convention and the delegates (complete with engravings) and the second largely concentrating on pictures and descriptions of floats and other contingents that had participated in the parade.

Zip Codes

Zip codes had not, of course, been invented at the time of the Constitutional Convention in 1787, but the zip code for Philadelphia, Pennsylvania, from which many of the U.S. Constitutional Bicentennial Covers were issued, is 19104. These commemorative covers were issued to designate 200 years from the time that Benjamin Franklin greeted delegates on May 13, 1787, through Convention debates, highlights of the ratification, and the establishment of the House of Representatives whose permanent site was first designated on July 10, 1790.

Stamps most frequently included on these covers included those depicting the U.S. flag (about 35, most in denominations of from 4 cents to 22 cents); George Washington (about 30, most in 18-cent denominations); the Preamble of the Constitution (four different versions); the spirit of independence; ratifications of the Bill of Rights; the Declaration of Independence; and U.S. states and cities. The stamp commemorating the earliest document was one commemorating the Magna Carta of 1215. Another stamp used was a purple one that had been issued to commemorate the sesquicentennial of the Constitution in 1937; it had unwisely attempted to include a picture of the collective delegates in space far too small for the purpose.

Delegates to the Constitutional Convention would not have had to purchase stamps since, like members of Congress, they were granted franking privileges.

FOR FURTHER READING

The United States Constitution Bicentennial Covers Collection. 1987–1990. Commemorative Postal Society.

1937

The sesquicentennial of the U.S. Constitution in 1937 was much better organized. Sol Bloom, a New York congressman who had headed a highly successful commemoration of the two hundredth anniversary of the birth of George Washington, in 1932, headed the sesquicentennial commission. Bloom had an active staff and received congressional funding for a host of commemorative and educational activities. Bloom eventually became known as "Mr. Constitution, U.S.A." (Kammen, 290). Celebrations of the sesquicentennial spanned the period from 1937 to 1939.

Popular attention was directed to the Constitution because of the ongoing conflict between President Franklin D. Roosevelt and the Supreme Court that resulted in Roosevelt's so-called court-packing plan. This conflict sometimes made it tricky for sesquicentennial organizers to proceed without displaying partisan biases. Celebrations featured the printing of a postage stamp featuring Junius Brutus Stearn's crowded portrait of the signers titled *Adoption of the Constitution*, the issuance of a poster titled *We the People* by Howard Chandler Christy with a female embodiment of liberty with features similar to those of his "Christy Girls," tree plantings, parades, and the opening of the 1939 World's Fair in New York.

With the help of ghostwriters, Bloom published *The Story of the Constitution*, which included a section labeled "Questions and Answers Relating to the Constitution." Another book, *The Federal Constitutional Celebration in Philadelphia, 1937–39*, detailed individuals who had worked on various committees. Bloom was eventually criticized for self-promotion, with one fellow congressman imagining the Founding Fathers exclaiming, "My God! Making a racket out of the Constitution" (Kammen, 310).

1976 and 1987

The bicentennial of the Declaration of Independence in 1976 clearly overshadowed the subsequent bicentennial of the U.S. Constitution, but the latter featured a variety of celebrations designed both to celebrate and to promote understanding of the Constitution. Chief Justice Warren Burger resigned from the U.S. Supreme Court in order to direct this latter celebration, which continued, in one form or another, into 1991, with ongoing celebrations of the ratification of the Bill of Rights. The American Political Science Association and the American Historical Association jointly sponsored "Project '87," which was designed to enhance scholarly understanding of the Constitution (Morris 1988). A number of scholarly publications, including Philip B. Kurland and Ralph Lerner's *The Founders' Constitution*, and Richard B. Bernstein and Kym Rice's *Are We to Be a Nation?* were timed to coincide with the bicentennial (for a review of publications from this time period, see Bernstein 1987). As in the case of earlier celebrations, scores of more popular commemorative items (stamps, coins, plates, posters, etc.) were produced for both bicentennials. It is perhaps not surprising that manufacturers sometimes confused the two celebrations. It was especially common to associate 1776 with the bicentennial of the Constitution rather than the Declaration of Independence.

In addition to special anniversaries, the week in which September 17 (the date the Constitution was signed) falls has in recent years been designated as Constitution Week, thus fairly well establishing this date over rival ones, like that on which the ninth state signed the Constitution. The Sons and Daughters of the American Revolution were especially influential in establishing September 17 as the appropriate one for commemoration.

See Also Declaration of Independence; Music; Philadelphia

FOR FURTHER READING

Bernstein, Richard B. 1987. "Charting the Bicentennial." *Columbia Law Review* 87 (December): 1565–1624.

Bernstein, Richard B., with Kym S. Rice. 1987. *Are We to Be a Nation? The Making of the Constitution.* Cambridge, MA: Harvard University Press.

"Bicentennial Events." 1987. *U.S. News and World Report* 102 (April 27): 32–33.

Bloom, Sol. 1937. *The Story of the Constitution.* Washington, DC: United States Constitutional Sesquicentennial Commission.

Carson, Hampton L., ed. 1889. *History of the Celebration of the One Hundredth Anniversary of the Promulgation of the Constitution of the United States.* 2 vols. Philadelphia, PA: J. J. Lippincott.

The Constitution of the United States with Tree Planting Instructions by the American Tree Association to Mark the Sesquicentennial: 1787–1937. Washington, DC: American Tree Association.

The Federal Constitutional Celebration in Pennsylvania, 1937–1938. 1938. Philadelphia, PA: Dunlap Publishing.

Kammen, Michael. 1987. *A Machine That Would Go of Itself: The Constitution in American Culture.* New York: Alfred A. Knopf.

Kurland, Philip B., and Ralph Lerner, eds. 1987. *The Founders' Constitution.* 5 vols. Chicago: University of Chicago Press.

Little, David B. 1974. *America's First Centennial Celebration: The Nineteenth of April 1875 at Lexington and Concord, Massachusetts.* 2nd ed. Boston: Houghton Mifflin.

Morris, Richard B. 1988. "The Genesis of Project '87." *this Constitution,* no. 18 (Spring/Summer): 76–77.

Rigal, Laura. 1996. "'Raising the Roof': Authors, Spectators and Artisans in the Grand Federal Procession of 1788." *Theatre Journal* 48, 3: 253–277.

Waldstreicher, David. 1995. "Rites of Rebellion, Rites of Assent: Celebrations, Print Culture, and the Origins of American Nationalism." *Journal of American History* 82 (June): 37–61.

COMMERCE POWER

Few, if any, provisions of the Constitution have done more to bolster the powers of Congress than the clause in Article I, Section 8 granting this body power "to regulate Commerce with foreign Nations, and among the several States, and with the Indian tribes."

Virginia and New Jersey Plans

There was general consensus that the lack of a similar power in the Articles of Confederation had led to state commercial discriminations against one another. The Virginia Plan concentrated more on structuring a new government than on delineating specific powers that this new government would exercise. However, provisions in the plan, introduced on May 19, granting Congress power "to legislate in all cases to which the separate States are incompetent, or in which the harmony of the United States may be interrupted by individual Legislation," would presumably have allowed Congress to exercise this power on behalf of the common good (see Farrand 1937, I, 21).

In describing the purposes of the Union on June 6, Roger Sherman of Connecticut listed the power of "regulating foreign commerce, & drawing revenue from it" as the fourth of four such purposes (I, 133). Significantly, although he thought the "objects of the Union . . . were few," he thought they included commercial regulation (I, 133). Similarly, in introducing the New Jersey Plan on June 15, New Jersey's William Paterson proposed adding the power "to pass Acts for the regulation of trade & commerce as well with foreign nations as with each other" along with several others (I, 243). By June 19, Maryland's Luther Martin had concluded that "because the States individually are incompetent to the purpose," there was "general Consent" to the view that "the United-States should also regulate the Commerce of the United States foreign & internal" (IV, 23).

Debates over the Report of the Committee of Detail

When the Committee of Detail reported the first draft of a Constitution to the Convention on August 6, it provided that Congress should have power "to regulate commerce with foreign nations, and among the several States" (II, 181). This draft also prohibited taxes on exports or on slave importations and provided that all navigation acts would require a two-thirds vote by Congress (II, 183).

Delegates from the Deep South states were the primary advocates of the last two provisions. They succeeded in blocking import restrictions on slaves until the year 1808 and in getting an outright ban on the taxation of exports. They did not succeed in getting approval for a provision that would have required a two-thirds vote of Congress for regulating interstate and foreign commerce.

When the Convention considered the provision in the report of the Committee of Detail requiring the assent of two-thirds majorities in Congress for adopting navigation acts, Charles Pinckney of South Carolina proposed instead "that no act of the Legislature, for the purpose of regulating the commerce of the U-S. with foreign powers, or among the several States, shall be passed without the assent of two thirds of the members of each House" (II, 449).

Citing the interest of the New England states in fishers and the West Indian trade; of New York in free trade; of New Jersey and Pennsylvania in wheat and flour; of Maryland, Virginia, and North Carolina in tobacco; and of South Carolina and Georgia in rice and indigo, he feared that such diversity of interests would "be a source of oppressive regulations if no check to a bare majority should be provided" (II, 449). Pinckney added that "the power of regulating commerce was a pure concession on the part of the S. States. They did not need the protection of the N. States at present" (II, 449). Luther Martin of Maryland seconded Pinckney's motion. Responding to the Northern concession allowing for the continuation of the slave trade, General Charles Cotesworth Pinckney of South Carolina opposed adding the two-thirds requirement. Pennsylvania's George Clymer added that the Northern and Middle states could be "ruined" if not permitted "to defend themselves against foreign regulations," while Sherman insisted that the very diversity of interests that Pinckney had cited was an obstacle to the abuse of power (II, 450). Pinckney replied that this still left the difference of interest between Northern and Southern states.

Gouverneur Morris of Pennsylvania opposed the two-thirds requirement on the basis that it would prevent preferences for Northern shipping, which, by multiplying such shipping, would drive down costs for the South. North Carolina's Hugh Williamson believed that a two-thirds vote would allay Southern fears, while Richard Spaight of the same state argued that it was unnecessary and that if regulations on behalf of U.S. shipping became oppressive, Southerners could build their own. Pierce Butler of South Carolina thought the South was making a concession, but he was willing to forgo the two-thirds requirement to conciliate the East. James Wilson argued that if all interests were to be placated, unanimity would be required, and he observed the difficulties that supermajority voting requirements had created under the Articles of Confederation.

If his own report is to be credited, James Madison then "went into a pretty full view of the subject" (II, 451), in which he appears ultimately to have concluded, consistent with his arguments elsewhere on behalf of representative government over a large land area, that the plurality of commercial interests was adequate to prevent abuse. John Rutledge of South Carolina also opposed Pinckney's motion on the basis that it did not "take a permanent view of the subject" (II, 452). Randolph used the occasion chiefly to prepare the ground for his decision not to sign the Constitution, while Nathaniel Gorham of Massachusetts argued: "If the Government is to be so fettered as to be unable to relieve the Eastern States[,] what motive can they have to join in it, and thereby tie their own hands from measures which they could otherwise take for themselves" (II, 453). The Convention voted 7-4 to strike the two-thirds requirement.

This certainly did not resolve all the issues related to the clause. Maryland's James McHenry opined in notes of September 4 that the Constitution did not appear to provide for the erection of lighthouses and the cleaning out of harbors. He also questioned whether it was proper "to declare all the navigable waters or rivers and within the U.S. common high ways?" but thought that the power to prohibit states from demanding tribute of one another might be "comprehended in the power to regulate trade between State and State" (II, 504).

On September 15, the Convention agreed to the provision in Article I, Section 10 prohibiting states from taxing imports or exports except for fees needed to execute state navigation laws. McHenry and Daniel Carroll, also of Maryland, subsequently moved that the states should be permitted to lay tonnage duties for the purpose of erecting lighthouses and clearing harbors. Mason supported this measure whereas Gouverneur Morris thought that states already had such power and that a proposal would thus detract from other implied powers.

Foreshadows of Future Issues

After the Constitution was ratified, judges and others had to decide on the degree to which congressional powers over commerce were exclusive and the degree to which they permitted the states to exercise concurrent jurisdiction. Madison probably came as close to addressing this issue at the Convention as anyone. Questioning whether the commerce clause restricted states from levying tonnage fees, he observed that this depended on the scope of the commerce clause:

> These terms are vague but seem to exclude this power of the States—They may certainly be restrained by Treaty. He observed that there were other objects for tonnage Duties as the support of Seamen &c. He was more & more convinced that the regulation of Commerce was in its nature indivisible and ought to be wholly under one authority. (II, 625)

While Madison contemplated the exercise of exclusive congressional powers, Sherman advanced the idea that state and national authorities might exercise some powers concurrently: "The power of the U. States to regulate trade being supreme can controul interferences of the State regulations [when] such interferences happen; so that there is no danger to be apprehended from a concurrent jurisdiction" (II, 625).

After New Hampshire's John Langdon insisted that regulating tonnage was equivalent to regulating trade and that states should be prohibited from doing so, the Convention voted 6-4-1 against McHenry and Carroll's motion.

Lighthouse Tax

One of the issues that generated pressure for a stronger national government was the commercial discrimination that was being practiced by states against one another. This discrimination stemmed from the fact that states were pursuing their own tariff policies with other nations. New York was among the states that, in attempting to enact tariffs on British goods, charged higher fees for foreign goods being brought into the state from Connecticut and New Jersey.

Unlike New York, New Jersey was pursuing a free trade policy that undercut New York's policies. After New York imposed its tariffs, New Jersey retaliated by taxing a lighthouse that New York had built on Sandy Hook at the rate of 30 pounds a month (Zornow 1954, 263). Although the states were coming to an accommodation and New Jersey ceased collection of the tax after about a year, the incident was sometimes used by early American historians as an example of the practices that had led to calls for the Constitutional Convention.

FOR FURTHER READING

Zornow, William Frank. 1954. "The Sandy Hook Lighthouse Incident of 1787." *Journal of Economic History* 24 (Summer): 261–266.

Later in the day, Mason expressed concern over the fact that Congress could enact navigation acts by a bare majority, but his motion to enact a provision, parallel to that dealing with slave importation, requiring the consent of two-thirds of both houses until the year 1808 lost by a vote of 7-3-1. Although Charles Pinckney shared Mason's reservation that the majority might abuse its power, unlike Mason, he had decided to support the Constitution. In opposing the document, Elbridge Gerry listed as one reason for his decision his belief that Congress might use its power over commerce to establish monopolies (II, 633).

Summary and Analysis

The decision to vest powers over commerce with foreign nations, with one another, and with the Indian tribes added substantially to the powers that Congress had exercised under the Articles of Confederation and helped the nation reap the economic benefits of a national market relatively free from state commercial restraints. Debates over the commerce clause had a distinct regional flavor, revealing existing and future fault lines among different regions, and especially between North and South. The delegates to the Convention limited congressional powers over commerce both by permitting states to import slaves for another 20 years and by prohibiting taxes on exports. Although the Convention adopted a provision requiring a two-thirds majority of the Senate to adopt treaties, it rejected a similar requirement that would have applied to all navigation acts. In light of subsequent controversies over tariffs, especially during the period from 1828 to 1832, many Southern states undoubtedly came to rue the day when they did not provide themselves with this security.

See Also Committee of Detail; Congress, Collective Powers

FOR FURTHER READING

Bittker, Boris I. 1999. *Bittker on the Regulation of Interstate and Foreign Commerce.* Gaithersburg, MD: Aspen Law and Business.

Crowley, John E. 1993. *The Privileges of Independence Neomercantilism and the American Revolution.* Baltimore, MD: Johns Hopkins University Press.

Farrand, Max, ed. 1937. *The Records of the Federal Convention.* 4 vols. New Haven, CT: Yale University Press.

Frankfurter, Felix. 1937. *The Commerce Clause under Marshall, Taney and Waite.* Chapel Hill: University of North Carolina Press.

COMMITTEE OF COMPROMISE ON REPRESENTATION IN CONGRESS (July 2)

One of the most divisive issues at the Constitutional Convention concerned representation in Congress.

Vote and Discussion Leading to Committee Formation

After weeks of acrimonious debate on the subject that culminated on Monday, July 2, with a 5-5-1 vote on whether states should be equally represented in the Senate, General Charles Cotesworth Pinckney of South Carolina proposed that the Convention appoint a committee consisting of a member from each state "to devise & report some compromise" (Farrand 1937, I, 511).

The intensity of the representation issue was evident in the reception that this idea itself received. Maryland's Luther Martin did not specifically object to the committee but said that "no modifications whatever could reconcile the Smaller States to the least diminution of the equal Sovereignty" (I, 511). By contrast, Connecticut's Roger Sherman thought that the committee would be "most likely to hit on some expedient" (I, 511). Gouverneur Morris of Pennsylvania also favored the committee, although he proceeded to deliver a long speech that would presumably guide committee members. Virginia's Edmund Randolph favored appointing a committee but did not expect much good to come from it; New York's John Lansing appears to have shared his sentiments. Caleb Strong of Massachusetts and Hugh Williamson of North Carolina expressed

their approval of the committee, but Pennsylvania's James Wilson objected that such a committee "would decide according to that very rule of voting which was opposed on one side" (I, 515). Virginia's James Madison expected nothing to result from the appointment of a committee except for delay. By contrast, Elbridge Gerry of Massachusetts favored creating the committee. Ultimately, the Convention accepted the committee by a vote of 9-2, with New Jersey and Delaware in dissent (I, 516). Only Pennsylvania opposed appointing one member from each state.

Committee Composition and Work

The committee consisted of Elbridge Gerry of Massachusetts, Oliver Ellsworth of Connecticut, Robert Yates of New York, William Paterson of New Jersey, Benjamin Franklin of Pennsylvania, Gunning Bedford of Delaware, Luther Martin of Maryland, George Mason of Virginia, William Davie of North Carolina, John Rutledge of South Carolina, and Abraham Baldwin of Georgia. The committee selected Elbridge Gerry as its chair; met on Tuesday, July 3, while the Convention recessed to prepare for Independence Day celebrations; and presented its report when the Convention reassembled on Thursday, July 5.

Apparently working in part from a motion by Benjamin Franklin, the committee proposed that each state be given one representative in the House of Representatives for every 40,000 inhabitants, with each state getting at least one representative. It revived an earlier proposal, which Elbridge Gerry had first proposed on June 13 but which the Committee of the Whole had rejected, by providing that all bills for "raising or apportioning money, and for fixing salaries" would originate in the House of Representatives and could not be altered by the second branch. It further specified that no money could be appropriated except from legislation originating in the first house. The capstone of the plan called for each state to have an equal vote in the Senate (I, 526).

Luther Martin, who left the Convention and opposed ratification of the Constitution within his home state of Maryland, there reported that feelings ran strong within the committee. He observed that the committee members considered their proposal to be an all-or-nothing proposition:

> However, the majority of the select committee at length agreed to a series of propositions, by way of compromise, part of which related to the representation in the first branch, nearly as the system is now published: And part of them to the second branch, securing in that, equal representation, and reported them as a compromise, upon the express terms, that they were wholly to be adopted, or wholly to be rejected: upon this compromise, a great number of the members so far engaged themselves, that, if the system was progressed upon agreeable to the terms of compromise, they would lend it their names, by signing it, and would not actively oppose it, if their States should appear inclined to adopt it. (III, 189–190, italics omitted in this and following quotations by Martin)

Martin further qualified his own support for the committee recommendations by observing that his support was tied to further progress on the document as a whole:

> Some, however, in which number was myself, who joined in the report, and agreed to proceed upon those principles and see what kind of a system would ultimately be formed upon it, yet reserved to themselves, in the most explicit manner, the right of finally giving a solemn dissent to the system, if it was thought by them inconsistent with the freedom and happiness of their country. (III, 190)

Martin further sought to explain why delegates had signed on to a system that they did not believe was perfect:

> This, Sir, will account why the members of the Convention so generally signed their names to the system; not because they thought it a proper one; not because they thoroughly approved, or were unanimous for it; but because they thought it better than the system attempted to be forced upon them. (III, 190)

Unresolved Issues

The committee report did not immediately settle the vexing issue of state representation. Indeed, on July 6, the Convention appointed a Committee of Five (Committee to Reconsider Representation in the House) specifically to consider the provision relative to giving each state one representative for every 40,000 inhabitants.

See Also Committee to Reconsider Representation in the House; Committees at the Constitutional Convention; Congress, House of Representatives, Representation in; Congress, Senate, Representation in; Connecticut Compromise; Gerry, Elbridge

FOR FURTHER READING

Farrand, Max, ed. 1937. *The Records of the Federal Convention*. 4 vols. New Haven, CT: Yale University Press.
Kromkowski, Charles A. 2002. *Recreating the American Republic: Rules of Apportionment, Constitutional Change, and American Political Development, 1700–1870*. Cambridge: Cambridge University Press.
Zagarri, Rosemarie. 1987. *The Politics of Size: Representation in the United States, 1776–1850*. Ithaca, NY: Cornell University Press.

COMMITTEE OF DETAIL (July 24)

By Monday, July 23, the Convention had been in near-continuous session for close to two months, and it had debated dozens of matters and adopted many resolutions. Elbridge Gerry of Massachusetts accordingly suggested that the Convention should refer its proceedings to a committee "to prepare & report a Constitution conformable thereto." After South Carolina's Charles Cotesworth Pinckney warned delegates that he was bound to reject any plan that did not provide security for states with slaves or that taxed exports, the states unanimously agreed to Gerry's motion (Farrand 1937, II, 95). Only Delaware voted for a committee of 10 members. After the Convention split equally on the desirability of a committee of seven members, it unanimously agreed to a committee of five members to be appointed the next day.

Committee Composition

On that day, the Convention selected Nathaniel Gorham of Massachusetts, Oliver Ellsworth of Connecticut, James Wilson of Pennsylvania, Edmund Randolph of Virginia, and John Rutledge of South Carolina. This ensured that each of the three major sections—the East (North), Middle, and South—would be represented, although the committee arguably underrepresented the smaller states (Thach 1922, 106). Rutledge served as the chair, on which every member, other than Gorham, was a lawyer (106).

Committee Work

The Convention continued to debate the presidency from Tuesday through Thursday (forwarding its new resolutions to the committee) and then adjourned for just over a week, until August 6, so that the committee would have time to prepare its report. In addition to examining the previous resolutions adopted by the Convention, the committee is believed to have drawn from the Pinckney Plan and from previous proposals that had been introduced in the Congress under the Articles of Confederation (Mabie 1987, 31–32). After going through two major drafts, one chiefly authored by Randolph and a second by Wilson (Thach, 111), the committee delivered its report on that date and presented copies to all the members. The report consisted of a preamble and 23 articles, one of which was repeated so that the last is Article XXII. Notably, the committee enumerated most of the powers of Congress that are in the current Constitution.

The Preamble did not contain the list of purposes found in the current Preamble (these are generally attributed to Gouverneur Morris and the later Committee of Style) and listed the states separately, somewhat optimistically including Rhode Island, which had not sent delegates to the Convention. Although it contains many more articles, the report from the Committee of Detail clearly foreshadows the final document, with the branches treated in order of the legislative (with the House of Representatives being first described and then the Senate), the executive, and the judicial and then proceeding to provisions dealing with the states, with the constitutional amending process, and with ratification of the document.

Analysis

In a study of this committee's work, John Hueston has suggested that it proposed a federal government significantly weaker than that promised by the preceding debate. He believes it did so both "by enumerating national powers and adding states' rights" (1990, 766). The judgment that the committee's enumeration of federal powers was intended to weaken national powers is based on the premise—which may not have been shared by all delegates—that powers not explicitly granted would be reserved to the states (Hueston, 770). Moreover, it needs to be balanced by the fact that the same committee added both the necessary and proper clause to the list of congressional powers and strengthened the supremacy clause by making it clear that federal law would also be supreme over state constitutions (Hueston, 770–771).

The committee enhanced states' rights by providing that the executive would not send troops to quell domestic rebellion except in cases where states requested them; that states would pay the salaries of members of Congress (a provision that was later changed by the Convention); and by giving states the power to set the qualifications for members of Congress, to help determine the time and manner of such elections, and the right to make emergency appointments to the House of Representatives (Hueston, 773). Hueston also believes that the committee somewhat weakened the power of the federal judiciary by providing that federal crimes would be tried by juries in the states where they were committed (Hueston, 774).

Number of Words in Original Constitution

Consistent with the Framers' desire to create a broad frame of government, the Constitution that emerged from the Convention of 1787 is, by contemporary standards, a relatively brief document. It contains 4,543 words. This includes the signatures of the signers but not the certificate that accompanied it. By contrast, the Declaration of Independence has 1,458 words.

The Framers, many of whom gained experience in writing constitutions at the state level, consciously chose to keep the Constitution relatively short. Notes from the Committee of Detail by Virginia's Edmund Randolph thus observed that two essentials in drafting a constitution were:

1. To insert essential principles only, lest the operations of government should be clogged by rendering those provisions permanent and unalterable, which ought to be accommodated to times and events. and

2. To use simple and precise language, and general propositions, according to the example of the (several) constitutions of the several states. (Farrand 1937, II, 137)

In assessing the constitutionality of the national bank in the case of *McCulloch v. Maryland* (1819), Chief Justice John Marshall contrasted the brevity of the U.S. Constitution with more prolix legal codes. He used the brevity of the Constitution as one rationale for interpreting the Constitution so as to encompass not only enumerated powers but also implied powers–like the establishment of a bank–that logically flowed from them.

Short framework-oriented documents like the U.S. Constitution are often favorably contrasted with the more prolix state constitutions, with their length sometimes associated with their shorter duration (see Amar 2000, 671). After examining the 145 state constitutions adopted since 1776, Christopher Hammons has recently challenged the assumption that shorter documents are necessarily more stable (1999).

FOR FURTHER READING

Amar, Akhil Reed. 2000. "Architexture +." *Indiana Law Journal* 77 (Fall): 671–700.
"Constitution of the United States: Questions and Answers." http://www.archives.gov/national_archives_experience/constitution_q_and_a.html
Farrand, Max, ed. 1937. *The Records of the Federal Convention.* 4 vols. New Haven, CT: Yale University Press.
Ferguson, Robert A. 1987. "1787: The Constitution in Perspective: 'We Do Ordain and Establish': The Constitution as Literary Text." *William and Mary Law Review* 29 (Fall): 2–25.
Hammons, Christopher W. 1999. "Was James Madison Wrong? Rethinking the American Preference for Short, Framework-Oriented Constitutions." *American Political Science Review* 93 (December): 837–849.

The Committee of Detail also appears to have significantly altered the presidency. Charles Thach has thus observed:

The executive which had gone into the committee with only the appointing power, the veto power, and the power to execute the laws, came out, not only with additional powers, but with all of them granted in terms which left no loophole for subsequent legislative interference. What have come to be known as the political powers were now the president's and the president's alone. (116)

Additional Work

On August 18, the Convention voted to send a number of proposed additional powers to the Committee of Detail (making it as close to a standing committee as any at the Convention). These appear to have originated with James Madison, Charles Pinckney, Elbridge Gerry, John Rutledge, and George Mason (II, 324–325). They included powers to dispose of unappropriated lands, provide temporary governments for new states, create and govern a national capital, grant charters of incorporations, secure copyrights, establish a university and/or other seminaries of learning, advance useful knowledge, procure lands needed for military facilities, secure payment of public debts, grant letters of marque and reprisal, regulate stages, and more (II, 321–322). On August 20, the Convention submitted additional resolutions to this committee. Among them were provisions for the writ of habeas corpus, freedom of the press, civilian control over the military, prohibitions against quartering troops in private homes, a great seal of the United States, and alterations of judicial jurisdiction (II, 341–342). It was also asked to look into the creation of a Council of State, consisting of secretaries of major departments who would give advice to the president.

The committee reported on these changes on August 22. It proposed adding a number of new congressional powers but not nearly as many as had been proposed. It ignored provisions like those relating to freedom of the press and quartering troops in private homes that would later make their way into the Bill of Rights. It set qualifications for the president that appeared in the Constitution with relatively minor changes. In a measure that the Convention eventually rejected, it also proposed the creation of a Privy Council to advise the president. It further proposed that the Senate should try judges on impeachment charges brought by the House, and it proposed an addition to the jurisdiction of the courts (II, 385–386).

See Also Congress, Collective Powers; Pinckney Plan; Rutledge, John; Supremacy Clause

FOR FURTHER READING

Farrand, Max, ed. 1937. *The Records of the Federal Convention.* 4 vols. New Haven, CT: Yale University Press.
Hueston, John C. 1990. "Altering the Course of the Constitutional Convention: The Role of the Committee of Detail in Establishing the Balance of State and Federal Powers." *Yale Law Journal* 100 (December): 765–783.
Mabie, Margot C. C. 1987. *The Constitution: Reflection of a Changing Nation.* New York: Henry Holt.
Thach, Charles C. 1922. *The Creation of the Presidency 1775–1789: A Study in Constitutional History.* Baltimore, MD: Johns Hopkins University Press.

COMMITTEE OF STYLE AND ARRANGEMENT (September 8)

On Saturday, September 8, the Constitutional Convention appointed a five-member committee to revise the style and to arrange the resolutions agreed upon into more coherent form. Members include Dr. William Samuel Johnson of Connecticut, Alexander Hamilton of New York, Gouverneur Morris of Pennsylvania, James Madison of Virginia, and Rufus King of Massachusetts. The committee reported back to the Convention on Wednesday, September 12, 1787, and, with few emendations, 39 of 42 remaining delegates signed this document on September 17, 1787.

Although Dr. Johnson, recently appointed as president of King's College (today's Columbia University), headed the committee, Gouverneur Morris was most responsible for the committee's work. He thus wrote a letter to Timothy Pickering dated December 22, 1814, in which he observed: "That instrument [the Constitution] was written by the fingers, which wrote this letter. Having rejected redundant and equivocal terms, I believed it to be as clear as our language would permit" (Farrand 1937, III, 420). Fellow committee member James Madison confirmed this authorship with greater explanation in a letter to Jared Sparks dated April 8, 1831:

The *finish* given to the style and arrangement of the Constitution fairly belongs to the pen of Mr. Morris; the task having, probably, been handed over to him by the chairman of the Committee, himself a highly respectable member, and with the ready concurrence of the others. A better choice could not have been made, as the performance of the task proved. It is true, that the state of the materials, consisting of a reported draft in detail, and subsequent resolutions accurately penned, and falling easily into their proper places, was a good preparation for the symmetry and phraseology of the instrument, but there was sufficient room for the talents and taste stamped by the author on the face of it. The alterations made by the Committee are not recollected. They were not such, as to impair the merit of the composition. (III, 499)

In notes that he made while serving as a member of the Committee of Detail, Edmund Randolph laid down two principles that the Committee of Style appears to have followed even more closely than the committee of which Randolph was a part. Randolph thus observed that in writing a Constitution, it was important:

1. To insert essential principles only, lest the operations of government should [be] clogged by rendering those provisions permanent and unalterable, which ought to be accommodated to times and events. and

2. To use simple and precise language, and general propositions, according to the example of the (several) constitutions of the several states. (II, 137)

A recent biographer of Morris has noted that he and the committee reduced 23 articles to seven. Morris consistently eliminated excess verbiage and substituted leaner and more precise prose. Morris's primary contribution to the document was the Preamble. Although substituting the words "We the People" for the names of individual states was designed in part to avoid the problem that would be posed if, as happened, the new government began without universal state approval, there is general agreement that these words also gave the document a more nationalistic focus (Brookhiser 2003, 91). Although Morris was a strong nationalist at the Convention, there seems to be relatively little to substantiate a later

charge by Congressman Albert Gallatin, who had not attended the Convention, that Morris had attempted to substitute a semicolon for a comma in the clause dealing with congressional imposition of taxes in order to enlarge national powers, but that Connecticut's Roger Sherman had detected this attempted alteration (Brookhiser, 90).

In addition to putting the final finish on the Constitution, the Committee of Style appears to have been responsible for writing the Letter of Transmittal to Congress that accompanied the document. William Jackson, the Convention secretary, reported in a letter to John Quincy Adams dated October 21, 1818, that Pennsylvania's Jared Ingersoll reported that he, Benjamin Franklin, and Gouverneur Morris had authored the letter (IV, 83), but this hearsay reflection is undercut by the fact that Ingersoll did not serve on the committee. Historian Ralph Ketcham (1971, 230) has attributed primary authorship of the letter to James Madison, who was a committee member.

See Also Authorship of the Constitution; Johnson, William Samuel; Letter of Transmittal; Morris, Gouverneur; Preamble; Signing of the Constitution

FOR FURTHER READING

Brookhiser, Richard. 2003. *Gentleman Revolutionary: Gouverneur Morris–The Rake Who Wrote the Constitution.* New York: The Free Press.

Farrand, Max, ed. 1937. *The Records of the Federal Convention.* 4 vols. New Haven, CT: Yale University Press.

Ketcham, Ralph. 1971. *James Madison: A Biography.* New York: Macmillan.

COMMITTEE OF THE WHOLE (May 30–June 19)

From May 30 through June 19, the Constitutional Convention resolved itself each day into a Committee of the Whole.

Functioning of the Committee

Perhaps in an attempt to provide some geographic balance (the Convention had just selected Virginia's George Washington as president), the Convention chose Nathaniel Gorham of Massachusetts, who had served successfully in the Congress under the Articles of Confederation, by ballot to chair this committee. The committee spent most of its time considering and debating the Virginia Plan. The committee of the whole mechanism developed in the British Parliament (Risjord 1992, 633) was used extensively in early Congresses (Galloway 1958, 457–459) and is still in use in the U.S. House of Representatives and in other legislative bodies. It enables a smaller number of members to act as a quorum and uses relaxed rules designed to expedite business (Plano and Greenberg 1989, 119).

Reports of Committee Progress

On almost every day that the Committee of the Whole met, the *Journal of the Convention* reflects that "Mr. Gorham reported from the Committee that the Committee had made a further progress in the matter to them referred; and had directed him to move that they may have leave to sit again" (Farrand 1937, I, 45, 62, 76, 93, 115, 130, 148, 162, 174, 192, 209, 223, 248, 281). This constant mention of "progress," while it might have been largely pro forma, added a note of optimism to the early Convention proceedings. On the last day of the committee's sitting, it reported its decision to reject the New Jersey Plan and continue discussion and modifications of the Virginia Plan.

Report of the Committee

Prior to the introduction of the New Jersey Plan, the Committee of the Whole prepared a report on June 13 consisting of 19 propositions, designed to summarize the work of the committee to that date. Most of these resolutions reflected the fact that much of the debate had centered on the legislative branch during this time.

The first resolution indicated the Convention's agreement that the new government should consist of three branches. Resolutions 2 through 8 dealt with the legislative branch. The committee had agreed that this body should be bicameral, that the first branch should be elected by the people for three-year terms and receive fixed stipends from the national treasury, and that they, as well as members of the Senate, would be ineligible for offices created by states during their service or by the United States for one year after leaving office. Members of the second branch were to be chosen by state legislatures, to be at least 30 years of age, and to serve for seven-year terms. According to the committee report, either house was to have power to originate acts. Congress would exercise not only the powers of the Congress under the Articles of Confederation but also would be able "to legislate in all cases to which the separate States are incompetent; or in which the harmony of the U.S. may be interrupted by the exercise of individual legislation" (I, 236). The committee report, like the original Virginia Plan, continued to contain a congressional negative of state laws. Representation in both branches was to be "according to some equitable ratio of representation," namely, one that was based on the proportion of white inhabitants and three-fifths of other persons (slaves).

Resolutions 9 and 10 described the executive branch. The committee had agreed on a single executive, selected by Congress for a single seven-year term. Removable by impeachment and conviction, the president was to receive a "fixed stipend" from the national treasury. He had the power to veto legislation, subject to an override by two-thirds of both houses of Congress.

Resolutions 11 through 13 dealt with the judicial branch. Consisting of at least one Supreme Court and other inferior tribunals created by Congress, the Senate was to appoint its members who would serve during good behavior and receive a fixed compensation. Its jurisdiction would extend to all cases involving "the collection of the Natl. revenue, impeachments of any Natl. Officers, and questions which involve the national peace & harmony" (I, 237).

Resolutions 14 through 19 dealt with other

matters. Resolution 14 provided for the admission of new states by less than unanimous congressional vote. The next resolution provided for the continuation of the existing Congress. Resolution 16 provided for guaranteeing each state a republican constitution. The seventeenth resolution specified that provision would be made for constitutional amendments. The next resolution provided that members of state governments would pledge to uphold the new Constitution, and the nineteenth resolution specified that, after being approved by Congress, the new Constitution would be ratified by special conventions within each state.

This committee report is helpful in summarizing agreements that the delegates made roughly during the first two weeks of the Convention, prior to serious consideration being given to any other plans. After the committee report was compiled, William Paterson introduced the New Jersey Plan, Alexander Hamilton outlined his own plans for government, and the committee engaged in a further day of debate. The Convention does not subsequently appear to have used the Committee of the Whole mechanism. It is unclear why the Convention abandoned this mechanism on June 20, although it is possible that the Convention thought that George Washington's more austere and prestigious presence as president of the Convention might help to moderate the increasing friction that was becoming evident with two plans now on the table and with partisans lining up more clearly on the side of the large states and the small ones.

Convention Rejects Resumption of Committee Mechanism

On August 7, the day after the Committee of Detail issued its report containing a preliminary draft of the Constitution to the Convention, Charles Pinckney of South Carolina proposed that it be referred to the Committee of the Whole. Nathaniel Gorham, chair of the original Committee of the Whole, was among those who feared that this would lead to further delay. The Convention rejected this proposal, with only Dela-

ware, Maryland, and Virginia favoring it (II, 196; the official report, at II, 193, indicates, however, that the Convention had taken an earlier 5-4 vote in favor of such a committee). The Committee of the Whole thus functioned only during the opening weeks of the Convention.

See Also Gorham, Nathaniel; New Jersey Plan; Virginia Plan

FOR FURTHER READING

Farrand, Max, ed. 1937. *The Records of the Federal Convention.* 4 vols. New Haven, CT: Yale University Press.

Galloway, George B. 1958. "Precedents Established in the First Congress." *Western Political Quarterly* 11 (September): 454–468.

Plano, Jack C., and Milton Greenberg. 1989. *The American Political Dictionary.* New York: Holt, Rinehart and Winston.

Risjord, Norman K. 1992. "Partisanship and Power: House Committees and the Powers of the Speaker, 1789–1801." *William and Mary Quarterly,* 3rd ser. 49 (October): 628–651.

COMMITTEE ON COMMERCIAL DISCRIMINATION (August 25)

On August 25, the Convention created a committee to examine a number of proposals regarding the regulation of commerce, most designed to see that Congress did not discriminate among U.S. ports. The committee consisted of the following 11 men: John Langdon of New Hampshire, Nathaniel Gorham of Massachusetts, Roger Sherman of Connecticut (the committee chair), Jonathan Dayton of New Jersey, Thomas Fitzsimmons of Pennsylvania, George Read of Delaware, Daniel Carroll of Maryland, George Mason of Virginia, Hugh Williamson of North Carolina, Pierce Butler of South Carolina, and William Few of Georgia.

The committee reported to the Convention on August 28. It provided that no commercial or revenue regulation should prefer one port to another or "oblige Vessels bound to or from any State to enter, clear, or pay duties in another" (Farrand 1937, II, 434). It also provided that "all tonnage, duties, imposts, and excises" exacted by Congress should be uniform throughout the nation. The Convention struck the word "tonnage" as redundant with duties, but otherwise adopted both proposals on August 31. These provisions are found in Article I, Sections 9 and 10.

See Also Sherman, Roger

FOR FURTHER READING

Hutchinson, David. 1975. *The Foundations of the Constitution.* Secaucus, NJ: University Books.

which such acts, records, and proceedings shall be proved, and the effect which judgments obtained in one State shall have in another. (Farrand 1937, II, 483–484)

The Convention adopted these provisions with minimal alterations on September 3 (II, 488–489).

See Also Bankruptcies; Full Faith and Credit Clause; Rutledge, John

FOR FURTHER READING

Farrand, Max, ed. 1937. *The Records of the Federal Convention.* 4 vols. New Haven, CT: Yale University Press.
Nadelmann, Kurt H. 1957. "On the Origin of the Bankruptcy Clause." *American Journal of Legal History* 1 (July): 215–228.

COMMITTEE ON INTERSTATE COMITY AND BANKRUPTCY (August 29)

The Convention took up discussion of the full faith and credit clause on August 29, at which time it committed this provision and a provision granting Congress power to establish uniform laws on bankruptcies to a committee. The committee consisted of five delegates: William Johnson of Connecticut, Nathaniel Gorham of Massachusetts, James Wilson of Pennsylvania, Edmund Randolph of Virginia, and John Rutledge of South Carolina (the chair).

On September 1, the committee proposed to grant Congress power over bankruptcy laws, and it reworded the full faith and credit clause so as to provide that

> full faith and credit ought to be given in each State to the public Acts, Records, and Judicial proceedings of every other State, and the Legislature shall by general laws prescribe the manner in

COMMITTEE ON ORIGINAL APPORTIONMENT OF CONGRESS (July 6)

Just one day after receiving a report from a Committee of a Member From Each State on representation in Congress (designated in this volume as the Committee on Representation in Congress), the Convention voted to create another committee, a Committee of Five, to reexamine its proposal that Congress be apportioned so that states would have a minimum of one representative for every 40,000 inhabitants. Gouverneur Morris of Pennsylvania offered the proposal, apparently thinking that a committee would more easily settle on the initial apportionment of the states than could the Convention as a whole.

James Wilson of Pennsylvania seconded Morris's motion, which initiated considerable discussion. Nathaniel Gorham of Massachusetts thought that setting representation for states would result in "great inconveniency," since state populations would subsequently change (Farrand

1937, I, 540). Elbridge Gerry, also of Massachusetts, favored a committee and hoped that it could come up with a formula for representation that would account for both wealth and population. Rufus King, yet another delegate from Massachusetts, wanted "the clause to be committed chiefly in order to detach it from the Report with which it had no connection" (I, 541). He did not believe that the standard of one representative would be able to adapt to future population growth. Pierce Butler of South Carolina disliked a standard based on population alone, and favored some balance between existing states and new ones. Charles Pinckney, also of South Carolina, could see no reason for a committee since he thought any rule other than population was impractical, but William Davie of North Carolina thought sending it to a committee was a good idea. The Convention voted 7-3-1 to do so.

Nathaniel Gorham and Rufus King of Masssachusetts, Gouverneur Morris of Pennsylvania, Edmund Randolph of Virginia, and John Rutledge of South Carolina were elected to the committee, giving it a distinct tilt to the large states (it seems especially unusual that Massachusetts had two representatives), with Rutledge being the only small-state representative. Morris served as committee chair.

The committee presented its report on Monday, July 9. It proposed that the first Congress would consist of 56 members. Rhode Island and Delaware were to have one representative; New Hampshire and Georgia to have two; New Jersey to have three; Connecticut and Maryland to have four; New York, North Carolina and South Carolina to have Five; Massachusetts to have seven; Pennsylvania to have eight; and Virginia to have nine. It further provided that the legislature be authorized to alter representation from time to time.

On the same day the committee report was introduced, the Convention created yet another committee to revisit the number of representatives entrusted to each state.

See Also Committee of Compromise on Representation in Congress; Committee to Reconsider Representation in the House; Morris, Gouverneur

FOR FURTHER READING

Farrand, Max, ed. 1937. *The Records of the Federal Convention*. 4 vols. New Haven, CT: Yale University Press.

Kromkowski, Charles A. 2002. *Recreating the American Republic: Rules of Apportionment, Constitutional Change, and American Political Development, 1700–1870*. Cambridge: Cambridge University Press.

Zagarri, Rosemarie. 1987. *The Politics of Size: Representation in the United States, 1776–1850*. Ithaca, NY: Cornell University Press.

COMMITTEE ON POSTPONED MATTERS (August 31)

On August 31, the Convention accepted a motion by Connecticut's Roger Sherman to take all the matters that it had previously postponed and assign them to a committee. The committee was known alternately as the Committee on Postponed Matters, the Committee on Unfinished Parts, or (because of its size) the Committee of Eleven. Its members consisted of Nicholas Gilman of New Hampshire, Rufus King of Massachusetts, Roger Sherman of Connecticut, David Brearly of New Jersey, Gouverneur Morris of Pennsylvania, John Dickinson of Delaware, Daniel Carroll of Maryland, James Madison of Virginia, Hugh Williamson of North Carolina, Pierce Butler of South Carolina, and Abraham Baldwin of Georgia (Farrand 1937, II, 481).

On September 1, Brearly issued a partial report on behalf of the committee proposing that members of Congress should be ineligible for any other civil offices during their tenure and prohibiting individuals in other civil offices from serving in Congress while maintaining such an office (II, 483). Brearly issued a much longer report on September 4. The committee report was the basis for the first clause in Article I, Section 8 providing Congress with the power of the purse; it provided for Congress to regulate commerce with the Indian tribes; it provided that trials for impeachment would require a two-thirds majority to convict; it established qualifications for the president; it provided that the vice president would preside over the Senate; it provided for presidential appointment and Senate confirmation of major officeholders; it provided for the president to get written opinions from cabinet officers; and it specified that treason and bribery would be grounds for presidential impeachments. Most of these provisions, some in modified form, became part of the Constitution upon which the Convention agreed.

The committee's most important work consisted in the formulation of the Electoral College. The plan incorporated provisions for representation in the Connecticut Compromise into the plan for selecting the president. By providing a method for selecting the president by a body other than Congress, the mechanism made it possible to allow for presidential re-eligibility for office without the fear of corruption.

The day that the committee issued its major report, the Convention also entrusted it with the task of preparing a report of defraying Convention expenses (II, 496). On September 5, it accordingly proposed that Congress pay the secretary and other Convention officials sums "in proportion to their respective times of service as are allowed to the Secretary and similar Officers of Congress," and ordered the secretary to send such an account to Congress. The Convention agreed to both measures (II, 506).

See Also Brearly, David; President, Selection

FOR FURTHER READING

Farrand, Max, ed. 1937. *The Records of the Federal Convention.* 4 vols. New Haven, CT: Yale University Press.

Slonin, Shlomo. 1986. "The Electoral College at Philadelphia: The Evolution of an Ad Hoc Congress for the Selection of a President." *Journal of American History* 73 (June): 35–58.

COMMITTEE ON RULES (May 25)

On Friday, May 25, the first day of deliberations at the Constitutional Convention, South Carolina's Charles Pinckney moved that the Convention should appoint a committee to recommend rules for the House. The Convention appointed a committee consisting of George Wythe of Virginia, Alexander Hamilton of New York, and Pinckney, thus effectively giving representation to the Eastern (Northern), Middle, and Southern states.

The Convention adjourned over the weekend (a rarity, as it generally met on Saturdays), and the committee, headed by George Wythe, a law professor at the College of William and Mary (only the second in the English-speaking world) and future Virginia judge, made its report on Monday, May 28. After a number of modifications and additions, the Convention subsequently adopted most of the committee's rules. This was the first, and smallest, of a number of committees used during the Constitutional Convention. The committee's amended work promoted deliberation and effectively channeled discussion and debate at the Convention.

See Also Hamilton, Alexander; Pinckney, Charles; Rules of the Constitutional Convention; Secrecy; Wythe, George

FOR FURTHER READING

Eidelberg, Paul. 1968. *The Philosophy of the American Constitution: A Reinterpretation of the Intentions of the Founding Fathers.* New York: The Free Press.

Lansky, Dana. 2000. "Proceeding to a Constitution: A Multi-Party Negotiation Analysis of the Constitutional Convention of 1787." *Harvard Negotiation Law Review* 5 (Spring): 279–338.

COMMITTEE ON SLAVE TRADE AND NAVIGATION (August 22)

At the Convention, the issue of continuing slave importation and the issue of the majorities that should be necessary in order to adopt navigation acts often pitted the Deep South states against the others. Delegates from South Carolina and Georgia were particularly insistent that states should be permitted to continue importing slaves, and they also favored supermajority requirements for levying navigation laws, which they feared might otherwise discriminate against the South.

Gouverneur Morris of Pennsylvania was among the delegates who thought that these matters might be linked so as to "form a bargain among the Northern & Southern States" (Farrand 1937, II, 374). On August 22, the Convention voted to send both of these matters, as well as the matter of capitation taxes, to a committee. The Convention chose John Langdon of New Hampshire, Rufus King of Massachusetts, William Johnson of Connecticut, William Livingston of New Jersey, George Clymer of Pennsylvania, John Dickinson of Delaware, Luther Martin of Maryland, James Madison of Virginia, Hugh Williamson of North Carolina, Charles Cotesworth Pinckney of South Carolina, and Abraham Baldwin of Georgia (II, 375). Eight members of this committee, including Livingston, its chair, had served on the earlier Committee on State Debts and Militia.

Livingston presented the committee report on August 24. It proposed that states should be permitted to continue to import slaves until 1800 but the only tax being permitted being one "not exceeding the average of the duties laid on imports" (II, 400). The committee further proposed keeping existing limitations on capitation taxes to proportions determined by the census and requiring that all navigation acts require a two-thirds majority.

In time the Convention voted to extend the period for importing slaves to 1808 and substituted a maximum $10 tax per person for the more ambiguous committee formulation. It kept the ambiguous limit on capitation taxes and dropped the two-thirds supermajorities for navigation acts.

See Also African Americans; Livingston, William; Slave Importation

FOR FURTHER READING

Berns, Walter. 1968. "The Constitution and the Migration of Slaves." *Yale Law Journal* 78 (December): 198–228.

Dellinger, Walter E., III. 1987–1988. "1787: The Constitution and 'The Curse of Heaven.'" *William and Mary Law Review* 29: 145–161.

Farrand, Max, ed. 1937. *The Records of the Federal Convention.* 4 vols. New Haven, CT: Yale University Press.

COMMITTEE ON STATE DEBTS AND MILITIA (August 18)

On August 18, the Convention voted to submit the issue of federal assumption of state debts to a committee. The Convention chose 11 men for this committee. They were John Langdon of New Hampshire, Rufus King of Massachusetts, Roger Sherman of Connecticut, William Livingston of New Jersey, George Clymer of Pennsylvania, John Dickinson of Delaware, James McHenry of Maryland, George Mason of Virginia, Hugh Williamson of North Carolina, Charles Cotesworth Pinckney of South Carolina, and Abraham Baldwin of Georgia (Farrand 1937, II, 322). Later that day the Convention entrusted this same committee with resolving how the militia would be governed (II, 323).

Livingston submitted the committee report on August 21. It provided that Congress should have power to discharge its debts as well as those incurred by the states in prosecuting the Revolutionary War, without apparently requiring Congress to assume such obligations. It also provided that Congress would have power "for organizing, arming, and disciplining the militia," while reserving to the states the power to appoint officers and train militia according to rules established by Congress (II, 352). This report was initially postponed. The Convention debated and accepted its proposals on August 23 (II, 384–389).

See Also Debts; Livingston, William; Militia, Congressional Power to Organize and Govern

FOR FURTHER READING

Farrand, Max, ed. 1937. *The Records of the Federal Convention*. 4 vols. New Haven, CT: Yale University Press.

Ferguson, E. James. 1951. "State Assumption of the Federal Debt during the Confederation." *The Mississippi Valley Historical Review* 38 (December): 403–424.

Fields, William S., and David T. Hardy. 1992. "The Militia and the Constitution: A Legal History." *Military Law Review* 136 (Spring): 1–42.

COMMITTEE ON SUMPTUARY LEGISLATION (September 13)

On August 20, and again on September 13, Virginia's George Mason, who was committed to republican principles, proposed giving Congress the power to adopt sumptuary legislation. On the second occasion, Mason proposed creating a committee to make a report on the matter, and Connecticut's William Samuel Johnson seconded him. The Convention appointed a committee of five, adding Benjamin Franklin, John Dickinson, and William Livingston to the two who had advocated the committee. There is no evidence that the committee offered a report, and the Constitution remains silent on the subject.

See Also Mason, George; Republicanism; Sumptuary Legislation

FOR FURTHER READING

Goodrich, Peter. 1998. "Signs Taken for Wonders: Community, Identity, and a History of Sumptuary Laws." *Law and Social Inquiry* 23 (Summer): 707–725.

COMMITTEE ON UNFINISHED PARTS

See COMMITTEE ON POSTPONED MATTERS

COMMITTEE TO RECONSIDER REPRESENTATION IN THE HOUSE (July 9)

This was the third of three committees that the Convention appointed between July 2 and July 9. The Convention appointed it to reconsider the first paragraph of a two-paragraph report prepared by a Committee of Five (generally referred to as the Committee on Original Apportionment of the Congress) and reported on July 9, which had suggested an initial allocation of 56 seats in the House of Representatives, giving states from one to nine delegates each.

Members of the Convention had immediately questioned the Committee of Five about what principle it had used in arriving at its figures. Delegates from Northern and Southern states further argued about how, if at all, slaves should be counted. Perhaps with a view to the manner in which the first committee had overrepresented the large states, Roger Sherman of Connecticut and Gouverneur Morris of Pennsylvania proposed the committee, with the latter, who had served on the Committee of Five, suggesting that "this was the only case in which such Committees were useful" (Farrand 1937, I, 560).

This committee consisted of the following: Rufus King of Massachusetts (the chair); Roger Sherman of Connecticut; Robert Yates of New York; David Brearly of New Jersey; Gouverneur Morris of Pennsylvania; George Read of Delaware; Daniel Carroll of Maryland; James Madison of Virginia; Hugh Williamson of North Carolina; John Rutledge of South Carolina; and William Houston of Georgia. Of these, Yates and Rutledge had served on the earlier Committee of Eleven, and King, Morris, and Rutledge on the Committee of Five.

The new committee submitted its report on the next day and proposed a House of 65 members rather than 56. It reached this number by raising New Hampshire's allocation from two to three; Massachusetts's from seven to eight; Connecticut's from four to five; New York's from five to six; New Jersey's from three to four; Maryland's from four to six; Virginia's from nine to ten; and Georgia's from two to three. Despite several attempts to alter this formula, it was the one the Convention ultimately adopted for the first Congress.

On July 13, when representation was linked to taxation, Read observed that he had sensed "a backwardness in some of the members from the large States, to take their full proportion of Representatives" (I, 601). He now openly wondered whether the advocates of these states had done so in an attempt to avoid their fair share of taxation. Madison believed that Read failed to remember that Massachusetts's Rufus King had advocated increased representation for his state in committee.

See Also Committee on Original Apportionment of Congress; King, Rufus

FOR FURTHER READING

Farrand, Max, ed. 1937. *The Records of the Federal Convention*. 4 vols. New Haven, CT: Yale University Press.

Kromkowski, Charles A. 2002. *Recreating the American Republic: Rules of Apportionment, Constitutional Change, and American Political Development, 1700–1870*. Cambridge: Cambridge University Press.

Zagarri, Rosemarie. 1987. *The Politics of Size: Representation in the United States, 1776–1850*. Ithaca, NY: Cornell University Press.

COMMITTEES AT THE CONSTITUTIONAL CONVENTION

Although only 55 delegates attended the Convention (and at no time were all of them present at once), the Convention, like similar bodies of its size, found it was more expedient to entrust some of its more specialized work to committees than to do all of it collectively. State legislatures had long used such committees, which had also been extensively utilized by the Continental Congresses (Risjord 1992, 632).

On May 25, its first full day of business, the Convention appointed a three-man Rules Committee, the smallest at the Convention. The committee, chaired by Virginia's George Wythe, issued its report on May 28 and 29. Largely adopted by the Convention, these rules proved to be vital to fostering the atmosphere of reason and compromise that prevailed through most of the proceedings. The rules included a provision specifying how committee members would be chosen. It provided that

> committees shall be appointed by ballot; and the members who have the greatest number of ballots, altho' not a majority of the votes present, shall be the Committee—When two or more members have an equal number of votes, the member standing first on the list in the order of taking down the ballots, shall be preferred. (Farrand 1937, I, 12)

The Convention further provided that committees would not meet while the Convention itself was in session (I, 15). In responding to an attack during the ratification debates, Maryland's Luther Martin indicated that "The business of the committees were not of a secret nature, nor were they conducted in a secret manner; I mean as to the members of the Convention" (III, 279). If true, this would suggest that other members of the Convention could attend committee meetings but not necessarily participate (Clarkson and Jett 1970, 108).

On May 30, the Convention resolved itself into a Committee of the Whole and continued so to meet until June 19. By adopting this mechanism, which is common in legislative bodies, the Convention was able to proceed without the same quorum and formality that would have been otherwise required. Nathaniel Gorham of Massachusetts served as chair of the Committee of the Whole. The committee discussed the Virginia Plan and witnessed the introduction both of the New Jersey Plan and of Alexander Hamilton's plan.

In a testament to the difficulty of the issue, the Convention selected three committees from July 2 through July 9, all dealing with representation in Congress. The first and third of these committees had 11 members, and the second had three. Elbridge Gerry of Massachusetts, Gouverneur Morris of Pennsylvania, and Rufus King of Massachusetts served as the respective chairs of these committees. The first committee, a Committee of Compromise on Representation in Congress, proposed the essence of what became the Connecticut Compromise, recommending that states have one representative in the House of Representatives for every 40,000 inhabitants and that states be represented equally within the Senate; it also provided that all money bills would originate in the House of Representatives. The second committee, a Committee on Original Apportionment of Congress, proposed that the first House of Representatives should consist of 56 members, and the third committee, the Committee to Reconsider Representation in the House, raised this number to 65.

On July 24, the Convention appointed a five-man Committee of Detail to prepare a draft of a Constitution. This committee was probably the most important to be selected by the Convention, and the power of its members was heightened by its small size. John Rutledge of South Carolina served as chair of this committee, which submitted its report on August 6 and was largely responsible for the delineation of the enumerated powers of Congress. On August 18 and 20, the Convention submitted further proposals for the committee's consideration, but it appears that a number of these matters found their way to the Committee on Postponed Matters created on August 31 and cited below (see II, 483).

The next four committees all had 11 members. These included a Committee on State Debts and Militia established on August 18, a Committee on Slave Trade and Navigation appointed on August 22, a Committee on Commercial Discrimination appointed on August 25, and a Committee on Postponed Matters created on August 31. There was a substantial overlap in membership (eight members) between the committees appointed on August 18 and August 22, including Robert Livingston of New Jersey, who chaired both. Roger Sherman of Connecticut and John Rutledge of South Carolina respectively chaired the other two committees.

The Committee on State Debts and Militia provided that Congress would have power to discharge state debts and that the nation and the states would share powers related to the militia. The Committee on Slave Trade and Navigation proposed allowing slave importation to continue until the year 1800 with states being allowed to enact limited taxes on such imports. The Committee on Commercial Discrimination prohibited preferences for ports and proposed uniform duties.

David Brearly of New Jersey chaired the Committee on Postponed Matters. Apart from the Committee of Detail, its work was one of the most far-ranging at the Convention.

Although William Johnson of Connecticut headed the five-man Committee of Style that the Convention created on September 8 to put the final touches on the Constitution, scholars generally agree that Pennsylvania's Gouverneur Morris was its most influential member. On September 13 the Convention appointed another five-man

Committee on Sumptuary Legislation, which never, however, appears to have issued a report.

Excluding the Committee of the Whole, which was open to all members, there were 12 committees at the Constitutional Convention. All were ad hoc, although the Committee of Detail was given assignments on more than one occasion. Of the 12 committees, one had three members, five had five members, and six had 11 members. Although it had the incidental advantage of having an odd number of members, the latter number was based on the practice often followed under the Articles of Confederation of providing one member from each state (of the 13 states, Rhode Island never sent a delegation, and the New Hampshire representatives arrived at about the time that New York representatives absented themselves). Since only one committee (that on Original Representation in Congress established on July 6) had two members from a single state, delegates from states with smaller delegations clearly had a better chance to serve on committees than those from states with more representatives.

It takes considerable care to trace committee assignments and reports through the Convention records because note takers often designated them by the number of members (a committee of five, a committee of 11, or a committee of a member from each state), rather than by the subject matter they were assigned, and several committees had the same number of members. Similarly, a number of the larger committees were designated as "grand" committees.

A total of 38 members served on committees sometime during the Convention. Virginia was the only state that had a member on every committee. By contrast, the states of New Hampshire and New York, whose delegates respectively arrived late and left early, were each represented on only four committees (and Rhode Island, which never sent delegates, was not represented on any). Rufus King of Massachusetts served on six different committees, the Convention record. John Rutledge of South Carolina and Hugh Williamson of North Carolina served on five; Roger Sherman, Nathaniel Gorham (who also chaired the Committee of the Whole), Gouverneur Morris, James Madison, and Abraham

Baldwin served on four and (if the Committee on Sumptuary Legislation that never issued a report is included) so did William Johnson, John Dickinson, and George Mason. John Langdon, Daniel Carroll, and Edmund Randolph served on three committees, as did William Livingston if the Committee on Sumptuary Legislation is included.

Although he served as president of the Convention, the Convention did not appoint George Washington to any committees. William Livingston and John Rutledge were the only delegates to chair, or issue the reports of, two committees. As Gouverneur Morris's powerful influence on the Committee of Style, which William Johnson chaired, indicates, however, designation as chair did not necessarily mean that a member was the most important individual on a committee. Similarly, some committees dealt with relatively modest matters while others shouldered far heavier responsibilities.

See Also Committee of Compromise on Representation in Congress; Committee of Detail; Committee of Style and Arrangement; Committee on Commercial Discrimination; Committee on Interstate Comity and Bankruptcy; Committee on Original Apportionment of Congress; Committee on Postponed Matters; Committee on Rules; Committee on Slave Trade and Navigation; Committee on State Debts and Militia; Committee on Sumptuary Legislation; Committee to Reconsider Representation in the House

FOR FURTHER READING

Clarkson, Paul S., and R. Samuel Jett. 1970. *Luther Martin of Maryland.* Baltimore, MD: Johns Hopkins University Press.

Farrand, Max, ed. 1937. *The Records of the Federal Convention.* 4 vols. New Haven, CT: Yale University Press.

Lansky, Dana. 2000. "Proceeding to a Constitution: A Multi-Party Negotiation Analysis of the Constitutional Convention of 1787." *Harvard Negotiation Law Review* 5 (Spring): 279–338.

Risjord, Norman K. 1992. "Partisanship and Power: House Committees and the Powers of the Speaker, 1789–1801." *William and Mary Quarterly,* 3rd ser. 49 (October): 628–651.

COMMON LAW

All but one American state (Louisiana, which, with its French and Spanish heritage, relies chiefly on civil, or code law) has a common law system. Because it is built from judicial precedents, such a system has often been described as "judge-made" law. At the time that judges were formulating decisions that would serve as "precedents" for other courts, however, most judges probably did not conceive of themselves as exercising will, or as "making" laws, at all. Rather, they understood themselves to be simply "discovering" the practices and procedures that were consistent with right reason, natural law (Stoner 1999, 179), or even Christianity (Stoner 2003, 24). At the time of independence from Great Britain, most American states accepted the idea of continuing with English common law, understanding that some changes in application would be required in the New World setting.

The Constitution was designed as a kind of foundational, or fundamental, law. Because the Constitution created a federal system of governance, however, delegates probably anticipated that most matters involving the judiciary would remain at the state level. Stoner thus observes:

> The American state constitutions and in particular the federal Constitution, then, not only established limited government but were themselves limited as forms of law. Federal law is supreme over state law, constitutions are supreme over state law, constitutions are supreme over statutes, and statutes are supreme over common law, but these hierarchies are not simple or absolute. Federal laws are supreme only if pursuant to the Constitution, and traditional common-law privileges and immunities are often embodied in constitutional bills of rights. More generally, although the federal Constitution might be said to have been formed largely on liberal republican principles—limited as it was, to providing security for peace, prosperity, and individual rights—and although the state constitutions became increasingly democratic in the early republican period, the persistent force of common law allowed for the continuation of traditional practices, not only in society, but in the law itself. (2003, 80)

Sir Edward Coke, English jurist (1552–1634)
(Pixel That)

Convention Discussions

In considering a provision on August 17 involving the congressional power to "declare the law and punishment of piracies and felonies &c" (Farrand 1937, II, 315), Pennsylvania's James Wilson, a well-educated lawyer who would later serve on the U.S. Supreme Court, responded to a proposal by Virginia's James Madison to insert "define" before the word "felonies," by saying that he "thought 'felonies' [was] sufficiently defined by Common law" (II, 316). Madison disagreed. He thought that the term "felony at common law is vague" and "defective" (II, 316). He feared that different states would enforce different laws, leading to lack of uniformity and stability. After further discussion that ranged over English statutes, the delegates adopted Madison's motion.

There was a somewhat similar discussion on August 22, when the delegates were discussing the prohibition on ex post facto (retroactive) criminal laws. Connecticut's Oliver Ellsworth indicated that such laws were "void of themselves," and that "it cannot be necessary to prohibit them" (II, 376). James Wilson indicated that if such a prohibition were to be included in the Constitution–as it eventually was–"It will bring reflexions on the Constitution–and proclaim that we are ignorant of the first principles of Legislation, or are constituting a Government which will be so" (II, 376). A week later, Delaware's John Dickinson observed that in examining the *Commentaries* of William Blackstone (1723–1780), one of the greatest English legal writers, he had discovered that the term "ex post facto" "related to criminal cases only; that they would not consequently restrain the States from retrospective laws in civil cases, and that some further provision for this purpose would be requisite" (II, 448–449).

Donald S. Lutz has identified Blackstone as the second-most-quoted European writer in America after the Baron de Montesquieu during the 1780s and 1790s (Lutz 1984). Blackstone had attempted to meld the idea of common law with that of the social contract (Zuckert 2003). Americans, however, did not always refer to Blackstone positively, in part because he had advocated parliamentary sovereignty in the New World during the conflict leading up to the Revolutionary War. Thus, none other than New York's Alexander Hamilton had cited earlier colonial opposition to this doctrine, which he specifically identified with Blackstone (II, 472). During the conflict with England over parliamentary sovereignty, the colonists had been more likely to quote Sir Edward Coke (1552–1634), who had provided an argument for the unconstitutionality of unjust legislation (Kirkham 1992, 8).

On August 27, Wilson again evoked common law when the Convention was discussing the jurisdiction of the judiciary. He responded to a query by Pennsylvania's Gouverneur Morris by observing that jurisdiction would extend "to cases of Common law as well as Civil law" (II, 431).

Some terms within the Constitution depend on an understanding of English common law. Thus, for example, Article III, Section 2 of the Constitution provides that the "Judicial Power shall extend to all Cases, in Law and Equity, arising under this Constitution, the Law of the United States, and Treaties made, or which shall be made, under their Authority." Law and equity were two classic divisions of English law, the first dealing with cases involving retroactive relief (damages or punishments) for wrongs committed, whereas equity was a more flexible system, sometimes involving the use of injunctions, designed to achieve justice in cases where the remedies provided under the first system were inadequate.

Virginia's George Mason objected to the Constitution in part on the ground that the new Constitution did not provide for the people to "be secured even in the enjoyment of the benefit of the common law" (II, 637). This prompted a perplexed letter from James Madison to George Washington dated October 18, 1787:

> What can he mean by saying that the Common law is not secured by the new Constitution, though it has been adopted by the State Constitutions. The Common law is nothing more than the unwritten law, and is left by all the Constitutions equally liable to legislative alterations. I am not sure that any notice is particularly taken of it in the Constitutions of the States. If there is, nothing more is provided than a general declaration that it shall continue along with other branches of law to be in force till legally changed. The Constitution of Virga. drawn up by Col. Mason himself, is absolutely silent on the subject. (III, 130)

Madison further observed that there were aspects of English law, like primogeniture (the provision that larger parts of inheritances would go to firstborn sons), or aspects of "ecclesiastical Hierarchy" that would be inappropriate to America. In a statement similar to one that Chief Justice John Marshall would later utter in *McCulloch v. Maryland* (1819), Madison went on to observe that if the delegates had attempted to delineate every case in which the common law would continue or not continue to apply, "they must have formed a digest of laws, instead of a Constitution" (III, 130).

The Convention's treatment, or relative silence, regarding the common law thus serves as a caution about expecting that the Constitution would directly address issues that delegates expected to remain for their implementation at the state level. The Seventh Amendment later referred specifically to "suits at common law," to which it extended the right to a jury trial.

Influences Identified

James R. Stoner, Jr., has identified four ways in which common law influenced the U.S. Constitution. Consistent with some of the discussions at the Convention examined above, he first observes that the common law provided some of the language of the document. He specifically cites the provisions related to habeas corpus, ex post facto laws, the provision that an individual be "natural born," and the term "good behavior" (2003, 17). He believes that, unless otherwise stated, the presumption was that such words would continue to maintain their existing meanings. Second, Stoner believes that the system of courts recognized in Article III of the Constitution presupposed a system like that in England—he notes the specific constitutional reference to courts of "law and equity" as well as to defenses of judicial review in *The Federalist* (Stoner 2003, 18–19). Stoner believes that it is not accidental that the judges' "power to set aside unconstitutional statutes [known as judicial review] remains unwritten, to be deduced on analogy to the rule for interpreting conflicting statutes a 'mere rule of construction, not derived from any positive laws, but from the nature and reason of the thing'" (Stoner 2003, 19, quoting Hamilton in *Federalist* No. 78). Stoner identifies the supremacy clause in Article VI as a third indication of common law thinking; he finds it especially significant that the federal Constitution and laws made under its authority were to be secured through the power of the courts. Fourth, he notes that many provisions within the Bill of Rights—especially those related to juries—recognized rights that had been established through the common law (Stoner 2003, 20).

A Caveat

The one danger of interpreting the Constitution to incorporate common law principles is that this doctrine might on occasion be used to import principles into the Constitution that are inconsistent with its specific language. In his "Report on the [Virginia] Resolution (1799–1800)," James Madison thus battled the idea that the U.S. Constitution had incorporated the English view, implicit in the Sedition Act of 1798, that the only protection for freedom of speech and press was a presumption against prior restraint (Sheldon 2001, 91–94). At least during the debates over the Sedition Act of 1798, Madison believed the protections of the First Amendment were much wider (Smolla 1992, 33–34), and later decisions by the U.S. Supreme Court have agreed.

See Also Ex Post Facto Laws; Federalism; Great Britain; Habeas Corpus; Judicial Jurisdiction; Judicial Review; Mason, George; Natural Rights; Reason and Experience

FOR FURTHER READING

Clinton, Robert L. 1997. *God and Man in the Law: The Foundations of Anglo-American Constitutionalism.* Lawrence: University Press of Kansas.

Cook, Edward. 2003. *The Selected Writings and Speeches of Sir Edward Coke.* Ed. Steve Sheppard. 3 vols. Indianapolis, IN: Liberty Fund.

Farrand, Max, ed. 1937. *The Records of the Federal Convention.* 4 vols. New Haven, CT: Yale University Press.

Kirkham, David M. 1992. "European Sources of American Constitutional Thought before 1787." *United States Air Force Academy Journal of Legal Studies* 3: 1–28.

Kreml, William P. 1997. *The Constitutional Divide: The Private and Public Sectors in American Law.* Columbia: University of South Carolina Press.

Lutz, Donald S. 1984. "The Relative Influence of European Writers on Late Eighteenth-Century American Political Thought." *American Political Science Review* 78 (March): 189–197.

Sheldon, Garrett Ward. 2001. *The Political Philosophy of James Madison.* Baltimore, MD: Johns Hopkins University Press.

Sherry, Suzanna. 1987. "The Founders' Unwritten Constitution." *University of Chicago Law Review* 54 (Fall): 1127–1177.

Smolla, Rodney A. 1992. *Free Speech in an Open Society.* New York: Alfred A. Knopf.

Stoner, James R., Jr. 1999. "Christianity, the Common Law, and the Constitution." *Vital Remnants: America's Founding and the Western Tradition.* Ed. Gary L. Gregg II. Wilmington, DE: ISI Books.

———. 1992. *Common Law and Liberal Theory: Coke,*

Hobbes, and the Origins of American Constitutionalism. Lawrence: University Press of Kansas.

——. 2003. *Common-Law Liberty: Rethinking American Constitutionalism.* Lawrence: University Press of Kansas.

Zuckert, Michael. 2003. "Social Compact, Common Laws, and the American Amalgam: The Contribution of William Blackstone." In Ronald J. Pestritto and Thomas G. West, eds., *The American Founding and the Social Compact.* Lanham, MD: Lexington Books, 37–74.

COMPROMISE

One of the keys to understanding the Constitutional Convention of 1787 is to recognize the importance that the spirit of compromise played in the proceedings. It is possible that this willingness to compromise in turn stemmed from a consensus on key issues. Benjamin Wright has thus observed:

> The most fundamental political or constitutional issues were taken for granted without debate, or they were only briefly discussed. These include such basic issues as representative government, elections at fixed intervals, a written constitution which is a supreme law and which contains an amending clause, separation of powers and checks and balances, a bicameral legislature, a single executive, and a separate court system. These principles could have been taken for granted in no other country in the eighteenth century, nor could they in combination have been accepted in any other country even after discussion and vote. (1958, 32)

Delegates certainly attempted to represent what they perceived as the special interests of their own states and regions. However, they recognized that not all interests could be equally accommodated, and they often proved to be quite flexible in regard to lesser matters. It would be difficult to find any delegate to the Convention who got everything that he wanted, but on the closing day, 39 of 42 delegates (one in absentia) signed the docu-

ment. When the Constitutional Convention submitted the Constitution to Congress it included a letter of transmittal, which portrayed the Constitution as "the result of a spirit of amity, and of that mutual deference and concession which the peculiarity of our political situation rendered indispensable" (Farber 1995, 649).

The most well-known compromise at the Convention was the Great, or Connecticut, Compromise between large-state representatives who wanted states to be represented according to population and/or wealth and representatives of the small states who favored continuing the equal state representation under the Articles of Confederation. Similarly, disputes between the slave and free states resulted in the three-fifths compromise, as well as compromises over slave importation and the return of fugitives.

Each of the three branches of government established in the Constitution represented scores of compromises in regard to qualifications for office, term lengths, powers, and limits. The Electoral College system of selecting the president was a result of numerous such compromises.

On some issues, slavery and state representation for example, the interests of delegates can be fairly easily ascertained from the states that they represented. On other matters, however, delegates often had to make decisions with regard to the power of the three branches or different layers of government without knowing in practice how these decisions would affect their own states. This uncertainty undoubtedly contributed to the spirit of moderation (Nelson 1987). Moreover at least one scholar has detected what he believes to have been fairly significant agreement on many matters, especially as regards economic issues and the need for more congressional powers (Schuyler 1916).

The strongest justification of compromise at the Convention was probably articulated by Benjamin Franklin's speech on the last day of the proceedings when he pleaded for unanimity. In that widely circulated speech, after first observing that "the older I grow, the more apt I am to doubt my own judgment, and to pay more respect to the judgment of others" (Farrand 1937, II, 642), Franklin observed:

I doubt . . . whether any other Convention we can obtain may be able to make a better Constitution. For when you assemble a number of men to have the advantage of their joint wisdom, you inevitably assemble with those men, all their prejudices, their passions, their errors of opinion, their local interests, and their selfish views. From such an Assembly can a perfect production be expected? It therefore astonishes me . . . to find this system approaching so near to perfection as it does; and I think it will astonish our enemies. (II, 642)

This theme was widely echoed during the ratification debates during which proponents of the Constitution pursued what Peter Knupfer has described as a "rhetoric of conciliation" during which they attempted "to defuse extremist, emotional, and dogmatic criticisms of the Constitution by stressing a moderate temperament as the necessary prelude to making important policy decisions" (1991, 317). Federalists further compromised during the course of the debates by indicating a willingness to consider the addition of a bill of rights, and Antifederalists in turn compromised by their willingness to give the new government a chance. This spirit of compromise stemmed logically from deference to reason and experience and regard for the rights of others.

See Also Coalitions; Connecticut Compromise; Letter of Transmittal; Parties, Factions, and Interests; Reason and Experience; Three-fifths Clause

FOR FURTHER READING

Donovan, H. H. 1937. "Making the Constitution." *Journal of the National Education Association* 26 (October): 219–234.

Farber, Daniel A. 1995. "The Constitution's Forgotten Cover Letter: An Essay on the New Federalism and the Original Understanding." *Michigan Law Review* 94 (December): 615–650.

Farrand, Max. 1904. "Compromises of the Constitution." *Annual Report of the American Historical Association* 1 (April): 71–84.

Farrand, Max, ed. 1937. *The Records of the Federal Convention.* 4 vols. New Haven, CT: Yale University Press.

Heckathorn, Douglas D., and Steven M. Maser. 1987. "Bargaining and Constitutional Contracts." *American Journal of Political Science* 31 (February): 142–168.

Knupfer, Peter B. 1991. "The Rhetoric of Conciliation: American Civic Culture and the Federalist Defense of Compromise." *Journal of the Early Republic* 11 (Fall): 315–337.

McCormick, Richard P. 1987. "The Miracle at Philadelphia." *Utah Law Review:* 829–846.

Nelson, William E. 1987. "Reason and Compromise in the Establishment of the Federal Constitution, 1787–1801." *William and Mary Quarterly,* 3rd ser. 44 (July): 458–484.

Roche, John P. 1961. "The Founding Fathers: A Reform Caucus in Action." *American Political Science Review* 55 (December): 799–816.

Schuyler, R. R. 1916. "Agreement in the Federal Convention." *Political Science Quarterly* 31 (June): 289–299.

Wright, Benjamin Fletcher. 1958. "Consensus and Continuity–1776–1787." *Boston University Law Review* 53 (Winter): 1–52.

CONFEDERAL GOVERNMENT

A confederation is a government, like that under the Articles of Confederation (1781–1789) and the later Confederate States of America (1861–1865), in which power is divided between a central government and constituent government or states, but in which the latter have primary power. Confederal governments are much like treaties. Small nations sometimes ally into a confederation to protect themselves against foreign governments. At the time of the Constitutional Convention, such an arrangement was sometimes known as a "federal" or "foederal" government.

In a confederation, the central authority does not act directly upon individual citizens but requests its constituent members to do so on its behalf. Thus, under the Articles of Confederation, Congress could requisition, or request, the states to raise taxes or to recruit soldiers, but it could not exercise such powers directly over citizens on its own authority. Moreover, under the Articles of

Confederation, nine of 13 states were required to agree on key matters involving revenue and other such measures. The consent of all the states was required to amend the Articles.

Over time, notable American leaders came to regard the Articles of Confederation as inadequate in either meeting the nation's domestic affairs or protecting it against foreign dangers. In part because of the former colonists' unhappy experience with Great Britain, a unitary government in which there were no permanent state divisions, and in part because of the great diversity of America and the separate histories of the constituent states, most leaders at the Convention were reluctant to advocate unitary government.

In time they invented the form of government that is today known as federalism. Because this system also preserved the states, albeit while granting greater powers to the national government, there was some initial confusion about what to call it. Although the usage was not completely new, supporters of the new Constitution appear to have preferred to call themselves Federalists, in part because it seemed to suggest that the changes for which they were calling were familiar. Ratification debates over the Constitution did not clear up precisely how the new federal government would differ from the older confederal one, and most such issues were left to be worked out in practice.

See Also Antifederalists; Articles of Confederation; Federalism; Federalists; Forms of Government; Sovereignty; Unitary Government

FOR FURTHER READING

Green, Jack P. 1987. "The Imperial Roots of American Federalism." *this Constitution: Our Enduring Legacy.* Washington, DC: Congressional Quarterly, 37–54.

CONGRESS, BICAMERALISM

The Congress established under the Articles of Confederation, like that of the Continental Congresses that preceded it, was unicameral. By contrast, the English Parliament was composed of two houses, the House of Commons and the House of Lords. By 1787, all the states except for Pennsylvania and Georgia had bicameral legislatures, and neither state with unicameral legislatures would keep them for long (Bowen 1966, 48). The new Constitution announced the principle of bicameralism in Article I, Section 1.

Resolution 3 of the Virginia Plan, proposed on May 29, provided "that the National Legislature ought to consist of two branches" (Farrand 1937, I, 20). By contrast, the New Jersey Plan, introduced on June 15, did not propose to alter the Articles of Confederation in respect to the number of houses. William Paterson explained on June 16 that there was no need for a check within the national legislature as within the states since "party heat" would be less likely within the former body and "the delegations of the different States are checks on each other" (I, 251). He further argued that having two houses (one of which he estimated would have 180 members and the other 90) would be too expensive.

Authors of both the Virginia and New Jersey Plans agreed on the need to entrust Congress with additional powers, but such powers presented the possibility for a greater degree of abuse. The Virginia Plan attempted to moderate the chance of abuse through bicameralism. After alluding to the possibility of "Legislative Despotism," Pennsylvania's James Wilson observed that "In order to controul the Legislative authority, you must divide it" (I, 254). Similarly, Virginia's Edmund Randolph observed that "If the Union of these powers heretofore in Congs. has been safe, it has been owing to the general impotency of that body" (I, 256). On June 20, George Mason, also of Virginia, cited a commitment to bicameralism (along with attachment to republican government) as one of two points on which the American people were agreed (I, 339). By contrast, Connecticut's Roger Sherman could not see the need for two branches. Sherman said that a second house could "serve to embarrass" (I, 342), presumably by delaying the passage of legislation. He was, however, willing to agree to a bicameral Congress if states could be guaranteed an equal vote in one of the houses. Wilson restated his belief in "the necessity of two branches" (I, 343).

On June 21, the Convention voted 7-3-1 for a bicameral legislature. On July 14, Maryland's Luther Martin restated his own opposition to bicameralism but, like Roger Sherman earlier, "was willing . . . to make trial of the plan, rather than do nothing" (II, 4). Rufus King of Massachusetts actually advocated three branches of the legislature, a second "to check the 1st. branch to give more wisdom, system, & stability to the Govt.," and a third to represent the states (II, 6–7). Under the terms of the Connecticut Compromise, the Senate was recognized as a body not simply to control and moderate the House but also to provide equal representation for the states to balance the proportional representation in the House of Representatives.

There is an anecdote that when over breakfast Thomas Jefferson questioned George Washington about the need for a second chamber of Congress, Washington asked Jefferson why he poured his coffee in his saucer. When Jefferson responded, "To cool it," Washington observed, "Even so we pour legislation into the senatorial saucer to cool it" (III, 359). Such a function was distinctly different from the upper house in some bicameral systems (in Britain, for example, the House of Lords provided representation for noblemen), where the upper house was designed to represent different classes of citizens (Appleby 1971, 279). Bicameralism has been revered throughout most of U.S. history but was sometimes questioned by advocates of populism and progressivism in the late nineteenth and early twentieth centuries. Today, Nebraska is the only state in the Union that does not have a bicameral legislature.

See Also Connecticut Compromise; Great Britain; Virginia Plan

FOR FURTHER READING

Appleby, Joyce. 1971. "America as a Model for the Radical French Reformers of 1789." *William and Mary Quarterly*, 3rd ser. 28 (April): 267–286.

Bowen, Catherine Drinker. 1966. *Miracle at Philadelphia: The Story of the Constitutional Convention May to September 1787.* Boston: Little, Brown.

Farrand, Max, ed. 1937. *The Records of the Federal Convention.* 4 vols. New Haven, CT: Yale University Press.

McGinnis, John O., and Michael B. Rappaport. 2002. "Our Supermajoritarian Constitution." *Texas Law Review* 80 (March): 703–806.

Wirls, Daniel, and Stephen Wirls. 2004. *The Invention of the United States Senate.* Baltimore, MD: Johns Hopkins University Press.

Wright, Benjamin Fletcher. 1958. "Consensus and Continuity–1776–1787." *Boston University Law Review* 38 (Winter): 1–52.

CONGRESS, COLLECTIVE POWERS

One of the central reasons for calling the Constitutional Convention was the widespread perception among governing elites, including many members of the existing Congress, that this legislature did not possess adequate powers. The delegates to the Convention listed most powers of Congress in Article I, Section 8 of the Constitution. It contains 18 different clauses delegating powers to Congress; some contain multiple powers.

Powers of Congress under the Articles

Rather than utilizing separate paragraphs, as under the new Constitution, the authors of Article IX of the Articles of Confederation had typically, albeit not uniformly, designated the individual powers of Congress by using dashes. The section listing the powers of Congress under the Articles lists at least 18 powers. However, the Articles severely restricted the practical exercise of a number of these powers by specifying that Congress could only exercise them by a two-thirds majority. Such powers are designated on the list that follows in italics.

The powers designated for Congress under the Articles included the powers to:

1. *determine matters of peace and war;*
2. send and receive ambassadors;
3. enter into treaties and alliances;
4. decide on the legality of, and division of, naval captures;
5. *grant letters of marque and reprisal in times of peace;*
6. appoint courts dealing with piracies and felonies on the high seas and for providing final appeals in such cases;
7. serve as the last resort for boundary disputes among the states;
8. *regulate the value of alloy and coin struck by Congress or by the states;*
9. fix the standard for weights and measures throughout the nation;
10. regulate trade with, and managing affairs with, Indian tribes;
11. establish post offices and exacting postage;
12. appoint officers of land forces serving the United States;
13. appoint officers of the navy and commissioning officers in U.S. service;
14. make rules for governing land and naval forces (limitations that follow indicate that this power included the right to name a commander-in-chief);
15. appoint "A Committee of the States" and other committees to meet during congressional recesses (a hyphen indicates that this committee may appoint a president);
16. ascertain the money to be raised for the U.S. and appropriate it (this section is set off by a semicolon rather than a hyphen);
17. *borrow money or emit bills on the credit of the U.S.* (this section is also set off by a semicolon);
18. build and equip a navy; and
19. *agree upon the number of land forces and requisition states for such soldiers.*

The Virginia and New Jersey Plans

The Virginia Plan that Edmund Randolph introduced to the Convention on May 29 devoted far less attention than had the Articles of Confedera-tion to listing the specific powers of Congress. In-stead it focused on reorganizing the new govern-ment and simply provided "that the National Leg-islature ought to be impowered to enjoy the Legislative Rights vested in Congress by the Con-federation & moreover to legislate in all cases to which the separate States are incompetent, or in which the harmony of the United States may be interrupted by the exercise of individual Legisla-tion" (Farrand 1937, I, 21). The Plan further pro-vided for Congress to have a negative on state laws and, in a measure that Madison would shortly thereafter repudiate, "call forth the force of the Union agst. any member of the Union failing to fulfill its duty under the articles thereof" (I, 21).

It is not surprising that the broad language of the Virginia Plan raised some red flags. Charles Pinckney and John Rutledge, both of South Car-olina, pointed out that the term "incompetent" was vague and said that they could not vote "until they should see an exact enumeration of the pow-ers comprehended by this definition" (I, 53). Al-though Randolph "disclaimed any intention to give indefinite powers to the national Legisla-ture," Madison was more equivocal:

he had brought with him into the Convention a strong bias in favor of an enumeration and defi-nition of the powers necessary to be exercised by the national Legislature; but had also brought doubts concerning its practicability.

His wishes remained unaltered; but his doubts had become stronger. What his opinion might ultimately be he could not yet tell. But he should shrink from nothing which should be found es-sential to such a form of Govt. as would provide for the safety, liberty and happiness of the Com-munity. (I, 53)

The Convention voted 9-0-1 (Connecticut be-ing divided and the delegates from South Car-olina apparently swallowing their objections) to uphold the general grant of power.

Consistent with the idea of amending, rather than reforming, the existing government, the New Jersey Plan proposed giving Congress a number of new powers. These included authorization to pass acts for raising revenue by levying duties on imports and by issuing stamp taxes; to adopt rules and regulations, subject to future emendation, for collecting these; and to regulate trade and commerce among the states and with foreign nations, with cases arising under such laws to originate within the state judiciaries (I, 243).

The sketchy plan that New York's Alexander Hamilton introduced to the Convention on June 18 followed the form of the Virginia Plan. Consistent with his expansive vision of national powers, Hamilton simply proposed that Congress be invested with a broad grant of power "to pass all laws whatsoever subject to the Negative [made by the chief executive of the nation in combination with state governors] hereafter mentioned" (II, 291).

The Committee of Detail

Although it had been previously raised, the idea of enumerating the specific rights of Congress along the order of the present Constitution appears to have emerged primarily from the five-man Committee of Detail, which John Rutledge of South Carolina chaired. It reported to the Convention on August 6. In listing the powers of Congress, it may have drawn in part from the earlier New Jersey Plan, in part from the Pinckney Plan, and in part from the list of congressional powers listed in the Articles of Confederation.

Much like the current Constitution, the committee proposed 18 specific powers, most, but not all of which, would make their way into the new Constitution. The committee included the power to:

1. lay and collect taxes;
2. regulate interstate and foreign commerce;
3. establish uniform rules of naturalization;
4. coin money;
5. regulate the value of foreign coin;
6. fix standards for weights and measures;
7. establish post offices;
8. borrow money and emit bills;
9. appoint a treasurer by ballot;
10. constitute inferior judicial tribunals;
11. legislate in regard to captures;

12. write laws dealing with and punish piracies and felonies; counterfeiting; and laws violating the laws of nations;
13. subdue rebellions within states;
14. make war;
15. raise armies;
16. build and equip fleets;
17. call out the militia to enforce laws and treaties and suppress insurrections and repel invasions; and
18. make all other necessary and proper laws for carrying out the above. (II, 181–182; the language closely tracks but is not identical to that in the plan).

Congressional Powers under the New Constitution

Below is a list of the powers that the Convention designated to Congress in Article I, Section 8 of the U.S. Constitution. Those powers that are found in this section of the Constitution but were not listed in the Articles of Confederation (and thus constitute new powers) are designated by bold print. The powers are as follows:

1. "to **lay and collect Taxes, Duties, imposts and Excises**, to pay the Debts and provide for the common Defence and general Welfare of the United States";
2. to borrow money;
3. **to regulate commerce with foreign nations, among the several States, and with Indian tribes;**
4. **to establish uniform rules of naturalization and uniform rules on bankruptcies;**
5. to coin money, regulate its value, and fix the standards of weights and measures;
6. **to provide for punishing counterfeiting;**
7. **to establish post offices and post roads;**
8. **to provide for copyrights and patents;**
9. **to constitute courts inferior to the U.S. Supreme Court;**
10. to define and punish piracies;
11. to declare war, grant letters of marque and reprisal; and govern captures;

12. **to raise and support armies;**
13. to establish and maintain a navy;
14. to govern and regulate land and naval forces;
15. to provide for calling forth the militia;
16. to organize, arm, and discipline the militia and govern that portion employed in U.S. service;
17. **to exercise exclusive jurisdiction over the nation's capital**; and
18. **to make all laws necessary and proper for carrying into effect the foregoing.**

Although they are not treated here, congressional powers under the Constitution are further refined by the designation of limits on the states that are included in Article I, Section 10. Thus, to cite a few examples, states may not under the new Constitution (as they could under the Articles) coin money, adopt laws impairing the obligation of contracts, tax imports or exports, or keep troops in time of peace.

The delegates to the Convention did not devote equal attention to each of the proposed powers; indeed some seemed to have been agreed to in an almost pro forma manner. This is especially true of powers that Congress was already exercising under the Articles.

Analysis

The list of powers in the Constitution can be somewhat deceptive. It is important to recognize that, beginning with the Virginia Plan, the Framers of the Constitution decided that rather than simply adding powers to the existing Congress, they would reform the entire governmental structure of government by dividing Congress into two houses and creating two additional branches of government.

The most significant additions to national powers are those providing for direct taxation (under the Articles, national authorities had to requisition the states for revenues); raising and supporting armies (under the Articles, national authorities had to requisition states for troops); regulating interstate and foreign commerce and commerce with the Indian tribes; providing for copyright and patent protections; establishing lower federal courts; establishing and governing a national capital; and making laws necessary and proper for carrying out the foregoing. By implicating the idea of implied powers—later confirmed by the U.S. Supreme Court in the case of *McCulloch v. Maryland*, 17 U.S. (4 Wheat.) 316 (1819)—the latter clause helps explain why the power to issue postage stamps was explicitly guaranteed under the Articles of Confederation but not under the new Constitution.

In contrast to the Articles of Confederation, none of the powers of Congress listed in Article I, Section 8 of the U.S. Constitution initially require two-thirds votes. However, laws implementing such powers must now be adopted by both houses of Congress and be either signed by the president or adopted by two-thirds majority votes over his veto.

Under the new Constitution, a number of powers previously assigned to Congress were now vested in the newly created executive and legislative branches. Thus, the power of sending and receiving ambassadors was entrusted to the president (with the Senate having the power of "advice and consent" in regard to ambassadorial appointments); the power to settle boundary disputes was entrusted to the newly appointed judicial branch; the power to appoint a commander-in-chief was no longer needed since the president was now so designated; the need for "a Committee of States" was negated by the creation of the presidency; and the need to serve as an arbiter of state boundaries was eliminated by the creation of a new system of federal courts.

The enumeration of congressional powers was arguably designed to strengthen the hand of Congress in areas where its powers had been inadequate while still ensuring that Congress would not have the authority to do whatever it chose. Especially since the New Deal (Pilon 2002, 33), congressional exercise of wider and wider powers, usually with judicial approval, suggests that enumeration has ultimately provided weaker restraint on the exercise of such powers than have specific constitutional prohibitions such as those embodied within the Bill of Rights and elsewhere in the document.

As of late, however, the Supreme Court has invalidated some laws on the basis that they exceeded a specifically designated power. In *United States v. Lopez*, 514 U.S. 549 (1995), for example, the Court invalidated provisions of the Gun-Free School Zones Act of 1990 on the basis that the law, designed to criminalize carrying a gun near a school, exceeded federal powers under the Commerce Clause. Similarly, in *United States v. Morrison*, 529 U.S. 598 (2000), the Court struck down a provision of the Violence against Women Act of 1994, which permitted civil suits in cases involving violence against women, again on the basis that this exceeded congressional authority under the commerce clause. It is too early to tell whether this represents a major shift in judicial thinking or simply an adjustment to past decisions.

See Also In addition to entries on individual powers (e.g., Commerce Power), Articles of Confederation; Committee of Detail; Congress, Power of the Purse; Hamilton Plan; Negative on State Laws; New Jersey Plan; Virginia Plan

FOR FURTHER READING

Cohn, Mary W., ed. 1991. *Guide to Congress*. 4th ed. Washington, DC: Congressional Quarterly.

Farrand, Max, ed. 1937. *The Records of the Federal Convention*. 4 vols. New Haven, CT: Yale University Press.

Hueston, John C. 1990. "Note: Altering the Course of the Constitutional Convention: The Role of the Committee of Detail in Establishing the Balance of State and Federal Powers." *Yale Law Journal* 100 (December): 765–783.

Pilon, Roger. 2002. "Madison's Constitutional Vision: The Legacy of Enumerated Powers." In John Samples, ed., *James Madison and the Future of Republican Government*. Washington, DC: Cato Institute, 25–42.

CONGRESS, COMPENSATION OF MEMBERS

Under the Articles of Confederation, states appointed and paid the salaries of their representatives in Congress. By contrast, Article I, Section 6 provides that members shall receive a salary "to be ascertained by Law, and paid out of the Treasury of the United States."

The original Virginia Plan, which Edmund Randolph introduced on May 29, specified that members of both proposed houses of Congress should "receive liberal stipends" (Farrand 1937, I, 20). It did not, however, specify the source of such salaries.

Discussions and Decisions in June

When the Committee of the Whole took up discussion of this provision on June 12, Virginia's James Madison proposed that such compensation also be "fixt," or established (I, 215). He also expressed the view that allowing states to provide salaries would lead to "an improper dependence" while allowing members to set their own wages would in time become "dangerous" (I, 216). He suggested some fixed measure of value—specifically, and perhaps somewhat quixotically, recommending wheat. George Mason, also from Virginia, seconded Madison's motion and agreed on the inappropriateness of allowing for state pay. He feared that states might provide different salaries leading to inequality and that state "parsimony" might end up limiting offices only to those who could afford them. Madison's motion then passed by an 8-3 vote.

After agreeing to "fixed" salaries, Pennsylvania's Benjamin Franklin objected to the word "liberal" and suggested that the term "moderate" might be more appropriate and probably more palatable to the public. Although the Convention did not accept the latter term, it did strike out the former, after which it agreed that the national government would pay such salaries (I, 216).

Later in the day, South Carolinians Pierce Butler and John Rutledge proposed that members of the Senate should serve without a salary. They may have hoped either that this would ensure that this body was more aristocratic, by seeing only that the wealthy could serve, or they may simply have intended that the states would supply such salaries. In any event the motion failed by a 7-3-1 vote (I, 219).

The Convention returned to the question of congressional salaries of members of the House on June 22. Connecticut's Oliver Ellsworth thought that states should provide salaries, reasoning the costs of living and "manners" would vary substantially from one state to another. North Carolina's Hugh Williamson expressed a far more selfish motive, arguing that it would be unfair to the existing states to have to subsidize representatives from future states admitted from the West who might "be employed in thwarting their measures & interests" (I, 372). By contrast, Nathaniel Gorham of Massachusetts thought that states would be likely to cut such salaries unduly. He thought that if salaries were fixed in the Constitution as liberally as they should be that this would excite opposition to the plan. He thought that Congress should have power, like existing state legislatures, to adjust their own salaries and did not expect an abuse of such power. Virginia's Edmund Randolph opposed taking popular prejudices into account on this point. The nation would have "an interest in the attendance & services of the members," and the nation should accordingly pay them (I, 372). Rufus King of Massachusetts agreed on the danger of allowing members of Congress to depend on the states, but he feared that a clause permitting Congress to set salaries would encounter more opposition than actually setting a salary in the Constitution itself.

Debate continued to revolve around old issues. Connecticut's Roger Sherman wanted states to set the pay of members of Congress and to provide it. Pennsylvania's James Wilson wanted members of Congress to be independent and thought it was impractical to set a specific salary. Madison again floated the idea of using wheat as a fixed measure, and responded to Williamson's previous observations by observing that if Westerners entered the Union, they "ought to be considered as equals & as brethren" (II, 373). New York's Hamilton thought it was "inconvenient" to set fixed salaries, and he opposed allowing states to become masters by setting such salaries. Madison thought it was "indecent" to allow members of Congress to set their own salaries—"to put their hands in the public purse for the sake of their own pockets" (I, 374). The Convention voted 7-2-2 against allowing states to pay salaries of House members.

Connecticut's Oliver Ellsworth then moved to strike payment from the national treasury, soon thereafter arguing that "if we are jealous of the State Govts. they will be so of us" (I, 374). Hamilton was characteristically opposed and the motion failed by a vote of 5-4-2. The Convention did agree to substitute a provision for "adequate compensation" in place of "fixt Stipends" (I, 374).

The Convention discussed senatorial salaries on June 26. This time South Carolina's Charles C. Pinckney, seconded by Benjamin Franklin, proposed striking senatorial salaries. Pinckney's intention was to guarantee that the Senate would represent wealth; Franklin was fearful that members of the Convention would be accused of having created lucrative positions for themselves. In any event, the motion narrowly failed by a 6-5 vote (I, 427).

The Convention then retread old ground. Williamson introduced a motion, agreed to by all states other than South Carolina, that eliminated the fixed salary provision. Ellsworth then proposed that states should directly pay the senators who were representing them. Madison feared that this would undermine their independence, leaving senators effectively serving during the pleasure of the state legislatures: "The motion would make the Senate like Congress, the mere Agents & Advocates of State interests & views, instead of being the impartial umpires & Guardians of justice and general Good" (I, 428). New Jersey's Jonathan Dayton also thought such dependence could prove "fatal" to the independence of senators. The Convention narrowly defeated the proposal by a 6-5 vote. After Mason raised the possibility of requiring a property qualification for members, the Convention then voted 6-5 against requiring that senators be paid out of the public treasury.

Discussions and Decision in August

In action that appears to have altered the Convention's previous distinction between the House and the Senate, a provision emerged from the report of the Committee of Detail of August 6 providing that "members of each House shall receive a compensation for their services, to be ascertained and paid by the State, in which they shall be chosen" (II, 180). The Convention reconsidered this issue on August 14. Oliver Ellsworth, who had served on the Committee of Detail, had changed positions. He now argued that state salaries would lead "to too much dependence on the States" (II, 290). Pennsylvania's Gouverneur Morris supported the motion, arguing that "there could be no reason to fear that they [members of Congress] would overpay themselves" (II, 290). South Carolina's Pierce Butler thought that state payment would be necessary to keep senators, who would be absent from their states for long periods, cognizant of their dependence on them. New Hampshire's John Langdon thought that it would be unfair to require the distant states to pay the greater expenses that would be necessitated by longer travel, while Madison feared undue dependence on states would lead to instability and, with his continuing concern about potential self-dealing, proposed establishing a range to guide Congress in setting salaries. After Delaware's David Broom expressed confidence that Congress, like state legislatures, would not give themselves overinflated salaries, Sherman expressed fears that they might set the salaries too low and proposed that salaries be set at $5 a day. In a colorful metaphor, Maryland's Daniel Carroll argued that a Congress in which members of both houses depended on the states for their support would be "nothing more than a second edition of Congress in two volumes, instead of one, and perhaps with very few amendments" (II, 292). Also concerned about "the necessity of making the Genl. Govt. independent of the prejudices, passions, and improper views of the State Legislatures" (II, 292), Delaware's John Dickinson proposed a plan whereby members of Congress would set their salaries every twelfth year. Ellsworth wanted to set a salary and add a provision specifying "or the present value thereof" (II, 292). Only Luther Martin was left to argue that the states should pay members of Congress, and he appeared to be arguing only for the Senate. The Convention thus voted 9-2 (with Massachusetts and South Carolina in dissent) to provide for payment out of the national treasury.

Ellsworth proposed to set the pay at $5 per day and per 30 miles of travel, a motion rejected by a vote of 9-2. Dickinson wanted to require that the pay of members of both houses be the same. Delaware's Jacob Broom seconded the motion, but Dickinson withdrew it after Gorham observed that members of the Senate might be obliged to meet longer, especially in times of war, and that states typically provided higher salaries for members of the upper house. The Convention then affirmed the provision specifying that Congress would set its own salaries.

Analysis

A review shows that debates over congressional salaries focused on a number of points. The main arguments were between those who wanted states to provide salaries and those who wanted Congress to set them. The first option appeared to open the possibility of inequality and of undue dependence of members of Congress on the states; the second opened the possibility of self-dealing. Members of Congress were unable to set a specific salary, or measure of value, that would have due permanence so they wisely left such specifications out of the Constitution. They left this power to specify salaries in the hands of Congress itself, subject to governmental checks and balances (the presidential veto) and electoral oversight. They further allowed, but did not require, differences between the salaries of those in the House and the Senate.

Postscript

The provision related to salaries provoked some criticism in the state ratifying conventions, especially on the part of those who feared that members of Congress were likely to establish an aristocracy. Madison subsequently proposed an amendment in the first Congress whereby its members should not be able to enact pay raises without an intervening election. This was one of two proposals that the states did not initially ratify when they adopted the Bill of Rights.

From time to time, however, critics accused Congress of "salary grabs," and over time, public sentiment mounted over the perception that members of Congress were feathering their own nests. States continued to ratify the original amendment, and after a push by Gregory Watson, an aide to a Texas legislator, in 1992 and a surge of new approvals in reaction to a congressional check-kiting scandal, Congress and the head of the National Archives both agreed that the requisite number of states had now ratified the amendment, which became the Twenty-seventh (Vile 2003, 478). Often dubbed "the Madison Amendment," this remains a constitutional anomaly, the only amendment ever to have been ratified over so long a time period and a timely testament to continuing concern over possible congressional self-dealing. Questions remain as to how effective the Twenty-seventh Amendment has been in addressing such concerns.

See Also Articles of Confederation; Judicial Organization and Protections; President, Compensation; Virginia Plan

FOR FURTHER READING

Bernstein, Richard B. 1991. "The Sleeper Wakes: The History and Legacy of the Twenty-seventh Amendments." *Fordham Law Review* 56 (December): 497–557.
Farrand, Max, ed. 1937. *The Records of the Federal Convention.* 4 vols. New Haven, CT: Yale University Press.
Levinson, Sanford. 1994. "Authorizing Constitutional Text: On the Purported Twenty-seventh Amendment." *Constitutional Commentary* 22 (Winter): 101–113.
Vile, John R. 2003. *Encyclopedia of Constitutional Amendments, Proposed Amendments, and Amending Issues, 1789–2002.* 2nd ed. Santa Barbara, CA: ABC-CLIO.

CONGRESS, CONTINTENTAL

See CONTINENTAL CONGRESSES

CONGRESS, CONTINUATION OF UNDER ARTICLES

Resolution 12 of the Virginia Plan, which Edmund Randolph introduced on May 29, provided that "provision ought to be made for the continuance of Congress and their authorities and privileges, until a given day after the reform of the articles of Union shall be adopted, and for the completion of all their engagements" (Farrand 1937, I, 22). Resolution 15 of the Committee of the Whole House, compiled about June 13, was almost identical (I, 231). The New Jersey Plan, which essentially proposed to strengthen the existing Congress, had no similar provision (see I, 242–245).

Three delegates discussed the provision that had first appeared in the Virginia Plan on July 18. Gouverneur Morris of Pennsylvania began. He was recorded as thinking that "the assumption of their engagements might as well be omitted; and that Congs. ought not to be continued till all the States should adopt the reform; since it may become expedient to give effect to it whenever a certain number of States shall adopt it" (II, 46–47). Virginia's James Madison attempted to clarify the provision by observing that it "can mean nothing more than that provision ought to be made for preventing an interregnum [a gap in government]; which must exist in the interval between the adoption of the New Govt. and the commencement of its operation, if the old Govt. should cease on the first of these events" (II, 47). Pennsylvania's James Wilson then observed that, although he had some concern about the way the clause was phrased, "he thought some provision on the subject would be proper in order to prevent any suspicion that the obligations of the Confederacy might be dissolved along with the Governt. under which they were contracted" (II, 47).

Notes indicate that the Convention then voted 6-3 against the provisions related to the continuation of Congress and without dissent against the provision related to the completion of congressional engagements. However, the Convention later voted to leave debts under the Articles of Confederation in the same position where they were under that arrangement.

The Convention's failure to adopt the transition provision leaves contemporary scholars to debate the precise point at which the authority of the Articles of Confederation ended and that of the new Constitution began. Kesavan has suggested that there may actually have been an interregnum between the two such as Madison expressed the hope of avoiding (see Kesavan 2002; Lawson and Seidman 2001; Lawson and Seidman 2002).

See Also Debts; Virginia Plan

FOR FURTHER READING

Farrand, Max, ed. 1937. *The Records of the Federal Convention.* 4 vols. New Haven, CT: Yale University Press.

Johnson, Calvin H. 2003–2004. "Homage to Clio: The Historical Continuity from the Articles of Confederation into the Constitution." *Constitutional Commentary* 20 (Winter): 463–513.

Kesavan, Vasan. 2002. "When Did the Articles of Confederation Cease to Be Law?" *Notre Dame Law Review* 78 (December): 35–82.

Lawson, Gary, and Guy Seidman. 2002. "The First 'Establishment' Clause: Article VII and the Post-Constitutional Confederation." *Notre Dame Law Review* 78 (December): 83–100.

———. 2001. "When Did the Constitution Become Law?" *Notre Dame Law Review* 77 (November): 1–37.

Madison observed that the right of expulsion was "too important to be exercised by a bare majority of a quorum: and in emergencies of faction might be dangerously abused" (Farrand 1937, II, 254). Madison proposed, and fellow Virginian Edmund Randolph seconded, a proposal raising the required majority to two-thirds in such cases. Gouverneur Morris of Pennsylvania thought that a majority could be trusted with the power of expulsion and, attempting to meet Madison on his own ground, observed: "A few men from factious motives may keep in a member who ought to be expelled" (II, 254). Maryland's Daniel Carroll weighed in on the side of the desirability of a two-thirds majority, and the motion carried by a 10-0 vote, with the state of Pennsylvania, from which Morris was serving as a delegate, divided. The Supreme Court relied on this provision in *Powell v. McCormack,* 395 U.S. 486 (1969), in invalidating the attempt by the U.S. House of Representatives to expel Representative Adam Clayton Powell.

See Also Committee of Detail

FOR FURTHER READING

Cohn, Mary. 1991. "Seating and Disciplining Members." *Guide to Congress.* 4th ed. Washington, DC: Congressional Quarterly, 759–784.

Farrand, Max, ed. 1937. *The Records of the Federal Convention.* 4 vols. New Haven, CT: Yale University Press.

CONGRESS, EXPULSION OF MEMBERS

Article I, Section 5, provides that each house may punish members for disorderly behavior and expel them by a two-thirds vote. This provision originated in the Committee of Detail, which had not initially specified a supermajority. When the Convention discussed this provision on August 10,

CONGRESS, HOUSE OF REPRESENTATIVES, QUALIFICATIONS OF MEMBERS

Article I, Section 2, Clause 2, outlines the qualifications for members of the U.S. House of Representatives. They are based on age, citizenship, and residency.

Age

The Virginia Plan, which Edmund Randolph introduced on May 29, had proposed that members of the House of Representatives be of a minimum, but unspecified, age, but the Constitution dropped this requirement on June 12. On June 22, Virginia's George Mason introduced a provision to require that members of the House of Representatives be at least 25 years of age. He reasoned that it was "absurd that a man to day should not be permitted by the law to make a bargain for himself, and tomorrow should be authorized to manage the affairs of a great nation" (Farrand 1937, I, 375). Reflecting on the immaturity of his own views at the age of 21—then the standard age for voting—Mason observed that Congress was not an appropriate place to provide schooling for such neophytes. By contrast, Pennsylvania's James Wilson opposed any such restriction, arguing that it would "damp the efforts of genius, and of laudable ambition" (I, 375). He observed that William Pitt and Lord Bolingbroke had both served Britain with distinction before they reached the age of 25. Despite these arguments, the Convention accepted the age restriction by a vote of 7-3-1.

Property-Related Qualifications

Mason moved to add another set of qualifications for congressional membership on July 26 and was seconded by South Carolina's Charles Pinckney. Specifically, Mason advocated requiring an unspecified amount of "landed property," of "citizenship," and a disqualification of individuals with "unsettled" accounts or who were indebted to the U.S. (II, 121). With a view to the situation of the states, Mason observed that debtors frequently sought election in order to "shelter their delinquencies" and that this same phenomenon appeared to be taking place in Congress (121). Gouverneur Morris of Pennsylvania observed that it would be better to raise the qualifications of the electors than of those whom they could select. He thought that the number of debtors in the United States was relatively small, but that those with un-

settled accounts were many. He observed that the latter group included patriots who had lent money to the government, and he asked whether they also were to be excluded from Congress.

Nathaniel Gorham of Massachusetts wanted to entrust Congress with the power to provide against abuses, although the records do not indicate how he intended for it to do so. Madison confirmed Mason's observations about self-interested legislators but wanted to alter Mason's suggestion so as to limit exclusions to individuals who had not accounted for money they had received from the public. Gouverneur Morris observed that Mason's proposal would allow the government to exclude worthy men from office and observed that a similar requirement had been used in Great Britain to favor the "landed" over "monied" interest (II, 122), an observation confirmed by Rufus King of Massachusetts. By contrast, Elbridge Gerry, also from Massachusetts, thought that Mason's proposals "did not go far enough" (123). Delaware's John Dickinson opposed "any recital of qualification in the Constitution," but he did so on the apparent basis that he believed that Congress should be able to set such qualifications on its own. Observing that republicanism had been associated with "a veneration for poverty & virtue," Dickinson opposed excluding any such men of merit (123). Gerry thought that since property was a key object of Government, it was appropriate to seek its protection through such qualifications. At this point, Madison moved, and Gouverneur Morris seconded a motion striking the word "landed" from Mason's proposal. Madison pointed out that the new republic would embrace a variety of interests including "the commercial" and "the manufacturing," and that a uniform property qualification would be difficult to formulate (124). Madison's motion carried by a vote of 10-1, and Mason's motion, as amended, by a vote of 8-3.

This latter victory proved relatively short-lived. Maryland's Daniel Carroll, seconded by Nathaniel Gorham, immediately moved to strike the provision excluding those with unsettled accounts from holding office. Gorham feared the effect of such a clause on "the commercial & manufacturing part of the people," but Luther Martin observed that this restriction and the one on debtors went together. Pennsylvania's James Wilson feared entrusting the auditors with the power to make such determinations while New Hampshire's John Langdon wanted to strike the entire clause, believing that the people would oppose it. Elbridge Gerry disagreed, fearing that, without such qualifications, "we might have a Legislature composed of public debtors, pensioners, placemen & contractors," but failed in his attempt to add pensioners to the list of the disqualified (125). After Gouverneur Morris renewed arguments about the effect of Mason's proposal on importers, the Convention voted 9-2 to strike the disqualification of those having unsettled accounts.

Discussion of property qualifications for members of Congress resumed on August 10, when the Convention discussed a provision emerging from the Committee of Detail allowing Congress to set property qualifications for its members. Charles Pinckney favored setting such a qualification within the Constitution itself, but Oliver Ellsworth thought that it would be impossible to set a uniform qualification throughout the country, and Franklin argued that such a qualification "tended to debase the spirit of the common people" (II, 249). After the Convention rejected Pinckney's proposal, it went on to strike out the provision allowing Congress to set any such property qualifications, a decision that also applied to the U.S. Senate.

Residency and Inhabitancy Requirements

On August 8 the Convention returned to the requirements of citizenship and residency for House members, considering a proposal by the Committee of Detail for a three-year citizenship requirement and for state residency. Although professing his desire to open a "wide door for emigrants," George Mason did not think that this length of time was sufficient either to guarantee "that local knowledge which ought to be possessed by the Representative" or to prevent foreign governments from sending over individuals "who might bribe their way into the Legislature

for insidious purposes" (II, 216). He proposed a seven-year citizenship requirement, which Gouverneur Morris seconded and which the Convention overwhelmingly adopted.

Roger Sherman then moved to substitute the term "inhabitant" for "resident," and Madison seconded him. Madison observed that the vaguer determination of inhabitancy had sometimes been used in Virginia to exclude individuals who had been out of the state on public business. Wilson favored the term "inhabitant," and Gouverneur Morris disfavored both requirements and observed that the people would "rarely chuse a nonresident" (217). South Carolina's John Rutledge wanted not only to specify seven years of residency but also to indicate that it should be within the state from which the representative was selected. George Read of Delaware and James Wilson both thought this was inconsistent with the desire for a national government, and Madison wondered what it might do in the case of new Western states. Maryland's John Mercer further thought that state residency requirements "would interweave local prejudices & State distinctions in the very Constitution which is meant to cure them" (217). After continuing discussion, Mason acknowledged that he now thought seven years was too long a time but still favored some residency requirement as a means of preventing rich men from nearby states from getting into the governments of neighbors. After a failed vote to postpone, the Convention unanimously adopted the term "inhabitant" in place of "resident." It then voted down requirements for three-year or one-year inhabitancy, requiring only that those elected be inhabitants at the time of their election.

Citizenship Requirements

On August 13, James Wilson and Edmund Randolph moved to strike the requirement for seven years of citizenship for House members and to replace it with a four-year requirement. Elbridge Gerry wanted to limit eligibility to "Natives"; his primary concern was that foreign powers would otherwise attempt to secrete their partisans into U.S. affairs. North Carolina's Hugh Williamson favored a nine-year citizenship requirement. His fear had a republican ring to it; he feared that "wealthy emigrants do more harm by their luxurious examples, than good, by the money, they bring with them" (268). New York's Alexander Hamilton, himself an immigrant who would become known as the first secretary of the Treasury for focusing on the bottom line, thought "the advantage of encouraging foreigners was obvious & admitted. Persons in Europe of moderate fortunes will be fond of coming here where they will be on a level with the first Citizens" (268). Moving for a simple requirement for citizenship and inhabitancy, he further observed that Congress could take care of any problems in providing for naturalization. Madison seconded Hamilton's motion and argued for a policy of "liberality." Pointing out that the U.S. "was indebted to emigration for her settlement & Prosperity" (268), Madison thought that there was little danger that many foreign governments would be able to get their agents elected to public office. James Wilson, an immigrant from Scotland, cited the growing population and prosperity of Pennsylvania as proof of the value of encouraging immigration, and observed that three other delegates from the state to the Convention were also immigrants. With no apparent sense of embarrassment, Pierce Butler, who had immigrated to South Carolina from Ireland, argued against "admitting foreigners into our public Councils" (269).

A series of votes followed. Hamilton's motion to delete a specified number of years was rejected by a vote of 7-4. Williamson's motion for a nine-year requirement failed 8-3. A renewed motion for a four-year requirement offered by Wilson was rejected by the same vote, thus leaving the seven-year requirement in place.

Retroactivity of Requirements

Gouverneur Morris moved that this requirement should not be applied to individuals who were already citizens, and Mercer seconded him. He argued that retroactive application of the provision would betray the nation's good faith to those who had been admitted into citizenship prior to such

requirements. Rutledge thought that the seven-year requirement could not be distinguished from the 25-year age requirement. Sherman observed that any promises that had been made had been offered by individual states. After Gorham suggested that naturalized citizens should "stand on an equal footing with natives" (270), Madison lambasted Sherman's reasoning as a potential excuse to allow the government to escape from a number of its obligations. Morris attempted to distinguish the requirements for a minimum age from those of a minimum time of citizenship. Charles Pinckney thought that existing state laws were too varied to bind the United States, and Mason attempted to defend Sherman's argument against Madison's broadside. Wilson responded by attempting to combine the provision in the Pennsylvania Constitution for citizenship with the privileges and immunities clause of the Articles of Confederation, and observed that foreign rulers would point to retroactive application of the citizenship provision as an example of American bad faith by which to discourage emigration. Mercer concurred with Wilson, and Baldwin repeated earlier arguments that a disqualification on citizenship was no different than the one adopted for age.

Morris's motion limiting retroactive application of the citizenship requirement subsequently failed in a narrow 5-6 vote. Carroll's motion for a five-year citizenship requirement failed 7-3-1, and the amended provision was thus unanimously accepted.

Summary

The provisions for House qualifications need to be considered in conjunction with the decision to allow states to set qualifications for voters rather than setting a single uniform national standard, which might have included provisions for a freehold. Compared to what they might have been, the formal requirements for members of the House are relatively minimal, leaving the voters with relatively broad choices as to who would represent them. Slightly longer citizenship requirements were established for senators and for the

Residency Requirements for Members of Congress, Learning from Experience

Rarely do scholars question the requirement that members of the House and Senate shall be inhabitants of the states that they represent, but in 1744, England, which would espouse the doctrine of "virtual representation" in the later dispute with the American colonies (who generally supported the idea that the only representation that counted was "actual representation" by real representatives from the areas being governed), had repealed such a requirement for members of the House of Commons, the lower and most popular branch of the Parliament (Munroe 1952, 167). Similarly, the government under the Articles of Confederation that preceded the existing Constitution had not required such residence requirements. Apparently attempting to remedy the unwillingness of some talented individuals to serve in this body and the poor attendance record of many that it had chosen, the state of Delaware elected four Philadelphians to the Congress in 1782.

Two of the four, Philemon Dickinson and Thomas McKean, had at one time resided in Delaware, but Samuel Wharton not only had never lived in Delaware but apparently did not own property there either (Munroe, 172). Moreover, although he represented Delaware at the Constitutional Convention of 1787, John Dickinson had held offices in both Delaware and Pennsylvania, and was at one point forced to resign his post as president of Delaware because he had accepted similar responsibilities in the neighboring state. When he was selected as Pennsylvania president, *The Freeman's Journal* in Pennsylvania, widely circulated in Delaware, compared the situation in Delaware to that of rotten boroughs (areas in England with almost no population that retained the right to elect representatives to Parliament) and said that Dickinson had brought "contempt and ridicule" on the state by making it "a mere stepping-stone . . . to the presidential chair of Pennsylvania" (quoted in Munroe, 183). Others questioned the propriety of a state allowing itself to be represented by "foreigners" (Munroe, 187).

Delaware appears to have been the only state to resort to the expedient of representation by out-of-state residents. By the time of the Convention (where both John Dickinson and Thomas McKean served as delegates, the first from Delaware and the second from Pennsylvania), Delaware had repudiated the practice, which was especially awkward in a legislative system where members of Congress were understood to represent both state and national interests.

FOR FURTHER READING

Munroe, John A. 1952. "Nonresident Representation in the Continental Congress: The Delaware Delegation of 1782." *William and Mary Quarterly*, 3rd ser. 9 (April): 166–190.

presidency. The latter office is the only constitutionally created office that is limited to native-born Americans, although with a view to the retroactivity issue, those who were citizens at the time of the writing of the Constitution were grandfathered in.

In *Powell v. McCormack*, 395 U.S. 486 (1969) and *U.S. Term Limits v. Thornton*, 514 U.S. 779 (1995), the U.S. Supreme Court decided that neither Congress nor the states had power to add to the constitutionally specified requirements for members of Congress.

See Also Congress, House of Representatives, Qualifications of Voters for; Congress, Senate, Qualifications; President, Qualifications; Religious Tests, Prohibition

FOR FURTHER READING

Cohn, Mary, ed. 1991. "Constitutional Beginnings." *Guide to Congress.* 4th ed. Washington, DC: Congressional Quarterly, 3–35.
Farrand, Max, ed. 1937. *The Records of the Federal Convention.* 4 vols. New Haven, CT: Yale University Press.

Munroe, John A. 1952. "Nonresident Representation in the Continental Congress: The Delaware Delegation of 1782." *William and Mary Quarterly,* 3rd ser. 9 (April): 166–190.

CONGRESS, HOUSE OF REPRESENTATIVES, QUALIFICATIONS OF VOTERS FOR

Article I, Section 2, Clause 1, establishes that the qualifications of voters for the U.S. House of Representatives shall be the same as those "qualifications requisite for Electors of the most numerous Branch of the State Legislature." This provision is similar to that included on August 6 in a report of the Committee of Detail to the Convention, which recommended that the electors of the House of Representatives should be the same, "as those of the electors in the several States, of the most numerous branch of their own legislatures" (Farrand 1937, I, 178). This provision thus avoided setting a single uniform national standard for such voters.

The next day, Gouverneur Morris, seconded by fellow Pennsylvania delegate Thomas Fitzsimmons, proposed replacing this provision with one limiting the right to vote to "freeholders," that is, to those with a certain amount of property. North Carolina's Hugh Williamson is recorded as opposing it. Pennsylvania's James Wilson observed that the Committee of Detail had found it difficult to arrive at a common standard and that it would be difficult to exclude individuals who voted for state legislators from congressional elections. Gouverneur Morris thought it would be little different than variations in requirements for governors and representatives or for different houses of the state legislatures; in any event, he did not think it was appropriate to leave the matter of qualifications to the states. By contrast, Connecticut's Oliver Ellsworth argued that "the right of suffrage was a tender point," that the people were not likely to agree to a system that would restrict their power

over the subject, and that "the States are the best Judges of the circumstances and temper of their own people" (II, 201). Virginia's George Mason observed that "eight or nine" states had already extended voting rights to those without a freehold, and observed that "a power to alter the qualifications would be a dangerous power in the hands of the Legislature" (202). South Carolina's Pierce Butler agreed and cited popular support of extensive suffrage. By contrast, Delaware's John Dickinson thought that freeholders were "the best guardians of liberty," and that restricting the vote to them was "a necessary defence agst. the dangerous influence of those multitudes without property & without principle, with which our Country like all others, will in time abound" (202). Most citizens were freeholders and would support a restriction to their own ranks. Ellsworth observed that the term "freeholder" would be difficult to define, and could end up excluding merchants and manufacturers.

Gouverneur Morris's arguments show that eighteenth-century thought could be complex. Instead of viewing limited suffrage as a way of promoting aristocracy, Morris argued that the reverse was true. At a time before the Australian secret ballot was invented, he reasoned that "mechanics & manufacturers" (who he and other delegates clearly anticipated would increase in the future) would sell their votes to those who employed them (202). There was little difference between restricting the vote of those who could not support themselves and in limiting it to children. Moreover, reflecting the prominence of the middle class in the United States, Morris calculated that restricting the vote to freeholders would affect less than one-tenth of the people and that merchants had enough wealth to buy property if they wanted to vote.

Mason responded with a fascinating argument of his own. He observed that although the freehold had been the qualification in Great Britain, it was hardly the only evidence that an individual had a stake in society. He questioned why "the merchant, the monied man, the parent of a number of children whose fortunes are to be pursued in their own [country]" should "be viewed as suspicious characters, and unworthy to be trusted with the common rights of their fellow Citizens" (203). Madison observed that aristocracies had been built upon erosions of the right of suffrage. Viewed simply on its merits, "the freeholders of the Country would be the safest depositories of Republican liberty" (203), but Madison expressed concern about how the states with wider suffrage would receive such a proposal.

Pennsylvania's Benjamin Franklin next entered the discussion with an appeal not to "depress the virtue & public spirit of our common people" many of whom had particularly distinguished themselves during the Revolutionary War (204). He also observed that the sons of freeholders, who did not yet have property of their own, would not look kindly upon such a restriction. Maryland's John Mercer objected to the whole idea of founding Congress in popular elections; he did not believe that they could "know & judge the characters of Candidates" (205). By contrast John Rutledge of South Carolina feared that voting restrictions would make enemies of those who were thus disenfranchised. Morris's motion was subsequently defeated by a vote of 7-1-1 and delegates engaged in no further debates on the subject.

The Convention thus left the determination of voting qualifications to the individual states, sacrificing uniformity to concerns about alienating nonfreeholders who already had the vote and leaving the foundation of the House on a broad base. Historically, the general trend in the United States has been for widening the suffrage often through constitutional amendments, as happened when states were respectively forbidden to discriminate in regard to voting against African American men (the Fifteenth Amendment), women (the Nineteenth Amendment), and eighteen-year-olds (the Twenty-sixth Amendment). Similarly, the Twenty-third Amendment provided votes in the Electoral College for residents of the District of Columbia, and the Twenty-fourth Amendment eliminated the poll tax, which a number of states, especially in the South, had used chiefly to restrict the voting rights of African Americans (see Grimes 1978).

See Also Committee of Detail; Suffrage

FOR FURTHER READING

Farrand, Max, ed. 1937. *The Records of the Federal Convention*. 4 vols. New Haven, CT: Yale University Press.

Grimes, Alan P. 1978. *Democracy and the Amendments to the Constitution*. Lexington, MA: Lexington Books.

CONGRESS, HOUSE OF REPRESENTATIVES, REPRESENTATION IN

The Virginia Plan proposed replacing the Congress under the Articles of Confederation, in which each state was represented equally, with a bicameral Congress in which "the rights of suffrage" would "be proportioned to the Quotas of contribution, or to the number of free inhabitants" (Farrand 1937, I, 20). The Convention spent considerable time considering how, if at all, slaves should be counted, but it spent far more time discussing representation in the Senate than it did in the House.

There was some generic discussion of representation in Congress on June 9, on a motion by William Paterson, seconded by David Brearly, who was also from New Jersey, to reconsider "the rule of suffrage in the Natl. Legislature" (I, 176). Brearly pointed to the settlement for equal representation that had been reached under the Articles of Confederation. Although proportional representation "carried fairness on the face of it," it was in fact "unfair and unjust" (I, 177). By Brearly's calculations, there were three large states (Virginia, Pennsylvania, and Massachusetts) and 10 small ones. The largest would have 16 votes to one vote by the smallest. Just as large counties overwhelmed smaller ones when they were combined in the same districts, so too, the large states would be likely to overwhelm the smaller ones. Brearly suggested a radical proposal. He proposed spreading out a U.S. map, erasing all boundaries and dividing it into "13 equal parts," with equality presumably referring to the number of inhabitants rather than to geographical sizes (I, 177).

Paterson joined in the argument that proportional representation struck "at the existence of the lesser States" (I, 177). He charged that the Convention was exceeding its commission in considering the Virginia Plan, but, like Brearly, suggested that "If we are to be considered as a nation [rather than as a confederation], the whole must be thrown into hotchpot, and when an equal division is made, then there may be fairly an equality of representation" (I, 178). Alluding to a comment by Pennsylvania's James Wilson, Paterson said that the larger states could not compel the smaller ones to join them. His emotion appeared to rise as his speech proceeded: "He had rather submit to a monarch, to a despot, than to such a fate. He would not only oppose the plan here but on his return home do everything in his power to defeat it" (I, 179).

Wilson proceeded to defend the justice of proportional representation by asking two rhetorical questions: "Are not the citizens of Pena. equal to those of N. Jersey? does it require 150 of the former to balance 50 of the latter?" (I, 180). North Carolina's Hugh Williamson joined in observing that as counties were proportionally represented within the states, so states should be so represented in national councils.

When the Convention resumed its meeting on Monday, June 11, Connecticut's Roger Sherman proposed the compromise that would make him famous by suggesting that the delegates should apportion the first branch according to population and provide for equal state representation in the second. However, it took the delegates more than a month of wrangling to agree to this formula. Most of the debate centered specifically on the Senate, but debates on June 27 and 28 focused specifically on the House. On the first day, Maryland's Luther Martin, who was known for his passion, delivered a three-hour speech, continued on the next day, in which he argued that states bore the same relationship to one another as did individuals in the state of nature and that smaller states needed security against the larger ones (I, 437–438). On June 28, John Lansing of New York and Jonathan Dayton of New Jersey

moved that states would be represented in the House as under the Articles of Confederation. Madison argued that equality was neither "just, nor necessary for the safety of the small States agst. the large States" (I, 446). He observed that the large states differed in "manners, Religion and the other circumstances, which sometimes beget affection between different communities" (I, 447). Their crops were different, and experience in other parts of the world showed that large states were more likely to be rivals than to be friends. Wilson further observed that giving states an equal voice would be to concur in a system like the justly lamented system of rotten boroughs in England. Sherman responded that the Convention was not dealing with natural rights but with the rights of men in society.

On June 28 Benjamin Franklin suggested that each day of the Convention should be opened with prayer. His description of the Convention as "groping as it were in the dark to find political truth" was undoubtedly influenced by the rising temper that Franklin sensed in the debate (I, 451). The Convention passed over Franklin's suggestion without taking a vote and resumed discussion of representation in the House on the next day.

Connecticut's Johnson concluded that "the controversy must be endless whilst Gentlemen differ in the grounds of their arguments" (I, 461). Gorham urged the small states to consider their positions with a view toward whether they could survive without union with the larger states. Read thought that the best solution was one like New York's Alexander Hamilton had proposed for abolishing the states. Madison urged the small states to "renounce a princle wch. was confessedly unjust, which cd. never be admitted, & if admitted must infuse mortality into a Constitution which we wished to last forever" (I, 464). Hamilton said that the issue involved "a contest for power, not for liberty" (I, 466). Georgia's William Pierce called for states to consider the union as a whole. Gerry likewise observed that "instead of coming here like a band of brothers, belonging to the same family, we seemed to have brought with us the spirit of political negociators" (I, 467). Martin lamented departure from the idea of states as sovereign and independent entities. The Convention subsequently voted 6-4-1 to reject equal representation in the House and went on to discussion of representation in the Senate. This issue was debated as strenuously as representation in the House and was not resolved until July 16, at which time the Convention voted both for proportional representation in the House (with slaves counted as three-fifths of a person) and for equal representation in the Senate.

See Also Congress, House of Representatives, Size; Congress, Senate, Representation in; Connecticut Compromise

FOR FURTHER READING

Farrand, Max, ed. 1937. *The Records of the Federal Convention.* 4 vols. New Haven, CT: Yale University Press.

Natelson, Robert G. 2002/2003. "A Reminder: The Constitutional Values of Sympathy of Independence." *Kentucky Law Journal* 91: 353–423.

Rakove, Jack N. 1987. "The Great Compromise: Ideas, Interests, and the Politics of Constitution Making." *William and Mary Quarterly,* 3rd ser. 44 (July): 427–457.

Zagarri, Rosemarie. 1987. *The Politics of Size: Representation in the United States, 1776–1850.* Ithaca, NY: Cornell University Press.

CONGRESS, HOUSE OF REPRESENTATIVES, SELECTION OF

Under the Articles of Confederation, members of Congress were selected by, and accountable to, state legislatures. The Virginia Plan proposed to change this by making the first branch of the legislature subject to popular election. This was intended to place Congress on a more popular base, but, in increasing democratic accountability, it also seemed likely to erode existing state powers.

The Convention first discussed selection of members of the House on May 31 as it contemplated the Virginia Plan. Connecticut's Roger Sherman opposed popular election, arguing that the people were too likely to be misled. Elbridge Gerry of Massachusetts agreed that "the evils we experience flow from the excess of democracy" (Farrand 1937, I, 48). By contrast, Virginia's George Mason viewed the first branch of the Congress as the American equivalent of the House of Commons, "the grand depository of the democratic principle of the Govt." (I, 48). As such, it should reflect the composition of the community that it represented. Similarly, Pennsylvania's James Wilson said that he favored "raising the federal pyramid to a considerable altitude and for that reason wished to give it as broad a basis as possible" (I, 49). Virginia's James Madison likewise considered popular election "as essential to every plan of free Government" (I, 49). He wanted to maintain the "necessary sympathy" between the people and their representatives and thought the idea of "successive filtrations" could be carried too far (I, 50). Gerry then appeared somewhat to modify his earlier position, saying that he did not object to popular election as long as "it were so qualified that men of honor & character might not be unwilling to be joined in the appointment" (I, 50). By contrast, South Carolina's Pierce Butler thought the mechanism would be impractical.

Delegates resumed discussion of the topic on June 6 when Charles Pinckney proposed that the first branch be chosen by state legislatures rather than by the people and was seconded by fellow South Carolinian John Rutledge. Again, Gerry seemed inclined to a compromise, suggesting that the state legislatures might make appointments from among nominees made by the people. By contrast, Wilson advanced the view that popular election would give "vigor" to the government. He argued that "the Legislature ought to be the most exact transcript of the whole Society" (I, 133). In his view, which appears to have been in significant tension with opinions expressed elsewhere in the Convention by other delegates including James Madison, representation was not a good in itself but was simply necessitated by the impossibility of the people "to act collectively" (133). He did suggest that elections would be better when carried out in large districts, where "bad men" would be less likely to succeed at intrigue (133). Sherman connected the idea of popular election to the abolition of state governments. Mason seemed at least partially to agree, noting that the Virginia Plan called for representing the people directly rather than the states as states. Like Wilson, Mason suggested that representatives "should sympathize with their constituents; shd. think as they think, & feel as they feel; and for that for these purposes shd. even be residents among them" (134). Like Wilson, he also favored elections from large districts. Madison thought that direct election of at least one branch of government was "a clear principle of free Govt." that would provide "more effectually for the security of private rights, and the steady dispensation of Justice" (134). He went on to justify his view with the theory of factions that he made so prominent in *Federalist* No. 10. Delaware's John Dickinson favored a system, like that proposed in the Virginia Plan, whereby members of one branch would be "drawn immediately from the people," with the other being chosen by state legislatures (136); Georgia's William Pierce shortly thereafter affirmed this idea. Delaware's George Read favored eliminating the states. By contrast, General Charles Cotesworth Pinckney thought that popular election was impractical and thought that states would resist giving up their appointment power. At the end of the discussion, Charles Pinckney's proposal for selection of the House by state legislatures was rejected by a vote of 8-3.

Pinckney was not yet willing to concede defeat. On June 21 he introduced a motion, seconded by Luther Martin of Massachusetts, that would allow for selection of members of the first branch "in such manner as the Legislature of each State should direct" (I, 358). New York's Alexander Hamilton expressed the fear that this mechanism would unwisely increase state powers, and Mason continued to argue that "the democratic principle" "must actuate one part of the Govt." in order to provide "security for the rights of the people" (I, 359). Sherman continued to favor state legislative selection but was willing to stick with the plan agreed upon. John Rutledge of South Carolina agreed with Pinckney in thinking that state legislatures were likely to make wiser choices than were

the people, and Wilson continued to insist that direct popular election was "not only the corner Stone, but . . . the foundation of the fabric" (359). Rufus King of Massachusetts added that state legislatures would attempt to select men subservient to their own views as contrasted to the general interest" (359). Pinckney's motion failed 6-4-1 and discussion was not resumed on this topic.

The decision for popular election of the House arguably ensured that it would be considered the part of government closest to the people. Such election also clearly undercut existing state legislative prerogatives. The debate over representation revealed tension between supporters of direct elections, who thought that such elections would more directly mirror the population, and those who hoped that such elections would filter out more partisan and selfish elements within the electors.

Although the Constitution provided that members of the House would be apportioned according to population, it provided that state legislatures would each choose two senators. The Seventeenth Amendment, ratified in 1913, provided that this mechanism would be replaced by popular elections, equalizing the way that both houses were selected.

See Also Congress, Senate, Selection

FOR FURTHER READING

Eidelberg, Paul. 1968. *The Philosophy of the American Constitution: A Reinterpretation of the Intentions of the Founding Fathers.* New York: The Free Press, 52–57.
Farrand, Max, ed. 1937. *The Records of the Federal Convention.* 4 vols. New Haven, CT: Yale University Press.

CONGRESS, HOUSE OF REPRESENTATIVES, SIZE

Under the Virginia Plan, which Edmund Randolph introduced at the Constitutional Convention on May 29, state representation in the House of Representatives was to be apportioned according to "the Quotas of contribution or to the number of free inhabitants" (Farrand 1937, I, 20). This contrasted with the Articles of Confederation under which each state had an equal vote. The Virginia Plan did not set a specific number of members in the House.

The Convention devoted considerable attention to the principle of representation in Congress, but the delegates accepted proportional representation in the House relatively early and focused on whether the same principle would be followed in the Senate. Ultimately, of course, the Convention resolved this issue in the Connecticut Compromise, which provided that states would be represented according to population (and three-fifths of the slaves) in the House and equally in the Senate.

From 56 to 65 Members

The Committee of Eleven eventually proposed that there be one representative for every 40,000 inhabitants. The committee report was then passed to a Committee of Five, which came up with a House of 56 members. A second Committee of Eleven, reporting to Congress on July 10, modified this to 65 representatives. Historian Edmund Morgan suggests that this number might have been formulated so as to see that the new Congress (including the 26 senators) would have a total of 91 members, the same size as the maximum allotted to the states (each with a maximum of seven delegates) under the Articles of Confederation (1988, 275). Significantly, only the states of Delaware and New Jersey had fewer than 65 representatives in their state legislatures, and the new House was about an eighth the size of the British House of Commons (275). The average size of state lower houses from 1776 to 1786 was 95 members (Kromkowski 2002, 230–231).

Proposed Changes in These Numbers

This may have been among the reasons leading James Madison to argue that the number of House members should be doubled in order to reflect the nation's diverse interests. Oliver Ellsworth objected, both because he thought such a plan would be expensive and because he thought the size would delay business (I, 568–569). Sherman said that he preferred a House of 50 members, while Elbridge Gerry and George Mason both wanted more than 65. Delaware's George Read observed that a Congress of 65 left Delaware and Rhode Island with only one member each whereas John Rutledge of South Carolina opposed expanding the number. The Convention subsequently rejected Madison's motion for doubling the size of the house by a vote of 9-2.

On the last day of the Convention, however, Rufus King of Massachusetts and Daniel Carroll of Maryland proposed altering the provision that there be no more than one representative for every 40,000 inhabitants to a provision saying there would be no more than one for every 30,000. This was adopted unanimously after George Washington made a rare speech on its behalf. This agreement, as well as the designation of representation from individual states, is found in Article I, Section 2, Clause 3 of the Constitution. Although this designation specified 65 seats in the first Congress, it allowed for relatively quick growth in that body.

Antifederalist Critique

This did not prevent Antifederalists from attacking the House as inadequately reflecting those whom it was intended to represent. Most such critiques were based on the idea that the House should be what John Rohr has described as "a microcosm of the society as a whole" (1986, 41). Federalists tended to place greater emphasis on the function of members of Congress in "filtering" public opinion.

Subsequent Size of the House

Congress conducted the first census in 1790, and it went into effect two years later. The size of the House of Representatives jumped from 65 to 106.

This was partly the result of the addition of Kentucky and Vermont (each with two seats), but largely stemmed from allocating seats by the new formula. Connecticut's representation jumped from 5 to 7; Maryland's from 6 to 8; Massachusetts's from 8 to 14; New Hampshire's from 3 to 4; New Jersey's from 4 to 5; New York's from 6 to 10; North Carolina's from 5 to 10; Pennsylvania's from 8 to 13; Rhode Island's from 1 to 2; South Carolina's from 5 to 6; and Virginia's from 10 to 19. Georgia dropped from 3 representatives to 2, and Delaware's remained constant at 1 (*Guide to Congress* 1991, 741). The most dramatic miscalculation in the original figures was that for the state of Virginia.

Although the United States population has continued to grow, in 1911 Congress capped the size of the current House of Representatives at 435 members (Vile 2003, 100). Members thus typically represent about 550,000 inhabitants. Because states are represented in the Electoral College according to the number of individuals to which they are entitled in Congress, and the Twenty-third Amendment has subsequently allocated 3 electors to the District of Columbia, it currently takes 270 or more electoral votes to become president, that is one-half plus one of 538; the sum of 435 members of the House; 3 electors allocated to Washington, D.C.; and 100 senators.

See Also Census; Congress, House of Representatives, Representation in; Three-fifths Clause

FOR FURTHER READING

Farrand, Max, ed. 1937. *The Records of the Federal Convention.* 4 vols. New Haven, CT: Yale University Press.

Green, Evarts B., and Virginia D. Harrington. 1966. *American Population before the Federal Census of 1790.* Gloucester, MA: Peter Smith.

Guide to Congress. 1991. 4th ed. Washington, DC: Congressional Quarterly.

Kromkowski, Charles A. 2002. *Recreating the American Republic: Rules of Apportionment, Constitutional Change, and American Political Development, 1700–1870.* Cambridge: Cambridge University Press.

Morgan, Edmund S. 1988. *Inventing the People: The Rise of Popular Sovereignty in England and America.* New York: W. W. Norton.

Return of the Whole Number of Persons within the Several Districts of the United States, 1802. Washington, DC: William Duane. Reprinted by New York: Arno Press, 1976.

Rohr, John A. 1986. *To Run a Constitution: The Legitimacy of the Administrative State.* Lawrence: University Press of Kansas.

Vile, John R. 2003. *Encyclopedia of Constitutional Amendments, Proposed Amendments, and Amending Issues, 1789–2002.* 2nd ed. Santa Barbara, CA: ABC-CLIO.

CONGRESS, HOUSE OF REPRESENTATIVES, TERMS

The Virginia Plan did not specify the length of terms for members of what became the House of Representatives. Eventually, the Convention settled for the two-year terms, which are specified in Article I, Section 2. This term fell midway between proposals that delegates advanced at the Constitutional Convention for annual and triennial elections.

Delegates first discussed House terms on June 12, with Connecticut's Roger Sherman and Oliver Ellsworth initially proposing one-year terms, John Rutledge of South Carolina proposing a two-year term, and Maryland's Daniel of St. Thomas Jenifer proposing three-year terms. The latter reasoned that overly frequent elections would make the office less appealing to "the best men," and Virginia's James Madison seconded the three-year proposal with the argument that a government as extensive as the one being formed would require that state delegates learn the interests of other states and, given the distances, it would almost require a year for some delegates to prepare for and to get to and from the seat of government (Farrand 1937, I, 214). Elbridge Gerry of Massachusetts said that New England voters would "never give up the point of annual elections" (214), prompting a mini-debate between Madison and him on the degree to which delegates should be guided by public opinion. Madison won the initial scrimmage, and the proposal for triennial elections was adopted by a vote of 7-4.

The issue was reconsidered on June 21 when Madison's fellow Virginia delegate Edmund Randolph proposed a two-year term. Like Gerry, Randolph believed that the people favored annual elections (he observed that all states except South Carolina had them), but he thought such elections would be inconvenient for a nation as large as the U.S. Delaware's John Dickinson favored triennial elections, with annual rotation of one-third of the membership each year, but Oliver Ellsworth, seconded by Caleb Strong of Massachusetts, proposed a one-year term. Pennsylvania's James Wilson supported this proposal as "most familiar & pleasing to the people," and as no more inconvenient than triennial elections (I, 361). Madison disagreed, focusing not on the inconvenience to the voters but to the representatives, who would be likely to desert their posts in order to return home during elections. Sherman did not think this was altogether bad as it forced the representatives "to return home and mix with the people" (362). Sherman made an argument about "inside the beltway" mentality before there ever was a Washington beltway, by expressing the fear that those who remained at the seat of Government would "acquire the habits of the place which might differ from those of their Constituents" (362). Still he could accept either annual or biennial elections. Alexander Hamilton's follow-up defense of three-year terms proved unavailing, and, after striking the three-year term, the Convention voted for biennial elections and did not further debate the subject.

Presidents serve for four-year terms, senators for six-year terms, and members of the federal judiciary "during good behavior," or for life. The term of the House is thus the shortest of any official specified in the Constitution. This short term indicates the delegates' desire to keep the members of the body "close to the people." Unlike the Senate, where a system of rotation was formulated with one-third of the seats up for election every two years, all members of the House are up for election every two years. After changes in the proposed term of the president (originally set at seven years), such elections correspond once every four years to elections for the presidency.

See Also Congress, Senate, Terms

FOR FURTHER READING

Eidelberg, Paul. 1968. *The Philosophy of the American Constitution: A Reinterpretation of the Intentions of the Founding Fathers.* New York: The Free Press, 93–105.

Farrand, Max, ed. 1937. *The Records of the Federal Convention.* 4 vols. New Haven, CT: Yale University Press.

Malbin, Michael J. 1986. "Framing a Congress to Channel Ambition." American Political Science Association, American Historical Association. *this Constitution: Our Enduring Legacy.* Washington, DC: Congressional Quarterly.

CONGRESS, HOUSE OF REPRESENTATIVES, VACANCIES

There is no recorded debate at the Convention on the provision in Article I, Section 2, providing that "when vacancies happen in the Representation from any State, the executive Authority thereof shall issue Writs of Election to fill such Vacancies."

The Committee of Detail formulated the content of this amendment and reported it to the Convention on August 6, and the delegates agreed to it without dissent three days later. The Committee of Style subsequently reworded this provision into the active voice.

Whereas state governors provide for writs of election in the case of House members, they may, according to the Seventeenth Amendment, actually appoint senators in similar cases. Fears of a terrorist attack that might kill large numbers of Representatives have recently led to discussion of a constitutional amendment to put members of the House on a similar footing to those in the Senate so that there would be no significant period during which the people would be significantly under-represented in the House (Vile 2003, 89–91).

See Also Committee of Detail; Congress, Senate, Selection

FOR FURTHER READING

Vile, John R. 2003. *Encyclopedia of Constitutional Amendments, Proposed Amendments, and Amending Issues, 1789–2002.* Santa Barbara, CA: ABC-CLIO.

CONGRESS, LEADERS DESIGNATED BY CONSTITUTION

The Constitution remains relatively silent in regard to the officers of Congress. Article I, Section 2 specifies that "The House of Representatives shall chuse their Speaker and other Officers." Article I, Section 3 further specifies that "the Vice President of the United States shall be President of the Senate," that the vice president shall vote only in cases of ties, and that "the Senate shall chuse their other Officers, and also a President pro tempore, in the Absence of the Vice President, or when he shall exercise the Office of President of the United States." One would hardly know from the sparse language of the Constitution that the Speaker of the House of Representatives is today often regarded as the second most powerful person in the United States (Patterson 2004, 336). Moreover, the Constitution makes no specific reference to the majority leaders, minority leaders, or whips (designated to round up party votes), who currently play such important roles in both houses.

The plan proposed by South Carolina's Charles Pinckney in the early days of the Convention and later forwarded for consideration by the Committee of Detail appears to be the first to suggest that "Each House shall appoint its own Speaker and other Officers, and settle its own Rules of Proceeding" (Farrand 1937, II, 158). The Committee of Detail, in turn, proposed in its report of August 6 that the House "shall choose its Speaker and other officers," and that the Senate "shall chuse its own President and other officers" (II, 179). The Convention unanimously accepted both provisions on August 9 (II, 231; II, 239). The lack of debate on this issue stems from the fact that the right asserted was taken from state constitutions. These had incorporated the claims of colonial assemblies to select their own speakers, sometimes in opposition to royal governors who asserted their prerogative to disallow them, as the royal governor of Massachusetts had done in 1766 when the Massachusetts house had chosen James Otis as its speaker (Hinds 1909, 156).

On August 22, the Committee of Detail, chaired by John Rutledge of South Carolina, proposed that the president should have a Privy Council. It was to include the president of the Senate, the Speaker of the House, the chief justice of the United States, and the heads of various departments (II, 367). The Convention rejected this proposal, just as it had rejected earlier proposals for a Council of Revision, which would have included select members of the judiciary.

The Committee of Detail had proposed that the president of the Senate should exercise the powers of the president in the case of his death or disability (II, 186). Gouverneur Morris of Pennsylvania objected to this provision on August 27, suggesting that the chief justice of the United States would be a more appropriate designee (II, 427). In time, of course, the Convention settled on a vice president who could assume this role. When the provision for designating the vice president as ex officio president of the Senate, Elbridge Gerry feared that "the close intimacy that must subsist between the President & vice-president makes it absolutely improper," while Gouverneur Morris said that in such a case, "the vice president . . . will be the first heir apparent that ever loved his father" (II, 537). He further observed that if the vice presidency were eliminated, as Gerry had suggested, "the President of the Senate would be temporary successor, which would amount to the same thing" (II, 537). The Convention voted to make the vice president the ex officio president of the Senate on September 7 (II, 538). On September 15, Gerry stated that this remained one of his objections to the proposed Constitution (II, 633).

On September 4, the Committee on Postponed Matters designated the president of the Senate as the individual who would open the electoral ballots for the president (II, 497–498). This was finalized two days later (II, 528). The result is that outgoing vice presidents, for example Richard Nixon in 1961 and Al Gore in 2001, sometimes have to certify the election of electoral opponents for the presidency.

See Also Council of Revision; President, Council; Vice Presidency

FOR FURTHER READING

Farrand, Max, ed. 1937. *The Records of the Federal Convention.* 4 vols. New Haven, CT: Yale University Press.

Hinds, Asher C. 1909. "The Speaker of the House of Representatives." *American Political Science Review* 3 (May): 155–166.

Patterson, Thomas E. 2004. *We the People: A Concise Introduction to American Politics.* 5th ed. New York: McGraw-Hill.

Risjord, Norman K. 1992. "Partisanship and Power: House Committees and the Powers of the Speaker, 1789–1801." *William and Mary Quarterly,* 3rd ser. 49 (October): 628–651.

limits the adoption of bills of attainder (legislative punishments without benefit of trials) or ex post facto laws. Paragraph four limits capitation or other direct taxes except in proportion to the census. Paragraph five prohibits Congress from laying taxes or duties on exports. Paragraph six prohibits Congress from preferring ports of one state over another or requiring states entering one state from paying duties in another. Paragraph seven provides that Congress shall not withdraw money except by law and requires regular accounting for such expenditures. Paragraph eight prohibits Congress from granting titles of nobilities and prohibits employees of the government from accepting such titles without congressional consent.

These limitations, along with limits on the states in Article I, Section 10, act as a miniature bill of rights and probably undercut the argument that Federalists initially advanced to the effect that such bills were unnecessary and possibly dangerous.

See Also Attainder, Bills of; Ex Post Facto Laws; Habeas Corpus; Slave Importation; Taxes on Imports and Exports; Titles of Nobility

FOR FURTHER READING

Cohn, Mary, ed. 1991. "Constitutional Beginnings." *Guide to Congress.* 4th ed. Washington, DC: Congressional Quarterly, 3–35.

CONGRESS, LIMITS ON

Article I, Section 8 grants powers to Congress while Article I, Section 9 provides limits on this institution. This section contains eight paragraphs.

Paragraph one, largely adopted by the Convention at the insistence of Georgia and South Carolina, prohibited Congress from limiting the importation of slaves (designated as "such Persons as any of the States now existing shall think proper to admit") until the year 1808. Paragraph two prohibits suspension of the writ of habeas corpus except in limited circumstances. Paragraph three

CONGRESS, MEMBERS' INELIGIBILITY FOR OTHER OFFICES

Article I, Section 6, of the Constitution contains what has become known as the emoluments clause. It provides that "no Senator or Representative shall, during the Time for which he was elected, be appointed to any civil Office under the Authority of the United States, which shall have been created, or the Emoluments whereof shall have been encreased during such time." It further prohibits an individual holding any other U.S. office from being a member of either house while holding such an office. This latter provision distinguishes the U.S. from parliamentary democracies where leaders of the cabinet are drawn from, and continue to serve in, the legislature.

The roots of Article I, Section 6 are found in the original Virginia Plan, under which members of both houses were to be ineligible for any offices created during their term of service or for an unspecified time period thereafter, by either the states or by the national government (Farrand 1937, I, 20–21). The Committee of the Whole filled in the unspecified blank with a one-year disability (I, 228), and discussion proceeded on this point on June 22, with the Convention answering key questions during the course of its debates.

How Long Should the Ineligibility Extend?

On that date Nathaniel Gorham, seconded by fellow Massachusetts delegate Rufus King, moved to strike out the one-year provision. King observed that "in this instance we refine too much by going to utopian lengths. It is a mere cobweb" (I, 379). By contrast South Carolina's Pierce Butler argued that the provision was a wise guard against corruption, which could be observed within the British system where individuals took seat in Parliament in order to procure jobs for themselves and their friends. James Wilson of Pennsylvania took Gorham's and King's position. He argued: "Strong reasons must induce me to disqualify a good man from office," and wondered what would happen in the event that a war broke out and some of the best military men were in Congress (I, 380–381). Virginia's James Madison favored excluding individuals from accepting only those offices created or augmented while they were serving in Congress. George Mason, also from Virginia, thought such a provision would not go far enough in guarding against corruption, which he, like so many other delegates, associated with the English system. He observed that the ineligibility clause was "the corner-stone on which our liberties depend—and if we strike it out we are erecting a fabric for our destruction" (I, 381). Arguing that men were motivated by "ambition and interest," Alexander Hamilton of New York argued that government should appeal to these interests. The only exclusion that he favored was one against holding more than one office at a time (I, 381–382).

Should the Ineligibility Extend to State Offices?

Discussion on this topic resumed the following day. South Carolina's General Pinckney proposed, and Connecticut's Roger Sherman seconded, a motion eliminating the disability of accepting state offices. Using a biblical analogy, both likened the establishment of such a restriction to designing a kingdom divided against itself (I, 386). Their resolution passed by a vote of 8-3 with Massachusetts, Pennsylvania, Delaware, and in dissent.

Should Ineligibility Extend to All Offices or to a More Limited Class?

Madison then proposed that the only offices to which members of Congress should be ineligible during their term or for one year thereafter were those offices created or augmented during their terms; North Carolina's Alexander Martin seconded the motion. This would allow members to aspire to other worthy offices. Pierce Butler and John Rutledge, both of South Carolina, thought this restriction would be too weak. George Mason agreed, pointing to examples of corruption both in his native Virginia and in Great Britain. King thought the delegates "were refining too much in this business" (I, 387). Wilson, however, thought that it was necessary for the Constitution not simply to remove the temptations implicit in legislative appointment to office but also from creating unnecessary ones that they could fill. Roger Sherman and Elbridge agreed. Gerry feared that Madison's proposal "would produce intrigues of ambitious men for displacing proper officers, in order to create vacancies for themselves" (I, 388).

Acknowledging difficulties, Madison observed that it was important not to disqualify good men from accepting offices for which they were qualified, but his motion was defeated by an 8-2-1 vote, carrying only New Jersey and Pennsylvania and dividing Massachusetts. The resolution was subsequently divided, and the Convention accepted congressional ineligibility to other offices during their terms while rejecting the continuing ineligibility for another year thereafter.

On June 26, the Convention considered whether ineligibility of senators (who were to be selected by state legislatures) should apply to both state and national offices or only to the latter. Butler proposed to strike out ineligibility to the former and was seconded by Williamson. Wilson observed that this would make members of Congress more dependent on their states. General Pinckney observed that "the States ought not to be barred from the opportunity of calling members of it into offices at home" and opined that a restriction on this would "discourage the ablest men from going into the Senate" (I, 429). The Convention voted unanimously to bar senators from federal offices created or augmented during their terms or for a year afterward but voted 8-3 against extending this prohibition to state offices.

In a speech on July 2, Gouverneur Morris argued that prohibiting senators from holding other offices was "a dangerous expedient" that would keep them from being "interested in your government" (I, 518). He observed that "If the state governments have the division of many of the loaves and fishes, and the general government few, it cannot exist" (I, 518).

On August 14, Charles Pinckney renewed objections against congressional ineligibility to office. He argued that the provision was "degrading," "inconvenient," and "impolitic" (I, 283) and moved to provide only that members could not hold other offices for which they received a salary. He hoped that Congress would "become a School of Public Ministers, a nursery of Statesmen" (I, 283). His motion brought a rare second from General Thomas Mifflin of Pennsylvania. Madison noted that George Mason then "ironically" proposed to strike the entire section, as a way to

encourage corruption, which he thought would be the effect of Pinckney's motion (II, 284)! By contrast, Maryland's John Mercer thought that the executive needed the power that could come by offering such offices. Gerry was opposed to making Congress into any sort of nursery of statesmen and feared that the temptation to office would create a government "of plunder" (I, 285). Morris feared that disqualifying members of the armed forces from congressional offices would give them an interest separate from that of the government—hence the eventual language limiting this disability to "civil" offices (Huntington 1956, 680). He disfavored any ineligibility to office. Wilson thought the new government was already too dependent on the states, and he argued that disqualifying members of Congress from other offices would further diminish its ability to attract talent (I, 288). Mercer also feared that such a qualification would encourage the best men to stay home and serve their own states while Morris again raised the possibility that a military man serving in Congress would be unable to aid his country effectively. Further action was deferred until the powers of the Senate were more clearly defined.

On September 3, Charles Pinckney moved to alter the provision at issue by restricting its impact so as only to limit the holding of two simultaneous offices, but only South Carolina and Georgia supported him. Rufus King then moved to limit exclusion only to offices created during a congressman's term. Sherman thought that such a prohibition needed to be extended not only to offices created but also increased during a member's term in office. Gerry feared that opening offices to congressmen would "have the effect of opening barriers agst. good officers, in order to drive them out & make way for members of the Legislature" (I, 491). Mason repeated his argument that the prohibition against accepting offices would exclude merit but "will keep out corruption" (II, 491). After continued discussion, the Convention agreed to exclude members only from offices created or the payment for which was increased during their terms.

This compromise was not altogether clear. Despite earlier suggestions to the contrary, on September 14, Georgia's Abraham Baldwin observed that this prohibition would not prevent members of the first Congress from being excluded from offices "*created by the Constitution;* and the salaries of which would be created, *not increased* by Congs. at the first session" (II, 613). Madison observed that "He was neither seconded nor opposed; nor did any thing further pass on the subject" (II 614).

The course of deliberations on this subject focused on the degree to which a provision designed to prevent corruption might lessen the inducement to accept public office. Congress came to a number of agreements. Members of Congress would be able to accept some other offices, but only if they gave up their seats. They could not accept federal civil offices created, or the emoluments of which were increased, during their terms. Members would face no continuing disqualifications once they left office, nor would they be barred from state offices.

Postscript

The public continues to be suspicious of those who hold public office and of the "revolving doors" in both the public and private sectors that seem to welcome ex-members of Congress. By the same token, former members of Congress continue to be welcomed into other positions of wealth and power because their previous jobs have provided them with such a valuable understanding of how power is wielded.

See Also Corruption; Virginia Plan

FOR FURTHER READING

Farrand, Max, ed. 1937. *The Records of the Federal Convention.* 4 vols. New Haven, CT: Yale University Press.

Huntington, Samuel P. 1956. "Civilian Control and the Constitution." *American Political Science Review* 50 (September): 676–699.

O'Connor, John F. "The Emoluments Clause: An Anti-Federalist Intruder in a Federalist Constitution." *Hofstra Law Review* 24 (Fall): 89–178.

CONGRESS, MILITIA POWERS

Article I, Section 8, Clause 16 of the Constitution vested Congress with the power "To provide for organizing, arming, and disciplining, the Militia, and for governing such Part of them as may be employed in the Service of the United States." Using language that anticipates that later used in the Tenth Amendment, the provision continues by "reserving to the States respectively, the Appointment of the Officers, and the Authority of training the Militia according to the discipline prescribed by Congress."

Mason Initiates Debate on August 18

This provision grew out of debates at the Constitutional Convention on August 18. Relatively early in the day's proceedings, Virginia's George Mason observed that the general government needed to have power over the militia. This need for congressional power would actually derive from federal reliance on the states:

> He hoped there would be no standing army in times of peace, unless it might be for a few garrisons. The Militia ought therefore to be the more effectively prepared for the public defence. Thirteen States will never concur in any one system, if the disciplining of the Militia be left in their hands. If they will not give up the power over the whole, they probably will over a part as select militia. (Farrand 1937, II, 326)

Apparently unsuccessful in getting this matter sent to the Committee of Detail, later in the day Mason proposed granting Congress the power "to make laws for the regulation and discipline of the Militia of the several States reserving to the States the appointment of the Officers" (II, 330). Connecticut's Roger Sherman later seconded the motion. Mason justified the addition of this provision on the need for uniformity. General Charles C. Pinckney of South Carolina affirmed that the lack of such uniformity had presented problems

The Battle of Lexington. *Print shows line of Minute Men being fired upon by British troops in Lexington, Massachusetts.*
(Library of Congress)

during the Revolutionary War, and he indicated that, without such a requirement, "States would never keep up a proper discipline of their militia" (II, 330).

Connecticut's Oliver Ellsworth feared that Mason's motion went too far. Although agreeing that the militia needed to have the same arms and be regulated by the U.S. when employed in its service, he feared that, if too much power were taken from the states, their "consequence would pine away to nothing after such a sacrifice of power" (II, 331). He also observed the difficulty that Congress would have of tailoring legislation "to the local genius of the people" (II, 331).

Gravely observing that the Convention was now dealing with "a most important matter, that of the sword," Delaware's John Dickinson offered a proposal whereby the national government would govern only one-fourth of the militia at a time, until, by rotation, it had trained the whole. Pierce Butler of South Carolina thought that Congress needed to govern the whole. This led Mason to withdraw his original proposal for one that would vest the national government with the regulating and disciplining of only one-tenth of the state militia each year but continue to reserve

to the states the right of appointing officers. General Pinckney instead renewed Mason's original motion, continuing to see the need for uniformity and arguing that there was no reason to distrust national authority in this area. In seconding him, New Hampshire's John Langdon said that he was more fearful of confusion flowing from different rules than from the power of either state or national governments.

James Madison argued that the power to regulate the militia was not easily "divisible between two distinct authorities." He thought that the general government could be as easily trusted with the use of military force as with the public monies. Madison argued that "the States would not be separately impressed with the general situation, nor have the due confidence in the concurrent exertions of each other" (II, 332). Ellsworth believed that the idea of a select militia was impractical and that state habits were too different to impose national authority. Charles Pinckney favored congressional control and expressed skepticism over the ability of militia to substitute for regular troops; he attributed the near state of "anarchy" in Massachusetts (see Shays's Rebellion) to reliance on militia troops.

Roger Sherman said that states needed militia to defend themselves and to enforce their own laws and said that, as in the case of taxation, they needed to maintain a concurrent power in this area. Gerry was almost apoplectic over the prospect of forcing the states to give up their militia—he described this "as black a mark as was set on Cain" (II, 332)—and believed that the states would share his lack of confidence in the new national government. For his part, Mason was willing to exempt that part of the militia that the states needed for their own use.

Delaware's George Read shifted attention to a somewhat different issue. He expressed concern over leaving the appointment of the officers of the militia to the states and insisted that, at the least, the Convention should require that state executives make such decisions (II, 333). The Convention then voted to commit these matters to the 11-man Committee on State Debts and Militia, which William Livingston of New Jersey headed.

Debate over Report of August 21

This committee reported back to the Convention on August 21, with a provision that contains all the elements, and most of the language, of the current provision (II, 352).

It provided that Congress would have power

> to make laws for organizing, arming & disciplining the Militia, and for governing such parts of them as may be employed in the service of the U.S. reserving to the States respectively, the appointment of the officers, and authority of training the militia according to the discipline prescribed." (II, 384–385)

The Convention began discussion of this provision on August 23. Sherman moved to strike the last phrase on the basis that states would have the authority to appoint and train militia even without such an express provision. Ellsworth thought the phrase might be needed but wanted clarification of the term "discipline" (II, 385). Rufus King of Massachusetts said that the committee had in-

tended for the term "organizing" to refer to "proportioning the officers and men," the term "arming" to "specifying the kind size and caliber of arms," and the term "disciplining" to "prescribing the manual exercise evolutions &c." (II, 385). Sherman then withdrew his motion.

Gerry feared that the provision left the states with little more than the power of "drill-sergeants." He further raised the specter of congressional "Despotism" (II, 385). Madison elicited further explanation from King over the intended meaning of terms.

A motion that Dayton offered to postpone in favor of a differently worded motion failed by a vote of 8-3. Ellsworth and Sherman then offered a motion "To establish an uniformity of arms, exercise & organization for the Militia, and to provide for the Government of them when called into the service of the U. States" (II, 386). Their stated purpose was "to refer the plan for the Militia to the General Govtr. but leave the execution of it to the State Govts." (II, 386). Langdon professed bewilderment over the distrust that delegates were expressing toward the proposed government, likening the power of the nation and states to the right and left hands. Gerry thought that the states should be considered as the former, and questioned whether national liberty could be safely reposed in the national government. Dayton questioned whether the proposal might lead to too much uniformity. General Pinckney preferred the committee's language, and Madison reiterated that the discipline of the militia was a national concern. Luther Martin did not think the states would ever part with this power, and he thought that they would be more likely to attend to it than the national government. Randolph did not think it likely that the militia would commit suicide. He feared that state legislators "courted popularity too much to enforce a proper discipline" and thought that leaving the states with the right to appoint officers would provide adequate security for their interests. The Convention thus rejected Ellsworth's motion by a vote of 10-1, then voted 9-2 to agree to the first part of the motion offered by the committee.

Madison subsequently proposed altering the part of the resolution relating to appointments so that states could only appoint those "under the rank of General officers" (II, 388). Sherman thought this would be "absolutely inadmissible" (II, 388). Similarly, Gerry "warned the Convention agst pushing the experiment too far," even predicting that insisting on federal powers that were too extensive could lead to civil war. By contrast, Madison argued that the greatest danger was that of "disunion of the States," and that if liberty were to be protected by guarding against standing armies, then the Convention needed effectually to provide for the militia" (II, 388). The Convention rejected Madison's motion by an 8-3 vote. It then unanimously accepted the reservation of state appointment of officers, and voted 7-4 to allow states to train militia under discipline prescribed by Congress. Finally, it unanimously voted to accept the entire clause.

Analysis

Debates over the governance of state militia seem relatively quaint, if not antiquated, at a time like today when the national government largely relies on troops recruited from throughout the nation. The Convention debates make it clear that many delegates were suspicious of the newly created government and were unwilling to concede full authority to it over even the most basic needs of national defense. Compromises allowing states to apply national rules of discipline and to appoint officers cooled but may not have completely assuaged such worries. There is continuing contemporary debate about the reference to state militias in the Second Amendment.

See Also Bill of Rights

FOR FURTHER READING

Cohn, Mary. 1991. "Constitutional Beginnings." *Guide to Congress*. Washington, DC: Congressional Quarterly, 3–35.

Farrand, Max, ed. 1937. *The Records of the Federal Convention*. 4 vols. New Haven, CT: Yale University Press.

Lofgren, Charles A. 1976. "Compulsory Military Service under the Constitution: The Original Under- standing." *William and Mary Quarterly*, 3rd ser. 33 (January): 61–88.

CONGRESS, ORIGINATION OF MONEY BILLS

Few disputes at the Constitutional Convention arguably generated such meager results from such intense debate as the one that resulted in the provision in Clause 1 of Article I, Section 7, for requiring that "all Bills for raising Revenue shall originate in the House of Representatives; but the Senate may propose or concur with amendments as on other Bills." The debate over this provision is significant in pointing to the vision that the delegates at the Convention had for the respective branches and to the role that determined delegates could play when they thought an issue was very important.

Original Proposal by Elbridge Gerry

During debates in the Committee of the Whole on June 13, Elbridge Gerry of Massachusetts introduced a proposal for restricting the Senate "from originating money bills" (Farrand 1937, I, 233), which he patterned after practice in the British Parliament and a majority of the states. Gerry observed that "The other branch was more immediately the representatives of the people, and it was a maxim that the people ought to hold the purse-strings" (I, 233). By contrast, Pierce Butler of South Carolina denied that the British example was relevant while Madison noted that it would be unwise to take such power from a body that would likely consist of "a more capable sett of men," and that such a restriction would be relatively worthless without a restriction on adding amendments to such legislation (I, 233–234). As various delegates supported or opposed Gerry's proposal, Sherman observed that as long as both houses had to agree, it would not matter where money bills originated. General Pinckney observed that a similar provision had led to evasion and disputes in South Carolina. This was followed by a vote rejecting Gerry's proposal 7-3.

Grand Committee Proposal and Discussion

On July 5, a Grand Committee (designated in this volume as the Committee on Compromise on Representation in Congress) headed by Gerry included his earlier proposal as part of a compromise designed to split the differences between the large and small states over representation in the two branches of Congress. Ironically, apart perhaps from George Mason and later Edmund Randolph, both of Virginia, other leading delegates from the larger states that it was purportedly designed to placate did not regard it as much of a concession except for Gerry, who was previously on record as favoring it! Virginia's James Madison thus argued that he "could not regard the exclusive privilege of originating money bills as any concession on the side of the small States. Experience proved that it had no effect" (I, 527). He argued that the plan had been "a source of frequent & obstinate altercations" in the states where it was used. While Butler also minimized the value of this provision, Delaware's Gunning Bedford (busy defending himself for suggesting that the smaller states might choose foreign allies) argued that if this did not please the larger states, it would not be likely that "they will ever accede to the plan" (I, 531).

Discussion resumed the following day. Gouverneur Morris opposed the money bill restriction, and James Wilson, also of Pennsylvania, "could see nothing like a concession here on the part of the smaller States." He explained: "If both branches were to say yes or no, it was of little consequence which should say yes or no first, which last" (I, 544). North Carolina's Williamson even argued that money bills would receive closer scrutiny from the branch without the benefit of "popular confidence" (I, 544). George Mason, a representative of a large state (Virginia), finally offered backup for Gerry's initial reasoning. He tied restricting the origin of money bills to the fact that the House would be the more immediate representative of the people and that allowing the Senate to have such a power would alienate them from its source and promote aristocracy. Gerry also tried to defend the provision as a genuine compromise. By his reasoning, it showed that the people did not trust this body, which would more directly represent the states with their money, and thus lessened its members' "weight & influence" (I, 545). Neither Charles Pinckney nor Gouverneur Morris was convinced although Franklin could see how the people would have greater confidence if money matters were handled by the branch that was closest to them.

Despite continuing protestations by Wilson and Pinckney that this was a meaningless concession, the Convention nonetheless supported it by a vote of 5-3, with 3 additional states being split. Of the largest states, Pennsylvania and Virginia voted no, and Massachusetts, the home of Gerry, was split.

Decision to Strike Provision

On August 8, Charles Pinckney proposed eliminating the limits on the origin of money bills as "giving no real advantage to the House of Representatives, and as clogging the Gov." (II, 224). Morris argued for the propriety of allowing the Senate to originate such bills. Mason repeated his earlier arguments about how this was a protection against aristocracy, and he argued that the motion could "unhinge the compromise of which it made a part" (II, 224). Mercer, Butler, and Ellsworth supported the existing limitation while Wilson and Madison continued to oppose it. The motion to strike the power passed by a 7-4 vote, with Massachusetts being the only large state to vote for retaining it.

The next day Edmund Randolph and Hugh Williamson raised the issue again. Randolph felt strongly enough that if the limitation were not restored, he thought that equal state representation in the Senate should be reconsidered. Delaware's George Read was among those who had no strong opinion but was willing to reinstate the provision if the delegates from the large states thought it was of value. Although Wilson, Ellsworth, and

Madison all denied it, Franklin and Williamson thought it had been a key part of the compromise, and Mason continued to argue that money bills should be left to "the immediate choice of the people" (II, 233). Soon thereafter Mason declared that if the limitation relating to money bills were not restored, he would oppose equal state representation in the Senate. Morris urged fellow delegates not to fall for such bluster; if the limitation on money bills were mistaken, they should not reinstate it.

Reconsideration of Decision to Strike

On August 11, Randolph succeeded in getting a vote to reconsider. He presented four arguments for reinstating the limitation on money bills. They were as follows: it was a necessary compensation for the large states; it would diminish fears of an aristocratic Senate and thus make the plan more acceptable to the people; it would give some advantage to the House; and small states were obligated to vote for it as it had been central to the Connecticut Compromise (II, 262–263).

When discussion of this provision resumed on August 13, Randolph reworded the language of the provision so that it now referred to "bills for raising money for the purpose of revenue," and reminded smaller states of the putative role that the earlier version of this provision had played in the Connecticut Compromise (II, 273). Mason supported the change in wording and gave a spirited speech on its behalf. He pointed out that the Senate represented the states rather than the people and argued that this made it improper for that body to tax them. He cited the length of senatorial terms as a reason for protection against senators, who might use their power to increase their salaries. In response, Wilson reiterated earlier arguments that such a restriction would be "a source of perpetual contentions" (II, 274). As to the power of the purse, "the purse was to have two strings; one of which was in the hands of the H. of Reps. the other in those of the Senate" (II, 275). Gerry joined Mason in believing that only the people's immediate representatives should tax them. By contrast, Morris observed that the Sen-

ate could just as easily wear out the House by refusing to concur in its measures as by originating revenue bills. Madison argued that, in the least, the Senate should be permitted "to *diminish* the sums to be raised" (II, 276). He thought the term "revenue" was ambiguous and thought that the words "amend" and "alter" could also lead to "doubt & altercation" (II, 276). He pointed out that the states that were supposed to benefit from the arrangement largely opposed it:

> Of the five States a majority viz. Penna. Virga. & S. Carola. have uniformly voted agst. the proposed compensation on its own merits, as rendering the plan of Govt. still more objectionable— Massts has been divided. N. Carolina alone has set a value on the compensation, and voted on that principle. What obligation then can the small States be under to concur agst. their judgments in reinstating the section? (II, 277)

Delaware's John Dickinson launched into a justly regarded speech on the value of experience over reason. In context, he argued that experience had vindicated the British practice of confining the taxing power to the branch that was closer to the people. Most state constitutions contained such a limitation, and having one in the U.S. Constitution would deflect arguments that it was designed to create an aristocracy; it would be adequate to allow the Senate to amend bills that it received. Randolph also thought that allowing the Senate to originate money bills would strengthen fears of an aristocracy. Responding to this argument, John Rutledge argued that the people would regard this restriction as "a mere tub to the whale," that is, as a worthless concession (II, 279); in an apparent attempt to meet Dickinson's argument from experience, he interposed the negative experience of his home state of South Carolina with this mechanism. After similar reflections from Daniel Carroll and James McHenry, both of Maryland, the Convention voted Randolph's measure down by a vote of 7-4.

The issue refused to die. Caleb Strong of Massachusetts reintroduced a motion on August 15 limiting the origination of revenue bills to the House. Mason seconded the motion, now tying it to his fears of senatorial power over treaties. Gorham feared that "The Senate will first acquire the habit of preparing money bills, and then the practice will grow into an exclusive right of preparing them" (II, 297). Moving to postpone the subject until consideration of senatorial powers, Hugh Williamson argued that since proponents of the restriction thought it to be essential and others thought it to be of no importance, the Convention should indulge the former. The matter was raised but postponed on September 5.

Provision Reinstated

The matter was finally resolved on September 8, just nine days before the delegates signed the Constitution, when a slightly amended version of the provision, allowing for alterations by the Senate, was adopted. Only Delaware and Maryland voted in opposition. There is no recorded debate, but it would appear that those who thought the measure was relatively useless thought it might calm popular fears over the Constitution. The measure clearly owed its existence largely to Gerry, Mason, and Randolph. No matter how frequently large-state delegates like Madison, Wilson, and Morris protested that the large states thought the provision was useless, the wily Gerry had persuaded fellow delegates that the provision was a vital part of the Connecticut Compromise, which might unravel if it were to be abandoned. Proponents of the limitation had the advantage of thinking the measure was necessary to prevent the formation of, or the perception of the formation of, an aristocracy. By contrast, opponents of the measure thought it was unnecessary and inconvenient, but not of great significance. Those opposed to the provision largely won the arguments but lost to appeals to experience and public prejudice.

See Also Congress, Power of the Purse

FOR FURTHER READING

Cohn, Mary ed. 1991. "Constitutional Beginnings." *Guide to Congress.* 4th ed. Washington, DC: Congressional Quarterly, 3–35.

Farrand, Max, ed. 1937. *The Records of the Federal Convention.* 4 vols. New Haven, CT: Yale University Press.

CONGRESS, POWER OF THE PURSE

The first provision in Article I, Section 8 of the U.S. Constitution provides that "the Congress shall have Power To lay and collect Taxes, Duties, Imposts and Excises, to pay the Debts and provide for the common Defence and general Welfare of the United States"; it further provides that "all Duties, Imposts and Excises shall be uniform throughout the United States." Article I, Section 9 provides limits on the taxation of slave importation to no more than $10 per person. Article I, Section 9 further prohibits laying capitation or other direct taxes except by enumeration, prohibits taxes on exports, and provides that money should only be drawn from the treasury by "Appropriations made by Law."

It is significant that the first power entrusted to Congress is what scholars frequently call "the power of the purse." The Patriot slogan of "no taxation without representation" during the Revolutionary War indicated that Americans had long associated the power of the purse with the legislative power. In the conflict with the British, the colonists had generally accepted duties on goods coming from England, so-called external taxes, and had generally rejected the authority of Parliament to impose other "internal" taxes (Slaughter 1984). Although the Congress under the Articles of Confederation had the power to appropriate money, it had to assess the states for this money rather than raising it directly. Under the circumstances, it is not surprising that states often met their requisitions slowly, if at all.

The Virginia and New Jersey Plans

More concerned with reforming the structure of government as a whole than with simply adding new powers to it, the Virginia Plan, which Edmund Randolph introduced on May 29, did not specifically list the power of Congress to raise revenue but simply specified "that the National Legislature ought to be impowered to enjoy the Legislative Rights vested in Congress by the Confederation & moreover to legislate in all cases to which the separate States are incompetent, or in which the harmony of the United States may be interrupted by the exercise of individual Legislation" (Farrand 1937, I, 21). The fact that this clause was intended to grant power to Congress to spend (and possibly to collect) revenue seems fairly evident from the fact that by June 13, delegates were introducing resolutions to restrict the Senate from introducing money bills. Consistent with its intention to link congressional representation to state size, the Virginia Plan had further proposed that the right to suffrage in Congress should be "proportioned to the Quotas of contribution, or to the number of free inhabitants, as the one or the other rule may seem best in different circumstances" (I, 20).

The New Jersey Plan, which was based on the idea of adding to the existing powers of Congress, listed the power "to pass acts for raising a revenue, by levying a duty or duties on all goods or merchandizes of foreign growth or manufacture, imported into any part of the U. States, by Stamps on paper, vellum or parchment, and by postage on all letters or packages passing through the general post-Office," as the first of several new powers to be vested in Congress (I, 243). When Congress instead exercised its power to requisition states, it was to do so "in proportion to the whole number of white & other free citizens & inhabitants . . . & three fifths of all other persons" (I, 243). Although the Convention proceeded with the Virginia Plan, many delegates might have continued to be more comfortable with the idea of enumerating the specific powers of Congress than with relying on a broad general statement.

The Committee of Detail

The first power enumerated by the five-man Committee of Detail, which reported to the Convention on August 6, was the power "to lay and collect taxes, duties, imposts, and excises" (II, 181). This clause stimulated intense debate, much of it on August 16, over whether it should include the power to tax exports. Largely as a result of opposition of the Southern states, the Convention accepted a prohibition on such taxes. On August 23 and August 25, the Convention further debated whether Congress should be obligated to pay off the debt or merely empowered to do so. Virginia's George Mason feared creating a right that the government might not be able to fulfill while other delegates were especially concerned about whether monies should be paid to the original holders of governmental securities or to those who had later purchased them, often at highly reduced prices. This issue was partly resolved (or, more accurately, evaded and postponed) by the eventual inclusion of a provision in Article VI of the Constitution providing that "all Debts contracted and Engagements entered into, before the Adoption of this Constitution, shall be as valid against the United States under this Constitution, as under the Confederation." The current wording of the first clause in Article I, Section 8, essentially emerged from the Committee on Postponed Matters, which reported to the Convention on September 4 (II, 493), with the Committee of Style later specifically designating "Congress" rather than the more generic "Legislature" (II, 594).

Postscript

In the early years of the republic, Congress relied almost solely on taxes on imports for raising revenue. In *Pollock v. Farmers' Loan & Trust Co.*, 157 U.S. 429 (1895), the U.S. Supreme Court read the limitation on direct taxation as a prohibition on the income tax. The ratification of the Sixteenth Amendment in 1913 subsequently authorized such taxes, which are currently the national government's chief source of revenue.

In other developments, the Supreme Court has upheld the view, which it attributed to Alexander Hamilton and Supreme Court Justice Joseph Story, that the clause grants Congress independent power to appropriate money and not simply, as James Madison had interpreted it after the Convention, as a redundant authorization to appropriate money to accomplish the goals of other specified powers. By the Court's reasoning, the power to tax and spend is subject only to the requirements that such appropriations must not violate specific constitutional prohibitions and that taxing and spending powers must be exercised on behalf of the general welfare—see *United States v. Butler*, 197 U.S. 65 at 66 (1936).

See Also Articles of Confederation; Committee of Detail; Committee on Postponed Matters; Congress, Origination of Money Bills

FOR FURTHER READING

Bullock, Charles J. 1900. "The Origin, Purpose and Effect of the Direct-Tax Clause of the Federal Constitution. I." *Political Science Quarterly* 15 (June): 217–239.

——. 1900. "The Origin, Purpose and Effect of the Direct-Tax Clause of the Federal Constitution II." *Political Science Quarterly* 15 (September): 452–481.

Edling, Max M. 2003. *A Revolution in Favor of Government.* New York: Oxford University Press.

Farrand, Max, ed. 1937. *The Records of the Federal Convention.* 4 vols. New Haven, CT: Yale University Press.

Slaughter, Thomas P. 1984. "The Tax Man Cometh: Ideological Opposition to Internal Taxes, 1760–1790." *William and Mary Quarterly,* 3rd ser. 41 (October): 566–591.

CONGRESS, PRIVILEGES OF MEMBERS

Article I, Section 6, specifies that members of Congress shall except in cases of "Treason, Felony and Breach of the Peace" be privileged against arrest during their attendance in Congress or their transit there and back. The corresponding speech and debate clause also specifies that they shall not be questioned outside the Congress for anything they say there. These provisions appear to have originated in the Committee of Detail (Farrand 1937, II, 180) and were adopted without any recorded discussion.

Toward the end of the Convention, South Carolina's Charles Pinckney provoked brief discussion when he proposed, and Pennsylvania's Gouverneur Morris seconded, a provision "that each House should be judge of the privilege of its own members" (II, 502). Edmund Randolph and James Madison, both of Virginia, expressed concerns about investing Congress with such power, and, ever the lawyer, Pennsylvania's James Wilson feared that including such an express provision "might beget doubts as to the power of other public bodies, as Courts &c." (II, 503). Madison instead proposed that such provisions should be established by law, the Convention adjourned for the day without any apparent further action, and Pinckney's provision was not adopted.

Even without further debate, it can be surmised that members of the Convention thought it would be essential for members of Congress to go about their business free from molestation or reprisals. The First Amendment later extended a more general freedom of speech against federal interference in the First Amendment.

See Also Committee of Detail

FOR FURTHER READING

Farrand, Max, ed. 1937. *The Records of the Federal Convention.* 4 vols. New Haven, CT: Yale University Press.

Greene, Jack P. 1969. "Political Mimesis: A Consideration of the Historical and Cultural Roots of Legislative Behavior in the British Colonies in the Eighteenth Century." *American Historical Review* 75 (December): 337–360.

CONGRESS, PUBLICATION OF APPROPRIATIONS

The Grand Committee of Eleven (designated in this volume as the Committee on Compromise on Representation), which the Convention appointed on July 2 to help find a compromise between the large and the small states, provided in its report of July 5 that "no money shall be drawn from the public Treasury but in pursuance of appropriations to be originated by the first Branch" (Farrand 1937, I, 524). The requirement that money bills originate in the House received considerable discussion at the Convention, but the provision in Article I, Section 9, Clause 7, that "a regular Statement and Account of the Receipts and Expenditures of all public Money shall be published from time to time" was almost an afterthought.

This provision emerged on September 14 from a motion introduced by Virginia's George Mason and seconded by Elbridge Gerry of Massachusetts (both of whom would decide not to sign the Constitution) requiring "that an Account of the public expenditures should be annually published" (II, 618). Pennsylvania's Gouverneur Morris thought this would sometimes be impossible, and Rufus King of Massachusetts thought that it would be impractical to account for every shilling. Virginia's James Madison moved to substitute the phrase "from time to time" for "annually," observing that an unrealistic requirement was likely to be ignored, as the Articles of Confederation had done with a requirement for semi-annual publications. Pennsylvania's James Wilson seconded Madison's motion, which was supported by Charles Pinckney of South Carolina and Roger Sherman of Connecticut and unanimously adopted in its present form.

The origins of the clause have been traced to English practices, to colonial practices, to state constitutions and state practices, and to the Articles of Confederation (Hutchinson 1975, 146–147).

See Also Congress, Origination of Money Bills

FOR FURTHER READING

Farrand, Max, ed. 1937. *The Records of the Federal Convention*. 4 vols. New Haven, CT: Yale University Press.
Hutchinson, David. 1975. *The Foundations of the Constitution*. Secaucus, NJ: University Books.

CONGRESS, QUORUMS

Article I, Section 5 of the Constitution provides that a majority of each house of Congress shall constitute a quorum. It also provides that members can compel the attendance of absent members. At the Convention, each state had a single vote; the Convention waited to begin its work until representatives from a majority of states (seven) arrived. It is therefore not surprising to find that the first mention of a quorum for Congress, which emerged from the Committee of Detail, specified that a quorum would consist of a majority of members, with a smaller number having the power to adjourn from one day to the next (Farrand 1937, I, 180; Hutchinson 1975, 62).

This Convention first discussed this provision on August 10. Perhaps with a view of the difficulties that the Confederation Congress had often faced in obtaining a quorum, Nathaniel Gorham of Massachusetts and John Mercer of Maryland, later joined by Rufus King of Massachusetts, both expressed the view that this number was too high. Gorham feared that such a quorum requirement would lead to delay. Mercer feared that it would vest power in the hands of members who decided to leave and advocated allowing Congress to set its own quorum. King later agreed that a majority quorum could lead to "public inconveniency" (I, 252).

Virginia's George Mason responded to Gorham and King with an argument focused on regional interests. Given the size of the nation, he feared that, without a majority quorum, the Central states might make laws in the absence of those at a distance. Although he knew that the secession of delegates could cause problems, "he had also known good produced by the apprehension of it" (I, 252). Moreover, if the legislature were to set the quorum too low, "the U. States might be governed by a Juncto" (252).

Pennsylvania's Gouverneur Morris, seconded by Maryland's John Mercer, appeared to arrive at something of a compromise in proposing that the quorums be set at 33 in the House and 14 in the Senate, thus establishing the initial majorities (the initial House was to consist of 65 members and the initial Senate of 26) as quorums. King offered a substitute motion making these numbers the lowest, but allowing Congress to set them higher as the population expanded. Oliver Ellsworth was opposed. He thought that the plan would secure greater popular confidence if the people knew "that no law or burden could be imposed on them, by a few men" (I, 253). Elbridge Gerry of Massachusetts reinforced Ellsworth's arguments by observing that under a bare majority quorum, as few as 17 members could carry a measure in the House and as few as 8 in the Senate. By his calculations, this would allow two large states to dominate in the House, and two large states allied with two small states to dominate in the Senate. He proposed allowing Congress to establish a range of between 33 and 50 in the House. King thought such a measure would be safe in that it would require presidential concurrence or a two-thirds override of a presidential veto. By contrast Maryland's Daniel Carroll feared that Congress would not raise the quorum numbers when it should do so. King's motion was defeated by a vote of 9-2, thus leaving the majority as the established quorum. James Madison and Edmund Randolph, both of Virginia, then proposed a motion, approved by all states but Pennsylvania (which was divided), allowing each House to compel the attendance of members who refused to attend.

The issue of congressional quorums resumed briefly on August 15 in the context of the presidential veto. Carroll thought that the small number of individuals within each house who could make legislation was an argument on behalf of an absolute presidential veto. Gorham thought there was little reason for concern: a majority "was the quorum almost every where fixt in the U. States" (I, 300).

See Also Rules of the Constitutional Convention

FOR FURTHER READING

Farrand, Max, ed. 1937. *The Records of the Federal Convention.* 4 vols. New Haven, CT: Yale University Press.
Hutchinson, David. 1975. *The Foundations of the Constitution.* Secaucus, NJ: University Books.

CONGRESS, RECALL

Under Article V of the Articles of Confederation, state legislatures appointed members of Congress and had power to recall them. The Virginia Plan provided for a similar recall for members of the first branch of Congress (Farrand 1937, I, 20), but it does not appear to have provided any details of how such a recall would work. Perhaps because of this ambiguity, the Committee of the Whole unanimously rejected this mechanism on June 12, albeit without recorded debate (I, 217).

Delegates may have associated legislative recall with legislative impotency. In arguing for the efficacy of the Virginia Plan over the New Jersey Plan, Virginia's Edmund Randolph thus observed that "If the Union of these powers heretofore in Congs. has been safe, it has been owing to the general impotency of that body" (I, 256). He went on to observe that "Congs. are moreover not elected by the people, but by the Legislatures who retain even a power of recall. They have therefore no will of their own, they are a mere diplomatic body, and are always obsequious to the views of the States, who are always encroaching on the authority of the U. States" (I, 256).

The Convention did not discuss the idea of recalling senators. Scholars have suggested that delegates may have thought that this mechanism would conflict with the idea of giving senators longer (six-year) terms (see Rossum 2001, 101, citing Jay S. Bybee). Convention delegates do appear to have anticipated that state legislatures would "instruct" senators on how they wanted them to vote. States exercised this practice until about the time of the adoption of the Seventeenth Amendment (1913), which provided for popular election of U.S. senators (Rossum, 99).

See Also Congress, Senate, Terms

FOR FURTHER READING

Farrand, Max, ed. 1937. *The Records of the Federal Convention.* 4 vols. New Haven, CT: Yale University Press.
Malbin, Michael J. 1986. American Political Science

Association, American Historical Association. "Framing a Congress to Channel Ambition." *this Constitution: Our Enduring Legacy.* Washington, DC: Congressional Quarterly.

Rossum, Ralph A. 2001. *Federalism, the Supreme Court, and the Seventeenth Amendment.* Lanham, MD: Lexington Books.

CONGRESS, SALARIES

See CONGRESS, COMPENSATION OF MEMBERS

CONGRESS, SENATE, QUALIFICATIONS

Article I, Section 3, of the U.S. Constitution provides that members of the U.S. Senate shall be 30 years of age, that they be nine years as U.S. citizens, and that they shall be inhabitants of the states that select them.

Age

The Virginia Plan proposed that members of both branches of Congress should be required to be of an unspecified minimum age. On June 12, the Committee of the Whole voted 7-4 to set this age for senators at 30 years (Farrand 1937, I, 238). The full Convention unanimously reaffirmed this decision on June 25 (I, 408). This age, which was five years higher than that set for the House of Representatives (and five years less than the age eventually set for the president), was designed to ensure greater maturity among its members. The only significant alternative suggestion appears to have been one offered by James Madison on June 26 supporting a nine-year term. Without suggesting a specific age but seeming to imply an age much higher than the one on which the Convention eventually settled, he offered the view that the

terms of senators "should not commence till such a period of life as would render a perpetual disqualification to be re-elected little inconvenient either in a public or private view" (II, 423).

Property Qualifications

Virginia's George Mason suggested on June 26 that senators should be required to have a certain amount of property. He reasoned that this body was being instituted in part to protect property, and that those with such possessions were most likely to provide for their security (I, 428). Mason did not introduce this observation as a motion and it received no more discussion on that day. Mason may have intended for his observation to support the idea, advanced earlier by South Carolina's General Pinckney, that members of the Senate, as representatives of wealth, would not need a salary (see Wirls and Wirls 2004, 109).

On July 26, the Convention extensively debated provisions for property qualifications for all members of Congress (a discussion included under the entry Congress, House of Representatives, Qualifications of Members), ultimately deciding not to impose any. The report of the Committee of Detail introduced on August 6 accordingly contained no such provision, although it did contain the minimum 30-year age requirement as well as a four-year citizenship requirement, and a requirement for state residency (II, 179).

On August 10 the Convention debated a provision, proposed by the Committee of Detail, allowing Congress to "establish such uniform qualifications of the members of each House, with regard to property, as the said Legislature shall seem expedient" (II, 248). South Carolina's Charles Pinckney wanted such qualifications fixed within the Constitution itself, suggesting that $50,000 might be appropriate. Oliver Ellsworth of Connecticut observed that the varied conditions of the nation made a uniform qualification impractical, and Franklin feared that such a qualification "tended to debase the spirit of the common people" (II, 249). The motion was rejected. Virginia's James Madison subsequently argued that if the legislature could set its own qualifications, it could "by degrees subvert the Constitution." He thought that "It was as improper as to allow them to fix their own wages, or their own privileges" and North Carolina's Hugh Williamson feared that a legislature might use such qualifications to favor members of a particular occupation, for example lawyers (II, 250). John Rutledge of South Carolina proposed making the qualifications for members of Congress the same as those for state legislature, but Pennsylvania's James Wilson carried the day in suggesting that the provision simply be struck.

Citizenship and Residency

The idea of specifying a minimum length of citizenship in the United States emerged from the report of the Committee of Detail on August 6, which proposed that senators be citizens for at least four years (II, 179). The Convention discussed the issue of citizenship for senators on August 9, at which time Gouverneur Morris of Pennsylvania proposed, and Charles Pinckney seconded, a motion inserting a 14-year citizenship requirement in place of the four-year requirement for senators—a proposal probably derived from doubling the proposed seven years required for members of the House (Wirls and Wirls, 112), to which the delegates had agreed on the previous day.

The debates over House and Senate terms were similar. Morris was motivated by "the danger of admitting strangers into our public Councils" (II, 235). By contrast, Oliver Ellsworth feared that such a provision would discourage "meritorious aliens" from coming to the U.S. (II, 235). Pinckney sought to distinguish the case of the Senate from that of the House by observing that "As the Senate is to have the power of making treaties & managing our foreign affairs, there is peculiar danger and impropriety in opening its door to those who have foreign attachments" (II, 235). Mason favored this reasoning and observed that, were it not for the exemplary contributions of immigrants during the Revolutionary War, he would favor limiting such offices to natural-born citizens. James Madison thought the 14-year require-

ment was too long. He thought that Congress could address the problem in regulating naturalization and feared that incorporating such a provision within the Constitution would give it "a tincture of illiberality" that would discourage immigration (II, 236). Pierce Butler of South Carolina, himself an immigrant, favored a long residence as being necessary to attain national habits, opinions, and attachments. Franklin did not completely oppose citizenship for a number of years, but, like Madison, "should be very sorry to see any thing like illiberality inserted in the Constitution" (II, 236). Randolph thought that inclusion of a 14-year requirement would break faith with immigrants who had entered the nation expecting more generous treatment. He said he could not support a period of more than seven years. James Wilson, another immigrant, observed the "mortification" he had felt when he found, on moving to Maryland, that his status of an immigrant incapacitated him from office (II, 237).

Gouverneur Morris responded with a notable speech, in which he urged that members of the Convention "should be governed as much by our reason, and as little by our feelings as possible" (II, 237) but in which he used an emotional example, calculated to appeal more to the latter than to the former. Observing that "we should not be polite at the expense of prudence" and arguing for "moderation in all things," Morris observed that hospitality could be carried too far by citing the alleged practice of certain Indians in offering their wives to visitors. He further argued for the necessity of emotional attachments in promoting patriotism:

As to those philosophical gentlemen, those Citizens of the World, as they called themselves, He owned he did not wish to see any of them in our public Councils. He would not trust them. The men who can shake off their attachments to their own Country can never love any other. These attachments are the wholesome prejudices which uphold all Government, Admit a Frenchman into your Senate, and he will study to increase the commerce of France; An Englishman, he will feel an equal bias in favor of that of England. (II, 238)

After Morris's speech, the Convention voted 7-4 against a 14-year requirement, 7-4 against a 13-year requirement, 7-4 against a ten-year requirement, and settled on a nine-year requirement after Rutledge pointed out that a longer period should be required for the Senate than for the House, which had been set at seven years. Randolph indicated that he was supporting this requirement, which passed by a vote of 6-4-1 with the understanding that it would be reduced if that of the House were.

See Also Congress, House of Representatives, Qualifications of Members; Religious Tests, Prohibition

FOR FURTHER READING

Farrand, Max, ed. 1937. *The Records of the Federal Convention.* 4 vols. New Haven, CT: Yale University Press.
Wirls, Daniel, and Stephen Wirls. 2004. *The Invention of the United States Senate.* Baltimore, MD: Johns Hopkins University Press.

CONGRESS, SENATE, REPRESENTATION IN

The Constitutional Convention created a Senate and provided that each state would have two members of that body.

The Virginia Plan Proposes a Departure

Scholars generally agree that the most contentious issue at the Constitutional Convention involved representation of the states in Congress. Under the Articles of Confederation, each state had been represented equally in a unicameral Congress, but the Virginia Plan proposed a bicameral Congress in which states would be represented proportionally. The plan further specified that members of this branch would be selected by members of the first branch from among nominees by the state legislators.

Because most delegates contemplated that the Senate would be a relatively small body, it is not altogether clear that the right to proportional representation in the Senate would have amounted to any more than the right of state legislatures to make nominations to this body. Indeed, when Pennsylvania's James Wilson later proposed that the people should directly elect senators, he contemplated that such elections would be held in interstate districts, leading some fellow delegates to complain that the smaller states would stand no chance in such a scheme.

Representation in the House of Representatives

Although the issue was not completely resolved until representation in the Senate was, the Convention appears to have settled rather early on that the House of Representatives would be apportioned according to population. It was clearly leaning in this direction before it cast a vote to this effect on June 29, about halfway through the debate on representation in Congress as a whole.

The Senate as the Battleground

The agreement to apportion the House of Representatives by population left the Senate as the primary battleground between those who wanted to establish proportionality, or something approximating it, in both houses and those who wanted at least one house to continue the equality of representation that states enjoyed under the Articles of Confederation. This debate was, in turn, linked both to the size of the Senate and to its method of selection. If the Senate were to be small, then it could not be proportioned according to population and accommodate representatives from every state. If state legislatures were to choose senators, then the smallest state would have to have at least one, and the size of the body, if it were apportioned according to population, would likely be 80 to 100 members (Farrand 1937, I, 51, 150), larger than some delegates thought was appropriate. During this debate, Charles Pinckney of South Carolina suggested that states should be divided into three classes, with the largest having three senators each, Middle states having two, and smaller states having only one (I, 155). The delegates do not appear to have voted on this proposal.

June 9

Small states mapped out their central arguments in a generic discussion of representation that took place on June 9. After observing that the Articles of Confederation had previously "settled" the issue by allowing each state one vote, New Jersey's David Brearly observed that proportional representation "carried fairness on the face of it; but on a deeper examination was unfair and unjust" (I, 176–177). He observed that proportional representation would allow the large states to dominate, and he rather gamely proposed that if large state representatives were serious about proportional representation, they should spread out a map of the U.S. and divide it in 13 equal divisions (presumably meaning 13 divisions that were equally populated rather than geographically the same size). William Paterson, also of New Jersey, argued less from theory than from practical considerations. He said that the delegates had no mandate to change the existing scheme of representation and argued that the people would oppose it.

June 11

As early as June 11, Connecticut's Roger Sherman offered what was to become the basis for what eventually became known as the Connecticut Compromise. On that date—he had proposed equal representation in the Senate as early as May 31 (I, 52)—he proposed that representation in the first branch should be on the basis of population but that states should be equally represented in the Senate. He specifically proposed that each state should have one vote, but, as the Articles of Confederation showed, this would not necessarily

have precluded states from having larger delegations (I, 196). Sherman's proposal met fierce resistance from delegates from the larger states who thought that deviations from proportionality were undemocratic and would embody a fatal weakness.

As discussion proceeded, Franklin observed "that till this point, the proportion of representation, came before us, our debates were carried on with great coolness & temper" (I, 197), suggesting that he sensed a clear change in tone once discussion of representation began in earnest. Although Sherman warned that the small states would not accept anything less than equal representation in the Senate (I, 201), the Convention rejected his motion, seconded by Ellsworth, to give each state an equal vote in the Senate. It then voted for a motion by James Wilson and Alexander Hamilton affirming that the Senate would be apportioned in the same manner as the House of Representatives. Both votes were 6-5 with Connecticut, New York, New Jersey, Delaware, and Maryland (all considered to be small states) favoring equal rather than proportional representation in the Senate.

June 15

When William Paterson offered the New Jersey Plan on June 15, he proposed a continuation of the unicameral Congress under the Articles of Confederation in which each state was represented equally (I, 243). On June 21, however, the delegates voted to proceed with a bicameral Congress. The fact that Paterson put up so little resistance might indicate that he was as concerned about reintroducing the issue of state representation in presenting his plan as he was about presenting a complete alternative to the Virginia Plan.

June 25

Discussion of Senate representation resumed on June 25. Nathaniel Gorham of Massachusetts said that he was "inclined to a compromise as to the rule of proportion" (I, 404). He observed that his home state of Massachusetts had devised a system whereby representation in the larger districts "should not be in an exact ratio to their numbers" and that experience had vindicated this policy (I, 405). Discussion, however, largely moved to the method of selection and the terms of senators, rather than to their apportionment.

June 27–30

On June 27 and June 28, the Convention focused on representation in the House. Serving again as a barometer of sentiment within the Convention, Franklin observed that the Convention was "groping as it were in the dark to find political truth and scarce able to distinguish it when presented to us" (I, 451). Although it may have been driven in part by lack of funds and by fear of causing popular alarm, it might also be appropriate to view the Convention's decision not to accept Franklin's motion for beginning each day with prayer as a further indication of the disagreement that was gripping the Convention.

On June 29, the Convention did reaffirm that the method of representation in the first branch should be different from that under the Articles of Confederation. Ellsworth then moved that representation in the Senate should be the same as that under the Articles. He professed to believe that although the vote just taken was appropriate, it needed to be balanced:

> He hoped it would become a ground of compromise with regard to the 2d. branch. We were partly national; partly federal. The proportional representation in the first branch was conformable to the national principle & would secure the large States agst. the small. An equality of voices was conformable to the federal principle and was necessary to secure the Small States agst. the large. He trusted that on this middle ground a compromise would take place. He did not see that it could on any others. And if no compromise should take place, our meeting would not only be in vain but worse than in vain. (I, 469)

Ellsworth went on to observe that among the Eastern states, Massachusetts alone was likely to accept a system that did not allow for equal state representation in the Senate. As to Ellsworth, "He was not in general a half-way man, yet he preferred doing half the good we could, rather than do nothing at all" (I, 469).

The Convention resumed discussion on the next day. Pennsylvania's James Wilson could see no reason for formulating contrary bases of representation for the two houses. He was more optimistic than Ellsworth about getting approval for proportional representation in both houses, but "if a separation must take place, it could never happen on better grounds" (I, 482). Wilson believed the "unalienable rights of men" were more important than the rights of artificial states, he thought it essential that the new system incorporate provisions for majority rule, and he disputed claims that equal state representation would be essential to the preservation of state sovereignty (I, 482–483).

Ellsworth responded that the smaller states did not want to rule over the larger ones but only to protect their own rights. He further accused the Convention of "razing the foundations of the building" when all that was needed was to "repair the roof" (I, 484). Madison, while commending Ellsworth's "able and close reasoning," pointed out that Connecticut had refused to comply with congressional requisitions. He reviewed the weaknesses of previous confederacies and concluded that the central differences in the United States were not between the large and small states but between those of the North and those of the South (I, 486). Madison had ruffled some feathers. Ellsworth replied that Connecticut had supplied more troops per capita during the Revolution than had Virginia before Sherman noted that this issue was a diversion. North Carolina's William Davie observed that allowing for proportional representation in the Senate would result in too large a body. Like Ellsworth, he wanted a solution that recognized that the new Union was to be "partly federal, partly national" (I, 488).

Wilson was willing to accept, as a ground of compromise, a plan whereby each state would be guaranteed at least one vote in the Senate, with states otherwise getting one senator for each 100,000 inhabitants. Franklin liked the idea of compromise, likening it, in a homespun analogy, to trimming the edges of planks to make a table. He proposed a plan whereby states would appoint an equal number of senators, with each state having an equal vote on matters related to state sovereignty but having proportional votes when it came to appropriations (I, 489). Rufus King said he could agree to a measure like Wilson's but that he could never accept the "vicious principle of representation" that would treat states equally (I, 490). By contrast, New Jersey's Jonathan Dayton did not believe any of the ills of the Articles could be linked to the principle of representation, and he thought the system on the table was "an amphibious monster" that "never would be recd. by the people" (I, 490).

Madison expressed his willingness to accept Wilson's proposal, but Gunning Bedford of Delaware saw "No middle way between a perfect consolidation and a mere confederacy of the States" (I, 491). Long before Charles Beard formulated his theory that members of the Convention were motivated by economic interests, Bedford proceeded to undermine the appeal to principle being advocated by representatives of the large states by portraying them as being more motivated by "interest" than by "right":

> Look at Georgia. Though a small State at present, she is actuated by the prospect of soon being a great one. S. Carolina is actuated both by present interest & future prospects. She hopes too to see the other States cut down to her own dimensions. N. Carolina has the same motives of present & future interst. Virga. follows. Maryd. is not on that side of the Question. Pena. has a direct and future interest. Massts. has a decided and palpable interest in the part she takes. Can it be expected that the small States will act from pure disinterestedness. (I, 491)

Bedford's passion increased as he continued to speak. Condemning the rhetoric of large state representatives who seemed to be telling the small states to take it or leave it, he observed: "The Large States dare not dissolve the confederation. If they do the small ones will find some foreign ally of more honor and good faith, who will take

them by the hand and do them justice" (I, 492). Robert Yates's notes further indicate that Bedford proclaimed to the delegates from the larger states: "*I do not, gentlemen, trust you.* If you possess the power, the abuse of it could not be checked; and what then would prevent you from exercising it to our destruction?" (I, 500).

If Bedford would issue implicit threats, Ellsworth preferred to think of the "domestic happiness" that his state had provided. He likened his link to his state as that of a newborn baby relying on its mother's milk (I, 492), indicating that, for him at least, states were organic entities (much like many nations are considered to be today) and not mere lines drawn on a map. King responded to Bedford by accusing him of intemperance in suggesting a foreign alliance.

July 2

As deliberations resumed on Monday, July 2, the Convention voted 5-5-1 on the proposition to give each state an equal vote in the Senate, with Georgia now joining the divided column. Charles Pinckney, professing still to believe that equal state representation in the Senate was inadmissible, said he could support a plan under which states were formed into different classes, each with different numbers of senators. General Pinckney preferred Franklin's earlier proposal and suggested a committee consisting of one member of each state to resolve the issue. Luther did not oppose such a committee but said that "no modifications whatever could reconcile the Smaller States to the least diminution of their equal Sovereignty" (I, 511). Sherman and Gouverneur Morris both supported formation of a committee, with the latter hoping that the Senate could be "a select & sagacious body of men, instituted to watch agst. them [the people] on all sides" (I, 514). Randolph, Strong, Williamson, and later Gerry added their support to a committee, with Wilson sagely objecting that such a committee would be weighted toward the very rule of Senate equality it was designed to discuss, and Madison fearing that a committee would simply result in additional delay. Only New Jersey and Delaware voted against forming a committee. The Convention elected Gerry, Ellsworth, Yates, Paterson, Franklin, Bedford, Martin, Mason, Davie, Rutledge, and Baldwin (I, 516).

July 5

After the Independence Day holiday, the committee, headed by Elbridge Gerry of Massachusetts, reported a compromise to the Convention whereby members of the first branch would, as previously agreed to, be represented according to population (one member for every 40,000 inhabitants), and states would have equal representation in the second. In a provision that most of the large-state representatives seemed to disdain as worthless, the plan also called for all money bills to originate in the House of Representatives (see Congress, Origination of Money Bills).

The compromise led to no immediate solution. Gouverneur Morris was among the delegates from large states who opposed conceding to the states: "He came here as a Representative of America; he flattered himself he came here in some degree as a Representative of the whole human race; for the whole human race will be affected by the proceedings of this Convention" (I, 529). Bedford was still defending himself for the passion he had expressed in an earlier speech, a passion which, as a lawyer, he attributed to "the habits of his profession, in which warmth was natural & sometimes necessary" (I, 531).

The debate continued and resulted in the formation of yet another committee to reexamine the formula for giving each state one member in the U.S. House of Representatives for every 40,000 inhabitants. The Convention agreed by a vote of 7-3-1 and appointed five members—Morris, Gorham, Randolph, Rutledge, and King. Wilson suggested that the committee should consider a system like that of Massachusetts that would give some advantage to the small states without representing them proportionally. The Convention then discussed the significance of the provision for originating money bills within the House.

July 7

Discussion resumed on July 7. Sherman urged equal representation in the Senate as a way to get consensus. Wilson thought that "firmness" was sometimes more highly to be valued than "a conciliating temper" (I, 550). The Convention voted 6-3-2 to keep equal representation in the Senate as part of the report of the Committee of Eleven.

July 9

On July 9, Gouverneur Morris delivered the report from the committee of 5 members as to the 40,000 formula; it suggested an initial House of 56 members. This matter was in turn referred to another Committee of Eleven. It consisted of King, Sherman, Yates, Brearly, Morris, Reed, Carroll, Madison, Williamson, Rutledge, and Houston.

Paterson and Madison subsequently engaged in a fascinating exchange. When Paterson attacked the three-fifths compromise as unfairly departing from proportionaltity, Madison responded that "his doctrine of Representation which was in its principle the genuine one, must for ever silence the pretensions of the small States to an equality of votes with the large ones" (I, 562). The next day the Committee of Eleven proposed a House of 65 members.

July 14

On July 14, the Convention resumed deliberation on the equality of votes in the Senate, after scrimmages over whether this matter should be considered alone or in combination with representation in the other house and the provision related to the origin of money bills. Perhaps sensing that the large states were losing the battle, Charles Pinckney introduced, and Wilson seconded, a proposal that the Senate should consist of 36 members, with states having from one to 5 votes. Jonathan Dayton of New Jersey said that "the smaller States can never give up their equality" (II, 5). Sherman argued that the states needed an equal vote in the

Senate to protect themselves. Madison favored Pinckney's compromise, as did Gerry, who saw no chance that it would pass. King continued to argue for proportional representation. Caleb Strong of Massachusetts argued that the time had come for the large states to concede. Madison and Wilson continued to protest. Ellsworth and Sherman pushed their advantage, and the Convention voted 6-4 against Pinckney's proposal, with Pennsylvania, Maryland, Virginia, and South Carolina in the minority.

July 16

On July 16, the Convention voted for the committee report, including equal representation in the Senate, by a vote of 5-4-1, with Massachusetts (one of the three large states) divided and Pennsylvania, Virginia, South Carolina, and Georgia voting negative. Randolph suggested that the Convention needed to adjourn so "that the large States might consider the steps proper to be taken in the present solemn crisis of the business, and that the small States might also deliberate on the means of conciliation" (I, 18). Purposely or not, Paterson incorrectly interpreted Randolph as calling for an adjournment sine die and suggested that the Convention should rescind its secrecy rule so that delegates should consult their constituents. Rutledge argued that there was "no chance of a compromise. The little States were fixt. They had repeatedly & solemnly declared themselves to be so. All that the large States then had to do, was to decide whether they would yield or not" (II, 19). Rutledge thought it was better to yield and hope for further changes than to disband permanently. The Convention adjourned overnight.

July 17

Madison observed that delegates from the large states met the following morning and were joined by some representatives from the smaller states. Opinions were far from unanimous. Some large state representatives favored continuing opposi-

tion but a majority decided to yield to the agreement "however imperfect & exceptionable." Madison further observed that the decision to yield "satisfied the smaller States that they had nothing to apprehend from a Union of the large, in any plan whatever agst. the equality of votes in the 2d branch" (II, 20).

A subsequent decision by the Convention provided in a clause found in the amending article (Article V) of the Constitution that "no State, without its Consent, shall be deprived of its equal Suffrage in the Senate."

Analysis of Debates

Debate over Senate representation arguably produced as much heat as light. Few, if any, new arguments were advanced after the first few days of debate, but delegates continued to search for a solution. The fact that they appointed three different committees to address issues connected to representation shows that they were struggling. Both sides seemed to go for all or nothing in the Senate. Although Franklin proposed dividing matters affecting states from those that did not, Wilson proposed a plan (somewhat echoing an earlier suggestion by Gorham) whereby each state would get at least one senator with others being apportioned according to population, and Pinckney suggested a plan whereby states would be divided into different categories and be awarded senators accordingly, the Convention does not appear to have taken any of these plans, except for Pinckney's, very seriously.

Today the Senate continues to epitomize the view that the Constitution created a federal system in which states were represented as states. However persuasive the arguments were on behalf of proportional representation, they floundered on the shoals of small-state intransigence. In their defense, they were leaving a system in which they were guaranteed complete equality in national councils, and once they had conceded proportional representation in the House of Representatives, there was little more that they could offer by way of compromise.

See Also Congress, House of Representatives, Representation in; Congress, Origination of Money Bills; Congress, Senate, Size; Connecticut Compromise

FOR FURTHER READING

Farrand, Max, ed. 1937. *The Records of the Federal Convention.* 4 vols. New Haven, CT: Yale University Press.

Natelson, Robert G. 2002/2003. "A Reminder: The Constitutional Values of Sympathy and Independence." *Kentucky Law Journal* 91: 353–423.

Rakove, Jack. 1987. "The Great Compromise: Ideas, Interests, and the Politics of Constitution-Making." *William and Mary Quarterly,* 3rd ser. 44 (July): 424–457.

Wirls, Daniel, and Stephen Wirls. 2004. *The Invention of the United States Senate.* Baltimore, MD: Johns Hopkins University Press.

CONGRESS, SENATE, SELECTION

The Virginia Plan proposed a bicameral legislature. Under this plan, the people were to elect members of the lower house. This house would in turn select members of the upper house from among "a proper number of persons nominated by the individual Legislatures" (Farrand 1937, I, 20). The authors of the Virginia Plan anticipated that the Senate would be a smaller, wiser body than the House. Accordingly, although the Virginia Plan proposed that states would be represented proportionally in both houses, it is not clear that the small size that was contemplated for the Senate would have accommodated representation for each state.

Proposed Alternatives

In any event, a number of alternatives were presented early in the Convention to the proposal in the Virginia Plan that the House choose members of the Senate from among nominees suggested by the state legislatures. When delegates first considered this provision on May 31, Richard Spaight of North Carolina proposed as an alternative that state legislatures should choose members of the Senate, but Rufus King of Massachusetts suggested that the method of selection would be impractical unless the upper house "was to be very numerous, or *the idea of proportion* among the States was to be disregarded" (I, 51). After King estimated that the body would have to have 80 to 100 members for Delaware, the least populous state, to have a single vote, Spaight withdrew his motion.

Pennsylvania's democratically inclined James Wilson followed by proposing that the people select members of both houses of Congress. Anticipating that the body would be kept small, he anticipated combining states, or parts of states, into electoral districts for the purposes of such election (I, 52). Madison argued that this would be unfair to those smaller states, or parts of states, that were affiliated with larger ones. Connecticut's Roger Sherman favored allowing each state legislature to select one, and presumably only one, member. The Convention then rejected a motion by South Carolina's Charles Pinckney to strike out nomination by state legislatures, but it also voted 7-3 against the proposal for senatorial selection in the Virginia Plan, thus leaving what Madison described as a "chasm . . . in this part of the plan" (I, 52).

The Convention returned to this discussion on June 7. Delaware's John Dickinson proposed that the state legislatures should choose members of the Senate, and Sherman seconded him on the basis that it would give the states a greater stake in the proposed government (I, 150). This time, when South Carolina's Charles Pinckney argued that this would require a Senate of at least 80 members, Dickinson said that this number, or even double this number, would be fine with him. Wilson again argued that the Senate should "be elected by the people as well as the other branch" and proposed dividing the people "into proper districts for this purpose" (I, 151), apparently contemplating that they would embrace more than one state. Pennsylvania's Gouverneur

Morris seconded him. Delaware's George Read made yet another proposal, which no one seconded, providing for the chief executive to select senators from "a proper number of persons to be nominated by the individual legislatures" (I, 151).

After Madison pointed to the problems with Dickinson's plan, Elbridge Gerry of Massachusetts reviewed the four options for selecting senators that had been proposed to that point—by the first branch, by the chief executive, by the people, or by the state legislatures—and indicated that he favored the latter. Dickinson argued that this mechanism was most likely to keep the states in place like planets, "to move freely in their proper orbits," and he accused Wilson of wanting to obliterate them (I, 153). Not surprisingly, Wilson denied this charge. Madison expressed fears that state legislatures would compound the bad propensities of Congress to issue paper money and engage in similar factious schemes. However, Sherman argued that state legislatures were more likely to select fit men than the people; Gerry thought that state commercial interests would be more secure if their legislatures made the selection; and Charles Pinckney thought that its members would be more "independent" if so selected. George Mason commended legislative selection of senators as a means of allowing state legislatures to defend themselves against "encroachment of the Natl. Govt." (I, 155). The Convention then unanimously adopted Dickinson's motion, and it was incorporated into the June 13 report of the Committee of the Whole.

The Size of the Senate and Other Convention and Post-Convention Decisions

The New Jersey Plan called for sticking with a unicameral Congress, so it did not raise questions related to selection of senators. This plan did raise the altogether critical question of how states were to be represented in Congress, and this debate overshadowed all others and was finally resolved by allowing states equal representation in this body, a number ultimately set at two per state. This decision undoubtedly negated earlier concerns that state selective selection would require a Senate that was too large effectively to fulfill its function of giving legislation a calm second look.

On August 9, the delegates decided that they would allow governors temporarily to fill vacancies in the Senate in cases where state legislatures were not in session, but they do not otherwise appear to have revisited the issue of Senate selection.

Analysis

Although there are some significant differences (most notably the fact that members are not qualified by wealth, and the positions are not hereditary), Elaine Swift has argued that the Senate was largely modeled on the upper house of the English Parliament, known as the House of Lords (1993). Swift argues that the indirect method of selection was designed to serve as a "filtration process," and that the six-year terms were designed to provide further for senatorial independence. As was true of the House of Representatives, Convention delegates made no explicit provision for state legislative recall or instruction of senators, and their salaries were set by Congress rather than by the states.

Subsequent Developments

In time, the Seventeenth Amendment vindicated Wilson's proposals at the Convention and further democratized the Constitution—arguably at the expense of state powers (see Hoebeke 1995)—by providing that the people of the states would directly elect members of the Senate. Legislatures in a number of states had previously specified that they would ratify the people's choice.

See Also Congress, Senate, Size; Connecticut Compromise

FOR FURTHER READING

Eidelberg, Paul. 1968. *The Philosophy of the American Constitution: A Reinterpretation of the Intentions of the Founding Fathers.* New York: The Free Press, 78–92.

Farrand, Max, ed. 1937. *The Records of the Federal Convention.* 4 vols. New Haven, CT: Yale University Press.

Hoebeke, C. C. 1995. *The Road to Mass Democracy: Original Intent and the Seventeenth Amendment.* New Brunswick, NJ: Transaction.

Swift, Elaine. 1993. "The Making of an American House of Lords: The U.S. Senate in the Constitutional Convention of 1787." *Studies in American Political Development* 7 (Fall): 177–224.

Wirls, Daniel, and Stephen Wirls. 2004. *The Invention of the United States Senate.* Baltimore, MD: Johns Hopkins University Press.

CONGRESS, SENATE, SIZE

The proposal for a bicameral Congress emerged from the Virginia Plan, which Edmund Randolph introduced on May 29. The plan did not initially designate the size of the upper house, or today's Senate, but its primary authors clearly envisioned that this body, which was designed to temper the passions of the lower house, would be smaller. On May 31, Randolph thus observed that in his opinion the second branch "ought to be much smaller than that of the first; so small as to be exempt from the passionate proceedings to which numerous assemblies are liable" (Farrand 1937, I, 51). Similarly, on June 7, James Madison, also from Virginia, argued that it was "inexpedient" to "admit into the Senate a very large number of members" (I, 151). He distinguished the House and Senate in this regard:

> The more the representatives of the people therefore were multiplied, the more they partook of the infirmaties of their constituents, the more liable they became to be divided among themselves either from their own indiscretions or the artifices of the opposite factions, and of course the less capable of fulfilling their trust. When the weight of a set of men depends merely on their personal characters; the greater the number the greater the weight. When it depends on the degree of political authority lodged in them the smaller the number the greater the weight. (I, 152)

The Virginia Plan had seemingly advocated proportional representation in both houses of Congress (with members of the first house—where states were represented according to population—choosing members of the second from among nominees made by the state legislatures and thus probably not guaranteeing that every state would have a Senate seat), but this goal seemed to conflict with the idea of keeping the Senate small. Significantly, when on May 31 North Carolina's Richard Spaight proposed that state legislatures elect senators, Rufus King of Massachusetts pointed out that the Senate would need to include 80 to 100 members to give every state legislature the choice of at least one senator, and Spaight withdrew his motion.

Not everyone thought that a large Senate was undesirable. On June 7, Delaware's John Dickinson said that he had no objection to a Senate composed of 80 members or even double this number (I, 150). By contrast, Hugh Williamson of North Carolina suggested that 25 would be a good number (a number that fell a single member short of the Senate's initial configuration).

Delegates offered a number of solutions during debates involving representation among the small states and the large ones that would have affected the size of the Senate. On June 7, South Carolina's Charles Pinckney proposed a plan whereby states would be divided into three classes, with each state being given one to three senators (I, 155). On June 30, Pennsylvania's James Wilson suggested that each state should have one senator per 100,000 inhabitants (by contrast, the House was to have no more than one representative for every 40,000 residents, a figure lowered on the last day of the Convention to 30,000), with each state having at least one (I, 488). Similarly, just days before the Great Compromise, Pinckney proposed that states be given from 1 to 5 votes each in the Senate, for a total number of senators at 36 (II, 5). Madison reported these numbers as follows: NH, 2; MA, 4; RI, 1; CT, 3; NY, 3; NJ, 2; PA, 4; DE, 1; MD, 3; VA, 5; NC, 3; SC, 3; GA, 3; total 36. In his address to the Maryland legislature after the Convention, Luther Martin reported a plan, also based on giving states from 1 to 5 votes, that would have resulted in 28 members (III, 177). Luther reports these numbers as: NH, 2; MA, 4; RI, 2; CT, 2; NY, 3; NJ, 1; PA, 4; DE, 1; MD, 2; VA, 5; NC, 2; SC, 2; GA, 1; total 28. Although it is possible that the delegates were reporting two different plans, it seems more likely that one or the other report, probably Martin's, was mistaken.

On July 23, the Convention returned to a discussion of the size of the Senate. A week earlier the Convention had agreed upon the Connecticut Compromise by which states were to be represented equally in that body. Delegates apparently feared that giving each state a single vote would make deliberation difficult; it would also leave states unrepresented in that body if their senator were absent (Wirls and Wirls 2004, 113). Pennsylvania's Gouverneur Morris accordingly proposed that each state should have three votes, with senators voting "per capita," that is, individually, instead of by state delegates as they had done under the Articles of Confederation. Morris reasoned that two members per state would allow too few men to constitute a quorum. Nathaniel Gorham of Massachusetts, however, favored two members per state as resulting in an overall number that would be more easily able to settle on matters of war and peace. He also observed that new states would be entering the Union, and some of the larger states might be divided, resulting in larger numbers of senators in the future. Virginia's George Mason also thought a Senate composed of three members from each state would be too numerous and would result in unneeded expense. Williamson thought it would be more difficult for distant states to send three senators. The motion for three senators was rejected, with only Pennsylvania voting in its favor, and the proposal for two senators per state was unanimously adopted (II, 94). Although Maryland's Luther Martin objected that per capita voting undermined the idea that states would be represented by states, the Convention approved of such voting with only Luther's home state in dissent.

Consistent with the desires of those who authored the Virginia Plan, the Senate was smaller than the House. In the first Senate created under the Constitution, there were 65 representatives and 26 senators. Today there are 435 voting mem-

bers in the House of Representatives and 100 senators. From 1776 to 1876 the average size of state senates, in those states that had them, had increased from 16 to 20 (Kromkowski 2002, 231).

See Also Congress, House of Representatives, Size; Connecticut Compromise

FOR FURTHER READING

Farrand, Max, ed. 1937. *The Records of the Federal Convention.* 4 vols. New Haven, CT: Yale University Press.

Kromkowski, Charles A. 2002. *Recreating the American Republic: Rules of Apportionment, Constitutional Change, and American Political Development, 1700–1860.* Cambridge: Cambridge University Press.

Wirls, Daniel. 2003. "Madison's Dilemma: Revisiting the Relationship between the Senate and the 'Great Compromise' at the Constitutional Convention." In Samuel Kernell, ed., *James Madison: The Theory and Practice of Republican Government.* Palo Alto, CA: Stanford University Press.

Wirls, Daniel, and Stephen Wirls. 2004. *The Invention of the United States Senate.* Baltimore, MD: Johns Hopkins University Press.

CONGRESS, SENATE, TERMS

The Virginia Plan had proposed that Congress be divided into two houses rather than continuing as a unicameral institution like that under the Articles of Confederation. Delegates reasoned that if Congress were to be entrusted with more powers, it would also need to have greater protections. They thought the Senate, generally conceived as a smaller and wiser body, would put the brakes on measures that were passed too precipitously by the House. One way to insulate the Senate from day-to-day political pressures and to provide greater stability to the system as a whole (Hammond and Miller 1987, 1156) was to give its members longer terms than those for the House, whose terms were eventually set at two years, and even for the president, whose term was set at four.

North Carolina's Richard Spaight appears to have been the first to suggest a term for members of the Senate. On June 12, he proposed that this term be set at seven years. Roger Sherman of Connecticut thought this was too long, reasoning that individuals who were not doing well should be replaced before this time whereas others could be reelected. He suggested a five-year term, as being set midway between the anticipated term of the executive—then generally contemplated at seven years—and the term of the House. Georgia's William Pierce proposed a three-year term and noted the alarm that the English septennial act, providing for seven-year terms, had provoked. By contrast, Virginia's Edmund Randolph thought a seven-year term was a necessary guard against "The Democratic licentiousness of the State Legislatures" (I, 218). Similarly, Virginia's James Madison concurred in the desirability of such a term to give the government due "stability" (I, 218). The Convention accepted this term by a vote of 8-1-2.

The Convention resumed consideration of Senate terms on June 25, with Nathaniel Gorham of Massachusetts then suggesting a four-year term, with one-fourth of the members to be rotated out each year (I, 408). Randolph liked the idea of rotation but still favored a seven-year term. North Carolina's Hugh Williamson suggested that six years would be a more convenient number for rotation purposes, and Roger Sherman (who had previously supported a five-year term) seconded this suggestion and moved to strike the seven-year provision. The Convention agreed to this by a 7-3-1 vote but then split 5-5-1 both on the question of a six-year term and a five-year term.

The Convention revisited the issue the next day, with Gorham proposing and Pennsylvania's James Wilson now seconding the six-year term. General Pinckney of South Carolina opposed this in favor of a four-year term. He feared that delegates, especially from distant states, would settle in the capital and develop interests different from those of the states that they represented. This argument apparently had little effect on Delaware's George Read and Jacob Broom who proposed a nine-year term but actually favored service "during good behavior" (I, 421), a proposal that New York's Alexander Hamilton, who wanted the Senate to be as aristocratic as possible, had made earlier. Madison launched into an extended speech favoring such a term as providing sufficient "wisdom & virtue" to the Senate but suggesting that members "should not commence till such a period of life as would render a perpetual disqualification to be re-elected little inconvenient either in a public or private view" (I, 423). Sherman favored more frequent elections and advocated a term of four or six years. Similarly, Elbridge Gerry of Massachusetts favored a term of four to five years. Wilson observed that senators would be making decisions in regard to both internal and external affairs. He thought a longer term would be especially helpful in providing respectability for members dealing with the latter and proposed a nine-year term with one-third being rotated every three years. The Convention then appears to have voted 8-3 in favor of a nine-year term and 7-4 in favor of a six-year term, each proposal calling for one-third of the membership to go out triennially (I, 426).

On July 2, Gouverneur Morris delivered an extended speech on behalf of a more aristocratic Senate in which he favored giving members a life term in order to give them adequate independence. Morris did not, however, make any specific motion on the subject, and the Convention does not appear to have taken this suggestion seriously.

The Convention thus discussed proposals for senatorial terms of three years, four years, five years, seven years, nine years, and good behavior. The term of six years on which the Convention settled was longer than that for either members of the House or the president. By choosing an even number of years, elections would fall in years in which members of the House and presidents would be selected. Senators would be accountable to the state legislatures that selected them, but they would presumably have greater leeway than would members of the other branch.

During the debates over ratification of the Constitution, Antifederalists argued that the Senate was too aristocratic. The Federalists arguably agreed in part with this critique by highlighting the wisdom and stability that this institution would bring to the new government (Rohr 1986, 33).

See Also Congress, House of Representatives, Terms; President, Term, Length, and Re-eligibility

FOR FURTHER READING

Hammond, Thomas H., and Gary J. Miller. 1987. "The Core of the Constitution." *American Political Science Review* 82 (December): 1155–1174.

Malbin, Michael J. 1986. American Political Science Association, American Historical Association. *this Constitution: Our Enduring Legacy.* "Framing a Constitution to Channel Ambition." Washington, DC: Congressional Quarterly, 55–72.

Rohr, John A. 1986. *To Run a Constitution: The Legitimacy of the Administrative State.* Lawrence: University Press of Kansas.

Wirls, Daniel, and Stephen Wirls. 2004. *The Invention of the United States Senate.* Baltimore, MD: Johns Hopkins University Press.

CONGRESS, TIME AND FREQUENCY OF MEETINGS

It was not until the Convention discussed the report of the Committee of Detail that it began to consider the time and frequency of congressional meetings (Hutchinson 1975, 57). This report proposed that the Congress would meet yearly on the first Monday in December.

On August 7, Virginia's James Madison inquired as to the specificity of this proposal, suggesting that it would be more appropriate for Congress to set such a date by law rather than stipulate such a date within the Constitution. Pennsylvania's Gouverneur Morris and South Carolina's Charles Pinckney agreed, with the former doubting even whether it would be necessary for Congress to meet yearly. By contrast Nathaniel Gorham, joined by Connecticut's delegate Oliver Ellsworth and Pennsylvania's James Wilson, thought that states would not be able to adjust their elections unless they knew when Congress would meet. Gorham further argued that at least one yearly meeting was required in order to

serve "as a check on the Executive department" (Farrand 1937, II, 198). By contrast, Rufus King of Massachusetts thought that yearly sessions would lead to unnecessary legislation; once Congress regulated commerce and revenue, he anticipated that it would have little to do.

James Madison foresaw practical problems with mandating a specific date within the Constitution. In cases where special sessions were required, one Congress might be just adjourning when the Congress mandated that another be called. He favored requiring an annual meeting, "but did not wish to make two unavoidable" (II, 198). Fellow Virginian Mason joined Madison in favoring an annual meeting but in opposing a constitutionally specified time. Unlike King, he anticipated that both the size of the country and the need for Congress to exercise its "inquisitorial powers" (presumably its powers of investigation, which are not directly specified within the Constitution) would give Congress plenty of business (II, 199). Connecticut's Roger Sherman favored fixing the time and frequent meetings of Congress. Indicating that he did not think that the Constitution should specify such a time but that some arrangement needed to be made prior to the first meeting of Congress, Edmund Randolph proposed modifying the provision for a meeting on the first Monday in December by allowing Congress to set a different date at its discretion. Seconded by Madison, the Convention adopted this motion by a vote of 8-2.

Gouverneur Morris of Pennsylvania then proposed setting the first meeting in May rather than in December. He observed that decisions in Europe were often made in the winter, and this would give Congress a chance to respond to such developments. Madison seconded the motion while noting that the weather would make May a more convenient time for travel. James Wilson, by contrast, thought the winter was more appropriate for business, and Connecticut's Oliver Ellsworth noted that many members of Congress would be involved in agriculture and that attending Congress in May would interfere with their private business. Randolph thought the December meeting would better accommodate the times that state legislatures met, and the Convention defeated Morris's motion to substitute May for December by a vote of 8-2.

Section 2 of the Twentieth Amendment, ratified in 1933 and designed to deal with the problem of "lame-duck" legislators, has subsequently altered the date. It provided that "The Congress shall assemble at least once in every year, and such meeting shall begin at noon on the 3d day of January, unless they shall by law appoint a different day."

See Also Committee of Detail

FOR FURTHER READING

Farrand, Max, ed. 1937. *The Records of the Federal Convention*. 4 vols. New Haven, CT: Yale University Press.
Hutchinson, David. 1975. *The Foundations of the Constitution*. Secaucus, NJ: University Books.

CONGRESS, TIMES, PLACES, AND MANNERS OF ELECTION

A provision for allowing state legislatures to set the "times and places and manner of holding election of each House" subject to alterations by Congress emerged from the Committee of Detail on August 6 (Farrand 1937, I, 179). The Convention debated this provision, which became Clause 1 of Article I, Section 4, on August 9.

At that time, Virginia's James Madison and Pennsylvania's Gouverneur Morris moved to substitute a reference to the House of Representatives for both houses. They reasoned that the state legislatures would effectively set their own election standards in choosing senators. The Convention rejected this motion without recorded debate.

Charles Pinckney and John Rutledge, both of South Carolina, subsequently moved that congressional supervening authority over this process be renounced, leaving elections totally in the hands of the states. Nathaniel Gorham of Massachusetts, James Madison, Rufus King of Massachusetts, and Gouverneur Morris all disagreed with Connecticut's Roger Sherman, who thought such a provision to be unnecessary but innocuous. Madison argued that, without such oversight, states might abuse their powers. He further observed that there was nothing to fear from Congress, since its members were drawn from the states. King feared that without such powers, Congress might find it difficult to judge disputed elections. Morris expressed apprehensions that, without such oversight, the states might make "false" returns (II, 241). The Convention thus rejected the motion offered by Pinckney and Rutledge, providing a major source of criticism during state ratification debates (Warren 1928, 408–410).

In a subsequent decision, the Court allowed Congress not only to "alter" but also to "make" provision for elections. Madison explained that this alteration was designed to allow Congress to "make regulations in case the States should fail or refuse altogether" (II, 242).

See Also Committee of Detail

FOR FURTHER READING

Farrand, Max, ed. 1937. *The Records of the Federal Convention*. 4 vols. New Haven, CT: Yale University Press.
Warren, Charles. 1928. *The Making of the Constitution*. Boston: Little, Brown.

CONGRESS, WAR POWERS

See WAR POWERS OF CONGRESS

CONGRESSIONAL CALL FOR CONSTITUTIONAL CONVENTION

When delegates from five states met at the Annapolis Convention in September 1787, they sent a letter to state governors and to Congress requesting that states appoint commissioners to meet on the second Monday in May. Its purpose was

> to devise such further provisions as shall appear to them necessary to render the constitution of the Foederal Government adequate to the exigencies of the Union; and to report such an Act for that purpose to the United States in Congress Assembled as well, when agreed to by them, and afterwards confirmed by the Legislatures of every State will effectively provide for the same. (Jensen 1976, 184–185)

Virginia authorized its delegation to the Convention on November 23, 1786. Much as he had done when he headed the delegation that called on an earlier occasion for the convening of the Annapolis Convention, Governor Edmund Randolph circulated this call for a constitutional convention to other states.

The document was notable for its explanation of why a convention was a preferable institution to Congress. It explained that Congress "might be too much interrupted by the ordinary business before them and where it would besides be deprived of the valuable counsels of sundry individuals, who are disqualified by the Constitution or Laws of particular States, or restrained by peculiar circumstances from a seat in that Assembly" (Jensen 1976, 176). The document is also notable for both its eloquent call for patriotism and its description of the need for action:

> the crisis is arrived at which the good people of America are to decide the solemn question, whether they will by wise and magnanimous efforts reap the just fruits of that Independence, which they have so gloriously acquired, and of that Union which they have cemented with so much of their common blood; or whether by giving way to unmanly jealousies and prejudices, or to partial and transitory interests, they will renounce the auspicious blessings prepared for them by the Revolution, and furnish to its enemies an eventual triumph over those by whose virtue and valour it has been accomplished. (Jensen, 197)

By February 1787, six states had heeded the call to appoint delegates. Undoubtedly prodded by unrest related to Shays's Rebellion in Massachusetts, a committee that Congress had appointed to consider the report of the Annapolis Convention voted by a narrow one-vote margin on February 19, 1787, to recommend that Congress accept the call of the Annapolis Convention. Congress considered this proposal on February 21, 1787, initially rejecting a request by the New York delegation that appeared designed to allow Congress to call its own convention at an unspecified time and place (rather than at Philadelphia on the second Monday in May) and instead adopted by a vote of 8-1 a Massachusetts resolution that more closely tracked the call of the Annapolis Convention. It is fascinating that Virginia's James Madison voted for the New York resolution, explaining that he "considered it susceptible of amendment when brought before Congress, and that if Congress interposed in the matter at all it would be well for them to do it at the instance of a state, rather than spontaneously" (Jensen, 189). It further appears from Madison's own notes of the event that he further doubted the friendliness of Nathan Dane, who sponsored the Massachusetts resolution, to a convention (189).

Although his observations may in part have reflected his own hopes for a stronger national authority, Madison's notes of the congressional debates further indicated that "It appeared from the debates and still more from the conversation among the members that many of them considered this resolution as a deadly blow to the existing Confederation." Citing Dr. William Samuel Johnson's concerns on this point, Madison observed that "Others viewed it in the same light, but were pleased with it as the harbinger of a better Confederation" (189).

After the congressional call, six additional states appointed delegates to the Constitutional Convention. Although some states might have appointed delegates anyway, congressional approval certainly helped add further legitimacy to what would otherwise have been a completely extralegal meeting. The Constitutional Convention reported its handiwork back to Congress without, however, either requiring its approval or following the process for constitutional amendment specified under the Articles of Confederation.

See Also Annapolis Convention; Articles of Confederation; Ratification in the States; Shays's Rebellion

FOR FURTHER READING

Jensen, Merrill, ed. 1976. *The Documentary History of the Ratification of the Constitution.* Vol. 1 of *Constitutional Documents and Records, 1776–1787.* Madison: State Historical Society of Wisconsin.

Rakove, Jack N. 1979. *The Beginnings of National Politics: An Interpretive History of the Continental Congress.* New York: Alfred A. Knopf.

CONNECTICUT

At the time of the American Revolution, Connecticut readopted the charter that Charles II had given to a group of merchants in 1662 (it was essentially a reiteration of the Fundamental Orders of Connecticut, often regarded as one of the first constitutions in America, which representatives from Connecticut and New Haven had approved on January 14, 1639) and simply deleted references to the king. This constitution remained in effect until 1818.

Politics within the State

In contrast to most other colonies, the people annually elected their governor, deputy governor, and their 12 assistants. The state's governor had favored the Patriot cause in the conflict with England and had been reelected when the state joined others in declaring its independence. Freemen with property selected delegates to the House of Representatives every six months. The legislature, in turn, selected judges annually, and freemen in the towns chose municipal officers annually. The Connecticut Constitution vested primary powers in the legislature. The governor's power came primarily from his power of persuasion.

Connecticut had a unique electoral system whereby voters wrote the name of the individual they most favored for governor on a piece of paper, and the legislature chose from among them. This system tended to favor a few prominent families who were often able to hold power for many decades. Such families were linked through education at elite schools and through intermarriage and were tied to members of the "Standing Order," consisting of prominent Congregational clergymen.

A gap between eastern and western parts of the state had emerged in the 1750s. At that time, easterners had organized the Susquehannah Company and settled in the Wyoming Valley over the opposition of both Connecticut westerners and residents of Pennsylvania. Easterners largely led the opposition to the British. Economically, the Revolutionary War proved to be a boon to the state, which was a major source of supplies, although it sometimes led to tension between the state's farmers and merchants.

Although the electoral system usually returned the same individuals for office, it still provided a "safety valve" that helped avoid disturbances like Shays's Rebellion in nearby Massachusetts by allowing voters to express sentiments at polling booths that might otherwise have broken out into violence. Economically and socially, the state was fairly homogenous, with some division tied to those areas of the state initially tied to Hartford and those tied to New Haven (the former being more favorable and the latter less favorable to the new Constitution). Under the Articles of Confederation, members of the state had been quite concerned about the congressional promise to pay Continental army officers half-pay for life. The subsequent organization of the Society of the Cincinnati, which included 250 Connecticut officers, also stirred some fears. Although Connecticut had been willing to approve congressional trade regulation and increased revenue powers for Congress, it had made it clear that it did not want these revenues to go to officer salaries. Faced with congressional requisitions, the state legislature instructed the governor in 1786 to indicate that, although the state was attached to the Union, it had no money to pay (Jensen 1978, 324). Interestingly, Connecticut was the only state delegation to vote against calling the Constitutional Convention (Collier 1988, 101).

Representation and Discussion at the Convention

Connecticut may have been the most ably represented of the small states at the Constitutional Convention. Its delegates included Oliver Ellsworth, William Samuel Johnson, and Roger Sherman—the latter had replaced Erastus Wolcott after he expressed fear that he might get smallpox in Philadelphia. In addition, Abraham Baldwin, who represented Georgia, had recently immigrated there from Connecticut and thus provided a critical link to the Southern states. Although Ellsworth left the Convention early and did not sign the document, all three Connecticut delegates supported the Constitution, and they gave their name to the compromise that settled the controversy over representation between the large and the small states.

On June 19, Virginia's James Madison observed that the delegates to Congress from Connecticut and Rhode Island were chosen not by the state legislatures, as in other states, but directly by the people (Farrand 1937, I, 314). Two days later, Madison cited Connecticut as a state in which all the townships had incorporated and had certain "limited jurisdiction" (I, 357). On June 26, Roger Sherman used his own state, where elections were frequent, to indicate that such elections did not necessarily lead to governmental instability (I, 423). Alexander Hamilton, in turn, indicated that government "had entirely given way to the people, and had in fact suspended many of its ordinary functions in order to prevent those turbulent scenes which had appeared elsewhere" (I, 425). Seemingly directing a question to Connecticut's Sherman, Hamilton asked, "whether the State at this time, dare impose & collect a tax on ye people?" (I, 425). When on June 30, Madison accused

Connecticut of not meeting its financial requisitions under the Articles of Confederation, Ellsworth responded that "the State was entirely federal in her disposition" and that she had fielded more troops during the Revolutionary War than had Virginia. He observed that, if the state had been delinquent in its payments, "it had been from inability, and not more so than other States" (I, 487).

Ratification of the Constitution

Governor Samuel Huntington followed the lead of Connecticut's representatives to the Constitutional Convention in advocating ratification of the Constitution. Roger Sherman and Oliver Ellsworth both published articles in the newspapers favoring the Constitution, and press coverage was almost uniformly positive. All three of Connecticut's representatives to the Constitutional Convention also attended the ratifying convention. Some scholars believe that the Connecticut delegates to the Constitutional Convention portrayed the document as giving greater deference to state sovereignty than it actually did. One scholar has even asserted: "It was this misperceived version of the new government that was sold to the Connecticut convention that ratified a document which would have been drummed out of the state if Hamilton's or Madison's or even Elbridge Gerry's or Luther Martin's version had come to light in Hartford" (Collier 1988, 107).

In any event, Connecticut became the fifth state to ratify the Constitution, which it did by a vote of 128 to 40 on January 9, 1788. Ratification appears to have stemmed chiefly from deference to state leaders, who almost uniformly favored the new Constitution. Connecticut residents living near Rhode Island overwhelmingly favored the Constitution, in part because Rhode Island had been forcing out-of-state creditors to accept the state's devalued paper money while refusing to accept payment in the same (Lutz 1989, 133), and the new Constitution prohibited the issuance of such money. Similarly, Connecticut citizens living near New York were especially favorable to the new Constitution because they realized that any imposts on state exports would now go into national coffers rather than, as previously, into New York's. As indicated above, sections of the state tied more closely to New Haven than to Hartford accounted for a disproportionate share of the votes that were cast against ratification.

With its ratification of the Constitution, Connecticut became a relatively strong Federalist stronghold for almost 30 years. In 1818, it adopted a new constitution that leaned more in the Republican direction.

See Also Baldwin, Abraham; Ellsworth, Oliver; Johnson, William Samuel; Ratification in the States; Sherman, Roger; Society of the Cincinnati

FOR FURTHER READING

Collier, Christopher. 2003. *All Politics Is Local: Family, Friends, and Provincial Interests in the Creation of the Constitution.* Hanover, NH: University Press of New England.

——. 1988. "Sovereignty Finessed: Roger Sherman, Oliver Ellsworth, and the Ratification of the Constitution in Connecticut." In Patrick T. Conley and John P. Kaminski, eds., *The Constitution and the States: The Role of the Original Thirteen in the Framing and Adoption of the Federal Constitution.* Madison, WI: Madison House, 93–112.

Farrand, Max, ed. 1937. *The Records of the Federal Convention.* 4 vols. New Haven, CT: Yale University Press.

"Fundamental Orders of Connecticut." *The American Republic: Primary Sources.* Ed. Bruce Frohnen. Indianapolis, IN: Liberty Fund, 12–14.

Jensen, Merrill, ed. 1978. *Ratification of the Constitution by the States Delaware, New Jersey, Georgia, Connecticut.* Vol. 3 of *The Documentary History of the Ratification of the Constitution.* Madison: State Historical Society of Wisconsin.

Lutz, Donald S. 1989. " Connecticut: Achieving Consent and Assuring Control." In Michael Allen Gillespie and Michael Lienesch, eds., *Ratifying the Constitution.* Lawrence: University Press of Kansas.

Steiner, Bernard C. 1915. *Connecticut's Ratification of the Federal Constitution.* Worcester, MA: American Antiquarian Society.

CONNECTICUT COMPROMISE

The issue of representation in Congress proved to be one of the most divisive issues at the U.S. Constitutional Convention. In contrast to the Articles of Confederation, in which states were equally represented in a unicameral Congress, the Virginia Plan, which was the first to be introduced at the Constitutional Convention, proposed a bicameral Congress in which states would be represented according to population in both houses. It is not entirely clear whether this hope would have been carried out in practice since under the original Virginia Plan, members of the House were to elect members of the Senate from nominees suggested by the state legislatures, and the number of senators contemplated appears to have been so small that it is not clear that each state would have had representation there.

In any event, debate over representation largely pitted the most populous states (usually designated as the large states), who favored representation in both houses of Congress on the basis of population, against members of the less populous or small states, who favored either continuing the system of equal representation under the Articles of Confederation or providing that such a method would at least be used for the Senate. Large-state advocates generally argued for the justice of using democratic principles of representation. Small-state advocates argued both for preserving their existing prerogatives under the Articles of Confederation and for allowing states to protect themselves as states.

Within two days after Randolph introduced the Virginia Plan on May 29, Roger Sherman of Connecticut (considered to be a small state) had suggested that the states should be equally represented within the Senate (Farrand 1937, I, 52). On June 11, he further linked this proposal to the idea of representation by population in the House, an idea that was seconded by his fellow Connecticut delegate, Oliver Ellsworth. The Convention rejected the proposal.

Although it was not the only difference, the central impetus for William Paterson's introduction of the New Jersey Plan on June 15 appears to have been his desire to keep the equal state representation for the states. Indeed, the judgment may have been overly harsh, but Charles Pinckney of South Carolina charged on the next day that "the whole comes to this. . . . Give N. Jersey an equal vote, and she will dismiss her scruples, and concur in the Natil. system" (I, 255). The New Jersey Plan initially failed, and the Committee of the Whole voted on June 19 to proceed with its consideration of the Virginia Plan.

Nonetheless, on June 29, Ellsworth reintroduced the earlier compromise that he and Roger Sherman had formulated:

> He hoped it would become a ground of compromise with regard to the 2d branch. We were partly national; partly federal. The proportional representation in the first branch was conformable to the national principle & would secure the large States agst. the small. An equality of voices was conformable to the federal principle and was necessary to secure the Small States agst. the large. He trusted that on this middle ground a compromise would take place. He did not see that it could on any others. And if no compromise should take place, our meeting would not only be in vain but worse than in vain. (I, 469)

It took until July 16 for the Congress to accept this idea, but it became the basis for an eventual compromise. In the meantime, Ellsworth had served on the Committee of Eleven that had been proposed to come up with a compromise on July 2 (Committee of Compromise on Representation in Congress), and Roger Sherman had served on a second Committee to Reconsider Representation in the House appointed on July 9.

Because of the role that Sherman and Ellsworth played, the compromise on representation in Congress, often simply called the Great Compromise, is also known as the Connecticut Compromise.

See Also Compromise; Congress, House of Representatives, Representation in; Congress, Senate, Representation in; New Jersey Plan; Virginia Plan

FOR FURTHER READING

Collier, Christopher. 1971. *Roger Sherman's Connecticut: Yankee Politics and the American Revolution.* Middleton, CT: Wesleyan University Press.

Dromkowski, Charles A. 2002. *Recreating the American Republic: Rules of Apportionment, Constitutional Change, and American Political Development, 1700–1870.* Cambridge: Cambridge University Press.

Farrand, Max, ed. 1937. *The Records of the Federal Convention.* 4 vols. New Haven, CT: Yale University Press.

Rakove, Jack N. 1987. "The Great Compromise: Ideas, Interests, and the Politics of Constitution Making." *William and Mary Quarterly*, 3rd ser. 44 (July): 424–457.

Zagarri, Rosemarie. 1987. *The Politics of Size: Representation in the United States, 1776–1850.* Ithaca, NY: Cornell University Press.

CONSTITUTION, DOCUMENT, PHYSICAL LOCATION OF

See NATIONAL ARCHIVES

CONSTITUTION, UNITED STATES

See U.S. CONSTITUTION

CONSTITUTIONAL CONVENTION MECHANISM

Americans more or less take it for granted that the U.S. Constitution was formulated by the Convention that met in Philadelphia and subsequently ratified by conventions in the states. However, the development of the Convention represented a unique achievement. Because thinkers of the day associated conventions with the people themselves, conventions had the authority to formulate new institutions and to divide power between existing institutions (for example, the nation and the states) in a manner that these individual institutions might not have been able to do on their own.

The Articles of Confederation were drafted in Congress (1777) and ratified by state legislatures (1781). When the American Revolution against Great Britain began in 1776, the Second Continental Congress encouraged states to rewrite their constitutions and most did so. Initially, state legislatures wrote most such constitutions. These legislatures suffered from a number of disadvantages. Not only did they have plenty of other business to do, which made it difficult to devote adequate time to constitution-making, but the people had not elected legislators for the purpose of rewriting the Constitution. Moroever, over time, critics, who envisioned the law of the Constitution as superior to other laws, questioned the authority of such bodies to adopt constitutional changes. How would such constitutions be any different than any other acts of ordinary legislation, which one legislature could enact and another repeal? If constitutions were no different from ordinary laws, what gave them special "constitutional" status, or status as "higher law"? Thomas Jefferson raised such points when he critiqued the constitution in Virginia in his *Notes on the State of Virginia* (1964, 115–119).

The term "convention" originated in England and initially referred simply to a meeting, often one outside duly constituted authority (Wood 1969, 310). Many such meetings were held throughout the colonies in the events leading up to the American Revolution, when existing institutions were often considered tainted by their association with the British Crown. Although some conventions were little more than mobs (conventions played a key role in the later events leading up to Shays's Rebellion), many were the locus of principled opposition to British policies.

Over time, the new states began to recognize the authority of such conventions, specifically elected by the people, apart from the legislature, to draw up state constitutions. The people, in turn, voted to accept or reject the work of such conventions, thus grounding the work of these conventions, as Jefferson had proclaimed (in the Declaration of Independence) that governments should be instituted, in "the consent of the governed." Massachusetts (1780) and New Hampshire (1781) were the first to propose and ratify new constitutions under this theory.

Although the Constitutional Convention of 1787 was originally called to revise and enlarge the Articles of Confederation, its members could justify its actions on the basis that they were recommendatory only and would not become final until ratified by the people; delegates were not in Philadelphia to "decide" but simply to "propose." Thus, when the Convention was debating whether to proceed with the Virginia Plan, the New Jersey Plan, or another, Alexander Hamilton was recorded as saying, "We can only propose and recommend—the power of ratifying or rejecting is still in the states" (Farrand 1937, I, 295). On July 23, Madison said that "the difference between a system founded on the Legislatures only, and one founded on the people, to be the true difference between a league or treaty and a *Constitution*" (II, 93). Late in the Convention Madison continued to insist on popular ratification:

> The people were in fact, the fountain of all power, and by resorting to them, all difficulties were got over. They could alter constitutions as they pleased. It was a principle in the Bills of rights, that first principles might be resorted to. (II, 476)

There is evidence from the debates that the idea of approving constitutions by conventions, rather than by state legislatures, was still evolving, and that not all delegates thought it was necessary. Thus, on July 23, Connecticut's Oliver Ellsworth observed that "a new sett of ideas seemed to have crept in since the articles of Confederation were established. [Prior to this] The Legislatures were considered as competent" (II, 91).

Had the Convention followed the procedure under the Articles of Confederation, the new

Constitution would have to have been accepted by Congress and unanimously ratified by the state legislatures. The delegates bypassed these mechanisms and specified that the Constitution would go into effect when ratified by conventions in nine or more states—such a ratifying convention mechanism was part of the original Virginia Plan (I, 22). Delegates thus bypassed legislative bodies slated to have their power diminished (for an articulation of this and other reasons for bypassing the existing Congress, see speech by Nathaniel Gorham on July 23 at II, 90) and rated approval of state conventions formed for this purpose as equivalent to the approval of the people themselves.

In devising procedures for amending the Constitution once it was established, the delegates provided a mechanism by which two-thirds of the states could petition Congress to call a special convention for the purpose of proposing amendments. To date, all amendments adopted since 1787 have utilized the alternate mechanisms outlined in Article V of the Constitution for proposal by two-thirds majorities in both houses of Congress and ratification by three-fourths of the states. James Madison and other Federalists worked hard to see that appropriate congressional majorities proposed and that appropriate state legislative majorities ratified the first 10 amendments, the Bill of Rights, rather than relying on a second convention, which they feared might undo the work of the first to propose these amendments or state conventions to approve them.

Especially in light of some claims that state constitutional conventions have made to be paramount to state legislative authority, some scholars have attempted to distinguish the Revolutionary Conventions that appeared during the conflict with England from Constitutional Conventions that are called under the authority of, and might therefore be considered subordinate to, the legislatures that called them (Jameson 1887, 6–10). Questions still remain as to the authority of a Constitutional Convention called under authority of Article V, but there is general agreement that nothing that such a convention proposed would become law until appropriately ratified.

See Also Amending Process; Bill of Rights; Ratification in the States; State Constitutions

FOR FURTHER READING

Adams, Willi Paul. 2001. *The First American Constitutions: Republican Ideology and the Making of the State Constitutions in the Revolutionary Era.* Lanham, MD: Rowman and Littlefield Publishers.
Farrand, Max, ed. 1937. *The Records of the Federal Convention.* 4 vols. New Haven, CT: Yale University Press.
Jameson, John A. 1887. *A Treatise on Constitutional Conventions: Their History, Powers, and Modes of Proceeding.* 4th ed. Chicago: Callaghan and Company. Reprinted in New York: Da Capo, 1974.
Jefferson, Thomas. 1964. *Notes on the State of Virginia.* New York: Harper and Row, Publishers.
Palmer. R. R. 1959. *The Age of the Democratic Revolution: A Political History of Europe and America, 1760–1800.* Volume I: *The Challenge.* Princeton, NJ: Princeton University Press.
Weber, Paul J., and Barbara A. Perry. 1989. *Unfounded Fears: Myths and Realities of a Constitutional Convention.* New York: Praeger.
Wood, Gordon S. 1969. *The Creation of the American Republic, 1776–1787.* Chapel Hill: University of North Carolina Press.

CONSTITUTIONAL MOMENTS

Bruce Ackerman, Sterling Professor of Law and Political Science at Yale University, has formulated a theory in which he has argued that the United States is a "dualist democracy" in which periods of ordinary politics are interrupted from time to time by periods of intense constitutional lawmaking, or constitutional moments. Ackerman believes that there have been three such moments in American history—the U.S. Constitutional Convention of 1787, the post–Civil War era in which the Thirteenth through Fifteenth Amendments were ratified, and the New Deal era, in which notions of a more expansive role for government was accepted. He contends that there have been other examples of failed constitutional moments.

Ackerman believes that during "constitutional moments" of "higher lawmaking," leaders sometimes ignore existing constitutional mechanisms. He thus joins scholars who have pointed to many of the extralegal or illegal features of the Constitutional Convention, which bypassed the requirements under the Articles of Confederation that Congress propose amendments and that they be unanimously ratified by the states. Ackerman thus claims that "Illegality was a leitmotif at the Convention from first to last" (Ackerman 1998, 49). Ackerman further argues that constitutional moments are characterized by five phases–"signaling, proposing, triggering, ratifying, and consolidating their constitutional authority" (66–67).

Ackerman's theories are widely debated in the scholarly community. Although Ackerman describes the Constitutional Convention as being illegal (for a critique, see Rakove 1999), he, like earlier historians who stressed the period of the Articles of Confederation as a "critical period," affirms its importance both in constituting the nation and in establishing a precedent for not following precise forms when major constitutional changes need to be effected. Ackerman's theories thus have particular relevance for the understanding of Article V of the Constitution, which provides for an amending process.

See Also Amending Process; Constitutional Convention Mechanism; Critical Period; Founding; Legality of the Convention

FOR FURTHER READING

Ackerman, Bruce. 1991. *We the People: Foundations.* Cambridge, MA: Belknap Press of Harvard University Press.

———. 1998. *We the People: Transformations.* Cambridge, MA: Belknap Press of Harvard University Press.

Ackerman, Bruce, and Neal Katyal. 1995. "Our Unconventional Founding." *University of Chicago Law Review* 62 (Spring): 475–573.

Kay, Richard S. 1987. "The Illegality of the Constitution." *Constitutional Commentary* 4 (Winter): 57–80.

Rakove, Jack N. 1999. "The Super-Legality of the Constitution, or, a Federalist Critique of Bruce Ackerman's Neo-Federalism." *Yale Law Journal* 108 (June): 1931–1958.

CONSTITUTIONALISM

The idea of a written Constitution did not originate at the Constitutional Convention of 1787; it had many state models from which to draw. Still, this Convention has probably done as much as any similar body to advance the idea of constitutionalism, especially as embodied in a single written document. It is a not altogether accurate commonplace that Great Britain does not have a written constitution. It is more correct to say that Britain does not trace its founding to a single event and does not attempt to outline the structure of its government in a single written document unchangeable by ordinary legislative means, since written documents like the Magna Carta (1215) and the English Bill of Rights (1689) have clearly played an important part in English history (Vile 1998). Moreover, a nation of laws has a "constitution," or regularized way of doing things, even though it may not have a written document that it identifies as its "Constitution" (Harris 1993, 46). Larry Kramer thus observes that American colonists phrased their arguments against Great Britain in terms of a "customary constitution," or set of rights that they believed all Englishmen shared, long before states began replacing their charters with new constitutions (2004, 40–41).

Compacts and Charters

Donald Lutz, a student of American constitutionalism, has traced the concept of a Constitution to a number of related terms including the contract, the compact, and the covenant. A contract, like its modern legal counterpart, was a document outlining mutual responsibilities on a specific issue. A compact was "an agreement between a large group of people creating a new community

A Constitution for Prisoners

At the time the Constitution was written, individuals who were unable to pay their debts could be sent to prison—as Robert Morris who attended the Convention on behalf of Pennsylvania would later discover—where they were expected to provide for their own upkeep. The widespread influence of constitutionalism is evident by the fact that in the 1790s the debtors housed on a floor of the New Gaol in New York City, typically about 30 to 35 men, drew up a constitution by which to govern themselves. William Duer, whose speculations had led to panic in 1792, was one of the prison's more prominent residents.

Although no copy of the Constitution has remained, scholars know that it created a three-man "Supreme Court" and was designed "to promote good Will, and Harmony, amongst the Prisoners, and 'to punish those who infringe on the Law of the Police, or Endeaver to disturb the public Peace'" (quoted with original spelling in Mann, 1994, 187). Other officers included an attorney general, a sheriff, a clerk, wardens and stewards.

The government thus created disciplined its members, evoking what has been described as "both the seriousness of Congregational church discipline and the mock seriousness of private gentlemen's clubs" (Mann, 191). Many of those in prison probably came from members of the upper strata of society who had fallen upon hard times. Consistent with social contract thinking, the constitution was held to bind only those who, on entering the prison, gave their consent to it. Thus, the Supreme Court dismissed a complaint against an inmate named Hutchinson who had lice on the basis that he had not signed the constitution and was thus outside its jurisdiction.

In time, the idea of imprisoning debtors was discontinued in part because it rarely succeeded in the payment of the debt for which individuals had been imprisoned. Using its authority under Article I, Section 1, Congress passed the Bankruptcy Act of 1800, after which it is recorded that the debtors in New Gaol "held a meeting during which, 'after a rich repast of social conversation, on the prospect of returning to the world and the bosom of our relatives and friends,' they drank sixteen toasts 'to celebrate the auspicious event,'" toasts that were published in a contemporary newspaper called *Forlorn Hope* (Mann, 202).

FOR FURTHER READING

Mann, Bruce H. 1994. "Tales from the Crypt: Prison, Legal Authority, and the Debtors' Constitution in the Early Republic." *William and Mary Quarterly*, 3rd ser. 51 (April): 183–203.

based upon their own consent" (Lutz 1988, 17). A covenant was similar (the terminology was actually older), but had religious origins, and was generally sanctioned by a higher religious or civil authority (Lutz, 17). These notions were also related to the idea of a charter (as in the Magna Carta), or a patent, or authorization, often for a monopoly, from the sovereign (Lutz, 20).

A "constitution" was, in turn, a term related to the idea of "constituent, which refers to being formative, essential, characteristic, or distinctive"; Lutz observes that "it is more immediately drawn from *constitute,* to establish, ordain, or appoint in legal form and status" (21). Compacts and covenants often embodied frames of government, or constitutions. Lutz argues that what is today designated the U.S. Constitution is actually "a compact dominated by a constitution" (34).

Despite its current name, the Mayflower Compact (1620), with its appeal to religious authority, was an early covenant, and fairly closely followed the structure of church covenants of its day, which appear to have been a source of colonial ideas of self-government. The Fundamental Orders of Connecticut had a similar structure. Lutz notes that the road from covenant to compact was often associated with the process of secularization (28).

Charters authorized most of the colonies in America. Most such charters contained a fairly predictable set of elements. These included

> the creation or identification of a grantee; a statement of the reason for the grant; a statement of what was being granted; the license or exclusive use given by the grant; a statement of how the grant was to be administered; specific restrictions or limits on the grant; and the required duties owed the grantor by the grantee. (35)

In the dispute with England that led to the Revolutionary War, colonists often tried to claim rights on the basis of their charters. In the initial dispute between the colonies and England, some colonists used these grants to claim loyalty to the English king but not the English Parliament, whose sovereignty the colonists disputed on the basis that they were not represented there.

State Constitutions

When the Continental Congress declared its independence from England and began formulating the Articles of Confederation, it encouraged states to replace the charters that had been issued by the king with constitutions, and most did so. These constitutions, often circulated in written form (Baum and Fritz 2000), in turn provided laboratories, as they continue to do, for the Constitution that the Convention formulated in 1787. With their declarations of rights, many state constitutions also provided a model for the first 10 amendments or Bill of Rights. One significant aspect of this government is the division of power between state and national authorities known as federalism. This term comes from the word *"foedus,"* the Latin word for covenant (Lutz, 43). Although it is thus possible to trace the current American government to a document drawn up by a specific convention, the idea of embodying the fundamental law in a document that is superior to ordinary legislation and enforceable in court actually predates the 1787 Convention.

Limits of "Parchment Barriers"

Because it was recognized that a written constitution was but part of the idea of constitutionalism, from time to time the Framers either expressed skepticism of, or responded to those who expressed skepticism about, such documents. On June 30, after commenting on the articles of union between England and Scotland as an example of a successful arrangement, Rufus King of Massachusetts observed:

> He was aware that this will be called a mere *paper security*. He thought it a sufficient answer to say that if fundamental articles of compact, are no sufficient defence against physical power, neither will there be any safety agst. it if there be no compact. (I, 493)

Similarly, on August 14, Maryland's John Mercer observed:

> It is a great mistake to suppose that the paper we are to propose will govern the U. States? It is The men who it will bring into the Governt. and interest in maintaining it that is to govern them. The paper will only mark the mode & the form—Men are the substance and must do the business. All Govt. must be by force or influence. (II, 289)

Such concerns extended into the debates over the Bill of Rights. After Thomas Jefferson wrote to James Madison on December 20, 1787, indicating that "a bill of rights is what the people are entitled to against every government on earth, general or particular, and what no just government should refuse, or rest on inference," Madison responded that he had "never thought the omission a material defect" (Mason and Stephenson 2002, 421). He observed:

> Experience proves the inefficacy of a bill of rights on those occasions when its control is most needed. Repeated violations of these parchment barriers have been committed by overbearing majorities in every State. In Virginia I have seen the bill of rights violated in every instance where it has been opposed to a popular current. (422)

Somewhat more receptively, however, Madison observed that "The political truths declared in that solemn manner acquire by degrees the character of fundamental maxims of free Governments, and as they become incorporated with the national sentiment, counteract the impulses of interest and passion" (422; for Madison's views, also see Leibiger 1993). Jefferson, in turn, responded that "tho it is not absolutely efficacious under all circumstances, it is of great potency always, and rarely inefficacious." He further observed that "A brace the more will often keep up the building which would have fallen with that brace the less" and suggested that language in a bill of rights would give judges power to use such guarantees as legal checks (422). In introducing the Bill of Rights before the House of Representatives on June 8, 1789, Madison observed that while "it is true, there are a few particular States in which some of the most valuable articles have not, at one time or other, been violated . . . it does not follow but they may have, to a certain degree, a salutary effect against the abuse of power" (423). Such discussion indicates that the Framers often supported written constitutional guarantees while recognizing that such paper barriers would not always prove efficacious. Significantly, much of the Constitution consists less of the delineation of abstract rights than of the creation of specific institutions.

See Also Great Britain; Magna Carta; Mayflower Compact; State Constitutions

FOR FURTHER READING

Anastaplo, George. 2000. "Constitutionalism, The Rule of Rules: Explorations." *Brandeis Law Journal* 39 (Fall): 17–217.

Baum, Marsha L., and Christian G. Fritz. 2000. "American Constitution-Making: The Neglected State Constitutional Sources." *Hastings Constitutional Law Quarterly* 27 (Winter): 199–242.

Bellamy, Richard, and Dario Castiglione. 1997. "Constitutionalism and Democracy–Political Theory and the American Constitution." *British Journal of Political Science* 27 (October): 595–618.

Borgeaud, Charles. 1892. "The Origin and Development of Written Constitutions." *Political Science Quarterly* 7 (December): 613–632.

Elazar, Daniel J. 1980. "The Political Theory of Covenant: Biblical Origins and Modern Developments." *Publius* 10 (Fall): 3–30.

Ferguson, Robert A. 1987. "1787: The Constitution in Perspective: 'We Do Ordain and Establish': The Constitution as Literary Text." *William and Mary Law Review* 3 (Fall): 3–25.

Fritz, Christian G. 2004. "Fallacies of American Constitutionalism." *Rutgers Law Journal* 35 (Summer): 1327–1369.

Griffin, Stephen M. 1996. *American Constitutionalism: From Theory to Politics.* Princeton, NJ: Princeton University Press.

Hall, Kermit L., and James W. Ely Jr. 1989. *An Uncertain Tradition: Constitutionalism and the History of the South.* Athens: University of Georgia Press.

Harris, William F., II. 1993. *The Interpretable Constitution.* Baltimore, MD: Johns Hopkins University Press.

Kammen, Michael. 1985. *The Problem of Constitutionalism in American Culture.* Irving, TX: University of Dallas.

——. 1980. "From Covenant to Constitution in American Political Thought." *Publius* 10 (Fall): 101–135.

——. 1988. *The Origins of American Constitutionalism.* Baton Rouge: Louisiana State University Press.

Kramer, Larry D. 2004. *The People Themselves: Popular Constitutionalism and Judicial Review.* New York: Oxford University Press.

Leibiger, Stuart. 1993. "James Madison and Amendments to the Constitution, 1787–1789: 'Parchment Barriers.'" *Journal of Southern History* 59 (August): 441–468.

Lutz, Donald S. 1988. *The Origins of American Constitutionalism.* Baton Rouge: Louisiana State University Press.

Mason, Alpheus Thomas, and Donald Drier Stephenson, Jr. 2002. *American Constitutional Law: Introductory Essays and Selected Cases.* 13th ed. Upper Saddle River, NJ: Prentice Hall.

McDowell, Gary L. 1998. "The Language of Law and the Foundations of American Constitutionalism." *William and Mary Quarterly,* 3rd ser. 55 (July): 375–398.

Murphy, Walter F., James E. Fleming, Sotirious A. Barber, and Stephen Macedo. 2003. *American Constitutional Interpretation.* 3rd ed. New York: Foundation Press.

Pennock, J. Roland, and John W. Chapman, eds. *Constitutionalism.* New York: New York University Press, 1979.

Riemer, Neal. 1980. "Covenant and the Federal Constitution." *Publius* 10 (Fall): 135–148.

Rothman, Rozann. 1980. "The Impact of Covenant and Contract Theories on Conceptions of the U.S. Constitution." *Publius* 10 (Fall): 149–164.

Vile, John R. 1992. "Three Kinds of Constitutional Founding and Change: The Convention Method and Its Alternatives." *Political Research Quarterly* 46 (December): 881–895.

Vile, M. J. C. 1998. *Constitutionalism and the Separation of Powers.* 2nd ed. Indianapolis, IN: Liberty Fund.

CONTINENTAL CONGRESSES

Prior to the Revolutionary War period, state assemblies dealt directly with British authorities, most visibly represented by British-appointed governors. In 1765, 28 delegates from nine states met together in the Stamp Act Congress in New York City in order collectively to protest parliamentary taxation. Following this model, 12 of the states (all but Georgia) sent a total of 56 delegates to the First Continental Congress, which met in Philadelphia from September 5 to October 26, 1774, to protest the Coercive Acts. The most creative work of this body was the adoption of a "Declaration and Resolves" articulating colonial rights (see Solberg 1958, 10–15).

The First Continental Congress provided a further basis for the calling of a Second Continental Congress, which began meeting in May 1775, just a month after the initiation of hostilities with the British at Lexington and Concord. This Congress transformed itself from a petitioning into a lawmaking body. It encouraged states to rewrite their constitutions; appointed one of its members, George Washington, as commander-in-chief of the Patriot forces, oversaw the writing of the Declaration of Independence (signed by 56 members), sought foreign alliances to fight the British, and eventually approved the treaty that ended the Revolutionary War. The Second Continental Congress also appointed the committee that drafted the Articles of Confederation and sent it to the states for approval.

This document essentially formalized the ad hoc government that the Second Continental Congress had created, and that body thus continued to be called a Continental Congress up to the implementation of the U.S. Constitution, after which it was called the federal, or U.S., Congress. States could send from two to seven delegates to the Continental Congress but had an equal vote in this body regardless of population. Much like diplomats, members were appointed, paid, and subject to recall by state legislatures. They served one-year terms and were limited to serving for three years during any six-year period. Congress lacked specific power to regulate interstate commerce, and key votes required agreement by nine or more states. Amendments required unanimous state consent.

Consistent with Article II of the Articles, added in congressional debates at the insistence of Thomas Burke of North Carolina, primary powers remained vested in the individual states. Attendance in Congress was sporadic, often making it difficult to muster the required majorities; Delaware even resorted to appointing residents of Pennsylvania to represent it (Cress 1975). As part of a confederal government, Congress could request states to supply tax monies and armed forces but could not force them to do so.

Over time, leaders in Congress and elsewhere in the nation came to believe that the government was inadequate to the domestic and foreign needs of the time. Meeting in September 1786, delegates from five states attending the Annapolis Convention to deal with problems of trade under the Articles issued a call for a convention to address broader issues under the Articles. Prompted by similar resolutions from the states and by the perception that Congress was dealing ineffectually with Shays's Rebellion (winter of 1786–1787), on February 21, 1787, Congress joined the call for a convention. It proposed that delegates should meet in Philadelphia "for the sole and express purpose of revising the Articles of Confederation and reporting to Congress and the several legislatures such alterations and provisions therein as shall, when agreed to in Congress and confirmed by the states render the federal constitution adequate to the exigencies of Government and the preservation of the Union" (quoted in Solberg,

64). Thirty-nine of the 55 men who attended the Convention had served in one or both of the Continental Congresses, and some were members of the Second Continental Congress at the time of their service at the Convention. They undoubtedly drew from their experience as members of this body. Some members traveled from one body to the other. One of Congress's most important acts, the adoption of the Northwest Ordinance of 1787, which provided for government in the territories that states had ceded to the Union largely as a condition of ratification of the Articles, actually occurred during Convention proceedings and may or may not have been partially coordinated with compromises adopted at the Convention itself.

Delegates from Virginia began proceedings at the Constitutional Convention by introducing a bold plan introducing separate executive and judicial branches and dividing the unicameral Congress into two houses, thus aligning it more closely with the structure of most existing state legislatures. They also proposed that both houses would be apportioned according to population. The first house would be directly elected by the people and the second chosen by the first house from nominees introduced by state legislatures. This Congress would not only inherit the powers of the Second Continental Congress but would also have power "to legislate in all cases to which the separate States are incompetent, or in which the harmony of the United States may be interrupted by the exercise of individual Legislation" as well as having power "to negative all laws passed by the several States, contravening in the opinion of the National Legislature the articles of Union" (Farrand 1937, I, 21).

Not all provisions of the Virginia Plan survived. The convention thus eliminated the veto of state legislation, a Committee of Detail later substituted a list of enumerated powers for the broad authority proposed in the original Virginia Plan, and the Connecticut Compromise provided that states would retain equal representation in the U.S. Senate. When its work was completed, the Convention further decided to bypass the requirement for congressional approval and unanimous state legislative consent and specified that the new Constitution would go into effect when ratified by special conventions called within nine or more of the states. Influenced in part by members who came back to Congress from the Convention, Congress, in turn, transmitted the Constitution to the states for approval without either opposing or specifically commending it. The Continental Congresses ceased with the inauguration of the government under the new Constitution.

See Also Annapolis Convention; Articles of Confederation; Declaration of Independence; Northwest Ordinance of 1787; Shays's Rebellion; Virginia Plan

FOR FURTHER READING

Cress, Lawrence Delbert. 1975. "Whither Columbia? Congressional Residence and the Politics of the New Nation, 1776 to 1787." *William and Mary Quarterly,* 3rd ser. 32 (October): 581–600.

Jensen, Merrill, ed. 1976. *Constitutional Documents and Records, 1776–1787.* Vol. 1 of *The Documentary History of the Ratification of the Constitution.* Madison: State Historical Society of Wisconsin.

Rakove, Jack N. 1979. *The Beginnings of National Politics: An Interpretive History of the Continental Congress.* New York: Alfred A. Knopf.

Solberg, Winton, ed. 1958. *The Federal Convention and the Formation of the Union of the American States.* Indianapolis, IN: Bobbs-Merrill.

Wilson, Rick K., and Calvin Jillson. 1989. "Leadership Patterns in the Continental Congress: 1774–1789." *Legislative Studies Quarterly* 14 (February): 5–37.

CONTRACT

See CONSTITUTIONALISM

CONTRACTS CLAUSE

Article I, Section 10, Clause 1, of the Constitution lists a number of restraints on the powers of the states. These include limits on powers exercised by Congress such as entering treaties, coining money, emitting bills of credit, and making anything but gold and silver legal tender. Like the corresponding provision in Article I, Section 9, limiting Congress, Article I, Section 10 also prohibits the states from passing bills of attainder, enacting ex post facto laws, or granting titles of nobility. The clause contains an additional limitation that the Constitution does not apply to Congress, namely the prohibition on passing any "Law impairing the Obligation of Contracts."

Many delegates were convinced that the states had abused this authority by adopting laws that made it too easy for debtors to pay off their creditors, often in inflated currency. Curiously, delegates did not raise the issue at the Convention until August 28 when Rufus King of Massachusetts suggested adding a prohibition on state interference in private contracts to other limitations on the states.

Pennsylvania's Gouverneur Morris objected that "this would be going too far" (Farrand 1937, II, 439). He pointed out that "there are a thousand laws relating to bringing actions—limitations of actions & which affect contracts" (II, 439). He further argued that the judicial power would protect against abuses (II, 439). Connecticut's Roger Sherman argued that, by this logic, the delegates should not be prohibiting states from emitting bills of credit.

Both Pennsylvania's James Wilson and Virginia's James Madison favored King's motion. Madison admitted "that inconveniences might arise" but "thought on the whole it would be overbalanced by the utility of it" (II, 440). Characteristically, he argued that a negative on state laws by the Council of Revision would be even better.

Virginia's George Mason feared that the contracts clause might be "carrying restraint too far" (II, 440). He explained that "Cases will happen that can not be foreseen, where some kind of interference will be proper, & essential." He cited the case of "bringing actions on open account—that of bonds after a certain [lapse of time]" (II, 440). Wilson responded that the clause would only apply to laws that were retroactively applied. Madison wondered whether the ex post facto

clause did not already make such provision. The Convention ended up adopting a provision against bills of attainder and retrospective laws by a vote of 7-3.

On August 29, Delaware's John Dickinson reported that he had read the *Commentaries* of William Blackstone (one of England's most prominent legal commentators). They revealed that the term "ex post facto laws" applied only to criminal cases. Dickinson concluded that such a prohibition accordingly would not prohibit retrospective laws in civil cases, and that "some further provision" would therefore be required (II, 448–449).

Perhaps responding to this observation, the Committee of Style, which included Rufus King who had introduced the original motion for such a clause, included a provision prohibiting states from adopting "laws altering or impairing the obligation of contracts" (II, 597), which the Convention accepted on September 14. That same day, Elbridge Gerry of Massachusetts indicated "the importance of public faith, and the propriety of the restraint put on the States from impairing the obligation of contracts" (II, 619). No one seconded his motion to extend a similar prohibition to the national government. It is probable that the states simply did not believe the Congress was likely to pose the same threats in this area; consistent with Madison's view of factions, Ralph Rossum has suggested that this was because the Framers expected less abuse from a government covering a larger land area with a wider variety of interests (Rossum 2001, 74).

Louis Potts has observed that the contract clause bears strong resemblance to a provision in the Northwest Ordinance of 1787. Article 2 of this Ordinance had provided that "no law ought ever to be made, or have force in the said territory, that shall in any manner whatever interfere with, or effect private contracts or engagements, bona fide, and without fraud previously formed" (1986, 147).

On November 29, 1787, Maryland's Luther Martin forwarded a critique of the Constitution to the Maryland state legislature. He indicated that he had opposed the contracts clause on the basis that there would be times of such great distress that it would be necessary to pass law "*totally or partially stopping* the courts of justice, or authorizing the debtor to pay by instalments, or by delivering up his property to his creditors at a *reasonable* and *honest* valuation" (III, 215). Ironically, in decisions from *Home Building and Loan Association v. Blaisdell*, 290 U.S. 398 (1934), to the present, the U.S. Supreme Court has interpreted the provision as having a flexible meaning similar to that which Martin favored. This decision was very different from decisions of the Marshall Court in cases like *Dartmouth College v. Woodward*, 4 Wheat. (17 U.S.) 518 (1819), which frequently invoked the contract clause to protect the rights of private property.

See Also Committee of Style and Arrangement; Ex Post Facto Laws; Northwest Ordinance of 1787

FOR FURTHER READING

Farrand, Max, ed. 1937. *The Records of the Federal Convention.* 4 vols. New Haven, CT: Yale University Press.

Potts, Louis W. 1986. "'A Lucky Moment': The Relationship of the Ordinance of 1787 and the Constitution of 1787." *Mid-America* 68 (October): 141–151.

Rossum, Ralph A. 2001. *Federalism, the Supreme Court, and the Seventeenth Amendment: The Irony of Constitutional Democracy.* Lanham, MD: Lexington Books.

COPYRIGHTS AND PATENTS

Article I, Section 8 grants Congress the power "To promote the Progress of Science and useful Arts, by securing for limited Times to Authors and Inventors the exclusive Right to their respective Writings and Discoveries." The term "science" in this provision is a reference to learning in general, rather than to the technical subjects that would today be identified as "scientific." Thus, the power to grant copyrights corresponds to the idea of promoting "the Progress of Science" while granting patents promotes the "useful Arts." By granting copyrights and patents, Congress essentially bestows a temporary monopoly on the profit from a writing or invention in the hope that such a monopoly, and the profits it generates, will encourage such activities.

There is little in the records of the Constitutional Convention to illuminate the copyright and patent provision. South Carolina's Charles Pinckney appears to have initiated this proposal with a list of governmental powers that he submitted for consideration of the Committee of Detail on August 18. These included powers to secure copyrights; establish a university; use "proper premiums and provisions" to advance useful knowledge; establish seminaries; grant charters of incorporation; grant patents; secure copyrights; and establish public institutions to promote "agriculture, commerce, trades, and manufactures" (Farrand 1937, II, 321).

The delegates passed these proposals on to the Committee on Postponed Matters, which they created on August 31, since the proposals for power over copyrights and patents was reported by New Jersey's David Brearly on behalf of this committee on September 5. There was no recorded debate to accompany its unanimous adoption on that day (II, 510). This suggests that these powers must have been relatively uncontroversial.

Congress had no enumerated grant of copyright power under the Articles of Confederation. However, on May 2, 1783, the Confederation Congress had recommended that states adopt legislation on the subject, and 12 of the 13 states had done so (Donner 1992, 373). Most had used the English copyright law of 1709, usually called the Statute of Anne (Donner, 367), as a model. It had in turn succeeded the earlier stationers' copyright and printing patent, which had initially favored printers over authors (366).

Noah Webster may also have influenced the adoption of this provision. He had met with many leaders in the states and had traversed the states seeking copyright protection for a school textbook he had written. Although he was not a delegate to the Constitutional Convention, he was teaching English and living in Philadelphia at the time of the Convention and was friends with many of those who were attending (Donner, 370–372).

The delegates clearly believed that protection for patents and copyrights required national uniformity. They also viewed such protection as a means of encouraging the production of scholarly and scientific works and protecting private property. Abraham Lincoln once described the resulting constitutional provision as one that "added the fuel of interest to the fire of genius, in the discovery and production of new and useful things" (quoted in Goldwin 1990, 40).

See Also Committee on Postponed Matters; Congress, Collective Powers; Property Rights

FOR FURTHER READING

Cohen, I. Bernard. 1995. *Science and the Founding Fathers: Science in the Political Thought of Jefferson, Franklin, Adams, and Madison.* New York: W. W. Norton.

Donner, Irah. 1992. "The Copyright Clause of the U.S. Constitution: Why Did the Framers Include It with Unanimous Approval?" *American Journal of Legal History* 36 (July): 361–378.

Farrand, Max, ed. 1937. *The Records of the Federal Convention.* 4 vols. New Haven, CT: Yale University Press.

Goldwin, Robert A. 1990. *Why Blacks, Women, and Jews Are Not Mentioned in the Constitution, and Other Unorthodox Views.* Washington, DC: AEI Press.

Markey, Howad T., Donald W. Banner, Beverly Pattishall, and Ralph Oman. 1988. *Celebrating the Bicentennial of the United States Constitution.* U.S. American Bar Association Section of Patent, Trademark and Copyright Law.

CORPORATIONS

Under the original Virginia Plan, which Edmund Randolph introduced at the Convention on May 29, Congress was to continue to "enjoy the Legislative Rights vested in Congress by the Confederation" and to be invested with broad powers to legislate in cases "in which the separate States are incompetent, or in which the harmony of the United States may be interrupted by the exercise of individual Legislation" (Farrand 1937, I, 21). By contrast, the New Jersey Plan proposed simply adding a number of new powers to the congressional quiver.

The Committee of Detail, which reported to the Convention on August 6, reverted to the method established under the Articles of Confederation, of listing individual powers of Congress (which it increased), although it further complicated matters by including the necessary and proper clause, which later served as the basis for the development of the doctrine of implied powers. This doctrine was used in the administration of George Washington to sanction the national bank, which Alexander Hamilton favored. Thomas Jefferson was among those who argued that such a bank exceeded the authority of Congress and violated the Tenth Amendment, reserving powers to the states (see Clarke and Hall 1832).

A debate in the Convention on September 14 presaged later controversies. When the delegates were considering vesting Congress with power over post offices, Benjamin Franklin proposed adding "a power to provide for cutting canals where deemed necessary" (II, 615), and James Wilson, also of Pennsylvania, seconded him. Connecticut's Roger Sherman objected that the expense would fall on the entire United States while benefits would accrue to specific localities, but Wilson thought canals might become a source of revenue.

In any event, Virginia's James Madison then proposed widening Franklin's proposal so as "to grant charters of incorporation where the interest of the U.S. might require & the legislative provisions of individual States may be incompetent" (II, 615), a provision quite similar to the broad grant of power included in the original Virginia Plan. Madison argued that his "primary object" was "to secure an easy communication between the States which the free intercourse now to be opened, seemed to call for" (II, 615). Fellow delegate Edmund Randolph seconded Madison's motion.

Rufus King of Massachusetts argued that the power was unnecessary. Wilson thought it would be useful in preventing a single state from obstructing the general welfare. King, however, persisted. He thought that the provision would divide cities like Philadelphia and New York that had already been torn by questions as to whether the government under the Articles had the right to establish a national bank. Elsewhere, he feared that it would stir fears of "mercantile monopolies" (II, 616). Wilson's answer was probably not very reassuring. He defended canals as a way of facilitating communications with the West, but he went on to doubt whether individuals would get very excited about banks and thought that "mercantile monopolies" were "already included in the power to regulate trade" (II, 616). Virginia's George Mason expressed his fear of such monopolies, said that he did not think that this power was implicit in any existing powers (although he would later argue otherwise when criticizing the Constitution), and wanted to limit the power of incorporation only to that of building canals. The wider question was considered rejected after the provision limited to canals was defeated by an 8-3 vote. The delegates further voted 6-4-1 against a proposal offered by Madison and Charles Pinckney—who seems to have proposed this, as well as a more general power "To grant charters of incorporation," to the Committee of Detail earlier (II, 325)—to establish a national university, although Gouverneur Morris seemed to believe that the power to establish such an institution might be implicit in the government's right to govern the nation's capital (II, 616).

Thomas Jefferson, whom Madison had granted access to his notes, appears to have summarized the debate pretty well on February 15, 1791, when he noted:

> A proposition was made to them [the Convention] to authorize Congress to open canals, and an amendatory one to empower them to incorporate. But the whole was rejected, and one of the reasons for rejection urged in debate was, that then they would have a power to erect a bank, which would render the great cities, where there were prejudices and jealousies on the subject, adverse to the reception of the Constitution. (III, 363)

However, one might also argue that the debates just as easily lend themselves to the view that the delegates simply remained silent on the subject. Responding that the debate had primarily concerned canals, Alexander Hamilton noted that no published records existed on the subject (the *Journal* of the Convention would not be published for another 15 years, and Madison's notes would not be published until after his death) and observed that, given the varied reports, the word of the Convention was inconclusive:

> Some affirm that it was confined to the opening of canals and obstructions in rivers; others, that it embraced banks; and others, that it extended to the power of incorporating generally. Some, again, allege that it was disagreed to because it was thought improper to vest in Congress a power of erecting corporations. Others, because it was thought unnecessary to *specify* the power, and inexpedient to furnish an additional topic of objection to the Constitution. In this state of the matter, no inference whatever can be drawn from it. (Quoted in Clarke and Hall, 101)

By this time, Madison, the author of broad congressional powers, was edging closer to Jefferson's theory of strict constitutional construction and was probably grateful that the delegates had not adopted his proposal to vest the power of incorporating in Congress.

See Also Banking; Committee of Detail; Congress, Collective Powers

FOR FURTHER READING

Clarke, M. St. Clair, and D. A. Hall. 1832. *Legislative and Documentary History of the Bank of the United States: Including the Original Bank of America.* Washington, DC: Gales and Seaton. Reprinted New York: Augustus M. Kelley, 1967.

Farrand, Max, ed. 1937. *The Records of the Federal Convention.* 4 vols. New Haven, CT: Yale University Press.

CORRUPTION

Fifteen delegates used the term "corruption" at least 54 times at the Constitutional Convention, with important delegates like James Madison, Gouverneur Morris, George Mason, and James Wilson using the term most frequently (Savage 1994, 177). Daniel Farber and Suzanna Sherry have observed that code words for symptoms of corruption included references to "placemen, standing armies, bishops, aristocrats, luxury, monopolies, [and] stock-jobbers" (1990, 7). They also observe that one of the arguments for a mixed government was that such a government was designed to provide a safeguard against corruption (7). The conflict between virtue and corruption had been a favorite theme of advocates of republicanism, especially of its "Country" advocates (see Hutson 1981, 361), and the use of these terms may therefore indicate lingering influences of this ideology, which some scholars believe had been largely superseded by liberalism, at the Convention.

James Savage, the closest student of the subject, believes that concerns about corruption were tied to at least four formal constitutional mechanisms. First, delegates developed the Electoral College mechanism for presidential selection after expressing fear that congressional selection of the president would lead to intrigue, cabal, and corruption. Second, the delegates instituted a mechanism for impeaching the president (who, as a single individual, was considered especially vulnerable to such a vice) should he become corrupt. They further decided to invest the power to try impeachments in the Senate rather than in the Supreme Court, believing that the Senate's larger size would make it less likely to be corrupted. Third, the delegates prevented members of Congress from holding other offices that the president might hold out as rewards to them and prohibited other officers from accepting gifts or emoluments from foreign governments. Fourth, the delegates approved of a House of Representatives with sufficient members that they believed it would be less subject to corruption.

The delegates often associated corruption with the influence of the English king in Parliament as well as with unequal representation in Parliament related to rotten boroughs, or localities that continued to elect members of Parliament even after their populations were largely gone. New York's

Alexander Hamilton was the only delegate who, sympathetic to the British system, defended what Americans considered to be corruption. He did so by observing that the English philosopher David Hume "had pronounced all that influence on the side of the crown, which went under the name of corruption, an essential part of the weight which maintained the equilibrium of the Constitution" (Farrand 1937, I, 376).

Corruption continues to be a concern in both the U.S. and other democracies. James Jacobs has recently argued both that the presence of corruption does not preclude the establishment of democracy and that tough anticorruption controls are neither necessarily effective nor do they necessarily increase government legitimacy (Jacobs 2004, 21).

See Also Congress, House of Representatives, Size; Great Britain; Hamilton, Alexander; Hume, David; Impeachment Clause; Mixed Government; President, Selection; Republicanism; Virtue; Whig Ideology

FOR FURTHER READING

Farber, Daniel A., and Suzanna Sherry. 1990. *A History of the American Constitution*. Saint Paul, MN: West Publishing.

Farrand, Max, ed. 1937. *The Records of the Federal Convention*. 4 vols. New Haven, CT: Yale University Press.

Hutson, James H. 1981. "Country, Court, and Constitution: Antifederalism and the Historians." *William and Mary Quarterly*, 3rd ser. 28 (July): 337–368.

Jacobs, James B. 2004. "Corruption and Democracy." *Phi Kappa Phi Forum* 84 (Winter): 21–25.

Savage, James D. 1994. "Corruption and Virtue at the Constitutional Convention." *Journal of Politics* 56 (February): 174–186.

Wood, Gordon S. 1982. "Conspiracy and the Paranoid Style: Causality and Deceit in the Eighteenth Century." *William and Mary Quarterly*, 3rd ser. 39 (July): 401–441.

COST OF CONSTITUTION

See EXPENSES OF DELEGATES

COUNCIL OF REVISION

One of the provisions in the original Virginia Plan, which did not directly make it into the final Constitution, was the proposal for a Council of Revision. This council was to consist of the president and "a convenient number of the National Judiciary" who were to have authority "to examine every act of the National Legislature before it shall operate, & every act of a particular [state] Legislature before a Negative [exercised by Congress under another section of the Virginia Plan] thereon shall be final" (Farrand 1937, I, 21). Congress would then have the opportunity to override this veto by an unspecified majority. Although the delegates did not adopt this measure, the Convention did vest the president with the veto power, and judges have subsequently exercised the power, called judicial review, to strike down legislation that they believe to be unconstitutional.

Arguments for and Against

The primary purpose of the Council of Revision was to fortify the president in countering legislative excesses. The primary concerns that delegates expressed over the Council of Revision centered on whether it was appropriate to join the executive and the judiciary together and on whether the judiciary should have any role in assessing legislation before it came before the judges in the course of cases and controversies. The first concern focused on separation of powers (clearly, delegates for and against the Council of Revision interpreted such powers in different ways), whereas the second focused on the proper role of the judiciary.

In debates that began on June 4, Elbridge Gerry of Massachusetts was the first of many delegates who expressed the view that judges should not be allied with the president in examining legislation since they would later have cause to do so in exercising their judicial powers. Fellow delegate Rufus King from Massachusetts thus observed that "the Judges ought to be able to expound the law as it should come before them, free from the bias of having participated in its formation" (I, 98). The Convention subsequently got sidetracked on

whether the veto should be subject to an override by a congressional supermajority, as the Virginia Plan had originally proposed, or whether it should be absolute. After the states unanimously rejected the idea both of an absolute veto and of simply allowing the president to "suspend" legislation by a unanimous vote, they subsequently voted 8-2 to vest the veto power in the executive alone rather than in the president and the council together (I, 104).

Two days later, Pennsylvania's James Wilson, seconded by Virginia's James Madison, moved to reconsider allying the president and members of the judiciary in a Council of Revision. Madison defensively argued that there would be relatively few occasions when judges would end up examining legislation both at the time the president was considering it and when the judges were determining whether laws were constitutional or not. He further argued that, if allied with the president, the judges would be able to lend their "perspicuity," "conciseness," and ability to systematize to their review (I, 139). By contrast, Gerry feared that judicial "sophistry" would mislead the president (I, 139), and other delegates argued that combining the president with judges would dissipate the idea of presidential accountability that had been incorporated in the decision to have a single executive. This time, the Convention rejected the proposal for a Council of Revision by a vote of 8-3.

Wilson and Madison reintroduced the proposal on July 21. Although Wilson thought that judges would be able to protect encroachments on their branch by exercising judicial review, he thought they should have additional power to protect the people against unjust and improvident laws. Similarly, Connecticut's Oliver Ellsworth argued that judges would "give more wisdom & firmness to the Executive" and possess a more "systematic and accurate knowledge of the laws" (II, 74). Madison thought that allying judges with the president would inspire "additional confidence & firmness in exerting the revisionary power" (II, 74), and George Mason agreed.

By contrast, Elbridge Gerry and Caleb Strong of Massachusetts both thought that it was improper to mix departments or to expect those whose purpose was to exposit the laws to participate in their making. Maryland's Luther Martin did not believe that judges had any better knowledge of legislative affairs than legislators and opposed giving the judges "a double negative" (II, 76). John Rutledge of South Carolina observed that there was nothing to prevent the president from consulting members of his cabinet when deciding whether or not to exercise a veto. Wilson's motion was narrowly defeated by a vote of 4-3-2.

On August 15, Madison proposed something of a variant to the Council of Revision. He suggested that before congressional laws went into effect they should be submitted to both the president and the Supreme Court. If either objected, Congress would have to override the law by a two-thirds vote for it to become law; if both objected, a three-fourths majority would be required. James Wilson seconded the motion (II, 298).

South Carolina's Charles Pinckney opposed the proposal on the basis that it would involve judges in party politics and "give a previous tincture to their opinions" (II, 298). Maryland's John Mercer approved the motion, indicating that he thought it would be preferable for courts to examine the wisdom of laws prior to their implementation rather than to examine their constitutionality afterward: "He thought laws ought to be well and cautiously made, and then to be uncontroulable" (II, 298). Gerry objected that the new proposal was like the one that the Convention had already rejected, and, in apparent agreement, the Convention voted 8-3 against the proposal. After discussing the possibility of vesting an absolute negative in the president, the Convention agreed to give the president the power to veto a law subject to being overridden by three-fourths majorities. The delegates later changed this to a two-thirds majority.

An Executive Council

On August 18, Ellsworth observed that the Convention had still not provided for an Executive Council. He suggested that such a council should be composed of "the President of the Senate–the Chief-Justice, and the Ministers as they might be establd." and that they "should advise but not conclude the President" (II, 329). South Carolina's Charles Pinckney, by contrast, wanted the president to be able to procure advice from anywhere but feared that "an able Council . . . will thwart him; a weak one . . . will shelter himself under their sanction" (II, 329). Gerry did not want to include the chief justice in such a council, whereas Dickinson thought such a council would be appropriate only if its members were selected by Congress (II, 329).

On August 20, Gouverneur Morris and Charles Pinckney submitted a proposal to the Committee of Detail for a Council of State to be composed of the chief justice and various departmental secretaries. The president would have the power to require opinions in writing from members of the council. "But he shall in all cases exercise his own judgment, and either Conform to such opinions or not as he may think proper" (II, 344–345). On August 22, the Committee of Detail proposed a "Privy-Council" similar to that which Morris and Pinckney had proposed (II, 367).

On September 7, George Mason proposed a Privy Council of six members, two from each of the nation's geographical sections, which the Senate would choose (II, 537). Wilson supported such a council "provided its advice should not be made obligatory on the President" (II, 539). Rufus King believed that "most of the inconveniencies charged on the Senate are incident to a Council of Advice" (II, 539). He expressed concern that "the people would be alarmed at an unnecessary creation of New Corps which must increase the expence as well as influence of the Government" (II, 539). As the Convention was considering the current provision for allowing the president to request the opinion of heads of departments in writing, Mason said that "in rejecting a Council to the President" the Convention was "about to try an experiment on which the most despotic Governments had never ventured–The Grand Signor himself had his Divan" (II, 541). Benjamin Franklin seconded Mason's renewed motion for a council of six. Franklin argued that such a council "would not only be a check on a bad President but be a relief to a good one" (II, 542). Gouverneur Morris observed that the Committee (presumably of Postponed Matters) had decided that "the Presidt. by persuading his Council—to concur in his wrong measures, would acquire their protection for them" (II, 542). Wilson preferred that a council consent to appointments rather than the Senate. Dickinson noted that "it wd. be a singular thing if the measures of the Executive were not to undergo some previous discussion before the President" (II, 542). Madison also favored such a council, which the Convention rejected by a vote of 8-3 (II, 542) in favor of allowing the president to ask for the advice of council members in writing.

Analysis

The idea of a Council of Revision suffered both from the perception that it violated the principle of separation of powers and from the perception that it would give judges not one, but two, bites at the apple. It may also have suffered from its general ambiguity since its proponents never specified how many judges would be involved, how they would be chosen, or the like. The presidential veto and the exercise of judicial review arguably achieved many of the same objectives as the proposed council without the same concerns. Likewise, the president's authority to ask department heads for their opinions in writing became a substitute for a Privy Council. Despite some worthy arguments on its behalf, delegates tended to believe that the president should be able to consult with whomever he wanted, without necessarily being required to heed or being able to hide behind the advice they had given. The failure to create such a council (especially one that may have included senators) has been credited with "refining the separation of powers and thereby accentuating the Senate's primary role as a legislative body" (Wirls and Wirls 1994, 125).

See Also Judicial Review; President, Council; Presidential Veto; Separation of Powers; Virginia Plan

FOR FURTHER READING

Farrand, Max, ed. 1937. *The Records of the Federal Convention*. 4 vols. New Haven, CT: Yale University Press.

Hobson, Charles F. 1979. "The Negative on State Laws: James Madison, the Constitution, and the Crisis of Republican Government." *William and Mary Quarterly*, 3rd ser. 36 (April): 214–235.

Wirls, Daniel, and Stephen Wirls. 2004. *The Invention of the United States Senate*. Baltimore, MD: Johns Hopkins University Press.

COURT AND COUNTRY PARTIES

Because the ideological origins of the U.S. Constitution and the period that surrounds it are so complex, scholars are continually seeking terms through which to explain it. "Classical liberalism" and "republicanism" are perhaps the two most prominent contemporary labels used to understand the thought of the Founders, although others have stressed classical influences; the role of the Scottish Enlightenment, Protestantism or Puritanism; or individual thinkers like John Locke or Charles Louis de Secondat de Montesquieu. One difficulty of broad terms describing the influences on the Constitution is that many embrace both the proponents and opponents of the document.

Another set of terms, derived from English usages, focuses on "Court" and "Country." The former group was associated with support of the British monarch and the monarch's policies, while the second was in opposition. Prior to the Glorious Revolution of 1688, which overthrew the Stuarts and installed William (III) and Mary, the court was associated with the Tory Party and the Whigs with its opposition. After William and Mary came to power, the roles were reversed, with Whigs supporting the monarchs and more radical Whigs, sometimes designated "Real Whigs" or "Commonwealthmen" (Wood 1969, 15; Robbins 1959), joining Tories in opposition. The Commonwealthmen included Richard Price and Joseph Priestley (Brewer 1980, 342), both of whom expressed support of the American cause during the Revolution. Significantly, both Whigs and Tories favored limited government, but their emphases differed. One writer has divided the

Country party into two groups. These consist of those like Algeron Sidney, James Harrington, Henry Neville, and John Milton, who grew up during the English Civil War, and the next generation, which included John Trenchard and Thomas Gordon (authors of the widely circulated *Cato's Letters*) and Henry St. John, Viscount Bolingbroke (Kirkham 1992, 10).

In order to finance the wars that the kings were waging, the Whigs instituted a series of revolutionary approaches to finance and administration that included "the establishment of a funded national debt, the creation of the Bank of England, the recoinage of the nation's money, and the rapid augmentation of the armed forces and bureaucracy" (Hutson 1981, 357). These associated the party with forces that favored both a strong central government that could take an important role on the world stage and rapid commercial growth. Both objectives were important to Federalist proponents of the U.S. Constitution.

Members of the English landed gentry, who feared inflation and rising property taxes, generally opposed such measures, and they were increasingly joined by members of the middle class, who often found themselves victims of high taxes and commercial speculation (Brewer, 342). Country party advocates stressed the need to be "jealous" of government power, to resist governmental "corruption," to have frequent elections, and to oppose "standing armies" (Hutson, 358–364). Country party advocates often highlighted what they considered to be "conspiracies" against liberty that they believed designing leaders in Britain and in America were hatching (McDonald 1985, 78–79). During the Revolutionary War period, many Patriots used these themes in developing an ideology to oppose British authority in the New World (Bailyn 1967).

One way of understanding the debate between Federalists and Antifederalists over the Constitution is to understand the former as a kind of "Court" party that desired to strengthen or replace the existing central government and the latter as members of a kind of "Country" party that largely feared such developments. Such a typology not only recognizes the way that Americans borrowed from contemporary English thinking of the day,

but also resists the temptation to resist viewing the conflict (as U.S. historians of the Progressive Era sometimes did) as a simple conflict between conservatives and liberals, between those who favored elites and those who favored democracy.

"Country" ideology and rhetoric came especially easy to Antifederalists (whose leaders tended to be older than Federalists) who had once used Country ideology in opposing what they considered to be English tyranny. Such tensions continue to be evident in the conflict between the emerging Federalist Party (and especially the Hamiltonian economic program that it advocated), with its more "Courtly" emphasis, and the Democratic-Republican Party, with its continuing jealousy of national powers (Hutson 360).

See Also Antifederalists; Armies, Standing; Corruption; Federalists; Liberalism; Price, Richard; Protestantism; Republicanism; Scottish Enlightenment; Whig Ideology

FOR FURTHER READING

Bailyn, Bernard. 1967. *The Ideological Origins of the American Revolution.* Cambridge, MA: Belknap Press of Harvard University Press.

Brewer, John. 1980. "English Radicalism in the Age of George III." In J. G. A. Pocock, ed., *Three British Revolutions: 1641, 1688, 1776.* Princeton, NJ: Princeton University Press, 323–367.

Hutson, James H. 1981. "Country, Court, and Constitution: Antifederalism and the Historians." *William and Mary Quarterly* 38 (July): 337–368.

Kirkham, David M. 1992. "European Sources of American Constitutional Thought before 1787." *United States Air Force Academy Journal of Legal Studies* 3: 1–28.

McDonald, Forrest. 1985. *Novus Ordo Seclorum: The Intellectual Origins of the Constitution.* Lawrence: University Press of Kansas.

Murrin, John M. 1980. "The Great Inversion, or Court versus Country: A Comparison of the Revolution Settlements in England (1688–1721) and America (1776–1816)." In J. G. A. Pocock, ed., *Three British Revolutions: 1641, 1688, 1776.* Princeton, NJ: Princeton University Press, 368–453.

Robbins, Caroline. 1959. *The Eighteenth-Century Commonwealthman: Studies in the Transmission, Development and Circumstance of English Liberal Thought from the Restoration of Charles II until the War with the Thirteen Colonies.* Cambridge, MA: Harvard University Press.

Wood, Gordon S. 1969. *The Creation of the American Republic 1776–1787.* Chapel Hill: University of North Carolina Press.

COVENANT

See CONSTITUTIONALISM

CRITICAL PERIOD

Scholars have long used the term "critical period" to describe the period during which the Articles of Confederation were in effect, essentially from the signing of the Treaty of Paris, officially ending the Revolutionary War, to the adoption and/or inauguration of the U.S. Constitution in 1788–1789. Historian William Henry Trescot appears to have originated the term in a book he wrote in 1857 entitled *Diplomatic History of the Administrations of Washington and Adams.* Historian John Fiske gave wider circulation to the term in 1888 in his book *The Critical Period of American History, 1783–1789* (Morris 1956, 144). Fiske used the term "critical" in two respects. First, this period was one in which the Framers had to decide whether there would be a national government or whether they would proceed independently as states. Second, Fiske used the term to describe what he considered to be the incompetence with which states were meeting the problems of the day (Morris, 145).

This description of the period as a critical period largely accepted the criticisms that leading nationalists like Alexander Hamilton, James Madison, Benjamin Franklin, and George Washington had in correspondence with one another—they appeared to temper their critiques when writing to foreigners (Morris, 142)—of the weaknesses of the existing government under the Articles of Confederation. The term "critical period" was therefore consistent with earlier nationalistic interpretations of the Constitution such as George Ticknor Curtis's *History of the Origin, Formation, and Adoption of the Constitution,* initially published in 1854, and the studies of historian George Bancroft, who did not publish his own study of this period *History of the Formation of the Constitution of the United States of America,* until 1882.

Later historians of the Progressive Era, most notably J. Allen Smith, author of *The Spirit of American Government,* published in 1911, and Charles Beard, author of *An Economic Interpretation of the Constitution of the United States,* first published two years later, cast some doubt on the Federalists' bleak assessment of government during this period. These Progressive historians focused less on the ideologies of the Founders and more on what they believed their economic interests to be, thus tending to portray the conflict not between those who favored stronger government and those who favored weaker but between those with one set of financial interests and those with another. In more recent times, historian Merrill Jensen has suggested, in his books *The Articles of Confederation* (1940) and *The New Nation* (1950), that those who wrote the Constitution were conservatives who feared democracy and exaggerated existing problems and ultimately betrayed the promise of the American Revolution.

This view suffers from the need to portray Federalists as elitists and Antifederalists as democrats, a view that does not seem consistent with the evidence. Historian Richard Morris has thus observed that "Unless one is ready to accept the thesis [which he considers implausible] that the group that started the war were libertarians and democrats and were supplanted by a conservative authoritarian party, one cannot give uncritical adherence to the Smith-Beard-Jensen approach to the Confederation period" (Morris, 153). Although acknowledging that the Framers built more checks and balances into the new government, Morris believes that the Federalists were in many respects more "radical" than their Antifederalist opponents (156).

Although they are not as likely to use the term "critical period," modern commentators are likely to portray Federalist critiques of the Articles as largely accurate while acknowledging the positive role of the government under the Articles of Confederation in concluding peace with England and in adopting the Northwest Ordinance of 1787. Bruce Ackerman's use of the term "constitutional moment" to describe the Constitutional Convention as well as the period following the Civil War and the inauguration of the New Deal fits earlier descriptions of the former period as critical.

See Also Articles of Confederation; Beard, Charles; Constitutional Moments; Revolutionary War

FOR FURTHER READING

Jensen, Merrill. 1966. *The Articles of Confederation.* Madison: University of Wisconsin Press.
——. 1950. *The New Nation: A History of the United States During the Confederation, 1781–1789.* New York: Vintage Books.
Morris, Richard B. 1956. "The Confederation Period and the American Historian." *William and Mary Quarterly,* 3rd Ser., 13 (April): 139–156.

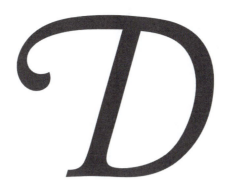

DAILY SCHEDULE OF THE CONSTITUTIONAL CONVENTION

Convention records indicate the Convention generally convened at either 10:00 or 11:00 most weekdays and Saturday mornings and adjourned at either 3:00 or 4:00. Delegates took off on Sundays, the Fourth of July, and occasional times for committees to formulate proposals. Although the hours of the day during which the Convention met were hotter than some, they would have afforded maximum light.

Because the Convention adopted a rule against simultaneous committee meetings, on those occasions when regular proceedings were not suspended it was necessary to allow time for committee members to work before or after regular hours. In addition, delegates would have personal affairs to which they needed to attend. Delegates were also probably cognizant that time for informal intercourse during which to develop and strengthen friendships, especially with members of other state delegations, would facilitate convention deliberations.

Although George Washington is among those whose diary often specified where he had supper, there is no indication that the delegates took a break during deliberations for lunch. It was common at the time to have two large meals during the day, one corresponding in time to a modern-day breakfast and the other in late midday, from about 2:00 to 4:00 (Phipps 1972, 72–73; Mitchell 1991, 7).

Recent research suggests that, however skilled they may have been in writing constitutions, the Founding Fathers probably did not set a good example for healthy eating. Melanie Polk, the director of Nutrition Education for the American Institute for Cancer Research, estimates that they consumed about 5,000 calories a day, much of them from fatty meats that were smoked or salted. They also often substitute hard cider, rum, and ale for water, which was often impure at the time (cited in American Institute for Cancer Research 2000). Such a high-calorie diet would have been ideally suited for individuals who spent most of the day working outdoors in fields but would be far too much for anyone doing less strenuous physical work today.

See Also Calendar

FOR FURTHER READING

American Institute for Cancer Research. 2000. "On Independence Day, Nutritionists Cast a Cold Eye on Eating Habits of Colonial America." June 24, http://www.charitywire.com/charity10/00210.html.

Mitchell, Patricia. 1991. *Revolutionary Recipes: Colonial Food, Lore, and More*. Chatham, VA: P. B. Mitchell.

Phipps, Frances. 1972. *Colonial Kitchens, Their Furnishings, and Their Gardens*. New York: Hawthorn Books.

DAVIE, WILLIAM RICHARDSON (1756–1820)

Born in Egremont, Cumberlandshire, England in 1756 to the family of a fabric manufacturer, the family of William Richardson Davie migrated to America where his mother's brother, a Presbyterian minister after whom he had been named, adopted him. After studying at Queen's Museum, he attended the College of New Jersey (today's Princeton), where he graduated with honors. He served in a number of important positions during the Revolutionary War, including captain of a cavalry unit and service as North Carolina's Commissary General. Davie was a model soldier to future president Andrew Jackson who served for a time under him. After completing his study of law, voters selected Davie to the state legislature where he served from 1786 to 1798, during which time he helped to found the University of North Carolina. Davie was present on May 25, the opening day of the Convention.

William Richardson Davie, delegate from North Carolina (Pixel That)

Congress

On June 30, the Convention was debating the possibility of granting each state equal representation in the Senate. Perhaps because other delegates were speaking of the conflict between the North and the South, because some were accusing some states (North Carolina does not appear to have been mentioned by name) of failing to fulfill their obligations, or, more likely, because he could not make up his mind, Davie professed to be "embarrassed" (Farrand 1937, I, 487). He indicated that he thought it would be impractical to allow state legislatures to choose members of the Senate on a proportional basis because he thought this would result in an initial body of at least 90 members (presumably based on the idea that the smallest state would get at least one senator), which would be too large to carry out the Senate's functions. Faced with a choice between proportional representation and equal representation, he would have to support the latter.

Davie disfavored a plan whereby senators would be chosen from larger districts (probably embracing more than one state) because he feared that the larger divisions would prevail over the smaller divisions with which they were paired. He realized that selection by state legislatures might be more likely to result in the representation of "local prejudices & interests," but he thought that such prejudices "would find their way into the national Councils" either way (I, 488). However, he feared that if the Senate were considered to be representative of the states, it would look like the Articles of Confederation and would not accomplish the objects the Convention was seeking. Thus, Davie groped for a middle way: "We were partly federal, partly national in our Union. And he did not see why the Govt. might [not] in some respects operate on the States, in others on the people (I, 488)."

Perhaps thinking that he was a conciliatory voice on this issue, the Convention appointed Davie on July 2 to the committee designed to formulate a mechanism for representation within the Senate; this was the only committee on which Davie served at the Convention. He may not have initially been completely satisfied with the Connecticut Compromise. Thus, on July 6, Madison reported that Davie wanted to recommit the issue of congressional representation. Madison believed that Davie favored a plan whereby "wealth or property ought to be represented in the 2d. branch; and numbers in the 1st. branch" (I, 542).

Davie further weighed in on the issue of representation on July 12, but at that time his primary concern was over how states with slaves should be represented. The summary of his comments appears to indicate considerable passion:

> Mr. Davie, said it was high time now to speak out. He saw that it was meant by some gentlemen to deprive the Southern States of any share of Representation for their blacks. He was sure that N. Carola. would never confederate on any terms that did not rate then at least as 3/5. If the Eastern States meant therefore to exclude them altogether the business was at an end. (I, 593)

Davie appears to have had an important role in North Carolina's acceptance of the Great Compromise (Robinson 1957, 186).

Presidency

On June 2, Davie seconded a motion by fellow North Carolina delegate Hugh Williamson providing that the executive should be removable on conviction of impeachment for "mal-practice or neglect of duty" (I, 78).

On July 24, Davie supported an eight-year term for the presidency (II, 102). Two days later, he seconded a motion by Virginia's George Mason providing that the executive should serve a single seven-year term (II, 120).

Life after the Convention

On August 23, Davie wrote to the governor of North Carolina indicating that he had left the Convention on the 13th. He observed that the other state delegates had agreed to stay, that "the general principles were already fixed," that he had other business to attend to, and that under the circumstances he felt "at liberty" to return home (III, 75).

Davie gave a reasoned defense of the Constitution at the North Carolina ratifying convention. Speaking in defense of the Connecticut Compromise, Davie there observed that "The protection of the small states against the ambition and influence of the larger members, could only be effected by arming them with an equal power in one branch of the legislature" (III, 341). He also observed that the Convention had represented a wide variety of interests and that "mutual concessions were necessary to come to any concurrence" (III, 341). Davie hoped that the same "spirit of amity, and of that mutual deference and concession which the peculiarity of their political situation rendered indispensable" would also pervade the North Carolina convention (III, 342). Davie helped publish the proceedings of the first North Carolina convention, which apparently helped set the stage for the state's eventual ratification of the Constitution.

In 1797, Davie became commander of North Carolina's militia, and the next year the state elected him as governor. The following year he served as a commissioner to France. Subsequent disagreements with the Democratic-Republicans over their preference for France over England sent him back to private life, and he retired to South Carolina.

Davie was involved from the beginning in the founding of the University of North Carolina in 1789. Much as Thomas Jefferson later involved himself with the University of Virginia, Davie is said to have been "intimately involved in every significant aspect of the university's evolution until his trustee term expired in 1807" (Johnson 1987, 135). He helped choose the site for the university at Chapel Hill, raised funds for the university and donated to it, laid out a curriculum that stressed practical knowledge, and helped secure state support. In 1811, the grateful university awarded Davie its first doctor of law degree. He died in 1820.

See Also North Carolina

FOR FURTHER READING

Bradford, M. M. 1994. *Founding Fathers: Brief Lives of the Framers of the United States Constitution.* 2nd ed. Lawrence: University Press of Kansas.

Farrand, Max, ed. 1937. *The Records of the Federal Convention.* 4 vols. New Haven, CT: Yale University Press.

Johnson, Eldon L. 1987. "The 'Other Jeffersons' and the State University Idea." *Journal of Higher Education* 58 (March-April): 127–150.

Robinson, Blackwell P. 1957. *William R. Davie.* Chapel Hill: University of North Carolina Press.

DAYTON, JONATHAN (1760–1834)

New Jersey's Jonathan Dayton, who was then 26, is chiefly known for having been the youngest man to attend the Constitutional Convention. Unlike South Carolina's Charles Pinckney, the

A profile portrait of Jonathan Dayton (1760–1834), delegate from New Jersey (Corbis)

next oldest delegate who dissembled about his age in order to make people believe he was the youngest, Dayton spoke relatively rarely at the Convention and was quite conscious that he was in the presence of men with far greater experience. Writing in June to fellow delegate David Brearly before Dayton had yet begun attending the Convention, he observed: "I feel about me on this occasion all that diffidence with which the consciousness of my youth and inexperience as well as inability to discharge so important a trust, cannot but impress me" (quoted in Hutson 1987, 59).

Background

Dayton was born in 1760 in Elizabethtown, New Jersey; his father later commanded a battalion of troops during the Revolutionary War. Despite his youth, Dayton, who had graduated from the College of New Jersey (today's Princeton University) in 1776 at the age of 16, had served throughout the Revolutionary War as an officer, being captured for a time by the British and being present at the British surrender at Yorktown. Elected in 1787 to the New Jersey legislature, his father declined nomination as a representative to the Constitutional Convention in deference to his son, who would eventually earn a law degree.

Positions Articulated at the Convention

Because the confirmation of the younger Dayton encountered delay, he was not seated at the Convention until June 21 (Farrand 1937, I, 353). The first position about which he is on record is that of senatorial pay. He observed on June 26 that he thought that state payment of senators would be "fatal to their independence" and therefore advocated that they should be paid out of the national treasury (I, 428).

Since the New Jersey Plan, advocating equal state representation in Congress, originated from his home state, it is not surprising to find that on June 28, Dayton supported a motion that representation in the first branch of Congress should be the same as it had been under the Articles of

Confederation (I, 445). On this occasion, he also wanted the vote postponed until Governor William Livingston from his state was able to attend. Objecting to the scare tactics that he thought advocates of change were advocating (substituting "assertion" for "proof" and "terror" for "argument"), and indicating a bit of his own impetuousness, on June 30 Dayton questioned whether the evils to which critics of the Articles of Confederation really stemmed from state equality in Congress. Perhaps more importantly, he came up with one of the Convention's most colorful analogies when he indicated that "he considered the system on the table as a novelty, an amphibious monster; and was persuaded that it never would be recd. by the people" (I, 490). On July 14, just two days before adoption of the Connecticut Compromise, Dayton indicated that "The smaller States can never give up their equality" (II, 5). Like other representatives of the smaller states, he connected such equality to "security for their rights" (II, 5).

On August 24, when the Convention was still contemplating that Congress would choose the president, Dayton was on record as opposing having this decision made by joint ballot. He feared that such a mechanism would effectively grant this power to the House of Representatives and thus sidestep the provision that had been made for the smaller states by granting them equal representation in the Senate (II, 402). When the Convention initially accepted such a joint ballot, Dayton unsuccessfully moved to provide that each state would have a single vote—a mechanism that has subsequently found its way in the mechanism by which the House of Representatives selects among the top three candidates for president in cases where no candidate gains a majority of the votes (II, 403).

After adoption of the Connecticut Compromise, delegates from the North and South continued to argue about how slaves should be counted in the formula for representation in the House. After Gouverneur Morris gave one of the Convention's most blistering speeches denouncing the institution of slavery and thus arguing that only free persons should be counted in apportioning representation in the U.S. House of Rep-

resentatives, Dayton, who owned slaves of his own but represented a state where slavery was dying out, seconded his motion. Recognizing that the delegates were unlikely to agree with him, he thought it was important "that his sentiments on the subject might appear whatever might be the fate of the amendment" (II, 223).

In assessing the relative strength of the Northern and Southern states, Dayton indicated on July 10 that he thought the balance was relatively equal. He considered Pennsylvania to be the state in the middle with six to its north and six to its south (I, 567).

On August 18, Dayton opposed providing a specific constitutional limit on the number of troops that could be kept in times of peace. He sagely observed that "preparations for war are generally made in peace, and a standing force of some sort may, for ought we know, become unavoidable" (II, 330). This subject evidently interested him since on August 23, he proposed a motion that would grant the national government the power to adopt laws "organizing, arming, disciplining & governing *such part of them as may be employed in the service of the U.S.*" (II, 385–386). Under this resolution, other powers related to the militia, including the right to appoint officers, would be reserved to the states. On that same day, Dayton opposed uniform regulations of the militia throughout the country in the belief that needs in terms of the kinds of troops and weapons would vary from one area of the country to another (II, 386). On September 8, Dayton made another foray into the area of foreign policy by moving along with Pennsylvania's James Wilson to strike the requirement for a two-thirds vote of the Senate to ratify treaties (II, 549).

The only committee on which Dayton served at the Convention was the 11-man Committee on Commercial Discrimination which was created on August 25. On a related matter, Dayton expressed concern that the provision allowing states to exact fees for inspection duties might be used to allow Pennsylvania to tax New Jersey under the guise of such duties (II, 589).

On August 24, Dayton concurred in a motion to strike a rather awkward mechanism, similar to a provision under the Articles, for deciding disputes between the states. He concurred with other delegates in believing that the establishment of a national judiciary would be adequate to deal with such problems (II, 401).

On August 30, Dayton opposed a provision that would require an application on the part of state legislatures before the national government could send in protection against domestic violence. In a sentiment in which other delegates must undoubtedly have concurred, he believed that the example of Rhode Island showed "the necessity of giving latitude to the power of the U-S. on this subject" (II, 467).

Life after the Convention

After the Convention, Dayton resumed his service in the New Jersey legislature and worked for adoption of the Constitution. He served from 1791 to 1799 as a delegate to the House of Representatives, where he supported Federalist policies and rose to the position of House Speaker. His election to the U.S. Senate subsequently brought him into close association with Vice President Aaron Burr. Dayton owned about a quarter of a million acres in Ohio, where the city of Dayton now bears his name. Perhaps in part because of these interests as well as his personal friendship, Dayton appears to have conspired with Burr to join western parts of the U.S. with Mexico in an empire. Charged but never tried for treason, Dayton's political career was effectively ended except for a year of service in the state legislature. Like George Washington and a number of other founders, Dayton was a member of the Society of the Cincinnati. He died in the town of his birth in 1834.

See Also Committee on Commercial Discrimination; New Jersey

FOR FURTHER READING

Farrand, Max, ed. 1937. *The Records of the Federal Convention*. 4 vols. New Haven, CT: Yale University Press.

Hutson, James H., ed. 1987. *Supplement to Max Farrand's* The Records of the Federal Convention of 1787. New Haven, CT: Yale University Press.

Whitney, David C. 1974. *Founders of Freedom in America: Lives of the Men Who Signed the Constitution of the United States and So Helped to Establish the United States of America*. Chicago: J. J. Ferguson Publishing.

DEBTS

Article VI of the Constitution specifies that "all debts contracted and Engagements entered into, before the adoption of this Constitution, shall be as valid against the United States under this Constitution as under the Confederation." Sometimes called the "Engagements Clause" (Kesavan 2002, 51), this provision was similar in sentiment, albeit shorter, than a provision in Section XII of the Articles of Confederation. The provision in the U.S. Constitution appears to have grown out of a short provision in the Virginia Plan calling "for the completion of all their [those of the Articles of Confederation] engagements" (Farrand 1937, I, 22).

Convention Debates

The main focus of debates on the subject at the Convention centered on the possible assumption of *state* debts and on the issue of whether the government was obligated to pay off federal obligations to the original holders of these securities or to those who had subsequently purchased them. The Convention left both issues to be decided under the new government rather than resolving them within the text of the new Constitution.

On August 18, the Convention appointed a committee of 11 to consider whether the national government should assume state debts. On August 21, New Jersey's William Livingston delivered the committee's report. It specified that

the Legislature of the U.S. shall have power to fulfil the engagements which have been entered into by Congress, and to discharge as well the debts of the U-S: as the debts incurred by the several States during the late war, for the common defence and general welfare. (II, 355–356)

Elbridge Gerry of Massachusetts feared that the language of this resolution by "giving the power only, without adopting the obligation," might destroy "the security now enjoyed by the public creditors of the U-States" (II, 356). He also observed that those states that had already redeemed their own debts, and that did not want to be saddled anew by the debts of other states, would not consider the provision to be fair.

The Convention resumed discussion the next day at which time it accepted an alteration that Pennsylvania's Gouverneur Morris proposed. It provided more affirmatively that "The Legislature *shall* discharge the debts & fulfil the engagements [of the U. States]" (II, 377), but did not address assumption of state debts. On August 23, Pierce Butler of South Carolina objected that this might "compel payment as well to the Blood-suckers who had speculated on the distresses of others, as to those who had fought & bled for their country," and indicated that he planned to offer the next day a motion distinguishing between the two groups of bondholders (II, 392). On that day, the Convention voted to consider the provision on the next.

On August 25, Virginia's George Mason objected that the term "shall" was too strong and might be impossible to honor. He further feared that the use of the term might "beget speculations and increase the pestilent practice of stock-jobbing," and while indicating that it would not be easy to distinguish between original and subsequent holders of bonds, he thought the attempt would be worth making (II, 413). Elbridge Gerry also expressed concern for the plight of the soldiers who had earned and sold their original securities at discounts. However, with a perspective that might have derived from his origin in a state where commerce was more influential than in South Carolina, he observed that instead of being censured, "Stock-jobbers" had "kept up the value of paper" and that, without them, "there would be no market" (II, 413). New Hampshire's John Langdon joined Pierce Butler in expressing a desire simply to keep the status quo in place.

At this point, Virginia's Edmund Randolph introduced a provision leaving debts to the United States in the same position that they had been under the Articles of Confederation. It provided that "All debts contracted & engagements entered into, by or under the authority of Congs. shall be as valid agst the U. States under this constitution as under the Confederation" (II, 414). Despite Gouverneur Morris's apparent concern that it would be better explicitly to say that the government "shall" pay its debts, the Convention voted 10 to 1 for Randolph's proposal. The Committee of Style slightly altered the language to that which is now found in the Constitution (II, 603).

Analysis

The delegates essentially left the status quo in place on dealing with debts. The new Constitution provided that the national government would accept the obligations of the previous one. However, it stated neither that the new government would take on state debts nor that it would not. Similarly, it did not specify whether the government would pay original holders of government securities or those who had subsequently purchased them. In the Washington administration, Alexander Hamilton (who had served as a delegate to the Constitutional Convention from New York) proposed the assumption of state debts and payment to existing bondholders. Although he ultimately prevailed, both issues were highly divisive and helped form the basis for the emerging Federalist and Democratic-Republican Parties.

See Also Committee on State Debts and Militia

FOR FURTHER READING

Farrand, Max, ed. 1937. *The Records of the Federal Convention.* 4 vols. New Haven, CT: Yale University Press.

Ferguson, E. James. 1951. "State Assumption of the Federal Debt during the Confederation." *The Mississippi Valley Historical Review* 38 (December): 403–424.

Holton, Woody. 2004. "'From the Labours of Others': The War Bonds Controversy and the Origins of the Constitution in New England." *William and Mary Quarterly,* 3rd ser. 61 (April): 271–305.

Kesavan, Vasan. 2002. "When Did the Articles of Confederation Cease to Be Law?" *Notre Dame Law Review* 78 (December): 35–82.

DECLARATION OF INDEPENDENCE

Although it had very different origins and purposes, the U.S. Declaration of Independence of 1776 is closely linked to the Constitution of 1787. The product of the Second Continental Congress rather than a special constitutional convention, the Declaration of Independence was commissioned to explain both to Americans and to other nations the colonists' reasons for declaring their independence from England. Adhering to the principle of "no taxation without representation," prior to 1776, the colonists had resisted parliamentary sovereignty, particularly in the area of taxation, but they had claimed to be loyal to the English king in pursuit of the protection of their rights as Englishmen. The publication of Thomas Paine's *Common Sense* in January of 1776, disputing the wisdom of kingship and hereditary succession, and King George's continuing intransigence turned the tide and promoted willingness to sever the one remaining legal tie. Paine's arguments, and King George III's behavior, further appear to have left an abiding bad taste for monarchy in America, which was frequently reflected in statements by delegates to the Constitutional Convention advocating "republican" government as opposed to either "monarchy" or "aristocracy."

The Writing of the Declaration

At the time the Convention was considering independence, it was also working to obtain foreign alliance and beginning to think about the need for a government to replace that of Great Britain. This need ultimately culminated in the writing of the Articles of Confederation. After Virginia's Richard Henry Lee introduced a resolution on

Text of the Declaration of Independence
(Pixel That)

June 7, 1776, stating that "these United Colonies are, and of right ought to be, free and independent States," the Congress appointed five men to write the Declaration of Independence. They were Thomas Jefferson, John Adams, Benjamin Franklin, Roger Sherman, and Robert Livingston. Jefferson did most of the writing of the document, which was then debated and modified on the floor of Congress. The Convention proclaimed independence on July 2, 1776, and adopted the Declaration of Independence in explanation of its actions on July 4, 1776. The signing of the document did not proceed, as many portrayals of the occasion indicate, on a single day, but during a period of several months.

The most important part of the Declaration of Independence is its second full paragraph. There Jefferson, and the Congress, declared their belief in certain "self-evident truths." These included a belief in the equality of all men and the recognition that governments are established to protect

Declaration of Independence, July 4th, 1776, *painted by J. Trumbull (Francis G. Mayer/Corbis)*

the inalienable rights of "life, liberty, and the pursuit of happiness." Reflecting the philosophy of the English philosopher John Locke, Jefferson portrayed government as a social compact rather than as a divine mandate. Jefferson further opined that when governments failed to secure individual rights, the people were entitled to replace such governments with institutions that would secure these blessings. The people should not revolt for "light and transient causes," and the colonists were not doing so. Rather, they were responding to a long series of "injuries & usurpations" designed to establish "an absolute tyranny over these states."

Most of the remainder of the Declaration of Independence is a set of approximately 25 grievances, written much like a legal brief, against the English king, whom Jefferson ultimately links to an unresponsive Parliament. The Declaration ends with a mutual pledge among the delegates of "our lives, our fortunes & our sacred honour." Fifty-six delegates signed the Declaration.

The Declaration of Independence stimulated not only a need to form the Articles of Confederation to replace the authority once exercised by the British government but also the movement for the adoption of new or revised state constitutions. Not only did these constitutions provide models for the delegates at the Constitutional Convention of 1787, but they also provided laboratories to test the effect of various provisions. Delegates were constantly citing their experiences within the states from the adoption of their new constitutions until the Convention met in 1787.

Six individuals—Roger Sherman, Robert Morris, Benjamin Franklin, James Wilson, George Clymer, and George Read—who signed the Declaration of Independence also signed the U.S. Constitution. Elbridge Gerry and George Wythe, both signers of the Declaration, attended the Convention but did not sign. Gerry did not sign because he did not agree with the document, and Wythe was unable to do so because he had gone home to a dying wife.

Relationship to the Constitution

Some Antifederalists like Mercy Otis Warren (Cohen 1983, 491) saw the Constitution as a betrayal of the ideals of the Declaration of Independence. Historians during the Progressive Era, in turn, believed that the Constitution represented a conservative reaction to the Declaration's more progressive ideals. It is probably more accurate to see the Constitution as a reaction both to the relative weakness of the Articles of Confederation and to some democratic excesses that were incorporated into the original state constitutions. There was certainly a shift in emphasis between 1776 and 1787 (Wood 1969). The *Pennsylvania Packet* thus observed on September 6, 1787, that "The year 1776 is celebrated . . . for a revolution in favor of liberty. The year 1787, it is expected, will be celebrated with equal joy, for a revolution in favor of Government" (cited in Kramnick 1988, 23). Steven C. Bullock has compared the Declaration of Independence to the Old Testament prophets and the Constitution to the Torah, or law (2002). Michael Lienesch has argued that "before 1787 Revolution and Constitution had been discontinuous. Afterward they became inseparable, Constitutionalists showing how Revolution had led inexorably to Constitution" (1980, 10; but see Carey 1980). Without the Constitution, the ideals of equality and the protection of human rights would not have been as effectively advanced. Significantly, the Journal of Convention begins by noting that the Convention was convening "in the eleventh year of the independence of the United States of America" (Farrand 1937, I, 1).

When delegates met at Seneca Falls, New York, in 1848 to demand equal rights (including the right to vote that would eventually be incorporated into the Nineteenth Amendment, adopted in 1920), they phrased their petition in the form of the Declaration, now declaring that men and women were created. The Fourteenth Amendment to the U.S. Constitution (ratified in 1868) ultimately provided for "equal protection of the laws" and defined citizenship so as to include all persons born or naturalized in the United States.

Some scholars have argued that, even apart from this, the Declaration of Independence should be considered to be a constitutional document. George Athan Billias has thus argued that American constitutionalism is more closely identified abroad with the Declaration of Independence than with the Constitution; the idea of the social compact was the basis for creating new state constitutions; many of these constitutions incorporated phrases from the document; and the document has been cited in U.S. Supreme Court decisions (Billias 1985; also see Gerber 1995).

References at the Constitutional Convention

Delegates to the Constitutional Convention frequently cited their opposition, which they believed the people shared, to monarchy. Although many of the grievances that Jefferson had stated against the British (for example, the lack of independent judges) were of undoubted concern to the delegates at the Constitutional Convention, the only recorded references to the Declaration of Independence at this Convention took place on June 19 and June 20. On the former date, James Wilson of Pennsylvania responded to the arguments of Luther Martin of Maryland that the separation from Britain had placed the colonies in a state of nature toward one another by referring to the Declaration's reference to "the *United Colonies*" and concluding that "they were independent, not Individually, but *Unitedly* and that they were confederated as they were independent States" (I, 324). On June 20, Martin nonetheless repeated his argument that Americans looked "for the security of their lives, liberties & properties" by "thirteen separate sovereignities instead of incorporating themselves into one" (I, 340–341). Ultimately, the delegates ended up with something of a compromise between the two views, although there is fairly clear authority for the proposition that sovereignty in foreign affairs is considered to be indivisible in a way that the exercise of authority in domestic affairs is not. In addition to references during debates, delegates to

---

"Founding Fathers": A Term with an Unlikely Origin

President Warren G. Harding is not generally considered to be among the more quotable presidents. Indeed, the journalist Hendrik Hertzberg has described him as "the patron saint of the unquotable" (2004). Harding was, however, the first president officially to employ a speechwriter, a gentleman by the name of Judson Welliver. According to Hertzberg, Welliver and Harding coined the phrase "Founding Fathers," which is now routinely used along with the terms "Founders" and "Framers" to describe the authors of the Declaration of Independence and the Constitution.

FOR FURTHER READING

Hertzberg, Hendrik. 2004. Interview by Terry Gross as recorded on National Public Radio, Wednesday, July 14.

---

the Constitutional Convention took a break during the July Fourth holiday.

The Convention appended a resolution developed by Gouverneur Morris and Benjamin Franklin to the Constitution for submission to the states. It indicated that the document had received the unanimous consent of the states "the Seventeenth Day of September in the Year of our Lord one thousand seven hundred and Eighty seven and of the Independence of the United States of America the Twelfth." They thus evoked a conscious reference back to the year of Independence, and by implication to the document that had proclaimed it.

See Also Adams, John; Critical Period; Equality; Jefferson, Thomas; Liberalism; Locke, John; Natural Rights; Paine, Thomas; Revolutionary War

FOR FURTHER READING

Bailyn, Bernard. 1976. "1776. A Year of Challenge–A World Transformed." *Journal of Law and Economics* 19 (October): 437–466.

Becker, Carl L. 1970. *The Declaration of Independence: A Study in the History of Political Ideas.* New York: Vintage Books.

Billias, George Athan. 1985. "The Declaration of Independence: A Constitutional Document." *this Constitution,* no. 6 (Spring): 47–52.

Bullock, Steven C. 2002. "Talk of the Past: American Midrash." *Common-Place* 2, no. 4 (July). http://www.common-place.org.

Carey, George W. 1980. "Comment: Constitutionalists and the Constitutional Tradition–So What?" *Journal of Politics* 42 (February): 36–46.

Cohen, Lester H. 1983. "Mercy Otis Warren: The Politics of Language and the Aesthetics of Self." *American Quarterly* 35 (Winter): 481–498.

Farrand, Max, ed. 1937. *The Records of the Federal Convention.* 4 vols. New Haven, CT: Yale University Press.

Gerber, Scott D. 1995. *To Secure These Rights: The Declaration of Independence and Constitutional Interpretation.* New York: New York University Press.

Kramnick, Isaac. 1988. "The 'Great National Discussion': The Discourse of Politics in 1787." *William and Mary Quarterly,* 3rd ser. 45 (January): 3–32.

Lienesch, Michael. 1980. "The Constitutional Tradition: History, Political Action, and Progress in American Political Thought 1787–1792." *Journal of Politics* 42 (February): 2–30.

Maier, Pauline. 1997. *American Scripture: Making the Declaration of Independence.* New York: Alfred A. Knopf.

Warren, Charles. 1945. "Fourth of July Myths." *William and Mary Quarterly,* 3rd ser. (July): 237–272.

Wills, Garry. 1978. *Inventing America: Jefferson's Declaration of Independence.* New York: Doubleday.

Wood, Gordon S. 1969. *The Creation of the American Republic, 1776–1787.* Chapel Hill: University of North Carolina Press.

Wright, Benjamin Fletcher. 1958. "Consensus and Continuity–1776–1787." *Boston University Law Review* 38 (Winter): 1–52.

DELAWARE

Founded by William Penn and governed by a charter long before it adopted a constitution, Delaware was one of the smallest states and was often overshadowed by its neighbor to the west, Pennsylvania. Like Pennsylvania, Delaware would have been identified as one of the Middle states. At the time of the Constitutional Convention, the northern county of New Castle served as the primary commercial center. Although this area was doing relatively well, other areas of the state were not faring so well and many counties, where specie was scarce, were petitioning the state legislature to issue paper money.

Historical and Political Background

Politically, the state was divided into two rival factions, the Whigs and the Tories (although the latter are probably better understood as moderates). The former had been readier to declare independence from Great Britain, while members of the latter had been more reluctant. Caesar Rodney, who had died in 1784, and Dr. James Tilton were leaders of the Whigs, while George Read, who attended the Constitutional Convention, was the chief leader of the Tories.

Delaware had held a constitutional convention in 1776. It replaced the unicameral colonial legislature with a bicameral body. The members of the House of Assembly served for one-year terms and those of the Legislative Council for three-year terms. The legislature chose the president, designated as commander-in-chief of the state militia, for a three-year term; he did not have the power to veto. A four-man Privy Council, whose members also served for three-year terms, advised the president. The judicial system was composed of justices of the peace, county courts of common pleas, and a supreme court. The president and the Privy Council had the power to appoint county sheriffs and coroners from among two candidates nominated by voters in each county. The Constitution required property ownership as a condition to voting (Jensen 1978, 38–39).

Delaware under the Articles of Confederation

Under the Articles of Confederation, Delaware had been one of the states that had insisted at the Continental Congress that the small states should be equally represented. Largely at the insistence of George Read, the delegates to the Constitutional Convention were mandated not to bargain this representation away. Like other small states, Delaware was concerned about the large states that held western lands; it was among the states that withheld ratification of the Articles of Confederation until the states agreed that the U.S. would hold such lands in common. Delaware worked for strengthening the government under the Articles, approving a congressional impost of 5 percent. Perhaps not altogether realistically, it also hoped to locate the nation's capital in Wilmington.

Delaware was among the states represented at the Annapolis Convention that preceded the Constitutional Convention. Although Delaware did better than average in meeting its requisitions for money under the Articles, Madison cited the state on debates on June 28 for having opposed an embargo at a time when other states thought this to be necessary (Farrand 1937, I, 476).

Representation at the Convention

All five of Delaware's delegates to the Constitutional Convention were from the Tory Party. They were Richard Bassett, Gunning Bedford, Jr., Jacob Broom, John Dickinson, and George Read. Although the states had previously selected all of them to attend the Annapolis Convention, only Bassett, Dickinson, and Read had done so. Of the delegates who attended the Constitution Convention, Dickinson, the "penman of the Revolution" and the initial author of the Articles of Confederation, was probably the most influential. Read's suggestion that the Convention should consider eliminating the states and Bedford's perceived threat to ally the small states with foreign governments were both notable aspects of the Convention. Bassett is the only one of the delegates who is not recorded as having said anything. Because

DELEGATES, COLLECTIVE ASSESSMENTS   213

of its size, Delaware was one of only two states (the other being Rhode Island) who started out in the first Congress with only one member of the U.S. House of Representatives, a number that it retains to this day.

Ratification of the Constitution

Like the Delaware delegates, all of whom signed the Constitution, the people of Delaware were solidly in its favor, and they ratified it quickly. Receiving the Constitution from Congress on October 23, the state legislature called elections for November 26 and the ratifying convention for December 3. The Convention was held in Dover. Each of three counties sent 10 delegates. They ratified the document by a vote of 30-0 on December 7, giving the state the honor (as its license plates still proclaim) of being "the first state." In contrast to other states, there is no record of convention debates and deliberations. In April 1788, Governor Thomas Collins sent Congress a message indicating that the state was offering land for a national capital along with its ratification, but it is not altogether clear whether the Convention had specifically voted on this motion (see Collins 2000).

A student of the ratification process in Delaware has outlined a number of reasons for the state's solid support of the Constitution. He observes first that the state was influenced by support for the document in neighboring Pennsylvania (although Delaware ratified five days before Pennsylvania, it was expecting its ratification). He further observes that the state was pleased with its continuing equality in the Senate under the new government; the state still had hopes that it might be the site of the new national capital; the state foresaw financial benefits in granting Congress power over western lands and in the possibility of a national impost; and that citizens anticipated that the state would have to pay less under the new system, relying on imposts, than it did under the system of requisitions then current under the Articles of Confederation. Leaders were also favorably impressed by the document's prohibition of paper money and its protection for contract rights (Saladino 1989, 45–46).

The parties that had divided Delaware under the Articles of Confederation continued after constitutional ratification. Delaware's former Tories, who succeeded in electing their members to the first Congress, tended to support the Federalist agenda while the Whigs generally supported Democratic-Republican policies (Jensen, 41).

See Also Bassett, Richard; Bedford, Gunning, Jr.; Broom, Jacob; Dickinson, John; Read, George

FOR FURTHER READING

Collins, Sheldon S. 2000. "A Delaware Initiative for Establishing the Federal Capital." *Delaware History* 29: 71–76.

Farrand, Max, ed. 1937. *The Records of the Federal Convention.* 4 vols. New Haven, CT: Yale University Press.

Hancock, Harold. 1988. "Delaware Becomes the First State." In Patrick T. Conley and John P. Kaminski, eds., *The Constitution and the States: The Role of the Original Thirteen in the Framing and Adoption of the Federal Constitution.* Madison, WI: Madison House.

Jensen, Merrill, ed. 1978. *Ratification of the Constitution by the States Delaware, New Jersey, Georgia, Connecticut.* Vol. 3 of *The Documentary History of the Ratification of the Constitution.* Madison: State Historical Society of Wisconsin.

Offutt, William M., Jr. 1995. *Of "Good Laws" and "Good Men": Law and Society in the Delaware Valley, 1680–1710.* Urbana: University of Illinois Press.

Saladino, Gaspare J. 1989. "Delaware: Independence and the Concept of a Commercial Republic." In Michael Allen Gillespie and Michael Lienesch, eds., *Ratifying the Constitution.* Lawrence: University Press of Kansas.

DELEGATES, COLLECTIVE ASSESSMENTS

Perhaps because the Constitution they wrote has lasted so long and has been the object of affection and national unity as well as a workable instrument of government, it is a commonplace for scholars and citizens to refer to the delegates to the Convention as, in words that Thomas Jefferson quoted in a letter to John Adams, "an assembly of demi-gods" (quoted in Farrand 1913, 39). One participant, Benjamin Franklin, reflecting his prior service as a diplomat to France, referred to the Convention as "une assemblée des notables[,] a convention composed of some of the principal people from the several States of our confederation" (Farrand 1937, III, 31). William Pierce of Georgia, who distinguished himself by writing short descriptions of most of the delegates, expressed satisfaction in having had "a seat in the wisest Council in the World" (III, 97). In writing to his wife Polly on June 15 of 1787, Delaware's John Dickinson said that the Convention was "of an excellent temper—and for Abilities exceeds, I believe any Assembly that ever met upon this Continent, except for the first Congress" (Hutson 1987, 75).

These impressions of the Convention were undoubtedly furthered in 1878 when William E. Gladstone, then an opposition member of Parliament attempting to further positive Anglo-American relations, observed that "as the British Constitution is the most subtle organism which had proceeded from the womb and the long gestation of progressive history, so the American Constitution is, so far as I can see, the most wonderful work ever struck off at a given time by the brain and purpose of man" (quoted in Kammen 1987, 162). Critics have, however, attacked Gladstone's quotation for its failure to recognize such antecedents of the U.S. Constitution as the English common law and the state constitutions of the Revolutionary period.

Moreover, not all contemporary observers of the Convention were as impressed either with its product or with the quality of the delegates who attended. New York Antifederalist Melancthon Smith thus wrote:

> I do not wish to detract from their merits, but I will venture to affirm, that twenty assemblies of equal number might be collected, equally respectable both in point of ability, integrity, and

patriotism. Some of the characters which compose it I revere; others I consider as of small consequence, and a number are suspected of being great public defaulters, and to have been guilty of notorious peculation and fraud, with regard to public property in the hour of our distress. (Quoted in Ford 1970, 115)

North Carolina's Hugh Williamson reported that Virginia's George Mason, one of three participants at the Convention who refused to sign the Constitution, said:

> You may have been taught . . . to respect the Characters of the Members of the late Convention. You may have supposed that they were an assemblage of great Men. There is nothing less true. From the Eastern States there were Knaves and Fools from the states Southward of Virginia They were a parcel of Coxcombs and from the middle States Office Hunters not a few. (Letter of June 3, 1788, cited in Hutson 1987, 295)

Farrand has observed that "the truth lies between the two opinions (1913, 40), and Walter Mead has described the delegates under the title "Mediocrity Amidst Merit" (1987, 36). The Convention included the two most notable men in the colonies, George Washington and Benjamin Franklin. The former, however, is known to have spoken out formally only on a single issue, while the second was not only infirm but found that other delegates listened to him with respect but rarely adopted his ideas (Garver 1936–1937, 549; however, see Carr 1990). Other men, like Alexander Hamilton of New York and George Wythe of Virginia did not attend frequently enough to exert significant influence. Robert Morris, the financier of the Revolution, attended consistently, but spoke rarely.

A student of the subject has evaluated convention delegates according to four criteria: "influence, ability, activity, and success in getting worth-while things done" (Garver, 545). In contrast to some bodies, Garver discovered that at the Convention, "the workers did the talking and the talkers did the work" (545). Judged by this and other standards, Virginia's James Madison and Pennsylvania's James Wilson and Gouverneur Morris clearly stand out. A second tier would include Roger Sherman, Elbridge Gerry, and Charles Pinckney. Somewhat behind them were George Mason, Hugh Williamson, Rufus King, Edmund Randolph, and Oliver Ellsworth. Garver believes that Washington and Franklin would fall into a second class behind these 12 men in terms of influence at the Convention, with most others falling into a relatively anonymous third class (Garver, 553). Although members of this third class may have had some behind-the-scenes influence, they appear to have been most important as "a sort of jury, accepting or rejecting the propositions advanced by the active members" (Garver, 546). Followers rather than leaders, many still were highly esteemed within their individual states, and their collective imprimatur undoubtedly gave legitimacy to the final document.

See Also Delegates, Individual Rankings; Speeches, Number of

FOR FURTHER READING

Carr, William G. 1990. *The Oldest Delegate: Franklin in the Constitutional Convention.* Newark: University of Delaware Press.

Farrand, Max. 1913. *The Framing of the Constitution of the United States.* New Haven, CT: Yale University Press.

——, ed. 1937. *The Records of the Federal Convention.* 4 vols. New Haven, CT: Yale University Press.

Ford, Paul Leicester. 1970. *Pamphlets on the Constitution of the United States Published during Its Discussion by the People, 1787–1788.* New York: Burt Franklin.

Garver, Frank H. 1936–1937. "Leadership in the Constitutional Convention of 1787." *Sociology and Social Research,* 544–553.

Hutson, James H., ed. 1987. *Supplement to Max Farrand's* The Records of the Federal Convention of 1787. New Haven, CT: Yale University Press.

Kammen, Michael. 1987. *A Machine That Would Go of Itself: The Constitution in American Culture.* New York: Alfred A. Knopf.

Mead, Walter B. 1987. *The United States Constitution: Personalities, Principles, and Issues.* Columbia: University of South Carolina Press.

DELEGATES, COLLECTIVE PROFILE

Of 74 men chosen by the states, 55 attended the Constitutional Convention. They represented each of the 13 states except for Rhode Island, which refused to send delegates.

Geographical Distribution

The colonies were often classified as falling in three sections: the East (also known as the North or as New England), the Middle states, and the South. Each section was represented at the Convention, with the Middle Atlantic and Southern states clearly predominating among delegates (each state, however, cast a single vote). New Hampshire, Massachusetts, and Connecticut sent a total of nine delegates; New York, New Jersey, Pennsylvania, and Delaware sent 21 delegates; and Maryland, Virginia, the Carolinas and Georgia sent 25 delegates. In addition, eight delegates had been born abroad (Lieberman 1987, 44). Some studies of collective characteristics single out the delegates to the Constitutional Convention for special treatment whereas others group them with delegates who were selected but did not attend or with individuals who signed the Declaration of Independence.

Natives and Immigrants

Eight of the 55 delegates who attended the Convention were born abroad. New Jersey's William Paterson, Pennsylvania's Thomas Fitzsimmons, Maryland's James McHenry, and South Carolina's Pierce Butler had all been born in Ireland. Pennsylvania's Robert Morris and North Carolina's William Davie had been born in England. Pennsylvania's James Wilson had been born in Scotland and New York's Alexander Hamilton in Nevis, West Indies. Pennsylvania's Benjamin Franklin was among those who were born to immigrant parents, but many other delegates were products of long-established American families (Carr 1990, 29).

Political Experience

Apart from the fact that they were all adult, white males (most of English dissent), perhaps the most obvious characteristic of the delegates that was relevant to their work at the Convention was that most were politically experienced. Political scientist Martin Diamond has thus observed that 6 of the 55 delegates had signed the Declaration of Independence; 6 had signed the Articles of Confederation; 24 had served in the Continental Congress; 46 had served in state or colonial legislatures; 10 had helped to draft state constitutions; 39 had served, or were then serving, in the federal Congress; and 3 had been confederal administrative officers (1981, 17). In addition, seven had been delegates to the Annapolis Convention, which had issued the call for the Convention, and others had served, or were serving, either as state governors or presidents (designations varied from state to state). Seven of the delegates to the Convention were members of the Congress at the time of their service (Potts 1986, 145).

Prior Military Service

Delegates had often supplemented their political experience with military service. Nearly two-thirds had served either in the Continental Army or in state militias (Carr, 27). Twenty-one of the delegates had fought in the Revolutionary War. The most renowned of these was, of course, George Washington, who had been commander-in-chief. New York's Alexander Hamilton had served as his aide-de-camp and had distinguished himself at the battle of Yorktown. Former brigadier-generals attending the Convention included Delaware's John Dickinson, Pennsylvania's Thomas Mifflin, and South Carolina's Charles Cotesworth Pinckney. North Carolina's Hugh Williamson had served as an army surgeon and Georgia's Abraham Baldwin as a chaplain. Such service was likely to have con-

tributed to the "continental" perspective of many of these delegates (see Risjord 1974, 626, confirming such an effect among members of Virginia's ratifying convention).

Age, Marriage, Children

Delegates ranged in age from New Jersey's Jonathan Dayton, who was 26 (seeking additionally glory, South Carolina's Charles Pinckney falsely claimed to be younger), to Pennsylvania's Benjamin Franklin, who was 81. George Washington was 55 at the time of the Convention; Madison was nineteen years younger. The average birth year of the delegates was 1743, and their average age was just over 43 (Brown 1976, 469).

The average Founding Father died at age 66.5 years, just about the same as the general average for that time period (Brown, 471). Some died within a year or two of the Convention. The last delegate who attended the Convention to die was James Madison (born in 1751), who passed away in 1836. Drawing from a list of prominent Federalists and Antifederalists compiled by Merrill Jensen, Stanley Elkins and Eric McKitrick have observed that the average age of the former was 10 to 12 years younger than the latter. They believe that, as "young men of the Revolution," many of the Federalist Founders had gained a more continental perspective than their Antifederalist contemporaries (1961, 203; see also Risjord, 624).

Although there were a few confirmed bachelors, most of the delegates to the Constitution were either married or, like Virginia's James Madison, were to become so. Delegates to both the Constitutional Convention and the Second Continental Congress tended to marry later (at the average age of 19.4 years) than members of the general population. They also had fewer children—an average of 4.8 rather than the more general average of six or seven (Brown, 469–470). Married delegates had from 0 (George Washington) to 15 children (Roger Sherman). Whereas members of the general population tended to marry individuals from the same state as themselves, almost half

Wives of the Delegates

Of the forty-seven delegates who attended the Constitutional Convention from out of town, 38 were married, and others, like James Madison, would later become so. Seven to nine of the others brought their wives with them. These included Charles Cotesworth Pinckney, who observed his first wedding anniversary with his second wife during the Convention; Elbridge Gerry and Rufus King from Massachusetts; New York's Alexander Hamilton; William Houston of New Jersey; Virginia's Edmund Randolph; and Pierce Butler of South Carolina. Maryland's Luther Martin and South Carolina's John Rutledge may also have brought their wives. Not all wives who accompanied their husbands stayed in the city throughout the entire summer (*Bicentennial Daybook*, June 24).

Although the strength of their marital bonds might have influenced whether delegates brought their wives, they also had to take into account the ages of their children and whether they could find help to care for them, possible health hazards of the city (including plagues), financial considerations, the need to have someone to look after the family farm or business, and their ability to attend to their families during the press of Convention business. American diplomats and other public servants often had to make similar decisions.

In an age before telegraphs and telephones, delegates often had to settle for short visits home or for letters—one reason that historians know as much as they do about the relationship between John and Abigail Adams is that we have correspondence from long periods during which they were separated. One of the more amusing letters from the Constitutional Convention is a letter that Oliver Ellsworth of Massachusetts sent to his wife on July 21. He observed: "I believe the older men grow the more uneasy they are [away] from their wives." He observed that in his wife's absence, he had clasped "the hand of a woman who died many hundred years ago" (Hutson 1987, 177). The hand in question was that of an arm that had been detached from an Egyptian mummy and brought to Philadelphia. Ellsworth described the arm in detail, noting that "the flesh, which I tried with my knife, cuts and looks much like smoked beef kept till it grows hard." He further speculated that their friend Dr. Stiles, the president of Yale, an Orientalist, would likely have tried to eat the entire arm (Hutson, 177).

FOR FURTHER READING

Bicentennial Daybook. Bicentennial of the Constitution of the United States. Research Project Working Files, 1783–1987. Library Archives. Independence National Historical Park, Philadelphia, PA.

Hutson, James H., ed. 1987. *Supplement to Max Farrand's* The Records of the Federal Convention of 1787. New Haven, CT: Yale University Press.

(46 percent) of the signers of the Declaration of Independence and members of the Constitutional Convention had married women from out of state, probably reflecting their more cosmopolitan outlooks (Brown, 470). John Adams had thus greeted news that Rufus King of Massachusetts had married Mary Alsop of New York the year before the Convention by observing that "It will be unnatural if federal purposes are not answered by all these intermarriages" (quoted in Roberts 2004, 197).

Education

Delegates were remarkably well educated for their day, with at least 30 having attended college, and others having been schooled at home. Nine had graduated from the College of New Jersey (today's Princeton), four from Yale, three from Harvard, and three from the College of William and Mary. A number had attended colleges abroad. Many had "read law," as was often then the custom, under other American attorneys.

Religious Affiliation

The most common religious identification, held by 28 of 55 delegates, was Episcopalian. Presbyterians and Congregationalists were next, with a smattering of other denominations, including two Roman Catholics (one was Daniel Carroll, whose brother served both as the first Roman Catholic bishop and as the first such archbishop in the United States), and a few known Deists (Bradford 1982, iv–v). Georgia's Abraham Baldwin had served the Continental Army as a chaplain during the Revolutionary War; Delaware's Richard Bassett was a onetime Methodist lay minister who was known for having religious meetings on his property.

Occupations

Given the nature of the Convention's work, it is not surprising that lawyers composed the most numerous group of delegates–34 of 55. Planters, merchants, career politicians, and doctors were also present. Bernstein (1987), whose figures may include delegates who did not attend, believes that 17 delegates held slaves. He classifies 14 as rich, 16 as well-to-do, 16 as comfortable, 5 as being of modest means, and three of being of very modest means. Historians have become particularly fond of classifying individuals according to their wealth and sources of income after historian Charles Beard advanced the controversial thesis that many of the delegates were chiefly motivated by economic concerns. It should be remembered, however, that circumstances sometimes changed rather precipitously, as in the case of Robert Morris who went from being one of the richest men in America to a debtor's prison (a fate similar to that of James Wilson).

Attendance and Participation

Delegates varied significantly in both their attendance and participation. Clinton Rossiter has classified 29 of the 55 delegates as "full-timers," 10 as "full-timers except for a few missed weeks," 12 delegates as having "missed long and critical portions of the Convention," and four as having missed so much that they can almost be classed with the absentees (Rossiter 1966, 164–165). A study of James Madison's notes concludes that Gouverneur Morris was the most talkative delegate, with 173 speeches, while a number of delegates never spoke at all ("Constitutional Convention, 1787," 18). William Pierce's character sketches of delegates indicate that they varied significantly in their skills in public speaking. The average attendance at the Convention appears to have been about 30 delegates a day. Forty-one delegates (and one proxy vote) remained on the final day of the Convention; although no one appears to have been completely satisfied with the outcome, of those remaining, 39 signed the document.

Future Achievements

Two delegates who attended the Convention (Washington and Madison) later served as president, and two others ran for the office. One (Elbridge Gerry) became a vice president (under Madison). Five subsequently served as U.S. Supreme Court justices, 13 as members of the House of Representatives, 19 as senators, one as a territorial governor, four as cabinet members (including a secretary of the treasury, Alexander Hamilton; a secretary of war, James McHenry; and two secretaries of state, Edmund Randolph and James Madison), and seven as ambassadors (Lieberman, 45).

See Also Attendance; Beard, Charles; Delegates, Collective Assessments; Education of Convention Delegates; Occupations of the Delegates; Oratory and Rhetoric; Religious Affiliations of the Delegates; Speeches, Number of

FOR FURTHER READING

Bernstein, David. 1987. "The Constitutional Convention: Facts and Figures." *History Teacher* 21 (November): 11–19.

Bradford, M. M. 1982. *A Worthy Company: Brief Lives of the Framers of the United States Constitution.* Marlborough, NH: Plymouth Rock Foundation.

Brown, Richard D. 1976. "The Founding Fathers of 1776 and 1787: A Collective View." *William and Mary Quarterly* 33 (July): 465–480.

Carr, William G. 1990. *The Oldest Delegate: Franklin in the Constitutional Convention.* Newark: University of Delaware Press.

"Constitutional Convention, 1787." 1861. *The Historical Magazine,* 1st ser., V (January): 18.

Diamond, Martin. 1981. *The Founding of the Democratic Republic.* Itasca, IL: F. F. Peacock Publishers.

Elkins, Stanley, and Eric McKitrick. 1961. "The Founding Fathers: Young Men of the Revolution." *Political Science Quarterly* 76 (June): 181–216.

Lieberman, Jethro K. 1987. *The Enduring Constitution: A Bicentennial Perspective.* Saint Paul, MN: West Publishing.

McDonald, Forrest. 1958. *We the People: The Economic Origins of the Constitution.* Chicago: University of Chicago Press.

Potts, Louis W. 1986. "'A Lucky Moment': The Relationship of the Ordinance of 1787 and the Constitution of 1787." *Mid-America* 68 (October): 141–151.

Risjord, Norman K. 1974. "Virginians and the Constitution: A Multivariant Analysis." *William and Mary Quarterly,* 3rd ser. 31 (October): 613–632.

Roberts, Cokie. 2004. *Founding Mothers: The Women Who Raised Our Nation.* New York: William Morrow.

Rossiter, Clinton. 1966. *1787: The Grand Convention.* New York: W. W. Norton.

DELEGATES, INDIVIDUAL RANKINGS

Ranking U.S. presidents and Supreme Court justices has long been a favorite pastime of American historians and political scientists (see, for example, Pederson and Provizer 2003). It is therefore no surprise that they have also attempted to assess the contributions of the 55 delegates who attended the Constitutional Convention of 1787.

Ranking Delegates According to Times They Spoke

The most objective way to do this is to count the number of times that an individual spoke at the Convention, but such a measure runs up against the obvious fact that loquaciousness does not always equate either with wisdom or with influence. Similarly, although delegates with spotty attendance were unlikely to exert significance influence, some delegates appear to have attended every day of the Convention and never even spoke. The most thorough study of the speeches at the Convention reveals that six speakers spoke more than 100 times–namely Gouverneur Morris (173 times), James Wilson (168), James Madison (161), Roger Sherman (138), George Mason (136), and Elbridge Gerry (119). Six other individuals spoke from 50 to 100 times, namely, Edmund Randolph (78), Hugh Williamson (75), Rufus King (75), Oliver Ellsworth (73), Nathaniel Gorham (68), and Charles Pinckney (61) ("Constitutional Convention, 1787," 18).

It is almost impossible to assess the work of delegates to the Convention apart from one's agreement with their proposals and from their other achievements (indeed, delegates like Washington and Franklin may have been useful precisely because of the prestige that they brought to the body). This too makes objective evaluation next to impossible. Moreover, a number of delegates, most notably James Madison and Alexander Hamilton, exerted significant influence both on calling the Convention and in arguing for its subsequent adoption. Analysts often attempt to place themselves at the Convention by deriving their own assessments from the character sketches of Georgia's William Pierce, but he did not himself attend the entire convention, and he gave significant, perhaps even inordinate, attention to the oratorical and rhetorical skills of the participants.

Early Assessments

Contemporaries of the Convention did not have the extensive knowledge that came with later publication of the Convention's records. They did know that Washington and Franklin had attended and that the former had served as the Convention's president, and the Federalist press often used the reputations of these two men to advance ratification of the Constitution.

George Ticknor Curtis, writing in 1861, identified nine delegates that he thought were most important at the Convention and six other men of distinction that he thought were quite important. His list of nine, in order, consisted of George Washington, Alexander Hamilton, James Madison, Benjamin Franklin, Gouverneur Morris, Rufus King, Charles Cotesworth Pinckney, James Wilson, and Edmund Randolph. The six others were Roger Sherman, Robert Morris, John Dickinson, John Rutledge, Charles Pinckney, and George Mason. The fact that Curtis included Robert Morris, who almost never spoke at the Convention, in the second list suggests that his evaluation may have centered more on the overall contributions that the individuals he identified made to the time period than on their specific contributions to the Convention (Curtis 1861, I, 380–486).

Early Twentieth-Century Assessments

Historian Max Farrand, who has compiled the most extensive records of the Convention before writing his own account of the proceedings, believed that Virginia's James Madison—often referred to, somewhat inaccurately, as *the* Father of the Constitution—was the most preeminent person at the Convention (1913, 197). He believed that Pennsylvania's James Wilson should rank second, and George Washington third (198). He also took note of Pennsylvania's Gouverneur Morris and South Carolina's Charles Pinckney. He placed Rufus King of Massachusetts, Charles C. Pinckney and John Rutledge of South Carolina, and Nathaniel Gorham of Massachusetts just below them, along with Virginia's Edmund Randolph and George Mason and apologies for not including Pennsylvania's Benjamin Franklin, who he thought was feeble and whose opinions he does not think carried much weight (199; but see

Carr 1990, 15–20). Reaching out to include those who did not support as strong a national government, Farrand also listed New Jersey's William Paterson, Delaware's John Dickinson, Elbridge Gerry of Massachusetts, Luther Martin of Maryland, and Oliver Ellsworth, William Samuel Johnson, and Roger Sherman of Connecticut (1913, 200).

Historian Charles Warren said that "the ablest delegations came from five states" and proceeded to list, by state: Washington, Madison and Randolph (VA); King, Gorham and Gerry (MA); Franklin, Wilson, and the two Morrises (PA); Sherman, Ellsworth, and Johnson (CT); and Rutledge, the two Pinckneys, and Butler (SC) (1928, 56). He put Hamilton, Brearly, Paterson, Dickinson, Williamson, Davie, Baldwin, and Martin in a second tier (56–57). Somewhat backtracking, he then attributed the final "form" of the Constitution to 10 delegates—"Madison, Randolph, Franklin, Wilson, Gouverneur Morris, King, Rutledge, Charles Pinckney, Ellsworth, and Sherman" (57).

In his account of the Convention published as part of the sesquicentennial, Sol Bloom ranked Washington as "the most important man in the convention" and Franklin as "the seer of the Convention" (1937, 19). Specifically noting that he was declining to list Hamilton as among those of significant influence, Bloom proceeded to name the following: Gouverneur Morris, Wilson, Sherman, Ellsworth, Gerry, King, Paterson, Dickinson, Martin, Rutledge, the two Pinckneys and Butler. This list seems especially generous to South Carolina (20).

Writing about the same time as Bloom, historian Frank Garver attempted to evaluate delegates according to "influence, ability, activity, and success in getting worth-while things done" (1936–1937, 545). Based on these criteria, Garver divided the influential delegates into three groups, the first tier of which is in turn subdivided into three parts. Garver listed Madison, Wilson, and Gouverneur Morris at the top of the top; followed by Sherman, Gerry, and Charles Pinckney; and Mason, Williamson, King, Randolph, Rutledge, and Ellsworth. Washington and Franklin compose a second tier, and the other delegates compose a third (553).

Mid-Twentieth-Century Assessments

Although he does not appear to have ranked the delegates, it may be significant that Carl Van Doren and his publisher included 10 illustrations of individual delegates to the Convention. They are, in order: George Washington, Benjamin Franklin, James Madison, Alexander Hamilton, George Mason, Roger Sherman, James Wilson, Gouverneur Morris, William Paterson, and Edmund Randolph (unnumbered pages at beginning of book). It is possible that this list reflects familiar faces as much as it does actual perceived influence.

Historian Merrill Jensen, writing in 1958, picked out 12 delegates for special commendation, listing them according to what he perceived to be their ideological orientation. Jensen classified James Madison, James Wilson, and Gouverneur Morris as "the outstanding nationalist leaders"; George Mason, John Dickinson, Oliver Ellsworth, and John Rutledge as middle men "who supported the idea of a strong central government, but who insisted on an important role for the states in the new system"; and Roger Sherman, William Paterson, Elbridge Gerry, and Luther Martin as among those "who wished to retain the federal structure of the old government, although believing it should be strengthened" (1958, 38). Acknowledging his relative silence during the Convention, Jensen further identified George Washington as "perhaps the single most important single member of the Convention," observing that "his presence . . . gave the Convention a 'national complexion,' and his support of the Constitution probably did more to secure its ratification than the hundreds of speeches and newspaper articles of men of lesser reputation" (39).

Sadly denying Alexander Hamilton a place in the group, historian Clinton Rossiter picked out a list of nine critical delegates to the Convention. They were Madison, Wilson, Gouverneur Morris, Sherman, Rutledge, Ellsworth, King, Franklin, and Washington (1966, 49).

With his typical thoroughness, Rossiter introduced what is probably the most comprehensive catalog of delegates to date in his book on the Convention two years later. Then he classified Madison, Wilson, Washington, and Morris as "*The Principals*"; Rutledge, Franklin, Sherman, Charles Pinckney, King, Charles C. Pinckney, Ellsworth, Gorham, Mason, Randolph, and Gerry as "*The Influentials*"; Dickinson, Williamson, Johnson, Read, Butler, Paterson, and Martin as "*The Very Usefuls*"; Brearly, Livingston, Spaight, Bedford, Baldwin, Carroll, Langdon, and Davie as "*The Usefuls*"; Blair, Daniel, Few, Broom, Strong, Houston, Clymer, Dayton, McHenry, and McClurg" as "*The Visibles*"; Bassett, Mifflin, Blount, Ingersoll, Fitzsimons, Gilman, and Martin as "*The Ciphers*"; William C. Houston, Pierce, Wythe, Mercer, Yates, and Lansing as "*The Dropouts and Walkouts*"; and Robert Morris and Hamilton as "*The Inexplicable Disappointments*" (247–252).

Taking a somewhat different approach, Broadus Mitchell and Louise Pearson Mitchell grouped the delegates to the Convention not so much by their contributions to the deliberations as by their abilities. They classified Hamilton, Franklin, Madison, Mason, the two Morrises, Washington, and Wilson as being in "the first order of ability"; Dickinson, Ellsworth, FitzSimmons, Gerry, Johnson, King, Langdon, Livingston, Martin, Paterson, the two Pinckeys, Randolph, Rutledge, and Sherman as "men of character and parts"; and others as "sincere, esteemed, and able" but as making "less impress on the gathering" (1964, 46–47).

In a biography of Rufus King, Robert Ernst listed Madison, Wilson, and Gouverneur Morris as being "in the first rank of those who forged the Constitution. He cited Washington as providing "a steadying influence" and Franklin for his "wit and experience." He then listed "King, Mason, Randolph, Rutledge, Charles Pinckney, Sherman, and Gorham" as "among the most influential secondary leaders" (1968, 116).

Assessments from the Bicentennial of the Constitution to the Present

In an article prepared for the bicentennial of the Constitution, historian Margaret Horsnell chose to highlight 11 delegates that she believed "played key roles in shaping and presenting plans of government, and in hammering out compromises that were crucial to the successful completion of that extraordinary document" (1987, 38). The individuals she chose to highlight were, in order: Washington, Randolph, Sherman, Rutledge, Wilson, G. Morris, Mason, Martin, Paterson, Johnson, and Madison.

More recently, Carol Berkin has identified 12 "critical participants in the convention, shaping the debates, igniting the controversies, and proposing the compromises that made a new constitution possible" (2002, 51). She lists these, presumably in order of importance, as follows: James Madison, Alexander Hamilton (albeit mentioning how "restricted . . . he was by the makeup of his delegation and his own outspoken extreme views"), Benjamin Franklin, Roger Sherman, Gouverneur Morris, James Wilson, Elbridge Gerry, William Paterson, John Dickinson, Charles Pinckney, Edmund Randolph, and George Mason (51). Perhaps because her focus is on direct participation, and he was largely silent, Berkin does not include Washington in this group.

Assessments of the Assessments

Washington and Franklin emerge as perhaps the most difficult delegates to evaluate, Washington because of his studied silence and Franklin because of concerns that delegates may have attended to his speeches more as a matter of respect than of agreement. Garver is the only one of the above analysts who lists North Carolina's Hugh Williamson as among the most influential delegates, a judgment that this writer would affirm on the basis of his own research. Williamson may be the Convention's most underappreciated delegate.

See Also Attendance; Delegates, Collective Assessments; Delegates, Collective Profile; Father of the Constitution; Oratory and Rhetoric; Press Coverage; Speeches, Number of

FOR FURTHER READING

Berkin, Carol. 2002. *A Brilliant Solution: Inventing the American Constitution*. New York: Harcourt.

Bloom, Sol. 1937. *The Story of the Constitution*. Washington, DC: United States Constitution Sesquicentennial Commission.

Carr, William G. 1990. *The Oldest Delegate: Franklin in the Constitutional Convention*. Newark: University of Delaware Press.

"Constitutional Convention, 1787." 1861. *The Historical Magazine*, 1st ser. V (January): 18.

Curtis, George Ticknor. 1861. *History of the Origin, Formation, and Adoption of the Constitution of the United States with Notices of Its Principal Framers*. 2 vols. New York: Harper and Brothers.

Ernst, Robert. 1968. *Rufus King: American Federalist*. Chapel Hill: University of North Carolina Press.

Farrand, Max. 1913. *The Framing of the Constitution of the United States*. New Haven, CT: Yale University Press.

Garver, Frank H. 1936–1937. "Leadership in the Constitutional Convention of 1787." *Sociology and Social Research* 21: 544–553.

Horsnell, Margaret. 1987. "Who Was Who in the Constitutional Convention? A Pictorial Essay of Its Leading Figures." *this Constitution*, no. 15 (Summer): 38–41.

Jensen, Merrill. 1958 (1979 reprint). *The Making of the American Constitution*. Malabar, FL: Robert E. Krieger Publishing Company.

Mitchell, Broadus, and Louise Pearson Mitchell. 1964. *A Biography of the Constitution of the United States: Its Origin, Formation, Adoption, Interpretation*. New York: Oxford University Press.

Pederson, William D., and Norman W. Provizer, eds. 2003. *Leaders of the Pack: Polls and Case Studies of Great Supreme Court Justices*. New York: Peter Lang.

Rossiter, Clinton. 1966. *1787: The Grand Convention*. New York: W. W. Norton.

———. 1964. *Alexander Hamilton and the Constitution*. New York: Harcourt, Brace and World.

Van Doren, Carl. 1948. *The Great Rehearsal: The Story of the Making and Ratifying of the Constitution of the United States*. New York: Viking Press.

Warren, Charles. 1928. *The Making of the Constitution*. Boston: Little, Brown.

DELEGATES WHO DID NOT ATTEND THE CONSTITUTIONAL CONVENTION

Altogether, 55 delegates from 12 states attended the Constitutional Convention at some point during the summer of 1787. An additional 18 men were chosen but did not attend. They were as follows:

> Charles Carroll of Carrollton (Maryland), Richard Caswell (North Carolina), Abraham Clark (New Jersey), Francis Dana (Massachusetts), Gabriel Duvall (Maryland), Robert Hansen Harrison (Maryland), Patrick Henry (Virginia), Willie Jones (North Carolina), Henry Laurens (South Carolina), Richard Henry Lee (Virginia), Thomas Sim Lee (Maryland), John Francis Mercer (Maryland), John Neilson (New Jersey), Thomas Nelson (Virginia), Nathaniel Pendleton (Georgia), John Pickering (New Hampshire), Thomas Stone (Maryland), and Benjamin West (New Hampshire). (Carson 1889, I, 138–139)

This list reveals that Maryland had the highest total (six) of delegates who were chosen but did not attend. All delegates chosen from Connecticut, New York, Pennsylvania, and Delaware who were chosen attended. New Hampshire's delegates would have doubled from two to four if all its delegates who were selected had attended.

Some delegates who had been selected to the Convention, most notably Patrick Henry and Richard Henry Lee of Virginia (both of whom became Antifederalists), refused to attend because they were opposed to what they thought the Convention would do. Others, as for example, members of the Maryland delegation, stayed home in order to attend to pressing legislative business. Still others were prevented from attending by personal circumstances.

Scholars generally agree that the two most important potential delegates who were missing from the Convention were John Adams of Massachusetts, who had played such an important role in the Second Continental Congress and would later become the second U.S. president, and Thomas Jefferson of Virginia, who was the primary author of the Declaration of Independence and who would go on to become the third U.S. president. Neither had been elected to the Convention since the former was serving as a diplomat in Great Britain and the latter in France.

See Also Adams, John; Henry, Patrick; Jefferson, Thomas

FOR FURTHER READING

Carson, Hampton L., ed. 1889. 2 vols. *History of the Celebration of the One Hundredth Anniversary of the Promulgation of the Constitution of the United States.* Philadelphia, PA: J. B. Lippincott.

DEMOCRACY

The word "democracy" is derived from two Greek words, "demos" and "kratis," meaning rule by the people. Today political scientists and politicians generally use the term positively. Classical philosophers warned, however, of the danger that democracy could degenerate into anarchy, or mob rule. Moreover, members of the Constitutional Convention, like their contemporaries in other nations (Palmer 1953), sometimes used the word more negatively to refer to abuses attributed to governments, like those typical in the states under the Articles of Confederation, in which almost all powers were concentrated in state legislatures, the members of which were often subject to annual election and to popular recall (Wood 1969). They associated such governments with "licentiousness" (Farber and Sherry 1990, 16).

Convention proceedings are full of examples of such criticisms. In surveying existing state constitutions Virginia's Edmund Randolph observed on May 29:

> Our chief danger arises from the democratic parts of our constitutions. It is a maxim which I

hold incontrovertible, that the power of the government exercised by the people swallows up the other branches. None of the constitutions have provided sufficient checks against the democracy. (Farrand 1937, I, 26–27)

On May 31, Randolph further traced evils under the Articles of Confederation to "the turbulence and follies of democracy" (I, 51). Somewhat earlier in debates of that day, Connecticut's Roger Sherman had opposed direct election of members of the U.S. House of Representatives on the basis that "the people [immediately] should have as little to do as may be about the Government" (I, 48). Elbridge Gerry of Massachusetts immediately followed these comments by observing that "The evils we experience flow from the excess of democracy. The people do not want virtue; but are the dupes of pretended patriots" (I, 48; also see comments at I, 123; I, 132). Virginia's George Mason, by contrast, observed that the House of Rep-

resentatives should be "the grand depository of the democratic principle of the Govt." (I, 48). Pennsylvania's James Wilson in turn argued:

He was for raising the federal pyramid to a considerable altitude, and for that reason wished to give it as broad a basis as possible. No government could long subsist without the confidence of the people. In a republican Government this confidence was particularly essential. (I, 49)

Similarly, Mason observed on June 4: "Notwithstanding the oppressions & injustice experienced among us from democracy; the genius of the people is in favor of it, and the genius of the people must be consulted" (I, 101).

On June 18, Alexander Hamilton of New York, who was an admirer of the English system of government, contrasted the few and the many, the former of which are rich, and the latter of which have the majority. He further observed: "The

Plato, a student of Socrates and teacher of Aristotle, is best known for writing The Republic, *his search for justice in an ideal state. (Corbis)*

voice of the people has been said to be the voice of God; and however generally this maxim has been quoted and believed, it is not true in fact. The people are turbulent and changing; they seldom judge or determine right" (I, 299). He therefore advocated granting the rich "a distinct, permanent share in the government" (I, 299).

Although the delegates did not adopt Hamilton's specific proposals, when they devised their own plans for a new national government, they provided a strong popular foundation by providing that the people would choose members of the lower house by direct popular elections and state legislatures would in turn choose members of the upper house. Delegates proceeded to divide Congress into two houses and to balance both houses with a single executive with conditional veto powers as well as with a judicial branch that over time asserted its power, today called judicial review, to invalidate laws that it considered to be unconstitutional. Delegates devised a form of indirect election, which they embodied in the Electoral College, for selecting the president. The president, in turn, appointed and the Senate confirmed members of the judiciary, who served for life terms.

In describing the government that they had created, the Framers of the Constitution began with the words "We the People," but instead of referring to their product as a democracy, they more generally referred to it as a "republic" or "free government." In *Federalist* No. 10, James Madison explained that a republic differed from a pure democracy in two respects. First, it filtered popular opinions through representatives, who were expected to take a broader view of the public interests. Second, because it used this mechanism, a republic was capable of expanding over a much wider land area. Turning the argument of Charles Louis de Secondat de Montesquieu, who had argued that republics were appropriate to small governmental entities and despotisms to large ones, on its head, Madison argued that larger entities would encompass more factions, or interests, and would therefore make it less likely that any such interests would dominate in the new government. Despite such distinctions, the uses of the terms "democracy" and "republic" tended then and thereafter to blend together.

See Also Aristocracy; *Federalist, The;* Forms of Government; Monarchy; Republicanism

FOR FURTHER READING

Adams, Willi Paul. 2001. *The First American Constitutions: Republican Ideology and the Making of the State Constitutions in the Revolutionary Era.* Lanham, MD: Rowman and Littlefield Publishers.

Farber, Daniel A., and Suzanna Sherry. 1990. *A History of the American Constitution.* Saint Paul, MN: West Publishing.

Farrand, Max, ed. 1937. *The Records of the Federal Convention.* 4 vols. New Haven, CT: Yale University Press.

Hamilton, Alexander, John Jay, and James Madison. *The Federalist.* Washington, DC: Robert B. Luce.

Palmer, R. R. 1953. "Notes on the Use of the Word 'Democracy' 1789–1799." *Political Science Quarterly* 68 (June): 203–226.

Pole, J. J. 1962. "Historians and the Problem of Early American Democracy." *American Historical Review* 67 (April): 626–646.

Wood, Gordon S. 1969. *The Creation of the American Republic, 1776–1787.* Chapel Hill: University of North Carolina Press.

DEMOCRATIC PARTY

See FEDERALIST AND DEMOCRATIC-REPUBLICAN PARTIES

DICKINSON, JOHN (1732–1808)

Delaware's John Dickinson was an attorney with a long history of service to two different states. Born in Talbot County, Maryland on November 8, 1732, to Samuel Dickinson and Mary Cadwalader

Dickinson, wealthy Quaker planters (his father also served as a judge), Dickinson finished his study of law under a Philadelphia attorney by attending the Middle Temple in London. Dickinson married Mary ("Polly") Norris, the daughter of a wealthy Philadelphian, in 1770, and he and his wife had two daughters.

Elected first to the Delaware colonial assembly and then to the assembly in Pennsylvania, Dickinson earned the reputation as the "penman of the Revolution." His works included the "Declaration of Rights" that the Stamp Act Congress adopted; "Letters from a Farmer in Pennsylvania to the Inhabitants of the British Colonies," in which he presented the colonial case against the Townsend Acts; and "Petition to the King" and "Declaration of the Causes and Necessity of Taking Up Arms," both of which the Second Continental Congress adopted. Although he justified the resort to force against the English, Dickinson continued to hope for reconciliation. He, and fellow delegate Robert Morris, absented themselves from the Second Continental Congress so that the Pennsylvania delegation on which he served could vote for independence, but Dickinson did not personally either vote for independence or sign the Declaration of Independence. A devoted Patriot, he did enlist in the militia, serving first in the capacity of a private and later being appointed as a brigadier general.

As a member of the Second Continental Congress, Dickinson wrote the first draft of what became the Articles of Confederation, but Congress modified his draft so as to give greater powers to the states that he had anticipated. Dickinson served from 1781 to 1782 as president of Delaware and from 1782 to1785 as president of Pennsylvania; during the latter term, he donated property for the establishment of what became Dickinson College. Having been a legislator and an executive in two states—one large and another small—Dickinson understood the respective positions of both states in regard to representation and other matters. The state that sent Dickinson to Philadelphia had specifically instructed its delegates not to change the method of representation under the Articles of Confederation.

When Dickinson arrived at the Constitutional Convention on Tuesday, May 29, he believed that "the confederation is defective" and "that it ought to be amended" (Farrand 1937, I, 42). Although professing to be obliged to Edmund Randolph for introducing the Virginia Plan, Dickinson believed the better way to proceed would be to ask what the legislative, executive, and judicial powers were then lacking and "then proceed to the definition of such powers as may be thought adequate to the objects for which it [the government] was instituted" (I, 42).

Dickinson prepared a plan of government, but he never presented it to the Convention. He did not speak from June 21 through July 25, presumably being sick and/or absent much of this time. On his return to the Convention, this absence might well have given him a perspective on intervening developments (including adoption of the Great Compromise) that other members did not have.

Congress

Representation

On June 2, Dickinson argued that it would be necessary for the large and small states to practice "mutual concession." He indicated that he thought that states should have equal representation in at least one house and favored apportioning the other according to state contributions to the national treasury (I, 87; also see I, 196). Dickinson later introduced the proviso that each state should have at least one representative in the branch to be apportioned according to tax contributions (II, 223).

Similarly, on August 21, Dickinson expressed concerns that the number of representatives of the large states should be limited; one reason he offered was that, without such a limitation, "encouragement" might be "given to the importation of slaves" (II, 356). Dickinson, who had freed his own slaves, returned to this theme the next day, saying that it was "inadmissible on every principle of honor & safety that the importation of slaves should be authorized to the States by the Constitution" and urging that Congress be given authority over this issue (II, 372). Although he may well

John Dickinson, delegate from Delaware
(Pixel That)

have been mistaken, Dickinson did not believe that the Southern states would refuse to join the new Union simply over this point. When the Convention decided to allow states to continue importation of slaves until 1808, Dickinson tried unsuccessfully to leave this power open only to the states that were currently exercising it (II, 416).

Dickinson favored drawing one branch "immediately from the people," but proposed that the other might be chosen by state legislatures (I, 136). Dickinson openly advocated forming the Senate as close to the English House of Lords as possible. Favoring state legislative choice of senators, Dickinson advocated giving them terms of three, five, or seven years and not making them (as were delegates under the Articles of Confederation) subject to recall (I, 136).

Selection and Qualifications of Senators

Dickinson elaborated on state legislative selection of senators on June 7, when he proposed this as a formal motion. He argued both that "the sense of the States would be better collected through their Government; than immediately from the people at large," and that such a mechanism would be more likely to result in a Senate "of the most distinguished characters, distinguished for their rank in life and their weight of property, and bearing as strong a likeness to the British House of Lords as possible" (I, 150). In contrast to a number of other delegates who anticipated that the Senate would gain weight if its numbers were relatively limited, Dickinson favored a Senate of 80 members, or even twice that. He feared that "if their number should be small, the popular branch could not be [ba]lanced by them. The legislature of a numerous people ought to be a numerous body" (I, 150). Similarly, he argued later in the day that "the Senate ought to be composed of a large number, and that their influence [from family weight & other causes] would be increased thereby" (I, 153).

On June 15, the day that William Paterson introduced the New Jersey Plan, Madison observed that Dickinson had upbraided him, accusing his intransigence of having led to the plan:

> Mr. Dickinson said to Mr. Madison you see the consequences of pushing things too far. Some of the members from the small States wish for two branches in the General Legislature, and are friends to a good National Government; but we would sooner submit to a foreign power, than submit to be deprived of an equality of suffrage, in both branches of the legislature, and thereby be thrown under the dominion of the large States. (I, 242)

On July 26, after George Mason had moved that the Convention specify "certain qualifications of landed property & citizenship" for members of Congress (I, 121), Dickinson indicated that he opposed specifying such qualifications within the Constitution. He observed that it was impossible to recite all qualifications that might be necessary and that a partial list "would by implication tie up the hands of the Legislature from supplying the omissions" (II, 123). Despite what he had earlier said about modeling the Senate on the English House of Lords, he now "doubted the policy of interweaving into a Republican constitution a veneration for wealth." Indeed, he sagely observed that "He had always understood that a veneration for poverty & virtue, were the objects of republican encouragement. It seemed improper that any man of merit should be subjected to disabilities in a Republic where merit was understood to form the great title to public trust, honors & rewards" (II, 123).

Nonetheless, on August 7, Dickinson indicated that he was willing to limit the vote to "freeholders," even though some states did not at the time have such a requirement:

> He considered them as the best guardians of liberty: And the restriction of the right to them as a necessary defence agst. the dangerous influence of those multitudes without property & without principle, with which our Country, like all others, will in time abound. As to the unpopularity of the innovation it was in his opinion chimerical. The great mass of our Citizens is composed at this time of freeholders, and will be pleased with it. (II, 202)

Powers of the Two Houses

Dickinson was among the delegates who supported the provision limiting the origination of money bills to the House of Representatives. In a frequently cited speech advocating this limitation that he gave on August 13, Dickinson argued that the delegates needed to be guided by "experience" rather than by "reason" (II, 278). He believed that experience both in Great Britain and in the states confirmed the policy of limiting the origination of such money bills to the lower houses, although he was willing to allow the upper house to make amendments. He further thought that such a provision would help inoculate the document against anticipated criticisms:

> When this plan goes forth, it will be attacked by the popular leaders. Aristocracy will be the watchword; the Shibboleth among its adversaries. Eight States have inserted in their Consti-

tutions the exclusive right of originating money bills in favor of the popular branch of the Legislature. Most of them however allowed the other branch to amend. This he thought would be proper for us to do. (II, 278)

Contrary to the Convention's eventual decision granting most appointment powers to the president subject to the "advice and consent" of the Senate, Dickinson believed that Congress should make the "great appointments" rather than the president (II, 329). He also opposed prohibiting Congress from taxing all exports, although he did not oppose designating "particular articles from the power" (II, 361).

Dickinson favored allowing both houses of Congress, and not simply the Senate, to make treaties. He did so despite believing that this would be "unfavorable to the little States" like the one he was representing (II, 393). As a way of protecting the small states, Dickinson believed that congressional consent should be required to any inspection duties (II, 589).

Presidency

Dickinson offered a plan on June 2 whereby "the Executive be made removeable by the National Legislature on the request of a majority of the Legislatures of individual States" (I, 85). He thought that this removal mechanism would be superior to impeachment. Dickinson indicated that although he favored separation of powers into three independent branches, he feared that a single executive was not consistent with a republic; "that a firm Executive could only exist in a limited monarchy" (I, 86).

Dickinson opposed the idea of a Council of Revision that would unite the executive with members of the judiciary. He feared that this would undermine executive responsibility and that it "involved an improper mixture of powers" (I, 140). However, on September 7, Dickinson indicated that he favored an Executive Council, which he apparently anticipated would act, much like today's cabinet, in a purely advisory capacity. He observed on this occasion that "It wd. be a singular thing if the measures of the Executive were not to undergo some previous discussion before the President" (II, 542).

The plan of government that Dickinson prepared had called for a tripartite executive to be selected by state legislatures. On his return to debates at the Convention on July 25, Dickinson indicated that he "had long leaned towards an election by the people which he regarded as the best and purest source" (II, 114), but he actually proposed a mediated form of election, not altogether dissimilar to the Electoral College that the Convention eventually adopted. Dickinson favored having each state nominate its best citizen and then allowing either Congress, or electors appointed by Congress for this purpose, to decide which of these would be president (II, 115). On September 5, Dickinson indicated that he thought the entire Congress, and not simply the Senate, should resolve deadlocks in the Electoral College when any individual failed to achieve a majority (II, 513).

Judiciary

When South Carolina's John Rutledge proposed on June 5 to eliminate the provision for lower federal courts—relying instead on courts within the states—Dickinson indicated that he thought that "if there was to be a National Legislature, there ought to be a national Judiciary, and that the former ought to have authority to institute the latter" (I, 125).

Dickinson agreed on August 15 with Maryland's John Mercer in believing that federal courts should not exercise the power, now known as judicial review, to invalidate acts of Congress. However, although "He thought no such power ought to exist," he also indicated that "He was at the same time at a loss what expedient to substitute" (II, 299).

When the Convention was discussing treason, Dickinson indicated that he thought the term "giving aid & comfort" to the enemy was too vague. He further proposed that the testimony of two witnesses should be required to an overt act (II, 346), and not simply to a series of events that

might be so interpreted. He also wanted to make it clear that war against any one state was war against the whole (II, 349).

On August 27, Dickinson indicated that he wanted to modify judicial service during good behavior so as to specify that the executive could remove judges on the application of Congress (II, 428). The Convention wisely rejected this proposal, which could have interfered with judicial independence. Dickinson appeared to believe that the division of Congress into two branches made it unlikely that the two "would improperly unite for the purpose of displacing a Judge" (II, 429). Dickinson successfully modified what became Article III of the Constitution by introducing the motion granting jurisdiction to federal courts "both as to law & fact" (II, 431).

Federalism

On June 2, Dickinson indicated that he "had no idea of abolishing the State Governments as some gentlemen seemed inclined to do. The happiness of this Country . . . required considerable powers to be left in the hands of the States" (I, 85). He reiterated this point later in the day, when he observed that one of the remedies for the diseases of republican government was the "division of this country into distinct States" (I, 87). He believed that such a division would lead to "stability" (I, 86); he seemed to believe that "A House of Nobles," which might also lead to stability, would be impossible in the United States since such nobles "were the growth of ages, and could only arise under a complication of circumstances none of which existed in this Country" (I, 87).

Perhaps as much as any delegate, Dickinson believed that the division between state and national governments was a vital part of checks and balances. Arguing on June 7 for retaining the states, Dickinson explained his view at length:

To attempt to abolish the States altogether, would degrade the Councils of our Country, would be impracticable, would be ruinous. He compared the proposed National System to the Solar System, in which the States were the planets, and ought to be left to move freely in their proper orbits. . . .

If the State Governments were excluded from all agency in the national one, and all power drawn from the people at large, the consequences would be that the national Govt. would move in the same direction as the State Govts. now do, and would run into all the same mischiefs. The reform would only unite the 13 small streams into one great current pursuing the same course without any opposition whatever. (I, 153)

Despite advocating state legislative selection of senators, Dickinson expressed support on June 8 for the congressional negative on state laws. Arguing that there was greater danger that the states would encroach on the national government than the reverse (at least, perhaps, under the system he favored whereby members of the Senate were to be chosen by state legislatures), he said that "To leave the power doubtful, would be opening another spring of discord, and he was for shutting as many of them as possible" (I, 167).

Similarly, on August 30, Dickinson indicated that he believed that Congress should be able to protect states against domestic violence whether the state legislatures requested such aid or not. He was apparently contemplating situations in which such controversies might "proceed from the State Legislature itself, or from disputes between the two branches where such exist" (II, 467). The Convention agreed to allow either the state legislature or the state executive to apply for such help (II, 467).

Dickinson indicated on August 14 that he disfavored leaving members of Congress dependent on state legislatures for their pay. He suggested that Congress might set wages every 12 years. He further observed that "If the Genl. Govt. should be left dependent on the State Legislatures, it would be happy for us if we had never met in this Room" (II, 292). Although Dickinson originally thought that the pay for both houses of Congress should be the same, he withdrew his motion after Nathaniel Gorham made an argument as to why senators should receive more (II, 293).

Dickinson wanted to preserve a role for the states in regulating militia. He favored a plan on August 18 that would invest the national government with the power to regulate only one-fourth of the militia at a time, hoping that through rotation, the entire militia would ultimately be so disciplined (II, 331).

Dickinson observed on August 29 that he had been reading William Blackstone's *Commentaries* and that he had discovered that a prohibition on states against adopting ex post facto laws would apply only to criminal laws. He accordingly suggested that some provision should be made against state adoption of retroactive civil laws as well (II, 449).

Perhaps with an eye to fears that Pennsylvania might seek to swallow Delaware, on August 30 Dickinson introduced the provision in the Constitution that provided that new states could not be formed within existing states or parts of states without their consent and that of Congress (II, 465).

Dickinson's Plan

At the time the Convention was comparing the Virginia and New Jersey Plans, Dickinson drafted a plan of his own. This plan combined elements of both plans as well as developing some mechanisms that were unique to Dickinson. Perhaps in deference to Alexander Hamilton who offered a plan at about the same time, or perhaps because Dickinson did not succeed in getting approval for a motion that would have introduced this plan, Dickinson never formally introduced this plan at the Convention. It nonetheless gives insight into what he and other delegates may have been thinking.

Dickinson's plan was divided into seven parts. The first called for a revision and an amendment of the Articles of Confederation, but the second recognized the need for three distinct branches of government. The third article further called, as in the Virginia Plan, for a bicameral Congress. Article 4 provided that members of one branch should be chosen, as under the Articles, by states, each to have one vote. Members were to be 30 years of age and to serve for seven-year terms;

members selected to fill a vacant term would only serve to the end of this term, thus ensuring the turnover of one-seventh of its members each year (Hutson 1987, 88).

Article 5 provided for the selection of the other house by people of the states for terms of three years, again to serve rotating terms. Members of this branch were to be apportioned according to the money that each state contributed to the common treasury, with new states to be treated identically to the original states.

Much as the Committee of Detail would later do, Article 6 proceeded to outline new powers for the government. These included powers "to pass Acts for enforcing an Observance of the Laws of Nations and an Obedience to their own Laws"; to levy duties, imposts, and stamps; to transfer suits from state to national courts; to emit money; to regulate "the Value and Alloy of Coin"; to negative state acts; to judge contests within states that might disturb the public peace; to secure "the Writ of Habeas Corpus and Trial by Jury in proper Cases"; and "for preventing Contests concerning the Authority of the United States and the Authority of individual states" (Hutson 1987, 90).

Article 7 contained a modified supremacy clause. It provided

> that all Laws and Resolves of any state in any Manner opposing or contravening the powers now vested or hereby to be vested in the United States or any Act of the United States made by Virtue and in pursuance of such powers or any Treaties made and ratified under the United States shall be utterly null and void (this nearly as in the proposals from New Jersey). (Hutson 1987, 90)

Article 7 further outlined the executive branch. Consistent with Dickinson's earlier reservations that a single executive might become a monarchy, Dickinson proposed that two-thirds of the state legislatures should be able to elect an executive of three persons, "one of them a Resident of the Eastern States, another of the Middle States and the third of the Southern States" (Hutson 1987, 90).

Initially, one would serve for two years, another for four years, and a third for seven years, with seven years becoming the eventual norm. The individual elected to the seven-year term, and thereafter the individual with the longest service, would be president. Members of the executive could be removed by Congress "if they judge it proper on Application by a Majority of the Executives of the several states" (Hutson 1987, 91). Members of the executive branch would also be impeachable "for Malconduct or Neglect of Duty" (Hutson 1987, 91). The members of the executive would be jointly responsible for everything they did, unless they recorded their dissents to the same. They would exercise the power of the veto subject to an override by two-thirds of Congress.

Dickinson further specified that the legislature would appoint members of the judiciary, and that "this Judiciary would have Authority to determine in the first Instance in all Cases touching the Rights of Ambassadors and other foreign Ministers" (Hutson 1987, 91). Congress would have power to establish inferior tribunals.

Dickinson then indicated that he favored the Report of the Committee of the Whole "from the 14th Resolution of the Report, inclusive to the End" (Hutson 1987, 91). These provisions respectively provided for the admission of new states; the continuance of Congress until a new government could be instituted; guaranteeing each state a republican form of government; an amending provision; state officials to be bound to the new Constitution by oath; and ratification of the new Constitution by special conventions within the states elected by the people (see I, 237).

Ratification

The plan that Dickinson prepared but never introduced at the Convention indicated that he favored ratification of the Constitution by ratifying conventions. He appeared to reiterate this point on August 30 when he questioned whether the Congress under the Articles of Confederation "could concur in contravening the system under which they acted" (II, 469).

Committees

Dickinson served on three committees at the Convention. He was appointed on August 18 to the Committee on State Debts and Militia, on August 22 to the Committee on Slave Trade and Navigation, and on August 31 to the Committee on Postponed Matters. It was this committee that was responsible for the invention of the Electoral College mechanism for choosing the president. Dickinson claimed in a letter of 1802 that his concern for a method of making the president accountable to the people was influential in creating this mechanism, although he attributed its actual writing to James Madison (see Flower 1983, 246–247).

Life after the Convention

Exhausted by ill health, Dickinson left Philadelphia before the Convention ended. Perhaps with a view to the criticism he had received for not signing the Declaration of Independence, Dickinson designated fellow delegate George Read to sign his name. Dickinson wrote some essays for the *Delaware Gazette* under the name of "Fabias" in support of the new Constitution (for analysis, see Ahern 1998). In 1792, Dickinson served as a delegate to the Delaware state constitutional convention, and was elected its president. He did some further writing, which did not, however, have the same force as his earlier works. He died in Wilmington, Delaware on February 14, 1808.

See Also Articles of Confederation; Committee on Postponed Matters; Committee on Slave Trade and Navigation; Committee on State Debts and Militia; Delaware; Dickinson Plan

FOR FURTHER READING

Ahern, Gregory S. 1998. "The Spirit of American Constitutionalism: John Dickinson's *Fabius Letters.*" *Humanitas* 11, no. 2. Center for Constitutional Studies. http://www.nhinet.org/ccs/ccs-res.htm.

Farrand, Max, ed. 1937. *The Records of the Federal Convention.* 4 vols. New Haven, CT: Yale University Press.

Flower, Milton E. 1983. *John Dickinson: Conservative Revolutionary.* Charlottesville: University Press of Virginia.

Hutson, James H. 1983. "John Dickinson at the Federal Constitutional Convention." *William and Mary Quarterly* 40, 3rd ser. (April): 256–282.

———, ed. 1987. Supplement to Max Farrand's The Records of the Federal Convention of 1787. New Haven, CT: Yale University Press.

Natelson, Robert G. 2003. "The Constitutional Contributions of John Dickinson." *Pennsylvania State Law Review* 108 (Fall): 415–477.

Webking, Robert H. 1988. *The American Revolution and the Politics of Liberty.* Baton Rouge: Louisiana State University Press.

DICKINSON PLAN

Although most students of the Constitution know about the Virginia and New Jersey Plans, far fewer know about the Dickinson Plan (by Delaware's John Dickinson), which is recorded in notes of the Constitutional Convention for June 18, 1787. This was the same day that Alexander Hamilton of New York presented the outlines of his own plan in a five-hour speech decrying both the Virginia and New Jersey Plans, although clearly leaning toward the former.

The Formulation and Significance of Dickinson's Plan

The reason so few are aware of the Dickinson Plan is that he apparently never presented it or a number of accompanying speeches that he had prepared to go with it. It is possible that Dickinson felt "preempted by" Hamilton (Hutson 1983, 262) or that he simply ended up being more pleased with the deliberations in the aftermath of that speech than he expected to be, but it seems more likely that his health was such that he felt unable to present it. James Hutson, who has written an illuminating article on the Dickinson Plan, observes that there is no evidence that Dickinson spoke at the Convention from June 21 to July 25. On the basis of this evidence, as well as letters indicating that he had left the Convention because of severe headaches, Hutson concluded that Dickinson never formally proposed the plan he had prepared.

The plan is nonetheless inherently interesting for a number of reasons: it gives insight into the architectonic schemes of another of the Framers; it highlights various elements of both the Virginia and New Jersey Plans; and it does so while also underlining some provisions that were unique to Dickinson. As an individual who represented Delaware at the Convention but who also had landholdings in Pennsylvania where he had previously served as a legislator and governor, Dickinson was in a unique position to see the virtues of the key arguments of both the large and small states.

The Content of Dickinson's Plan

Dickinson divided his plan into seven parts. The first followed the New Jersey Plan in suggesting that the Articles needed to "be revised and amended, so as to render the Government of the United States adequate to the Exigencies, the preservation, and the prosperity of the Union" (a phrase that at least dimly foreshadows the Preamble to the Constitution). However, the next two resolutions immediately follow by echoing the Virginia Plan's calls for a tripartite government and for a bicameral Congress. Dickinson proposed that senators (members of what he calls the "first Branch") be chosen, as under the Articles, by state legislatures, with members being at least 30 years of age and states having an equal vote (Hutson 1983, 267). Dickinson proposed that they serve seven-year terms. Similarly, in Dickinson's plan, members of today's House of Representatives would be selected for terms of three years. Dickinson's plan for congressional rotation is as complex as any introduced at the Convention. He proposed grouping senators into seven classes with approximately one-seventh being elected each year and placing House members on similar three-year rotations.

A unique feature of Dickinson's plan was his proposal to base representation in the House "in proportion to the sum of Money collected in each state and actually paid into the Common Treasury within the preceding 3 Years" (Hutson, 267). He decided to exclude imposts from this calculation, in apparent response to previous arguments by Rufus King of Massachusetts that their inclusion would be unfair to states without major ports (261). Additionally, Dickinson sought to guarantee that each state would have at least one vote in that body and that the state contributing the most should not exceed the state contributing the least by a certain ratio, which he does not appear to have determined at the time he developed his plan.

Dickinson showed himself to be a friend to the West. He specified that any new state would initially have the same representation as the state containing the least number in Congress. However, after the next apportionment, each state would be represented on the same basis as the others.

In Section 6, Dickinson attempted to enlarge the powers of Congress. He would have entrusted Congress with power to enforce observance of "the Laws of Nations and an Obedience to their own Laws," and for taxing imports and exports. He included a provision that all such laws should be publicized six months in advance and that although suits concerning such matters must originate in "the Common Law Judiciary" of the states, they might be removed to U.S. courts on appeal. Although he favored broader congressional powers than those under the Articles of Confederation, his proposal stating that "all other proper Objects of the legislative Assembly of the United States, if any, ought to be accurately defined" demonstrated his concern over broad grants of power, perhaps like the one that eventually became the necessary and proper clause. Dickinson favored enumerating congressional powers (Natelson 2003, 456). Dickinson thus would have entrusted Congress with the sole power to emit money, regulate the value of coin, veto state laws, and resolve conflicts within states that could "disturb the public Peace." He sought protection for the writ of habeas corpus and for trial by jury as well as "for preventing Contests concerning the Authority of the United States and the Authority of individual states" (Hutson 268–269). Arguably, this last power could have ended up being one of the general clauses to which Dickinson had expressed an aversion.

Section 7 of Dickinson's plan began with a provision like the supremacy clause that first appeared in the New Jersey Plan; indeed, Dickinson wrote that it was to be "nearly in the proposals from New Jersey" (269). Dickinson proceeded to propose a plural executive, selected by Congress and consisting of one delegate from the Eastern (Northern), one from the Middle, and a third from the Southern states. Hutson describes this as a "Rube Goldberg magistracy" (260), perhaps in part because Dickinson proceeded to attempt to establish a two-year, four-year, and seven-year rotation system. Dickinson would have granted Congress authority not only to provide for vacancies but also to remove members of the magistry on petition from "a Majority of the Executives of the several states and to be impeachable for Malconduct or Neglect of Duty" (269). The executive would operate a bit like modern courts, with each executive being individually responsible for all decisions made, unless they recorded dissents in writing. The executive veto would be subject to a two-thirds override by Congress.

Under the Dickinson Plan, as under the Virginia Plan, the legislature would appoint the judges. Their jurisdiction would be similar to that in the New Jersey Plan except that they would have original jurisdiction involving ambassadors and foreign ministers. Dickinson indicated that he concurred in Resolutions 14 and following of the report of the Committee of the Whole of the Virginia Plan. These provisions had called for the admission of new states, for the continuation of the Congress under the Articles until the new government was initiated, for guaranteeing each state a republican form of government, for binding state officials by an oath to uphold the Constitution, and for ratification of the Convention results by state conventions (see Farrand 1937, I, 237).

It is interesting to speculate how Dickinson's plan, had he introduced it, might have affected the Convention's outcome. Absent its introduction at the Convention, the plan serves primarily to give insight into the positions that a member who apparently absented himself in the following weeks might have taken.

See Also Delaware; Dickinson, John; Hamilton Plan; New Jersey Plan; Virginia Plan

FOR FURTHER READING

Farrand, Max, ed. 1937. *The Records of the Federal Convention.* 4 vols. New Haven, CT: Yale University Press.
Hutson, James H. 1983. "John Dickinson at the Federal Constitutional Convention." *William and Mary Quarterly* 40, 3rd ser. (April): 256–281.
Natelson, Robert G. 2003. "The Constitutional Contributions of John Dickinson." *Pennsylvania State Law Review* 108 (Fall): 415–477.

DIRECT TAXES

See THREE-FIFTHS CLAUSE

DISTRICT OF COLUMBIA

Article I, Section 8, Clause 17 of the Constitution vests Congress with the power "To exercise exclusive Legislation in all Cases whatsoever, over such District (not exceeding ten Miles square) as may, by Cession of Particular States, and the Acceptance of Congress, become the Seat of the Government of the United States." The clause further vests Congress with similar authority over places purchased "for the Erection of Forts, Magazines, Arsenals, dock-Yards, and other needful Buildings."

Concerns over Utilizing an Existing State Capital

Virginia's George Mason appears to have made the first mention of a nation's capital at the Constitutional Convention. On July 26, he suggested

An Ambulatory Capital?

Although Americans today take it for granted that there shall be a single national capital, the site of the capital during the Articles of Confederation was ambulatory. It moved from place to place partly because of exigencies created during the British occupation of Philadelphia during the Revolutionary War, partly because of fears that U.S. militiamen might capture the Congress, and partly out of republican fear of allowing any one state or region (or the lobbyists gathered there) to gain special influence.

In 1783, the Congress under the Articles of Confederation decided to alternate the U.S. capital between Trenton and Annapolis, thus providing for one capital on the Delaware River and the other on the Potomac. Perhaps remembering the story of the fall of Troy, Philadelphia's Francis Hopkinson ironically responded by suggesting that Congress should create an equestrian statue of George Washington that could serve as a building and be floated from one capital to the other through the Chesapeake Bay. He further suggested that other governmental buildings could be constructed of light wood and fitted with sails and bellows to travel between the two sites (Cress 1975, 595).

Under the new Constitution, the capital began in New York, moved to Philadelphia, and then was moved to a site on the Potomac not more than ten miles square. The location of the capital appears to have been highly influenced by the wishes of George Washington and by a "logrolling" between Federalists and Democratic-Republicans over the location of the capital, which Southerners wanted in the South, and the assumption of state debts which Alexander Hamilton and other northern representatives wanted to be undertaken by the national government.

FOR FURTHER READING

Cress, Lawrence Delbert. 1975. "Whither Columbia? Congressional Residence and the Politics of the New Nation, 1776 to 1787." *William and Mary Quarterly*, 3rd ser. 32 (October): 581–600.

---

that the Convention should guard against allowing the nation's capital to be established in the same city as one of the state capitals. He argued that such a prohibition was needed both to guard against disputes by the two governments over jurisdiction and as a way of avoiding giving "a provincial tincture to ye Natl. deliberations" (Farrand 1937, II, 127). Alexander Martin of North Carolina seconded this motion.

Pennsylvania's Gouverneur Morris said that he was not necessarily opposed to the idea but thought that such an explicit provision might make enemies of Philadelphia and New York, both of which hoped to become the capital—a view that North Carolina's Hugh Williamson would later echo. New Hampshire's John Langdon raised the possibility that a state might move its capital to the national site *after* the new government had erected buildings there, prompting Nathaniel Gorham of Massachusetts to suggest

that the national government might avoid the problem by refusing to construct such buildings! Gerry then stated that he wanted to construct the new government not only away from a state capital but away from any existing big city, whereas South Carolina's Charles Pinckney thought large cities would be appropriate as long as they were not state capitals.

Mason, professing not to want "to excite any hostile passions agst. the system" (II, 128), withdrew his motion although South Carolina's Pierce Butler expressed his hope that the Convention would fix a central place for the national government. The Convention appears to have passed this matter along, with other matters discussed on that day, to the Committee of Detail. When it reported to the Convention on August 6, however, this committee did not include the right to establish a national capital in the list of the enumerated powers of Congress.

Discussion over Making the Site of the Capital Permanent

On August 11, the Convention was discussing the right of one or both houses of Congress to adjourn to another place. Rufus King of Massachusetts said: "The mutability of place had dishonored the federal Govt. [that is, the government under the Articles of Confederation], and would require as strong a cure as we could devise" (II, 261). He recommended that the capital could not be moved without a law to this effect, and Madison seconded the motion. North Carolina's Richard Spaight feared that this would keep the government in New York (the existing capital of the Articles) forever, especially if the first president should be from the North.

Although Morris thought that such "distrust" was unbecoming, James Madison, who probably had the interests of Virginia in mind, expressed his view that it was desirable to locate the new capital in a central location–many states, especially the larger ones, had moved their own capitals from the coast to more centrally located sites (Zagarri 1987, 8–35). He pointed out that the new government would have more members, would exercise greater powers, and would thus draw more private individuals to its business. He proposed a provision whereby Congress would determine at its first meeting where its future sessions would be held and specifying that neither house could meet elsewhere. Gerry did not want the president to have a veto power over this choice. North Carolina's Hugh Williamson and Maryland's Daniel Carroll feared that this would keep the capital in New York. Maryland's John Mercer did not think the two houses would be able to agree on a common meeting place. The Convention left the matter unresolved.

Development of the Current Provision

On August 18, the Convention forwarded a proposal to grant Congress power over a seat of government, which is remarkably like that in the current Constitution, to the Committee of Detail. It provided that Congress should have power "To exercise exclusively Legislative authority at the seat of the General Government, and over a district around the same, not exceeding (?) square miles; the Consent of the Legislature of the State or States comprising the same, being first obtained" (II, 325).

The Convention in turn appears to have turned this provision over to the Committee on Postponed Matters. This committee reported the provision to the Convention on September 5 along with a proposal for congressional exercises of power over places purchased for forts and other governmental establishments. This clause now specified that Congress would have power

> to exercise exclusive legislation in all cases whatsoever over such district (not exceeding ten miles square) as may by Cession of particular States and the acceptance of the Legislature become the seat of the Government of the U-S–and to exercise like authority over all places purchased for the erection of Forts, Magazines, Arsenals, Dock-Yards, and other needful buildings. (II, 509)

The Convention accepted the provision related to the national capital without emendation. After Gerry raised fears that Congress might use its power to purchase territory for forts to buy up its territory and using the strongholds as "a means of awing the State into an undue obedience to the Genl. Government," the Convention unanimously voted to accept the reservation that states would have to consent to such purchases (II, 510). The Committee of Style did not further alter the wording of this provision.

Analysis and Consequences

During the Convention a number of delegates expressed concerns about locating the capital in existing state capitals or major cities, and Madison had expressed the desire to locate the nation's capital in a central place. The Convention did not alienate any existing states or regions by designating the site of a new capital, although cities reading between the line would probably have realized that the provision for national governance of an area of up to 10 miles square would preclude existing cities that did not choose to part with self-governance. The decision to carve a capital out of lands ceded by Virginia and Maryland was left to the future and was ultimately influenced both by George Washington (whose house at Mount Vernon was nearby) and by congressional leaders who were willing to trade votes, a process called "log-rolling," to fulfill their wishes.

Convention debates hint at concerns that national business might be unduly influenced by state business. They do not directly express the delegates' apparent fears that members of the legislature might be threatened, as ex-militiamen had done during the Articles of Confederation, if the government did not have a designated area that it could protect and defend (Report to the Attorney General 1987, 52–55).

In authorizing the creation of a fairly sizeable federal entity that was not a state, the delegates created problems of voting, self-government, and representation that continue to be worrisome. It took the ratification of the Twenty-third Amendment in 1961 to guarantee presidential electoral votes to residents of the district, but states subsequently rejected an amendment proposed in 1978 that would have treated the district as a state for purposes of representation. Congress thus continues to oversee the government in the District of Columbia, and members of the district still do not have voting rights within Congress. The fact that the delegates to the Constitutional Convention did not even discuss the issues of voting and representation for the district suggests that these effects may have been largely, if not completely, unintentional. This has not kept them from being long-lasting.

See Also Delaware; Philadelphia; President, Selection

FOR FURTHER READING

Cress, Lawrence D. 1975. "Whither Columbia? Congressional Residence and the Politics of the New Nation, 1776 to 1787." *William and Mary Quarterly,* 3rd ser. 32 (October): 581–600.

Farrand, Max, ed. 1937. *The Records of the Federal Convention.* 4 vols. New Haven, CT: Yale University Press.

Fortenbaugh, Robert. 1948. *The Nine Capitals of the United States.* York, PA: Maple.

Report to the Attorney General. 1987. *The Question of Statehood for the District of Columbia.* April 3. Washington, DC: U.S. Government Printing Office.

Zagarri, Rosemarie. 1987. *The Politics of Size: Representation in the United States, 1776–1850.* Ithaca, NY: Cornell University Press.

DOMESTIC VIOLENCE, PROTECTION AGAINST

See GUARANTEE CLAUSE

DOMINION OF NEW ENGLAND

The Dominion of New England (1686–1689) was among the precursors to the Articles of Confederation and the U.S. Constitution. It differed primarily in the fact that Britain's James II imposed this alliance, rather than it being home growth. In attempts both to control colonial resistance to the Navigation Acts and to form an alliance against the French and Indians, James initially united the New England colonies, which had already joined on their own in the New England Confederation, and then added New York and the two New Jerseys two years later.

Joseph Dudley briefly headed the Dominion and was then followed by Sir Edmund Andros, but the alliance was never popular in the colonies. Opposition was especially strong in Massachusetts and Connecticut. In the latter, colonists hid their charter in the crevice of an oak tree (hence designated as the Charter Oak). The Dominion was not very successful and was ended when the colonists expelled Andros after finding that

William and Mary had deposed James II in England in the Glorious Revolution of 1688.

See Also Albany Plan of Union; Articles of Confederation; New England Confederation

FOR FURTHER READING

"Dominion of New England, 1686–1689." u-s-history. com. http://www.u-s-history.com/pagesh546.html.
Long, Breckinridge. 1926. *Genesis of the Constitution of the United States of America.* New York: Macmillan.

DOOR-KEEPER OF THE CONVENTION

See FRY, JOSEPH

DUNLAP AND CLAYPOOLE

John Dunlap, the same printer who had printed the first issues of the Declaration of Independence and the Articles of Confederation for the Continental Congresses, was also commissioned to print the first edition of the U.S. Constitution. Dunlap and his assistant, David C. Claypoole, first printed copies of the report of the Committee of Detail, which were distributed to the Convention on August 6. In what has to be an unusual example of journalistic discretion, Dunlap and Claypoole proved they were worthy of confidence by keeping the draft of this document secret, even though they owned a newspaper, the *Pennsylvania Packet* (Rossiter 1966, 202).

The Convention subsequently instructed Dunlap and Claypoole to print a few hundred copies for the delegates and for members of Congress and the state legislatures from a completed document that they received on September 15. When, on September 17, the delegates decided to alter the minimum representation in the House of Representatives from one per every 40,000 inhabitants to one per every 30,000, these copies became obsolete and were destroyed. Dunlap and Claypoole printed new versions that afternoon; they included copies of the authorizing resolution and the accompanying letter to Congress. They also published these documents in the *Pennsylvania Packet and Daily Advertiser,* which they printed on September 19. The document was quickly copied, and was printed in England within the month (Bernstein with Rice 1987, 186–191). The documents, as originally printed, consisted of four parchment pages measuring 23.5 by 27.5 inches (Farrand 1937, II, 651).

See Also Shallus, Jacob

FOR FURTHER READING

Bernstein, Richard B., with Kym S. Rice. 1987. *Are We to Be a Nation? The Making of the Constitution.* Cambridge, MA: Harvard University Press.
Farrand, Max, ed. 1937. *The Records of the Federal Convention.* 4 vols. New Haven, CT: Yale University Press.
Rossiter, Clinton. 1966. *1787: The Grand Convention.* New York: W. W. Norton.

DUTIES

See TAXES ON IMPORTS AND EXPORTS

EDUCATION OF CONVENTION DELEGATES

At a time when college education was not widespread, 30 of the 55 delegates who attended the Constitutional Convention had attended college, most within the United States. At the time there were about 25 such institutions in the nation, 10 of which–Harvard, 1636; William and Mary, 1693; St. Johns 1696; Yale, 1701; University of Pennsylvania, 1740; Moravian College, 1742; University of Delaware, 1743; Princeton, 1746; Washington and Lee, 1749 (called Liberty Hall Academy at the time of the Convention); and Columbia, 1754–had been founded in 1754 or earlier ("U.S. Colleges and Universities"). The numbers give only a partial view, however. One scholar has thus observed that of the colleges in existence in 1789

> all . . . were pathetically small in size (Harvard, the largest, had a mere 150 students), badly straitened in finances, and severely limited in curriculum. Some of them, in fact, were hardly more than backwoods grammar schools, and all of them were devoted mainly to preparing young men for the ministry. (Castel 1964, 281)

Pennsylvania's Benjamin Franklin, who had a worldwide reputation for his discoveries in electricity, was among the delegates to the Convention without such a formal education. Although he had studied surveying, George Washington was not a college graduate. George Wythe, who would do so much to educate others, was among those who had been brilliantly taught at home (in his case, largely by his mother), as was fellow Virginian George Mason. As was common at a time before law schools had been formally established, many of the delegates had learned law by "reading" under other attorneys.

The college with the single greatest number of graduates was the College of New Jersey (today's Princeton University), which had nine; this figure was especially impressive given the relatively late founding of the school. Most of these had graduated during the presidency of John Witherspoon, the highly esteemed Presbyterian cleric who was one of the signers of the Declaration of Independence. Significantly these included James Madison, who was most responsible for the Virginia Plan; William Paterson, who was most responsible for the New Jersey Plan; and Oliver Ellsworth, who was among those who significantly influenced the formulation of the Connecticut Compromise. Princeton had the further distinction of having educated delegates from the most states (six). Princeton was particularly successful in recruiting from the South, where its graduates founded several other colleges (Come 1945), and apart from Connecticut's Oliver Ellsworth and the three of New Jersey's delegates (Paterson, William C. Houston, and Jonathan Dayton), all the rest

Nassau Hall at the College of New Jersey (today's Princeton University) (Pixel That)

were from states southward–Gunning Bedford from Delaware, Luther Martin from Maryland, Madison from Virginia, and Alexander Martin and William Davie from North Carolina. In addition to graduating from Princeton, William C. Houston had served as a mathematics professor there. In addition to graduates, Daniel Brearly attended Princeton and was awarded an honorary M.A. in 1781 and John Dickinson was awarded an honorary LL.D. (Lloyd and Sammon).

Seven delegates at the Convention had spent some time in London's Middle Temple, one of the Inns of Court designed to provide legal training. These included John Dickinson of Delaware (for whom Dickinson College had been named when he was serving as president of Pennsylvania), William Livingston of New Jersey, Jared Ingersoll of Pennsylvania, John Blair of Virginia, and John Rutledge, Charles Cotesworth Pinckney, and Charles Pinckney of South Carolina (Bedwell 1920, 681–682).

Five delegates at the Convention had attended Virginia's College of William and Mary. They included John Francis Mercer of Maryland; John Blair, James McClurg (who got a medical degree

in Edinburgh), and Edmund Randolph of Virginia; and William Pierce of Georgia; Blair, McClurg, and Mercer received degrees. In addition, George Wythe was the school's, and the nation's, first professor of law, and James McClurg had been appointed to a chair of medicine there in 1779, a position he appears to have filled only briefly, if at all.

Five delegates had attended Yale, although one of these (Ellsworth) graduated from Princeton. Yale's graduates included Connecticut's William Samuel Johnson, Pennsylvania's Jared Ingersoll, New Jersey's William Livingston, and Georgia's Abraham Baldwin. Yale awarded an honorary M.A. to Roger Sherman and an honorary LL.D. to William Livingston.

Harvard provided three graduates–Elbridge Gerry, Rufus King, and Caleb Strong. All three represented Massachusetts at the Convention. In addition, William Samuel Johnson earned an M.A. there, and George Washington was awarded an honorary LL.D. (Lloyd and Sammon).

Leitch lists King's College (today's Columbia University) as having three Convention alumni. He appears, however, to be including Connecti-

John Witherspoon (1723?–1794)

Although he did not attend the Constitutional Convention, the Rev. John Witherspoon had a significant impact on the thought of the Founding era. Witherspoon was born in Scotland, where he earned a master's and a divinity degree at the University of Edinburgh and established himself as a spokesman for Presbyterian orthodoxy. The College of New Jersey (today's Princeton University) invited Witherspoon to be its president, and he immigrated to America and served in this capacity from 1768 until his death in 1794, during which time many of the delegates to the Constitutional Convention were educated. Despite his foreign roots, Witherspoon quickly joined the Patriot cause. He served in the New Jersey state legislature; was a delegate to both the Continental and Confederation Congresses, where he served on a large number of committees; and was a member of the New Jersey convention that ratified the U.S. Constitution.

Witherspoon signed both the Declaration of Independence (the only clergyman to do so) and the Articles of Confederation, and he drew up three religious proclamations for Congress (Morrison 2004, 119). Witherspoon is credited with bringing unity to American Presbyterians, who had been split into New Side and Old Side divisions that arose from disputes over the emotional religious manifestations accompanying the Great Awakening.

Witherspoon's students are a virtual *Who's Who* of the Revolutionary and early U.S. Constitutional periods. They included 5 delegates at the Constitutional Convention, one of whom (James Madison) went on to become a U.S. secretary of state and president; a future vice president (Aaron Burr); 12 representatives to the Continental Congress; 28 U.S. senators; 49 members of the U.S. House of Representatives; 3 U.S. Supreme Court justices; 8 U.S. district judges; 26 state judges; 17 members of conventions that drew up state constitutions; and 14 members of conventions that the states called to ratify the U.S. Constitution (119).

An embodiment of the Protestant work ethic, Witherspoon stressed the manner in which politics, like service to the church, could be a calling by which individuals glorified God. Garrett Ward Shelton, a Madison biographer, is among the scholars who believe that James Madison embodied this conviction in his own career (2004, 88–89). Despite his own orthodoxy, Witherspoon stressed freedom of conscience and focused on ecumenical principles in the political realm. Although he did not advocate a theocracy, Witherspoon believed that clergymen should have the same right as others to be elected to public office. Reacting in 1789 to a provision in the Georgia state constitution barring clergymen from serving in the state legislature, Witherspoon published a satirical newspaper article in which he suggested that perhaps the state would prefer to select individuals who had been defrocked for a "deposition for cursing and swearing, drunkenness or uncleanness" (quoted in Morrison, 123).

FOR FURTHER READING

Morrison, Jeffry H. 2004. "John Witherspoon's Revolutionary Religion." In Daniel L. Dreisbach, Mark D. Hall, and Jeffry H. Morrison, eds. *The Founders on God and Government.* Lanham, MD: Rowman and Littlefield Publishers, 117–146.

Shelton, Garrett Ward. 2004. "Religion and Politics in the Thought of James Madison." In Daniel L. Dreisbach, Mark D. Hall, and Jeffry H. Morrison, eds. *The Founders on God and Government.* Lanham, MD: Rowman and Littlefield Publishers, 83–116.

cut's William Samuel Johnson, who served for a time as the college's president. The two graduates were New York's Alexander Hamilton and Pennsylvania's Gouverneur Morris.

Two delegates had attended the University of Pennsylvania, which Benjamin Franklin had helped to establish (Pennsylvania also named Franklin College, which it chartered in 1787, in

Franklin's honor). They were Thomas Mifflin of Pennsylvania and Hugh Williamson of North Carolina. In addition, the university awarded an honorary degree to James Wilson, who also taught there.

In addition to delegates who had received some education at London's Middle Temple, James Wilson had been educated in Scotland, Charles Cotesworth Pinckney had been educated at Oxford, Daniel Carroll had been educated in French Flanders, and Richard Dobbs Spaight had graduated from the University of Glasgow.

A number of delegates continued to be associated with higher education. Investments donated by George Washington continue to fund tuition for students attending Washington and Lee University (once Washington College). James Madison (after whom a university in Harrisonburg, Virginia, is now named) later served as a trustee at the University of Virginia, which his friend, Thomas Jefferson, founded in Charlottesville. Hugh Williamson served as one of the first trustees of the University of North Carolina and later as a trustee of the University of the State of New York. Abraham Baldwin was the principal founder of the University of Georgia. William Richardson Davie helped found the University of North Carolina. Charles Cotesworth Pinckney helped found the University of South Carolina. George Clymer served as a trustee of the University of Pennsylvania and as president of the Pennsylvania Academy of Fine Arts.

See Also Delegates, Collective Profile; National University

FOR FURTHER READING

Bedwell, C. E. A. 1920. "American Middle Templars." *American Historical Review* 25 (July): 680–689.

Castel, Albert. 1964. "The Founding Fathers and the Vision of a National University." *History of Education Quarterly* 4 (December): 280–302.

Come, Donald R. 1945. "The Influence of Princeton on Higher Education in the South before 1825." *William and Mary Quarterly*, 3rd ser. 2 (October): 359–396.

"The Founding Fathers: A Brilliant Gathering of Rea-

son and Creativity." Special Issue of *Life, The Constitution* (Fall 1987): 51–58.

Leitch, Alexander. "Constitutional Convention of 1787, The." http://etc.princeton.edu/CampusWWW/Companion/constitutional_convention.html. From 1978. *A Princeton Companion*. Princeton, NJ: Princeton University Press.

Lloyd, Gordon, and Jeff Sammon. "The Educational Background of the Framers." http://teachingamerican history.org.

Robson, David W. 1983. "College Founding in the New Republic, 1776–1800." *History of Education Quarterly* 23 (Autumn): 323–341.

"U.S. Colleges and Universities." http://www.dean.usma.edu/math/people/rickey/dms/OldestSchools.html.

Vine, Phyllis. 1976. "The Social Function of Eighteenth-Century Higher Education." *History of Education Quarterly* 16 (Winter): 409–424.

ELECTORAL COLLEGE

See PRESIDENT, SELECTION

ELLSWORTH, OLIVER (1745–1807)

Born to Captain David Ellsworth and his wife Jemima Leavitt Ellsworth on April 29, 1745, in Windsor, Connecticut, Ellsworth attended Yale before finishing a degree at the College of New Jersey (today's Princeton University). There he met William Paterson, who would also attend the Constitutional Convention and with whom he would later serve on the U.S. Supreme Court. After abandoning the study of theology, Ellsworth took up law and was admitted to the Connecticut bar. In 1772 he married then 16-year-old Abigail Wolcott.

As his legal business began to pick up, Ellsworth also began participating in politics. He was elected as a state representative, served on the Council of Safety, and was elected in 1777 to the

Oliver Ellsworth, delegate from Connecticut
(Pixel That)

The Great Compromise

The first time that Ellsworth's name appears in relation to Convention debates, he is seconding a motion by fellow Connecticut delegate Roger Sherman recommending that each state have an equal vote in the U.S. Senate (I, 201). Significantly, after weeks of exasperating debate over representation in Congress, Ellsworth said on June 29 that "I do not despair but that we shall be so fortunate as to devise and adopt some good plan of government" (I, 471).

It was on June 29, after the Convention had agreed to allow for proportional state representation in the House of Representatives, that Ellsworth proposed that representation in the Senate should remain like representation under the Articles of Confederation, that is, with each state having an equal vote. Professing that he was not opposed to the motion that had just been adopted, Ellsworth hoped that it might become the basis of a compromise. He further introduced a formulation for describing the new government that James Madison (who strongly opposed it at the time) would later use in *Federalist* No. 39 in describing and justifying the new Constitution:

> We were partly national; partly federal. The proportional representation in the first branch was conformable to the national principle & would secure the large States agst. the small. An equality of voices was conformable to the federal principle and was necessary to secure the Small States agst. the large. He trusted that on this middle ground a compromise would take place. He did not see that it could on any other. (I, 468–469)

Ellsworth did not think the small states would accept a plan that did not give them equality in at least one house, and he did not think such equality would undermine the large states. He offered an analysis designed to appeal to both groups of states:

> He could never admit that there was no danger of combinations among the large States. They will like individuals find out and avail themselves of the advantage to be gained by it. It was true

Continental Congress, where he served on the Committee on International Treaties and on the Committee of Appeals, which has been described as "the first forerunner of the present Supreme Court of the United States" (Brown 1905, 754). He was subsequently selected to the Connecticut Supreme Court of Errors and to the state's superior court. For this reason, he is often referred to at the Constitutional Convention as "Judge" Ellsworth. He was a large man who was about six feet, two inches in height and who was known for dressing elegantly.

Oliver Ellsworth began attending the Convention on May 28, and although he was not present for the signing of the document, he participated significantly in its formulation. He is perhaps best known for being one of those delegates who helped effect a compromise between the large states and the small states on representation in Congress and for formulating a description of the new government as "partly national, partly federal" (Farrand 1937, I, 468).

the danger would be greater, if they were contiguous and had a more immediate common interest. A defensive combination of the small States was rendered more difficult by their greater number. (I, 469)

Ellsworth further argued that states had some obligation to recognize the equality that states enjoyed at the time under the Articles. Ellsworth urged caution:

Let a strong Executive, a Judiciary & Legislative power be created; but Let not too much be attempted; by which all may be lost. He was not in general a half-way man, yet he preferred doing half the good we could, rather than do nothing at all. The other half may be added, when the necessity shall be more fully experienced. (I, 469)

When Pennsylvania's James Wilson attacked Ellsworth's proposal as allowing for minority rule, Ellsworth held his ground. Strengthened by the fact that the Convention had already provided for majority rule in the House of Representatives, Ellsworth presented equal representation within the Senate as a defensive mechanism: "The power is given to the few to save them from being destroyed by the many" (I, 484). Citing the House of Lords in Britain, which a number of delegates had commended, Ellsworth said that equal representation in the Senate would provide for a similar check. He moved from theory to practice, with a homey, but effective, example: "We are running from one extreme to another. We are razing the foundations of the building. When we need only repair the roof" (I, 484). Ellsworth further outlined a case where the three largest states might attempt to favor themselves, and he again cited representation under the Articles as a kind of faith into which the states had mutually entered. He further defended Connecticut's contributions under the Articles of Confederation—he said that Connecticut had fielded more troops during the Revolution than had Virginia—indicating that "If she had been delinquent, it had been from inability, and not more so than other States" (I, 487).

Later in the day, Ellsworth indicated that it was possible to appreciate the objects both of general Union and of an individual's own state. Acknowledging that the general government would provide for national security, he demonstrated even greater attachment to his state:

I want domestic happiness, as well as general security. A general government will never grant me this, as it cannot know my wants or relieve my distress. My state is only as one out of thirteen. Can they, the general government, gratify my wishes? My happiness depends as much on the existence of my state government, as a new-born infant depends upon its mother for nourishment. (I, 502)

The Convention appointed Ellsworth to the committee that developed the Great Compromise but he was apparently unable to attend. Not surprisingly, however, he supported it (I, 532). Ellsworth posed two critical questions on July 14, just two days before the Convention adopted the Great Compromise. He asked Wilson whether he had ever known a measure to fail in Congress for lack of a majority of states in its favor, and he asked Madison whether the negative by the Senate "could be any more dangerous" than the negative over state laws that Madison had proposed investing in Congress (II, 11). Far later in the Convention, Ellsworth stated that he did not believe the privilege of originating money bills in the House of Representatives amounted to much but that "he was willing it should stand" (II, 224; also see II, 233).

Congress

Terms

On June 12, Ellsworth joined Roger Sherman in proposing to set terms for members of the U.S. House of Representatives at one year. At least in Sherman's case, however, he appears to have introduced the motion to hasten convention business rather than because he favored it (I, 214). The fact that Ellsworth reintroduced this motion on June 21 suggests that he may have felt more strongly on the matter than Sherman (I, 361).

On June 16, Ellsworth proposed "that the Legislative power of the U.S. should remain in Congs" (I, 255). He apparently hoped that this would be a substitute for William Paterson's motion introducing the New Jersey Plan which had called for revising, correcting, and enlarging the Articles so as "to render the federal Constitution adequate to the exigencies of Government, & the preservation of the Union" (I, 242). Along a similar line, on June 20, Ellsworth proposed dropping the word "national" out of the resolution introducing the revised Virginia Plan (I, 335). On this occasion, Ellsworth further denied that a breach of one of the Articles would dissolve the whole. He expressed the view that what changes were needed in the Articles could go forward as amendments, which state legislatures could then ratify.

Pay of Members

On June 22, Ellsworth proposed that members of Congress should be paid out of state treasuries rather than by Congress. He observed that standards of living varied within the states, and he feared that what would be deemed reasonable in one state would be regarded as unreasonable in others, thus undermining confidence in the proposed system (I, 371–372). In opposing New York's Alexander Hamilton on this point, Ellsworth argued that "If we are jealous of the State Govts. they will be so of us" (I, 374). On June 26, Ellsworth attempted to see that the states would at least maintain control over the salaries of senators. He deftly combined a theoretical with a practical argument by observing: "If the Senate was meant to strengthen the Govt. it ought to have the confidence of the States. The States will have an interest in keeping up a representation and will make such provision for supporting the members as will ensure their attendance" (I, 427).

By August 14, Ellsworth had changed his mind on the subject. He feared that state payment of members of Congress would lead to overdependence on the state legislatures. He proposed that members should be paid an unspecified per diem payment out of the national treasury (II, 290). He hoped to tie it to its current exchange value so as to obviate concerns over granting Congress unlimited authority to set its own salary (II, 292). He proposed an initial salary of $5 per day and for every 30 miles (II, 293).

Choice of Senators

On June 25, Ellsworth favored allowing state legislatures, rather than electors chosen directly by the people, to choose U.S. senators. He believed that senators would reflect views distinctive to their states, no matter how they were chosen. He thought that legislative selection was more likely to result in getting senators who were wise. He further advanced his view that, given the size of the United States, it would be necessary to preserve the states:

> He urged the necessity of maintaining the existence & agency of the States. Without their cooperation it would be impossible to support a Republican Govt. over so great an extent of Country. An army could scarcely render it practicable. . . . If the principles & materials of our Govt. are not adequate to the extent of these single states [Virginia, Massachusetts, and Pennsylvania]; how can it be imagined that they can support a single Govt. throughout the U. States. The only chance of supporting a Genl. Govt. lies in engrafting it on that of the individual States. (II, 406–407)

Size of Congress

Ellsworth opposed a motion by James Madison to double the size of the initial House of Representatives from 65 to 130 members. He objected both because of the expense of so many representatives and because he thought such a size would slow congressional business. He further argued "that a large number was less necessary in the Genl. Legislature than in those of the States, as its business would relate to a few great, national Objects only" (I, 569). Ellsworth indicated that he favored allowing members of the Senate to vote on a "per capita" basis rather than casting a single vote for each state delegation (II, 94).

Three-fifths Provision

Just as he had smoothed the way for a compromise on representation of the large and small states, so too, Ellsworth attempted to reconcile differences between free and slave states. He proposed that the three-fifths formula be used for representation in the House "until some other rule shall more accurately ascertain the wealth of the several States" (I, 594). Ellsworth subsequently withdrew this motion in deference to a motion by Virginia's Edmund Randolph that gave greater security to the rule by making it permanent (I, 595). Ellsworth thought this same formula could be used for levying poll taxes, although he did not anticipate that any would be needed (II, 597). He thought requiring taxes to be apportioned in the interim according to representation in the House of Representatives was an unwise attempt to micromanage the new government (I, 602).

When delegates proposed that Congress should be able to tax slave importations, Ellsworth expressed his opposition. Consistent with earlier expressions of deference to state decision-making, he believed that the "morality or wisdom of slavery" was a state matter that should be left to them. He further believed that what helped states individually would help the whole and that there was no more reason for the proposed government to regulate this matter than there would have been for the government under the Articles of Confederation (II, 364).

Although he professed not to believe this was a national matter, there is some indication that Ellsworth reacted negatively to George Mason's speech against slavery, possibly because Ellsworth regarded it as hypocritical. Mason, a slave owner, had argued that "Every master of slaves is born a petty tyrant" (II, 370). Ellsworth observed that "As he had never owned a slave" he "could not judge of the effects of slavery on character" (II, 371). He suggested that if slavery was as bad as Mason said, however, the Convention should consider not only excluding their future importation but free-

ing those that were already in the country. He went on to make a poor prophecy, but probably one that other delegates shared at the time:

> Let us not intermeddle. As population increases; poor laborers will be so plenty as to render slaves useless. Slavery in time will not be a speck in our Country. Provision is already made in Connecticut for abolishing it. And the abolition has already taken place in Massachusetts. (II, 371)

Finding a silver lining in what was otherwise a fairly dark cloud, Ellsworth further observed that fears of slave insurrections would serve to motivate their masters to good behavior (II, 371).

Qualifications of Members

Ellsworth opposed a provision to disqualify individuals with debts from running for Congress. He thought it better to leave "to the wisdom of the Legislature and the virtue of the Citizens, the task of providing agst. such evils" (II, 126). He further observed that the reason the British had excluded pensioners from running for office was that they were dependent upon the Crown, and thus increased the influence of the monarch (II, 126). Ellsworth later elaborated on his opposition of specifying qualifications within the Constitution. His arguments indicate continuing sensitivity to state differences:

> The different circumstances of different parts of the U.S. and the probable difference between the present and future circumstances of the whole, render it improper to have either *uniform* or *fixed* qualifications. Make them so high as to be useful in the S. States, and they will be inapplicable to the E. States. Suit them to the latter, and they will serve no purpose in the former. In like manner what may be accommodated to the existing State of things among us, may be very inconvenient in some future state of them. (II, 249)

Ellsworth thought it would be less dangerous to allow Congress to set qualifications for its own members than for their electors (II, 250).

Ellsworth believed that one year of residency within a state should be an adequate time for individuals running for Congress (II, 218). Similarly, Ellsworth opposed a motion by Gouverneur Morris to raise the citizenship requirement from four to 14 years for senators. Ellsworth feared that this would discourage "meritorious aliens from emigrating to this Country" (II, 235).

Voting Qualifications

Ellsworth opposed fixing voting qualifications within the Constitution. He observed that voting rights were "a tender point" and that "The people will not readily subscribe to the Natl. Constitution, if it should subject them to be disfranchised" (II, 201). This fit nicely with his view of the functions of the states, which he regarded as "the best Judges of the circumstances and temper of their own people" (II, 201). He also anticipated practical problems in defining the freehold, especially in commercial areas: "Shall the wealthy merchants and manufacturers, who will bear a full share of the public burdens be not allowed a voice in the imposition of them" (II, 202).

Powers of Congress

Ellsworth opposed granting Congress power to tax exports (II, 307). He later offered three reasons against such taxation. He argued that it would discourage industry, that it would be difficult to apportion such taxes equitably since states had different products, and that it would "engender incurable jealousies" (II, 360). He did not think that the provision related to exports would prevent Congress from imposing complete embargoes if such became necessary (II, 361).

Ellsworth thought that the Convention represented a propitious time "to shut and bar the door against paper money" and that doing so would gain support for the new Constitution (II, 309). He argued that "Paper money can in no case be necessary—Give the Government credit, and other resources will offer—The power may do harm, never good" (II, 310). Ellsworth introduced

the motion granting Congress power "to define and punish piracies and felonies committed on the high seas, counterfeiting the securities and current coin of the U. States, and offences agst. the law of Nations" (II, 316).

Ellsworth indicated that he did not generally think Congress should have the power to intervene in force within states unless requested to do so. However, he was willing to allow the governor to request such aid when the legislature was not in session (II, 317).

Ellsworth thought that a distinction should be made between making war and making peace. Specifically, he argued that "It shd. be more easy to get out of war, than into it." His reasoning, however, did not necessarily appear to support this assertion: "War also is a simple and overt declaration. peace attended with intricate & secret negociations" (II, 319).

Ellsworth thought that Congress should assume state debts to the degree that it could equitably do so (II, 327). He later became a strong supporter of Alexander Hamilton's economic plan which was introduced in the first Congress.

Ellsworth opposed a motion by George Mason granting Congress power to regulate the militia as going too far:

> The whole authority over the Militia ought by no means to be taken away from the States whose consequence would pine away to nothing after such a sacrifice of power. He thought the Genl. Authority could not sufficiently pervade the Union for such a purpose, nor could it accommodate itself to the local genius of the people. It must be vain to ask the States to give the Militia out of their hands. (II, 331)

Ellsworth opposed the idea of a select militia as impractical and did not believe the states would agree to it (II, 332). Ellsworth favored leaving a provision in the Constitution specifying that states retain the right to train their militia as well as to appoint their officers (II, 385). He later introduced a provision the object of which was "to refer the plan for the Militia to the General Govt. but leave the execution of it to the State Govts." (II, 386).

When George Mason proposed granting Congress the power to enact sumptuary legislation, Ellsworth said that it would be sufficient simply to allow Congress "to enforce taxes & debts. As far as the regulation of eating & drinking can be reasonable, it is provided for in the power of taxation" (II, 344).

When the Convention discussed the issue of treason, Ellsworth spoke out for allowing both the states and the national government to protect their respective sovereignties (II, 349). He further proposed that Congress should carry out the first census within three, rather than within six, years (II, 350). He did not believe it would be fair to apportion taxes according to the initial number of congressional representatives since he did not believe the initial apportionment would be that accurate (II, 358).

Ellsworth opposed a congressional veto of state laws. He believed that it would either require that states submit all such legislation beforehand to Congress or require the general government to appoint state governors (II, 391).

Other Matters Related to Congress

Ellsworth was among those who favored fixing the time of congressional meetings in the Constitution. He thought this was a matter about which "the Convention could judge . . . as well as the Legislature" (II, 198). He believed that summer would not be a good time since he anticipated that most members of Congress would be tied in some manner to agriculture (II, 200). Ellsworth opposed a motion setting one-half of the initial membership of Congress as a quorum on the basis that this number would prove to be inadequate in the future. He favored granting each house the power to compel absent members to attend (II, 253). Ellsworth agreed with Roger Sherman in opposing congressional roll call votes since the reasons that members of Congress voted as they did would not be recorded along with their votes (II, 255). After the requirement that Congress publish its proceedings was qualified, Ellsworth thought that it would be better to strike it out completely arguing that the people would ensure that Congress published its records (II, 260).

Ellsworth saw no problem with requiring that members of Congress be ineligible to accept other offices. He observed both that "merit will be most encouraged, when most impartially rewarded," and that "if rewards are to circulate only within the Legislature, merit out of it will be discouraged" (II, 288).

Ellsworth favored leaving in a provision that would have required a two-thirds majority of Congress to enact navigation acts at a time when some wanted to eliminate the provision and others wanted to make the majority even larger. His motivation was purely practical:

> If we do not agree on this middle & moderate ground he was afraid we should lose two States, with such others as may be disposed to stand aloof, should fly into a variety of shapes & directions, and most probably into several confederations and not without bloodshed. (II, 375)

Ellsworth did not favor the prohibition on ex post facto (retroactive criminal) laws, but for a fairly lawyerly reason. He believed they were "void of themselves" and that it could not therefore "be necessary to prohibit them" (II, 376). Similarly, he thought it unnecessary to grant Congress the power to fulfill the engagements of the Articles of Confederation since it would automatically become the agent of this former body (II, 377).

Presidency

Ellsworth attempted to resolve the issue of presidential selection somewhat as he had proposed resolving representation in Congress. When the Convention was still contemplating allowing Congress to select the president, he proposed that states should choose electors, having one, two, or three according to whether their populations had up to 200,000 residents, from 200,000 to 300,000 residents, or above 300,000 (II, 57). He believed that New Hampshire and Georgia should both be entitled to two electors (II, 63). Ellsworth thought that members of Congress should be barred from serving as electors, but he did not think this disability needed to be further extended (II, 58).

On July 19, Ellsworth indicated that he thought the president should serve for a six-year term. His central objective was to give the office sufficient firmness. He further observed that "if the Elections are too frequent, the best men will not undertake the service and those of an inferior character will be liable to be corrupted" (II, 59).

Even when the Convention was contemplating a plan whereby Congress would elect the president, Ellsworth favored allowing the president to be re-eligible for election. He explained:

> The Executive . . . should be reelected if his conduct proved him worthy of it. And he will be more likely to render him[self] worthy of it if he be rewardable with it. The most eminent characters also will be more willing to accept the trust under this condition, than if they foresee a necessary degradation at a fixt period. (II, 101)

Somewhat later Ellsworth proposed a plan whereby a sitting president would be chosen by electors appointed by state legislatures rather than by Congress (II, 108–109). Ellsworth was concerned, however, that the systems of election being discussed at the Convention tilted too much in the direction of the most populous states (II, 111).

Ellsworth favored a provision whereby the president could supply vacancies in the U.S. Senate but did not anticipate that the president would need to exercise such a power when the state legislature was in session (II, 231). He did not oppose allowing either state governors or state legislatures to make such appointments, but he did not want to divide the power between them (II, 232).

Just as he had supported a Council of Revision (see below), Ellsworth favored establishing a presidential council. He wanted it to consist of the president of the Senate, the chief justice and the ministers of leading departments. He anticipated that they "should advise but not conclude the President" (II, 329).

Judiciary

Ellsworth, a Connecticut judge who later served as chief justice of the U.S. Supreme Court, approved of the plan to associate members of the judiciary with the executive in a Council of Revision. He saw several advantages:

> The aid of the Judges will give more wisdom & firmness to the Executive. They will possess a systematic and accurate knowledge of the Laws, which the Executive can not be expected always to possess. The law of Nations also will frequently come into question. Of this the Judge alone will have competent information. (II, 74)

In discussing judicial appointments on July 21, Ellsworth indicated that he could support allowing the Senate to nominate judges, subject to a presidential veto, which could be overridden by a two-thirds vote, but that he would prefer a system whereby the Senate had the absolute appointment power. He seemed concerned in part about popular reaction, and in part about a number of practical problems:

> The Executive will be regarded by the people with a jealous eye. Every power for augmenting unnecessarily his influence will be disliked. As he will be stationary it was not to be supposed he could have a better knowledge of characters. He will be more open to caresses & intrigues than the Senate. The right to supersede his nomination will be ideal only. A nomination under such circumstances will be the equivalent to an appointment. (II, 81)

Ratification

On June 20, Ellsworth expressed the view that what changes were needed in the Articles could go forward by amendments that states could ratify. He feared that if state conventions were to be used, it would take a number of them. He further observed that "He did not like these conventions. They were better fitted to pull down than to build up Constitutions" (I, 335). Ellsworth repeated his support for state legislative ratification on July 23, when he portrayed the idea that constitutions needed to be ratified by conventions as a new idea. He attempted to answer arguments by George Mason that legislatures had no authority to ratify constitutions, and that if they exercised such authority, future legislatures could rescind it. As to the first argument, Ellsworth argued that legislatures had until recently been accepted as competent to ratify constitutions as the very existence of the Articles demonstrated: "The fact is that we exist at present, and we need not enquire how, as a federal Society, united by a charter one article of which is that alterations therein may be made by the Legislative authority of the States" (II, 91). Intentionally or perhaps unintentionally sidestepping the second issue, Ellsworth argued that legislative ratification did not need, as some delegates had argued, to be unanimous:

> If such were the urgency & necessity of our situation as to warrant a new compact among a part of the States, founded on the consent of the people; the same pleas would be equally valid in favor of a partial compact, founded on the consent of the Legislatures. (II, 91)

Life after the Convention

Ellsworth left the Constitutional Convention on August 25. He appears to have done so in order to attend to his judicial duties rather than, as in the case of some other delegates, because he opposed the direction that the Convention had taken. He emerged as a defender of the Constitution during the debates over ratification in his state.

Selected as one of Connecticut's first two U.S. senators, Ellsworth gravitated toward the Federalist Party. Ellsworth chaired the Senate Judiciary Committee. In this capacity he was the primary author of the Judiciary Act of 1789 when he put flesh on the bare bones of Article III of the Constitution (the sketchiest of the three distributing articles, allocating powers to the branches of the national government) by creating a three-tier system of federal courts, with circuit and district courts below the Supreme Court. President Washington appointed Ellsworth as the third chief justice of the United States Supreme Court in 1796, whereas Ellsworth often expressed his admiration for the English common law. Ellsworth served in this capacity until 1800 but issued few landmark rulings.

President John Adams appointed Ellsworth and two other Americans to France to negotiate over its interference in American shipping. Although the trip resulted in a treaty that Congress ratified, the trip and Ellsworth's prior circuit-riding duties as a justice were not good for Ellsworth's health. After a brief sojourn in England, Ellsworth returned to Connecticut and became a member of the Governor's Council and the state's Supreme Court of Errors. He died at his farm in Windsor, Connecticut, on November 26, 1807.

See Also Connecticut; Connecticut Compromise

FOR FURTHER READING

Brown, William Garrott. 1905. "A Continental Congressman: Oliver Ellsworth, 1777–1783." *American Historical Review* 10 (July): 751–781.

Cushman, Clare, ed. 1995. *The Supreme Court Justices: Illustrated Biographies, 1789–1995.* 2nd ed. Washington, DC: Congressional Quarterly.

Farrand, Max, ed. 1937. *The Records of the Federal Convention.* 4 vols. New Haven, CT: Yale University Press.

EMBOSSING OF CONSTITUTION

See SHALLUS, JACOB

ENLIGHTENMENT

See REASON AND EXPERIENCE

ENTREPRENEURS, CONSTITUTIONAL

Constitutional entrepreneurs have been defined as "individuals who perceive opportunities for altering the constitutional framework of a political order, who envision alternatives to the constitutional status quo, who bear the personal risk of promoting these alternatives, and who possess the interpersonal skills to persuade others to follow in the wake of their visions" (Kromkowski 2002, 238). In addition to being motivated by patriotism, such individuals may be spurred to action by the desire for fame. A number of such talented constitutional entrepreneurs, most notably James Madison and Alexander Hamilton, as well as James Wilson, George Washington, and Benjamin Franklin, helped initiate the movement for the U.S. Constitution. They also helped formulate a new Constitution and worked for its ratification and implementation.

Entrepreneurs of one period may become highly resistant to major constitutional change in another. Once the new government was formed, James Madison was among those who sought to surround the new government with an aura of veneration that would make it less susceptible to future replacement (Vile 1992, 36–39). Thus, in *Federalist* No. 49, Madison opposed a proposal suggested by Thomas Jefferson in his *Notes on the State of Virginia* for periodic constitutional revision by arguing that "as every appeal to the people would carry an implication of some defect in the government, frequent appeals would, in general measure, deprive the government of that veneration which time bestows on everything, and without which perhaps the wisest and freest governments would not possess the requisite stability" (Hamilton, Madison, and Jay 1961, 314).

See Also Constitutional Moments; Fame; Franklin, Benjamin; Hamilton, Alexander; Madison, James, Jr.; Washington, George; Wilson, James

FOR FURTHER READING

Hamilton, Alexander, James Madison, and John Jay.

1961. *The Federalist Papers*. Ed. Clinton Rossiter. New York: New American Library.
Kromkowski, Charles A. 2002. *Recreating the American Republic: Rules of Apportionment, Constitutional Change, and American Political Development, 1700–1870*. Cambridge: Cambridge University Press.
Vile, John R. 1992. *The Constitutional Amending Process in American Political Thought*. New York: Praeger.

EQUALITY

One of the most striking omissions of the U.S. Constitution of 1787 is arguably an explicit commitment to equality. Indeed, the only specific mention of equality in the document is found in Article V, which guarantees "that no State, without its Consent, shall be deprived of its equal Suffrage in the Senate" (a point noted by Katz 1988, 747), thus focusing on governmental entities rather than persons. By contrast, in the opening paragraph of the Declaration of Independence Thomas Jefferson had announced that "all men are created equal." Even this document, however, had rested such equality on the equal possession of rights rather than on an equality of results. It was not until the ratification of the Fourteenth Amendment in 1868 that the Constitution itself incorporated the aspiration of legal equality into the Constitution by guaranteeing all persons "equal protection of the laws," and this amendment itself was not vigorously enforced until the advent of the Warren Court in the 1950s and 1960s.

The Declaration of Independence and the Constitution

Although historians from the Progressive Era often distinguished between what they considered to be a liberal revolutionary Declaration of Independence and a "conservative" Constitution, it appears that the central difference between the documents was that of purpose. The former was designed to announce American aspirations for independence so that Americans could assume "the equal station to which nature and nature's laws entitle them," whereas the latter was responsible for creating, or re-creating, specific governmental structures.

Inequalities

The greatest obstacle to recognizing equality in the Constitution was the status of slaves, who were specifically acknowledged, for purposes of taxation and representation, to count for "three-fifths of a person." Although women were not specifically singled out in the Constitution, contemporary state laws relegated them to positions of inferior rights. Similarly, the Constitution identified Native American Indians as distinct from others.

Both liberalism (with its emphasis on a state of nature in which all men are equal) and republicanism (with its opposition to aristocracy and to hereditary privilege) had strong strains of equality. This was embodied in part in the provision in Article I, Section 9 prohibiting Congress from granting titles of nobility.

Equality in America

For the most part, Americans probably believed that they had already achieved far greater equality than Europeans by creating a society where (apart from slaves) most people could expect to enjoy the fruits of their own labor (Hutson [1993] has observed the frequent recurrence of this value). South Carolina's Charles Pinckney called attention to this equality at the Constitutional Convention on June 25 when he spoke out on the Senate, pointing to widespread equality among American "freemen":

The people of the U. States are perhaps the most singular of any we are acquainted with. Among them there are fewer distinctions of fortune & loss of rank, than among the inhabitants of any other nation. Every freeman has a right to the same protection & security; and a very moderate share of property entitles them to the possession

of all the honors and privileges the public can bestow; hence arises a greater equality, than is to be found among the people of any other country, and an equality which is more likely to continue. (Farrand 1937, I, 398)

In what Hutson has identified as another favorite theme of the Founding Fathers (1993), Pinckney pointed to "the destruction of the right of primogeniture [special inheritance rights for firstborn sons] & the equal division of the property of Intestates [those who die without written wills]," both developments in state laws of the time, as factors that were likely to "have an effect to preserve this mediocrity [by which he meant equality]" (I, 400).

Inequality in America

If America were characterized by more widespread equality than was found in the monarchies of Europe, delegates recognized that there were distinctions among Americans that were likely to continue. In referring back on June 26 to Pinckney's speech, Virginia's James Madison thus observed that although "we had not among us those hereditary distinctions, of rank which were a great source of the contests in the ancient Govts. as well as the modern States of Europe, nor those extremes of wealth or poverty which characterize the latter," still

We cannot however be regarded even at this time, as one homogeneous mass, in which every thing that affects a part will affect in the same manner the whole. In framing a system which we wish to last for ages, we shd. not lose sight of the changes which ages will produce. (I, 422)

Madison went on to foresee the possibility of increased economic inequality. He did not so much seek to prevent this increased inequality as to prepare for it by granting due stability to the Senate:

An increase of population will of necessity increase the proportion of those who will labour under all the hardships of life, & secretly sigh for a more equal distribution of its blessings. These may in time outnumber those who are placed above the feelings of indigence. According to the equal laws of suffrage [not then to be specifically guaranteed by the Constitution], the power will slide into the hands of the former. No agrarian attempts have yet been made in this Country, but symptoms of a leveling spirit, as we have understood, have sufficiently appeared in a certain quarter [presumably a reference to Shays's Rebellion] to give notice of the future danger. (I, 422–423)

Madison further elaborated on this theme in defending the Constitution in *Federalist* No. 10. Scanning the diversity of interests that divided citizens, Madison attributed some interests to "the diversity in the faculties of men, from which the rights of property originate" (Hamilton, Madison, and Jay 1961, 78). Similarly, Madison grounds faction in what he describes as "the various and unequal distribution of property":

Those who hold and those who are without property have ever formed distinct interests in society. Those who are creditors, and those who are debtors, fall under a like discrimination. A landed interest, a manufacturing interest, a mercantile interest, a moneyed interest, with many lesser interests, grow up of necessity in civilized nations, and divide them into different classes, actuated by different sentiments and views. (1961, 79)

Madison was among the Framers who opposed allowing states to emit paper money whereby he thought debtors could unjustly escape their debts.

Although ultimately focusing more on political than on social or economic equality, the Constitution initially left out some groups, especially African Americans, women, and Indians. Pointing to continuing problems in implementing ideas of equality in modern times, Historian Herman Belz argues that instead of condemning the Founders, "we might more appropriately praise them for establishing a constitutional framework, in which every person has an opportunity to pursue his or her interests under guarantees of freedom and equal rights, a framework through which blacks, women, and a wide variety of ethnocultural groups have gained inclusion in the political community" (1992, 275).

See Also African Americans; Aristocracy; Declaration of Independence; Indians; Money, State Coining and Emissions of; Republicanism; Social Contract; Three-fifths Clause; Women

FOR FURTHER READING

Belz, Herman. 1992. "Liberty and Equality for Whom? How to Think Inclusively about the Constitution and the Bill of Rights." *The History Teacher* 25 (May): 263–277.

Farrand, Max, ed. 1937. *The Records of the Federal Convention.* 4 vols. New Haven, CT: Yale University Press.

Hamilton, Alexander, James Madison, and John Jay. 1961. *The Federalist Papers.* Ed. Clinton Rossiter. New York: New American Library.

Hutson, James L. 1993. "The American Revolutionaries, the Political Economy of Aristocracy, and the American Concept of the Distribution of Wealth, 1765–1900." *American Historical Review* 98 (October): 1079–1900.

Katz, Stanley N. 1988. "The Strange Birth and Unlikely History of Constitutional Equality." *Journal of American History* 75 (December): 747–762.

EUROPEAN INFLUENCES ON DELEGATES TO THE CONVENTION

The intellectual roots of the American Constitution are truly legion. The delegates to the Convention were men who were well educated and well read in the history and culture of Western civilization. In addition to their familiarity with statesmen from their own continent, the delegates would have been familiar with a variety of thinkers, most from Europe. The author of this encyclopedia has attempted to limit entries to individuals whose names are known to have been actually mentioned or discussed on a number of occasions at the Convention. They include David

Hume, John Locke, the Baron de Montesquieu, Richard Price, and others.

The Framers made frequent reference to both classical thinkers (like Polybius) and leagues (most notably the Achaean and Amphictyonic) with which Europeans would have been familiar as well as to the examples of such modern governments and leagues as those of Holland, Poland, and Germany. The Framers were also concerned about European governments—namely those of Great Britain, France, and Spain—with interests in the New World. Especially in the case of Great Britain, the colonists had inherited a number of ideas and institutions, most notably the idea of rights, representative government, and the system of common law, which they would adapt to and refine in the American setting.

Because so many individuals who influenced the Framers may not have been mentioned at all, or only in passing, in the notes of the Convention, it is often useful to examine ideologies that influenced the Framers. Schools of thought with European origins that are known to have influenced the American Framers included liberalism, republicanism, the Court and Country Parties in England, Scottish Enlightenment thinkers, and thinkers influential in Puritan and Protestant thought.

See Also Common Law; Court and Country Parties; France; Germany; Great Britain; Holland; Hume, David; Liberalism; Locke, John; Montesquieu, Charles Louis de Secondat de; Poland; Price, Richard; Protestantism; Puritanism; Republicanism; Scottish Enlightenment; Spain

FOR FURTHER READING

McDonald, Forrest. 1985. Novus Ordo Seclorum: *The Intellectual Origins of the Constitution.* Lawrence: University Press of Kansas.

EX POST FACTO LAWS

Among other limits on Congress, Article I, Section 9, prohibits ex post facto laws. Article I, Section 10, applies this same limitation to the states. Ex post facto laws are generally defined as retrospective criminal laws. They may punish an individual for something that was not a crime when the act was committed, aggravate the penalty for such a crime, or allow for evidence in a case to be admitted that was not admissible at the time of such a crime (see Schultz and Vile I 2005, 342–344).

Elbridge Gerry of Massachusetts and James McHenry of Maryland proposed limiting Congress from adopting either ex post facto laws or bills of attainder on August 22. In an argument that somewhat turned Madison's arguments elsewhere at the Convention for the advantages of an extended republic on its head, Gerry stated that the prohibitions were more necessary at the national level because, having fewer legislators, they were more to be feared. Gouverneur Morris of Pennsylvania thought the prohibition against ex post facto laws was unnecessary. Oliver Ellsworth of Connecticut supplied Morris's likely reasoning: he thought such laws were "void of themselves" (Farrand 1937, II, 376). James Wilson, a future U.S. Supreme Court justice, agreed: "It will bring reflexions on the Constitution—and proclaim that we are ignorant of the first principles of Legislation, or are constituting a Government which will be so" (II, 376). The Convention thus voted to divide the question, agreeing unanimously to the prohibition against bills of attainder but continuing to discuss the ex post facto law prohibition.

Maryland's Daniel Carroll argued that "experience overruled all other calculations" (II, 376). However invalid ex post facto laws might be in theory, state legislatures had passed them, and they needed to be guarded against. Wilson responded that this simply showed that state prohibitions had been useless. He further observed that "both sides will agree to the principle & will differ as to its application" (II, 376). North Carolina's Hugh Williamson responded that, if there were a prohibition within the Constitution, "the Judges can take hold of it" (II, 376). Connecticut's William Johnson thought the clause was unnecessary and implied "an improper suspicion of the National Legislature," but South Carolina's John Rutledge favored it, and the Convention subsequently adopted it by a vote of 7-3-1.

On August 28, Rufus King of Massachusetts proposed adding a prohibition restricting states from interfering in private contracts. This elicited a discussion as to whether this would be going too far. The Convention ended up adopting by a 7-3 vote a prohibition against bills of attainder or ex post facto laws (II, 435)–Madison's notes appear incorrectly to refer to these as "retrospective laws" (II, 440). On August 29, Delaware's John Dickinson mentioned that he had examined William Blackstone's *Commentaries on the Law of England* (the most comprehensive and widely read analysis of English law), that Blackstone had indicated that the term "ex post facto" referred only to criminal laws, and that some other provision would therefore be needed if the states were to be restricted from adopting other retrospective laws (II, 448–449).

By contrast, on September 14, just three days before the delegates signed the Constitution, Virginia's George Mason moved to strike the ex post facto clause. He argued that it was not clear that this provision was confined to criminal cases, and "no Legislature ever did or can altogether avoid them in Civil cases" (II, 617). Elbridge Gerry actually wanted to extend the prohibition to civil cases, but the state unanimously rejected this proposal.

On September 15, Mason cited the two provisions prohibiting ex post facto laws as one of the grounds for his opposition to the Constitution. Apparently believing that these provisions would apply to all retrospective legislation, he observed that "there never was nor can be a legislature but must and will make such laws, when necessity and the public safety require them; which will hereafter be a breach of all the constitutions in the Union, and afford precedents for other innovations" (II, 640).

The provisions against ex post facto laws foreshadow the Bill of Rights in that they attempt to place limits on Congress and the states in an effort to protect individual rights. The central debate over the clause both at the Convention and in subsequent ratifying debates focused on "whether one read the key phrase as a lawyer or as a layperson" (Nelson 2002, 578). In *Calder v. Bull*, 3 Dall. (3 U.S.) 386 (1798), the U.S. Supreme Court established the view, shared by most lawyers, limiting ex post facto laws to retroactive criminal laws, rather than to laws in general. Other provisions in the Constitution and the Bill of Rights, including the takings and due process clauses of the Fifth Amendment, arguably prohibit some civil laws that might not be covered by the ex post facto provisions (Natelson 2003, 491).

See Also Attainder, Bills of; Congress, Limits on; Contracts Clause; States, Limits on

FOR FURTHER READING

Farrand, Max, ed. 1937. *The Records of the Federal Convention*. 4 vols. New Haven, CT: Yale University Press.

Natelson, Robert G. 2003. "Statutory Retroactivity: The Founders' View." *Idaho Law Review* 39: 489–528.

Nelson, Caleb. 2002. "Originalism and Interpretive Conventions." *University of Chicago Law Review* 70 (Spring): 519–598.

Schultz, David, and John R. Vile, eds. 2005. *The Encyclopedia of Civil Liberties in America* (Armonk, NY: M. E. Sharpe).

EXECUTIVE BRANCH OF GOVERNMENT; EXECUTIVE POWER

See Entries beginning with PRESIDENT

EXPENSES OF DELEGATES

At least for most of the delegates, attending the Constitutional Convention does not appear to have been a lucrative proposition. This undoubtedly limited the individuals who were able to attend. Congress did not pay a salary to the delegates, although, consistent with its treatment of its own members, Congress appears to have extended franking (free mailing) privileges to them (Farrand 1937, III, 17).

North Carolina's Richard Spaight wrote to the state governor on June 12, 1787, asking for "a further advance of two months' Salary" (III, 46) and received a positive response (III, 52); the state assembly had voted "the same allowance to be made the Deputies as is granted to the Delegates to Congress" (III, 568 n.). Maryland also voted to pay the delegates "as delegates in congress were paid" (III, 586 n.; Steiner 1899, 25). Similarly, Virginia's Edmund Randolph inquired about his "wages," although he may have been referring to the salary he would normally have received as governor (III, 74).

On the whole, however, states appear only to have provided the delegates with expense allowances. New Jersey paid $4 per delegate per day; Virginia paid $6 a day (III, 57); Delaware paid 40 shillings a day; because its delegates already lived in Philadelphia, Pennsylvania apparently did not pay any expenses (*1787*, 23). Some states paid in advance and others reimbursed the delegates later. New Hampshire's two delegates, John Langdon and Nicholas Gilman, who did not arrive until July 23, would probably never have arrived had John Langdon not proved able to front the money for their expenses. With states paying their bills (as they had paid the salaries of members of Congress under the Articles of Confederation), it is no wonder that many delegates thought their primary obligation was to the states. Significantly, the delegates provided that the salaries of members of Congress who were selected under the new Constitution would be paid directly from the national treasury rather than depending on the states. By contrast, states remained responsible for paying for whatever expenses they chose to reimburse for members of state ratifying conventions.

The Constitution should probably rank with the Louisiana Purchase as one of the nation's best bargains. Congressional costs for the Convention, which were spent on paying the secretary, doorkeeper, messenger, and stationer, came to only $1,586.00 (*1787*, 24). Apparently, Congress did not have to pay for the use of the Pennsylvania State House. Congress did later appropriate about $30,000 to purchase Madison's *Notes* of the Convention's proceedings.

See Also Congress, Salaries

FOR FURTHER READING

1787: The Day-to-Day Story of the Constitutional Convention. 1987. Compiled by historians of the Independence National Historical Park. New York: Exeter Books.

Farrand, Max, ed. 1937. *The Records of the Federal Convention.* 4 vols. New Haven, CT: Yale University Press.

Steiner, Bernard C. 1899. "Maryland's Adoption of the Federal Constitution I." *American Historical Review* 5 (October): 22–44.

EXPORT TAXES

Congress exercises the "power of the purse." The first clause in Article I, Section 8 accordingly vests Congress with the power "to lay and collect Taxes, Duties, Imposts, and Excises." However, Article I, Section 9 prohibits Congress from laying any "Tax or Duty" on exports while Article I, Section 10 limits states from laying "Imposts or Duties on Imports or Exports, except what may be absolutely necessary for executing its inspection laws." It further provides that "the net Produce of all Duties and Imposts, laid by a State on Imports or Exports, shall be for the Use of the Treasury of the United States; and all such Laws shall be subject to the Revision and Controul of the Congress."

As early as June 18, New York's Alexander Hamilton had suggested that national revenue might be drawn from export taxes (Farrand 1937, I, 286), but the issue received little attention until July 12. After proposing that taxation should be proportioned according to representation, Gouverneur Morris indicated that he intended for this formula to apply only to forms of direct taxation and not to taxes "on *exports* & imports & on consumption" (I, 592). Approving Morris's idea of linking taxation and representation, South Carolina's General Charles Cotesworth Pinckney nonetheless expressed concern about the idea of taxing exports and, by the opposition that Morris expressed the previous day, counting slaves in the representation formula. Pinckney calculated that South Carolina exported goods valued at about 600,000 pounds sterling a year, "which was the fruit of the labor of her blacks." If the state were not to be represented by blacks, then neither should it be taxed according to their labor. Accordingly, he expressed the hope that "a clause would be inserted in the system restraining the Legislature from a taxing [of] Exports" (I, 592). When the Convention established a Committee of Detail headed by fellow South Carolinian John Rutledge, the general said that he would vote against any report that did not limit such taxes (II, 95). The committee report allowed Congress to lay "taxes, duties, imposts and excises," but contained a prohibition on Congress against levying any "tax or duty" laid "on articles exported from any State" and required congressional consent to any such state impositions (II, 181, 183, 187).

On August 16, a question arose as to the difference between "duties" and "imposts." Pennsylvania's James Wilson suggested that "duties" was the broader term, extending to some objects like stamp duties that were not specifically in commerce (II, 305). Wilson expressed concern that the Convention should not ratify congressional power over the former without a guarantee that it would not tax exports: "He was unwilling to trust to its being done in a future article. He hoped the Northn. States did not mean to deny the Southern this security. It would hereafter be as desirable to the former when the latter should become the most populous" (II, 305). Connecticut's Roger Sherman and South Carolina's John Rutledge did not oppose such a provision, but they thought it properly belonged under the section limiting the powers of Congress.

By contrast, Gouverneur Morris of Pennsylvania thought that a provision was "radically objectionable"; he thought there were cases where it would be inequitable to tax imports without also taxing exports and that taxes on exports would often be "the most easy and proper of the two" (II, 306). Virginia's James Madison agreed. He observed that export taxes could often be used as a means of leveraging foreign markets. Raising an issue that did not appear to be under discussion (namely *state* imposition of export taxes which were forbidden

in another section), Madison said that he would be "unjust" to allow states to tax exports produced in neighboring states. He also said that it would not be improper if the South paid more export taxes since they were most in need of naval protection.

Delegates began to line up on two sides. North Carolina's Hugh Williamson thought the prohibition against taxing exports was "reasonable and necessary" (II, 307). Ellsworth agreed but was content to leave the restriction elsewhere in the Constitution. Wilson, like Madison, opposed a restriction on congressional imposition of export taxes but denounced state taxation of exports of other states. Elbridge Gerry of Massachusetts feared that Congress could "ruin the Country" if it had the power to tax exports (II, 307). Morris reiterated his view that there were occasions when taxing exports would be "highly politic" (I, 307). Such taxes would be preferable to direct taxes. Maryland's John Mercer opposed allowing Congress to tax exports, but he did so in the apparent belief that this would allow states to exercise the power; he further denied that the South contributed more to the need for national defense. Almost always the conciliator, Connecticut's Roger Sherman thought the Convention had already arrived at the conclusion that imports could be taxed but exports not. Export taxes were only appropriate on "such articles as ought not to be exported," and "A power to tax exports would shipwreck the whole" (II, 308). The Convention voted to leave the restriction on taxing exports where it was. When the Convention voted on allowing Congress the power to collect taxes and levy imposts, only Elbridge Gerry dissented.

When the Convention resumed discussion of the congressional prohibition against taxing exports, New Hampshire's John Langdon objected that this left the states at liberty to do so. He wanted to require supermajority approval from Congress in such cases (II, 359). Connecticut's Oliver Ellsworth thought that states would be protected by the congressional power to regulate interstate trade. Ellsworth went on to argue that Congress should be restrained from taxing exports since such taxes would discourage industry, would be "partial & unjust," and "would engender incurable jealousies" (II, 360). Williamson said that his state could never agree to such a power, and Sherman later agreed that all such congressional powers should be prohibited. Gerry feared that congressional powers over commerce could allow the national government to oppress the states, and Mason connected this fear to that of taxing states differentially (II, 362–363).

By contrast Gouverneur Morris continued to favor national taxation of exports. Without such a power, he doubted that Congress could levy embargoes. Such taxes might further encourage U.S. manufacturers (II, 360). John Dickinson of Delaware later argued that although such taxes might be "inconvenient at present," it would be unwise to prohibit them for all times (II, 361). Madison agreed, also fearing that a restriction might affect future embargoes. Ellsworth, however, did not think the section restricted the embargo power, and Maryland's James McHenry thought that embargoes fell under the war power. Wilson thought that it was foolish to deny Congress power over half of trade and thought that export taxes could be helpful in obtaining "beneficial treaties of commerce" (II, 362).

Perhaps reaching back to a distinction that the colonists had sometimes made in their quarrel with Great Britain that led to the Revolutionary War, George Clymer of Pennsylvania proposed that Congress should be able to tax for the purpose of regulating trade but not for the purpose of revenue. Ths motion failed by a vote of 7-3. Madison and Wilson then suggested substituting a two-thirds majority requirement for the absolute prohibition on taxing exports. The Convention defeated this proposal by a vote of 6-5, and then passed the motion for prohibiting all such congressional-imposed taxes by a vote of 7-4.

When the Convention continued discussion of taxation of imported slaves on the next day, Gouverneur Morris resolved to commit the clauses related to taxes on exports to the committee, hoping that "These things may form a bargain among the Northern & Southern States" (II, 374). South Carolina's Pierce Butler observed that he would never "agree to the power of taxing exports" (II, 374).

On August 28, Madison proposed that the prohibition against state taxation of imports should be absolute, and Williamson seconded him. Sherman thought that Congress should retain power to allow for such taxation, and Mason observed that states might want to keep such taxes as a means of encouraging products, like hemp, for which they had a natural advantage. Madison responded that this was exactly why such a prohibition was needed, lest it "revive all the mischiefs experienced from the want of a Genl. Government over commerce" (II, 441). Madison's motion, however, failed by a 7-4 vote.

The Convention proceeded to extend the prohibition of state taxation of state imports without congressional consent to exports as well, and the Convention agreed by a vote of 6-5. It then voted 9-5 to require that any such taxes would go into the common treasury, arguably defeating any incentive for it.

On September 12, Virginia's George Mason recommended that the prohibition against state taxation of exports not be interpreted to prevent "the incidental duties necessary for the inspection & safe-keeping of the produce," and was seconded by Madison in making an exception for such. Gouverneur Morris had no objection, although Jonathan Dayton of New Jersey, Nathaniel Gorham of Massachusetts and John Langdon of New Hampshire all expressed fears that this might provide a subterfuge for states to tax their neighbors, to which Madison responded that the Supreme Court would prevent this, although putting in a plug for the preferably of his negative on state laws. Mason's motion was adopted on September 13, and the language of the Constitution was accordingly adjusted on September 15, with only Virginia dissenting (II, 624).

The Convention handled the taxation on the importation of slaves in a separate clause of Article I, Section 9, permitting such importation until 1808 and limiting taxation to $10 per person.

Perhaps the greatest irony of the debates on export taxes is that, for all the attempts of the states, especially those of the South, to protect themselves against taxes on exports, tariffs (taxes on imports), became a major cause of division in the early republic. Southern states had to import almost all manufactured goods. Southern states found that tariffs designed to foster industrial development in the Northeast raised consumer prices in the South. Many undoubtedly regretted that they had not incorporated a provision in the Constitution that would have required that such tariffs be levied by supermajorities or prohibited them altogether. It is difficult to know, however, how the national government would have raised money in the days before the income tax had there been such a prohibition.

See Also Congress, Power of the Purse; Slave Importation

FOR FURTHER READING

Farrand, Max, ed. 1937. *The Records of the Federal Convention.* 4 vols. New Haven, CT: Yale University Press.
Taylor, George R., ed. 1993. *The Great Tariff Debate, 1820–1830.* Boston: D. D. Heath.

EXTRADITION

Article IV, Section 2 of the Constitution provided that "a Person charged in any State with Treason, Felony, or other Crime, who shall flee from Justice, and be found in another State, shall on Demand of the executive Authority of the State from which he fled, be delivered up, to be removed to the State having Jurisdiction of the Crime." The process of extraditing criminals is essential to a nation of states. Not surprisingly, then, the provision in the U.S. Constitution is almost identical to that under the Articles of Confederation. It had provided that "if any Person guilty of, or charged with, treason, felony, or other high misdemeanor in any state, shall flee from Justice, and be found in any of the united states, he shall, upon demand of the governor or

executive power, of the state from which he fled, be delivered up and removed to the state having jurisdiction of his offence" (Solberg 1958, 43).

The New Jersey Plan, which William Paterson introduced, appears to have been the first to mention an extradition provision. It had "resd. that a Citizen of one State committing an offence in another State of the Union, shall be deemed guilty of the same offence as if it had been committed by a Citizen of the State in which the Offence was committed" (Farrand 1937, I, 245). In presenting its draft of a Constitution to the Convention on August 6, the Committee of Detail chose to follow the language of the Articles of Confederation, even using the term "high misdemeanor" (II, 287). The Convention substituted the term "other crime" for this on August 28, believing that the meaning of high misdemeanor was too technical and limited (II, 443). Pierce Butler and Charles Pinckney, both of South Carolina, wanted "to require fugitive slaves and servants to be delivered up like criminals," but Pennsylvania's James Wilson questioned the propriety of using public monies for this purpose and Connecticut's Roger Sherman observed that he "saw no more propriety in the public seizing and surrendering a slave or servant, than a horse" (II, 443). The Convention dealt with the fugitive slave question in the subsequent clause.

See Also Articles of Confederation; Committee of Detail; Fugitive Slave Clause; New Jersey Plan

FOR FURTHER READING

Farrand, Max, ed. 1937. *The Records of the Federal Convention.* 4 vols. New Haven, CT: Yale University Press.
Solberg, Winton U. 1958. *The Federal Convention and the Formation of the Union of the American States.* Indianapolis, IN: Bobbs-Merrill.

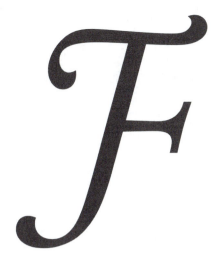

FACTIONS

See PARTIES, FACTIONS, AND INTERESTS

FAME

Whereas other analysts have focused on economic motives or other motives that may be considered to be relatively plebeian, historian Douglass Adair observed in a highly regarded essay that many of the American Founding Fathers had been motivated by a desire for fame (Adair 1974). Attempting in part to account for the large number of extraordinary leaders who emerged from such a thinly populated continent during the Revolutionary and early nation-building periods, Adair observed that during this time individuals like George Washington, John Adams, Thomas Jefferson, Alexander Hamilton, and others had raised their sights from relatively modest goals in their youth to being actors on the world stage.

Further distinguishing fame from mere popularity in a way that contemporaries do not always do, Adair explained that whereas popularity refers largely to contemporary appraisals by the masses, fame seeks the regard of wise men and of posterity: "The love of fame encourages a man to make history, to leave the mark of his deeds and his ideals on the world; it incites a man to refuse to be the victim of events and to become an 'event-making' personality–a being never to be forgotten by those later generations that will be born into a world his actions helped to shape" (Adair, 11). Adair argued that by focusing on "the psychic reward of fame, honor, [and] glory" these key leaders, a number of whom attended the Constitutional Convention, transformed "egotism and self-aggrandizing impulses into public service" (8). Adair further tied the desire for fame to a "desire for immortality" (12), and observed how well it tied to classical conceptions of greatness (with which many of the Founding Fathers were familiar), which included the founding and preservation of nations. Adair tied the use of the pen name Publius in *The Federalist* and Madison's comparison of the Founders to ancient lawgivers like Lycurgus in *Federalist* essay No. 38 to the desire for fame, and believes that Madison's posthumous publication of his notes was a further attempt at secular immortality.

Convention references to posterity, which another essay in these volumes documents, confirm that many of those at the Convention were looking not simply to the immediate future but to the judgment of future generations. The most explicit reference to fame at the Constitutional Convention is the speech that Gouverneur Morris, who largely authored the stirring Preamble to the Constitution, delivered on July 19 in opposing presidential ineligibility for a second term. In this speech, Morris observed that the proposal will destroy the great incitement to merit public esteem by taking away the hope of being rewarded with a reappointment. It may give a dangerous turn to one of the strongest passions in the human breast. The love of fame is the great spring to noble & illustrious actions. Shut the Civil road to Glory & he may be compelled to seek it by the sword. (Farrand 1937, II, 53)

Although other members disputed his argument, none appear to have contradicted his arguments about the role of fame as "the great spring to noble & illustrious actions." In a subsequent speech delivered on September 3, Charles Pinckney opposed restricting offices that former members of Congress could hold, observing that the delegates should emulate the Romans "in making the temple of virtue the road to the temple of fame" (II, 490). In *Federalist* No. 72, Alexander Hamilton called "the love of fame, the ruling passion of the noblest minds" (Hamilton, Madison, and Jay 1961, 437). He used the existence of this passion to argue for presidential re-eligibility for office, observing that a single term would deter presidents from undertaking "extensive and arduous enterprises for the public benefit, requiring considerable time to mature and perfect" when a president "foresaw that he must quit the scene before he could accomplish the work, and must commit that, together with his own reputation, to hands which might be unequal or unfriendly to the task" (437).

Despite this strain of the thought of the Founding Fathers, many Enlightenment figures criticized the desire for fame and honor among the ancients for leading to aggression and conquest. Moreover, the desire for immortality, if not tied to the esteem of good men, could lead men seeking to be remembered to "care more about simply being remembered, rather than by whom or for what" (Treanor 1997, 733). Roman history thus offered the warning of Herostratus, who had burned the magnificent Temple of Diana at Ephesus in order to become immortal (Treanor, 733).

Similarly, at times the Framers of the U.S. Constitution indicated that they recognized that the desire for fame, like other passions, could be insatiable (McNamara 1999, 25). Moreover, unlike

the ancients, the American Framers "tended to treat politics as an instrument for the protection of inherent human rights and not as an end in itself" (26). Much more than the ancients, the Americans often spoke of the "burdens" of public service (26–29).

To the extent that fame was among the rewards that many of the delegates hoped to receive, they succeeded. Books continue to document their lives, the proceedings of the Convention, and interpretations of the document they wrote, with most commentators and citizens alike focusing on the nobility of their enterprise and the wisdom and public-spiritedness of their work.

See Also Delegates, Collective Assessments; Human Nature; Posterity and Perpetuity

FOR FURTHER READING

Adair, Douglass. 1974. "Fame and the Founding Fathers." In Trevor Colbourn, ed. *Fame and the Founding Fathers: Essays*. New York: W. W. Norton, 3–26.

Farrand, Max, ed. 1937. *The Records of the Federal Convention*. 4 vols. New Haven, CT: Yale University Press.

Hamilton, Alexander, James Madison, and John Jay. 1961. *The Federalist Papers*. Ed. Clinton Rossiter. New York: New American Library.

McNamara, Peter. 1999. *The Noblest Minds: Fame, Honor, and the American Founding*. Lanham, MD: Rowman and Littlefield Publishers.

Miroff, Bruce. 1986. "John Adams: Merit, Fame, and Political Leadership." *Journal of Politics* 48 (February): 116–132.

Treanor, William Michael. 1997. "Fame, the Founding, and the Power to Declare War." *Cornell Law Review* 82: 695–772.

FARRAND, MAX (1869–1945)

Study of the U.S. Constitutional Convention would be much more difficult were it not for the work of Professor Max Farrand. Born in Newark,

New Jersey, he graduated from Newark Academy, where his father served as headmaster, and then earned a number of degrees, including a Ph.D. in history from Princeton University. He subsequently taught history at Wesleyan University, chaired the Department of History at Stanford University, and taught at Cornell (1905–1906) and Yale Universities (1908–1925) before planning the Huntington Library, and becoming its first research associate and later director of research until he retired in 1941 (Kesavan and Paulsen 2003, 1121–1122).

While he was at Yale, Farrand edited *The Records of the Federal Convention* in 1911, which he subsequently revised in 1937. James H. Hutson in turn updated Farrand's fourth volume in 1987. These volumes remain the standard compilation of notes of debates of the Constitutional Convention, letters to and from convention delegates, and other relevant information, organized in chronological fashion, and containing numerous notes. Farrand drew from the *Official Journal of the Convention* by William Jackson, from James Madison's extensive notes, and from notes and letters from other delegates.

In addition to this compilation of original sources, Farrand authored a book on the Convention titled *The Framing of the Constitution* (1913). In addition to other books and articles, he authored *The Fathers of the Constitution* (1921). Farrand served in 1940 as president of the American Historical Society and was the recipient of numerous honorary degrees. He died of cancer in Reef Point, Bar Harbor, Maine, in 1945.

See Also Jackson, William; Madison, James, Jr.; Records of the Constitutional Convention

FOR FURTHER READING

Farrand, Max. 1921. *The Fathers of the Constitution: A Chronicle of the Establishment of the Union.* New Haven, CT: Yale University Press.

———. 1913. *The Framing of the Constitution of the United States.* New Haven, CT: Yale University Press.

———, ed. 1911, 1937. *The Records of the Federal Convention.* 4 vols. New Haven, CT: Yale University Press.

Hutson, James H., ed. 1987. *Supplement to Max Farrand's* The Records of the Federal Convention of 1787. New Haven, CT: Yale University Press.

Kesavan, Vasan, and Michael Stokes Paulsen. 2003. "The Interpretive Force of the Constitution's Secret Drafting History." *Georgetown Law Journal* 91 (August): 1113–1214.

FATHER OF THE CONSTITUTION

When what has been described as an "admiring citizen" described James Madison in 1834 as "*the writer of the Constitution of the U.S.*" (quoted in Rutland 1984, 23), Madison responded modestly, "You give me a credit to which I have made no claim." Madison further noted that the Constitution "was not, like the fabled Goddess of Wisdom, the offspring of a single brain. It ought to be regarded as the work of many heads & many hands" (Rutland, 23).

Still, following the lead of Madison's admirer, many people have designated James Madison as the "Father" of the Constitution. Certainly, Madison has as great a claim to such paternity as any individual. He helped arrange the Mount Vernon Conference, was influential in using the Annapolis Convention as a springboard to the Philadelphia meeting, helped convince George Washington to attend the Convention, is believed to be the primary author of the Virginia Plan, was among the most vocal and articulate members of the Convention, helped author *The Federalist Papers,* led the action in the Virginia ratifying convention for approval of the document, pushed in the first Congress for the Bill of Rights to quiet discontent with the document, and went on to guide the nation as both secretary of state and fourth president. After his death, Madison bequeathed the most complete and accurate records of the Convention to the nation.

Still, as Madison pointed out to his admirer, the Constitution was not the work of a single mind but a collective achievement. Moreover, a number of Madison's key proposals, most notably his plan for a "negative" of state legislation and for representation in both houses of Congress on the basis of population did not make it into the final plan. It is therefore more accurate to refer to the "Founding Fathers" than to a single founding father. Although it too was a collective achievement, given his prominent role in the adoption of the Bill of Rights, Madison can probably better be called the "Father" of these additions to the Constitution than of the document itself.

See Also Delegates, Collective Assessments; Delegates, Individual Rankings; Founding; Madison, James, Jr.

FOR FURTHER READING

Meyers, Marvin, ed. 1973. *The Mind of the Founder: Sources of the Political Thought of James Madison.* Indianapolis, IN: Bobbs-Merrill.
Rutland, Robert A. 1984. "The Virginia Plan of 1787: James Madison's Outline of a Model Constitution." *this Constitution,* no. 4 (Fall): 23–30.

FEDERAL RATIO

See THREE-FIFTHS CLAUSE

FEDERALISM

The U.S. Constitutional Convention, and the Constitution it produced, are often associated with the idea of federalism. Federalism involves a division of power between a national government and various subgovernments, designated in the United States as states. The colonies arguably had a federal relationship with Great Britain, but one the dimensions of which were never fully understood or articulated. Generally, the British understood the Parliament to be sovereign in the New World, whereas the colonists believed that local legislatures should exercise the power in America that Parliament exercised in Britain (Greene 1986).

When the American colonies declared their independence from Great Britain, they wanted to keep their previous identity. Retaining state boundaries and adding a national authority to replace British rule enabled them to do so. A government divided into states with some independent authority enables greater adaptation to local needs than might otherwise be possible.

Political scientists often distinguish a federal government from a confederal government or a unitary government. The government under the Articles of Confederation (like that later created under the Confederate States of America) was a confederal government in which the national government requested money and troops from states who alone had the power to operate on individual citizens. By contrast, unitary governments, like, for example, those in Great Britain and France, use administrative subdivisions but do not have permanent entities like states with guaranteed boundaries.

Federal governments are generally associated with three characteristics. These are a division of power between a general government and various subgovernments, authority on the part of both governments to act directly on individual citizens, and a written constitution to help establish the respective powers of these governments and the boundaries between them (Vile 2001, 103–104).

Terminology was not always uniform (the term "Federalist" had already sometimes been used under the Articles of Confederation to designate individuals who favored strengthening the existing "federal" government), but there is general agreement that the designation of a "federal" or "foederal" government underwent a change in meaning at about the time of the Constitutional Convention and its immediate aftermath. The current idea of a federal government, largely invented by the Convention, did not previously exist. Thus, at the Constitutional Convention the term "federal" was used to designate a government that political scientists would today designate as a "confederal government," and the term "national" (or the negative term "consolidated") was sometimes used to designate a unitary government and at other times, a government with strengthened powers.

When on May 29, Edmund Randolph attempted to introduce a resolution to describe the proposal of the Virginia Plan, he thus resolved "that an union of the States, merely federal, will not accomplish the objects proposed by the articles of confederation" (Farrand 1937, I, 30). Using the terminology of the day, proponents of the new Constitution argued in *Federalist* No. 39 that the new government was neither "wholly *national* nor wholly *federal*" (Hamilton, Madison, and Jay 1961, 246). Many critics of the new Constitution believed that it was inadequately federal and that it therefore threatened the existence of the states.

Perhaps with such critics in mind, the advocates of the new Constitution dubbed themselves "Federalists" and their opponents "Antifederalists." Not only did this take some of the sting out of criticism of the new document, but it also enabled supporters of the new Constitution to indicate that they were advocating a positive solution while accusing their opponents of being less constructive. In an address to his state not long after the Convention, Maryland's Luther Martin, one of three delegates present on the last day of the Convention (September 17) who refused to sign, was among those who objected to such usage:

> Afterwards the word "*national*" was struck out by them [supporters of the Constitution], because they thought the *word* might tend to *alarm;* and although, *now,* they who *advocate* the system pretend to call themselves *federalists,* in convention the distinction was quite the reverse; those who *opposed* the system were *there* considered and styled the *federal party,* those who advocated it, the *antifederal.* (III, 195)

Convention Discussions

Prior to the Constitutional Convention, Virginia's James Madison wrote a letter on April 16, 1787, arguing that the relationship between the national government and the states needed to be reworked:

> Conceiving that an individual independence of the States is utterly irreconcileable with their aggregate sovereignty, and that a consolidation of the whole into one simple republic would be as inexpedient as it is unattainable, I have sought for middle ground, which may at once support a due

supremacy of the national authority, and not exclude the local authorities wherever they can be subordinately useful. (Quoted in Meyers 1973, 95)

The provisions of the Virginia Plan, in which Madison is believed to have played a key role, clearly anticipated increased national powers. The plan provided

> that the National Legislature ought to be impowered to enjoy the Legislative Rights vested in Congress by the Confederation & moreover to legislate in all cases to which the separate States are incompetent, or in which the harmony of the United States may be interrupted by the exercise of individual Legislation. (I, 21)

It further provided that Congress would have the power "to negative all laws passed by the several States, contravening in the opinion of the National Legislature the articles of Union" (I, 21).

Although containing the seeds of what would become the supremacy clause, the New Jersey Plan envisioned far less national power. The report of the Committee of Detail later substituted a list of enumerated congressional powers in place of the rather general provisions for congressional authority contained in the original Virginia Plan (a development modified in part by the presence of the "necessary and proper clause"), and the Convention also rejected the idea of a negative on state laws (although the institution of judicial review—the power of courts to invalidate unconstitutional legislation—arguably eventually played a somewhat similar role). The issue of federalism was one of the most prominent at the Convention and can better be traced through individual clauses cited below than generically. What is clear is that, by the Convention's end, the status of the powers of the new national government were far more ambiguous than had the Virginia Plan been adopted. Antifederalists could point to continuing questions as to the relation of the state and national governments, while Federalist supporters of the new document had ample justification, as noted above, for describing the new government as both "partly national" and "partly federal," rather than as wholly federal (confederal) or national (unitary).

Constitutional Provisions

A myriad of provisions in the Constitution address the relation of the state and national governments. In accord with provisions of the Great Compromise, Article I, Sections 2 and 3 specify that members of Congress are chosen from states, with states being represented according to population in the House of Representatives and equally in the Senate. Article I, Section 8, outlines the powers of Congress, with the "necessary and proper clause" indicating that Congress would have implied powers in addition to those specifically designated. Articles II and III further delineate the powers of the executive and judicial branches, with the number of presidential electors from each state being chosen on the basis of state representation within Congress.

Article I, Section 9 lists a number of restraints on congressional powers including many designed to protect the states. Thus, states were permitted to import slaves for an additional twenty years. Congress was prohibited from taxing exports or from preferring the ports of one state to those of another.

Article I, Section 10 further limited the rights of the states. It indicated that a number of the powers that the Convention entrusted to the national government were exclusive powers. Thus, states are prohibited from entering into treaties, coining money, laying imposts on imports and exports, or keeping troops or warships in peacetime.

Other powers, most notably the power of taxation, are understood to be concurrent powers, jointly exercised by state and national governments. State and national governments both exercised some power over the militia.

Many provisions related to federalism are found in Article IV. Sections 1 and 2 of this Article outline the obligations that states have to one another. These include giving "full faith and credit" to the acts of other states, recognizing the "privileges and immunities" of citizens of other states, extraditing criminals to other states, and returning fugitives.

Section 3 of Article IV outlines a process for the admission of new states, which the Convention wisely decided would be admitted on an equal basis with the original 13, and for congressional regulation of federal territory. Section 4 further outlines the duty of the national government to guarantee each state a "republican" form of government and to protect them against invasion or domestic violence.

The amending provision in Article V of the Constitution has a federal dimension in that two-thirds of the states may petition Congress to call a constitutional convention. Similarly, three-fourths of the states are required to ratify amendments—the Articles of Confederation had required unanimous state consent.

Article VI further describes the relationship between the state and national governments in the supremacy clause. It provides that the U.S. Constitution and laws and treaties made under it are the supreme law of the land. Section 3 of this Article further requires all state officials to uphold the Constitution. Article VII provides that the new Constitution would go into effect when ratified by conventions in nine or more of the states.

The Bill of Rights further addressed federalism issues with the Tenth Amendment indicating the existence of certain undesignated powers "reserved" to the states. The Eleventh Amendment subsequently recognized some immunity by states against prosecutions, whereas the Fourteenth Amendment and others have subsequently limited various state powers.

Ratification Debates

As the quotation from Luther Martin above should demonstrate, concerns about the nature of the new government were prominent in the Federalist/Antifederalist debates over the Constitution. Antifederalists charged that the new government was unduly consolidated, or national, in character. They feared that it concentrated governmental sovereignty in the national government. Federalists generally followed the argument outlined by Virginia's James Madison, who (as noted above) had advocated a more powerful national government than the one that actually emerged from the Convention, in *Federalist* No. 39 in arguing that the new government was "in strictness, neither a national nor a federal Constitution, but a composition of both" (Hamilton, Madison, and Jay, 246).

E Pluribus Unum

The Latin phrase "*e pluribus unum,*" meaning "from many, one," that appears on American coins is a fitting description of American federalism. In a unitary system, like that with which the colonists were familiar in England, previous governmental entities lose or suppress their individual identities, resulting in a governmental *unum,* or whole. In a confederal system, like that under the Articles of Confederation, individual governmental entities dominate, thus emphasizing *pluribus,* or many. By contrast, a federal system, like that established by the Constitution, was designed to direct the powers of states toward common goals while leaving the states themselves intact.

Pennsylvania's official state quarter (United States Mint)

FOR FURTHER READING

Wolin, Sheldon S. 1989. "*E Pluribus Unum:* The Representation of Difference and the Reconstruction of Collectivity." *The Presence of the Past: Essays on the State and the Constitution.* Baltimore, MD: Johns Hopkins University Press, 120–136.

Madison's argument came close to tracking Oliver Ellsworth's description of the new government at the Convention on June 29 when he indicated that "We were partly national; partly federal" and described this arrangement as a "middle ground" on which he hoped the delegates could agree (I, 468). In answering Antifederalist arguments that sovereignty could not be divided, Madison argued that it was possible for the sovereign people to divide sovereignty between the national government and the states.

Federalism Today

Delegates at the Convention argued passionately over the relationship between the national government and the states. There was general agreement that the states were too powerful in relation to the Congress under the Articles of Confederation, but there was far less consensus, and perhaps some wishful thinking, as to what the relationship between these two levels of government should be. Disputes over federalism erupted into the Civil War from 1861 to 1865. Although the result of this war appeared to invalidate the claim by the Southern states that they had a right to secede (or the earlier claim that they had the authority to "nullify" national laws with which they disagreed), other issues of state and national power remain long after.

See Also Amending Process; Antifederalists; Articles of Confederation; Bill of Rights; Confederal Government; Congress, Collective Powers; Congress, Limits on; Connecticut Compromise; Extradition; Federalists; Full Faith and Credit Clause; Guarantee Clause; Madison, James, Jr.; Negative on State Laws; New Jersey Plan; Privileges and Immunities Clause; Sovereignty; States, Admission and Creation; States, Limits on; States, Police Powers; Supremacy Clause; Unitary Government; Virginia Plan

FOR FURTHER READING

Beer, Samuel H. 1993. *To Make a Nation: The Rediscovery of American Federalism.* Cambridge, MA: Belknap Press of Harvard University Press.

Farrand, Max, ed. 1937. *The Records of the Federal Convention.* 4 vols. New Haven, CT: Yale University Press.

Greene, Jack P. 1987. "The Imperial Roots of American Federalism." *this Constitution: Our Enduring Legacy.* Washington, DC: Congressional Quarterly, 37–54.

———. 1986. *Peripheries and Center: Constitutional Development in the Extended Politics of the British Empire and the United States, 1607–1788.* Athens: University of Georgia Press.

Hamilton, Alexander, James Madison, and John Jay. 1961. *The Federalist Papers.* Ed. Clinton Rossiter. New York: New American Library.

McDonald, Forrest. 2000. *States' Rights and the Union: Imperium in Imperio, 1776–1876.* Lawrence: University Press of Kansas.

McLaughlin, Andrew C. 1918. "The Background of American Federalism." *American Political Science Review* 12 (May): 315–340.

Meyers, Marvin, ed. 1973. *The Mind of the Founder: Sources of the Political Thought of James Madison.* New York: Bobbs-Merrill.

Murrin, John M., David E. Narrett, Ronald L. Hatzenbuehler, and Michael Kammen. 1988. *Essays on Liberty and Federalism: The Shaping of the U.S. Constitution.* College Station: Texas A and M University Press.

Ranney, John C. 1946. "The Bases of American Federalism." *William and Mary Quarterly,* 3rd ser. 3 (January): 1–35.

Rossiter, Clinton, ed. 1961. *The Federalist Papers.* Alexander Hamilton, James Madison, and John Jay. New York: New American Library.

Vile, John R. 2001. *A Companion to the United States Constitution and Its Amendments.* 3rd ed. Westport, CT: Praeger.

Vile, M. J. C. 1961. *The Structure of American Federalism.* London: Oxford University Press.

FEDERALIST AND DEMOCRATIC-REPUBLICAN PARTIES

The term "Federalist" is applied to those individuals who favored ratification of the U.S. Constitution. In terminology that can sometimes be confusing, this name was also used to identify adherents of one of the first two political parties that developed during the Washington administration. When the new government went into effect, not all Federalist supporters of the Constitution became members of the Federalist Party, and individuals like James Madison and Alexander Hamilton, as well as many others, who had once worked cooperatively for adoption of the Constitution, split into different parties. These two parties, in turn, significantly influenced the early understandings of the work of the Constitutional Convention and the document it had produced (see Powell 1985). Significantly, both parties supported the new Constitution, arguing that their conception of this document was the most proper (Banning 1974; Powell 1985).

Consistent with contemporary beliefs that associated political parties with partial interests, President Washington did not officially identify himself as a member of the Federalist Party, but he generally supported the policies of the party's founder, his secretary of state, Alexander Hamilton, especially in regard to the establishment of a national bank and the national assumption of state debt. Although he had many differences with Hamilton, John Adams, the second president of the United States, did identify himself as a Federalist, and the party continued to run candidates through the second decade of the nineteenth century.

The Federalist Party was largely formed around the idea of supporting a strong national government such as would be competent to exercise its powers under the necessary and proper clause to establish a national bank. By contrast, the Democratic-Republican Party, largely founded by Thomas Jefferson (the first secretary of state) and James Madison (an early congressional leader), was generally more supportive of states' rights. One of the clearest articulations of this view, which was sometimes difficult to distinguish from the view that the United States remained a confederation, was found in the Virginia and Kentucky Resolutions, which Madison and Jefferson secretly authored in opposition to the Alien and Sedition Acts (making citizenship more difficult and punishing critics of the government) of 1798.

As a general rule, Federalists supported strong exercises of executive power and looked to the judiciary to advance national interests and to strike down acts of unconstitutional legislation at both state and national levels. By contrast, although there was often a gap between their stated beliefs and their actions when in power, Democratic-

Republicans tended to emphasize the primacy of Congress in national decisionmaking and to denigrate acts of the judiciary as being undemocratic.

Federalists were strongest in the New England states and tended to represent the commercial interests in this region. Democratic-Republicans were typically stronger in the South and West, and put more emphasis on agrarian concerns.

Federalists and Democratic-Republicans often differed on matters of foreign policy. The former were generally more supportive of Britain and sympathetic to its form of government, while the latter were more sympathetic to the French, who had been allied with the U.S. during the Revolutionary War and who reiterated some American principles in waging their own revolution against their king.

One of the Federalist Party's greatest contributions to constitutional interpretation came with John Adams's appointment in 1801 of John Marshall as chief justice of the United States. Although he had not attended the Constitutional Convention of 1787, Marshall had served at the Virginia ratifying convention and had been a strong supporter of George Washington. In his 35 years as chief justice, Marshall established the doctrine of judicial review (the power to invalidate unconstitutional legislation), upheld the supremacy of federal laws over conflicting state legislation, enforced the contract clause as a limit on state action, and affirmed Hamilton's earlier broad reading of congressional powers under the necessary and proper clause.

The Federalist Party largely died out when it became associated with opposition to the War of 1812 and even (in contrast to its earlier nationalism) with the possibility of disunion. The Whig Party succeeded it in the 1820s and was, in the 1850s, replaced by today's Republican Party. The Democratic-Republican Party underwent considerable changes of its own when Andrew Jackson initiated a movement for popular democracy. It is the forebear of today's Democratic Party.

Although the Constitution does not specifically address the issue of political parties, the Framers often expressed concern over factional interests. The Twelfth Amendment adjusted the Electoral College to deal with an unanticipated problem—a tie between candidates for president and vice president—brought about by the development of such parties.

See Also Hamilton, Alexander; Jefferson, Thomas; Madison, James, Jr.; Marshall, John; Parties, Factions, and Interests

FOR FURTHER READING

Banning, Lance. 1974. "Republican Ideology and the Triumph of the Constitution, 1789 to 1793." *William and Mary Quarterly*, 3rd ser. 31 (April): 167–188.

Hofstadter, Richard. 1972. *The Idea of a Party System: The Rise of Legitimate Opposition in the United States, 1780–1840*. Berkeley: University of California Press.

Powell, H. Jefferson. 1985. "The Original Understanding of Original Intent." *Harvard Law Review* 98 (March): 885–948.

White, Leonard D. 1948. *The Federalists: A Study in Administrative History, 1789–1801*. New York: The Free Press.

FEDERALIST, THE

The Federalist, sometimes also called *The Federalist Papers*, was one of the most important products of the debate between Federalist supporters and Antifederalist opponents of the Constitution that the Constitutional Convention had formulated for popular consideration. Initially published as a series of 85 articles in New York newspapers from October 17, 1787, to August 16, 1788 (Rossiter 1961, viii), a volume containing the first 36 essays was first published in March 1788. The second volume, containing essays 37 through 85, was published on May 28 of that year.

Authorship

The Federalist was the brainchild of Alexander Hamilton, one of New York's delegates to the Constitutional Convention who recognized that the fight for constitutional ratification in New York would be an uphill contest. *The Federalist* was the collective work of Hamilton; James Madison,

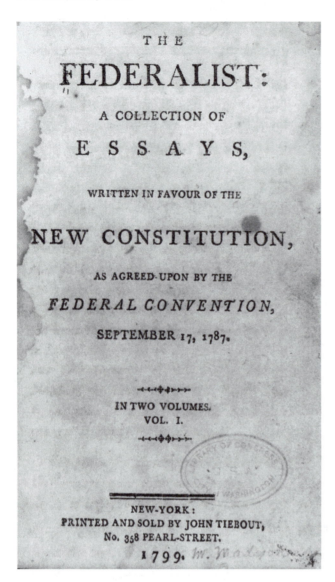

THE

FEDERALIST:

A COLLECTION OF

E S S A Y S,

WRITTEN IN FAVOUR OF THE

NEW CONSTITUTION,

AS AGREED UPON BY THE

FEDERAL CONVENTION,

SEPTEMBER 17, 1787.

IN TWO VOLUMES.
VOL. I.

NEW-YORK:
PRINTED AND SOLD BY JOHN TIEBOUT,
No. 358 PEARL-STREET.
1799.

Title page of The Federalist, *1799 printing*
(Library of Congress)

a delegate to the Constitutional Convention from Virginia who was in New York as part of his congressional duties; and John Jay, another New Yorker who was an American diplomat and future first chief justice of the U.S. Supreme Court and whose essays dealt mostly with foreign affairs. Hamilton had attempted to recruit Gouverneur Morris, who had represented Pennsylvania at the Convention, to help with *The Federalist,* but, despite his flair for writing, Morris had declined. Hamilton had in turn refused the services of William Duer (Brookhiser 2003, 93), a New York banker, three of whose essays, signed "Philo-Publius," were published in an appendix to an

1810 edition of *The Federalist* edited by J. C. Hamilton (Carey and McClellan 2001, xliv, note 4).

Although Hamilton and Madison disputed authorship of some of the essays, it now appears that Hamilton wrote 51 essays, Madison 26, and Jay 5, with Hamilton and Madison coauthoring 3 (Rossiter, xi). The authors wrote under the nom de plume of Publius, a prominent Roman statesman.

Outline of The Federalist

Written to defend both the initiative that the delegates had taken in proposing a new Constitution and the government this document proposed to create, Hamilton used the initial essay to pose the question "whether societies of men are really capable or not of establishing good government from reflection and choice, or whether they are forever destined to depend for their political constitutions on accident and force" (33). Hamilton further outlined the central themes that subsequent essays would outline, roughly in the order that the volumes would present them:

> The utility of the UNION to your political prosperity–The insufficiency of the present Confederation to preserve that Union–The necessity of a government at least equally energetic with the one proposed, to the attainment of this object–The conformity of the proposed Constitution to the true principles of republican government–Its analogy to your own State constitution–and lastly, The additional security which its adoption will afford to the preservation of that species of government, to liberty, and to property. (36)

David Epstein has identified essays 2 through 14 as demonstrating the utility of the Union, essays 15 through 22 as showing the insufficiency of the Articles, and essays 23 through 36 with the necessity of a government as energetic as the one proposed (1984, 7). The essays in the second volume, which treat each of the respective branches of the new government, largely correspond to the attempt to show the conformity of the new government with republican principles, while essay 85 serves as a concluding essay (9).

Publius

The use of pen names was common in political writings that were published at the time the Constitution was being debated. Such names conveyed authors' broad intentions without identifying them by name and thus drawing attention to their personalities rather than to arguments (see Bernstein with Rice 1987, 218). Writers often chose names from classical history. At the time that Alexander Hamilton was considering publication of *The Federalist*, essays critical of the Constitution, probably written by Robert Yates, were being published in New York under the pen name of Brutus. This name was derived from that of Lucius Brutus, who had overthrown Tarquin, the last Roman king, and was the forebear of Marcus Junius Brutus, the ringleader in the assassination of the future dictator Julius Caesar.

In entering the fray with *The Federalist*, Alexander Hamilton drew from his knowledge of Plutarch to come up with the name Publius. Publius Valerius was the statesman who established a worthy republican government after Lucius Brutus overthrew Tarquin. The Romans had called Publius "Publicola," or "people-lover," as a way of symbolizing his commitment to republican government. Hamilton wanted to convey this same commitment to republicanism in his and his collaborators' essays (Bernstein with Rice 231).

FOR FURTHER READING

Bernstein, Richard B., with Kym S. Rice. 1987. *Are We to Be a Nation? The Making of the Constitution.* Cambridge, MA: Harvard University Press.

Hamilton, Alexander, James Madison, and John Jay. 1961. *The Federalist Papers.* Ed. Clinton Rossiter. New York: New American Library.

The Federalist *as a Work of Theory*

Although written with the specific objective of defending the new Constitution, *The Federalist* has frequently been cited as an example of a work of advocacy that transcended its immediate purpose to outline a more general theory of government and its problems and even of human nature. The work has also been one of the most quoted sources of information for ascertaining the intentions of the Founding Fathers in regard to specific provisions of that document—Madison's *Notes* of the Convention, which might have had a greater claim, were not published until after his death, whereas *The Federalist* was available to contemporaries.

Federalist *No. 10: The Role of Republican Government in Combating Factions*

Federalist No. 10 remains one of the most important and most quoted essays (but see Kramer 1999 for doubts about its contemporary influence). In this essay, James Madison portrayed the republican government that he thought the new Constitution had created as a cure for self-interest, or faction. Madison believed the causes of faction lay deep within human nature:

> A zeal for different opinions concerning religion, concerning government, and many other points, as well of speculation as of practice; an attachment to different leaders ambitiously contending for pre-eminence and power; or to persons of other descriptions whose fortunes have been interesting to the human passions, have, in turn, divided mankind into parties, inflamed them with mutual animosity, and rendered them much more disposed to vex and oppress each other than to co-operate for their common good. (79)

Madison further connected faction—indeed, he believed it to be its most common source—to "the various and unequal distribution of property" (79).

Arguing that it is impossible to remove the causes of faction without destroying liberty,

Madison instead advocated attempting to control its effects. He argued that the new government would do so both by substituting the considered judgment of the people's representatives for the people themselves and by embracing a larger land area than that of earlier democracies. Madison theorized that, unlike a pure democracy, this republic would encompass so many factions that no single faction would be likely to dominate. In so arguing, Madison addressed one of the most prominent concerns of the Antifederalists who, following the philosophy of the Baron de Montesquieu on this point, had argued that republican government would not be possible over a large land area. Madison's essay provided much of the theoretical rationale for America's subsequent westward expansion, most notably in the Louisiana Purchase. Somewhat more negatively, some scholars of the Progressive Era later seized on *Federalist* No. 10, with its concern for property rights, as an indication of what they believed to be the prominence of economic motives and class biases of the Framers.

Federalist *Nos. 37, 39, and 40*

In *Federalist* No. 37, without revealing that he had attended the Constitutional Convention, Madison explored the difficulties that the delegates faced in constituting a new government. He portrayed the delegates' task as that of "combining the requisite stability and energy in government with the inviolable attention due to liberty and to the republican form" (226). Madison pointed to the difficulties of dividing power among the three branches of government and of satisfying both the small and large states. He opined:

The real wonder is that so many difficulties should have been surmounted, and surmounted with a unanimity almost as unprecedented as it must have been unexpected. It is impossible for any man of candor to reflect on this circumstance without partaking of the astonishment. It is impossible for any man of pious reflection not to perceive in it a finger of that Almighty hand which has been so frequently and signally ex-

tended to our relief in the critical stages of the revolution. (230–231)

Although Madison and Hamilton had both argued for a stronger national government than that which the Constitutional Convention created, *Federalist* No. 39 is notable for presenting the new government as being partly national and partly federal in nature. *Federalist* No. 40, in turn, argued that it was important to keep a door open to future constitutional change without providing for such frequent changes that they would undermine public confidence in, and respect for, existing laws.

Federalist *No. 51: Separation of Powers and Human Nature*

Federalist 51 presented an elaborate defense of the doctrine of separation of powers based on a realistic, or even a pessimistic, view of human nature. In explaining the division of the new government into three separate branches, Madison argued:

Ambition must be made to counteract ambition. The interest of the man must be connected with the constitutional rights of the place. It may be a reflection of human nature that such devices should be necessary to control the abuses of government. But what is government itself but the greatest of all reflections on human nature? If men were angels, no government would be necessary. If angels were to govern men, neither external nor internal controls on government would be necessary. In framing a government which is to be administered by men over men, the great difficulty lies in this: you must first enable the government to control the governed; and in the next place oblige it to control itself. (322)

Defense of Each of the Three Branches

Publius addressed the structure of each of the three branches of the new government. In a government that would exercise significantly greater powers than that under the Articles of Confederation, Publius portrayed the Senate as a necessary mechanism for calming the impetuousness of the House of Representatives, which would be closest to the people.

Hamilton wrote most of the essays dealing with the executive and judicial branches. Essays 67 through 77 cover the executive branch. They stress the need for executive energy (furthered by its unitary character) and defend the qualified veto and the four-year presidential term. Essays 78 through 83 defend the judicial branch. *Federalist No. 78* is notable for defending the judicial power, now called judicial review, to invalidate legislation it considers to be unconstitutional. In contrast to the Congress, which will exercise the power of the purse, and the president, who will exercise the power of the sword, Hamilton argued that the judges would not be exercising their own "will," but would be merely enforcing the Constitution to which the people have agreed. Hamilton argued that expertise that could only come through appointment would best meet this need, as would service "during good behavior."

Defense of the Omission of a Bill of Rights

In his penultimate essay, Hamilton attempted, with seemingly less success, to defend the Constitution's omission of a bill of rights. He observed that "The truth is, after all the declamations we have heard, that the Constitution is itself, in every rational sense, and to every useful purpose, A BILL OF RIGHTS" (516). This argument was undercut, however, by the fact that the proposed Constitution already contained a number of provisions similar to those that a bill of rights would add. In the final essay, Hamilton, who was quite concerned about heading off yet a second convention that might undo the work of the first, further suggested that the new amending process would be adequate to adopt any needed changes, *after* the Constitution had been ratified.

One Publius or Two?

Although New York did vote to ratify the Constitution, the specific effect of *The Federalist* on this process is still disputed. Less disputed is the role of *The Federalist* as a political classic that provided both enduring theoretical and practical defenses of the new Constitution.

It is fascinating that Hamilton and Madison, the two primary authors of *The Federalist*, soon divided into rival political parties. Hamilton, the first secretary of the Treasury, formed the Federalist Party, which favored a strong national government (Jay also became a prominent member of the Federalist Party). Madison, a key player in the first Congress, joined Thomas Jefferson in the Democratic-Republican Party, which placed greater emphasis on states' rights and opposed many Hamiltonian initiatives, including the creation of the national bank. Although this has fueled scholarly attempts to divide Publius (and especially Hamilton and Madison) into rival persona, it seems more indicative of the unique opportunity for nation-building that the Constitutional Convention of 1787 presented.

See Also Antifederalists; Federalists; Hamilton, Alexander; Jay, John; Madison, James, Jr.; New York; Parties, Factions, and Interests; Ratification in the States; Separation of Powers

FOR FURTHER READING

Brookhiser, Richard. 2003. *Gentleman Revolutionary: Gouverneur Morris, the Rake Who Wrote the Constitution.* New York: The Free Press.

Carey, George W. 1989. *The Federalist: Design for a Constitutional Republic.* Urbana: University of Illinois Press.

Carey, George W., and James McClellan. 2001. "Editors' Introduction." *The Federalist.* Alexander Hamilton, James Madison, and John Jay. Indianapolis, IN: Liberty Fund.

Diamond, Martin. 1981. "The Federalist, 1787–1788." In Leo Strauss and Joseph Cropsey, eds., *The History of Political Philosophy.* Chicago: University of Chicago Press, 37–57.

Epstein, David F. 1984. *The Political Theory of* The Federalist. Chicago: University of Chicago Press.

Hamilton, Alexander, James Madison, and John Jay. 1961. *The Federalist Papers.* Ed. Clinton Rossiter. New York: New American Library.

Kramer, Larry D. 1999. "Madison's Audience." *Harvard Law Review* 112 (January): 611–679.

Rossiter, Clinton. 1961 "Introduction." *The Federalist Papers*. Alexander Hamilton, James Madison, and John Jay. New York: New American Library.

FEDERALISTS

The term "Federalist" can be confusing because it was used to denote both those individuals who emerged from the Constitutional Convention defending the new Constitution and somewhat later, for members of the political party formed by Alexander Hamilton during conflicts over the constitutionality of the national bank in George Washington's first administration (see Federalist and Democratic-Republican Parties). The Federalist supporters of the new Constitution emphasized that they were advocating a positive solution to perceived weaknesses of the government under the Articles of Confederation in both domestic and foreign affairs, and they appear to have been partly responsible for designating their opponents Antifederalists.

Federalists came out of the Convention with their fists swinging, hoping to capitalize both on their superior knowledge of the new document (the proceedings in Philadelphia had been kept secret) and on the illustriousness of the delegates, especially George Washington and Benjamin Franklin. The delegates to the Convention had been fairly united with 39 of the 42 delegates who remained at the end of the Convention willing to sign the new document (Delaware's John Dickinson signing in absentia). Many of the Federalist arguments for the new Constitution were, however, shaped by emerging Antifederalist critiques of the document, some of which individuals like Luther Martin of Maryland, Elbridge Gerry of Massachusetts, and George Mason of Virginia had already raised within the Convention itself and others of which would be printed in newspapers and argued in state ratifying conventions, where opposition to the new Constitution was sometimes stiff.

Defense of Proposing a New Constitution

One objection that Federalist supporters of the Constitution faced was that the delegates to the Constitutional Convention had exceeded their mandates when they decided to construct a new form of government rather than simply revising the existing one and increasing the powers of the Congress under the Articles of Confederation. Federalists generally conceded the charge, arguing that perilous times called for extraordinary actions. They also pointed out that the delegates to the Convention had no authority to adopt anything and that they were simply *proposing* a new government for the people's consideration.

Defense of Republican Government over a Large Land Area

One of the key arguments that Antifederalists made against the new Constitution was the argument, borrowed from the French philosopher the Baron de Montesquieu, that republican government, such as the one the Federalists were proposing, would be impossible over a land area the size of the existing 13 states, and with the potential for still further expansion. Virginia's James Madison argued in response, most notably in *Federalist* No. 10, that a large land area actually had the potential to be more republican. Madison associated republican government with popular representation. He argued that representatives would moderate popular passions in a way that they would not be moderated in a direct, or pure, democracy, and that a larger nation, which representation made possible, would encompass more factions, therefore making it less likely that any one such faction would dominate.

Whereas Antifederalists feared that the new government was too national, or too consolidated, the Federalists responded that the new government was partly national and partly federal and that the states and national authorities would tend to preserve liberty by keeping one another in check. Federalists indicated that state governments would remain strong as long as they had the affection and confidence of their citizens. The division of authority between the national authority and the states appeared to be a further way of accommodating republican government to a large nation.

Separation of Powers

Similarly, the Federalists defended a more complex government of three branches (the legislative branch was the only real branch under the Articles of Confederation) as providing for checks and balances that would help preserve liberty. Although the new government would grant the increased powers that it was necessary for Congress to possess, it would guard against these powers not only by counterposing strong executive and judicial branches but also by dividing the new Congress into two branches. The Founders had designed the smaller size of the Senate and the longer terms of senators to enable them to resist temporary currents of public opinion and provide greater wisdom and stability than would otherwise be possible.

Federalists had to defend the presidency against concerns that it leaned toward a monarchy like that which the colonists had rejected in Great Britain. Federalists pointed to the popular basis on which the presidency rested via the Electoral College (which had the advantage of making the president largely independent of Congress) while portraying the unity, energy, and terms of office of the presidency as essential to accountability and strength, especially in the area of foreign affairs. Instead of rejecting Antifederalist charges that the judiciary would void acts of legislation that it considered to be unconstitutional—a power known today as judicial review—Federalists generally acknowledged that the courts would exercise this power. Rather than portraying this power as one that would enable unelected judges

to establish an aristocracy to dominate the citizenry, Federalists portrayed such a power as essential to preserving the paramount nature of a written constitution.

Defense against the Lack of a Bill of Rights

The single most important criticism that Federalists had to meet was the charge that the proposed Constitution was inadequate because it failed to contain a bill of rights. Initially, Federalists generally argued that the entire Constitution served, through its structure, as a kind of bill of rights. They also argued that the new government would be one of enumerated, or listed, powers, that the Constitution already contained some prohibitions on government, and that a listing of rights could prove dangerous if it were taken to mean that all rights not reserved were granted to the new government. These arguments, however, proved inadequate. Federalists themselves had often argued for generous constructions of governmental powers. The fact that the Constitution contained some guarantees already indicated that such guarantees were hardly likely to prove dangerous and might even do some good. In time, key Federalists agreed to support a bill of rights *after* the Constitution was adopted, and James Madison, a key Federalist, subsequently led the fight for the first 10 amendments in the first Congress. In constructing these guarantees, Madison took care to focus on guarantees for individual rights rather than, as some Antifederalists appear to have preferred, on restructuring the new government or increasing the power of the states.

Federalist Success in Getting the Constitution Adopted

The Convention had specified that the new Constitution would go into effect when conventions in nine or more states ratified it. Federalists thus had to defend the new Constitution in each of the states. Although there were some initial successes, debates were particularly heated in some of the larger states like Massachusetts, Virginia, and New York. Federalists eventually prevailed, and the requisite number of states ratified the new Constitution. Scholars generally agree that the Federalists prevailed in part by the strength of their arguments, in part because the people generally perceived that *something* needed to be done and Federalists offered a solution, and in part because of their superior organization, furthered by the shared experiences many of the Federalists had had by their association at the Constitutional Convention. Federalists were generally stronger in more urban and cosmopolitan areas, especially those that were tied into the national economy, and an initial economic upswing further cemented support for the new Constitution.

Of the many writings in support of the Federalist position, the most important was *The Federalist*, a two-volume work defending the new Constitution, which was originally published in New York as 85 newspaper essays. Alexander Hamilton, James Madison, and John Jay authored this work under the pen name of Publius. Scholars and judges still frequently consult these essays as a guide to Federalist thought and constitutional intentions. Although united in support of the new Constitution, Federalists eventually split into rival parties, with one party claiming the Federalist moniker and the other, calling itself the Democratic-Republican Party, often picking up support not only from Federalist advocates of adoption of the new Constitution but also from individuals who had once identified themselves as Antifederalists.

See Also Antifederalists; *Federalist, The;* Federalist and Democratic-Republican Parties; Ratification in the States

FOR FURTHER READING

Bailyn, Bernard. 1993. *The Debate on the Constitution: Federalist and Antifederalist Speeches, Articles, and Letters During the Struggle over Ratification.* 2 vols. New York: Library of America.

Hamilton, Alexander and James Madison and John Jay. 1961. *The Federalist Papers.* New York: New American Library.

Sheenhan, Colleen A., and Gary L. McDowell. 1998. *Friends of the Constitution: Writings of the "Other" Federalists 1787–1788.* Indianapolis, IN: Liberty Fund.

St. John, Jeffrey. 1990. *A Child of Fortune: A Correspondent's Report on the Ratification of the U.S. Constitution and the Battle for a Bill of Rights.* Ottawa, IL: Jameson Books.

Wooten, David, ed. 2003. *The Essential Federalist and Anti-Federalist Papers.* Indianapolis, IN: Hackett Publishing.

FEW, WILLIAM (1748–1828)

William Few was born near Baltimore, Maryland, in 1748 to a farm family and subsequently moved with his family first to North Carolina and later to Georgia. Given a small tract of land in Georgia by his father, Few, who had little formal education, punctuated his farm tasks with reading. After serving at the state's constitutional convention of 1777, Few entered the North Carolina militia where he became a lieutenant colonel before being elected to the state legislature.

Admitted to the bar without ever receiving formal training in law, Few was serving at the time of the Constitutional Convention, to which he had been appointed, as a member of Congress. He appears to have attended the Convention the first few weeks but to have spent most of his time during the summer of 1787 on his congressional duties. As a consequence of this and of what appears to have been a timidity in the presence of men more educated than he (a French observer noted that "Il est tres timide et embarassant dans la societe, a moins qu'on ne lui parle d-affaires" III, 238), he is not recorded as having spoken a single time at the Convention. He was present for the opening day of business on May 25, and he did sign the document.

In a short autobiography that he wrote in 1816, Few discussed the "incalculable difficulties" of the Convention, especially the problems in addressing states' rights. Few confirmed that the Conven-

William Few, delegate from Georgia
(Pixel That)

scorching climate of Georgia, under all the accumulating evils of fevers and Negro slavery, those enemies to humane felicity" (quoted in Whitney 1974, 90). He subsequently moved to New York, where the people elected him to the state legislature. He served in a number of governmental posts, including inspector of state prisons, and was director of New York City's Manhattan Bank and later of the City Bank in New York City. He was a strong proponent of manufacturing and was president of the National Institution for the Promotion of Industry. He died in New York in 1828.

See Also Georgia

FOR FURTHER READING

Bradford, M. M. 1994. *Founding Fathers: Brief Lives of the Framers of the United States Constitution.* Lawrence: University Press of Kansas.

Farrand, Max, ed. 1937. *The Records of the Federal Convention.* 4 vols. New Haven, CT: Yale University Press.

Whitney, David C. 1974. *Founders of Freedom in America: Lives of the Men Who Signed the Constitution of the United States and So Helped to Establish the United States of America.* Chicago: J. J. Ferguson Publishing.

tion did not adopt Benjamin Franklin's proposal to bring in a chaplain each day to begin the meeting in prayer. Few observed that the Convention had progressed on the "principle of accommodations" and that "It was believed to be of the utmost importance to concede to different opinions so far as to endeavor to meet opposition on middle ground, and to form a Constitution that might preserve the union of the States" (Farrand 1937, III, 423). Few further observed that "after about three months' arduous labor, a plan of Constitution was formed on principles which did not altogether please anybody, but it was agreed to be the most expedient that could be devised and agreed to" (III, 423).

After the Convention, Few served as one of Georgia's first two senators and as a Georgia judge. Defeated in a reelection bid for the Senate, he later viewed the outcome favorably: "if I had obtained that appointment I should have most probably spent the remainder of my days in the

FITZSIMONS, THOMAS
(1741–1811)

Born in Ireland in 1741, Fitzsimons immigrated to Philadelphia in 1760. He started as a clerk, married well, and became a merchant. He is believed to have been the first Roman Catholic elected to public office in Pennsylvania, and he was, with Maryland's Daniel Carroll, one of two Catholics to sign the Constitution. In addition to serving as a member of Pennsylvania's provincial Congress, he served as a militia captain during the Revolutionary War, was one of the directors of the Bank of America, represented Pennsylvania at the Continental Congress, served on the state's Council of Censors, and attended the Annapolis Conven-

Thomas Fitzsimons, delegate from Pennsylvania
(Pixel That)

tion as one of its representatives. Fitzsimons did not speak frequently at the Convention, and most of what he said related fairly directly to his knowledge of mercantile affairs.

A Man of Few Words

Fitzsimons was present on May 25. He is believed to have attended almost every session of the Convention. However, his first recorded action took place on August 7 when he seconded a motion by Gouverneur Morris for a provision limiting the suffrage to freeholders (Farrand 1937, II, 201). Individuals like Morris, who hoped to give a more "high-toned" or "aristocratic" character to the new government, generally favored this provision.

Appropriately enough for a merchant, Fitzsimons offered his second recorded statement in reaction to observations by Virginia's James Madison that it would be inconvenient to adopt a provision prohibiting vessels entering one state to pay duties in another. Fitzsimons agreed that this could be "inconvenient," but "thought it would

be a greater inconvenience to require vessels bound to Philada. to enter below the jurisdiction of the State" (II, 48). Significantly, the only committee on which Fitzsimons served at the Convention was the committee appointed on August 25 to deal with commercial discrimination.

On September 6, Maryland's James McHenry reported in his notes that Fitzsimons had indicated in personal conversation that he favored adding a provision allowing Congress "to erect piers for protection of shipping in winter and to preserve the navigation of harbours" (II, 529). On September 7, Fitzsimons further seconded a motion by fellow Pennsylvania delegate James Wilson requiring consent by both houses of Congress (and not simply the Senate) to treaties negotiated by the president. The Convention defeated the motion by a vote of 10 to 1.

On September 10, Fitzsimons explained to fellow delegates that the proposal for ratification of the Constitution had omitted the words "for their approbation" so as "to save Congress from the necessity of an Act inconsistent with the Articles of Confederation under which they held their authority" (II, 560). About the same time, when the Convention was discussing the legitimacy of incidental state duties, Fitzsimons observed that such duties, like those on flour and tobacco, "never have been & never can be considered as duties on exports" (II, 589). Finally, on September 14, when the delegates were discussing whether congressional expenditures could be published at stated times each year, Fitzsimons observed that "It is absolutely impossible to publish expenditures in the full extent of the term" (II, 619).

Life after the Convention

After the Convention, Fitzsimons served as one of Pennsylvania's first delegates to the U.S. House of Representatives, where he served until 1795. He sat on committees dealing with finance and supported the financial policies of Alexander Hamilton, who had represented New York at the Constitutional Convention. Fitzsimons founded the Insurance Company of North America and was president of the Philadelphia Chamber of Commerce. Generous to his friends, including Robert Morris, another delegate to the Convention from Pennsylvania, Fitzsimons was brought to financial ruin by their inability to repay loans he had made to them and by his own speculation in western lands. He died in Philadelphia in 1811.

See Also Pennsylvania

FOR FURTHER READING

Bradford, M. M. 1994. *Founding Fathers: Brief Lives of the Framers of the United States Constitution.* Lawrence: University Press of Kansas.

Farrand, Max, ed. 1937. *The Records of the Federal Convention.* 4 vols. New Haven, CT: Yale University Press.

FOREIGN AFFAIRS AND THE CONVENTION

Scholars who study the formation of the Constitutional Convention typically stress the financial distress and domestic instability within the states (especially Shays's Rebellion in Massachusetts) that led to that meeting, but it is important to remember that delegates were also concerned about international security. The U.S. had found that it was unable to uphold its requirements under the Treaty of Paris that had ended the Revolutionary War, and the British had in turn refused to withdraw their forces from forts in the American West. Relations with Britain, which controlled Canada to the north, were therefore still strained, and the English had cut American commerce with the West Indies. Spain, which was cutting off American commerce on the Mississippi River, owned title to land to America's south and west (the latter later being transferred to the French). Indians posed threats to most of the Southern states, especially Georgia, and throughout the inland frontier.

States themselves were regulating commerce and imposing imposts on one another as though the individual colonies were foreign powers, and

some delegates feared that sections of the continent might group together in defense pacts or even join foreign governments to such an end. The nation had almost no army or navy, and the Articles of Confederation required that states raise troops and revenue at the request of the Congress. Fortunately, the nation was not, as in 1776, facing imminent war, and delegates therefore had more time to devote themselves to long-running problems.

Critiques of the Articles of Confederation Related to Foreign Affairs

In listing "the Vices of the Political System of the United States" in April 1787, Virginia's James Madison included "violations of the law of nations and of treaties," specifically noting violations of treaties with Great Britain, France, and Holland (1973, 83). In presenting the Virginia Plan to the Constitutional Convention, Governor Edmund Randolph listed five defects of the existing Articles of Confederation. First on his list was the accusation "that the confederation permitted no security again[st] foreign invasion; congress not being permitted to prevent a war nor to support it by th[eir] own authority" (Farrand 1937, I, 19). Elaborating, he observed that the Articles "could not cause infractions of treaties or of the law of nations, to be punished; that particular states might by their conduct provoke war without controul; and that neither militia nor draughts being fit for defence on such occasions, enlistments only could be successful, and these could not be executed without money" (II, 19). After pointing to the difficulty of the government under the Articles in checking quarrels among the states, Randolph went on to observe that "there were many advantages, which the U. S. might acquire, which were not attainable under the confederation—such as a productive impost—counteraction of the commercial regulations of other nations—pushing of commerce ad libitum—&c &c." (II, 19).

In defending the Virginia Plan over the rival New Jersey Plan on June 19, Madison cited a number of ways in which he thought the former was superior. He observed that, despite a grant of power giving Congress power over the Indians, "in several instances, the States have entered into compacts, without previous application or subsequent apology" (I, 316). He further expressed the fear that a stronger union was needed in order to "secure the Union agst. the influence of foreign powers over its members" (I, 319), a concern that Gouverneur Morris of Pennsylvania and others expressed later in the Convention (I, 530). Madison further predicted that if the union of states were dissolved, this would result either in individual state sovereignty or in the formation of "two or more Confederacies . . . among them" (I, 320).

Important Convention Decisions Related to Foreign Affairs

The Convention made a number of decisions impinging on foreign affairs. It vested Congress with power to declare war and created an executive whom it designated as commander-in-chief of the armed forces. The Constitution permitted Congress to act directly on individual citizens in raising revenue and in mustering troops rather than remaining dependent upon the states. Congress was granted power to regulate interstate and foreign commerce, and the president had power to negotiate treaties subject to confirmation of two-thirds majorities in the Senate. Despite some republican concerns about the issue, delegates ultimately resisted the temptation to prohibit a standing army. Delegates provided citizenship and residency requirements for members of the legislative and executive branch in attempts to lessen foreign influences, and they specified that presidents not in the United States at the time would have to be "native-born."

On the last day of the Constitutional Convention, Benjamin Franklin of Pennsylvania pleaded for delegates to set aside their reservations and sign the document. He observed:

> I think it will astonish our enemies, who are waiting with confidence to hear that our councils are confounded like those of the Builders of Babel;

and that our States are on the point of separation, only to meet hereafter for the purpose of cutting one another's throats. (II, 642–643)

The Role of Foreign Affairs in Ratification Debates

Frederick Marks has observed that Federalist proponents of the new Constitution often cited the anticipated role of the new Constitution in protecting the nation. Antifederalists generally conceded that this was so but tended to worry more about the possible implications of a stronger national government for the protection of domestic freedoms (Marks 1971). Marks observed that the new Constitution received especially strong support from men who had dealt with foreign affairs under the Articles of Confederation, among individuals who had studied abroad, among men of foreign birth, and among men with experience on the national level, including involvement with the military (Marks, 466–468), all of whom were presumably more cosmopolitan in outlook than those without similar experiences.

Further Observations

David Hendrickson has likened the federal convention to "an international conference, conducted in secrecy among diplomatic plenipotentiaries of the states" (2003, 259). He further observes that "the Constitution also incorporated, while domesticating, the hoary doctrine of the balance of power, and indeed projected it into the interior of federal government" (259).

Foreign affairs remained an important issue during the early years of the new republic when the Federalist Party found itself more frequently allying with Great Britain and the Democratic-Republican Party more frequently expressing its sympathy for France.

See Also Articles of Confederation; Canada; France; Great Britain; Indians; Jay-Gardoqui Negotiations; Shays's Rebellion; Spain; Treaty-Making and Ratification

FOR FURTHER READING

Farrand, Max, ed. 1937. *The Records of the Federal Convention.* 4 vols. New Haven, CT: Yale University Press.

Hendrickson, David C. 2003. *Peace Pact: The Lost World of the American Founding.* Lawrence: University Press of Kansas.

Madison, James. 1973. "Vices of the Political System of the United States, April 1787." *The Mind of the Founder: Sources of the Political Thought of James Madison.* Ed. Marvin Meyers. Indianapolis, IN: Bobbs-Merrill.

Marks, Frederick W., III. 1971. "Foreign Affairs: A Winning Issue in the Campaign for Ratification of the United States Constitution." *Political Science Quarterly* 86 (September): 444–469.

Moore, John Allphin, Jr. "Empire, Republicanism, and Reason: Foreign Affairs as Viewed by the Founders of the Constitution." *The History Teacher* 26 (March): 297–315.

FORMS OF GOVERNMENT

Classical political theorists categorized governments by whether they were ruled by the one, the few, or the many. Such theorists further divided each of these three types into both a good and a bad form depending on whether the ruler or rulers served public or private interests. In a typical scheme, rule by a single individual on behalf of the common good was called a monarchy, and on behalf of self-interest, a tyranny. Rule by the few could be either an aristocracy or an oligarchy, while rule by the many could be classified as democracy or as mob rule or anarchy. John Adams showed his knowledge of this classification system in an essay he wrote in 1763 (see Lint and Ryerson 1986, 25).

A Digression on Three Other Forms of Government

Modern political scientists also classify governments according to the manner in which nations divide power between national and subnational authorities. Today scholars recognize three such divisions. One is a unitary government, like that of Great Britain or France, where there are no permanent sovereign subunits, and the national government can operate directly on individuals. A second type is a confederal government, like the states had under the Articles of Confederation, in which power is divided between the national authorities and various subunits, with the former having to act through the latter, which are considered to be sovereign. A third type is a federal government, which the Framers essentially invented at the Constitutional Convention. In such a government, both national and state authorities can act directly on individuals.

The American Founders essentially invented the federal form of government as a halfway house between the unitary, or "national," government with which they were familiar in Great Britain, and the confederal government, or what, prior to the invention of the modern federal government, they labeled the "federal" government, under the Articles of Confederation. Seeking the rhetorical advantage of familiar terminology, the defenders of the new government took the name "Federalist" and dubbed their opponents Antifederalists, but the defenders of the new Constitution recognized that the form of government they created was new. In defending the new government in *Federalist* No. 39, James Madison thus described it as being neither "wholly *national* nor wholly *federal*" but as a combination of the two (Hamilton, Madison, and Jay 1961, 246). Maryland's Luther Martin who had attended the Convention and went on to oppose the new Constitution observed the shift in language when he observed that "although, *now*, they who *advocate* the system pretend to call themselves *federalists*, in convention the distinction was quite the reverse; those who *opposed* the system were *there* considered and styled the *federal* party, those who advocated it, the *antifederal*" (Farrand 1937, III, 195).

Terminology at the Convention

In contrast to the ancients, the delegates to the Constitutional Convention generally associated rule by one or the few as inherently undesirable and unsuited to the American situation. Similarly, although "democracy" can be an almost sacred word in today's political context in the United States, with a recent book by a prominent political scientist asking *How Democratic Is the American Constitution?* and critiquing the document because it does not fully reach the democratic ideal (Dahl 2001), the Framers, who believed that government rested on the consent of the governed, still often used the word in less flattering terms. In fact, they sometimes used the term much as classical writers had used the term "mob rule."

No discussion of such a subject can be complete, but a review of the use of the terms "monarchy," "aristocracy," and "democracy" (at least to a degree) at the Constitutional Convention helps point to the kind of government they were seeking to avoid while an analysis of the term "republic" helps show the government they were trying to create. The Virginia Plan for a tripartite government in part resembled Roman ideas of a mixed constitution, as well as the British idea of balancing the rule of the one, the few, and the many in different parts of the government (without, however, relying, as the British did in their monarchy and in the House of Lords, on hereditary distinctions). Although there were obvious differences between the developed class systems in England and Europe and those in the United States, the Framers were willing to allow individual parts of their proposed government to reflect certain monarchical or aristocratic features, but they were adamantly opposed to allowing any single such feature to dominate. This approach was consistent with the Framers' general distrust of power that was exercised by any single individual or group of individuals.

Monarchy

Given the colonists' experience with King George III and their positive reception of Thomas Paine's indictment of monarchy in *Common Sense,* their general antipathy toward monarchy is fairly easy to understand. The delegate who most admired the British system and its accompanying monarchy was Alexander Hamilton. In his five-hour-long speech to the Convention on June 18 in which he introduced his own plans for government, which most delegates enjoyed but then proceeded politely to ignore, he argued that hereditary monarchy was desirable because the king's reputation was tied to that of his people (I, 310), but he was clearly in a distinct minority.

South Carolina's Charles Pinckney wanted a "vigorous Executive" but feared that if the executive had the powers of war and peace, it would "render the Executive a Monarchy, of the worst kind, to wit an elective one" (I, 64–65). On the same day, Pennsylvania's James Wilson said that he favored an executive with "energy[,] dispatch and responsibility" (I, 65), but he did not think the prerogatives of the English king provided the appropriate model. In a novel speech in which Benjamin Franklin proposed that the executive should not receive a salary (a practice voluntarily followed by Presidents George Washington and John F. Kennedy), Franklin said there "is scarce a king in a hundred who would not, like the Biblical Pharoah, get first all the peoples money, then all their lands, and then make them and their children servants forever." He further warned, however, that "there is a natural inclination in mankind to Kingly Government. It sometimes relieves them from Aristocratic domination. They had rather have one tyrant than five hundred. It gives more of the appearance of equality among Citizens, and that they like" (I, 83). Delaware's John Dickinson (who never formally presented his own plan for a tripartite executive to the Convention) observed that "such an Executive as some seemed to have in contemplation was not consistent with a republic; that a firm Executive could only exist in a limited monarchy" (I, 86).

On June 4, Virginia's George Mason, who later advocated a plural executive, expressed his fear of the danger of an "elective" monarchy. He also registered his hope that "nothing like a monarchy would ever be attempted in this Country," observing that "A hatred to its oppressions had carried the people through the late Revolution" (I, 101–102).

After Madison argued that members of the Convention should do what was just and proper and present it to the people without worrying about public opinion, Elbridge Gerry of Massachusetts sought to refute him by arguing that, by such logic, if members "supposed a limited Monarchy the best form of itself, we ought to recommend it, tho. the genius of the people was decidedly adverse to it, and having no hereditary distinctions among us, we were destitute of the essential materials for such an innovation" (I, 215). Gerry, in turn, estimated that fewer than one in a thousand citizens would support a monarchy (I, 425). Later in the Convention, Gouverneur Morris of Pennsylvania observed that under the U.S. Constitution the executive would be less like a "king" than a "prime-Minister," and that "the people are the King" (II, 69).

Aristocracy

If the members of the Convention thought that monarchy was bad, they considered a pure aristocracy to be little better. Elbridge Gerry observed that "He was not disposed to run into extremes. He was as much principled as ever agst. aristocracy and monarchy" (I, 132). James Madison observed on August 7 that "the right of suffrage is certainly one of the fundamental articles of republican Government," and ought not be left to legislative regulation lest the ruin of popular government form the basis for an aristocracy (II, 203). Connecticut's Oliver Ellsworth made a similar observation on the same day (II, 207).

Debates over whether the suffrage should be confined to freeholders (those who owned a certain amount of land) show how the context of debates sometimes changes from one century to another. Gouverneur Morris attempted to justify such a limitation, not as a way of limiting the power of ordinary people but of curbing the influence that aristocrats might have on them at a time prior to secret voting. Madison summarized:

He had learned not to be the dupe of words. The sound of Aristocracy therefore, had no effect on him. It was the thing, not the name, to which he was opposed, and one of his principal objections to the Constitution as it is now before us, is that it threatens the Country with an Aristocracy. The aristocracy will grow out of the House of Representatives. Give the votes to people who have no property, and they will sell them to the rich who will be able to buy them. (II, 202)

A day later, in opposing counting the slave population in apportioning representatives, Morris raised an issue that was especially touchy for Southern delegates by observing: "Domestic slavery is the most prominent feature in the aristocratic countenance of the proposed Constitution" (II, 222).

Morris's speech on behalf of the freehold, although couched in anti-aristocratic language, concerned Benjamin Franklin, who without apparently directly referring to democracy, commended "the virtue & public spirit of our common people" (I, 204). As evidence, he cited the refusal of captured American seamen to fight for the British and favorably contrasted American treatment of common people with the less favorable treatment they received in England. Ironically, Franklin supported measures withholding salaries from both the president and senators, making it highly unlikely that common people could have held such posts.

Opposing the Senate origination of money bills on the same day, George Mason argued that it would tend toward aristocracy, which he defined as "the governt. of the few over the many." Using a mechanical analogy not altogether remote from modern lingo, he further observed that "An aristocratic body, like the screw in mechanics, working its way by slow degrees, and holding fast whatever it gains, should ever be suspected of an encroaching tendency" (II, 224).

Virginia's Edmund Randolph argued that because people would regard the Senate as the more aristocratic body, they "will expect that the usual guards agst its influence be provided according to the example in G. Britain" (II, 263). John Dickinson prophetically predicted that "When this plan goes forth, it will be attacked by the popular leaders. Aristocracy will be the watchword; the Shibboleth among its adversaries" (II, 278). Fearing that the members of the legislature would become aristocratic, Maryland's John Mercer advocated giving the executive a council with which to counterbalance such influence (II, 285).

Democracy

If the experience under George III had prompted Americans to fear monarchy, their experience, especially at the state level, under the Articles of Confederation had taught them the dangers of democratic, and especially legislative, excesses (Wood 1969). Delegates received constant warnings about legislative abuses, as in issuing paper money (thus favoring debtors over creditors) or in abusing individual rights, a theme that Antifederalists renewed in their demands after the Convention for a bill of rights limiting the power of the newly established government. Although members of the Convention expressed the need to rest the foundations of Congress, and especially of the lower house (as well as the Constitution itself) on popular approval, they also accepted the tripartite system of government and bicameralism in part to counterbalance such influence. Citing the inadequacy of the Virginia Senate, the Maryland Senate, and the New York and Massachusetts Constitutions, Edmund Randolph introduced his plan, which called for popular selection of the lower house, by observing:

> Our chief danger arises from the democratic parts of our constitutions. It is a maxim which I hold incontrovertible, that the powers of government exercised by the people swallow up the other branches. (I, 26–27)

Connecticut's Roger Sherman was among those who thought the plan went too far in this respect. In opposing direct election of the House (under the Articles of Confederation, state legislatures had chosen members of Congress), he observed that the people were lacking in information and "are consistently liable to be misled" (I, 48). Elbridge Gerry was of a similar mind: "The evils we experience flow from the excess of democracy. The people do want virtue; but are the dupes of pretended patriots" (I, 48). Professing still to being "republican," he also said that experience had

taught him "the danger of the leveling spirit" (I, 48). George Mason, in turn, "admitted that we had been too democratic but was afraid we sh. incautiously run into the opposite extreme" (I, 49). Moreover, although he later equated democracy with some "oppression & injustices," he thought "the genius of the people is in favor of it, and the genius of the people must be consulted" (I, 101). New York's Alexander Hamilton disputed the proposition that the voice of the people is the voice of God by observing that "the people are turbulent and changing; they seldom judge or determine right" (I, 299). Elbridge Gerry, in turn, noted that although democracy was the worst political evil, others in his state were "as violent in the opposite extreme" (II, 647).

Republican Government

If the Framers thus expressed skepticism of government of the one, the few, and the many, what exactly were they seeking? The answer is almost as elusive as the terms that have been examined so far, but can probably be summarized in what delegates, and scholar Alpheus T. Mason, called "free government" or "popular government" (Mason and Baker 1985, 178), what political scientist Martin Diamond called a "democratic republic" (1981), or, simply, "republican" government.

Significantly, when he presented the rationale for the Virginia Plan, Edmund Randolph said that the remedy for the Articles needed to be based on "the republican principle" (I, 19). Delegates talked constantly about their desire for "liberty," and they expressed this goal in the Preamble of the Constitution. On June 1, Pennsylvania's James Wilson noted that the extent of the country was so great that "the manners so republican, that nothing but a great confederated Republic would do for it" (I, 66). Acknowledging that "improper elections" were an element of "Republican Govt's," George Mason noted "the advantage of this Form in favor in the rights of the people, in favor of human nature" (I, 134). Similarly, he later recognized "the superiority of the Republican form over every other" while acknowledging that it had "its evils," the chief being "the danger of the majority oppressing the minority, and the mischievous influence of demagogues" (II, 273). On June 26, James Madison observed that "as it is more than probable we were now digesting a plan which in its operation wd. decide forever the fate of Republican Govt we ought not only to provide every guard to liberty that its preservation cd. require, but be equally careful to supply the defects which our own experience had particularly pointed out" (I, 423). Alexander Hamilton, acknowledging that he was not himself a friend to such government, "addressed his remarks to those who did think favorably of it, in order to prevail on them to tone their Government as high as possible" (I, 424). Yates's notes further summarize Hamilton's argument as saying:

> We are now forming a republican government. Real liberty is neither found in despotism or the extremes of democracy, but in moderate governments. Those who mean to form a solid republican government, ought to proceed to the confines of another government. As long as offices are open to all men, and no constitutional rank is established, it is pure republicanism. But if we incline too much to democracy, we shall soon shoot into a monarchy. (I, 432)

Edmund Randolph later cited the Baron de Montesquieu to the effect that suffrage is "a fundamental article in Republican Govts." (I, 580). James Madison observed that "A Republic may be converted into an aristocracy or oligarchy as well by limiting the number capable of being elected, as the number authorized to elect" (II, 250). In a nice transition to later debates over constitutional ratification, Madison argued that "One of the greatest evils incident to Republican Govt. was the spirit of contention & faction" (II, 276).

Although the delegates to the Constitutional Convention did not use the word "republican" uniformly, they generally used the term to refer to a moderated democracy without hereditary titles or massive class distinctions. A chief mechanism for accomplishing moderation in democracy was the tripartite system of government which would provide checks and balances. The division of Congress into two branches was yet another means of moderating the impetuousness of the House of Representatives.

Constitutional Provisions

The Constitution does not employ the term "monarchy," "aristocracy," or "democracy." In language that leans toward a democratic interpretation, it does, however, begin with the words "We the People of the United States." Similarly, Article IV, Section 4 guarantees to each state a "republican" form of government. The fact that members of the Convention sought not to change such governments but to guarantee their existence is a fairly good indication that, with all their faults, the delegates recognized that the term "republican" was a fairly broad term that could cover the existing state representative arrangements with which the Framers were familiar.

It is probably also significant that, although they hoped that the Senate would moderate the passions of the lower house, the Framers did not impose a wealth requirement for this office. Similarly, although the Convention created a single executive, this president was indirectly elected by the people via the Electoral College and serves for distinct terms, rather than for life. Largely through amendments that have widened suffrage and provided for direct election of U.S. senators, the U.S. Constitution has become increasingly more democratic than when it was first adopted (Grimes 1978).

Consistent with these developments, today's common usage refers to the U.S. government as a democracy. Significantly, however, the Pledge of Allegiance to the U.S. flag refers specifically to the "republic," rather than the "democracy," for which it stands.

Further Illumination from the Ratification Debates

One problem that the advocates of the Constitution faced was that "republican" government was generally associated, most notably in the respected writings of Montesquieu and in the existing states, with the governments of relatively small geographical entities. By contrast, the Framers were attempting to provide greater unity over an area of land already larger than most European nations, with sound prospects of further expansion into the South and West. If it were impossible to establish "republican" government over a large land area, then the Founders were either pursuing an illusion or being less than candid with the public about their intentions. One of the Antifederalists' most popular charges against the new Constitution was either that Congress, or more specifically the Senate, was too aristocratic or that the presidency was too monarchical.

James Madison's *Federalist* essay No. 10 represents the most famous response to these critiques. There he argued, contrary to Montesquieu, that a large republic actually provided a better way to combat the injustices of faction than a smaller one. In making his argument, Madison drew two distinctions between the government of a "republic" and that of a "pure democracy." The first distinction centered on representation, or what Madison referred to as "the delegation of the government, in the latter, to a small number of citizens elected by the rest" (Hamilton, Madison, and Jay, 82). Madison argued that representatives would "refine" public opinion on behalf of common interests and add greater wisdom to government councils. The second distinction between a pure democracy and republican government focused on size. Although a pure democracy was confined to a small space from which all citizens could be gathered for public meetings, a republic could cover a vaster territory (Hamilton, Madison, and Jay, 83). Madison went on to argue that the larger the land area a republic covered, the more factions, or what today's contemporaries would call interest groups, it would embrace. The greater number of factions in turn made it less likely that any single faction could form a majority to oppress the others. Significantly, Madison defended the new Constitution as providing "a republican remedy for the diseases most incident to republican government" (84).

See Also Aristocracy; Classical Allusions and Influences; Confederal Government; Democracy; Federalism; *Federalist, The;* Guarantee Clause; Madison, James, Jr.; Mixed Government; Monarchy; Paine, Thomas; Separation of Powers; Republicanism; Unitary Government

FOR FURTHER READING

Dahl, Robert. 2001. *How Democratic Is the American Constitution?* New Haven, CT: Yale University Press.

Diamond, Martin. 1981. *The Founding of the Democratic Republic.* Itasca, IL: F. F. Peacock Publishers.

Farrand, Max, ed. 1937. *The Records of the Federal Convention.* 4 vols. New Haven, CT: Yale University Press.

Grimes, Alan P. 1978. *Democracy and the Amendments to the Constitution.* Lexington, MA: Lexington Books.

Hamilton, Alexander, James Madison, and John Jay. 1961. *The Federalist Papers.* Ed. Clinton Rossiter. New York: New American Library.

Lint, Gregg L., and Richard Alan Ryerson. 1986. "The Separation of Powers: John Adams' Influence on the Constitution." *this Constitution,* no. 11 (Summer): 25–31.

Mason, Alpheus T., and Gordon E. Baker. 1985. *Free Government in the Making: Readings in American Political Thought* 4th ed. New York: Oxford University Press.

Montesquieu, Baron de. 1949. *The Spirit of the Laws.* Trans. Thomas Hugent. New York: Hafner Press.

Paine, Thomas. 1986 (first published 1776). *Common Sense.* New York: Penguin Books.

Wood, Gordon S. 1969. *The Creation of the American Republic, 1776–1787.* Chapel Hill: University of North Carolina Press.

FOUNDING

The Constitutional Convention of 1787 is frequently tied to the idea of the "Founding" period. The delegates at the Constitutional Convention are, in turn, often referred to as the "Founding" Fathers, or the constitutional "Framers." These terms indicate that the delegates played a role in the establishment or constituting of the United States. The Baron de Montesquieu recognized the importance of such foundings when he observed that "At the birth of societies, the rulers establish

The Forefathers' Forefathers

The idea of honoring forefathers is an ancient one. It did not begin, even in America, with the adulation of those who signed the Declaration of Independence or gathered to write the U.S. Constitution. In 1769, Plymouth held its first annual "Forefathers' Day" to honor "the first landing of our worthy ancestors in this place" (quoted from documents from the period in Stavely and Fitzgerald 2004, 60). Like modern Fourth of July picnics, the day often consisted of eating and speechmaking.

Like those who compare modern "politicians" with the "statesmen" who wrote the Constitution, speakers at this event often delivered a "jeremiad," a speech condemning modern evils and often unfavorably comparing moderns with those who had preceded them. Daniel Webster continued this tradition in 1820 in a historic speech commemorating the landing of the pilgrims. In this speech, he argued that the "free nature of our institutions" had "come down to us from the Rock of Plymouth" (Stavely and Fitzgerald, 60).

Although they varied in significant ways, historians still often emphasize the "Pilgrim" roots of men like Connecticut's Roger Sherman and Pennsylvania's Benjamin Franklin, who attended the Constitutional Convention, and John Adams, a contemporary of theirs who did not. Historians still continue to debate the manner in which American Protestantism (as reflected in Puritanism) coexisted with Enlightenment rationalism to produce the unique blend of American politics (Dreisbach, Hall, and Morrison 2004).

FOR FURTHER READING

Dreisbach, Daniel L., Mark D. Hall, and Jeffry H. Morrison, eds. 2004. *The Founders on God and Government.* Lanham, MD: Rowman and Littlefield Publishers.

Stavely, Keith, and Kathleen Fitzgerald. 2004. *America's Founding Food: The Story of New England Cooking.* Chapel Hill: University of North Carolina Press.

---

institutions; and afterwards, the institutions mould the rulers" (quoted in Rohr 1986, 5).

Although people throughout the world cherish their histories, most nations cannot trace their origins to a single specific event, but trace their foundings back to a whole series of developments. Similarly, some nations, like Great Britain, do not have a single constitutional document that they identify as their "constitution." By contrast, the U.S. can trace its origins as a nation back to the Declaration of Independence from Great Britain in 1776 and the subsequent war to secure this independence, and the origin of its written Constitution to the Convention of 1787. This leaves two potential sets of Founding Fathers, who are, in fact, often confused in the popular mind.

Thomas Jefferson had asserted in the Declaration of Independence that government rested "on the consent of the governed." The attempt by the Constitutional Convention to draw up a new gov-

ernment was in turn an application of this idea. Like the Declaration of Independence, it rested on the belief, prominent in the political philosophy of the Founding period (and particularly that of the British philosopher John Locke) that legitimate government rests on a social contract, based on popular consent rather than on force or conquest. Future generations assent to this original contract by participating in government and by electing its leaders.

The idea of founding goes at least as far back as Greek and Roman historians and political thinkers who often cited the works of prominent lawgivers—Solon and Lycurgus, for example—who established regimes; Moses provided a similar example from Jewish history (Wildavsky 1984). Ancient writers on politics often portrayed the act of lawgiving or founding as one of the most important tasks to which an individual could aspire. The example of the U.S. attributes to a group of men what other nations have often attributed to a single individual, sometimes portrayed as having had divine sanction.

Frank W. Fox, a contemporary historian, has identified five elements of a founding. These are a connection with a specific name of a country (but, for reservations about whether there was such a name for the United States, see De Grazia 1997) and a place; the development of a system of fundamental law creating "an essential political order"; a decision as to who will share in constituting the polity; the creation of a sense of nationhood; and what Fox calls a "founding myth," that is, a story that imparts a sense of legitimacy to the government (2003, 9–10).

Under this typology the Constitutional Convention represented a founding, or refounding, of the United States of America, over the area occupied by the 13 former British colonies, to be governed by a new Constitution that represented a significant departure from the previous government under the Articles of Confederation. This event has played a major role in the delineation of American identity. The mythical elements of the Framing focus on the idea that if the Founders were not demigods, they were at least an extraordinary group of men who pursued the common good and may even have been aided by divine providence.

The original Founding was probably incomplete, as in the Constitution's initial failure to provide a definition of citizenship—a development that would occur when the Fourteenth Amendment overturned the *Dred Scott* decision of 1857 by declaring that all persons born or naturalized within the United States are citizens. However, the Founders were wise enough to have included an amending provision to remedy initial mistakes in the nation's blueprint and to cope with future exigencies.

The immortality of the Framers is confirmed by, and depends in part on, the success and durability of the form of government they created. The provision of such a government for its own amendment leaves a place for members of future generations to establish continuity with the original set of Founders by following the provisions for constitutional change that the original Founders outlined.

Thus, individuals like Abraham Lincoln can, in turn, achieve greatness both by defending the Union and by contributing to the expansion or reformulation of the principles for which it stands.

See Also Declaration of Independence; Father of the Constitution

FOR FURTHER READING

De Grazia, Sebastian. 1997. *A Country with No Name: Tales from the Constitution.* New York: Pantheon Books.

Fox, Frank W. 2003. *The American Founding.* Boston: Pearson Custom Publishing.

Jordan, Cynthia S. 1988. "'Old Words' in 'New Circumstances': Language and Leadership in Post-Revolutionary America." *American Quarterly* 40 (December): 491–513.

Lienesch, Michael. 1980. "The Constitutional Tradition: History, Political Action, and Progress in American Political Thought 1787–1793." *Journal of Politics* 42 (February): 2–30.

Rohr, John A. 1986. *To Run a Constitution: The Legitimacy of the Administrative State.* Lawrence: University Press of Kansas.

Vile, John R. 1992. "Three Kinds of Constitutional Founding and Change: The Convention Model and Its Alternatives." *Political Research Quarterly* 46: 881–895.

Wildavsky, Aaron B. 1984. *The Nursing Father: Moses as a Political Leader.* University: University of Alabama Press.

FRAMERS

Just as scholars sometimes refer to those who participated in the writing of the U.S. Constitution as "Founding Fathers," or simply "Founders," so too, they sometimes refer to them as "Framers," and to the Constitution as a "frame" of government. Robert Ferguson observes that Samuel Johnson's much-touted *Dictionary of the English Language* defined "frame" to include "'to form or fabricate by orderly construction and union of various parts,' 'to make,' 'to regulate,' 'to invent,' and, from the verb, 'a fabrick, any thing constructed of various parts or members,' 'any thing made so as to inclose or admit something else,' 'order; regularity; adjusted series or disposition,' 'scheme,' 'contrivance,' 'projection'" (1987, 11). Akhil Ree Amar has observed that architectural imagery is often used to describe the making of the Constitution. Not only are the delegates to the Constitutional Convention often called "Framers" or likened to builders but the most substantial reordering of the Constitution via constitutional amendment has been described as a "Reconstruction" (2002, 671).

Somewhat objecting to the idea of completeness that is sometimes associated with the idea of a Constitution frame, Michael Benedict has observed that the *Oxford English Dictionary* also defines a frame as "'a structure which serves as an underlying support or skeleton,' or a structure 'of which the parts form an outline or skeleton not filled in'" (1987, 32). Following this definition, Benedict further likens the Constitution to "a sketch" rather than "a painting" (33).

FOR FURTHER READING

Amar, Akhil Ree. 2002. "Architexture +." *Indiana Law Journal* 77 (Fall): 671–700.

Benedict, Michael L. 1987. "1787: The Constitution in Perspective: 'We Do Ordain and Establish': The Constitution as Literary Text: Our 'Sacred' Constitution–Another View of the Constitution as Literary Text." *William and Mary Law Review* 29 (Fall): 27–34.

Ferguson, Robert A. 1987. "The Constitution in Perspective: 'We Do Ordain and Establish': The Constitution as Literary Text." *William and Mary Law Review* 29 (Fall): 3–25.

FRANCE

Great Britain, France, and Spain were the three European powers that most influenced the development of America. With forts in the American Northwest and control over Canada, Britain continued to pose a military threat to the new nation, and Spain's control of Florida, Louisiana, and Mississippi posed potential problems to American expansion. The Americans had joined the British in opposition to France and its Native American allies in the French and Indian War (during which France ended up forfeiting Canada to Great Britain), but when the former colonies and Britain split, France became America's ally in the Revolutionary War, French ministers participated actively in American politics (Ketcham 1963, 205–209), the Marquis de Lafayette volunteered for service in the American Revolution, and French support was essential to the critical victory at Yorktown, Virginia. The Baron de Montesquieu, of France, was a major philosophic influence on the American Founding Fathers. Benjamin Franklin, John Adams, Gouverneur Morris, and Thomas Jefferson all spent time in France as American diplomats.

America, however, was delinquent in its debts to France, and Americans had negotiated an end to the Revolutionary War without taking the French into their full confidence. In his "Preface" to the debates at the Convention, Madison observed that one of the defects of the Articles of Confederation was the fact that states were ignoring treaty obligations with France and Holland (Farrand 1937, III, 548).

The French chargé d'affaires, Louis Guillaume Otto, took a keen interest in the U.S. Constitutional Convention and sent a number of letters to France analyzing this event (III, 15, 39, 61). Delegates to the Convention in turn occasionally referred to France during their deliberations. In justifying the novel proposition that presidents should serve without pay, Pennsylvania's Benjamin Franklin (who had served as an ambassador to France) cited the French office of counsellor as one that individuals were willing to take a financial loss on in return for being able to serve their country (I, 84). In assessing the respective powers of the Virginia and New Jersey Plans, Edmund Randolph of Virginia thus observed that "France, to whom we are indebted in every motive of gratitude and honor, is left unpaid the large sums she has supplied us with in the day of our necessity" (I, 262). Virginia's James Madison cited the rivalry between Austria and France as what one would expect at a time when the two were the major powers in Europe (I, 448). George Mason, also of Virginia, opposed the idea of allowing the Senate to initiate money bills by arguing that this power could render the House "like the Parliament of Paris, the mere depository of the decrees of the Senate" (II, 274). Maryland's John Mercer observed that "It is not the king of France—but 200,000 janisaries of power that govern that Kingdom" (II, 289). Gouverneur Morris of Pennsylvania cited French taxation of exported "wines and brandies" (II, 307), and Madison cited an agreement between Robert Morris (presumably as superintendent of finance under the Articles of Confederation) and France regarding tobacco as a justification for maintaining the power to tax exports (II, 306). In a draft speech, now believed to have been prepared by Pennsylvania's Jared Ingersoll, he further observed that "France our great & good Ally resents the Conduct of our Ministers in the course of the negotiations for a peace, & immediate Interest unites all the powers of Europe, in a combination to exclude from their West-India Islands" (Hutson 1987, 101).

Not long after the Constitutional Convention, France became the site of a major revolution, which drew in part on American revolutionary ideals, but carried many of them much farther (see Appleby 1971). Decisions about what support to give France in its almost perpetual war with Britain was a major issue in early American politics that often divided the Federalists, who generally favored Great Britain, and Democratic-Republicans, who generally favored France. In time the French acquired the Louisiana Territory from Spain, which the United States purchased in Thomas Jefferson's administration in 1803, thus helping to realize the dream of an expanded commercial republic.

See Also Canada; Federalist and Democratic-Republican Parties; Great Britain; Montesquieu, Charles Louis de Secondat de; Spain

FOR FURTHER READING

Appleby, Joyce. 1971. "America as a Model for the Radical French Reformers of 1789." *William and Mary Quarterly*, 3rd ser. 28 (April): 267–286.

Farrand, Max, ed. 1937. *The Records of the Federal Convention.* 4 vols. New Haven, CT: Yale University Press.

Higonnet, Patrice. 1988. *Sister Republics: The Origins of French and American Republicanism.* Cambridge, MA: Harvard University Press.

Hutson, James H., ed. 1987. *Supplement to Max Farrand's* The Records of the Federal Convention of 1787. New Haven, CT: Yale University Press.

Ketcham, Ralph L. 1963. "France and American Politics, 1763–1793." *Political Science Quarterly* 78 (June): 198–223.

Spurlin, Paul M. 1976. "The Founding Fathers and the French Language." *The Modern Language Journal* 60 (March): 85–96.

FRANKLIN, BENJAMIN (1706–1790)

With the possible exception of General Washington, Benjamin Franklin was the most widely known member of the Constitutional Convention of 1787. Born in Boston on January 17, 1706, at 81 years of age Franklin was also the Convention's eldest, and probably its most widely traveled, member. Franklin had left Boston as a youth for Philadelphia (and briefly for England). A self-educated man—described as one of the "least-schooled, and the most broadly educated" member of the Convention (Carr 1990, 29)—who had arrived in Philadelphia with almost nothing and spent most of his life as a printer, Franklin had authored *Poor Richard's Almanack*, and described his life in a famous autobiography published after his death. Inventor of the Franklin stove, bifocals, and the lightning rod, Franklin had established the first subscription library and helped found the University of Pennsylvania. Franklin had served as a representative to the Albany Congress, where he had proposed the Albany Plan of Union, represented the colonies in England in the disputes leading up to the U.S. Revolutionary War, served on the five-man committee responsible for drafting the Declaration of Independence, served as postmaster general under the Continental Con-

Benjamin Franklin, 1782, delegate from Pennsylvania
(Library of Congress)

Capitol has a picture from the Constitutional Convention portraying Franklin entertaining Alexander Hamilton, James Wilson, and James Madison under his mulberry tree.

At the time of the Convention, Franklin's health was not good. Although it does not appear that he arrived by this mode of conveyance every day, gout and kidney stones were among the problems that required that he be carried into the Convention at least on May 28 in a sedan hoisted by four prisoners from the nearby Walnut Street jail. Although Franklin appears to have composed his own speeches, his colleagues, usually James Wilson, usually delivered them on his behalf. Most of Franklin's most notable contributions to the Convention appear to have been in the form of speeches and short vignettes rather than debates with other delegates. Franklin often attempted to play the role of a conciliator.

Unable to attend the first session of the Convention, Franklin agreed with other delegates from the Pennsylvania convention that Robert Morris would nominate George Washington as president of the Convention (Farrand 1937, I, 4). Franklin was somewhat mortified, however, that Alexander Hamilton's nomination of William Jackson as convention secretary prevailed over Franklin's own hope that the position might go to his grandson, Temple Franklin (Hutson 1987, 1).

gress, presided over the Pennsylvania Constitutional Convention of 1776, helped negotiate the Treaty of Paris that ended the Revolutionary War, and later served as a diplomat to France, where he received almost universal adulation.

In 1787, Franklin was serving as president of Pennsylvania, and the next year he was chosen to head the nation's first antislavery society. It is unlikely that anyone in the former colonies, with the possible exception of Thomas Jefferson (then serving as an ambassador in France), would obtain Franklin's breadth of knowledge.

Franklin had adopted the city of Philadelphia as his home, and he enjoyed entertaining a number of delegates to the Convention at his residence on Market Street. Washington made a call shortly after arriving in town. A mural in the U.S.

Congress

Franklin was known to favor a unicameral legislature, like that in Pennsylvania. He had likened a bicameral legislature to a specimen he had of a snake with two heads (Isaacson 2003, 453). Madison attributed Pennsylvania's sole vote against the Virginia Plan's proposal to a bicameral Congress to Franklin's influence (I, 48). This set something of a pattern whereby on many occasions delegates appeared to treat Franklin's proposals with respect because of his authorship, but were not thereby persuaded of their utility.

On June 11, Franklin expressed concern that the issue of representation in Congress was destroying the calm that was needed for deliberation. He had hoped that delegates to the Convention might consider themselves to be "rather as a representative of the whole, than as an Agent for the interests of a particular State" although he now realized that this goal was no longer "to be expected" (I, 197). Franklin's view, however, was that "the number of Representatives should bear some proportion to the number of the Represented; and that the decisions shd. be by the majority of members, not by the majority of States" (II, 197–198). Franklin thought that there was little cause to fear that the large states would swallow the small, and he cited the union of England and Scotland to support this proposition (I, 198). He believed, however, that if states were not represented proportionally, the minority might dominate. Franklin said that he would not oppose equalizing the states in regard to population if this were practical, but he did not think that it was practical and observed that even if it could be done, boundaries would continually have to be changed as population altered. Franklin's speech on this subject has been characterized as "long, complex, and at times baffling" (Isaacson, 450), and it did not appear directly to address the problem. He proposed that the smallest state should specify the amount of money and the number of troops it could supply and that each of the other states would agree to the same. In such circumstances (which, perhaps, Franklin thought impossible to fulfill), states could be equally represented in Congress. If Congress needed more than these requisitions, it could petition states to give more, leaving them, much as under the Articles of Confederation, to decide whether they could or would provide more (I, 199–200). Immediately after having made this proposal (could Franklin therefore have intended for it to be ironic?), however, Franklin observed that the original decision to grant states equal representation in the First Continental Congress had stemmed from its inability to ascertain "the importance of each colony" (I, 200).

Two days after he proposed that the Convention should start the day with prayer, Franklin returned to the subject of state representation, and tried to appeal for compromise by a homely example. Observing that small states feared for their "liberties" and large ones feared for their "money,"

he observed that "When a broad table is to be made, and the edges [of the planks do not fit] the artist takes a little from both, and makes a good joint. In like manner here both sides must part with some of their demands, in order that they may join in some accommodating proposition" (I, 488). His proposal was similar to what became the Connecticut Compromise but with some interesting wrinkles. He proposed that states would be represented equally in one house and that "in all cases or questions wherein the Sovereignty of individual States may be affected, or whereby their authority over their own Citizens may be diminished, or the authority of the General Government within the several States augmented, each State shall have equal suffrage" (I, 489). Similarly states would have an equal vote in the appointment of civil officers. However, on the issue of salaries and expenditures, states would be represented "in proportion to the Sums which their respective States do actually contribute to the treasury" (I, 489). Franklin commended this approach as consistent with the rule that was used when a ship had many owners. Robert Yates later identified Franklin as the individual who introduced the motion in the Committee on Representation in Congress (appointed on July 2) that eventually resulted in the Great Compromise (I, 523).

Franklin's very presence on the committee indicated that he was considered to be one of the conciliatory voices on the subject at the Convention (the only other committee to which he was appointed was the Committee on Sumptuary Legislation, appointed on September 13, which never appears to have met). Because this compromise involved the origination of money bills within the House, Franklin felt obligated to continue to vote for that measure in subsequent deliberations (I, 543; also see II, 233). Franklin defended this provision, the utility of which James Madison and James Wilson had both questioned, by observing that "It was a maxim that those who feel, can best judge. This end would, he thought, be best attained, if money affairs were to be confined to the immediate representatives of the people" (I, 546).

Just as he expressed concern over the magnitude of presidential salaries (see below), Franklin successfully proposed striking a provision that would have specified "liberal" salaries for members of Congress. Preferring the word "moderate," Franklin had observed "the tendency of abuses in every case, to grow of themselves when once begun," and illustrated by the "development of modest benefices enjoyed by the early apostles as compared to those of later popes" (I, 216).

Similarly, Franklin later seconded a proposal by South Carolina's Charles Cotesworth Pinckney that would have disallowed members of the Senate from receiving salaries. Observing that the Convention contained a number of "young men who would probably be of the Senate," he feared that "If lucrative appointments should be recommended we might be chargeable with having carved out places for ourselves" (I, 427).

Toward the end of the Convention, Franklin proposed that Congress should be entrusted with the power to cut canals (II, 615). The Convention rejected this proposal, leaving future congresses to decide on the constitutionality of government corporations.

Presidency

Franklin prompted the Convention to further discussion when delegates appeared reluctant to discuss fellow delegate James Wilson's proposal that the executive should be unitary (I, 65). Franklin introduced a far more novel proposal on June 2 when he proposed that the president should not receive a salary, although his expenses should be paid. More important than the suggestion, which received deference only out of regard for its author, was the logic by which Franklin attempted to justify this provision and the insight that it cast on Franklin's view of human nature. He observed that men were motivated by two powerful influences: "ambition and avarice; the love of power, and the love of money" (I, 82). He feared the conjunction of these two motives, for as he indicated, "place before the eyes of such men a post of *honour* that shall at the same time be a place of *profit*, and they will move heaven and earth to obtain it" (I, 82). Tracing factions to struggles for such objects, Franklin feared that they would stimulate "the bold and the violent, the men of strong passions and indefatigable activity in their selfish pursuits" (I, 82). Franklin believed that there would be a natural pressure within government to increase the emoluments that presidents would receive. Indeed, he feared that this tendency would push the presidency toward monarchy. Again, his explanation says a great deal about his view of human nature and shows some affinity with those, like George Mason, who consistently advocated a republican ideology: "there is a natural inclination in mankind to Kingly Government. It sometimes relieves them from Aristocratic domination. They had rather have one tyrant than five hundred. It gives them more of the appearance of equality among Citizens, and that they like" (II, 83).

Franklin thought this descent into monarchy might be slowed, and that the nation could see that it did not nourish "the foetus of a King" by separating ambition from avarice. Acknowledging that some individuals would regard it as "utopian" to think that individuals would serve their nation without salary, Franklin cited the examples of sheriffs in England and Quaker committeemen who served without such compensation. He also pointed to Washington's service as commander-in-chief during the Revolutionary War (I, 84). Franklin did not believe that the nation would ever "be without a sufficient number of wise and good men to undertake and execute well and faithfully the office in question" (I, 85).

The irony of this speech is that Franklin appears to have written it with no thought that many individuals of merit, but without sufficient financial resources, would be unable to serve as president without a salary. This seeming equation of wealth and merit appears inconsistent with Franklin's acknowledgment elsewhere of the merit of the common people.

When the Convention was discussing the possibility of investing the president with an absolute negative, Franklin argued that such a mechanism had not worked well in Pennsylvania. Indeed, in comments depicting atrocities by American Indians, he observed that the royal governors had used their veto to extort increases in their salaries (I, 99). Franklin did indicate that he thought such a power would be less objectionable were the

Convention to vest it in the president in conjunction with a council, much as James Madison had previously proposed (I, 99). Franklin continued to fear, however, that the executive would be constantly increasing in power, and, in this particular at least, his words were not especially reassuring about the long-range future. Undoubtedly anticipating, like many other delegates, that George Washington would serve as the nation's first president, Franklin observed: "The first man, put at the helm will be a good one. No body knows what sort may come afterwards. The Executive will be always increasing here, as elsewhere, till it ends in monarchy" (II, 103). After the Convention rejected the absolute veto, Franklin seconded a motion to grant the executive power to suspend legislation for a period still to be specified (I, 103).

On July 20, Franklin indicated that he favored a provision for presidential impeachment, but his argument seems bizarre, in part because it seems to have been based upon a hereditary monarch rather than on an individual serving as chief executive for a fixed term. Arguing that "History furnishes one example only of a first Magistrate being formally brought to public Justice" (presumably England's Charles II, who was beheaded in 1649), Franklin advocated impeachment as preferable to assassination, which deprived an executive not only of his life but also of the possibility of vindicating his character. Franklin observed that "It wd. be the best way therefore to provide in the Constitution for the regular punishment of the Executive when his misconduct should deserve it, and for his honorable acquittal when he should be unjustly accused" (II, 65). Shortly thereafter, Franklin cited King William, the former Prince of Orange, as someone whose power was diminished by accusations that he did not have the opportunity publicly to refute, as he would have had Parliament impeached him.

When George Mason reintroduced a motion limiting the president to one term, Franklin supported it with the observation that it was no disgrace in republican government for a ruler to return to live among the people. He argued that this was not, in fact, "to *degrade* but to *promote* them" (II, 120). This prompted Gouverneur Morris to observe, with a touch of sarcasm, that "he had no doubt that our Executive like most others would have too much patriotism to shrink from the burden of his office, and too much modesty not to be willing to decline the promotion" (II, 120).

On September 7, Franklin supported George Mason's proposal for a Council of State to consist of six persons from three different geographical regions appointed by the Senate to advise the president. Franklin said that he thought that "a Council would not only be a check on a bad President but be a relief to a good one" (II, 542).

Judiciary

Franklin often added humor to the Convention proceedings. One such occasion occurred on June 5 when he suggested that he would like to hear a suggestion for appointing judges other than by Congress or the president. He then told about procedures in Scotland where lawyers made the selection and, according to Franklin, "always selected the ablest of the profession in order to get rid of him, and share his practice" (I, 120).

On July 18, Franklin was among those who supported a motion allowing for future increases in judicial salaries. He observed that "Money may not only become plentier [a time of inflation], but the business of the department may increase as the Country becomes more populous" (II, 44–45).

Franklin supported the provision in the Constitution requiring the testimony of two witnesses to an overt act of treason. He observed that "prosecutions for treason were generally virulent; and perjury too easily made use of against innocence" (II, 348).

Prayer

One of Franklin's most notable actions at the Constitutional Convention was that of calling for the Convention to open with prayer. He proposed this on June 28 at a time when the dispute over representation for the large and small states was particularly intense. At a Convention where members are perhaps best known for their faith in human reason, Franklin saw this disagreement as "a melancholy proof of the imperfection of the Human Understanding" (I, 451). Indicating that the delegates had scoured history for examples, he wondered why no one had "hitherto once thought of humbly applying to the Father of lights to illuminate our understanding" (I, 451). Citing supplications that the colonists had made in the war against Great Britain, Franklin said that the longer he lived the more convinced he was "*that God governs in the affairs of men*" (I, 451). Citing the observation (made by Jesus) that a sparrow could not perish without God's knowledge, the injunction that "except the Lord build the House they labour in vain that build it," and the example from the Old Testament of the Tower of Babel, Franklin proposed that the Convention bring in a clergyman to lead each day's proceedings with prayer. When Hamilton suggested that it would be embarrassing to do this at this stage of the proceedings, Franklin was among those who observed that "the past omission of a duty could not justify a further omission—that the rejection of such a proposition would expose the Convention to more unpleasant animadversions than the adoption of it: and that the alarm out of doors that might be excited for the state of things within would at least be as likely to do good as ill" (II, 452). Still unsuccessful, Franklin seconded a motion by Virginia's Edmund Randolph requesting that a sermon be preached for the celebration of July 4. Even this motion appears to have failed, but Franklin's motion remains a frequently told story and is part of the lore of the Convention. It seems ironic that a man known for his Deism would cite so many scriptural authorities, and it seems likely that, however he may have viewed the need for divine assistance, Franklin might have hoped that a Convention that prayed together would be likely to stay together.

Defense of the Common Man

When James Madison proposed that the right to vote should be confined to "freeholders," Frank-

lin responded that this would "be injurious to the lower class of Freemen" (II, 208). He further observed that this group had shown its virtue and integrity in the Revolutionary War. Indeed, American seamen had refused to serve in the English navy in order to gain their freedom. Franklin wanted to ensure that "Americans were all free and equal to any of yr. fellow Citizens" (II, 208).

Franklin returned to this theme on August 10. Expressing "his dislike of every thing that tended to debase the spirit of the common people," Franklin observed:

> If honesty was often the companion of wealth, and if poverty was exposed to peculiar temptation, it was not less true that the possession of property increased the desire for more property— Some of the greatest rogues he was ever acquainted with, were the richest rogues. (II, 249)

Franklin argued that if the nation betrayed "a great partiality to the rich" it would not only lower the nation in the esteem of European thinkers but would also "discourage the common people from removing to this Country" (II, 249).

Franklin displayed a similar attitude in regard to restricting the offices for which immigrants could qualify. Although he favored "a reasonable time," he observed that he "should be very sorry to see any thing like illiberality inserted in the Constitution" (II, 236). Observing that America had many friends in Europe and that immigrants had served the nation favorably, he wanted America to remain on good terms with those who wanted to come here. He also observed that simply allowing immigrants to be eligible for offices did not guarantee that they would be elected to the same (II, 239).

Ratification of the Constitution

On September 10, Franklin seconded a motion by Virginia's Edmund Randolph proposing that the Convention send the Constitution to Congress for its approval and subsequently to state conventions that would have the power either to ratify the document or to propose amendments.

This was not, of course, the manner in which the delegates proceeded.

One of Franklin's most notable speeches at the Convention was a speech that he gave on the final day of Convention deliberations. He subsequently circulated it in the form of a pamphlet. It is a model of Franklin's reasoning, and displays a worldly wisdom that must have had widespread appeal among those who questioned one or another aspect of the new government but who thought that it was an improvement over the Articles of Confederation.

Franklin began his speech by observing that "there are several parts of this constitution which I do not at present approve," but that he could not be sure that "I shall never approve them" (II, 641). He explained that, although individuals found it difficult to admit mistakes, as he had aged, he had become more willing to doubt his own individual judgment. He was willing to accede to the document, flawed though it might be, because of what he hoped it could achieve:

> I agree to this Constitution with all its faults, if they are such; because I think a general Government necessary for us, and there is no form of Government but what may be a blessing to the people if well administered, and believe rather that this is likely to be well administered for a course of years, and can only end in despotism, as other forms have done before it, when the people shall become so corrupted as to need despotic Government, being incapable of any other. (II, 642)

Franklin thought it unrealistic to anticipate a perfect document:

> For when you assemble a number of men to have the advantage of their joint wisdom, you inevitably assemble with those men, all their prejudices, their passions, their errors of opinion, their local interests, and their selfish views. (II, 642)

He hoped that the document would "astonish our enemies" abroad who were expecting the Confederation to fall apart much like the project on which builders of the Tower of Babel had worked (II, 642). He further urged other delegates to swallow their reservations, like him, rather than reporting their own disappointments and stirring opposition to the document. He proposed that the Convention adopt the Constitution unanimously by the "consent of the States present" and offered a motion to this effect (apparently authored by the less popular fellow Pennsylvania delegate Gouverneur Morris) that would allow delegates the option of signing in witness to this unanimity rather than to their own individual consent (II, 643). Perhaps a bit too clever, this ploy did not succeed in convincing all the remaining delegates to sign. Surprisingly, however, Franklin responded to a statement by South Carolina's General Pinckney by indicating that he thought it was "too soon to pledge ourselves before Congress and our Constituents shall have approved the plan" (II, 647).

The Rising Sun

The final story in Madison's reports is based on a reminiscence about Franklin that confirms the image of the elder sage seeking to leave his mark on the mythology of a document under which he could expect to offer limited, if any, service. As president of the Convention, George Washington had been seated in a Chippendale chair on the top slat of which had been painted a sun (this chair is one of the few original items still on display at Independence Hall). Observing that painters had found it difficult to distinguish a rising from a setting sun, Franklin observed:

> I have . . . often and often in the course of this Session, and the vicissitudes of my hopes and fears as to its issue, looked at that behind the president without being able to tell whether it was rising or setting: But now at length I have the happiness to know that it is a rising and not a setting Sun. (II, 648)

James McHenry of Maryland later reported that Franklin responded to a question by a lady of Philadelphia (a Mrs. Powel) as to what kind of government the Convention had created by saying, "A republic, if you can keep it" (III, 85).

Benjamin Franklin and the Two-Headed Snake

Franklin enjoyed the role of entertaining guests of the Constitutional Convention at his house, and he loved telling stories. Manasseh Cutler, who was not a Convention delegate but who visited Franklin on July 13, 1787, close to the time that the Convention was about to resolve the issue of representation between the large states and the small ones by adopting the Connecticut Compromise, reported that he found Franklin at his residence under the mulberry tree conversing with a number of people. Cutler also related that Franklin had shown him a snake with two heads, which he had preserved, and that his scientific enthusiasm almost caused him to breach Convention secrecy:

> The Doctor mentioned the situation of this snake, if it was traveling among bushes, and one head should choose to go on one side of the stem of a bush and the other should prefer the other side, and that neither of the heads would consent to come back or give way to the other. He was then going to mention a humorous matter that had that day taken place at the Convention, in consequence of his comparing the snake to America, for he seemed to forget that everything in Convention was to be kept a profound secret; but the secrecy of Convention matters was suggested to him, which stopped him, and deprived me of the story he was going to tell. (Farrand 1937, III, 59)

FOR FURTHER READING

Farrand, Max, ed. 1937. *The Records of the Federal Convention.* 4 vols. New Haven, CT: Yale University Press.

The knowledge that Franklin supported the document, like the knowledge that the document had the support of Washington, undoubtedly helped to convince individuals who might be wavering. It was certainly difficult to cast aspersions on a body that had the assent of the two most distinguished men in the hemisphere.

Impact on the Convention

Although Franklin has often been portrayed as an individual who was hobbled by physical illness and whose central ideas were largely rejected by the Convention, his mind remained sharp during the Convention, and he appears to have had a larger influence than is often recognized. Not only did he lend prestige to the event and foster necessary compromises, but many of his ideas were adopted. One study has shown that of 27 recorded proposals that Franklin is known to have introduced or supported, 16 (some of which were later modified or reversed) were approved, only six were rejected, and four were not acted upon (Carr 1990, 131). Franklin made one of his most quoted statements five months before his death when he wrote to Jean Baptiste Leroy, a former French neighbor, and observed: "Our new Constitution is now established and has an appearance that promises permanency; but in this world nothing can be said to be certain except death and taxes" (quoted in Carr, 142).

See Also Albany Plan of Union; Pennsylvania; Prayer at the Convention

FOR FURTHER READING

Carr, William G. 1990. *The Oldest Delegate: Franklin in the Constitutional Convention.* Newark: University of Delaware Press.

Farrand, Max, ed. 1937. *The Records of the Federal Convention.* 4 vols. New Haven, CT: Yale University Press.

Hutson, James H., ed. 1987. *Supplement to Max Farrand's* The Records of the Federal Convention of 1787. New Haven, CT: Yale University Press.

Isaacson, Walter. 2003. *Benjamin Franklin: An American Life.* New York: Simon and Schuster.

Wood, Gordon. 2004. *The Americanization of Benjamin Franklin.* New York: Penguin Books.

FREE-MASONS

See MASONS

FRY, JOSEPH

Records of the Constitutional Convention report that delegates appointed Joseph Fry as the doorkeeper on May 25, the same day that they appointed Nicholas Weaver as a messenger (Farrand 1937, I, 2). Fry received $133.30 for his services ($33.00 more than Weaver), this amount being figured as four months' pay at $400.00 per year (Hutson 1987, 277). Fry is recorded as having been the doorkeeper of the Pennsylvania House of Representatives and as having lived in the West Wing of Independence Hall (Cabinet 2, Drawer 2, Files at the Archives and Library of the Independence Historical National Park, Philadelphia, PA).

Both Fry and Frye appear to have been fairly common names of the period. It is possible that Fry was a military officer who lived from 1711 to 1794, took part in military engagements in 1745 and 1757, was appointed by Congress as a brigadier-general in 1775, and resigned in the spring of 1776 because of ill health (his ill health in 1776 would not necessarily exclude him since he lived for another 18 years, although it seems a bit surprising that if this was the same man, he was not designated by his military title). If so, this individual was born in Andover, Massachusetts, and passed away in Fryeburg, Maine (*Harper's Encyclopaedia*, II, no page number).

The *Pennsylvania Gazette* of June 23, 1768, has a dispatch from Kittery, dated June 2, noting that a Joseph Fry was struck by lightning with several others in a house and that, although he apparently survived, the bolt has "made a breach thro' Mr. Fry['s] clothes on his shoulder the bigness of a dollar, set his shirt on fire, split the seam of his coat, broke some skin on his arm, and left it black, and past into the seam of his breeches, and split it open, marking the same as it went, cut off his garter, tearing his stocking to rags, and leaving a sulphurous matter on it, and taking away one quarter of his shoe, and leaving the like mark all the way" (1768). Ten years later the *Pennsylvania Packet* posted a $6.00 reward by a man named Joseph Fry for "a small dark brown COW, with a slit in one if not both ears." This Fry, who may again not be the man hired by the Constitutional Convention, was listed as living in Loxley Alley, Philadelphia.

Historian Max Farrand cites but does not footnote "a contemporary account of the Convention" that states that "sentries are planted without and within—to prevent any person from approaching near—who appear to be very alert in the performance of their duty" (1913, 58). It seems likely that these "sentries" were Fry and Weaver. Given the press description of them (if indeed these are the men to which the press was referring) as "sentries," it is possible that one or both were in uniform. Both must have been considered extremely trustworthy to be given the opportunity to hear debates that were not accessible to any other nondelegates other than William Jackson, the Convention secretary.

See Also Sentries; Weaver, Nicholas

FOR FURTHER READING

Farrand, Max. 1913. *The Framing of the Constitution of the United States.* New Haven, CT: Yale University Press.

Farrand, Max, ed. 1937. *The Records of the Federal Convention.* 4 vols. New Haven, CT: Yale University Press.

Harper's Encyclopaedia of United States History: From 458 A.D. to 1915. 1915. Ed. Benson John Lossing. New York: Harper and Brothers Publishers.

Hutson, James H., ed. 1987. *Supplement to Max Farrand's* The Records of the Federal Convention of 1787. New Haven, CT: Yale University Press.

The Pennsylvania Gazette, June 23, 1768. http://www.accessible.com/search/fhit.htw?CiWebHitsFile=%Faccessible%2Ftext%2Fga ...

The Pennsylvania Packet. "Six Dollars Reward." December 15, 1778. http://www.accessible.com/search/fhit.htw?CiWebHitsFile=%2Faccessible%Ftext%2Fga ...

FUGITIVE SLAVE CLAUSE

The institution of slavery brought with it measures to secure those who owned them against runaways. Such legislation has a long history that precedes the establishment of the U.S. Constitution (David 1924). Article IV, Section 2 of the Constitution specifies that "No Person held to Service or Labour in one State, under the Laws thereof, escaping into another, shall, in Consequence of any Law or Regulation therein, be discharged from such Service or Labour, but shall be delivered up on Claim of the Party to whom such Service or Labour may be due."

This clause developed out of a discussion of the extradition clause, which directly precedes it. During consideration of that clause on August 28, Pierce Butler and Charles Pinckney, both of South Carolina, moved "to require fugitive slaves and servants to be delivered up like criminals" (Farrand 1937, II, 443). Pennsylvania's James Wilson objected that this would require public expenditures, and New Jersey's Roger Sherman said that he could see "no more propriety in the public seizing and surrendering a slave or servant, than a horse" (II, 443). Butler withdrew his motion in order that it might be treated in a different clause.

The next day Butler introduced a provision that "if any person bound to service or labor in any of the U-States shall escape into another State, he or she shall not be discharged from such service or labor, in consequence of any regulations subsisting in the State to which they escape, but shall be delivered up to the person justly claiming their service or labor," and this was unanimously approved (II, 454). The Committee of Style recommended a provision that "No person legally held to service or labour in one state, escaping into another, shall in consequence of regulations subsisting therein be discharged from such service or labor, but shall be delivered up on claim of the party to whom such service or labour may be due" (II, 601–602). On September 15, this provision was altered by striking the word "legally" and inserting "under the laws thereof" after "State"; Madison explained that this was done "in compliance with the wish of some who thought the term [legal] equivocal, and favoring the idea that slavery was legal in a moral view" (II, 628). Madison's language is not transparent. It *could* mean that delegates were acknowledging the morality of slavery, but it seems, on close reading, to indicate that members of the Convention thought that, by eliminating the word "legal," they were avoiding this implication.

In any event, like other references to the subject in the Constitution, the fugitive slave clause studiously avoided mentioning the word "slave" or "slavery." William Wiecek has further observed that "the clause was drafted entirely in the passive voice, leaving the location of responsibility for its enforcement entirely unclear and ambiguous," and that the clause was included not in Article I, which listed the powers of Congress, but in Article IV, which dealt with interstate relations (1987, 181).

The new Congress adopted a Fugitive Slave Law in 1793. This law became a bitter bone of contention between Northern and Southern states in the time leading up to the Civil War.

See Also African Americans; Extradition; Northwest Ordinance of 1787; Slavery; Three-fifths Clause

FOR FURTHER READING

David, C. W. A. 1924. "The Fugitive Slave Law of 1793 and Its Antecedents." *Journal of Negro History* 9 (January): 18–25.

Farrand, Max, ed. 1937. *The Records of the Federal Convention*. 4 vols. New Haven, CT: Yale University Press.

Morris, Thomas D. 1996. *Southern Slavery and the Law, 1619–1860*. Chapel Hill: University of North Carolina Press.

Wiecek, William M. 1987. "The Witch at the Christening: Slavery and the Constitution's Origins." *The Framing and Ratification of the Constitution.* Leonard W. Levy and Dennis J. Mahoney, eds. New York: Macmillan Publishing, 167–184.

FULL FAITH AND CREDIT CLAUSE

Article IV, Section 1, of the Constitution provides that "Full Faith and Credit shall be given in each State to the public Acts, Records, and judicial Proceedings of every other State. And the Congress may by general Laws prescribe the Manner in which such Acts, Records, and Proceedings shall be proved, and the Effect thereof."

The first sentence of this provision appears to have originated in the report of the Committee of Detail, which was reported to the Convention on August 6. The committee consisted of Nathaniel Gorham of Massachusetts, Oliver Ellsworth of Connecticut, James Wilson of Pennsylvania, Edmund Randolph of Virginia, and John Rutledge of South Carolina, the last of whom served as chair. The committee report provided that "Full faith shall be given in each State to the acts of the Legislatures, and to the records and judicial proceedings of the Courts and Magistrates of every other State" (Farrand 1937, II, 188).

The Convention discussed this provision on August 29. At that time, North Carolina's Hugh Williamson said that he could not understand the meaning of this provision and moved to substitute the words of the Articles of Confederation, which had provided that "Full faith and credit shall be given in each of the states to the records, acts and judicial proceedings of the courts and magistrates of every other state" (Solberg 1958, 43). James Wilson of Pennsylvania and William Johnson of Connecticut said that the provision was intended to indicate that "the Judgments in one State should be the ground of actions in other States, & that acts of the Legislatures should

be included, for the sake of Acts of insolvency &c" (II, 447). Charles Pinckney of South Carolina wanted to add a provision providing for uniform laws on bankruptcies and damages arising "on the protest of foreign bills of exchange" (II, 447). Virginia's James Madison said that "He wished the Legislature might be authorized to provide for the *execution* of Judgments in other States, under such regulations as might be expedient" (II, 448). Indicating that "there was no instance of one nation executing judgments of the Courts of another nation," Randolph proposed sending a much more complicated proposal to committee providing that

Whenever the Act of any state, whether Legislative Executive or Judiciary shall be attested & exemplified under the seal thereof, such attestation and exemplification, shall be deemed in other States as full proof of the existence of that act—and its operation shall be binding in every other State, in all cases to which it may be related, and which are within the cognizance and jurisdiction of the State, wherein the said act was done. (II, 448)

Delegates recommitted these matters to the Committee of Detail. Rutledge presented the committee report to the Convention on September 1, and, with only modest differences (for example, a reference to "the Legislature" rather than to "Congress"), the Convention adopted the current language of both the full faith and credit clause and a provision granting Congress power to establish uniform laws on bankruptcies.

See Also Committee of Detail

FOR FURTHER READING

Farrand, Max, ed. 1937. *The Records of the Federal Convention.* 4 vols. New Haven, CT: Yale University Press.

Solberg, Winton. 1958. *The Federal Convention and the Formation of the Union of the American States.* New York: Liberal Arts Press.

GALLOWAY PLAN

At the First Continental Congress in 1774, Joseph Galloway (1731?–1803) of Pennsylvania introduced a plan of continental government, based in part on Benjamin Franklin's earlier Albany Plan of Union, which was designed to quell the growing conflict between the colonies and the mother country. At the heart of Galloway's plan was a "grand council," or colonial parliament, whose members were to be selected to three-year terms by each of the state legislatures to address interests, like commerce, that the colonies and Britain had in common, but leaving existing state governments in place to legislate on purely local matters. A president general was to be designated to head the grand council and to serve "during the pleasure of the King" (Boyd 1970, 114). Under this plan, Parliament would have to approve all measures of the council.

Although individuals like James Duane, John Jay, and Edward Rutledge praised this plan, others opposed it. Virginia's Patrick Henry, for example, feared that the British king would be able to corrupt this body just as effectively as Henry and other colonials believed that the king had already corrupted the British Parliament. Opponents also disliked the provision that referred to the president general and the grand council as "an inferior and distinct Branch of the British Legislature united and incorporated with it" (Boyd, 114). This plan was tabled by a narrow 6-5 vote (Mid-

dlekauff 1982, 245). The Galloway Plan appears to foreshadow both the U.S. Congress under the Articles of Confederation and the current Constitution and the idea of dividing power between central and state authorities.

Galloway, who remained an English Loyalist, continued to look for a plan that would continue to unite Great Britain and the colonies even after the Revolutionary War began. One such plan proposed establishing an American branch of Parliament. It would have included two houses, the upper house consisting of members appointed by the crown for life (see Schuyler 1942, 282).

New Jersey's William Paterson cited the Galloway Plan on June 9 of the Convention in opposing the Virginia Plan's proposal for representation in both houses of Congress on the basis of state population. Paterson observed that just as granting the colonies 200 of 500 members in Parliament would not have secured colonial liberties, so too, under the Virginia Plan "neither wd. the smaller States be secured in their Liberties" (Farrand 1937, I, 184; see also I, 178–179).

See Also Albany Plan of Union; Franklin, Benjamin; New England Confederation

FOR FURTHER READING

Boyd, Julian B. 1970. *Anglo-American Union: Joseph Galloway's Plan to Preserve the British Empire, 1774–1788.* New York: Octagon Books.

Farrand, Max, ed. 1937. *The Records of the Federal Convention.* 4 vols. New Haven, CT: Yale University Press.

Middlekauff, Robert. 1982. *The Glorious Cause: The American Revolution, 1763–1789.* New York: Oxford University Press.

Schuyler, Robert Livingston. 1942. "Galloway's Plans for Anglo-American Union." *Political Science Quarterly* 57 (June): 281–285.

GENERAL WELFARE CLAUSE

The Preamble of the U.S. Constitution refers to one of the purposes of the new government as that of promoting "the general welfare." The opening provision of Article I, Section 8 further vests Congress with power to "collect Taxes, Duties, Imposts and Excises, to pay the Debts and provide for the common Defence and general Welfare of the United States."

The general welfare provision of this clause has been traced to Delaware's John Dickinson who, borrowing from an earlier proposal by Benjamin Franklin, included a general welfare provision in his draft of the Articles of Confederation. Under this provision, found in Article VII, "All charges of war, and all other expences that shall be incurred for the common defence or general welfare, and allowed by the United States in congress assembled, shall be defrayed out of a common treasury."

On August 18, Dickinson served on an 11-man Committee on State Debts and Militia chaired by William Livingston. That committee proposed on August 21 that

> The Legislature of the U.S. shall have power to fulfil the engagements which have been entered into by Congress, and to discharge as well the debts of the U-S: as the debts incurred by the several States during the late war, for the common defence and general welfare. (Farrand 1937, II, 356)

On August 25, Connecticut's Roger Sherman indicated that he "thought it necessary to connect with the clause for laying taxes duties &c an express provision for the object of the old debts &c—and moved to add 'for the payment of said debts and for the defraying the expences that shall be incurred for the common defence and general welfare'" (II, 414). Defeated on this occasion, Sherman's proposal reemerged from the Committee on Postponed Matters on which he served. The committee, which was formed on August 31, was chaired by New Jersey's David Brearly. On September 4 it reported a provision specifying that "The Legislature shall have power to lay and collect taxes duties imposts & excises, to pay the debts and provide for the common defence & general welfare" (II, 497). The Convention voted to accept this provision on the same day (II, 499; see Hutchison 1975, 98).

According to the report of Maryland's James McHenry, on September 6, Gouverneur Morris of Pennsylvania argued against a provision designed to allow Congress to erect piers to protect winter shipping "and to preserve the navigation of harbours" by saying that he thought Congress could exercise such power under its power to provide for the common defence and general welfare (II, 529). At least one commentator, however, believes that Morris may simply have been saying that such a provision could be placed under this provision within the Constitution (Natelson 2003, 28). This same author doubts the authenticity of a story that in putting the final polish on the Constitution, Morris attempted to substitute a semicolon for a comma in the taxing clause, thus attempting to make the general welfare clause independent of the clause that preceded it (Natelson, 28). If this had been Morris's attempt, it did not succeed.

Commentators generally agree that the general welfare provision is specifically tied to the power to levy taxes and pay the debts rather than intended to serve as a general grant to Congress to do anything it chooses to advance the defense or general welfare. There is continuing dispute, however, as to whether the general welfare provision was intended to be an additional grant of power to Congress, as Alexander Hamilton and Supreme Court Justice Joseph Story later argued—a position the U.S. Supreme Court endorsed in *United States v. Butler,* 297 U.S. 1 (1936)—or whether it was designed to refer, as James Madison later argued, only to the enumerated powers that followed in Article I, Section 8. A recent commentator has even suggested that the provision was intended to be a limit rather than a grant of power (Natelson, 17–20).

See Also Committee on Postponed Matters; Committee on State Debts and Militia; Congress, Power of the Purse; Dickinson, John

FOR FURTHER READING

Farrand, Max, ed. 1937. *The Records of the Federal Convention.* 4 vols. New Haven, CT: Yale University Press.

Hutchison, David. 1975. *The Foundations of the Constitution.* Secaucus, NJ: University Books.

Natelson, Robert G. 2003. "The General Welfare Clause and the Public Trust: An Essay in Original Understanding." *Kansas Law Review* 52 (November): 1–56.

GEOGRAPHY

The geography of North America has significantly influenced U.S. history and the individual states. Numerous debates and decisions at the Constitutional Convention reflected this influence, which continues to this day.

Geography and Revolution

The geography of the New World arguably contributed to the development of liberty. Because the 13 colonies were an ocean away from the mother country, they quickly developed representative institutions whereby they could immediately take care of many of their own affairs, often subject to the eventual approval or disapproval of Britain. Prior to the end of the French and Indian War in 1763, the British furthered this independence through a policy of "salutary neglect," which allowed them to concentrate their attention elsewhere. When the British ended this policy, became more active in American affairs, and asserted their right to tax the colonists, who were not represented in the British Parliament. Thomas Paine was among those who argued, in *Common Sense,* that it was absurd for an island to govern a continent and who feared that continuing association with European nations would involve the American colonies in their wars. Colonists ultimately declared their independence in 1776 and fought a revolutionary war to preserve what they considered to be their liberties. Despite a provision within the Articles of Confederation that would have allowed this, the 13 southern colonies proved unsuccessful in getting Canada to join them.

Although Dutch, Germans, and Swedes had brought their own languages and cultures to the New World, Britain's eventual dominance had contributed to the development of a common mother tongue in the colonies. When the Revolution broke out, the colonists were aided in their fight by the fact that to defeat the colonists, the British had to project their power across an ocean, whereas the colonists only had to avoid allowing Britain to strike a fatal blow. George Washington clearly understood and utilized this dynamic in his role as commander-in-chief of colonial forces, but his efforts at opposing the British were often hindered by congressional weakness and by state jealousies, and he was among those who had awaited the opportunity to create a more effective central government.

The Articles of Confederation

Consistent with the states' separate historical development and their desire to maintain control over their own affairs, the first continental government that the former colonies instituted, the Articles of Confederation, was designed to vest primary sovereignty within the individual states. Although the plan was formulated by the Second Continental Congress in 1777, it was not ratified until 1781, as states (like Maryland) with no western lands waited for states like Virginia to cede

The United States of North America, with the British and Spanish territories according to the treaty of 1784.
Engraving by William Faden. (Library of Congress)

their lands to the national government. Even when ratified, this confederation was in part defective because it did not adequately provide for national regulation of interstate commerce, which would have helped the new nation reap the potential economic results of its large size. Under the Articles, states also continued to coin their own money, and the power of the central government to raise money and recruit armies was largely limited to its power to make requests of the states.

Not surprisingly, leaders doubted that the new nation could adequately defend itself. The outbreak of Shays's Rebellion in the winter of 1786–1787 further seemed to call into question

the ability of some states, especially larger ones like Massachusetts, to keep order within their own territories. States like New York and Georgia could not be sure that the national government would be able to rally sister states to come to their defense in the case of Indian attacks, and Britain (which retained forts in the Northwest Territory), France, and Spain (which controlled modern Florida and lands west of the Mississippi River that it later ceded to France) continued to pose potential threats not only to the nation's hopes of continental expansion but also to its very survival. Americans who had served abroad as diplomats were especially cognizant that other nations were questioning the strength and durability of the government that the onetime colonists had established in North America.

Philadelphia

The Constitutional Convention was held in Philadelphia, then the largest city on the continent (soon to be overtaken by New York City) and the second-most populous (next to London) in an English-speaking country in the world. As a Middle state, Pennsylvania was fairly well centered geographically between the states to the north and the south. Because its port was accessible by sea, Philadelphia's location facilitated maximum participation by the 55 delegates, and especially by the largest delegation from Pennsylvania, all of whose members lived in the city. Founded by William Penn, a Quaker who had sought religious and political freedom, the state had a good record of tolerating rival viewpoints that undoubtedly facilitated freewheeling discussion at the Convention.

Despite its role in hosting the Convention, it was not to become the nation's permanent capital, a role for which a number of states were vying. This capital began in New York, moved to Philadelphia, and then moved again to the District of Columbia, where it remained largely because of its central location relative to the North and South and because of its potential access to the West via the Potomac River. The deal was cemented by a bargain between Southern Republican members of Congress who were willing to allow for federal debt assumption (as Federalists wanted) if the capital were placed near them. At the state level, many states moved their capitals from the coast to more central locations, believing that accessibility to the people was especially important (see Zagarri 1987).

Geographical Issues at the Convention

Twelve of the 13 states (all but Rhode Island), spread up and down the Atlantic Coast from New Hampshire (Maine was not yet a state, and states like Tennessee and Kentucky had not yet been

birthed) to Georgia, sent delegates to the Constitutional Convention. Despite population differences, each state delegation present cast a single vote at the Convention, with equally divided states losing their voice. In the absence of established political parties, state and regional differences often predominated during the Convention debates.

The most contentious issue at the Convention centered on differences between states generally geographically larger, with larger populations, and those generally geographically smaller, with smaller populations—of 3,893,635 persons reported in the first census, populations ranged from a low of 59,094 in Delaware to a high of 747,610 in Virginia, the latter of which included 292,627 slaves. These divisions were represented at the Convention by respective provisions in the Virginia Plan (favoring the large states by calling for proportional representation in both houses of a proposed bicameral Congress) and the New Jersey Plan (favoring equal state representation in a unicameral Congress). This division ultimately led to the Connecticut Compromise whereby states were represented according to population in the U.S. House of Representatives and equally in the U.S. Senate, where each was granted two votes.

A more enduring issue centered on states that permitted slavery and those that did not. This division was increasingly becoming a North-South issue. Representatives of the Deep South states of Georgia and South Carolina were particularly adamant about protecting slavery by permitting the continuing importation of slaves and by providing that slaves would be counted as three-fifths of a person for purposes of representation within the U.S. House of Representatives. Although the majority of the population lived in the Northern states, a number of delegates believed that population trends pointed to future growth in the South and West (Farrand 1937, I, 605).

Contemporaries tended to divide the 13 former colonies into three regions: East (really the Northeast), Middle, and South. Each region had distinct interests that their representatives sought to protect at the Convention. The East, for example, was often associated with fisheries, the Middle states with grain, and the South with slavery and tobacco. In notes that Jared Ingersoll of Pennsylvania prepared for a speech he planned to give on or about June 19, he noted some of the more important regional differences, his emphasis on crops indicating the primarily rural nature of most of the states—the 1790 census indicates that 95 percent of the population was rural (Martis 2001, 155):

> the Fisheries & Manufacturers of New-England, The Flour Lumber Flaxseed & Ginseng of New York New Jersey Pennsylvania & Delaware The Tobacco of Maryland & Virginia the Pitch Tar, Rice & Indigo & Cotton of North Carolina South Carolina & Georgia, can never be regulated by the same Law nor the same Legislature, nor is this diversity by any means confined to Articles of Commerce, at the Eastward Slavery is not acknowledged, with us it exists in a certain qualified manner, at the Southward to its full extent. (Hutson 1987, 103)

Although the nation long remained predominantly rural, statesmen in the early republic debated whether the nation's future was predominately agricultural or mercantile, with Jeffersonian Republicans, who were fearful that city dwellers would not be sufficiently independent, often advocating the former and Hamiltonian Federalists the latter.

Further geographical divisions showed themselves between the Eastern states and potential new states to the west. In part to deter future conflicts with Native Americans, the British had established the Proclamation Line of 1763 to hem in white expansion east of the Appalachian Mountains (Martis, 143), but this line did not stem the tide of western settlers, and the Treaty of Paris which ended the Revolutionary War recognized American claims westward to the Mississippi River. Alerted by the Jay-Gardoqui negotiations, Westerners feared that the new government might bargain away their rights, most notably to navigate the Mississippi River, in exchange for fishing or other rights. Although many of the Eastern delegates feared that a growing number of Westerners might assume the savage qualities that they attributed to their Native American neighbors and overwhelm the interests of representatives from the East, they ultimately provided that

new states from this region would enter the Union on the same basis as those that were already members. Vermont, the first state to be so admitted, had awaited settlement of claims between New York and New Hampshire. Carved from western Virginia, Kentucky entered as the fifteenth state in 1792. Carved from North Carolina, Tennessee became the sixteenth in 1796. Delegates to the Convention provided for the House of Representatives to be reapportioned after each decennial census, thus preventing new states from being held in a position of continuing dependence. The delegates provided that existing states could not be carved up into new states without their consent.

One of the Convention's most important innovations was the system of federalism whereby the delegates divided powers between the national government and the states, in some ways reflecting former divisions between the mother country and the colonies. Modern citizens who are familiar with a nation of 50 states that spreads from coast to coast and beyond sometimes forget that the 13 colonies were already far larger than most European states of the day and that there were genuine concerns, heightened by the primitive conditions of transportation and communication of the time, about whether any centralized authority, especially one that professed to be democratic or republican, could govern over so wide an area. One of the Constitution's most important roles was to establish at least a general framework for relationships between the new national government and the existing states. Answering concerns that had been raised by Antifederalists who had cited the writings of the French philosopher Montesquieu, Virginia's James Madison was among those who argued (most notably in *Federalist* No. 10) that the size of the new nation would better enable it to protect individual liberties by making it less likely that minority factions would dominate than they might do within the states. Others hoped to reserve significant powers to the states in the fear that the national government would be too distant from the people.

The delegates rejected proposals for a plural executive that might internally represent different regions of the country. In part because of concerns that 13 states spread out over such a large territory would be unable to tally ballots effectively and in part because of concerns that individuals within individual states would not adequately know politicians from other parts of the country and states would accordingly vote only for favorite sons, however, the delegates to the Convention established an Electoral College to select the president and vice president. This mechanism provided that electors would nominate two candidates for president, one of whom had to be from a state other than that of the delegate who cast the ballot. Even with this provision, four of the first five presidents hailed from Virginia, the nation's most populous state, which received an additional electoral bonus because of its slaves.

Ratification

Bypassing the requirement under the Articles of Confederation by which constitutional changes had to be adopted unanimously, the Framers specified that the new Constitution would go into effect when affirmatively ratified by conventions within nine or more of the states. Although the small states had been extremely wary of changes that would deprive them of their equal representation within Congress, they largely embraced the Constitution with the adoption of the Connecticut Compromise. With the exception of Rhode Island, most ratified the Constitution fairly quickly, with Delaware being the first to do so. Divisions within states were often as great as the divisions among them. Studies show that Federalists tended to be stronger in commercial centers that would likely benefit from increased national commerce and Antifederalists stronger in the backwaters and frontiers, where people were more suspicious of centralized authority. Although formal constitutional ratification required only nine states, realistically, the new nation could not have made it without the approval of large states like Pennsylvania, Virginia, and Massachusetts, so ratification controversies within these states, which were closely divided, proved especially important.

As it was, North Carolina and Rhode Island did not ratify the Union until it had already gone into effect. The new nation actually had to threaten sanctions against Rhode Island to get it to join.

Subsequent Developments

The nation expanded significantly during its early years, most notably with the acquisition from France in 1803 and later exploration of the Louisiana Territory during the administration of Thomas Jefferson. Adhering to strict constitutional construction, Jefferson believed that this acquisition would most legitimately be made under authority of a constitutional amendment but ultimately decided that the purchase was worth making, with or without explicit constitutional approval. Regional divisions were a major problem during the first 100 years of the nation's history (and included incidents like the Hartford Convention, in which Northeastern states threatened secession during the War of 1812). Divisions between political parties often reflected geographical interests. Ultimately, these divisions resulted in a bitter war between the North and South that ended slavery and reaffirmed the principle that the Union established under the Constitution was designed to be perpetual.

Today the nation has expanded from 13 states to 50. The technology associated with nuclear weapons and delivery systems has arguably deprived it of some of the protection that being an ocean away from Europe and Asia once provided, but this distance still provides some defense against invasion. The idea of the American frontier continued to shape America's self-understanding for generations. Historian Frederick Jackson Turner was among those to emphasize this in the late nineteenth century. In the second half of the twentieth century, President John F. Kennedy would later refer to his own programs as "the New Frontier."

Modern scholars frequently question the effect of the Electoral College, and especially state "winner-take-all" provisions, on state and regional influence within the United States. Questions raised by federalism about the proper relationship between the national government and the states persist into modern times, with the Supreme

Court often arbitrating between state and national claims.

See Also Antifederalists; Articles of Confederation; Canada; Census; Congress, House of Representatives, Representation in; Congress, Senate, Representation in; Connecticut Compromise; District of Columbia; Federalism; Federalists; Foreign Affairs and the Convention; France; Great Britain; Land Disputes; Mississippi River; Parties, Factions, and Interests; Philadelphia; Population of the United States; President, Selection; Ratification in the States; Revolutionary War; Sectionalism; Slavery; Spain; States, Admission and Creation; Territory of the United States; Three-fifths Clause

FOR FURTHER READING

Davis, Joseph L. 1977. *Sectionalism in American Politics, 1774–1787.* Madison: University of Wisconsin Press.

Greene, Jack P. 1986. *Peripheries and Center: Constitutional Development in the Extended Politics of the British Empire and the United States, 1607–1788.* Athens: University of Georgia Press.

Linklater, Andro. 2002. *Measuring America: How the United States Was Shaped by the Greatest Land Sale in History.* New York: Plume.

Martis, Kenneth C. 2001. "The Geographical Dimensions of a New Nation, 1780s–1820s." In Thomas F. McIlwraith and Edward K. Muller, eds. *North America: The Historical Geography of a Changing Continent.* 2nd ed. Lanham, MD: Rowman and Littlefield Publishers.

Ohline, Howard A. 1972. "Republicanism and Slavery: Origins of the Three-fifths Clause in the United States Constitution." *William and Mary Quarterly,* 3rd ser. 18 (October): 563–584.

Onuf, Peter S. 1986. "Liberty, Development, and Union: Vision of the West in the 1780s." *William and Mary Quarterly,* 3rd Ser. 53 (April): 179–213.

Zagarri, Rosemarie. 1987. *The Politics of Size: Representation in the United States, 1776–1850.* Ithaca, NY: Cornell University Press.

GEORGIA

The last of the 13 states to have been settled (James Oglethorpe had established it in 1732),

Georgia started as a charter colony but became a royal colony in 1754 with the arrival of the first British governor. He worked with a council that the Crown appointed and an assembly that the voters elected. In contrast to other colonies, the British paid the governor directly so that he did not need to depend on appropriations by the assembly for his salary.

Political and Constitutional Situation

Georgia did not elect delegates to the First Continental Congress, but a state provisional congress sent delegates to the second such Congress and adopted a temporary constitution for the state in April 1776. The president of this government called for a state constitutional convention, which met in October 1776 and wrote a constitution, which the Convention adopted in February 1777.

This constitution provided for a governor and executive council, a chief justice and a unicameral legislature called the House of Assembly (Pennsylvania was the only other state with such a unicameral body). White Protestant property owners elected members of the Assembly annually. The governor could serve no more than one year in any three-year period. He was required to heed the council in carrying out his responsibilities, and although he had the power to issue temporary reprieves, he did not have the power to veto legislation. The constitution protected individual rights but had a weak judiciary, with the chief justice serving for annual terms and associate justices serving at the good graces of the Assembly.

Georgia was known for deep sectional divisions between the upper and lower parts of the state. Led by Savannah, the lower portion of the state relied on commerce and looked eastward whereas the upper portion, represented by Augusta, looked westward. Western forces had largely dominated the state since the time of the American Revolution. They had little regard for the rights of Loyalists, who were more respected on the coast, leading to continual conflicts. In 1786, the legislature moved the state capital permanently to Augusta (it had previously alternated between there and Savannah) and issued paper money, which quickly declined in value and which Eastern merchants were rightfully disinclined to accept.

The British captured Savannah in December 1778 and reinstituted Sir James Wright as the royal governor, but this government disintegrated, and the Constitution of 1777 came back into effect with the British evacuation of the state in July 1782. The Assembly quickly proclaimed that the state boundaries extended to the Mississippi River and began a policy of western expansion, fueled by the promise of free land to settlers, that brought the state into constant conflict with Native Americans, particularly the Creeks.

Georgia sometimes appeared to be part of the Articles of Confederation in name more than in fact. Although the state delegates signed on to the Articles in July 1778, it often ignored congressional requests and rarely sent more than two delegates, often leaving the state completely without representation. Initially rejecting the call for the Convention issued by the Annapolis Convention, the state relented after receiving a letter from Virginia's Edmund Randolph.

Representation and Discussion at the Constitutional Convention

Abraham Baldwin, William Few, William Pierce, and William Houston represented Georgia at the Constitutional Convention, but Pierce and Houston left early, and only Baldwin and Few signed the document. Nathaniel Pendleton and George Walton were selected but did not serve. Three of the four delegates who attended were lawyers; Pierce was a merchant. None of the four delegates contributed to Convention deliberations in a particularly outstanding way. The better-known and more vocal delegates from South Carolina did far more of the work in representing the interests of the Deep South states and, especially, their interests in the perpetuation of slavery.

Although it was not, at the time of the Convention, one of the most populous states, Georgia continued to aspire to this status and its delegates believed its western lands, and its rapid growth in population, gave it the potential for being one. Delaware's Gunning Bedford thus observed on June 30 that although Georgia "is a small State at present, she is actuated by the prospect of soon being a great one" (Farrand 1937, I, 491). Similarly, Maryland's Luther Martin explained Georgia's alliance with the large states in supporting the Virginia Plan by observing that

> Georgia has the most extensive territory in the Union, being larger than the whole island of Great Britain, and 30 times as large as Connecticut. This system being designed to preserve to the States their whole territory unbroken, and to prevent the erection of new States within the territory of any of them, Georgia looked forward when, her population being increased in some measure proportioned to her territory, she should rise in the scale, and give law to the other States, and hence we found the delegation of Georgia warmly advocating the proposition of giving the States unequal representation. (Quoted in III, 187)

Georgia's allocation of three seats in the initial House of Representatives appears to have been based as much on the state's future prospects as on its present population (see I, 562). As a state that looked westward, Georgia was especially concerned about having a national government that could protect it from the Indians and that could guarantee its access to the Mississippi River, access that had been threatened by the proposed Jay-Gardoqui negotiations of 1786.

The Georgia government was mentioned at least twice at the Convention, and both mentions were negative. James Madison observed on July 17 that one reason his proposed congressional negative of state laws was needed was that state courts could not be expected to protect national interests. One evidence he cited for this was the fact that the Georgia state legislature appointed such judges annually (II, 28). Similarly Georgia's own William Houston expressed concern on July 18 about the provision whereby Congress would guarantee existing state governments. He observed that he "was afraid of perpetuating the existing Constitutions of the States. That of Georgia was a very bad one, and he hoped [it] would be revised & amended" (II, 48).

Ratification of the Constitution

Georgia ratified the Constitution with a dispatch hindered only by the fact that, because of its geographical location, it had taken longer than most states to be informed of the new document. The state legislature was in session when the news arrived. At the time, the state was troubled by disputes between the eastern and western parts of the state over conflicts with Alexander McGillivray, a Creek chief who was refusing to agree to a treaty ceding lands coveted by the state. The state legislature called for elections for a convention. That convention met in August beginning on Saturday, December 28. It considered the document for a day, recessed on Sunday, unanimously adopted the document the following Monday, and signed a formal resolution to this effect on January 2. Georgia thereby became the fourth state (and the first in the South) to ratify the Constitution.

Georgia's haste in ratifying the U.S. Constitution appears primarily to have stemmed from its hope that a strengthened national government could help it secure itself from the Indians, on whose land it was continually encroaching, and negotiate favorably with the Spanish who controlled the Mississippi River. These concerns were especially prominent in the western part of the state where republican-minded politicians with their suspicions of centralized authority might otherwise have been expected to oppose the new government.

Georgia and the New Government

Many of the delegates who served at the ratifying convention were also at the convention that revised the Georgia state constitution beginning on November 4, 1788. The convention is notable for patterning the new constitution on that of the United States. Perhaps most notably, it created a general Assembly with a senate and house of representatives in place of its previous unicameral legislature. It also adopted a mechanism for representing counties similar to that incorporated into the Great Compromise and increased the powers of the governor to issue pardons and to veto legis-

lation. It other ways the new constitution also appeared to reflect the interests of the eastern part of the state.

Although the new government provided greater security, western supporters of the new government quickly became disillusioned when they discovered that it did not always uphold its land claims in disputes with Native Americans. After ratification of the new Constitution, Georgia quickly asserted its sovereignty against the new government. George Washington was alleged to have asserted that "the United States are at peace with all the world except the state of Georgia" (quoted in Jensen 1978, 211). In actions that eventually led to the Eleventh Amendment, securing immunity of states against suits by citizens of other states, Georgia resisted paying debts it had incurred during the Revolutionary War. Georgia's continuing fascination with western lands was also reflected in an early contract case, *Fletcher v. Peck*, 10 U.S. (6 Cranch) 87 (1810), in which Chief Justice John Marshall refused to uphold a revocation of a large land grant by Georgia by a subsequent legislature.

See Also Baldwin, Abraham; Few, William; Houston, William; Indians; Mississippi River; Pierce, William

FOR FURTHER READING

Abbott, William W. 1957. "The Structure of Politics in Georgia: 1782–1789." *William and Mary Quarterly*, 3rd ser. 14 (January): 47–65.

Cashin, Edward J. 1989. "GEORGIA: Searching for Security." In Michael Allen Gillespie and Michael Lienesch, eds. *Ratifying the Constitution*. Lawrence: University Press of Kansas.

Farrand, Max, ed. 1937. *The Records of the Federal Convention*. 4 vols. New Haven, CT: Yale University Press.

Griffin, J. David. 1977. *Georgia and the United States Constitution, 1787–1789*. Georgia Commission for the National Bicentennial Celebration and Georgia Department of Education.

Jensen, Merrill, ed. 1978. *Ratification of the Constitution by the States Delaware, New Jersey, Georgia, Connecticut*. Vol. 3 of *The Documentary History of the Ratification of the Constitution*. Madison: State Historical Society of Wisconsin.

GERMANY

Although Germans from Hesse-Cassel and other regions had fought as mercenaries against the former colonies during the American Revolution (Ingrao 1982), numerous Germans had settled in America (Weaver 1957, 538 says that there were more than 100,000 Germans in colonial Pennsylvania alone), Baron von Steuben (1730–1794) had come to America where he helped bring discipline to the U.S. forces during the Revolution and remained in the United States as a citizen, and many German intellectuals had been sympathetic to the American cause (Douglass 1960). Led by Benjamin Franklin, in 1785 America had negotiated a highly successful trade treaty with Prussia (Reeves 1917), the dominant German state in the remains of the old Holy Roman Empire, which dated back to Charlemagne in A.D. 800 and to Otto I, king to the Germans, crowned in Rome in A.D. 962 and which technically lasted until Napoleon defeated it in 1804. Americans correctly viewed Germany as a confederation of principalities rather than a modern nation state (see Reeves). Delegates made about a dozen recorded references to Germany at the Constitutional Convention of 1787. It served, like ancient Greek leagues, Holland, and the Swiss cantons, as a point of a largely cautionary reference for delegates concerned about foreign influences on state governments and groping for a new federal system.

On June 18, New York's Alexander Hamilton referred to the German Diet as an example of a confederacy that exercised power over individuals (Farrand 1937, I, 283). Going all the way back to the heyday of the Holy Roman Empire, he further observed that, although Charlemagne appeared to have exercised necessary power, "The great feudal chiefs . . . exercising their local sovereignties, soon felt the spirit & found the means of, encroachments, which reduced the imperial authority to a nominal sovereignty" (I, 285). On that same day, he cited the German empire as an example of a nation where "Electors & Princes, who have equal motives & means, for exciting cabals & parties" (I, 290) selected the monarch.

On June 19, Virginia's James Madison cited the Germanic League both as an example of the "ten-

dency of the parts to encroach on the authority of the whole" (I, 317) and as an example of the interferences or "intrigues" by foreign powers (I, 319; also see notes for a speech by John Dickinson, June 30, Hutson 1987, 138). He further cited the German empire, along with the Amphyctionic League, as an example of the danger of allowing the national government to use force against individual states (I, 320).

On June 20, Pennsylvania's James Wilson attributed the German confederacies "to the influence of the H. of Austria" (I, 343). Like Madison, he used this illustration in a group that included the Amphyctionic, the Achaean, and other such leagues.

On June 25, South Carolina's Charles Pinckney distinguished the situation of the U.S. from that of "the unwieldy, unmeaning body called the Germanic Empire" (I, 402). On June 28, James Madison argued that "The contentions, not the combinations of Prussia & Austria, have distracted & oppressed the Germanic empire" (I, 448). He further argued that "the lesser States in the German Confederacy" "are exceedingly trampled upon and . . . owe their safety as far as they enjoy it, partly to their enlisting themselves, under the rival banners of the preeminent members, partly to alliances with neighbouring Princes which the Constitution of the Empire does not prohibit" (I, 449). On June 30, Madison further cited the German example in which states were not equally representing, observing that "the K. of Prussia has nine voices" (I, 485).

On July 5, Pennsylvania's Gouverneur Morris cited Germany as exhibiting "the melancholy picture of foreign intrusions" (I, 530). On July 7, Morris further cited Germany as an illustration of the need to consider fair representation in national counsels. He observed that

Germany alone proves it. Notwithstanding their common diet, notwithstanding the great prerogatives of the Emperor as head of the Empire, and his vast resources as sovereign of his particular dominions, no union is maintained: foreign influences disturbs every internal operation, & there is no energy whatever in the general Governmt. (I, 552)

Asking, "Whence does this proceed?", Morris responded: "From the energy of the local authorities; from its being considered of more consequence to support the Prince of Hesse, than the Happiness of the people of Germany" (I, 552).

Madison further cited Germany, with Poland, as an example of the danger of allowing the national legislature to choose the executive. He observed that, in Germany, "the election of the Head of the Empire, till it became in a manner hereditary, interested all Europe, and was much influenced by foreign interference" (II, 109–110).

A study of the Founders' treatment of the Netherlands has demonstrated that it served chiefly as "an Awful Example" (Riker 1957, 513) of dangers that the proponents of the new Constitution were attempting to avoid. Germany appears to have served as a similar example, and it is possible that the Framers' understanding of Germany was just as incomplete as that of Holland.

See Also Achaean League; Amphictyonic League; Federalism; Holland; Swiss Cantons

FOR FURTHER READING

Douglass, Elisa P. 1960. "German Intellectuals and the American Revolution." *William and Mary Quarterly,* 3rd ser. 17 (April): 200–218.

Farrand, Max, ed. 1937. *The Records of the Federal Convention.* 4 vols. New Haven, CT: Yale University Press.

Hutson, James H., ed. 1987. *Supplement to Max Farrand's* The Records of the Federal Convention of 1787. New Haven, CT: Yale University Press.

Ingrao, Charles. 1982. "'Barbarous Strangers': Hessian State and Society during the American Revolution." *American Historical Review* 87 (October): 954–976.

Reeves, Jesse S. 1917. "The Prussian-American Treaties." *American Journal of International Law* 11 (July): 475–510.

Riker, William H. 1957. "Dutch and American Federalism." *Journal of the History of Ideas* 18 (October): 495–521.

Umbach, Maiken. 1998. "The Politics of Sentimentality and the German Furstenbund, 1779–1785." *The Historical Journal* 41(3): 679–704

Weaver, Glenn. 1957. "Benjamin Franklin and the Pennsylvania Germans." *William and Mary Quarterly,* 3rd ser. 14 (October): 536–559.

GERRY, ELBRIDGE
(1744–1814)

Elbridge Gerry was born in Marblehead, Massachusetts, to Thomas and Elizabeth Greenleaf Gerry in 1744. His father was a merchant who had immigrated from England. Members of the local clergy educated Gerry before he attended and graduated from Harvard College in 1762, after which he joined his father's business.

Gerry became involved in the U.S. Revolution, becoming friends with Samuel Adams, serving on Marblehead's Committee of Correspondence, writing the Essex Resolves, chairing the Massachusetts Committee of Supply, and serving in the Second Continental Congress, where, however, he attended sporadically after his conduct was criticized in 1779 and 1780. Gerry became further involved in developing the Northwest Territory, and in attempts to reduce the nation's standing army and to abolish the Society of the Cincinnati (Bradford 1981, 7). Gerry developed a reputation for honesty and a distaste for either pure popular democracy or rule by elites.

Although he had signed both the Declaration of Independence and the Articles of Confederation, Elbridge Gerry of Massachusetts was one of three men who remained at the Constitutional Convention on September 17, 1787, and refused to sign the document, but his opposition could not have come as much of a surprise to those who listened to him closely. On May 30, just one day after his arrival, Gerry observed that it was necessary to distinguish "between a *federal* and *national* government" (Farrand 1937, I, 42). He observed that if the Convention were intending to pursue the latter option, it might be exceeding its commission, since, by his understanding Congress had commissioned the Convention with the understanding that it would operate agreeably to its recommendations. Throughout the Convention, Gerry was continually concerned not simply about what proposals were best but about which such proposals the people were likely to accept. Although he professed to be wary of direct democracy, as much as any delegate, he appears to have been guided by his view of what the public wanted.

Elbridge Gerry, delegate from Massachusetts
(Pixel That)

Congress

Selection of Members

James Madison, the putative author of the Virginia Plan, argued that it was essential for the people to elect members of at least one branch of Congress. By contrast, Gerry said that "he did not like the election by the people" (I, 50). He did not think that the people actually trusted the legislators that they elected, although he had no objection if the people's election was so restrained "that men of honor & character might not be unwilling to be joined in the appointments" (I, 50). He suggested that this might be accomplished by allowing the people to make nominations from which the Senate would choose.

By June 6, Gerry appears to have changed his position somewhat. He feared that the U.S. was running into an excess of democracy and indicated that the people in his home state of Massachusetts had recently selected some individuals of the legislature who had been convicted of crimes. Opposed to both monarchy and aristocracy, he now acknowledged that "It was necessary . . . that

the people should appoint one branch of the Govt. in order to inspire them with the necessary confidence" (I, 132). He apparently hoped that such a popular house could be balanced by another house chosen (as the Senate was initially to be) by the state legislatures thereof from nominees suggested by the people. Interestingly, Gerry indicated during this speech that "He was not disposed to run into extremes" (I, 132). On June 7, after reviewing four methods that delegates had proposed for selecting senators, Gerry again recommended that this be done by state legislatures, adding to earlier arguments the hope that "The elections being carried thro' this refinement, will be most likely to provide some check in favor of the commercial interest agst. the landed; without which oppression will take place, and no free Govt. can last long when that is the case" (I, 152). Later that day, Gerry observed that the people were more likely to favor schemes for paper money than the legislatures. He also argued that using interstate districts to select members of the Senate was impractical, would work against the small states, and would increase tensions within the districts themselves (I, 155).

Apportionment of Representation

On June 11, Gerry indicated that he opposed considering property in apportioning congressional representation. He wondered why blacks "who were property in the South" should be entitled to any more representation "than the cattle & horses of the North" (I, 201). On June 13, Gerry opposed allowing the Senate to originate money bills. He observed that "The other branch was more immediately the representatives of the people, and it was a maxim that the people ought to hold the purse-strings" (I, 233).

On July 2, Gerry was one of the delegates who favored committing the issue of representation within Congress to a committee (I, 515). The fact that Gerry was not only appointed to this committee (the only one on which he served during the Convention) but selected as its chair indicated that fellow delegates probably considered him to be one of the more moderate members in respect to this issue. Gerry delivered the committee report on July 5. It recommended granting states one representative for every 40,000 persons in the lower house, with each state having at least one vote. It further provided that bills "for raising or appropriating money, and for fixing the Salaries of the Officers of the Governt. of the U. States shall originate in the 1st branch of the Legislature, and shall not be altered or amended by the 2d branch" and that states would have an equal vote in the Senate (I, 526).

In responding to a question about the report, Gerry indicated that the conditions were meant to be mutually reinforcing and that "Those opposed to the equality of votes have only assented conditionally; and if the other side do not generally agree will not be under any obligation to support the Report" (I, 527). Gerry later indicated that "tho' he had assented to the Report in the Committee, he had very material objections to it." He believed however that compromise was necessary if "secession" were to be avoided (I, 532). Gerry disfavored splitting the large states. In what may have represented some backtracking in regard to slave representation, however, on July 6, he indicated that he was willing that representation "ought to be in the Combined ratio of number of Inhabitants and of wealth, and not of either singly" (I, 541). On July 11, he supported counting blacks as three-fifths of a person for purposes of representation rather than counting them equally (I, 580). He subsequently favored using this same formula for both taxation and representation (I, 601; also see II, 275, and II, 350).

Gerry had previously favored restricting the origination of money bills to the House, and he continued to insist that this was a vital part of the compromise his committee had offered. Acknowledging on July 6 that we "would not say that the concession was a sufficient one on the part of the small States," he said that "he could not but regard it in the light of a concession. It wd. make it a constitutional principle that the 2d. branch were not possessed of the Confidence of the people in money matters, which wd. lessen their weight & influence" (I, 545). By July 14, Gerry was describing this measure as "the corner stone of the accommodation" (II, 5).

Gerry indicated, however, that the "critical question" decided by the committee was to grant states equal representation in the Senate (I, 550). Professing to favor a motion by South Carolina's Charles Pinckney giving states from 2 to 5 senators based on their populations, Gerry did not think this could be accomplished at the Convention (II, 5). Engaged in something of a chicken-or-egg debate (which should come first?) with Virginia's James Madison, Gerry indicated that he thought "it would be proper to proceed to enumerate & define the powers to be vested in the Genl. Govt. before a question on the report should be taken as to the rule of representation in the 2d. branch" (I, 551). Gerry did favor allowing senators to vote individually, rather than by state delegation, as a way of preventing "the delays & inconveniences that had been experience in Congs." (II, 5).

Length of Terms

Consistent with the republican ideology of his day, Gerry favored annual elections for members of the House of Representatives. He argued that such elections were widely favored in the East and constituted "the only defence of the people agst. tyranny" (I, 214–215). Madison said that the delegates should do what they considered best and not worry overmuch about public opinion. Gerry responded that by such reasoning the delegates might establish a limited monarchy, even though they knew that "the genius of the people was decidedly adverse to it" (I, 215).

Representation of Western States

Gerry was among the delegates to the Convention (Gouverneur Morris was another) who feared the dangers posed by admitting new states from the West. Saying on July 14 that "He was for admitting them on liberal terms," he indicated that he was "not for putting ourselves into their hands" (II, 3). Reasoning that, like other men, they would abuse power if they had it and "will oppress commerce, and drain our wealth into the Western Country," he proposed limiting the number of new states "in such a manner, that they should never be able to outnumber the Atlantic States" (II, 3).

Qualifications

Gerry favored excluding public debtors for election to office. Moreover, he favored a property qualification in the belief that "if property be one object of Government, provisions for securing it can not be improper" (II, 123). He observed that, without qualifications, "we might have a Legislature composed of public debtors, pensioners, placemen & contractors" (II, 125).

Gerry was similarly concerned about foreigners. He wanted to restrict future eligibility to Congress to natives lest foreign governments conspire to influence U.S. policies (II, 268).

Powers and Limits

As a merchant, Gerry was unwilling to trust Congress with the power to tax imports. He argued that "It might ruin the Country. It might be exercised partially, raising one and depressing another part of it" (II, 307). Gerry's view of the powers of Congress was related to his concern for states' rights. He indicated that Congress could use a power over exports "to compel the States to comply with the will of the Genl Government, and to grant it any new powers which might be demanded" (II, 362). He feared that the national government might become as oppressive over state governments as Great Britain had been over Ireland (II, 362).

Gerry proposed adding the power to Congress of establishing post roads, as well as post offices (II, 308). He believed that the Constitution should grant the power of concluding peace through treaties to the entire Congress rather than to the Senate, which he believed would be more subject to corruption (II, 319). Gerry later argued that the Senate should have to vote for treaties of peace by larger majorities since there was a greater danger that such treaties would sacrifice "the extremities of the Continent . . . than on any other

occasions" (II, 541). He also continued to fear that the Senate would be subject to foreign influence (II, 548). Gerry joined South Carolina's John Rutledge in proposing that two-thirds of the senators should have to approve all treaties (II, 549). Gerry thought that Congress should have power over public securities and that it should be given specific power to issue letters of marque (II, 326).

Although the notes are arguably subject to different interpretations, Gerry apparently indicated on August 21 that he thought states should retain both the power and the responsibility to pay off their debts. He believed this was needed to provide for the security of existing "public creditors," focusing on both "the merit of this class of citizens, and the solemn faith which had been pledged under the existing Confederation" (II, 356). Gerry believed that if Congress assumed these obligations, the states that had already paid off most of their debts "would be alarmed, if they were now to be saddled with a share of the debts of States which had done least" (II, 356). However, on August 22, Gerry indicated that he favored some explicit constitutional statement regarding fulfillment of existing obligations "so that no pretext might remain for getting rid of the public engagements" (II, 377). Observing on August 25 that "as the public had received the value of the literal amount, they ought to pay that value to some body," he expressed sympathy for those who had to sell their securities at a discount, and said that "If the public faith would admit, of which he was not clear, he would not object to a revision of the debt so far as to compel restitution to the ignorant & distressed, who have been defrauded" (II, 413). On this occasion, he made a rare stand on behalf of stock-jobbers—often derided at the time by republican spokesmen who associated them with "corruption"—who he observed "keep up the value of the paper" and without whom "there would be no market" (II, 413).

Gerry did not believe that it was the business of Congress to interfere with state control over slaves, but he indicated that he thought the delegates should "be careful not to give any sanction to" slavery (II, 372). Gerry favored provisions prohibiting Congress from adopting bills of attainder or ex post facto laws (II, 375). In an argument that was almost the inverse of Madison's approach, Gerry thought that such provisions were more necessary at the national than at the state level since there would be fewer legislators in Congress than in the states, and they were therefore more to be feared (II, 375). Gerry later indicated that he also favored extending the ban on ex post facto laws to civil as well as criminal cases (II, 617).

By the end of the Convention, Gerry was becoming more and more suspicious of the government that the Constitution was creating. When the Convention was considering a resolution to grant Congress power over places purchased for forts and the like, Gerry objected that Congress might attempt to use this power to "enslave any particular State by buying up its territory, and that the strongholds proposed would be a means of awing the State into an undue obedience to the Genl. Government" (II, 510).

Other Legislative Matters

Gerry disfavored allowing members of Congress to accept any offices during their terms or for a year afterward. He feared that "it would produce intrigues of ambitious men for displacing proper officers, in order to create vacancies for themselves" (I, 388). Gerry expounded at length on this subject on August 14. He argued that reposing confidence in legislators, rather than tying them down by law, "is the road to tyranny" (II, 285). He feared that if the Senate were responsible for appointing ambassadors, as was then being considered, "they will multiply embassies for their own sakes" (II, 285). Gerry observed that "If men will not serve in the Legislature without a prospect of such offices, our situation is deplorable indeed. If our best Citizens are actuated by such mercenary views, we had better chuse a single despot at once. It will be more easy to satisfy the rapacity of one than of many" (II, 285). Gerry had apparently become increasingly concerned that the Senate as it had been constituted was too aristocratic, and he did not think the people would tolerate this (II, 286). On September 3, Gerry indicated that if members of Congress were eligible for existing offices they would use their power to drive existing

officeholders away to make way for themselves (II, 491).

In the discussion of the length of Senate terms, Gerry favored terms of four or five years. He observed that less than one in a thousand persons in the United States favored monarchy. Acknowledging Madison's observation that the majority would violate justice when it had an incentive to do so, Gerry had hopes that "there would be a sufficient sense of justice & virtue for the purpose of Govt." (I, 425).

When the Convention proposed that the initial House of Representatives should consist of 65 members, Gerry indicated that he favored more. He thought that there would be less chance of corrupting a larger body. Consistent with his emphasis elsewhere at the Convention on popular opinion, Gerry also believed that "The people are accustomed to & fond of a numerous representation, and will consider their rights as better secured by it" (I, 569).

Gerry favored allowing members of the Senate to vote "per capita," or individually, rather than as a delegation. On July 14, he thus observed that this "would prevent the delays & inconveniences that had been experienced in Congs. and would give a national aspect & Spirit to the management of business" (II, 5). The Convention accepted this idea on July 23 (II, 95).

Gerry favored allowing Congress to set the initial quorum for the House of Representatives somewhere between 33 and 50, out of the initial 65 seats (II, 253). Possibly with a view to the Senate's anticipated role in foreign affairs, he thought there were occasions when the Senate should not be required to publish its proceedings (II, 255–256). However, he later favored publication of all proceedings in the House of Representatives (II, 613).

Gerry saw difficulties in whether members of Congress collectively set their own salaries or whether the states set their salaries. He observed that state legislatures might attempt to turn their senators out of office by reducing their salaries (II, 291).

Gerry disfavored requiring three-fourths majorities in Congress to override a presidential veto. He feared that this would grant too much power to too few senators who might combine with the president "and impede proper laws" (II, 586). He argued that this likelihood was increased by the role of the vice president as president of the Senate.

Presidency

Council

Gerry indicated on June 1 that he favored "annexing a Council [to the Executive] in order to give weight & inspire confidence" (I, 66). Consistent with his opposition to combining the executive and members of the judiciary in a Council of Revision, however, Gerry said that he disfavored "letting the heads of the departments, particularly that of finance have any thing to do in business connected with legislation. He mentioned the Chief Justice also as particularly exceptionable" (II, 329). Gerry reasoned that judges would have too many judicial duties to accept others.

Selection

On June 2 Gerry indicated that he opposed legislative selection of the president as likely to lead to "constant intrigue" (I, 80). In theory he liked the idea of an Electoral College, but he feared that "it would alarm & give a handle to the State partisans, as tending to supersede altogether the State authorities" (I, 80). It sounds, however, as though Gerry was less concerned about the prospect of abolishing the states than about the fact that he did not think the states were yet ready for such a step, and he wanted to wait until the people would "feel more the necessity of it" (I, 80). He continued to oppose direct elections even of electors, suggesting this time that the legislatures might nominate electors and let them make the choice (I, 80). On June 9, Gerry suggested a plan whereby state governors would choose the president. He observed that "the Executives would be most likely to select the fittest men, and that it would be their interest to support the man of their own choice" (I, 176).

Gerry offered a variant of this proposal on July 19. Vigorously opposing allowing presidential reeligibility if he were to be chosen by Congress, he also continued to oppose popular election as vesting selection in individuals who were uninformed and "would be misled by a few designing men" (II, 57). He suggested that state governors should choose the electors who would choose the president. This plan would have the advantage of attaching state governments more strongly to the Union. He reiterated that "The popular mode of electing the chief Magistrate would certainly be the worst of all" (II, 57; also see II, 100 and II, 109). He subsequently supported a plan whereby state legislators would choose 25 electors, who would select the president (II, 58; also see II, 63 for breakdown as to how these electors would be allocated). Gerry also proposed that presidential electors should neither be officeholders nor eligible for the presidency themselves (II, 69; also see II, 521). On September 5, Gerry recommended that in cases when no individual got a majority of the Electoral College six senators and seven members of the House of Representatives chosen by a joint ballot should be entrusted with the eventual selection of the president (II, 514). Gerry strongly opposed allowing the Senate, rather than the Congress as a whole, to select presidents in cases when no candidate got an Electoral College majority (II, 522).

Other Executive Matters

Gerry opposed a tripartite executive. He believed that it would be inconvenient, especially in military matters. He likened such an executive to "a general with three heads" (I, 97). When Pierce Butler of South Carolina suggested that the executive should have the power to suspend legislation for a time period still to be ascertained, Gerry observed that such a power "might do all the mischief dreaded from the negative of useful laws; without answering the salutary purpose of checking unjust or unwise ones" (I, 104).

Gerry favored an impeachment mechanism for presidents. He observed that "A good magistrate will not fear them. A bad one ought to be kept in fear of them" (II, 66). He further thought this was a way of establishing the principle that the U.S. did not agree that the president could do not wrong (II, 66). Gerry seconded a motion by Virginia's George Mason to extend the grounds of impeachment of the president to "maladministration," a motion that Mason subsequently withdrew in place of "other high crimes and misdemeanors" (II, 550), the current constitutional language.

Gerry opposed allowing the vice president to preside over the Senate. He feared that the president and vice president would be too intimate. Gerry, who would later serve in this position under the presidency of James Madison, actually opposed having a vice president at all (II, 536–537).

Presidential Term

Vigorously opposed to presidential selection by Congress, Gerry said that it would be better to give the president a term of 10, 15, or 20 years than to make the executive dependent on this branch (II, 102). He specifically proposed a 15-year term (II, 102). He later supported a motion offered by South Carolina's Charles Pinckney limiting the president to six years of service out of every 12 years (II, 112). Gerry continued to oppose popular election. Identifying this mechanism as "radically vicious," he feared that it would give power to groups like the Society of the Cincinnati to "elect the chief Magistrate in every instance, if the election be referred to the people" (II, 114).

Gerry strongly opposed a motion that would allow the president power to declare war. He believed this to be inconsistent with government "in a republic" (II, 318).

Judiciary

Although he had favored an Executive Council, Gerry opposed joining the executive with members of the judiciary in a Council of Revision as James Madison had proposed. Gerry believed that judges would already have the ability to void legislation that was unconstitutional (the power now known as judicial review) in their capacity as judges, and thought that this power was far different from that of making members of the judiciary "judges of the policy of public measures" (I, 98). He also questioned giving so great a control over a body–the Congress–that he anticipated would consist of "the best men in the Community" (I, 98). Later arguments indicate that Gerry might have shared in a suspicion of judges as a group. He thus observed on June 6 that "the Executive, whilst standing alone wd. be more impartial than when he cd. be covered by the sanction & seduced by the sophistry of the Judges" (I, 139).

Gerry reiterated this view on July 21, when he opposed reconsideration of the Council of Revision. His critique of this proposal indicated that he viewed the judicial function as distinct from that of the other two branches:

> The motion was liable to strong objections. It was combining & mixing together the Legislative & the other departments. It was establishing an improper coalition between the Executive & Judiciary departments. It was making Statesmen of the Judges; and setting them up as the guardians of the Rights of the people. He relied for his part on the Representatives of the people as the guardians of their Rights & interests. It was making the Expositors of the Laws, the Legislators which ought never to be done. (II, 75; also see II, 298)

Gerry suggested that the Convention might follow the example of Pennsylvania and appoint an individual skilled in drafting laws to aid the legislature (II, 75). He indicated, however, that he would prefer investing the president with an absolute veto rather than mix the powers of the two departments together in what might become "an offensive and defensive alliance agst. the Legislature" (II, 78).

Gerry opposed a plan whereby the president would appoint judges with two-thirds of the Senate having the power to block such appointments. He did not believe that this plan as constructed would satisfy either the people or the states. He feared that the president would not be as informed of candidates throughout the Union as would members of the Senate, and he argued that appointments under the Articles of Confederation had been generally good (II, 82). On September 7, Gerry reiterated his view that the responsibility expected from presidential appointments would be "chimerical" since the president could not possibly know everyone he appointed, and he could "always plead ignorance" (II, 539).

On August 27, Gerry seconded a motion offered by Delaware's John Dickinson, which would have arguably undercut judicial independence. It would have allowed the president to remove judges on an application by Congress (II, 428). On September 12, Gerry advocated guaranteeing the right to jury trials in civil cases. He thought such juries were a necessary guard against "corrupt Judges" (II, 587). This was one of the reasons that Gerry made the proposal, seconded by Virginia's George Mason, on behalf of adding a bill of rights (II, 588). Somewhat later, he joined South Carolina's Charles Pinckney in advocating that a provision be added "that the liberty of the Press should be inviolably observed" (II, 617). Gerry favored putting the same restraints on congressional interference with the obligations of contracts as had been imposed on the states (II, 619).

Federalism

Gerry opposed Madison's proposal to allow Congress to veto state laws. Gerry observed that he "cd. not see the extent of such a power, and was agst. every power that was not necessary" (I, 165). He suggested that Congress could remonstrate against state laws that it disapproved and could, if necessary, use force (I, 165). He feared that such a negative would extend to regulation of the militia, which he thought the states should control. He further observed: "The States too have different interest and are ignorant of each other's interests. The negative therefore will be abused. New States too having separate views from the old States will never come into the Union" (I, 166). On August 18, Gerry renewed his opposition to granting Congress control over state militia. He observed that such a decision would give the

Constitution "as black a mark as was set on Cain." He further observed that "He had no such confidence in the Genl. Govt. as some Gentlemen possessed, and believed it would be found that the States have not" (II, 332). Again on August 232, Gerry said that he would just as soon see the citizens of his state disarmed "as to take the command from the States, and subject them to the Genl Legislature." He observed that this "would be regarded as a system of Despotism" (II, 385). He further asked whether anyone would think their liberty as secure "in the hands of eighty or a hundred men taken from the whole continent, as in the hands of two or three hundred taken from a single State" (II, 386). When the Convention was debating whether state or national governments should appoint officers of the militia Gerry "warned the Convention agst pushing the experiment too far." He explained that "Some people will support a plan of vigorous Government at every risk. Others of a more democratic cast will oppose it with equal determination. And a Civil war may be produced by the conflict" (II, 388).

On June 11, Gerry illumined his view of the relation between the nation and the states when he opposed requiring state officials to support the national constitution. He argued that "there was as much reason for requiring an oath of fidelity to the States, from Natl. officers, as vice versa" (I, 203). When the Convention adopted a proposal on July 23 requiring that state officials pledge to uphold the national Constitution, Gerry successfully proposed that national officials should have to take the same oath (II, 87).

By contrast, Gerry's speech on June 29 appeared quite nationalistic. Then observing that "The States & the advocates for them were intoxicated with the idea of their *sovereignty*," Gerry indicated that he thought the Articles were dissolving. He further "lamented that instead of coming here like a band of brothers, belonging to the same family, we seemed to have brought with us the spirit of political negociators" (I, 467).

When the Convention discussed the possibility of allowing Congress to send troops into a state even without its request, Gerry showed considerable agitation. He said that he was "agst. letting loose the myrmidons [warriors] of the U. States on a State without its own consent" (II, 317). With an eye to his own state, he argued that more blood would have been shed during Shays's Rebellion had the general government intervened.

Standing Armies

On August 18, Gerry rose to express his concern that the Constitution did not prohibit standing armies in times of peace. Referring, as he so frequently did, to public opinion, Gerry observed: "The people were jealous on this head, and great opposition to the plan would spring from such an omission" (II, 329). He clearly agreed with what he considered to be public sentiment and suggested that a limitation to 3,000 men under arms might be appropriate in peacetime (II, 329–330).

On September 5, Gerry tied his fear of standing armies in peacetime to his concern that military appropriations could be made for two-year periods. Again, he argued that "The people would not bear it" (II, 509). He subsequently argued for annual publication of all public expenditures (II, 618).

Gerry may have been an intense man, but he was not without a sense of humor. He is reported to have likened a standing army to an organ of the male anatomy with similar properties. He observed that such a standing organ was "an excellent assurance of domestic tranquility, but a dangerous temptation to foreign adventure" (quoted in Isaacson 2003, 456).

Other Matters

On August 20, Gerry opposed authorizing Congress to establish sumptuary laws regulating food and clothing purchases and the like. He argued quite practically that "the law of necessity is the best sumptuary law" (II, 344).

Amendment and Ratification

Gerry indicated on June 5 that he favored including an amending process in the Constitution. He

observed both that "the novelty & difficulty of the experiment requires periodical revision" and that "the prospect of such a revision would also give intermediate stability to the Govt." (I, 122). He further thought that state experience confirmed the utility of such mechanisms.

On September 10, Gerry moved for a reconsideration of the amending clause. He feared that the provision whereby two-thirds of the states could request that Congress call a convention to propose amendments might be used to allow a majority of a convention "which can bind the Union to innovations that may subvert the State-Constitutions altogether" (II, 557–558). He subsequently seconded a motion by Connecticut's Roger Sherman allowing Congress to propose amendments, which would not go into effect until the states ratified them (II, 558).

Consistent with his distrust of election of governmental officials, Gerry said on June 5 that he feared allowing the people to ratify the Constitution. He observed that the people, at least those he knew in the Eastern states, had "the wildest ideas of Government in the world" (I, 123). He cited the desire of the people of Massachusetts to abolish the state Senate and give all power to the more popular house. On July 23, Gerry reiterated his opposition to submitting ratification of the Constitution to the people:

> Great confusion he was confident would result from a recurrence to the people. They would never agree on any thing. He could not see any ground to suppose that the people will do what their rulers will not. The rulers will either conform to, or influence the sense of the people. (II, 90)

On August 31, Gerry indicated that he did not think the Articles of Confederation could be dissolved except by "the unanimous Consent of the parties to it," by which he referred to the state government thereof (II, 478). He further observed on September 10 that "If nine out of thirteen can dissolve the compact, Six out of nine will be just as able to dissolve the new one hereafter" (II, 561). He thus seconded Alexander Hamilton's motion to send the Constitution first to Congress

Gerry the Lightweight

Elbridge Gerry was among the delegates to the Constitutional Convention who had been a strong supporter of independence from Great Britain. Gerry was a small wiry man sometimes likened to one of the seabirds that were so common in his hometown of Marblehead, Massachusetts. When the two were signing the Declaration of Independence, the more corpulent Benjamin Harrison of Virginia had engaged in some true "gallows humor" with Gerry by remarking that "I shall have a great advantage over you, Mr. Gerry, when we are hung for what we are doing. From the size and weight of my body I shall die in a few minutes, but from the lightness of your body you will dance in the air an hour or two before you are dead" (cited in Billias 1990, 68). Although Gerry chose not to sign the Constitution, his willingness to sign the Declaration is an indication that his refusal to sign was not from any fear of personal consequences but from heartfelt concern about a number of perceived problems with the new document, including the absence of a bill of rights. After the Constitution was ratified, Gerry went on to serve as a two-term governor of Massachusetts and as vice president of the United States in the administration of James Madison.

FOR FURTHER READING

Billias, George Athan. 1990. "Elbridge Gerry." *Constitution* 2 (Spring-Summer): 68–74.

and then to the states, which would have authority to determine whether they were willing to join the new Union only when nine other states so consented (II, 562). Gerry proposed a change in the amending clause that required Congress to call a convention on the application of two-thirds of the states (II, 629). He was not successful, however, in striking a provision (only used to date in the case of the Twenty-first Amendment overturning national alcoholic prohibition) allowing amendments to be ratified by special state ratifying conventions.

Gerry's Decision Not to Sign

On September 15, Gerry presented eight reasons why he had decided not to sign the Constitution; most were issues on which he had previously taken positions. These included "the duration and re-eligibility of the Senate;" "the power of the House of Representatives to conceal their journals;" congressional control over "the places of election;" congressional power to set their own salaries; inadequate representation for the state of Massachusetts; representation of blacks according to the three-fifths ratio; his fear that Congress might use its power over commerce to establish monopolies; and his objection to the vice president's role in presiding over the Senate. He indicated that these objections would not alone have been sufficient for him to withhold his signature:

> If the rights of the Citizens were not rendered insecure 1. by the general power of the Legislature to make what laws they may please to call necessary and proper. 2. raise armies and money without limit. 3. to establish a tribunal without juries, which will be a Star-chamber as to Civil cases. (II, 633)

He indicated that, under the circumstances, he favored calling a second convention (II, 633).

Two days later Gerry alluded to "the painful feelings of his situation and the embarrassment under which he rose to offer any further observations" (II, 646). He feared that the nation was headed toward civil war. He observed that there were two parties within his own home state, "one devoted to Democracy, the worst he thought of all political evils, the other as violent in the opposite extreme" (II, 647). He had hoped that the Constitution might have been proposed "in more mediating shape" but assured delegates that "if it were not otherwise apparent, the refusals to sign should never be known from him" (II, 647).

Life after the Convention

Despite his opposition to the Constitution, Gerry also feared domestic strife. Once the states had ratified the Constitution, he joined other Antifederalists in deciding to accept it and to continue to push for amendments protecting individual rights. Massachusetts elected Gerry to the first Congress under the new Constitution; Gerry defeated fellow delegate Nathaniel Gorham in this election.

Gerry served as a presidential elector for John Adams in 1797, but subsequently lost favor with Adams after he pursued a pro-French policy as one of three U.S. emissaries to France (the others were John Marshall and Charles Cotesworth Pinckney) to be caught up in the so-called XYZ Affair, in which the Americans turned aside French attempts to bribe them. Gerry continued to stay in France to negotiate after his colleagues had left. Later serving as an elector for Thomas Jefferson in the election of 1804, he was selected in 1810 as the governor of Massachusetts. The term "gerrymandering" (referring to drawing district lines for partisan advantage) grew from this time period when a district that Gerry designed so as to favor his own party was shaped so bizarrely that it was likened to a salamander. Gerry served briefly as vice president under James Madison before passing away in 1814.

See Also Antifederalists; Committee of Compromise on Representation in Congress; Massachusetts

FOR FURTHER READING

Billias, George Athan. 1990. "Elbridge Gerry." *Constitution* 2 (Spring-Summer): 68–74.
——. 1976. *Elbridge Gerry: Founding Father and Republican Statesman.* New York: McGraw Hill.
Bradford, M. M. 1981. *Founding Fathers: Brief Lives of the Framers of the United States Constitution.* 2nd ed. Lawrence: University Press of Kansas.
Farrand, Max, ed. 1937. *The Records of the Federal Convention.* 4 vols. New Haven, CT: Yale University Press.
Isaacson, Walter. 2003. *Benjamin Franklin: An American Life.* New York: Simon and Schuster.
Morison, S. S. 1929. "Elbridge Gerry, Gentleman-Democrat." *The New England Quarterly* 2 (January): 6–33.

GILMAN, NICHOLAS (1755–1814)

Nicholas Gilman was born in Exeter, New Hampshire in 1755 to a family that had long-established roots within the state. His father was a relatively wealthy merchant who had served in the French and Indian War. Gilman served in the Revolutionary War and rose to the rank of assistant adjutant general. He inherited a sizeable estate when his father died in 1783, the same year Gilman helped found the Society of the Cincinnati. Regarded as a handsome man, Gilman was a lifelong bachelor who devoted much of the rest of his life to politics. From 1786 to 1788, Gilman represented New Hampshire in the Congress under the Articles of Confederation, and he was among those who voted to forward the Constitution to the states for approval.

Nicholas Gilman and fellow delegate John Langdon did not arrive at the Constitutional Convention to represent New Hampshire until July 23, a week after the delegates had resolved the issue of representation. Arguably, his attendance did not make much difference. Although Gilman was one of the signers of the Constitution, he is not recorded as having made a single comment during Convention deliberations.

After the Convention, Gilman served for eight years in the U.S. House of Representatives, where he established a reputation as a Democratic-Republican. During this time, he made only one recorded speech (Saladino 1999, 9: 62). Although he had stepped down from office, Gilman sup-

Nicholas Gilman, delegate from New Hampshire
(Pixel That)

Nathaniel Gorham, delegate from Massachusetts
(Pixel That)

ported John Langdon, his fellow delegate from New Hampshire to the Constitutional Convention, in the 1805 race for New Hampshire, who succeeded in winning over Gilman's elder brother. The New Hampshire legislature subsequently appointed Gilman to the U.S. Senate where he served until his death in Philadelphia in 1814. Although he had initially supported Thomas Jefferson's administration, Gilman turned against Jefferson and his successor James Madison and opposed both the embargo against England and the War of 1812.

See Also New Hampshire

FOR FURTHER READING

Saladino, Garpare J. 1999. "Gilman, Nicholas." In John A. Garraty and Mark C. Carnes, eds. *American National Biography.* New York: Oxford University Press, 9: 62–63.

GORHAM, NATHANIEL (1738–1796)

Born in Charlestown, Massachusetts, in 1738, the son of a packet boat operator, Nathaniel Gorham was apprenticed to a Connecticut merchant before opening his own merchant house. He began attending the Constitutional Convention on May 28, the day after his forty-ninth birthday, having stayed in New York for a time to help keep the Congress, of which he was president, running. Gorham was a successful merchant who had served his state and nation. Previous positions had included a stint from 1771 to 1775 in the Massachusetts legislature, service from 1774 to 1775 in the Massachusetts Provincial Congress, participation in the Massachusetts Constitutional Convention of 1779–1780, and two periods of service in the Congress under the Articles of Confederation. Gorham was extremely concerned about Shays's Rebellion within Massachusetts and wrote to Prussia's Prince Henry to see if he might be willing to serve as a U.S. king if the rebellion spread and the nation decided on a monarchy (Lettieri 1999, 9, 306).

Likely because of the prominence he had achieved in Congress, the Convention chose Gorham on May 30 by a 7-1 vote to chair the Committee of the Whole at the Convention. He served in this role through June 19, taking a position at the front of the Convention that George Washington otherwise occupied. Perhaps as a consequence, Gorham's first recorded comments at the Convention were not made until June 22 during a discussion of congressional salaries. From that time forward, he participated in Convention discussions on a fairly regular basis. In addition to chairing the Committee of the Whole, Gorham served on the Committee on Original Apportionment of Congress, which the Convention created on July 6, on the important Committee of Detail that the Convention formed on July 24, and on the Committees on Commercial Discrimination and on Interstate Comity and Bankruptcy that the delegates created on August 25 and 29.

Congress

Salaries of Members

Gorham opposed allowing the states to set the salaries of members of Congress. He observed that the state legislatures "were always paring down salaries in such a manner as to keep out of offices men most capable of executing the functions of them" (Farrand 1937, I, 372). He further opposed specifying this salary in the Constitution, "because we could not venture to make it as liberal as it ought to be without exciting an enmity agst. the whole plan" (I, 372). He favored allowing Congress to "provide for their own wages from time to time; as the State Legislatures do" (I, 372). Gorham opposed a motion that would require that members of both houses be paid the same. He pointed out that senators would need more since members "will be detained longer from home, will be obliged to remove their fami-

lies, and in time of war perhaps to sit constantly" (II, 293).

Eligibility for Other Offices

Gorham opposed a motion that would have prevented members of the House of Representatives from being ineligible to offices during their tenure and for one year after as "unnecessary & injurious" (I, 375). He later argued that "the eligibility was among the inducements for fit men to enter into the Legislative service" (II, 491).

Representation

On June 25, Gorham indicated that he favored a compromise in the representation of the small states and the large ones. He observed that in his state of Massachusetts, the large counties were not given representation "in an exact ratio to their numbers," and he expressed the view that a similar approach might be "expedient" in regard to Congress (I, 405).

On June 29, Gorham made a strong speech directed to the small states urging them to consider the price of disunion. He observed that the smaller states would be far less capable of taking care of themselves in such a situation than the large ones. He observed that Delaware would lie at the mercy of Pennsylvania and that New Jersey would suffer from its lack of commerce. He also anticipated that the large states were through growing and might, like Massachusetts—which anticipated that Maine would become independent—split (I, 462–463). He concluded that "a Union of the States [was] as necessary to their happiness, & a firm Genl. Govt. as necessary to their Union" (I, 463). On July 6, Gorham repeated the idea that it would be good for the larger states to split, in which case their representation in Congress should be reduced. He favored a strong national government, and thought that a further division of the states would help accomplish this goal:

> He conceived that let the Genl. Government be modified as it might, there would be a constant

tendency in the State Governmts. to encroach upon it: it was of importance therefore that the extent of the States shd. be reduced as much & as fast as possible. The stronger the Govt. shall be made in the first instance the more easily will these divisions be effected; as it will be of less consequence in the opinion of the States whether they be of great or small extent. (I, 540)

On July 6, the delegates appointed Gorham to the second of three committees designed to examine representation in Congress. This committee, chaired by Gouverneur Morris of Pennsylvania, proposed on July 9 a House of 56 members apportioned according to wealth and numbers (roughly one representative for every 40,000 inhabitants), with the number of representatives reapportioned to states if they broke up (I, 559). In explaining this plan, Gorham observed that "The number of blacks & whites with some regard to supposed wealth was the general guide" (I, 559). His explanation indicated that he must have shared Morris's reluctance to grant equal representation to equal numbers of persons in the Western states. Gorham thus observed that "the Atlantic States having ye. Govt. in their own hands, may take care of their own interest, by dealing out the right of Representation in safe proportions to the Western States" (I, 560). By July 11, Gorham indicated that if the current Convention were perplexed as to how to apportion new states, the new government "under the full biass of those views" would be even more so; he thus favored fixing a standard (I, 583).

Gorham had earlier indicated his support for the three-fifths clause as a provision "fixed by Congs. as a rule of taxation" and as "pretty near the just proportion" (I, 580). He continued to support this provision on July 11. Acknowledging that the people of the Eastern states might take some "umbrage" to allowing slaves to count as three-fifths of a person, he observed that when Massachusetts considered this proportion under the Articles of Confederation, "the only difficulty then was to satisfy them that the Negroes ought not to have been counted equally with whites instead of being counted in the ratio of three fifths only" (I, 587).

It would appear that Gorham did not have particularly strong views against slavery. On August 25, Gorham seconded a motion by South Carolina's Charles Cotesworth Pinckney to extend the time that states could import slaves from 1800 to 1808 (II, 415). When Connecticut's Roger Sherman objected that allowing a duty on slaves implied that they were property, Gorham preferred a more positive interpretation. Such duties were simply to be regarded "as a discouragement to the importation of them" (II, 416).

The committee that reported the compromise granting differential modes of representation in the House and Senate also proposed barring the Senate from proposing money bills. Gorham indicated his agreement with this compromise on August 8 (II, 224) and again on August 13 (II, 297).

One of Gorham's more fascinating statements was made in the context of the formula for representation in the U.S. House of Representatives. When Madison objected that apportioning the House according to the rule of one for every 40,000 inhabitants would one day result in a House that was too big, Gorham said that "It is not to be supposed that the Govt will last so long as to produce this effect?" He openly questioned: "Can it be supposed that this vast Country including the Western territory will 150 years hence remain one nation?" (II, 221).

Long after the Convention had settled on a formula for representation in the two houses and John Rutledge and Roger Sherman opposed a joint ballot for selecting the president, Gorham indicated that he thought the delegates were focusing too much on who the respective houses were representing:

> It was wrong to be considering, at every turn whom the Senate would represent. The public good was the true object to be kept in view— Great delay and confusion would ensue if the two Houses shd vote separately, each having a negative on the choice of the other. (II, 402)

On the last day of the Convention, Gorham was the delegate who proposed that his colleagues should change representation from a minimum of one representative for every 40,000 inhabitants to one for every 30,000 (II, 643–644). Significantly, this motion proved the occasion for one of only two recorded speeches by George Washington—in favor of Gorham's proposition, which then passed unanimously.

Number of Senators

Gorham favored granting each state two rather than three senators. He feared that a larger number of senators would find it difficult to decide on matters of peace and war. He also anticipated that new states would enter the Union and that existing states would split. As on other occasions at the Convention, Gorham observed that "The strength of the general Govt. will lie not in the largeness, but in the smallness of the States" (II, 94).

Western Lands

Gorham, who spent much of his life speculating in Western lands, did not favor including an adjustment of Western land claims within the new Constitution. He believed that Congress was already working on the subject and that "The best remedy would be such a Government as would have vigor enough to do justice throughout" (I, 405). He argued that such a strengthened government would give the smaller states their "best chance" at justice (I, 405).

Terms

On June 25 Gorham proposed a four-year term for senators (I, 408). On June 26, he proposed to lengthen this to a six-year term (I, 421)—the solution that the Convention ended up adopting. Both proposals were even numbers, allowing for equal numbers of terms to end each year.

Powers

Perhaps with a view to the disturbances that had rocked Massachusetts during Shays's Rebellion, Gorham thought that the national government needed to have power to quash rebellions within the states. He observed that if the government did not have this power, "an enterprising Citizen might erect the standard of Monarchy in a particular State, might gather together partisans from all quarters, might extend his views from State to State, and threaten to establish a tyranny over the whole & the Genl. Govt. be compelled to remain an inactive witness of its own destruction" (II, 48). Acknowledging that individuals should be able to say what they wanted, he said that "If they appeal to the sword it will then be necessary for the Genl. Govt., however difficult it may be to decide on the merits of their contest, to interpose & put an end to it" (II, 48).

Pointing to the British experience, Gorham also believed that Congress should have the power to regulate elections (II, 240). Gorham feared that requiring a majority for a quorum in each house would lead to unnecessary delays.

Gorham favored striking a provision allowing Congress to emit bills of credit, but he also opposed specifically prohibiting such bills (II, 309). He later argued that "an absolute prohibition of paper money would rouse the most desperate opposition from its partisans" and favored simply prohibiting states from issuing such money without congressional consent (II, 439). At a time when the Convention was suggesting that Congress should appoint the national treasurer, Gorham proposed that this should be done by joint ballot rather than by the houses jointly (II, 314; also see II, 615). Gorham also moved to grant Congress power not only to "raise" but also to "support" armies (II, 329). Gorham supported the provision granting Congress power to make uniform laws regarding bankruptcies and legislating in regard to damages arising "on the protest of foreign bills of exchange" (II, 447).

Gorham did not see any need for a requirement that two-thirds of Congress should have to consent to navigation acts. He may have ruffled some feathers when on August 22 he observed that "the Eastern States had no motive to Union but a commercial one. They were able to protect themselves. They were not afraid of external danger, and did not need the aid of the Southn. States" (II, 374).

The next day, Gorham joined Virginia's James Madison in opposing a provision whereby treaties would have to be ratified by law—apparently by both houses. He observed that it would be difficult to get such previous ratification, which would make it difficult for American diplomats (II, 392). Somewhat later in the day, however, he said that "it is necessary to guard against the Government itself being seduced" (II, 393).

On August 29, Gorham again opposed a two-thirds requirement for navigation bills. Once again, he wondered what motives this would give the Eastern states to join the Union. Although "he deprecated the consequences of disunion," he believed that the South would lose the most in such circumstances. He said that it was improbable that the Northern states would combine against those of the South (II, 453).

Gorham did not see any necessity for allowing two-thirds of the Senate to make peace treaties without presidential consent. He observed that Congress would already have control over the "means of carrying on the war" (II, 540; also see II, 549).

Other Matters Related to Congress

Gorham preferred to allow Congress to adopt legislation to prevent abuses by debtors and others who might get elected to office in order to advance their own individual interests rather than to rely on property qualifications for members of Congress or those who elected them (II, 122). He thought a provision barring members with "unsettled accounts" from running from office would unfairly fall on "the commercial & manufacturing part of the people" (II, 125). On August 8, he opposed a freehold requirement for voting, observing that merchants and mechanics were just as qualified as small landowners. Moreover, "The people have been long accustomed to this right in various parts of America, and will never allow it to be abridged. We must consult their rooted prejudices if we expect their concurrence in our propositions" (II, 216). Similarly, Gorham opposed applying durational citizenship requirements on immigrants retroactively: "When foreigners are naturalized it wd. seem as if they stand on an equal footing with natives" (II, 270).

Gorham thought that requiring the nation to establish a capital in a place other than a city with an existing state capital could be evaded by a congressional refusal to construct buildings elsewhere (II, 127). Gorham believed that the Constitution should specify the meeting time for Congress to avoid future disputes on the subject. He observed that the New England states had fixed such times, and that "no inconveniency had resulted" (II, 198). He believed that state legislatures should meet at least once each year.

On August 10, Gorham opposed a provision that would have allowed a single member of Congress to ask for a roll-call vote. Based on his experience with such a mechanism in Massachusetts, he observed that members "stuffed the journals" with such requests and that "they are not proper as the reasons governing the voter never appear along with them" (II, 255).

Presidency

When the Convention discussed a provision whereby Congress would select the president, Gorham wanted Congress to act by joint ballot. He thought that separate ballots would lead to "great delay, contention & confusion" (II, 196). Acknowledging that a joint ballot would advantage the larger states, he thought this was preferable to disturbing the public tranquillity.

Once the Convention established the Electoral College mechanism, Gorham said that he did not want the vice presidency going to the person with the second-highest number of votes unless that individual had a majority. Otherwise, he feared that the office might go to "a very obscure man" (II, 499). He did not, however, believe that a supermajority should be required for the presidential office (II, 526–527).

Judiciary

On July 18, Gorham proposed that the president should appoint members of the judiciary with the advice and consent of the Senate. Gorham said that this measure, which was the eventual plan on which the Convention settled, "had been long practiced" in Massachusetts (he later claimed the practice had been in effect for 140 years [II, 44]) "& was found to answer perfectly well" (II, 41). He defended this plan by saying that the president would look as widely as the Senate for judges, and that senators would be more likely to be attached to the seat of government and, as a public body, to "give full play to intrigue & cabal" (II, 42). He observed that if senators "can not get the man of the particular State to which they may respectively belong, they will be indifferent to the rest" (II, 42). He further observed that "The Executive would certainly be more answerable for a good appointment, as the whole blame of a bad one would fall on him alone" (II, 43).

Gorham observed that national courts already operated in the states to deal with matters of piracy and commerce. He believed that "Inferior tribunals are essential to render the authority of the Natl. Legislature effectual" (II, 46).

On July 21, Gorham opposed allying the judges with the executive in a Council of Revision. He observed that "As Judges they are not to be presumed to possess any peculiar knowledge of the mere policy of public measures. Nor can it be necessary as a security for their constitutional rights" (II, 73). His solution was "to let the Executive alone be responsible, and at most to authorize him to call on Judges for their opinions" (II, 73). Later in the day, Gorham observed that "the Judges ought to carry into the exposition of the laws no prepossessions with regard to them" (II, 79). He also feared that the judges would outweigh the executive in number and that "instead of enabling him to defend himself" they "would enable the Judges to sacrifice him" (II, 79).

In a discussion of judicial oaths, Gorham did not think they were particularly effective, but he sought to rebut the argument that such oaths would inhibit constitutional change. He opined that "A constitutional alteration of the Constitution, could never be regarded as a breach of the Constitution, or of any oath to support it" (II, 88).

On August 24, Gorham indicated that he favored keeping a mechanism similar to that under the Articles of Confederation for resolving disputes among the states to granting this power to the Courts. He feared that such judges might be connected to the states that had claims in such cases (II, 401).

On September 12, Gorham joined delegates who believed that it was impossible to specify conditions within the Constitution where civil juries should be required from cases where they would not be (II, 587). Such reservations were among the reasons that the Convention decided not to add a bill of rights.

Ratification

On July 23, Gorham used five different arguments to oppose allowing the existing Congress and state legislatures to ratify the new Constitution. He argued first that members chosen specifically for the purpose of ratifying a Constitution would discuss the matter more candidly than those who stood to gain or lose power. He next observed that most state legislatures had two houses, both of which would have to approve. He further noted that some state legislatures excluded members of the clergy who were "generally friends to good Government" (II, 90). He observed that legislatures would have plenty of other business, by which "designing men" would "find means to delay from year to year" (II, 90). Finally, he noted the unlikelihood of getting unanimous state consent, especially when Rhode Island had not even sent delegates to the Convention and New York was enjoying commercial advantages under the existing system (I, 90). Such arguments must have come with particular force from a man who was president of the Congress under the Articles of Confederation.

Gorham reiterated his support for ratification of the Constitution by state conventions on August 31 (II, 476). He opposed a measure by Alexander Hamilton of New York that would have left it to the states to decide how many consenting votes should be necessary for the new Union. He feared that "the different and conditional ratifications will defeat the plan altogether" (II, 560).

Life after the Convention

Gorham was selected as a member of the Massachusetts ratifying convention but he lost a bid to be elected to the new Congress to Elbridge Gerry, who had refused to sign the document. Gorham subsequently became involved in a massive land deal involving over six million acres. This led to his financial ruin and may have hastened his death, by apoplexy, on June 11, 1796.

See Also Committee of the Whole; Committee on Interstate Comity and Bankruptcy; Committee on Original Apportionment of Congress; Massachusetts

FOR FURTHER READING

Farrand, Max, ed. 1937. *The Records of the Federal Convention.* 4 vols. New Haven, CT: Yale University Press.
Lettieri, Ronald J. 1999. "Gorham, Nathaniel." In John A. Garraty and Mark C. Carnes, eds. *American National Biography.* New York: Oxford University Press, 9: 306–307.
Whitney, David C. 1974. *Founders of Freedom in America: Lives of the Men Who Signed the Constitution of the United States and So Helped to Establish the United States of America.* Chicago: J. J. Ferguson Publishing.

GOVERNORS, STATE

Under the British, the Crown had designated individuals who served as state governors and represented the Crown's interest in the colonies. Upon independence, states generally continued with some executive authority who thus served as one model for the presidency. A number of delegates to the Constitutional Convention either had served, were serving, or would go on to serve as state governors, or presidents (the designation was not, at the time, uniform).

Opinion leaders in 1787 generally agreed that the state constitutions under the Articles generally did not accord sufficient authority to the executives (who were generally dominated by the state legislatures), but some states, most notably New York and Massachusetts, had taken steps to strengthen this office. The delegates to the Convention discussed state governors in a number of contexts.

Governors and the Electoral College

One such context involved the possibility of using such governors to select the chief executive. Elbridge Gerry of Massachusetts announced his intention to introduce such a motion on June 7 (Farrand 1937, I, 149), and he did so two days later (I, 175). At a time when the Convention was contemplating congressional selection of the president, Gerry argued that his proposal would be a way of freeing the executive from undue dependence on the legislature. He further "supposed the Executives would be most likely to select the fittest men, and that it would be their interest to support the man of their own choice" (II, 176). By contrast, Virginia's Edmund Randolph thought that state executives would be "little conversant with characters not within their own small spheres," that they would be too much influenced by their state legislatures, and that they would prefer in-state favorites (I, 176). Perhaps most tellingly, he argued that "They will not cherish the great Oak which is to reduce them to paltry shrubs" (II, 176). The Convention defeated Gerry's proposal by a vote of 9-0, with the state of Delaware divided on the matter (I, 176). Gerry later reintroduced his suggestion on July 25, at which time he suggested that state councils or "Electors chosen by the Legislatures" could aid governors in their selection of the president (II, 109). Virginia's James Madison objected that "An appointment by the State Executives, was liable among other objections to this insuperable one, that being standing bodies, they could & would be courted, and intrigued with by the Candidates, by their partizans, and by the Ministers of foreign powers" (II, 110). The invention of the Electoral College made such a plan unnecessary but did not exclude gubernatorial candidates. Since 1976, four governors (Jimmy Carter, Ronald Reagan, Bill Clinton, George W. Bush) have served as president.

Filling Congressional Vacancies

Two provisions in the Constitution relate to congressional vacancies. Article I, Section 2 provides that "the Executive Authority" within each state shall issue writs of elections to fill vacancies in the House of Representatives. Article I, Section 3 further allows the president to make temporary appointments to the Senate until the legislature meets to fill such vacancies (the Seventeenth Amendment modified this to reflect the time of the next general election). These provisions emerged from the report of the Committee of Detail, which it submitted to the Convention on August 6 (II, 179).

On August 9, Pennsylvania's James Wilson opposed allowing governors to fill vacancies in the Senate. He stated a number of objections:

> It was unnecessary as the Legislatures will meet so frequently. It removes the appointment too far from the people; the Executive in most of the States being elected by the Legislatures. As he had always thought the appointment of the Executives by the Legislative department wrong: so it was still more so that the Executive should elect into the Legislative department. (II, 231)

Virginia's Edmund Randolph responded that such appointments were required in order "to prevent inconvenient chasms in the Senate," especially in those states where the legislature met only once a year. Oliver Ellsworth of Connecticut further observed that when the legislature was meeting, it could make the appointments on its own. North Carolina's Hugh Williamson pointed out that senators might resign their posts or refuse to accept them, and the Convention thus voted not to strike the provision for executive appointments of vacancies (II, 231). There does not appear to be a corresponding discussion of the provision related to members of the House, probably because the terms were much shorter. The terrorist attacks of September 11, 2001, on domestic targets have recently renewed concerns about whether the provision for filling vacancies in the U.S. House of Representatives would be adequate in the case of mass vacancies (Vile 2003, 89–91).

Presidential Correspondence with State Executives

The Committee of Detail suggested that the president should have power to correspond with state executive officials (II, 185). The Convention struck this provision by a 9-1 vote on August 25 after Gouverneur Morris of Pennsylvania, seconded by Delaware's Jacob Broom, argued that the provision was unnecessary and would falsely imply "that he could not correspond with others" (II, 419).

Prior to the time the Convention entrusted state boundary disputes to the judicial branch, the Committee of Detail also proposed that state governors should memorialize the Senate to deal with such problems (II, 183–184). Any such role that state governors would play today would be the result of being parties to lawsuits.

Auxiliary Role in Appointment Power

When debating appointments of federal officials on August 24, Delaware's John Dickinson proposed that the Constitution might vest some appointments either in state legislatures or state executives (II, 406). The delegates rejected the motion after Gouverneur Morris said: "This would be putting it in the power of the States to say, 'You shall be viceroys but we will be viceroys over you'" (II, 406).

Provisions against Domestic Insurrections

Article IV, Section 4 of the Constitution provides that the United States shall protect states against domestic violence upon the application of the state legislature or the state executive. This provision originally provided only for such application on the part of the state legislatures. John Dickinson proposed adding the state executive by observing that domestic violence "might hinder the Legislature from meeting" (II, 467). After refusing to limit such requests to state legislative recesses, the Convention accepted this motion by a vote of 9-2.

Other Discussions

The New Jersey Plan, which William Paterson introduced on June 15, proposed that Congress should be able to remove such executives "on application by a majority of the Executives of the several States" (I, 244). The Convention does not appear to have discussed this provision.

Delegates mentioned governors in other contexts as well. James Wilson observed on June 4: "All the 13 States tho' agreeing in scarce any other instance, agree in placing a single magistrate at the head of the Governmt." (I, 96).

That same day, Benjamin Franklin expressed concern over the proposal of a congressional negative of state laws by observing that the governor had used such a veto under the Propriety Government "to extort money" from the legislature (I, 99). Many delegates expressed concern that, unlike most governors, or leaders of foreign nations, the president was not granted a Council of State with whom he had to consult.

Federal Appointment of Governors

All of the ideas above appear predicated on keeping state executives pretty much as they were or allowing them to evolve as needs dictated–Article IV, Section 4 thus provided only that the U.S. should guarantee states a "Republican Form of Government," leaving them to fill in the details. By contrast, New York's Alexander Hamilton suggested in the plan that he introduced to the Convention on June 18 that "the Governour or president of each state shall be appointed by the General Government and shall have a negative upon the laws about to be passed in the State of which he is Governour or President" (I, 293).

On August 23, when the Convention was debating a congressional negative of state law, Oliver Ellsworth observed that this would "require either that all laws of the State Legislatures should previously to their taking effect be transmitted to the Genl Legislature, or be repealable by the Latter; or that the State Executives should be appointed by the Genl Government, and have a controul over the State laws" (II, 391). Clearly

opposed to this, he affirmed: "If the last was meditated let it be declared" (II, 391). Charles Pinckney of South Carolina was willing to do so: "he thought the State Executives ought to be so appointed with such a controul, & that it would be so provided if another Convention should take place" (II, 391). Gouverneur Morris did not support such a proposal but wanted to refer it to a committee. The Convention narrowly defeated this idea by a vote of 6-5.

See Also Congress, House of Representatives, Vacancies; Guarantee Clause; Hamilton Plan; President, Selection

FOR FURTHER READING

Farrand, Max, ed. 1937. *The Records of the Federal Convention.* 4 vols. New Haven, CT: Yale University Press.

Vile, John R. 2003. *Encyclopedia of Constitutional Amendments, Proposed Amendments, and Amending Issues, 1789–2002.* 2nd ed. Santa Barbara, CA: ABC-CLIO.

GREAT BRITAIN

Individuals who chronicle the Constitutional Convention sometimes portray the delegates as political theorists. Although men like James Madison, James Wilson, and Gouverneur Morris were undoubtedly better versed than most contemporary politicians in knowledge of theories of government, they and other delegates were also imminently practical men who often referred to history and to experience. The history of previous confederacies had particular interest not only for James Madison, who had used books Thomas Jefferson had purchased for him in France to write an essay on the subject, but for all those who were concerned about the future of the Articles of Confederation. References to confederacies in Greece, Switzerland, Belgium, and Germany are sprinkled throughout the Convention proceedings. At a time when those who were educated were likely to study the classics, the delegates also referred frequently to lessons from Greek and Roman history.

The most common references that the delegates made, however, were to the experiences with government with which they were personally familiar. These included their knowledge of their own and surrounding states, of the government under the Articles of Confederation, and of the government of Great Britain. Indeed, of approximately 400 historical references that delegates made at the Convention, about 125 were to events in American history and another 100 to those in Great Britain (Narroll 1953, 3–4). Even the youngest delegates present had spent more years under British rule than under the government of the Articles and of their own state constitutions. Delegates were both proud of their resistance to what they considered to be developing British tyranny and concerned about the continuing presence of British troops in the Northwest Territory and about England's ability to restrain American trade. At times, as in the construction of a bicameral national legislature, Britain provided an example to follow; at other times, it was an example to be avoided (see Colbourn 1965, 40–56). For the most part, delegates were wary of creating either a monarchy or an aristocracy, and yet they had admiration for the "energy" of the British monarch.

Expressions of Admiration for the British System

Several themes recur in the delegates' discussion of Britain. Some openly admired the British system. Most notable was New York's Alexander Hamilton, who asserted in one of the longest speeches at the Constitutional Convention, which he made on June 18, that "In his private opinion he had no scruple in declaring, supported as he was by the opinions of so many of the wise & good, that the British Govt. was the best in the world: and he doubted much whether any things short of it would do in America" (Farrand 1937, I, 288). Hamilton was surely not alone. Madison observed that in one of his speeches,

Delaware's John Dickinson "repeated his warm eulogiums on the British Constitution" (I, 136). Pierce Butler observed that "We are constantly running away with the idea of the excellence of the British parliament, and with or without reason copying from them; when in fact there is no similitude in our situations" (I, 238). Fellow South Carolinian Charles Pinckney noted that "Much has been said of the Constitution of G. Britain. I will confess that I believe it to be the best constitution in existence; but at the same time I am confident it is one that will not or can not be introduced into this Country, for many centuries" (I, 398). Gouverneur Morris of Pennsylvania further observed that "We should either take the British Constitution altogether or make one for ourselves" (I, 545).

Critiques of the English System

If some admired the British system, others, many of whom had first come into prominence during the American Revolution, could not fail to remember that Britain had once been a mortal enemy. Many of the charges that the colonists had once hurled against the British reemerged during Convention debates. English suffrage and English "corruption" were frequent objects of comment. Pennsylvania's Benjamin Franklin, who had once represented colonial interests in England, explained that the English king had not in some time exercised his veto power, but he attributed this to the fact that "The bribes and emoluments now given to the members of parliament rendered it unnecessary, everything being done according to the will of the Ministers" (I, 99). Elbridge Gerry of Massachusetts thought that the people of England "will probably lose their liberty from the smallness of the proportion having a right of suffrage" (I, 132). He later observed that, "If we dislike the British government for the oppressive measures by them carried on against us, yet he hoped we would not be so far prejudiced as to make ours in everything opposite to theirs" (I, 238). Butler noted that the scramble for offices by member of the British Parliament "was the source of the corruption that ruined their Govt." (I, 376).

Pennsylvania's James Wilson referred to the English boroughs, which sent representatives to Parliament quite disproportional to their populations, as "the rotten part of the Constitution" (I, 450). Virginia's James Madison observed that in England, "The power there had long been in the hands of the boroughs, of the minority; who had opposed & defeated every reform which had been attempted" (I, 584). Telling delegates that they were unduly influenced by the British example in thinking about who should have the right to vote, Virginia's George Mason observed that "there a Twig, a Turf is the Elector" (II, 208), initiating several further references to the source of "corruption" in England.

Britain as a Source of Examples

Because it was so familiar, delegates were constantly comparing institutions that they were considering with institutions in England. Delegates compared the House of Commons and the House of Lords to the emerging House and Senate, but they did not always agree on how well the institutions matched. In discussing whether the new Congress should emulate the British example and limit the origination of money bills to the lower house, as some delegates had proposed, South Carolina's Pierce Butler complained: "We were always following the British Constitution when the reason of it did not apply. There was no analogy between the Ho[use] of Lords and the body proposed to be established" (I, 233).

The delegates contrasted the British system of mixing powers with the emerging system of separated powers. Pierce cited the "mischiefs" of the "septennial act" of Britain (I, 218) in arguing against long legislative terms. The British practice became an argument for restricting the origin of money bills to the lower house, just as differences between the Parliament and the emerging Congress provided reasons for ignoring this example. The British allocation of power to the king over foreign policy was cited in discussing the presidency. Delegates cited the role of the judges in England, with James Wilson tying two arguments together by contending that "the secu-

George III, king of Great Britain and Ireland, 1738–1820 (Library of Congress)

rity of private rights is owing entirely to the purity of her tribunals of Justice, the Judges of which are neither appointed nor paid by a venal Parliament" (I, 253–254). He and other delegates produced examples from the reign of Cromwell (Hutson 1987, 136), from the reign of Queen Anne (I, 546; II, 275), from the prime ministries of Pitt and Fox (II, 104), from the English Revolution (II, 199), from the reign of Edward III (II, 345), and others.

The Legacy of English Rights

These frequent references serve as a reminder that many of the colonists had considered themselves to be English citizens until shortly before the final break with the mother country in July 1776. Until this Revolution, those who studied English history would have been studying their own history. American conceptions of rights, and of representative government, were grounded in English rights, and in their experience under the British. American institutions were consciously or unconsciously borrowed largely from British examples. Although the English tradition was not the exclusive tradition under which the colonists had been nurtured, debates at the Convention indicate that it, and the brief experience of independence at both the state level and the level of the Articles of Confederation, were primary. A student of the demographics of the signers of both the Declaration of Independence and the Constitution observed: "Collective analysis suggests that the shared British political culture of the Founding Fathers was more important than economic interests, occupation, or provincial origin in shaping American unity" (Brown 1976, 473). British political culture also helped provide a common political language and a common store of experiences.

Margaret Banks has observed that a number of provisions in the U.S. Constitution were patterned after British practices. She says that provisions in the U.S. Constitution allowing each house of Congress to judge the elections, returns, and qualifications of its own members; to punish members for disorderly behavior; to decide on its own rules; to be free to debate matters without fear of arrest; and to keep a journal of its proceedings were all based on British parliamentary practice (1966, 23). The U.S. Constitution designated the president, like the British monarch, as commander-in-chief of the armed forces. Similarly, the president exercises clemency powers and delivers an annual message similar to that which the monarch gives at the beginning of every session of the Parliament (27).

Postscript

In part because they share a common language, Americans continue to follow affairs in Britain, and students of government continue to study the British parliamentary system. Woodrow Wilson was among those who was a great admirer of this system and who arguably altered at least some elements of the American system in this direction; as president, for example, he resumed the English practice of speaking directly to the national legislature rather than simply sending a written address. Although America and Britain fought against one another in the War of 1812, in the twentieth century they were allied in two world wars, through the long Cold War, and in both wars in the Persian Gulf. Laws in every state except Louisiana, which is based on European-style civil law, continue to mimic the English common law tradition, based on carefully crafted judicial precedents, designed to fill in gaps left by acts of legislation.

One of the most important decisions of twentieth-century American jurisprudence was a series of cases dealing with state and congressional apportionment. In a notable decision in *Reynolds v. Sims,* Chief Justice Earl Warren decided that representation in both houses of state legislatures needed to be based on population. He opined:

> Legislators represent people, not trees or acres. Legislators are elected by voters, not farms or cities or economic interests. As long as ours is a representative form of government, and our legislatures are those instruments of government elected directly by and directly representative of the people, the right to elect legislators in a free and unimpaired fashion is a bedrock of our political system. (562, opinion)

Dissenters questioned whether Warren's preference for relying almost solely on population was grounded in text of the Constitution. However one choose to answer (and Warren himself had to distinguish representation in the states from the example of the U.S. Senate), Warren's opinion arguably at least reflects concerns that members of the Constitutional Convention frequently expressed about the adequacy of representation in the English system in which unequal districts had been given similar weight.

See Also Classical Allusions and Influences; Declaration of Independence; Hamilton, Alexander; Magna Carta; Reason and Experience

FOR FURTHER READING

Banks, Margaret A. 1966. "Drafting the American Constitution–Attitudes in the Philadelphia Convention towards the British System of Government." *American Journal of Legal History* 10 (January): 15–33.

Bradford, M. M. 1993. *Original Intentions: On the Making and Ratification of the United States Constitution.* Athens: University of Georgia Press.

Brown, Richard D. 1976. "The Founding Fathers of 1776 and 1787: A Collective View." *William and Mary Quarterly,* 3rd ser. 33 (July): 465–480.

Colbourn, H. Trevor. 1965. *The Lamp of Experience: Whig History and the Intellectual Origins of the American Revolution.* Chapel Hill: University of North Carolina Press.

Farrand, Max, ed. 1937. *The Records of the Federal Convention.* 4 vols. New Haven, CT: Yale University Press.

Hutson, James H., ed. 1987. *Supplement to Max Farrand's* The Records of the Federal Convention of 1787. New Haven, CT: Yale University Press.

Narroll, Raoul Soskin. 1953. *Clio and the Constitution: The Influence of the Study of History on the Federal Convention of 1787.* Ph.D. diss. University of California, Los Angeles.

Rodick, Burleigh Cushing. 1953. *American Constitutional Custom: A Forgotten Factor in the Founding.* New York: Philosophical Library.

GREAT COMPROMISE

See CONNECTICUT COMPROMISE

GREECE

See CLASSICAL ALLUSIONS
AND INFLUENCES

GUARANTEE CLAUSE

Article IV, Section 4 of the Constitution guarantees each state a "Republican Form of Government." The clause further specifies that the United States shall "protect" each state against "Invasion," and, on the application of state legislatures (or governors when the former cannot be convened) "against domestic violence."

Initial Discussions of the Virginia Plan

Virginia's James Madison listed the omission of a guarantee for preserving the state governments in the Articles of Confederation as one of the "vices" of this system, and many of the delegates who attended the Convention had been disturbed by the lax reaction to Shays's Rebellion in Massachusetts. Not surprisingly, the Virginia Plan provided "that a Republican Government & the territory of each State, except in the instance of a voluntary junction of Government & territory, ought to be guaranteed by the United States to each State" (Farrand 1937, I, 22). When the Committee of the Whole initially considered this provision on June 5, New Jersey's William Paterson asked that the issue be postponed until after the matter of state representation was decided, and the Convention agreed.

On June 11, on a motion by Madison, the Committee of the Whole acknowledged the possibility of a "voluntary junction" of states as well as of state divisions. It appeared, however, to have ignored a suggestion by George Read of Delaware to eliminate states altogether, rather than worrying about securing their territory. Yates's notes for the day further indicate that Virginia's Edmund Randolph associated "republican" government with government that was not monarchical (I, 206).

The Convention resumed consideration of the amended provision on July 18. Gouverneur Morris probably reflected more than his personal opinion when he openly wondered whether the Convention should agree to protect "such laws as exist in R. Island," which was known for partisan legislation on behalf of debtors and which had never sent delegates to the Convention (II, 47). Fellow Pennsylvanian James Wilson responded that "The object is merely to secure the States agst. dangerous commotions, insurrections and rebellions" (II, 47). Virginia's George Mason noted that a general government unable to protect its individual components "will be in a bad situation indeed" (II, 47). Somewhat denying Wilson's attribution of a single intention to this clause, Randolph indicated that it was designed both "to secure Republican Government" and "to suppress domestic insurrections" (II, 47). Madison offered a substitute motion guaranteeing "the Constitutional authority of the States" against both domestic and foreign violence, and fellow Virginian James McClurg seconded him. William Houston of Georgia did not want the government perpetuating existing constitutions, like the one in his home state, which he thought needed changing. He also thought the national government would find it difficult to choose between contending governments, both of whom claimed constitutional sanction. Luther Martin of Maryland wanted to allow states to suppress their own rebellions. Nathaniel Gorham, a delegate from the state that had witnessed Shays's Rebellion, "thought it strange that a Rebellion should be known to exist in the Empire, and the Genl. Govt. shd. be restrained from interposing to subdue it" (II, 48), and he painted a scenario in which monarchy might spread from one state to another in such circumstances. He was willing to allow individuals to say what they wanted but thought that when parties appealed to the sword, "it will then be necessary for the Genl. Govt., however difficult it may be[,] to decide on the merits of the contest, to interpose & put an end to it" (II, 48). Maryland's Daniel Carroll also thought that such a provision was essential.

Randolph then moved to amend Madison's motion by adding a provision specifying "that no State be at liberty to form any other than a Republican Govt." and Madison seconded him (II, 48). John Rutledge of South Carolina argued that by the very nature of things, Congress already had the power "to cooperate with any State in subduing a rebellion" (II, 48). James Wilson then offered a substitute motion providing "that a Republican [form of Govnmt. shall] be guarantied to each State & that each State shall be protected agst. foreign & domestic violence" (II, 48–49). Madison and Randolph withdrew their motions, and Wilson's was unanimously adopted.

Discussions of the Report of the Committee of Detail

When the Committee of Detail reported to the Convention on August 6, it contained a provision under the powers of Congress granting this body authority "To subdue a rebellion in any State, on the application of its legislature," and a separate provision providing that the U.S. would guarantee states a republican form of government, protect each state against foreign invasion, and "on the application of its Legislature, against domestic violence" (II, 182, 188).

The Convention considered the provision related to the power of Congress on August 17. Charles Pinckney of South Carolina and Gouverneur Morris wanted to strike the provision requiring state legislatures to apply for federal help. By contrast, Luther Martin and John Mercer, both of Maryland, thought that state consent was essential to the introduction of national force. When Oliver Ellsworth of Connecticut suggested that either the state legislatures or the state executive should be able to ask for national help, Gouverneur Morris observed that the state executive might be heading the rebellion. Elbridge Gerry opposed "letting loose the myrmidons of the U. States on a State without its own consent" and argued that there would have been greater bloodshed in his home state of Massachusetts had the national government intervened (II, 317). New Hampshire's John Langdon thought that the "apprehension of the national force, will have a salutary effect in preventing insurrections" (II, 317). Randolph questioned whether the national government should be deciding whether or not a state legislature could meet, while Morris thought that Congress could certainly be trusted with this power. The Convention agreed to Pinckney's motion to drop the requirement that the state legislature ask for help was agreed to be a vote of 5-3-2. By a vote of 4-2-2, the Convention then approved a motion offered by Madison, and seconded by Gerry, to add, by way of explanation, "against the Government thereof" (II, 318).

The Convention considered the next set of powers in the report of the Committee of Detail on August 20. It began by unanimously voting to delete the word "foreign" before "invasion," as being unnecessary (II, 466). Delaware's John Dickinson then moved to strike out the provision for state legislative applications for help, believing that the U.S. should be free to suppress violence from whatever source, including the legislature itself. The Convention rejected Dickinson's motion by a vote of 8-3. The Convention further voted against substituting the word "insurrections" for "domestic violence" and for allowing either the executive or legislature to appeal for help. With minor revisions by the Committee of Style, this provision found its way into the Constitution.

Analysis

Delegates agreed that the term "republican" was a suitable designation for the governments they were trying to protect and defend. Most delegates thought it was essential for the national government to agree to protect the state, but some also attempted to guard against the introduction of national forces without state consent. Ultimately, delegates authorized both the state legislature and governor to request national intervention. Although the Convention initially listed this provision under congressional powers, it ended up in Article VI. This did not keep the Supreme Court from ruling in *Luther v. Borden,* 48 U.S. (7 How.) 1 (1849), that the issue of deciding which governments were republican in character was a "political question" for the elected branches of government to make rather than a matter for judicial resolution.

See Also Republicanism; Shays's Rebellion

FOR FURTHER READING

Farrand, Max, ed. 1937. *The Records of the Federal Convention.* 4 vols. New Haven, CT: Yale University Press.

Lerche, Charles O., Jr. 1949. "The Guarantee of a Republican Form of Government and the Admission of New States." *Journal of Politics* 11 (August): 578–604.

Maier, Pauline. 1970. "Popular Uprisings and Civil Authority in Eighteenth-Century America." *William and Mary Quarterly,* 3rd ser. 27 (January): 3–35.

HABEAS CORPUS

The writ of habeas corpus is a mechanism, deeply rooted in English history, that provides a means for prisoners to require that the government either release them from prison or specify the charges against them. Article I, Section 9, of the Constitution, a section designed to limit the powers of Congress, specifies that "The Privilege of the Writ of Habeas Corpus shall not be suspended, unless when in Cases of Rebellion or Invasion the public Safety may require it."

Charles Pinckney of South Carolina submitted a proposal for such a provision among a number of propositions that he introduced on August 20. The Convention forwarded these to the Committee of Detail. Pinckney's proposal would have provided for the enjoyment of the writ "in the most expeditious and ample manner" but would have made an exception for suspending the writ on "the most urgent and pressing occasions" and for "a limited" but unspecified time (Farrand 1937, II, 341).

Although this committee did not incorporate this idea into its draft of the Constitution, Pinckney reintroduced this proposal on August 28, at which time he specified a 12-month maximum suspension of the writ. Fellow South Carolinian John Rutledge apparently wanted to go farther. He hoped that the right of habeas corpus could be declared "inviolable" and doubted that it would ever be necessary to suspend the writ throughout the whole nation (II, 438). Gouverneur Morris then moved for adoption of the current constitutional language, making an exception for cases of rebellion or invasion. Although fellow Pennsylvania delegate James Wilson doubted that such a suspension should ever be necessary since judges always had the discretion to deny bail, the Convention nonetheless accepted the first part of Morris's provision unanimously and the part related to suspension during rebellion or invasion by a vote of 7-3.

Protections for the writ of habeas corpus, like a number of other limitations on Congress, are a prelude to the Bill of Rights in specifically limiting the power of the government over individual civil liberties.

See Also Bill of Rights; Common Law; Congress, Limits on; Great Britain

FOR FURTHER READING

Chemerinsky, Erwin. 1987. "The Individual Liberties within the Body of the Constitution: A Symposium: Thinking About Habeas Corpus." *Case Western Reserve Law Review* 37: 748–793.

Farrand, Max, ed. 1937. *The Records of the Federal Convention.* 4 vols. New Haven, CT: Yale University Press.

HAMILTON, ALEXANDER (1755?–1804)

Alexander Hamilton was born in Nevis, in the British West Indies, in 1755 or 1757; his parents were never legally married, his father abandoned the family, and his mother died when Hamilton was eight. After serving as a merchant's apprentice, a minister's family helped bring Hamilton to the U.S. where he was aided by William Livingston (a future delegate to the U.S. Constitutional Convention from New Jersey) before becoming a student at King's College, today's Columbia University.

Hamilton quickly became involved in the Revolutionary cause and wrote an influential pamphlet entitled "A Full Vindication of the Measures of the Congress from the Calumnies of Their Enemies." He went on to serve as an aide-de-camp to General

Alexander Hamilton, delegate from New York
(Pixel That)

Washington and to fight at the battle of Yorktown. Delegates to the Convention thus addressed him as "Colonel." Hamilton was a strong nationalist who was convinced early on that the government of the Articles of Confederation was inadequate. He had entered the field of law and married Elizabeth Schuyler, the daughter of a wealthy businessman from a prominent New York family, by whom he fathered seven children who survived into adulthood. Although he had been an ardent Patriot, Hamilton was engaged in a number of cases defending the rights of loyalists and quickly distinguished himself for his legal skills.

Perhaps in part because he had been born and raised abroad rather than in one of the states, Hamilton was an avowed nationalist. He may well have been the first individual explicitly to call for a constitutional convention, a sentiment that he expressed in a letter of September 3, 1780, to James Duane (see Rossiter 1964, 36), even before the Articles of Confederation had been ratified. He tried at one point to apply military pressure on the Congress under the Articles before George Washington nixed the plan. On another occasion, Hamilton tried to get New York to ratify an amendment granting Congress power to enact import duties. He was a major figure at the Annapolis Convention, and he went on to become an important figure at New York's ratifying convention.

Given this background, Alexander Hamilton must have been very frustrated at the Constitutional Convention. Fellow New York delegates John Lansing and Robert Yates, both of whom favored states' rights, constantly checked him at the Convention. He left the Convention for long periods. Still, he returned to sign the document and went on to argue for its adoption as one of three authors who wrote the *Federalist Papers* under the name of Publius.

Hamilton was present when the Convention opened on May 25. Maryland's James McHenry observed in his notes of May 29 that Hamilton asked whether the Convention should conduct an inquiry as to "whether the united States were susceptible of one government, or required a separate existence connected only by leagues offensive and defensive and treaties of commerce" (Farrand 1937, I, 27).

Congress

On May 30, Hamilton introduced a resolution whereby "the rights of suffrage in the national Legislature ought to be proportioned to the number of free inhabitants" (I, 36). On June 11, he further moved that the right of suffrage in the second branch should be the same as in the first (I, 202). On June 21, Hamilton opposed state legislative selection of senators.

On June 21, Hamilton advocated a three-year term for members of the House of Representatives at a time when others were advocating annual or biennial terms. Hamilton reasoned that "there ought to be neither too much nor too little dependence, on the popular sentiments" (II, 362). He indicated that septennial elections had not quenched "the democratic spirit" of the English constitution and that "Frequency of elections tended to make the people listless to them; and to facilitate the success of little cabals" (I, 362).

Not unexpectedly, Hamilton opposed allowing states to pay members of Congress. He sagely observed that "Those who pay are the masters of those who are paid" (II, 373). He further observed that states might pay unequally. Undoubtedly anticipating the need for future adjustments, Hamilton opposed fixing the wages within the Constitution (I, 373).

Hamilton continued to support state representation in both houses of Congress on the basis of population. On June 29, shortly before he left the Convention for an extended period, Hamilton indicated that he regarded the small state quest for equal representation in one or both houses to be "a contest for power, not for liberty" (I, 466). He argued that the rights of the people individually, rather than the rights of the states as entities, should be the Convention's central concern:

> The state of Delaware having 40,000 souls will *lose power,* if she has 1/10 only of the votes allowed to Pa. having 400,000: but will the people of Del: *be less free,* if each citizen has an equal vote with each citizen of Pa. (I, 466)

Consistent with his focus on economics, Hamilton argued that the real distinction between states involved the "carrying & non-carrying States" rather than the distinction between the large and small ones (I, 466). Hamilton feared that America could divide into partial confederacies that would ally with European governments and give them a foothold. Hamilton viewed the creation of a stronger government as thus a necessary measure for both domestic and foreign concerns, and he viewed the time as peculiarly ripe for positive actions:

> No Governmt. could give us tranquility & happiness at home, which did not possess sufficient stability and strength to make us respectable abroad. This was the critical moment for forming such a government. As yet we retain the habits of union. We are weak & sensible of our weakness. Henceforward the motives will become feebler, and the difficulties greater. It is a miracle that we were now here exercising our tranquil & free deliberations on the subject. It would be madness to trust to future miracles. A thousand causes must obstruct a reproduction of them. (I, 467)

Hamilton did not take part in Convention debates from June 30 through August 12. When he returned to the Convention, he opposed specifying the number of years of citizenship and residency for members of Congress as "embarrassing the Govt. with minute restrictions" (II, 268). He thought that an overly restrictive number of years would discourage immigration and wanted to leave the determination of how many years should be required to future Congresses to decide.

On September 8, Hamilton came out in support of a larger House of Representatives than the Convention had provided. Favoring "a broad foundation" for this body, he observed that it "was on so narrow a scale as to be really dangerous, and to warrant a jealousy in the people for their liberties" (II, 554).

Hamilton's Plan

By June 18, the Convention had two major plans before it—the Virginia Plan and the New Jersey Plan. The first favored the large states and the second favored the smaller; the first called for a complete overhaul in the governmental system and the second stuck more closely to the existing Articles of Confederation. On this day, however, Hamilton took to the floor for an address that lasted the entire session. He observed that he had previously been largely silent out of deference to the "superior abilities age & experience" of others as well as because of "his delicate situation with respect to his own State, to whose sentiments as expressed by his Colleagues, he could by no means accede" (I, 282). Proclaiming that the "crisis" obliged him to contribute his own efforts to forming a new Constitution, he professed to be "unfriendly to both plans" (I, 283), and especially to the New Jersey Plan. Convinced that "no amendment of the confederation, leaving the States in possession of their sovereignty could possibly answer the purpose," he took a more negative view of the nation's large extent than did James Madison, the putative author of the Virginia Plan. By contrast, Hamilton said that "he was much discouraged by the amazing extent of Country in expecting the desired blessings from any general sovereignty that could be substituted" (I, 283).

Hamilton thought that those who debated the meaning of federalism had become too subtle. He believed that a federal government was simply "an association of independent Communities into one," and he did not believe such a system precluded direct action on individuals as well as on communities. The emergency dictated that the delegates act according to what they thought proper, and if states had no authority to ratify what they did, the people could assume this authority, presumably in state ratifying conventions.

Hamilton proceeded to the question "what provision shall we make for the happiness of our Country?" (I, 284). He thought the answer was a provision for a national government. Such a government would be based on five principles, which indicated that Hamilton had a realistic, perhaps even pessimistic, view of human motivations. These were:

- "an active & constant interest in supporting it";
- "the love of power";
- "an habitual attachment of the people";
- "*force* by which may be understood *a coertion of laws or coertion of arms*"; and
- "influence. he did not [mean] corruption, but a dispensation of those regular honors & emoluments, which produce an attachment to the Govt." (I, 284–285)

Hamilton did not think the current government had such supports. Under the Articles, states had developed "the esprit de corps" in favor of their individual interests rather than those of the nation as a whole (I, 284). Under the Articles, power rested with the states and "the ambition of their demagogues is known to hate the controul of the Genl. Government" (I, 284). Moreover, the people were more firmly attached to their states than to national authority. Under the present system state sovereignty "is immediately before the eyes of the people: its protection is immediately enjoyed by them. From its hands distributive justice, and all those acts which familiarize & endear Govt. to a people, are dispensed to them" (I, 284). Under the Articles it was impossible to exert national force upon the states. Moreover the state governments had the dispensation of honors within their hands: "All the passions when we see, of avarice, ambition, interest, which govern most individuals, and all public bodies, fall into the current of the States, and do not flow in the stream of the Genl. Govt." (I, 285).

Hamilton then offered a series of examples of past confederations including the Amphyctionic Council, the German Confederacy, the reign of Charlemagne, the German diet, and the Swiss cantons. He concluded that the only solution was to invest " such a compleat sovereignty in the general Govermt. as will turn all the strong principles & passions above mentioned on its side" (I, 286).

Hamilton argued that the New Jersey Plan was inadequate on this account. He focused on the plan's need to requisition the states for money. He observed that experience proved such requisitions to be unreliable. He believed that the national government should rely instead on taxation of commerce, including exports (I, 286). Hamilton also faulted the New Jersey Plan for proposing equal state representation within Congress. He observed that "It is not in human nature that Va. & the large States should consent to it, or if they did that they shd. long abide by it. It shocks too much the ideas of Justice, and every human feeling" (I, 286). Hamilton did not believe that the New Jersey Plan provided for proper defense in peacetime. He also believed that the Congress proposed under this plan would represent "local prejudice" (I, 287). He observed:

It is agst. all the principles of a good Government to vest the requisite powers in such a body as Cong. Two Sovereignties can not co-exist within the same limits. Giving powers to Congs. must eventuate in a bad Govt. or in no Govt. (I, 287)

It was at this point that Hamilton returned to his concerns over the extent of the nation, and came close to suggesting that states, at least as semisovereign entities, should be abolished:

The extent of the Country to be governed, discouraged him. The expence of a general Govt. was also formidable; unless there were such a diminution of expence on the state of the State Govts. as the case would admit. If they were extinguished, he was persuaded that great economy might be obtained by substituting a general Govt. He did not mean however to shock the public opinion by proposing such a measure. On the other [hand] he saw no *other* necessity for declining it. (I, 287)

Hamilton recognized the need for lesser administrative units, but not for the states, qua states:

Subordinate authorities he was aware would be necessary. There must be district tribunals: corporations for local purposes. But cui bono, the vast & expansive apparatus now appertaining to the States. (I, 287)

Hamilton wondered however how representatives would be drawn "from the extremes to the center of the Community" (I, 287). Indeed, "this view of the subject almost led him to despair that a Republican Govt. could be established over so great an extent" (I, 288). Still, "he was sensible at

the same time that it would be unwise to propose one of any other form" (I, 288).

As to his private views, Hamilton "had no scruple in declaring, supported as he was by the opinions of so many of the wise & good, that the British Govt. was the best in the world; and that he doubted much whether any thing short of it would do in America" (I, 288). He knew that the public did not currently agree, but he observed that public opinion was progressing, and anticipated that it would one day recognize the British system as "the only Govt. in the world 'which unites public strength with individual security'" (I, 288). Whereas Madison stressed the multifarious factions that arise within society, Hamilton saw a primary division between "the few & the many" (I, 288), and he thought that government needed to be devised so as to protect both classes. In England, the House of Lords performed this balancing function:

Having nothing to hope for by a change, and a sufficient interest by means of their property, in being faithful to the National interest, they form a permanent barrier agst. every pernicious innovation, whether attempted on the part of the Crown or of the Commons. (I, 288–289)

Hamilton did not believed that the Senate proposed would be adequate to these purposes. He thought that the seven-year term then under discussion would not give that body adequate "firmness" in the face of "the amazing violence & turbulence of the democratic spirit" (I, 289). Similarly, Hamilton did not have confidence in the proposed executive. Again, England provided an example of what was needed:

The Hereditary interest of the King was so interwoven with that of the Nation, and his personal emoluments so great, that he was placed above the danger of being corrupted from abroad—and at the same time was both sufficiently independent and sufficiently controuled, to answer the purpose of the institution at home. (I, 289)

He therefore favored service for life in both the Senate and the chief executive offices.

Hamilton knew that his listeners would wonder whether the government he was proposing qualified as a republican government. He answered that it would so qualify "if all the Magistrates are appointed, and vacancies are filled, by the people, or in a process of election originating with the people" (I, 290).

Hamilton then proceeded to outline his plan. It called for a bicameral Congress, with the members of the lower house elected to three-year terms and senators to serve during good behavior. The president would also be elected by the people and would serve during good behavior. He would have a negative on all laws, would direct war, would make treaties, would appoint the heads of departments, and could pardon all offenses other than treason (I, 292). The Senate would declare war and advise on and approve treaties. Members of the judiciary would serve during good behavior. All U.S. officers would be subject to impeachment. The general government would appoint the governors of each state who would have power to negative state laws. States would further be prohibited from having any land or sea forces, and their militia would be under national control.

Two days after Hamilton's speech, Connecticut's William Johnson observed that although Hamilton "has been praised by every body, he has been supported by none" (I, 363). Hamilton seemed to understand his position. On June 26, he apparently indicated, or at least this is how Madison interpreted his remarks, that he did not himself favor republican government (he said however that he was "as zealous an advocate for liberty as any man whatever" [I, 424]) but recognized that he needed to address his remarks to those that did in the hopes that they would "tone their Government as high as possible" (I, 424). The rest of his remarks followed up on the theme of the speech by which he had introduced his plan of government. He pointed out that as long as liberty existed, the distribution of property would vary, and such inequality would result in distinctions between rich and poor that were mirrored in Roman society by the distinction between patricians and plebeians. Hamilton thought that the House of Representatives would be the guardian of the poor and the Senate, of the rich (I, 424).

Human Nature

One of the fascinating aspects of Hamilton's plan was the way that it attempted to rely on human motives for the support of government. New York's Robert Yates cited Hamilton as having said that "the science of policy is the knowledge of human nature" (I, 378). Hamilton cast further light on this view in opposing the provision limiting members of Congress from accepting other offices. After observing that "We must take man as we find him, and if we expect him to serve the public must interest his passions in doing so" (I, 376), Hamilton cited David Hume's view that the "corruption" in Great Britain was essential to the operation of the system there (I, 376).

Federalism

Hamilton had gone just about as far as anyone at the Convention in suggesting that the states be abolished or reorganized. Apparently responding to a comment by Pennsylvania's James Wilson who had indicated that he did not favor the establishment of a national government "that would swallow up the State Govts. as seemed to be wished by some gentlemen" (I, 322), Hamilton had to explain himself the day after his long-winded speech, but it is likely that his explanation aroused even greater suspicion:

> He had not been understood yesterday. By an abolition of the States, he meant that no boundary could be drawn between the National & State Legislatures; that the former must therefore have indefinite authority. If it were limited at all, the rivalship of the States would gradually subvert it. Even as Corporations the extent of some of them as Va. Massts. &c. would be formidable. *As States,* he thought they ought to be abolished. But he admitted the necessity of leaving in them, subordinate jurisdictions. (II, 323).

On June 19, Hamilton joined Wilson in disagreeing with the view of Maryland's Luther Martin that Independence had put individual states in a "state of nature" in which each was on an equal footing. Although admitting that states were now on an equal footing, he "could see no inference from that against concerting a change of the system in this particular" (I, 325). He believed that small states would be protected by the fact that the three largest states were "separated from each other by distance of place, and equally so by all the peculiarities which distinguish the interests of one State from those of another" (I, 325). He also pointed out that states did not fall simply into the category of "large" and "small" but that there were all kinds of gradations in size between these.

In opposing a motion whereby one branch of Congress would be selected by state legislatures, Hamilton feared that this "would increase that State influence which could not be too watchfully guarded agst." (I, 358–359). In what might well have been a case of wishful thinking, Hamilton said that there was always the possibility that under the new system "the State Govts. might gradually dwindle into nothing," and that delegates should beware of engrafting the national government onto that which "might possibly fail" (I, 359).

Hamilton opposed allowing states to pay members of Congress because he wanted to avoid dependency of that body on them. He observed that state governments were distinct from the people of the states (I, 373–374).

Presidency

On June 2, Hamilton seconded the motion by Benjamin Franklin of Pennsylvania that the president should serve without pay, but it was clear that he did so as a way of honoring its author rather than because Hamilton agreed with the proposal (I, 85). Hamilton moved on June 4 that the president should have an absolute veto of legislative acts, but, in doing so, he observed that the British king, who had similar authority, had not exercised it since the American Revolution (I, 98). On September 12, Hamilton indicated that the provision in the New York legislature to override the governor by a two-thirds vote had proven to be ineffectual (II, 585).

On September 6, Hamilton said that he preferred the Electoral College mechanism to the previous proposal of allowing members of Congress to select the president for a single term. He referred to the previous plan negatively as one in which:

the president was a Monster elected for seven years, and ineligible afterwards; having great powers, in appointments to office, & continually tempted by this constitutional disqualification to abuse them in order to subvert the Government– Although he should be made re-eligible, Still if appointed by the Legislature, he would be tempted to make use of corrupt influence to be continued in office. (II, 524)

Because he feared that such corruption might also occur between the president and the Senate, Hamilton favored allowing the individual with the highest number of electors to be president rather than having this choice devolve on the Senate (II, 525).

Critique of Madison's Extended Republic

On June 6, Hamilton made some notes of a speech that Madison gave in which Madison argued that large districts were less likely to allow factions and demagogues to predominate. Interestingly, Hamilton, with whom Madison would join forces in writing *The Federalist*, appended a note indicating that "An influential demagogue will give an impulse to the whole–Demagogues are not always *inconsiderable* persons–Patricians were frequently demagogues–Characters are less known & a less active interest taken in them–" (I, 147).

Prayer

Toward the end of his life, Hamilton became an extremely pious man, leading his family in devotions, and joining the Episcopal Church on his deathbed. Earlier in life, Hamilton was often associated, correctly or not, with impiety. These associations might have been formed in part from Hamilton's objection to Benjamin Franklin's motion that each day of the Convention be opened in prayer. Despite later stories that Hamilton objected to the impropriety of calling in foreign aid, Madison's notes suggested that Hamilton was among those who argued that "however proper such a resolution might have been at the beginning of the convention, it might at this late day, 1. bring on it some disagreeable animadversions. & 2. lead the public to believe that the embarrassments and dissentions within the convention, had suggested this measure" (I, 452).

Amendment and Ratification of the Constitution

On September 10, Hamilton seconded a motion to reconsider the amending provision which called, up to this point, for Congress to call a convention to propose amendments on the application of two-thirds of the states. Whereas Elbridge Gerry of Massachusetts had favored reconsideration for fear that the national government might invade the powers of the states, Hamilton had a different concern. He favored "an easier mode for introducing amendments" (II, 558). Fearing that state legislatures would only apply for conventions with a view toward increasing their own powers, Hamilton wanted Congress to be able to propose amendments on its own: "The National Legislature will be the first to perceive and will be most sensible to the necessity of amendments, and ought also to be empowered, whenever two thirds of each branch should concur to call a Convention" (II, 558). Hamilton subsequently seconded a motion by James Madison that closely resembles the current amending mechanism (II, 559).

Curiously, Hamilton thought that Congress should have to approve the new Constitution. He further proposed allowing states to decide whether they felt comfortable entering into a union to which only nine states had consented (II, 560).

Hamilton urged all members of the Convention to sign the Constitution. Indicating that the plan proposed was far from what he desired, Hamilton still thought the choice was clear:

> A few characters of consequence, by opposing or even refusing to sign the Constitution, might do infinite mischief by kindling the latent sparks which lurk under an enthusiasm in favor of the Convention which may soon subside. No man's ideas were more remote from the plan than his own were known to be; but it is possible to deliberate between anarchy and Convulsion on one side, and the chance of good to be expected from the plan on the other. (II, 646)

Life after the Convention

Hamilton was the chief author of *The Federalist*, and was responsible for recruiting James Madison and John Jay as coauthors. This work explained and defended the government, which the Philadelphia convention had proposed. In these papers, Hamilton emerged as a particularly powerful critic of the weaknesses of the Articles of Confederation. He was also a proponent of strong presidential powers and of the power of judicial review whereby courts can invalidate legislation that they consider to be unconstitutional. Hamilton also successfully led the Federalist forces at New York's ratifying convention.

Washington subsequently appointed Hamilton to be the first secretary of the Treasury. Much as in the English model of government that he so admired, Hamilton practically converted this position into a position as prime minister. In this capacity, Hamilton proposed stretching the powers of the new government to their utmost by assuming state debts and establishing a national bank; he was a powerful defender of the idea of implied powers, which federal courts later affirmed in the case of *McCulloch v. Maryland* (1819). Hamilton took a leading role in suppressing Pennsylvania's Whiskey Rebellion. He founded the Federalist Party, which put him at odds with James Madison and Thomas Jefferson, who founded the rival Democratic-Republican Party. Hamilton resigned from the cabinet in 1795 and returned to his law practice but continued to advise Washington's administration. At one point, Hamilton admitted to an affair with the wife of an individual who was attempting to blackmail him in an attempt to refute charges that he had misused his office as secretary of the Treasury.

At odds with the Federalist administration of John Adams whom he had tried to maneuver out of the presidency in 1796, when the presidential electors for Thomas Jefferson and Aaron Burr (the intended vice president) were tied in the election of 1800, Hamilton advocated Jefferson as the lesser of two evils. This, and subsequent comments about Burr's character, which Hamilton made when Burr ran for governor of New York in 1804, eventually led to a duel with Burr at Weehawken, New Jersey in 1804 that left Hamilton (like a son who had died on a previous occasion, also in a duel) mortally wounded. After he fell out of political power, Hamilton appears to have turned to religion for consolation (Adair and Harvey 1955). In 1802 he proposed the establishment of a "Christian Constitutional Society," and he received communion on his deathbed from an Episcopal bishop.

See Also Annapolis Convention; Banking; Federalist and Democratic-Republican Parties; *Federalist, The;* Great Britain; Hamilton Plan; New York

FOR FURTHER READING

Adair, Douglass, and Harvin Harvey. 1955. "Was Alexander Hamilton a Christian Statesman?" *William and Mary Quarterly,* 3rd ser. 12 (April): 308–329.

Chernow, Ron. 2004. *Alexander Hamilton.* New York: Penguin.

Farrand, Max, ed. 1937. *The Records of the Federal Convention.* 4 vols. New Haven, CT: Yale University Press.

Ferguson, E. James. 1983. "Political Economy, Public Liberty, and the Formation of the Constitution." *William and Mary Quarterly,* 3rd ser. 40 (July): 389–412.

Rossiter, Clinton. 1964. *Alexander Hamilton and the Constitution.* New York: Harcourt, Brace and World.

Vile, John R., ed. 2001. *Great American Lawyers: An Encyclopedia.* 2 vols. Santa Barbara, CA: ABC-CLIO.

Walling, Karl. 2003. "Alexander Hamilton and the Grand Strategy of the American Social Compact." In Ronald J. Pestritto and Thomas G. West, eds. *The American Founding and the Social Compact.* Lanham, MD: Lexington Books, 199–230.

HAMILTON PLAN

On June 18, 1787, after Edmund Randolph had introduced, and the Committee of the Whole had refined, the Virginia Plan and William Paterson had proposed his New Jersey Plan, Alexander Hamilton of New York gave a speech that lasted throughout the entire session of the day. Hamilton professed respect for those of "superior abilities[,] age & experience" at the Convention and admitted "his delicate situation with respect to his own State" (Farrand 1937, I, 282) where largely by design of New York's Governor George Clinton, Hamilton was the only nationalist among New York's three delegates. Nonetheless, he proposed an 11-part plan toward the end of his speech. The delegates then adjourned and politely ignored just about every proposal he made.

Hamilton's Concern with Both Plans

The delegate's reception of Hamilton's plan was fairly predictable since Hamilton acknowledged that he was "unfriendly" to both plans that had been proposed. He thought the New Jersey Plan was especially inadequate as he was "fully convinced, that no amendment of the confederation, leaving the States in possession of their sovereignty could possibly answer this purpose," but he also acknowledged that "he was much discouraged by the amazing extent of [the] Country in expecting the desired blessings from any general sovereignty that could be substituted" (I, 283).

Hamilton proceeded to argue that it was relatively useless to make overly subtle arguments as to the meaning of a federal government and that the delegates owed it to their country to do whatever they needed to do to secure its happiness.

Having said that the term "federal" was not in and of itself important, perhaps he was thinking more of substance when he argued that both plans under consideration were defective compared with "a *national* one" (I, 284).

Five Basic Principles

Hamilton proceeded to outline five principles necessary for the support of government. First, it required "an active & constant interest in supporting it" that states did not then have in the perpetuation of the general government. Second, government was based on "the love of power," and, in the existing scheme of things, states had an interest in asserting their own powers at the expense of the general government while individuals could see the benefits of, and were thus more attached to, the former than the latter. The third requisite of "an habitual attachment of the people" currently thus rested at the state level, where state sovereignty "is immediately before the eyes of the people: its protection is immediately enjoyed by them." Fourth, governments depend on force, and, although states could sometimes muster such force, the central authority could not exercise such power over the states in their collective capacities. Fifth, governments depended on influence. Like economists who rely on self-interest to drive the engine of capitalism, Hamilton wanted to tap into the passions of "avarice, ambition, [and] interest, which govern most individuals and all public bodies" (I, 285). Under the Articles, he believed that the weight of all these incentives and attachments rested with the states. Hamilton illustrated with reference to Greek, German, late Roman, and Swiss history. To succeed, the general government required "a compleat sovereignty" such "as will turn all the strong principles & passions above mentioned on its side" (286).

Judged by such standards, the New Jersey Plan was inadequate. Its chief defects were its inability to raise adequate resources and its continuing reliance upon states for fiscal requisitions, which were almost impossible to allot on principles that the states would consider to be proper. It was, moreover, shocking to "the ideas of Justice, and every human feeling" to expect the larger states to settle for equal legislative representation in the national legislature. Hamilton doubted whether the Congress under the Articles of Confederation had power "to keep Ships or troops in time of peace" (I, 287). With its members being selected by state legislatures and subject to recall, its members represented "local prejudices." Ultimately, either the state governments or the general government would perish as "Two Sovereignties can not co-exist within the same limits" (I, 287).

Hamilton's Solution

If the New Jersey Plan were inadequate, it was less easy to point to a viable solution. Hamilton did not want "to shock public opinion by proposing such a measure," but he could see no reason other than public opinion for keeping the states in any capacity other than as "subordinate authorities" (I, 287). Personally, Hamilton doubted whether republican government, presumably as outlined in the Virginia Plan, was adequate to the crisis. He believed "that the British Govt. was the best in the world" and that someday something like it would prove necessary in America. The seven-year term proposed for members of the Senate did not favorably compare to the nobility of the English House of Lords. Hamilton further commended the British king. In Hamilton's opinion, the king's "Hereditary interest . . . was so interwoven with that of the Nation, and his personal emoluments [were] so great, that he was placed above the danger of being corrupted from abroad—and at the same time was both sufficiently independent and sufficiently controuled, to answer the purpose of the institution at home" (I, 289).

Following the British example, Hamilton advocated life terms both for the executive and for members of one house of the legislative body. He argued that such a government could still be classified as "republican" as long as "all the Magistrates are appointed, and vacancies are filled, by the people, or a process of election originating with the people" (I, 290).

Hamilton acknowledged that his plan "went beyond the ideas of most members" (I, 291). He believed, however, that the Union was on the verge of dissolution and that evils evident in the states would "soon cure the people of their fondness for democracies." He further speculated: "the people will in time be unshackled from their prejudices; and whenever that happens, they will themselves not be satisfied at stopping where the plan of Mr. R.[andolph] wd. place them, but be ready to go as far at least as he proposes" (I, 291).

He presented his own 11-point plan not so much as an independent proposal as a source for suggested amendments to the Virginia Plan.

Outline of Hamilton's Plan

The first three articles of Hamilton's plan, as well as the sixth, dealt with the legislative branch. Hamilton proposed investing it with the "Supreme Legislative power of the United States of America," and, as in the Virginia Plan, making it bicameral. The people would elect members of the Assembly for three-year terms, while senators would serve "during good behavior," a euphemism, used in the Constitution to refer to the terms of judges, essentially meaning "for life." Electors chosen by the people in individual districts would select the senators. Given his earlier critique of the New Jersey Plan and indications that he intended for his proposals to be amendments to the Virginia Plan, both houses would presumably be apportioned according to population. The Senate would have the "sole power of declaring war," advising on treaties, and the power of confirming officers whose appointment was not vested exclusively in the chief executive.

Articles IV and V outlined the role of the chief executive, prudently designated as governor, rather than as a king or monarch. Although he would serve during good behavior, the office would not be hereditary; electors chosen by the people would select him. He would have a veto, apparently absolute, "on all laws about to be passed, and the execution of all laws passed." He would "have the direction of war when authorized or begun." He would make all treaties subject to senatorial counsel. He would have the sole power of appointing the heads of "the depart-

ments of Finance, War and Foreign Affairs" and make other nominations subject to senatorial approval. He could pardon all offenses on his own authority except for cases of treason, which would require Senate concurrence.

Given Hamilton's later defense of the judiciary in the *Federalist Papers,* Hamilton's proposals for judges are especially interesting. Articles VII and VIII outlined a "Supreme Judicial authority" to be vested in judges serving during good behavior and given "adequate and permanent salaries." Congress would have further powers "to institute Courts in each State for the determination of all matters of general concern" (I, 292).

Article IX further provided that the governor, members of the Senate, and all other officers would be subject to impeachment for mal- or corrupt conduct. The court of impeachment would consist of the chief judge from each state's top court, providing that each was serving during good behavior and on a fixed salary.

Article X took Madison's idea for a negative of state laws to a new level. It not only declared that any state laws adopted contrary to the U.S. Constitution would be void but also allowed the general government to appoint the governor or president of each state with power to veto any laws about to be passed.

Article XI further prohibited states from having any land or naval forces and declared that the U.S. would have exclusive authority over state militia as well as power to appoint and commission their officers.

Analysis

Hamilton's plan appeared to represent a unique voice at the Convention, the nationalist counterpart to delegates like Luther Martin of Maryland and Elbridge Gerry of Massachusetts who feared such national encroachment. Hamilton's plan, with both a chief executive and senators serving during good behavior, was easily subject to misrepresentation—by 1801 his plan had been "leaked" and printed in an effort to undermine his influence (Farrand 1907, 46)—and it is a measure of his courage that he gave it. Hamilton seemed to realize that most aspects of his plan were unlikely to be adopted, but whether he intended such a result or not, it seems likely that his plan made the Virginia Plan appear as the moderate plan, with the New Jersey Plan calling for inadequate national powers and his own calling for more powers than delegates were likely to give.

The speech that Hamilton gave in support of his plan presents a dour, albeit arguably realistic view of human nature. He put his hope to tie individual personal interests to the perpetuation of the national government into practice when he advocated the assumption of state debts and the founding of the national bank as the nation's first secretary of the Treasury.

See Also Great Britain; Hamilton, Alexander; Human Nature; New Jersey Plan; Virginia Plan

FOR FURTHER READING

Chernow, Ron. 2004. *Alexander Hamilton*. New York: Penguin Books.

Eidelberg, Paul. 1968. *The Philosophy of the American Constitution: A Reinterpretation of the Intentions of the Founding Fathers*. New York: The Free Press, 106–136.

Farrand, Max. 1907. "The Records of the Federal Convention." *American Historical Review* 13 (October): 44–65.

Farrand, Max, ed. 1937. *The Records of the Federal Convention*. 4 vols. New Haven, CT: Yale University Press.

HENRY, PATRICK (1736–1799)

Although he was selected as a delegate, Virginia's Patrick Henry professed that he "smelt a rat" (Peters 1987, 23) and refused to attend the Constitutional Convention in 1787. He subsequently led the fight against ratification in Virginia. His dazzling displays of oratory only gradually yielded to the steady arguments that James Madison, John Marshall, and others raised.

Patrick Henry delivering his speech, "Give me liberty or give me death!" (Pixel That)

Born in Hanover, Virginia, Henry passed the bar without a college education and quickly went on to establish his reputation in the parsons' case. In that case he succeeded in persuading a jury to award only a penny to Anglican parsons whose salaries (due in tobacco) had been altered. Henry continued to take on some of the most notorious cases that arose before the Virginia bar (McDaniel 2001).

Henry went on to distinguish himself in the Virginia House of Burgesses. He opposed the Stamp Act and became an early advocate for independence. Disappointed at not being selected to head Virginia's military, Henry, who was very popular within the state, went on to serve a number of terms as state governor.

Henry appears only to have left his native Virginia for service in the Continental Congress, and, like others who had been active in the American Revolution, he was deeply suspicious of increased national power. Henry was perhaps the most oratorically gifted of the Antifederalists, but, in retrospect, his bombastic speeches raising a multitude of fears about the new government (Banning 1988, 63, likens some of his rhetoric to "verbal terrorism") do not stand up as well as more reasoned published arguments. The core of his arguments emphasizing the primacy of liberty—albeit he also raised concerns that Northerners might use the new Constitution to abolish slavery (Einhorn 2002)—may well have been helpful, however, in furthering the cause of a bill of rights.

After the adoption of the Constitution, Henry's political views shifted and he became a Federalist. He turned down offers from George Washington to be secretary of state or serve on the U.S. Supreme Court (O'Brien 1991, 188), although he did heed Washington's request to run for the Virginia state legislature, in order to oppose the Virginia and Kentucky Resolutions. Although he was elected, he died at his home before being able to take his seat. His reconstructed house, Red Hill, and an accompanying museum are now open near Lynchburg, Virginia.

See Also Antifederalists; Virginia

FOR FURTHER READING

Banning, Lance. 1988. "1787 and 1776: Patrick Henry, James Madison, the Constitution and the Revolution." *Toward a More Perfect Union: Six Essays on the Constitution.* Provo, UT: Brigham Young University, 59–90.

Einhorn, Robin L. 2002. "Patrick Henry's Case against the Constitution: The Structural Problem with Slavery." *Journal of the Early Republic* 22 (Winter): 549–573.

McDaniel, Robb A. 2001. "Henry, Patrick." In John R. Vile, ed. *Great American Lawyers: An Encyclopedia.* 2 vols. Santa Barbara, CA: ABC-CLIO, 1: 357–364.

O'Brien, Steven G. 1991. *American Political Leaders from Colonial Times to the Present.* Santa Barbara, CA: ABC-CLIO.

Peters, William. 1987. *A More Perfect Union.* New York: Crown Publishers.

HISTORIOGRAPHY

See MOTIVES OF THE FOUNDING FATHERS

HISTORY, DELEGATES' USE OF

See REASON AND EXPERIENCE

HOLLAND

The Framers of the Constitution, among them Virginia's James Madison, gathered information about foreign governments, especially confederacies, that might prove instructive in addressing the problems of the Articles of Confederation. Benjamin Franklin had some familiarity with Holland from his experience as a foreign diplomat, and, indeed, appears to have been the best informed individual at the Convention on the subject. Although the political information he acquired appears to have been largely inaccurate, South Carolina's Pierce Butler had also visited there.

Political scientist William Riker has counted a total of 37 references to the United Netherlands at the Constitutional Convention of 1787 and in subsequent state ratifying conventions. He cites substantive discussions of the United Netherlands, the Statholder, at the Constitutional Convention relating to the executive (Pierce Butler), to Dutch history (Benjamin Franklin), to legislative unanimity (James Wilson), and to Holland (James Madison).

Riker further traces the Framers' information about Holland to three primary written sources. They were as follows: Sir William Temple's *Observations upon the United Provinces of the Netherlands*, the most commonly available edition of which was from 1676; John De Witt's *Political Maximums of the State of Holland: Comprehending a General*

View of the Civil Government of that Republic, and the Principles on which it is Founded: the Nature, Rise, and Progress of the Commerce of its Subjects, and of their True Interests with Respect of all their Neighbors, published in 1743; and a published letter to his son that Philip Dormer Stanhope, the Fourth Earl of Chesterfield, authored entitled "Some Account of the Government of the Republic of the Seven United Provinces," written in about 1745 and subsequently published in London and in the colonies (Riker 1957, 499–500). This knowledge was supplemented by word of mouth, by visits, and by speeches such as the one Franklin gave on the subject at the Constitutional Convention.

The Framers were chiefly drawn to the United Netherlands because of its apparent similarities to the government of the Articles of Confederation. Not only was Holland part of a confederation, but commentary (much of it outdated) suggested that key matters required unanimity of all the provinces, that all had equal legal weight, and that Holland (as Virginia and Massachusetts had often been under the Articles of Confederation) was often saddled with major financial requisitions. In point of fact, Holland largely dominated key institutions of the confederation, and the requirement for unanimity largely applied to diplomatic affairs and does not appear to have even been uniformly followed in this area (Riker, 509). Moreover, the entire seven provinces of the Netherlands would have fit into an area the size of New York (512), arguably limiting still further the value of any cross-oceanic comparisons.

William Riker has concluded that the Netherlands served chiefly to provide "an Awful Example" (513) of the dangers of supermajorities and of weak confederations for proponents of a new Constitution. Antifederalists, who had no more information than proponents of the new Constitution, were left to argue not so much that their opponents were wrong, but that the example did not apply. Riker concluded that the experience from which proponents of the new Constitution drew was "only slightly Dutch and mostly American" (516). It was "a metaphor for domestic experience [under the Articles of Confederation] from which they had *already* learned very much" (517).

Riker does not believe that the Framers deliberately manipulated the truth about the Netherlands. He does believe that the Framers' general misinformation on the subject suggests that, here as in other examples that they cited, they drew more from their own experience under the Articles of Confederation and less from foreign examples than is generally supposed.

In addition to serving as a possible model, or antimodel, Holland had been important in loaning money to keep the Articles of Confederation afloat.

See Also Articles of Confederation; Confederal Government

FOR FURTHER READING

Riker, William H. 1957. "Dutch and American Federalism." *Journal of the History of Ideas* 18 (October): 495–521.

HOLY ROMAN EMPIRE

See GERMANY

HOUSTON, WILLIAM (1757–1812)

William Houston was born in Scotland. His father, a baronet, immigrated to Georgia with his wife. William was privately educated before attending the English Inns of Court. On his return to the United States, he was able to secure the properties of his Tory brothers and was clearly a member of the landed elite. Elected to the Georgia legislature in 1782, Houston subsequently served in the Continental Congress, where he earned a reputation as an ardent supporter of Southern interests.

Congress

Houston was seated at the Convention on June 1, but he did not participate extensively in Convention deliberations, and he left before the document was signed. On July 2, Houston was recorded as having voted against a motion to grant each state a single senator (Farrand 1937, I, 510), thus dividing his state since Abraham Baldwin had voted the other way. Houston was subsequently appointed to the Committee to Reconsider Representation in the House which was created on July 9, the only such Convention committee on which he served. He may not have been happy with the results since, the next day, Houston joined South Carolina's General Pinckney in unsuccessfully urging that Georgia's representation in the first Congress be raised from three to four representatives (I, 568)–the committee on which Houston had served had already raised representation from two to three.

Although associated with love for his state, Houston opposed a federal guarantee to the states against domestic violence on the basis that this might perpetuate bad constitutions, among which he counted that of Georgia. Expressing the hope that this constitution "would be revised & amended," he also observed that it might be difficult for the general government to decide between contending parties (II, 48).

Presidency

On July 20, the Convention was debating a plan, which Elbridge Gerry of Massachusetts had proposed, whereby there would be 25 presidential electors with states having from one to three. Houston seconded a motion by Oliver Ellsworth of Connecticut to add one elector each to New Hampshire and Georgia–each of which had, along with Delaware, been allocated one vote (II, 64).

On July 23, Houston proposed reconsideration of the proposal for allowing state legislatures to choose presidential electors. His reasoning undoubtedly reflected the feeling that Georgia was on the periphery of the nation. He thus pointed to "the extreme inconveniency & the considerable expense, of drawing together men from all the States for the single purpose of electing the Chief Magistrate" (II, 95). With a similar objective, the next day, Houston proposed that state legislatures should select the president, arguing for "the improbability, that capable men would undertake the service of Electors from the more distant States" (II, 99). Although the Convention did not choose the method of legislative selection, the Convention does appear to have taken Houston's concern into account in the eventual design of the Electoral College, which specifies that electors meet within individual states to cast their ballots rather than assembling collectively at the nation's capital.

On July 17, Houston joined Gouverneur Morris of Pennsylvania in successfully postponing a motion that the presidential term be seven years (II, 32). That same day he succeeded in getting a motion adopted that would strike presidential reeligibility to a second term (II, 33).

Life after the Convention

Houston was plagued by illness during the Convention and is believed to have left, probably in late July, or after fellow delegate William Few arrived after August 6. Houston married in 1788 and subsequently spent much of his life in New York living a fairly private life. He died in New York City in 1812.

See Also Committee to Reconsider Representation in the House; Georgia

FOR FURTHER READING

Bradford, M. E. 1981. *Founding Fathers: Brief Lives of the Framers of the United States Constitution.* 2nd ed. Lawrence: University Press of Kansas.
Farrand, Max, ed. 1937. *The Records of the Federal Convention.* 4 vols. New Haven, CT: Yale University Press.

HOUSTON, WILLIAM CHURCHILL (1746–1788)

William Churchill Houston was born into a family of small planters in South Carolina's Sumner District in 1746. He attended the University of New Jersey (today's Princeton) where he later taught mathematics and natural philosophy and served as the college's treasurer and part-time administrator before undertaking the study of law. Houston married Jane Smith, who bore him five children. Prior to attending the Constitutional Convention, Houston had served in the New Jersey state legislature, as a delegate to the Continental Congress where he was deputy secretary from 1785 to 1786, as a clerk of the New Jersey Supreme Court, and as a delegate to the Annapolis Convention.

Afflicted with the tuberculosis that would soon kill him, Houston was present at the Constitutional Convention on May 25 but was gone by June 6. He is not recorded as having made any statements during this time. Houston died in 1788 but had signed the report of his delegation to the New Jersey legislature.

See Also Annapolis Convention; New Jersey

FOR FURTHER READING

Bradford, M. M. 1984. *Founding Fathers: Brief Lives of the Framers of the United States Constitution*. 2nd ed. Lawrence: University Press of Kansas.

Clemens, Paul G. G. "Houston, William Churchill." In John A. Garraty and Mark C. Carnes, eds. *American National Biography*. New York: Oxford University Press, 11: 281–283.

HUMAN NATURE

The Constitution was written during a century touted for its "enlightenment" and its faith in reason. The willingness of delegates to spend a summer in Philadelphia devising a Constitution is partial testament to their belief, which Alexander Hamilton expressed in *Federalist* No. 1, that the people were capable of establishing government "from reflection and choice" rather than relying "on accident and force" (Hamilton, Madison, and Jay 1961, 33).

Throughout the Convention, however, the delegates who expressed their views on the subject articulated views of human nature that are more frequently associated with the pessimism, or realism, of St. Augustine, the fifth-century church father whose view of man was based on the idea of original sin, and of some of their Puritan forebears than with the optimism of the Enlightenment (Dunn 1984, 12). Because most delegates tended to limit their speeches to more mundane views, those who explicitly addressed issues related to human nature tended to be the Convention's more prominent members, and their views are thus entitled to special consideration.

Statements at the Constitutional Convention

On June 6 Virginia's James Madison outlined a view of factions that he later reiterated in his justly famous *Federalist* No. 10. According to this view, men tended to form factions that sought to oppress one another in pursuing their own self-interests. Madison thought that institutional devices would have to be utilized in place of pious hopes that individuals might restrain themselves. In examining such motives, Madison thus observed:

> A prudent regard to the maxim that honesty is the best policy is found by experience to be as little regarded by bodies of men as by individuals. Respect for character is always diminished in proportion to the number among whom the blame or praise is to be divided. Conscience, the only remaining tie, is known to be inadequate in individuals: In large numbers, little is to be expected from it. Religion itself may become a motive to persecution & oppression. (Farrand 1937, I, 135)

In his lengthy speech to the Convention on June 18, New York's Alexander Hamilton further asserted that "Men love power" (I, 284). He observed: "Give all power to the many, they will oppress the few. Give all power to the few they will oppress the many" (I, 288). In statements that appear consistent with his later policies as secretary of the Treasury, he asserted that it was necessary for successful governments to appeal to the passions of men, which he identified as including "avarice, ambition" and "interest" (I, 285).

Few individuals at the Convention could have had more disparate views of Hamilton's politics than Virginia's George Mason, who was a consistent advocate of republicanism. However, in a speech of July 11 in which he attempted to make a case for the interests of new Western states, he agreed with Hamilton's view of power. Mason observed that "From the nature of man we may be sure, that those who have power in their hands will not give it up while they can retain it. On the Contrary we know they will always when they can rather increase it" (I, 578).

Later that same day, James Madison opposed a proposal by Pennsylvania's Gouverneur Morris to allow Congress to determine future methods of representation. He too, however, appeared to appeal to an understanding of human nature that he believed the two held in common. He thus said that he "was not a little surprised to hear this implicit confidence urged by a member who on all occasions, had inculcated So strongly the political depravity of men, and the necessity of checking one vice and interest by opposing to them another vice & interest" (I, 584). Madison went on to add that "The truth was that all men having power ought to be distrusted to a certain degree" (I, 584). Somewhat later that day, Morris observed that he would vote against additional representation for states that had slaves on the basis that he must either do "injustice to the Southern States or to human nature [by which he appears to have meant human equality], and he must therefore do it to the former" (I, 588).

The Influence of Fame

One human sentiment that the Framers did appear to believe could counteract the basest forms of human self-striving was the desire for fame. Ac-

knowledging in a speech on July 19 that "Wealth tends to corrupt the mind & to nourish its love of power, and to stimulate it to oppression," Gouverneur Morris thought that the executive could be fashioned into an office that would protect the people if he were made re-eligible to office. Morris argued that taking away this eligibility would "destroy the great incitement to merit public esteem by taking away the hope of being rewarded with a reappointment" (II, 53). He continued:

> The love of fame is the great spring to noble & illustrious actions. Shut the Civil road to Glory & he may be compelled to seek it by the sword. 2. It will tempt him to make the most of the Short space of time allotted to him, to accumulate wealth and provide for his friends. 3. It will produce violations of the very constitution it is meant to secure. (II, 53)

Given such a view, it would not be unlikely to find that many of the more illustrious members of the Convention, as well as other early statesmen (John Adams comes particularly to mind), anticipated that they would be rewarded by the esteem, if not the adulation, not only of contemporaries but also of future generations.

Ratification Debates

Although scholars sometimes contrast the pessimism of the Federalists with more optimistic liberal views (Lea 1982, 24–25), concern over human nature appears to have united rather than divided Federalist supporters of the Constitution and Antifederalist opponents. Federalists believed that they had constructed mechanisms—separation of powers, federalism, bicameralism, representative government, and the like—that could channel the human thirst for power and control its adverse effects, whereas Antifederalists feared that they had not adequately done so.

Given this background, it is not surprising that *The Federalist* is replete with references to human nature. In asserting in *Federalist* No. 51 that "Ambition must be made to counteract ambition" and that "The interest of the man must be connected with the constitutional rights of the place," Madison responded to anticipated charges that he was being overly pessimistic about human nature by contrasting the government of men with that of angels:

> It may be a reflection on human nature that such devices should be necessary to control the abuses of government. But what is government but the greatest of all reflections on human nature? If men were angels, no government would be necessary. If angels were to govern men, neither external nor internal controls on government would be necessary. In framing a government which is to be administered by men over men, the great difficulty lies in this: you must first enable the government to control the governed; and in the next place oblige it to control itself. (Hamilton, Madison, and Jay, 322)

See Also Antifederalists; Fame; Protestantism; Puritanism

FOR FURTHER READING

Curti, Merle. 1953. "Human Nature in American Thought." *Political Science Quarterly* 68 (September): 354–375.

Dunn, Charles W., ed. 1984. *American Political Theology: Historical Perspectives and Theoretical Analysis.* New York: Praeger.

Farrand, Max, ed. 1937. *The Records of the Federal Convention.* 4 vols. New Haven, CT: Yale University Press.

Hamilton, Alexander, James Madison, and John Jay. 1961. *The Federalist Papers.* Ed. Clinton Rossiter. New York: New American Library.

Ketcham, Ralph L. 1958. "James Madison and the Nature of Man." *Journal of the History of Ideas* 19 (January): 62–76.

Lea, James F. 1982. *Political Consciousness and American Democracy.* Jackson: University Press of Mississippi.

Sheldon, Garrett Ward. 2001. *The Political Philosophy of James Madison.* Baltimore, MD: Johns Hopkins University Press.

Spicer, Michael W. 1995. *The Founders, the Constitution, and Public Administration: A Conflict in World Views.* Washington, DC: Georgetown University Press.

HUME, DAVID (1711–1776)

David Hume's name is only once recorded in the minutes of the Constitutional Convention. Moreover, this is a citation by Alexander Hamilton of New York trying to justify the influence of the British king in Parliament (Farrand 1937, I, 376), something that most other delegates, especially those advocating republicanism, classified as "corruption." However, there is solid evidence that the Scottish philosopher, like other Scottish intellectuals of his day (Wills 1978), may have had a fairly profound influence on a number of the Founding Fathers.

Hume was best known for his skepticism of metaphysical arguments and for reliance on "experience," which generally had the effect of reaffirming scientific method (Werner 1972, 440). Similarly, in one of the most quoted statements at the Constitutional Convention, Delaware's John Dickinson said:

> Experience must be our only guide. Reason may mislead us. It was not Reason that discovered the singular & admirable mechanism of the English Constitution. It was not Reason that discovered or ever could have discovered the odd & in the eye of those who are governed by reason, the absurd mode of trial by Jury. Accidents probably produced these discoveries, and experience has give[n] a sanction to them. This is then our guide. (II, 278)

Although he had been a proponent of the American Revolution, Hume was not always admired in the colonies where his *History of England,* which is today recognized for its relative impartiality, was thought to be too sympathetic to the English monarchy. In the judgment of American Founders like John Adams and Thomas Jefferson, Hume's *History* was regarded as presenting the "Tory" rather than the "Whig" view of the subject. Hume was himself, however, a proponent of "republican" government. Hume believed that governments of the past had largely arisen through custom, but because he took this view, he would have agreed with Jefferson and other authors of the Declaration of Independence that specific rulers were not divinely sanctioned and could be overthrown when they did not secure the liberty of the people.

Hume's most direct influence on the Framers may have been his influence on James Madison (for reservations about this influence, however, see Conniff 1980). Historian Douglass Adair has shown that Hume's 1752 essay entitled "Idea of a Perfect Commonwealth," served as the foundation for Madison's argument in *Federalist* No. 10 that, contrary to the views of another influential philosopher, Charles Louis de Secondat de Montesquieu, it was possible to establish republican government over a large land area. In arguments similar to Madison's, Hume had observed in "Idea of a Perfect Commonwealth":

> In a large government, which is modeled with masterly skill, there is compass and room enough to refine the democracy, from the lower people who may be admitted into the first elections or first concoction of the commonwealth, to the higher magistrates who direct all the movements. At the same time, the parts are so distant and remote that it is very difficult, either by intrigue, prejudice, or passion, to hurry them into any measures against the public interest. (Hume 1948, 385)

In a recent article, Mark G. Spencer has further argued that Madison's view of factions may also have been influenced by Hume's *History of England* (Spencer 2002).

See Also Dickinson, John; *Federalist, The;* Madison, James, Jr.; Montesquieu, Charles Louis de Secondat de; Reason and Experience; Republicanism; Scottish Enlightenment

FOR FURTHER READING

Adair, Douglass G. 1951. "The Tenth Federalist Revisited." *William and Mary Quarterly,* 3rd ser. 8 (January): 48–67.

Conniff, James. 1980. "The Enlightenment and American Political Thought: A Study of the Origins of Madison's *Federalist* Number 10." *Political Theory* 8 (August): 381–402.

Farrand, Max, ed. 1937. *The Records of the Federal Convention.* 4 vols. New Haven, CT: Yale University Press.

Hume, David. 1948. *Hume's Moral and Political Philosophy.* Ed. Henry D. Aiken. New York: Hafner Publishing Co.

Manzer, Robert A. 2001. "A Science of Politics: Hume, *The Federalist,* and the Politics of Constitutional Attachment." *American Journal of Political Science* 45 (July): 508–518.

Spencer, Mark G. 2002. "Hume and Madison on Faction." *William and Mary Quarterly,* 3rd ser. 59 (October): 869–896.

Watson, Bradley C. C. 2003. "Hume, Historical Inheritance, and the Problem of Founding." In Ronald J. Pestritto and Thomas G. West, eds. *The American Founding and the Social Compact.* Lanham, MD: Lexington Books.

Werner, John M. 1972. "David Hume and America." *Journal of the History of Ideas* 33 (September): 439–456.

Wills, Garry. 1978. *Inventing America: Jefferson's Declaration of Independence.* Garden City, NY: Doubleday.

IMPEACHMENT CLAUSE

Although often confused in the popular mind, the U.S. Constitution bifurcates the system of impeachment (or bringing a charge, or indictment, against a public official) and conviction. The former rests according to Article I, Section 2, Clause 3, in the U.S. House of Representatives, and the latter is vested by Article I, Section 3, Clause 3, in a two-thirds vote of the U.S. Senate.

Key Issues Identified

A foremost student of the subject has identified five major areas of controversy regarding impeachment at the Convention. Delegates had to decide on the interrelated questions of "the proper forum for impeachment trials and the means for judicial removal," "the impeachability of the president," "the scope of impeachable offenses," and "the number of votes necessary for conviction and removal" (Gerhardt 1996, 5, 7, 8–9).

The Virginia Plan Discussed

The Virginia Plan, the first that the delegates debated at the Convention, had provided that the national legislature would hear and try "impeachments of National officers" (Farrand 1937, I, 22). On June 1, Delaware's Gunning Bedford objected to a seven-year term for the president on the basis that impeachments would be inadequate to cover cases in which an unqualified president were elected or a president became unqualified after taking office. Bedford observed that "an impeachment would reach misfeasance only, not incapacity" (I, 69).

On June 2, Delaware's John Dickinson advanced, and fellow delegate Gunning Bedford seconded, a motion providing that the president should not be removable by judges but by Congress "on the request of a majority of the Legislatures of individual States" (I, 85). Perhaps much like a modern parliamentary system, Connecticut's Roger Sherman proposed that Congress should be able to remove the president "at pleasure" (86). Although Virginia's George Mason agreed on the necessity of "displacing an unfit magistrate," with a likely view toward the idea of separation of powers, he "opposed decidedly the making [of] the Executive the mere creature of the Legislature" (86). Focusing on the trigger mechanism, Virginia's James Madison and Pennsylvania's James Wilson feared that it would enable smaller states to have too much control, and might "open a door for intrigues agst. him in States where his administration tho' just might be unpopular" (86). John Dickinson followed with a discursive speech, which appeared directed more to the issue of representation in the two houses of Congress than to the issue at hand. Only his home state of Delaware voted for Dickinson's motion.

This decision apparently left the judiciary both to initiate and try impeachments. On a motion made by Hugh Williamson and seconded by William Davie, both from North Carolina, the Convention now added some mention of what offenses would be impeachable. It voted to make the president removable "on impeachment and conviction of mal-practice or neglect of duty" (I, 78).

New Jersey and Hamilton Plans

The New Jersey Plan, which William Paterson introduced on June 15, provided for the judiciary to "have authority to hear & determine in the first instance on all impeachments of federal officers" (I, 244). Correctly or not, in comparing the Virginia and New Jersey Plans, Pennsylvania's James Wilson interpreted the latter as first requiring requests of a majority of state executives (I, 252). Under the plan offered by Alexander Hamilton of New York, which the Convention largely ignored, state governors, senators and other U.S. official would "be liable to impeachment for mal- and corrupt conduct." Such impeachments were to result in removal and disqualification from office and, in an interesting twist, would be tried by a tribunal consisting of the chief judge of each state (I, 292–293).

July Discussions

On July 19, during a speech directed largely to presidential re-eligibility, Gouverneur Morris of Pennsylvania expressed dissatisfaction with the provision for impeaching the president. He feared that "it will hold him in such dependence that he will be no check on the Legislature," and that "he will be the tool of a faction, of some leading demagogue in the Legislature" (II, 53). Debate proceeded on the length of the president's term, on who should choose him, and on whether he should be re-eligible for office. Discussion of impeachment resumed the next day. Morris and South Carolina's Charles Pinckney then moved to strike the provision for impeaching the president for malpractice or neglect of duty, with

Pinckney voicing the position that the president could not be impeachable while in office (perhaps reflecting the English view that "the King can do no wrong"). Morris subsequently observed that if impeachment were to result in suspending the president's functions, it would render him dependent on the impeaching body whereas if it did not, it would not correct the perceived "mischief."

Morris and Pinckney were in a distinct minority. On July 20, North Carolina's William Davie argued that without an impeachment mechanism, the president "will spare no efforts or means whatever to get himself re-elected" (II, 64). Wilson thought that such impeachment was a "necessity" (II, 64). Mason tied the necessity of a power of impeachment with the rule of subjecting all men to the law. In a somewhat novel argument (perhaps intended to provide some comic relief?), Pennsylvania's Benjamin Franklin defended impeachment as preferable to assassination. He also argued that impeachment was a means not only of removing the guilty but also for vindicating individuals who were innocent, an argument he later backed up with an illustration from the Dutch experience with the prince of Orange. Madison perceived impeachment as a necessary guard against "the incapacity, negligence or perfidy" of the president (II, 65). Elbridge Gerry of Massachusetts saw the mechanism as a necessary corrective to the idea "that the chief Magistrate could do no wrong" (II, 66). Rufus King, also of Massachusetts, expressed the view that the president should only be subject to impeachment if he held office, as he favored, during good behavior (reasoning by which federal judges are subject to this mechanism), but he argued that, in any event, the legislature should not be the body with responsibility for such trials. Virginia's Edmund Randolph thought the need for an impeachment mechanism was linked to the idea that "Guilt wherever found ought to be punished," and he commended Hamilton's idea for trial by state justices or at least for "some preliminary inquest" (II, 67).

Gouverneur Morris, who had earlier suggested the need for defining any impeachable offenses, then indicated that he had changed his mind on the need for impeachment. Professing his belief that the president should be more like a prime minister than a king (a position he thought should be reserved to the people), he still reiterated his view that the impeachment mechanism should not make the president "dependent on the Legislature" (II, 69). Eight states then voted to retain impeachment of the president, with only Massachusetts and South Carolina voting in the negative.

August and September Discussions

On August 6, the Committee of Detail proposed that the president could be "removed from his office on impeachment by the House of Representatives, and conviction in the supreme Court, of treason, bribery, or corruption" (II, 186). On August 27, Gouverneur Morris asked that this motion be postponed. He reiterated his concern about the role of the Supreme Court in the process, "particularly, if the first judge was to be of the privy Council" (II, 427).

On September 4, the Committee on Postponed Matters proposed vesting the Senate, which no longer had a role in presidential selection, with the power to try impeachments and specifying treason or bribery as impeachable offenses (II, 499). In a momentous development that was accepted but never appears to have been debated by the Convention as a whole, the committee also provided that conviction by the Senate would require a two-thirds vote (II, 497).

The delegates debated the grounds for impeachment on September 8. Seconded by Elbridge Gerry, George Mason proposed to add "maladministration" to treason and bribery as causes for impeachment (II, 550). Mason observed that the delegates had defined treason restrictively and that they had limited bills of attainder. Madison thought the term "maladministration" was too vague, and Gouverneur Morris argued that the people would vote every four years on the president's administrative abilities. Although it is not clear that they therefore significantly added to the clarity of the provision they were accepting (questions have been raised during discussions of impeaching Presidents Andrew Johnson, Richard Nixon, and Bill Clinton), the delegates then accepted Mason's substitute motion for substituting the words "other high crimes & misdemeanors" for maladministration (II, 550).

Madison moved to strike the provision for trials by the Senate, preferring that this power rest in the Supreme Court or in a body of which it formed a part (II, 551). By contrast, Gouverneur Morris argued that the Senate would be better than the Supreme Court, whose numbers would be so small that they "might be warped or corrupted" (II, 551). Charles Pinckney supported Madison in thinking that granting power to the Senate would make the president too dependent on that body, but Hugh Williamson of North Carolina thought that given their close working relationship, the Senate was more likely to be lenient than not. Connecticut's Roger Sherman further noted that the Supreme Court would be an improper body for this task since the president would appoint its members. Only Pennsylvania and Virginia voted for Madison's motion. That same day, the Convention voted to make the vice president and other civil officers also subject to impeachment and to require that senators be under oath when judging such matters.

On September 10, Edmund Randolph listed the president's trial by the Senate as one of his objections to the new Constitution. On September 14, South Carolina's John Rutledge and Gouverneur Morris proposed that individuals on trial for impeachment be suspended from office until being acquitted. Madison objected that this would make the president overly dependent on the legislature and Rufus King concurred. Only Connecticut, South Carolina, and Georgia voted for the motion.

Assessment

In assessing Convention debates, Professor Michael Gerhardt has observed that the Convention broke with English precedents on impeachment in at least five ways. It thus defined impeachable offenses, limited such proceedings to public officials, required a supermajority, limited punishment to removal from and disqualification to office, and applied it to the nation's chief executive official. He believes the resulting mechanisms were thus "uniquely American" (1996, 11). To date, two presidents, Andrew Johnson and Bill Clinton, have been impeached; neither has been convicted; Richard Nixon resigned the presidency in 1974 under the pending threat of an impeachment. Congress has used the impeachment mechanism to remove a number of judges from office, some in recent years (Volcansek 1993). William Blount, a delegate to the Convention from North Carolina who later became one of Tennessee's first two U.S. senators, was subsequently impeached for participation in a plot with the British to invade Florida and Louisiana, then held by Spain, but the Senate later dismissed charges, largely in the belief that members of Congress were not subject to this mechanism (Melton 1998).

See Also Committee of Detail; Committee on Postponed Matters

FOR FURTHER READING

Farrand, Max, ed. 1937. *The Records of the Federal Convention.* 4 vols. New Haven, CT: Yale University Press.

Gerhardt, Michael J. 1996. *The Federal Impeachment Process: A Constitutional and Historical Analysis.* Princeton, NJ: Princeton University Press.

Hoffer, Peter C., and N. E. H. Hull. 1979. "Power and Precedent in the Creation of an American Impeachment Tradition: The Eighteenth-Century Colonial Record." *William and Mary Quarterly,* 3rd ser. 36 (January): 51–77.

Melton, Buckner F., Jr. 1998. *The First Impeachment: The Constitution's Framers and the Case of Senator William Blount.* Macon, GA: Mercer University Press.

Volcansek, Mary L. 1993. *Judicial Impeachment: None Called for Justice.* Urbana: University of Illinois Press.

IMPLIED POWERS

See POWERS, IMPLIED

INCOMPATABILITY AND INELIGIBILITY CLAUSES

See CONGRESS, MEMBERS' INELIGIBILITY FOR OTHER OFFICES

INDENTURED SERVANTS

Although scholars understandably have devoted greater attention to the status of slaves under the Constitution, this document also recognized the institution of indentured servitude. Article I, Section 1 thus provided that the formula used for representation and the apportionment of direct taxes shall include "the whole Number of free Persons, including those bound to Service for a Term of Years." Similarly, Article IV, Section 2, often called the "fugitive slave clause," also refers to a person "held to Service," a category associated with, but apparently distinct from, "a Person held . . . to Labour."

As many as one-half to two-thirds of the European immigrants to America during the colonial era probably arrived as indentured servants (Menard 1991, 542). Although the institution somewhat resembled apprenticeship, indentured servitude appears to have grown out of the British institution of "service in husbandry." Unlike slaves, indentured servants voluntarily accepted their positions of service in exchange for lodging and for the promise of freedom within a term of years—although this did not apparently stop a good many from attempting to get out of their responsibilities early (Prude 1991). Years of service varied depending on age, skills, and local law. Servants had greater legal protections than slaves. Indentured servants could sometimes be sold from one master to another, and they could not marry without their employer's consent. The institution continued as late as the 1830s but appears largely to have died out by 1800 (Menard, 543). As in the case of slave owners, employers of indentured servants sometimes sought governmental help in capturing runaways—an offense for which the time of servitude could be increased.

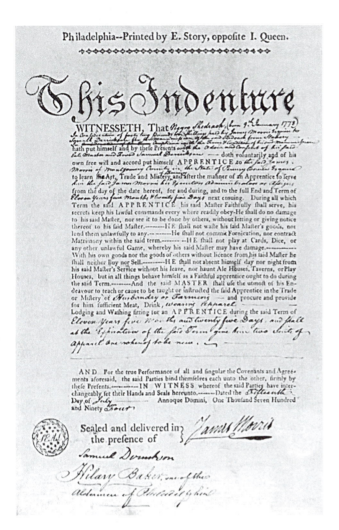

Paper documenting the term of service for an indentured servant (Hulton Archive/Getty Images)

One of the most fascinating such cases involved Sarah Wilson, who arrived in Maryland in 1771 as an indentured servant and was purchased by William Duvall. Unbeknownst to Duvall, Wilson had been a personal maid to one of the ladies in Queen Charlotte's court, whose sentence had been commuted from death to indentured servitude after she was discovered to have stolen jewelry and a miniature of the Queen, which had not been recovered. Carrying this booty to America, the beautiful and resourceful Wilson had escaped and pretended to be Lady Susannah Caroline Matilda, Queen Charlotte's sister. She used the portrait and jewels, which she had carried with her, to establish her credentials. Successful in carrying out this disguise in Virginia where she was lavishly hosted in the homes of elite planters, many of whom generously lent her money, she fled to New

York after her identity was discovered. She was caught in New York and returned to Maryland.

She appears to have later escaped to South Carolina. Again, she succeeded for a time in brazenly parading as the Queen's sister before once again being discovered and presumably again returned to her employer.

See Also African Americans; Slavery

FOR FURTHER READING

Biehl, Katharine L. 1945. "The Indentured Servant in Colonial America." *The Social Studies* 36 (January): 316–319.

Fogelman, Aaron S. 1998. "From Slaves, Convicts, and Servants to Free Passengers: The Transformation of Immigration in the Era of the American Revolution." *Journal of American History* 85 (June): 43–76.

Menard, Russell R. 1991. "Indentured Servitude." In Eric Foner and John A. Garraty, eds. *The Reader's Companion to American History.* Boston: Houghton Mifflin, 542–543.

Prude, Jonathan. 1991. "To Look upon the 'Lower Sort': Runaway Ads and the Appearance of Unfree Laborers in America, 1750–1800." *Journal of American History* 78 (June): 124–159.

INDEPENDENCE HALL

See PENNSYLVANIA STATE HOUSE

INDIAN QUEEN

See LODGING OF THE DELEGATES

INDIANS

American Indians, or Native Americans, as they are now generally called, were not represented at the U.S. Constitutional Convention. However, one delegate, New Jersey's William Livingston, who is not recorded as having participated in Convention debates, is known to have spent a year of his youth with a Moravian missionary among New York's Mohawk Indians.

References to Indians at the Convention

A number of delegates to the Constitutional Convention mentioned Indians, albeit never in a complimentary fashion. Instead, consistent with security concerns, the delegates cited Indians as a threat to the states against which the central government should be helping or as an example of uncivilized conduct. Pennsylvania's Benjamin Franklin used Indian attacks as an argument against an absolute executive veto, observing on June 4, 1787, that the governor of Pennsylvania under the propriety government had refused to concur in means of self-defense, "when the Indians were scalping the western people," until his estate was "exempted from taxation" (Farrand 1937, I, 99). New York's Alexander Hamilton noted that one of the objects of union was that of protecting the Western frontier "against the savages" (I, 297). In a view that appears to reflect a generally more sympathetic attitude to the Indians (see Levy 2002), Virginia's James Madison observed that, although the government under the Articles of Confederation had been designed to handle "transactions with the Indians," states had in several cases "entered into treaties & wars with them" (I, 316).

Reinforcing the theme of Indians as "American savages," Madison used them as examples of "ye situation of the weak compared with the strong in those stages of civilization in which the violence of individuals is least controlled by an efficient Government" (I, 448). In discussing whether foreigners should be eligible to the presidency, Gouverneur Morris of Pennsylvania argued that "we should be governed as much by our reason, and as little by our feelings as possible" (II, 237). The illustration that he offered, which would have been especially outrageous to the sensibilities of his day, centered on reports that "some tribes of

Indians carried their hospitality so far as to offer to strangers their wives and daughters." There was no doubt that he intended for his fellow delegates to answer his rhetorical question, whether "this is a proper model for us?" (II, 238), negatively.

Constitutional Provisions

Two provisions in the Constitution of 1787 dealt directly with Indians. A provision in Article I, Section 2 excluded "Indians not taxed" (these being those Indians who were living on Indian territories or reservations and thus not integrated into the nation as a whole) from the figures used in apportioning state representation. A second provision, found in Article I, Section 8 among the powers of Congress, extended such powers to the regulation of commerce "with the Indian Tribes." This provision was much broader than a comparable provision under the Articles of Confederation that did not extend federal power to deal with Indians who lived within state boundaries (Levy, 122).

Other provisions also affected relations with Indian tribes. By providing for the admission of new states, Article IV, Section 3 pointed to the hope of many Framers for westward expansion into territories then occupied by Indian tribes. Similarly, Article II, Section 2 grants powers to negotiate treaties to the president, subject to consent of two-thirds majorities in the Senate, and Article I, Section 10 denies this same power to the states. Article II, Section 3 grants Congress exclusive power to govern U.S. territories. The supremacy clause in Article VI further recognized that the U.S. Constitution and "all Treaties made, or which shall be made under the Authority of the United States, shall be the supreme Law of the Land."

Impact of the Constitution

Some delegates expressed concerns over Western settlers that almost portrayed them as sharing in the uncivilized conduct attributed to the Indians. Gouverneur Morris thus observed: "The Busy haunts of men not the remote wilderness, was the proper School of political Talents. If the Western

America, 1772–title page ornamentation showing Native wearing skirt made of feathers pointing to a map of America. Augustae Vindelicorum, 1772. (Library of Congress)

U.S. [5 Pet.] 1 [1831]), with some, but not all, elements of sovereignty attributable to foreign countries (see Rossum and Tarr 2003, 415–449). Congress did not grant American Indians the rights of citizenship until 1924.

See Also Iroquois

FOR FURTHER READING

Claiborne, Louis F. 1987–1988. "Black Men, Red Men, and the Constitution of 1787: A Bicentennial Apology from a Middle Templar." *Hastings Constitutional Law Quarterly* 15: 269–293.

Farrand, Max, ed. 1937. *The Records of the Federal Convention*. 4 vols. New Haven, CT: Yale University Press.

Johansen, Bruce E. 1990. "Native American Societies and the Evolution of Democracy in America, 1600–1800." *Ethnohistory* 37 (Summer): 279–290.

Levy, Jacob T. 2002. "Indians in Madison's Constitutional Order." In John Samples, ed. *James Madison and the Future of Limited Government*. Washington, DC: Cato Institute, 121–133.

Payne, Samuel B., Jr. 1996. "The Iroquois League, the Articles of Confederation, and the Constitution." *William and Mary Quarterly*, 3rd ser. 53 (July): 605–620.

Rossum, Ralph A., and G. Alan Tarr. 2003. *The Structure of Government*. Vol. 1 of *American Constitutional Law*. Belmont, CA: Wadsworth/Thomson Learning.

Smith-Rosenberg, Carroll. 1992. "Dis-Covering the Subject of the 'Great Constitutional Discussion, 1786–1789." *Journal of American History* 79 (December): 841–873.

Wunder, John R. 2000/2001. "'Merciless Indian Savages' and the Declaration of Independence: Native Americans Translate the Ecunnaunuxulgee Document." *American Indian Law Review* 24: 65–92.

———. 1994. *"Retained by the People": A History of American Indians and the Bill of Rights*. New York: Oxford University Press.

people get the power into their hands they will ruin the Atlantic interests" (I, 583).

These references, as well as the weight of historical research, suggest that what impact Indian governments may have had on the Constitution–historians sometimes cite the Iroquois government, which was confederal in character, as one such influence–was probably indirect (Payne 1996; Johansen 1990). Sadly, Convention delegates appear to have had little concern for Native American tribes. However it benefited much of the rest of the nation, the Constitution probably made the plight of the Indians worse by strengthening the national government.

Subsequent U.S. Supreme Court decisions have recognized that Indian tribes fall into a special position under the Constitution as "domestic dependent nations" (*Cherokee Nation v. Georgia*, 30

INGERSOLL, JARED (1749–1822)

Jared Ingersoll was born in New Haven, Connecticut, in 1749. His father was a lawyer who fa-

Jared Ingersoll, delegate from Pennsylvania
(Pixel That)

vored the Loyalists during the Revolution. After Ingersoll graduated from Yale, his father sent him to London where he studied law at the Middle Temple before going to Paris and returning to the U.S. during the Revolution to establish a law practice in Philadelphia. Ingersoll represented Pennsylvania at the Continental Congress from 1780 to 1781.

A Largely Silent Participant

Pennsylvania's Jared Ingersoll was seated at the Constitutional Convention on May 28, 1787, and he signed the document on September 17. Unlike some who were somewhat more equivocal about their signing of the document, Ingersoll said that he "did not consider the signing, either as a mere attestation of the fact, or as pledging the signers to support the Constitution at all events; but as a recommendation, of what, all things considered, was the most eligible" (Farrand 1937, III, 647). He was not appointed to any committees at the Convention and he was otherwise silent.

An Undelivered Speech

There is, however, a draft of a speech, once attributed to Maryland's Luther Martin or to Connecticut's Roger Sherman, that appears to be in Ingersoll's handwriting and which he appears to have prepared for delivery sometime after June 19. Such an attribution seems consistent with the speech's somewhat apologetic beginning in which the author attributes his silence to "my Inferiority, to the members of this hon[orab]le convention, in an acquaintance with the political history of this Country" and to the fact that "a laborious application to the business of my profession has not afforded me much Opportunity for attendance here in order to collect Information, nor time for reflecting on the few Ideas with which my Mind was stored relative to the Object of our present meeting" (Hutson 1987, 101).

Ingersoll saw the dilemma of the Convention as that of being able "to introduce a System unexceptionable in itself & relatively so, authorized & yet efficacious" (101). He identified the central issue as that of whether the Convention would settle on a "national" or a "federal" government (101). Ingersoll further attempted to trace the cause of the nation's problems. He believed that many of these problems were attributable not so much to the weakness of Congress as to the situation that the nation faced after winning independence. Many of these problems he traced to British pride and to the interest of European nations to keep the U.S. weak.

Ingersoll identified three powers that Congress should exercise. These were the power to get sufficient revenue to discharge its debts, to regulate foreign and internal commerce, and to fix the currency. Ingersoll expressed doubts as to whether Congress also needed to be granted "physical power" to carry its will into execution or whether it needed power to act directly upon individual citizens.

In addressing this question, Ingersoll thought it necessary to examine abstract principles, practical concerns, and what the Convention was authorized to do. In looking at abstract principles, Ingersoll developed an argument as to why, even if the Convention were starting from scratch, a federal government might be preferable to a unitary one. His central theme was diversity. Laws needed to differ for

> the Fisheries & Manufacturers of New-England, The Flour Lumber Flaxseed & Ginseng of New York New Jersey Pennsylvania & Delaware The Tobacco of Maryland & Virginia the Pitch Tar, Rice & Indigo & Cotton of North Carolina South Carolina & Georgia. (103)

Similarly there were differences between slave states and free, and other differences that stemmed from "the Climate, Produce, Soil, & even Genius of the people" (103).

Ingersoll feared that "the present System," by which he appeared to be speaking of the proposals under consideration by the Convention, might be "more objectionable much than a general Government" (104). He observed that those opposed to a "general government" would also oppose the proposals under consideration, citing criticisms that had already been raised within the Convention itself to the effect that the new government would result either in monarchy or the abolition of the states (104). Ingersoll himself had doubts about the plan under consideration: "I cannot but think that the present System is more objectionable much than a general Government" (104). Ingersoll continued:

> Others will say & I must be of the Number that this Government is consonant to no principle whatever, on the principle of the Union it is too much on the Idea of a general Government it is too little—that it has all the expence of a National Government without its *energy*—will give equal Alarm, equal opportunity to excite prejudice, without affording any dignity to Government or securing Obedience to obtaining any of the primary Objects of Government, that an eternal contest will be excited between the several Governments & this monstrous sluggard, that the activity of the latter will be able to thwart the overgrown lubber [?], that all that can be expected from it is securing a Revennue, the whole of which will be absorbed in the collection that so much might be obtained nearly in the present

> system & a great part of the expence saved that it is [?]. (104)

Unfortunately, the speech soon becomes difficult to follow (perhaps because it was not complete), addressing what the people might be likely to accept but failing to examine, as promised, what the Convention was authorized to do. What is most notable about the speech is the candid observation that the very attitudes that propelled the nation to war against Britain (attitudes similar to those that the British philosopher Edmund Burke had identified during the Revolutionary War) were now making it difficult–impractical–to form a new government in which the national government was given too much power:

> The people of the united-States, excited to Arms by the insidious designs of the then Mother Country have become admirers of liberty warmly & passionately so—they snuff Tyranny in every tainted Gale—they are jealous of their liberty—they are pleased with their present Governments, they think them as energetick as they ought to be framed, they are continually planning subdivisions of the present Governments, they are complaining of the expence of the present Governments—they are jealous of designs to introduce a Monarchy, under specious pretences & different names . . . they are apprehensive of designs to abridge the liberties of the common people . . . they are prejudiced each against the neighboring State—of no humour to coalesce. (104–105)

The lesson would appear to be that the delegates should do more to work to strengthen the present system than to alter it. The writer of this speech would appear especially unlikely to favor the proposed congressional veto of state laws or any other measures that might be associated with a national bureaucracy. Again, it is important to remember that the speech began by observing that the current plight of the nation might not be as attributable to the weakness of the general government as to the animosity of European powers.

Pennsylvanians were, of course, at the forefront of the movement toward a stronger central government, a stronger presidency, and a reconfigured Congress based on proportional representation—witness the influence of Gouverneur Morris and James Wilson. Perhaps this is the reason Ingersoll never delivered his speech. If it had been delivered, this speech would arguably have been as strong as any such speech at the Convention in portraying the continuation of significant state powers not simply as practical necessity but as desirable in and of itself as a way of adapting to the wide variety of local interests. If, in fact, Ingersoll was the author of this speech, it would appear that Convention deliberations would have been even stronger had he participated.

Life after the Convention

After the Convention, Ingersoll served in a number of governmental positions to which Federalists appointed him. These included serving as Pennsylvania's attorney general, as Philadelphia's city solicitor, and as judge. Ingersoll ran for vice president in 1812 with New York's Governor DeWitt Clinton but the two lost to James Madison and Elbridge Gerry (all the candidates except Clinton had attended the Constitutional Convention). Ingersoll died in 1822, financially ruined by his speculation in Western lands. His son, Charles Jared Ingersoll, served in the U.S. Congress from 1813 to 1815 and from 1841 to 1849.

See Also Pennsylvania

FOR FURTHER READING

Farrand, Max, ed. 1937. *The Records of the Federal Convention.* 4 vols. New Haven, CT: Yale University Press.

Hutson, James H. 1987. *Supplement to Max Farrand's* The Records of the Federal Convention of 1787. New Haven, CT: Yale University Press.

Whitney, David C. 1974. *Founders of Freedom in America: Lives of the Men Who Signed the Constitution of the United States and So Helped to Establish the United States of America.* Chicago: J. J. Ferguson Publishing.

IROQUOIS

Although the thesis is not new, Donald A. Grinde, Jr., and Bruce E. Johansen have been among the better-known scholarly advocates of the view that the Framers of the U.S. Constitution were influenced by the Iroquois, who had formed a confederation of six nations (see Grinde and Johansen 1977 and 1996). Indeed, in a dubious contribution to the problems of historiography that falsely suggests that such issues can be resolved by legislative mandate, the U.S. Congress weighed in on the matter in 1988. At that time, it adopted a resolution proclaiming that "the confederation of the original Thirteen Colonies into one republic was influenced by the political system developed by the Iroquois Confederacy as were many of the democratic principles which were incorporated into the Constitution itself" (quoted in Payne 1996, 606).

Grinde and Johansen provided some evidence of Founding Fathers who were presumably aware of Indian institutions, including those of the Iroquois. However, the weight of the evidence from the Convention itself would suggest that the Framers held deep prejudices against Indians, whom they often referred to as "savages," and were generally ill informed about them. The members of the Constitutional Convention are not once recorded at the meeting lauding Indian institutions or citing them as positive examples. The sources the Framers cite for their own illustrations and ideas are instead drawn from their knowledge of Greek and Roman classics, of the government of Great Britain, of European nations and commentators on such governments, and on their own experience under state constitutions and under the Articles of Confederation.

American Framers knew about confederacies from these sources before they ever became familiar with the institutions of the Iroquois. However it might appeal to those with Native American constituencies to proclaim their influence, most historians believe the influence was minimal to nonexistent.

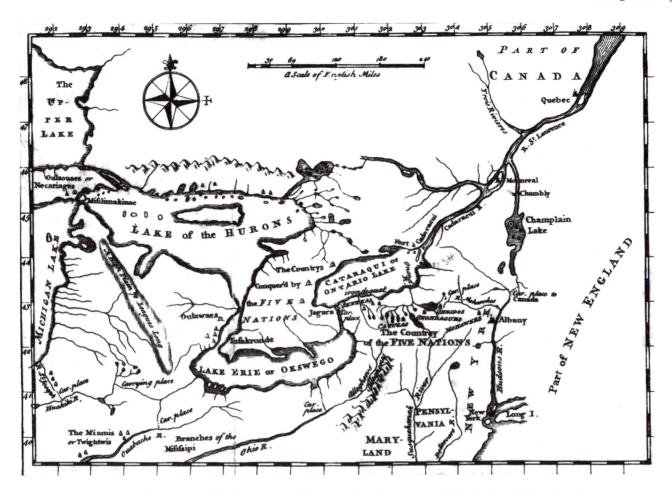

A map of the country of the Iroquois Confederacy, or Five Nations, ca. 1650 (Hulton Archive/Getty)

See Also Indians; New England Confederation

FOR FURTHER READING

Grinde, Donald A., Jr., and Bruce E. Johansen. 1977. *The Iroquois and the Founding of the American Nation.* San Francisco: Indian Historian Press.

——. 1996. "Sauce for the Goose: Demand and Definitions for 'Proof' Regarding the Iroquois and Democracy." *William and Mary Quarterly,* 3rd ser. 53 (July): 621–636.

Levy, Philip A. 1996. "Exemplars of Taking Liberties: The Iroquois Influence Thesis and the Problem of Evidence." *William and Mary Quarterly,* 3rd ser. 53 (July): 588–604.

Payne, Samuel B., Jr. 1996. "The Iroquois League, the Articles of Confederation, and the Constitution." *William and Mary Quarterly,* 3rd ser. 53 (July): 605–620.

JACKSON, WILLIAM (1759–1828)

In addition to the 39 delegates who attended the Convention and signed the Constitution, William Jackson, the Convention secretary, also signed. Fellow Revolutionary War veteran Alexander Hamilton of New York nominated Jackson on May 25, the Convention's first day of business. James Wilson of Pennsylvania had previously nominated Temple Franklin, Benjamin Franklin's grandson, who had served as secretary to American diplomats, including his grandfather, who had negotiated the Treaty of Paris that had ended the Revolutionary War. The state delegations then in attendance voted for Jackson by a vote of 5-2.

Jackson had written to George Washington prior to the Convention seeking this appointment (Farrand 1937, III, 18). A contemporary letter written by William Shippin to his son indicates that Jackson was "extremely delighted" with his appointment and "thinks his forture and fame are both established." By contrast, Benjamin Franklin was reported to be "much mortified he had not interest [influence] enough to procure the place for his Grandson" (quoted in *1787*, 1987, 10). Congress paid Jackson for four months of work at an annual pay of $2,600; he thus received $866.80 for his work as secretary at the Convention (Hutson 1987, 277).

The day after it selected Jackson, the Convention rejected a motion providing that a committee be appointed to "superintend the minutes" (Farrand I, 17). Morris objected that a single individual was likely to be more impartial and that "A committee might have an interest & bias in moulding the entry according to their opinions and wishes" (I, 17). The Convention barely rejected the motion by a vote of 5-4.

Jackson had been born in Cumberland, England in 1759, but when his parents died when he was still a youth, he was sent to Charleston, South Carolina, where Owen Roberts, a merchant and family friend, raised him. Roberts was a veteran of the French and Indian War, who later died fighting for the Patriot cause in 1779. Jackson is believed to have volunteered prior to his seventeenth birthday and was commissioned as a second lieutenant in May of 1776. On the recommendation of his regimental commander, Charles Cotesworth Pinckney, who would later serve as a delegate to the Constitutional Convention, Major General Benjamin Lincoln of Massachusetts appointed Jackson as an aide, and he was promoted to the rank of major. Captured when the Patriots surrendered in Savannah in 1780, he became a staff officer to Lieutenant Colonel John Laurens, an aide to George Washington, after being exchanged. Jackson accompanied Laurens to France to negotiate for war supplies and, on arriving back in Philadelphia, served again under Benjamin Lincoln as assistant secretary of war.

Initially intent on becoming a merchant, Jack-

William Temple Franklin

On May 25, Pennsylvania's James Wilson nominated William Temple Franklin to be secretary of the Constitutional Convention. Temple was the illegitimate son of William Franklin, Benjamin's loyalist son, who had served as the royal governor of New Jersey at the outbreak of the American Revolution. Although William and his father were at loggerheads, Temple had served as the secretary to Benjamin Franklin and other Americans who had negotiated a treaty of peace with Great Britain. Temple Franklin returned to America with Benjamin, returned to England after Franklin's death, quarreled with his father, and died childless in Paris in 1823 (Fleming 1997, 374).

To the apparent embarrassment of Benjamin Franklin, the position of Convention secretary went instead, by a vote of 5 states to 2, to Major William Jackson. Jackson was a former secretary to George Washington, whom New York's Alexander Hamilton nominated. Jackson's notes were not very complete, and serve mostly to confirm more extensive notes that James Madison took of the Convention.

FOR FURTHER READING

Fleming, Thomas. 1997. *Liberty! The American Revolution.* New York: Viking.

---

son instead studied law, and was accepted into the Philadelphia bar the year after the Constitutional Convention. He served as George Washington's private secretary when Washington was president, later married a daughter of a Philadelphia merchant named Thomas Willing and was appointed as surveyor of customs for the Philadelphia port. A strong Federalist who was displaced from this position when the Jeffersonian Republicans gained power in 1801, Jackson served for a time as editor of Philadelphia's *Political and Commercial Register.* Jackson also served for more than 25 years as the national secretary of the Society of the Cincinnati. Jackson took part in ceremonies welcoming General Lafayette to Philadelphia in 1824, and died in Philadelphia in 1828.

Although Jackson has been described as "the quintessential civil servant" (Wright and MacGregor 1987, 128), scholars have been generally disappointed with the notes he took of the Constitutional Convention. For the most part, they consist simply of records of motions and the votes of states on each one, and the notes were in relative disarray when, as secretary of state, John Quincy Adams made the first attempt to publish them. Madison had access to Jackson's notes when correcting his own records, but his original records are often more accurate than Jackson's. Serious students of the Convention have received far more help from the summaries of actual deliberations and debates taken by James Madison and other participants than from Jackson's sketchy records of yeas and nays, but Jackson's records often confirm that debates occurred on the days and with the results that others have reported.

See Also Records of the Constitutional Convention; Society of the Cincinnati

FOR FURTHER READING

1787: The Day-to-Day Story of the Constitutional Convention. 1987. Compiled by historians of Independence National Historical Park, National Park Service. New York: Exeter Books.

Farrand, Max, ed. 1937. *The Records of the Federal Convention.* 4 vols. New Haven, CT: Yale University Press.

Hutson, James H., ed. 1987. *Supplement to Max Farrand's* The Records of the Federal Convention of 1787. New Haven, CT: Yale University Press.

Wright, Robert K., Jr., and Morris J. MacGregor, Jr. 1987. *Soldier Statesmen of the Constitution.* Washington, DC: Center of Military History, U.S. Army.

JAY, JOHN (1745–1829)

The only one of the three authors of *The Federalist* who did not attend the Constitutional Convention, John Jay nonetheless exercised an important role in achieving American independence. Jay was born in New York City in 1745 to the family of a merchant with French Huguenot (dissenting Protestant) roots. He graduated from King's College (today's Columbia University), read law, began a legal career, and married Sarah Livingston, the daughter of William Livingston, who became the longtime governor of New Jersey and attended the Constitutional Convention as one of the state's delegates.

Jay was elected in 1774 to the New York City Committee of Correspondence and was later selected as a delegate to the First and Second Continental Congresses. Although he wrote the "Address to the People of Great Britain," in which he justified colonial actions, as well as a later appeal to Canada to join the lower colonies, Jay moved more cautiously toward independence than many of the other delegates. After returning to New York from Congress, he even helped draft instructions from New York to the congressional delegation asking that it oppose such a move.

Once Congress declared Independence, however, and his home state was threatened, Jay helped supply George Washington with cannon, engaged in espionage against the British, and was one of the moving forces behind the New York state constitution, which contained a number of features that later found their way into the U.S. Constitution. Upon his return to Philadelphia, Congress selected him as president, during which time he insisted that the Articles of Confederation were in effect, even though Maryland had not ratified them. After this service, Congress sent him on the exasperating missions of attempting to get support for the Revolution from royalist Spain. After two years of fairly fruitless efforts, Jay became, along with Benjamin Franklin and John Adams, one of the principal negotiators of the Treaty of Paris that ended the Revolutionary War and in which the British recognized American sovereignty in the New World to the borders of the Mississippi River. Upon his

*John Jay, first chief justice of the U.S. Supreme Court
(1789–1795)
(Collection of the Supreme Court
of the United States)*

return, he was selected as the secretary for foreign affairs.

In this capacity, Jay came to an agreement with Diego de Gardoqui of Spain to concede U.S. rights to navigate the Mississippi River for 30 years in exchange for certain trade concessions. The Southern states stoutly and successfully resisted this measure, which continued to be a point of suspicion and controversy during the Constitutional Convention.

Although Jay was not chosen to attend, he was known to favor increased congressional powers and separation of powers. He thus wrote a letter to Jefferson in 1786 in which he said:

To vest legislative, judicial, and executive powers in one and the same body of men and that, too, in a body daily changing its members, can never be wise. In my opinion, these three great departments of sovereignty should be forever separated, and so distributed as to serve as checks on one another. (Quoted in Morris 1985b, 190)

Jay was also known to oppose a king but favor a strong executive. Jay wrote a letter to Washington during the Convention in which he suggested that congressional offices, as well as the presidency, should be limited to native-born citizens. The Convention agreed to a measure similar to the second half of this proposal, albeit with an escape clause for individuals who were citizens at the time the Constitution was adopted. Jay was serving at the time of the Convention as president of the New York Society for the Manumission of Slaves and drafted a motion asking the New Yorkers at the Convention to oppose its continuation, but fellow New Yorker Alexander Hamilton persuaded the Society that such a petition would prove counterproductive, and the Society did not send it (Morris 1985b, 193–194).

After the Convention, Hamilton recruited Madison and Jay to help him author *The Federalist*. Jay's contribution, a total of five essays (numbers 2–4 and 64), was cut short by attacks of rheumatism. As befitted his own experience, most of the essays he wrote dealt with the need for a stronger government to deal with foreign affairs. Jay also wrote a highly influential pamphlet in favor of the Constitution called an "Address to the People of the State of New York."

President Washington appointed Jay as the nation's first chief justice, during which time most of his decisions were nationalistic. Jay advised the president on foreign policy issues and even served for a time as an envoy to London. The Jay Treaty which he helped negotiate in 1794 to head off conflict with the English, who had been attacking American shipping, was adopted, but was widely criticized for not gaining more concessions. It stirred almost as much passion as Jay's earlier agreement with the Spanish and further widened the rift that had been developing between Federalists and Democratic-Republicans.

Jay resigned from the Supreme Court after being elected as New York's governor. Ironically, Jay later refused John Adams's offer to reappoint him as chief justice largely because he did not believe that this body (which John Marshall would soon so effectively muster) was capable of supporting the new government. Jay undoubtedly remem-

bered that the Eleventh Amendment had overturned the decision in which he had participated in *Chisholm v. Georgia* (1783), declaring that states could be sued by citizens of other states.

Jay and the wife to whom he was so devoted retired to New York, where she died in 1802. Jay survived until 1829. Jay was a proud and prickly but devout and honest man who helped establish the American Bible Society, over which he served for a time as president.

See Also *Federalist, The;* Jay-Gardoqui Negotiations; Mississippi River; New York

FOR FURTHER READING

Morris, Richard B. 1985a. "The Constitutional Thought of John Jay." *this Constitution*, no. 9 (Winter): 25–33.
——. 1985b. *Witnesses at the Creation: Hamilton, Madison, Jay, and the Constitution.* New York: New American Library.
Stahr, Walter. 2005. *John Jay: Founding Father.* London: Hambledon and London.

JAY-GARDOQUI NEGOTIATIONS

After the former colonies entered into a peace treaty with Great Britain, the Spanish, who controlled the port of New Orleans, became alarmed by American power and blocked navigation of the Mississippi River by Americans. This action had a serious effect on the economic well-being on the American frontier (mountain ranges often prevented easy transport and marketing of agricultural products eastward), and it depressed Western land values in which many individuals, especially in the South, had speculated.

After initial negotiations proved fruitless, Spain sent Don Diego de Gardoqui in 1785 as a minister plenipotentiary to negotiate this matter with John Jay, the U.S. secretary of foreign affairs. Although Congress had instructed Jay not to give up American rights to navigate the Mississippi, he asked for permission to conclude a treaty that would give up such claims for the next 25 to 30 years in exchange for the right to market grain and fish to Spain, a measure that he believed would help the ailing New England economy.

This request led to a bitter congressional debate in which all five Southern states, including North Carolina and Virginia (with Western lands that would later become the states of Tennessee and Kentucky), voting as a block, narrowly stopped this reversal in policy. Northerners thought that conceding what the nation did not have was a small price to pay for other commercial advantages, whereas Southerners saw this attitude as an indication that Northern states would pursue sectional interests over national ones (see McDonald and McDonald 1968, 77–80).

The memory of this event appears to be largely responsible for the constitutional provision that treaties would have to be ratified by a two-thirds majority of the Senate. It was also the impetus for less successful proposals to require a similar majority for all matters related to the taxation of exports. Throughout the Convention, Southern delegates were more closely tied to Western interests and generally took a much more positive view of eventually admitting the Western states into the Union on an equal basis with the old.

See Also Mississippi River; Sectionalism; States, Admission and Creation; Treaty-Making and Ratification

FOR FURTHER READING

McDonald, Forrest, and Ellen Shapiro McDonald. 1968. *Confederation and Constitution 1781–1789.* New York: Harper and Row Publishers.

Merritt, Eli. 1991. "Sectional Conflict and Secret Compromise: The Mississippi River Question and the United States Constitution." *American Journal of Legal History* 35 (April): 117–171.

JEFFERSON, THOMAS
(1743–1826)

Thomas Jefferson was one of the most famous Founding Fathers who was *not* present at the Constitutional Convention of 1787. Born in Shadwell (near present-day Charlottesville), Virginia, in 1743, Jefferson attended the College of William and Mary and read law under George Wythe, who later briefly attended the U.S. Constitutional Convention. Elected to the Virginia House of Burgesses in 1769, Jefferson wrote *A Summary View of the Rights of British America,* which strongly supported the Patriot cause in the developing struggle with England and established Jefferson's credentials for lucid writing.

Life prior to the Convention

Subsequently appointed to the Second Continental Congress, Jefferson made his most important mark in writing the first draft of the Declaration of Independence. There he proclaimed that all men are created equal and are entitled to certain unalienable rights. He further contended that when government becomes destructive of such liberties, the people have the right to replace it with one that is more responsive.

Returning to Virginia where he was elected to the House of Delegates, Jefferson had a major role in revising the state's laws. One of his most important contributions was the Virginia Statute for Religious Freedom (disestablishing the Anglican Church in the state), which was not, however, adopted until 1786. Jefferson served as Virginia's governor at a trying time during the Revolution, and later served in Congress where he helped draft the Ordinance of 1784, which provided a model for the later Northwest Ordinance. Notably, Jefferson, who owned slaves, tried to keep slavery out of the territories. Jefferson also wrote his *Notes on the State of Virginia,* explaining and critiquing (among other things) the constitution of Virginia and indicating that he supported the idea of separation of powers and arguing that constitutions should not be adopted by, or amended by, simple majorities of the state legislature.

Congress appointed Jefferson to succeed Benjamin Franklin as the nation's minister to France, and his five years there included the period during which the Constitutional Convention met. He sent scores of books to his friend James Madison, who was preparing for this event and who would influence its outcome so greatly, and subsequently corresponded with Madison about the outcome. In contrast to many supporters of the Constitution, Jefferson does not appear to have been as shaken by Shays's Rebellion. Indeed, he wrote that "I hold it that a little rebellion now and then is a good thing, and as necessary in the political world as storms in the physical" (quoted in Koch 1950, 45).

Reaction to the Constitution

Jefferson was generally pleased with the document but, with many Antifederalists, was strongly convinced that the Constitution needed to have a bill of rights. He stated: "Were I in America, I would advocate it warmly till nine should have adopted, and then as warmly take the other side to convince the remaining four that they ought not to come into it till the declaration of rights is annexed to it" (quoted in Vile 1992, 69).

Jefferson wrote to Madison suggesting that "a bill of rights is what the people are entitled to against every government on earth, general or particular, and what no just government should refuse, or rest on inferences" (quoted in Koch, 41). He sent a series of letters to Madison between October 1787 and March 1789 advocating such a bill and especially commending it for the power that it would give to members of the judiciary to strike down unconstitutional legislation. Jefferson specifically recommended including guarantees of "freedom of religion, freedom of the press, protection against standing armies, restriction against monopolies, the eternal and unremitting force of the habeas corpus laws, and trials by jury in all matters of fact triable by the laws of the land and not by the law of Nations" (quoted in Mayer 1994, 155). This correspondence appears to have been one of the factors that influenced Madison's decision to support such a bill of rights, and Madison specifically used some of the arguments that Jefferson had made when he defended this bill on the floor of the U.S. House of Representatives.

Although Madison did not inform Jefferson of his work on *The Federalist* at the time he was writing it, Jefferson later praised the work as "the best commentary on the principles of government which ever was written" (quoted in Koch, 54). He wrote this despite the fact that Madison had used the essays to oppose one of Jefferson's suggestions that constitutions should be rewritten every generation.

In addition to advocating a bill of rights, Jefferson had feared the constitutional provision that had allowed for reelection of the presidency. Jefferson later helped reinforce the precedent that George Washington had established of not seeking a third term in this office. Largely in reaction to the long presidential tenure of Franklin D. Roosevelt, the nation would eventually adopt an amendment (the Twenty-second) limiting presidents to two terms.

Service in National Offices

George Washington asked Jefferson to serve as his first secretary of state. Although Jefferson did his job well, it brought him into increasing conflict with Secretary of the Treasury Alexander Hamilton. In contrast to Hamilton, Jefferson opposed the federal assumption of state debt and the establishment of a national bank and feared the growth of national power. His opposition, together with that of James Madison, eventually led to the establishment of the Democratic-Republican Party. Jefferson resigned from Washington's cabinet but was chosen as vice president in 1796, serving under John Adams, whose policies he largely opposed. In 1798, Jefferson penned the Kentucky Resolution in opposition to the Alien and Sedition Acts; this resolution, like Jefferson's earlier statements on the establishment of the national bank, put key emphasis on the idea that the Tenth Amendment had reserved major powers to the states.

Located outside Charlottesville, Virginia, Monticello was the home of Thomas Jefferson, who served as U.S. president from 1801 to 1809. (PhotoDisc)

Swept into office by the election of 1800 (where, however, he initially tied in the Electoral College vote with fellow Republican Aaron Burr), Jefferson went on to serve two terms as president (1801–1809). He attempted to moderate some of the party strife that had helped get him elected, noting at his inauguration that "We are all republicans—we are all federalists." His administration was marked by the successful purchase of the Louisiana Territory from France and the quite unpopular embargo, designed to pressure Great Britain and avert war. Ironically, both measures appeared to press the limits of constitutional powers. In another irony, Jefferson found himself increasingly at odds with the national judiciary, then led by fellow Virginian Chief Justice John Marshall, and dominated by Federalists. James Madison served as Jefferson's secretary of state, and, after choosing not to seek reelection after two terms, Jefferson helped him to secure the presidency.

Jefferson in Retirement

In retirement, Jefferson helped found the University of Virginia. A quintessential example of enlightenment rationality, Jefferson distinguished himself as a statesman, a diplomat, a man of letters, an architect (especially known for designing his home, Monticello, the Virginia State Capitol Building and the grounds of the University of Virginia), an inventor, and an educator. A planter who died near bankruptcy, his reputation has been marred in part by his failure to implement his professed belief in human equality by freeing his own slaves (see Wills 2003) as well as by allegations that he may have fathered children by one of his slaves, named Sally Hemmings. Jefferson died on July 4, 1826, fifty years to the day after Congress had adopted the Declaration of Independence.

See Also Adams, John; Bill of Rights; Declaration of

Independence; Federalist and Democratic-Republican Parties; Madison, James, Jr.; Northwest Ordinance of 1787; Shays's Rebellion; Virginia

FOR FURTHER READING

Cunningham, Noble E., Jr. 1987. *In Pursuit of Reason: The Life of Thomas Jefferson*. Baton Rouge: Louisiana State University Press.

Jefferson, Thomas. 1964. *Notes on the State of Virginia*. New York: Harper and Row, Publishers.

Koch, Adrienne. 1950. *Jefferson and Madison: The Great Collaboration*. New York: Oxford University Press.

Malone, Dumas. 1948–1977. *Jefferson and His Time*. 6 vols. Boston: Little, Brown.

Mayer, David M. 1994. *The Constitutional Thought of Thomas Jefferson*. Charlottesville: University Press of Virginia.

Vile, John R. 1992. *The Constitutional Amending Process in American Political Thought*. New York: Praeger.

Wills, Garry. 2003. *"Negro President": Jefferson and the Slave Power*. Boston: Houghton Mifflin.

the only two Maryland delegates in attendance. Because Martin was a strong proponent of states' rights who ultimately refused to sign the Constitution and Jenifer was a nationalist who signed it, the two often split the state's vote. The two did join on July 6 in urging postponement of the vote related to state equality in the Senate until a committee appointed to look into the matter had made its report (Farrand 1937, I, 543). It would have been highly likely that as a representative of a relatively small landlocked state, Jenifer would have agreed with Martin on the necessity for equal state representation. Jenifer missed a vote on the issue on July 2 (I, 510). He was reported by James McHenry to have responded privately to criticisms by Martin by saying that he had voted with him against the new system until he realized that it was useless to oppose it; he was reported on this same occasion, August 6, to believe that mere amendments of the Articles of Confederation would prove inadequate (II, 190–191). There were other signs of tension between Jenifer and Martin (see III, 85).

JENIFER, DANIEL, OF ST. THOMAS (1723–1790)

Born in Charles County, Maryland, in 1723 to a wealthy planter family, Jenifer grew up at the family plantation, named Retreat. Establishing himself as both a planter and a merchant, Jenifer occupied a number of posts in the colonial government, including service on the commission that established the Mason-Dixon line between the North and South. As the conflict with the British arose, Jenifer joined the Patriot side and served both as president of Maryland's Committee of Safety and of the state senate. A friend of George Washington, Jenifer had attended the meeting at Mount Vernon designed to settle issues of navigation between the states of Maryland and Virginia. From 1782 to 1788, Jenifer tried to bring fiscal stability to Maryland in his service as the intendant of revenue.

Jenifer, who arrived at the Convention on June 2, often found that he and Luther Martin were

Daniel of St. Thomas Jenifer, delegate from Maryland (Pixel That)

Jenifer's best-known position at the Convention may have been his first. On June 12, he was recorded as favoring a three-year term for members of the U.S. House of Representatives, a motion that Virginia's James Madison seconded. Jenifer had favored a three-year term in preference to terms of one or two years on the basis that "too great frequency of elections rendered the people indifferent to them, and made the best men unwilling to engage in so precarious a service" (I, 214). Although Jenifer's motion succeeded at the time, the Convention later voted to reduce the term of service from three years to two.

On June 23, Jenifer observed that the senators of Maryland, who served five-year terms, were prohibited from holding other offices. He said that "this circumstance gained them the greatest confidence of the people" (I, 390). On August 31, Jenifer joined fellow delegates James McHenry and Daniel Carroll in urging adoption of a provision prohibiting states from obliging vessels going to or from one state to pay duties in another. Jenifer was reported as having agreed to Carroll's assertion that "this was a tender point in Maryland" (II, 481).

After the Convention, Jenifer advocated the Constitution in his home state. He died in Annapolis, Maryland in 1790, a lifelong bachelor who provided that his slaves would be freed in 1796. Jenifer willed all his French books to Virginia's James Madison.

See Also Maryland; Martin, Luther; Mount Vernon Conference

FOR FURTHER READING

Farrand, Max, ed. 1937. *The Records of the Federal Convention.* 4 vols. New Haven, CT: Yale University Press.

Hoffman, Ronald. "Jenifer, Daniel of St. Thomas." 1999. In John A. Garraty and Mark C. Carnes, eds. *American National Biography.* New York: Oxford University Press, 11: 931–933.

William Samuel Johnson, delegate from Connecticut (Pixel That)

JOHNSON, WILLIAM SAMUEL (1727–1819)

Johnson was born in Stratford, Connecticut. His father was an Anglican pastor who would later head King's College (today's Columbia University). Johnson studied Latin and Greek at an early age and went on to earn two degrees from Yale, with Harvard and Oxford later awarding him honorary degrees.

After studying law, Johnson married a wealthy woman, Ann Beach, whose dowry helped launch him into a highly successful legal career. The people elected him to the Connecticut legislature, the Stamp Act Congress, and to the governor's council. Subsequently sent to England to represent Connecticut in the growing dispute with England, he made the acquaintance of Benjamin Franklin. Unlike Franklin, Johnson opposed the colonial decision to split with the mother country, declined appointment to the Continental Congress, and did not take an oath of allegiance to the new state government until 1779.

Johnson was, however, elected to the Congress under the Articles of Confederation. In the same month that the Constitutional Convention began, Johnson was asked to fill the shoes that his father once filled as president of King's College. Although he was one of the most educated men at the Constitutional Convention, he was not among the more active participants. He is chiefly known for his role in effecting the Connecticut Compromise and the compromise related to slave importation, taxation, and duties. During the Convention, he served on committees to look into the slave trade and navigation (August 22), interstate comity and bankruptcy (August 29), and, as discussed below, he chaired the Committee of Style and Arrangement (September 8) and was appointed to a Committee on Sumptuary Legislation (September 13). Coming relatively late in the Convention, these appointments might suggest either that Johnson was more available and/or that he had risen in the eyes of his fellow delegates as the Convention progressed.

The Issue of Sovereignty

Johnson was seated at the Convention on June 2, after the Virginia Plan had been sent to the Committee of the Whole for consideration. Johnson's first recorded comments took place on June 21, after William Paterson had introduced the New Jersey Plan and after Alexander Hamilton had outlined his own plans for a new government. What is fascinating about Johnson's first speech is that it focused not so much on the effect each plan would have had on state representation but on state sovereignty itself. Johnson observed that the primary difference between the Virginia Plan and the New Jersey Plan was that the latter was "calculated to preserve the individuality of the States" (Farrand 1937, I, 355). Although the authors of the Virginia Plan had not professed the destruction of the states as an object, critics had made this accusation, and Hamilton had advanced the idea of abolishing the states as desirable.

According to Johnson, the issue thus posed was whether the Virginia Plan's allocation of "general

sovereignty and jurisdiction" in the central government was compatible with allowing the states to retain "a considerable, tho' a subordinate jurisdiction" (I, 355). If the proponents of the Virginia Plan could demonstrate that these two goals were compatible, it would relieve proponents of the New Jersey Plan. Johnson said the issue for consideration was therefore

> whether in case the States, as was proposed, shd. retain some portion of sovereignty at least, this portion could be preserved, without allowing them to participate effectually in the Genl. Govt., without giving them each a distinct and equal vote for the purpose of defending themselves in the general Councils. (I, 355)

Johnson's speech evoked a response from Pennsylvania's James Wilson who noted his "respect" for him.

Johnson further expostulated on the differences between the Virginia and New Jersey Plans on June 29. Almost like a schoolteacher, Johnson attempted to demonstrate to each side the arguments of the other. Supporters of the Virginia Plan, Johnson believed, were viewing the situation from the perspective of a single political society, whereas proponents of the New Jersey Plan were viewing it from the perspective of a society of states. Johnson correctly perceived that a compromise might be achieved by combining the two ideas:

> In some respects the States are to be considered in their political capacity, and in others as districts of individual citizens, the two ideas embraced on different sides, instead of being opposed to each other, ought to be combined; that in *one* branch the *people*, ought to be represented; in the *other*, the *States*. (I, 461–462)

Just four days before adoption of the Connecticut Compromise, as the Convention was discussing how slaves should be counted, Johnson indicated his preference for providing for representation in the lower house of Congress on the basis of population, which he thought would also provide a good measure of wealth. In contrast to many Northern delegates, Johnson was willing to count slaves on an equal basis with whites, rather than counting them by the discounted three-fifths formula (I, 593).

On August 20, the Convention was debating the definition of treason against the United States. Johnson appeared to take an academic position in suggesting that treason could not take place against both the national government and the states since sovereignty "can be but one in the same community" (II, 346). He joined Wilson in proposing that the phrase "or any of them" thus be struck out after the words "United States" (I, 346), but continued to insist that any treason that would occur, under the Articles or under the new Constitution, would be against the whole rather than against particular states (I, 347).

Legislative Powers

On August 22, Johnson opposed a limitation prohibiting Congress from passing ex post facto, or after-the-fact, laws. He believed the clause was "unnecessary" and implied "improper suspicion" of that body (II, 376).

Three days later, in a view that would be especially compatible with his emphasis on sovereignty, Johnson said that it would not be necessary to indicate that the new Congress would assume the debts of the old. He observed that "Changing the Government cannot change the obligation of the U-S—which devolves of course on the New Government" (II, 414).

On August 29, Johnson joined James Wilson in attempting to explain the full faith and credit clause, after North Carolina's Hugh Williamson asked for explanation. They believed that it provided that "Judgments in one States should be the ground of actions in other States, & that acts of the Legislatures should be included, for the sake of Acts of insolvency &c" (II, 447; also see II, 488). That same day, Johnson indicated that he believed the faith of the existing Congress should be recognized in granting Vermont its independence of New York (II, 456). The next day, he introduced language exempting this process from the consent of the new Congress (II, 463).

On September 13, Johnson seconded a motion by Virginia's George Mason for the appointment of a Committee on Sumptuary Legislation (I, 606). Although the motion was subsequently agreed to and Johnson was appointed as one of its five members, it does not appear that the committee issued any subsequent report.

Judiciary

On August 24, Johnson seconded a motion by South Carolina's John Rutledge striking out a mechanism, similar to one used under the Articles of Confederation, for resolving disputes among the states. Presumably he agreed with Rutledge that the establishment of a national judiciary would make such a mechanism unnecessary (II, 401).

Johnson appears to have made at least a small mark on the actual language of the U.S. Constitution on August 27 when he successfully proposed that the federal judicial power should extend to cases of "equity" as well as "law" (II, 428). In Britain, these two areas of law, the first of which was designed to provide for more just and flexible remedies than those that were available in the regular courts of law, were distinct. That same day, Johnson was also responsible for inserting the words "this Constitution and the" before the word "laws" so that what would become Article III of the new Constitution vested judicial power to all cases "in Law and Equity, arising under this Constitution, ["and" later deleted] the Laws of the United States" (II, 430).

Ratification of the Constitution

Although Pennsylvania's Gouverneur Morris was the primary mover on the committee, the Convention appointed Johnson to chair the Committee of Style. In his capacity as chair Johnson reported the committee recommendations that the Constitution should be "laid before" the U.S. Congress and then submitted to ratifying conventions in each of the states (II, 608). This resolution further provided that nine states should be sufficient to ratify the document, and that once they had done so, Congress should fix a day for the electors to meet and for the new Constitution to commence.

Life after the Convention

Johnson returned to the Continental Congress in New York after the Convention and accepted the position as president of King's College that had been previously offered to him. This did not keep him from attending the Connecticut ratifying convention, where he supported adoption of the new Constitution. At one point he observed at the Convention that

> I cannot but impute it to a signal intervention of divine providence, that a convention from States differing in circumstances, interest, and manners should be so harmonious in adopting one grand system. If we reject a plan of government, which with such favorable circumstances is offered for our acceptance, I fear our national existence must come to an end. (Quoted in McCaughey 1980, 226–227)

Similarly, Johnson accepted a position as one of Connecticut's first two senators–it helped that King's College and the nation's first capital were both in New York City. Johnson remained in the Senate for only two years, where he supported the admission of Vermont (where he had investments, and where a city was named in his honor), and the congressional assumption of state debts, from which he and his sons profited financially. Shortly after Congress adopted the latter bill, part of Hamilton's fiscal package, Johnson resigned and devoted full time to his responsibilities as a college president. Ill health forced him to resign in 1800, but he lived until 1819, dying in the city where he was born.

See Also Committee of Style and Arrangement; Committee on Interstate Comity and Bankruptcy; Committee on Slave Trade and Navigation; Connecticut Compromise; Sovereignty

FOR FURTHER READING

Calhoun, Robert M. 1999. "Johnson, William Samuel." In John A. Garraty and Mark C. Carnes, eds. *American National Biography.* New York: Oxford University Press, 12: 144–145.

Farrand, Max, ed. 1937. *The Records of the Federal Convention.* 4 vols. New Haven, CT: Yale University Press.

McCaughey, Elizabeth P. 1980. *From Loyalist to Founding Father: The Political Odyssey of William Samuel Johnson.* New York: Columbia University Press.

Whitney, David C. 1974. *Founders of Freedom in America: Lives of the Men Who Signed the Constitution of the United States and So Helped to Establish the United States of America.* Chicago: J. J. Ferguson Publishing.

JOURNAL OF THE CONSTITUTIONAL CONVENTION

See RECORDS OF THE CONSTITUTIONAL CONVENTION

JUDICIAL JURISDICTION

One of the more prosaic sections of the Constitution is Article III, Section 2. This clause extends the "judicial Power" of the United States to a variety of cases "in Law and Equity [the two grand divisions of English law]." Scholars often divide these cases into those based on subject matter jurisdiction and those based on the parties involved (see Abraham 1998, 170). In the former category are included cases "arising under this Constitution, the Laws of the United States and Treaties made, or which shall be made, under their Authority;–to all Cases affecting Ambassadors, other public Ministers and Consuls; [and] to all Cases of admiralty and maritime Jurisdiction." In the latter category, jurisdiction is extended "to

The Eleventh Amendment and Judicial Jurisdiction

In outlining the jurisdiction of federal courts, Article I, Section 2 provided that judicial power would extend to cases involving controversies "between a State and Citizens of another State." In *Federalist* No. 81, Alexander Hamilton argued that these words did not mean what some had taken them to mean. Responding to Antifederalist criticisms that individuals might prosecute a state for payment of its securities, Hamilton articulated the widely accepted doctrine of state sovereign immunity by responding:

It is inherent in the nature of sovereignty, not to be amenable to the suit of an individual without its consent. This is the general sense and the general practice of mankind; and the exemption, as one of the attributes of sovereignty, is now enjoyed by the government of every state in the Union. Unless therefore, there is a surrender of this immunity in the plan of the convention, it will remain with the states, and the danger intimated must be merely ideal.

He thus concluded that "there is no colour to pretend that the state governments, would by the adoption of that plan, be divested of the privilege of paying their own debts in their own way, free from every constraint but that which flows from the obligations of good faith" (quoted in Kurland and Lerner 1987, IV, 244).

Pointing to the "unusual vehemence" with which critics had "decried" vesting jurisdiction in such cases, John Marshall took a similar stance in defending the new Constitution at the Virginia ratifying convention. Working from a similar assumption of state sovereign immunity, he observed: "It is not rational to suppose, that the sovereign power shall be dragged before a Court.

The intent is, to enable States to recover claims of individuals residing in other States" (Kurland and Lerner, IV, 248).

Despite such reassurances, the Supreme Court decided in *Chisholm v. Georgia*, 2 U.S. 419 (1793), that Article III did permit out-of-state citizens to bring a suit against Georgia for unpaid debts from the Revolutionary War. Georgia balked, and within two years the necessary number of states had ratified the Eleventh Amendment. It provided that "the Judicial power of the United States shall not be construed to extend to any suit in law or equity, commenced or prosecuted against one of the United States by Citizens of another State, or by Citizens or Subjects of any Foreign State." This amendment reinforced the idea of checks and balances by affirming the continuing power of the people to alter the Constitution in cases where they thought that the Supreme Court had improperly interpreted it. Other amendments that have modified Supreme Court decisions include the Thirteenth and Fourteenth (1865 and 1868), which overturned the *Dred Scott* decision of 1857 and provided citizenship for African Americans; the Sixteenth Amendment (1913), which overturned a Supreme Court decision invalidating the income tax; and the Twenty-sixth Amendment (1971), which overturned a Supreme Court decision that Congress could lower federal voting rights to the age of 18 only in federal elections.

FOR FURTHER READING

Kurland, Philip B., and Ralph Lerner. 1987. *The Founders' Constitution.* 5 vols. Chicago: University of Chicago Press.

Controversies to which the United States shall be a Party;—to Controversies between two or more States;—between a State and Citizens of another State;—between Citizens of different States;—between Citizens of the same State claiming Lands under Grants of different States, and between a State, or the Citizens thereof, and foreign States, Citizens or Subjects."

The Judicial Article goes on to provide that the U.S. Supreme Court will have "original jurisdiction" in "Cases affecting Ambassadors, other public Ministers and Consuls, and those in which a State shall be Party." The U.S. Supreme Court is granted "appellate Jurisdiction, both as to Law and Fact, with such Exceptions, and under such Regulations as the Congress shall make" in all other cases.

Origins in the Virginia Plan

Compared to many provisions, those related to judicial jurisdiction were the subject of relatively little debate but considerable evolution at the Convention. The distinction between cases of original and appellate jurisdiction was clearly outlined in the Virginia Plan (with lower trial courts to hear the former and the Supreme Court to hear the latter), but the cases designated were quite different than those that eventually appeared in the Constitution. The plan called for federal courts to hear cases involving "all piracies & felonies on the high seas, captures from an enemy; cases in which foreigners or citizens of other States applying to such jurisdictions may be interested, or which respect the collection of the National revenue; impeachments of any National officers, and questions which may involve the national peace and harmony" (Farrand 1937, I, 22). The last clause was the most ambiguous and clearly had the most potential for future growth. The Virginia Plan also contained a provision for a Council of Revision in which the president and select members of the judiciary were to review the wisdom of state and national laws (see Council of Revision; also see President, Council).

Suggestions and Alterations

On June 12, the Convention decided to strike out the provisions related to piracies and felonies on the high seas or to captures from an enemy, but no debate is recorded over these measures, which today would be subsumed under admiralty and maritime law (I, 211). The next day, the Convention voted to affirm jurisdiction over issues related to national revenue, impeachments of fed-

eral officials, and matters related to national peace and harmony, but, again, little debate was recorded on the subject (I, 224). In fact, Randolph said that at this point he was most interested in establishing the principle of "the security of foreigners where treaties are in their favor, and to preserve the harmony of states and of the citizens thereof," leaving a subcommittee to iron out details (I, 238).

When William Paterson offered the New Jersey Plan on June 15, he proposed vesting greater powers in Congress. He further proposed that cases arising under such laws would begin "in the first instance . . . in the superior Common law Judiciary in such State . . . subject nevertheless, for the correction of all errors, both in law & fact in rendering judgment, to an appeal to the Judiciary of the U. States" (I, 243). Madison critiqued this plan in part on the basis that federal appeals would come after acquittals and would thus be too late (I, 317). In offering his own plan, which the Convention largely ignored, New York's Alexander Hamilton, who later defended judicial powers in the *Federalist*, suggested that the U.S. Supreme Judicial authority (he did not distinguish the Supreme Court from others) would have original jurisdiction in cases involving capture [presumably on the high seas] and appellate jurisdiction on cases involving revenue or foreign citizens (I, 292). Curiously, he provided that impeachments would be tried by the chief judge "of the Superior Court of Law of each State, provided such Judge shall hold his place during good behavior, and have a permanent salary" (I, 282–293) rather than before federal courts. On July 18, a day when delegates were discussing judicial appointments, they voted to strike the provision in the Virginia Plan whereby federal judges would try cases of impeachment (II, 39). This decision was probably designed to make the appointment and/or confirmation process less problematic by minimizing possible conflicts of interest.

The Committee of Detail

The Committee of Detail formulated several versions of a Constitution before presenting its findings to the Convention on August 6. Later versions became increasingly detailed. The version reported to the Convention contained an elaborate provision designed to resolve controversies between states "respecting jurisdiction or territory." Under this plan, which was largely patterned on a similar procedure employed under the Articles of Confederation, the U.S. Senate would appoint seven to nine commissioners or judges in individual cases, who would resolve such matters (II, 183–184). The Convention eventually struck this measure on August 24 in preference to judicial resolution of such issues (II, 400–401).

Another section of the committee's report came quite close to the current designation of judicial jurisdiction, with designations of the kinds of cases the courts would hear and a distinction between cases of original and appellate jurisdiction. A provision for the Supreme Court to preside over impeachments was, however, included. The section provided for Congress to make exceptions to the Supreme Court's jurisdiction. It also provided that "The Legislature may assign any part of the jurisdiction above mentioned (except the trial of the president of the United States) in the manner, and under the limitations which it shall think proper, to such Inferior Courts, as it shall constitute from time to time" (II, 186–187).

On August 20, the Convention submitted to the Committee of Detail a provision for a Council of State that would include the chief justice of the Supreme Court who would preside in the president's absence (II, 342). John Rutledge reported such a provision for a Privy Council on August 22 (II, 367), but, just as the Convention rejected the Council of Revision proposed in the original Virginia Plan, so too, it did not create such a Privy Council.

On August 27, the Convention voted to add to the Committee of Detail's list of cases of jurisdiction those cases to which the U.S. would be a party. By precedents established in the early years of the Constitution, U.S. courts do not issue advisory opinions. Such a policy, at least in embryonic form, was raised after William Johnson of Connecticut proposed adding a provision giving courts power to hear cases that arose under the U.S. Constitution as well as U.S. laws. Madison indicated that he thought this might be going too far, believing judicial jurisdiction should "be limited to cases of a Judiciary Nature. The right of expounding the Constitution in cases not of this nature ought not to be given to that Department" (II, 430). Although Johnson's motion was accepted, Madison observed that delegates "generally supposed that the jurisdiction given was constructively limited to cases of a Judiciary nature" (II, 430). On this same day, the Convention voted to extend judicial appellate jurisdiction to issues of both law and fact, and voted to substitute the words "the Judicial power" for "supreme court" (II, 431). It also tinkered with the provision relating to the judicial resolution of land grants. The Committee of Style later made other minor alterations.

Analysis

As in the original Virginia Plan, the Constitution attempted specifically to define those categories of cases over which federal courts would have jurisdiction. The Constitution also preserved the distinction in the Virginia Plan between cases of original and appellate jurisdiction. The Convention's most important decision relative to judicial jurisdiction was its decision providing that lower federal courts would hear cases involving the U.S. Constitution and U.S. laws rather than leaving these decisions with state courts. This differed significantly from the proposal in the New Jersey Plan to vest such decisions initially in state courts.

Throughout the Convention, but especially with the work done by the Committee of Detail, delegates added new categories of cases that federal courts would hear. The most significant power that the delegates withdrew from the judiciary was that of trying impeachments (the chief justice's role in presiding over Senate trials of presidential impeachments is perhaps a remnant of this power), which they entrusted to the Senate. The Convention, however, settled on judicial resolution of disputes about land claims rather than entrusting these to special bodies specifically established for this purpose.

See Also Articles of Confederation; Committee of Detail; Council of Revision; Judicial Review; President, Council; Supremacy Clause; Virginia Plan

FOR FURTHER READING

Abraham, Henry J. 1998. *The Judicial Process.* 7th ed. New York: Oxford University Press.

D'Amato, Anthony. 1988. "The Alien Tort Statute and the Founding of the Constitution." *American Journal of International Law* 82 (January): 62–67.

Farrand, Max, ed. 1937. *The Records of the Federal Convention.* 4 vols. New Haven, CT: Yale University Press.

JUDICIAL ORGANIZATION AND PROTECTIONS

Article III of the Constitution vests the judicial power "in one supreme Court, and in such inferior Courts as the Congress may from time to time ordain and establish." It provides that all federal judges shall serve "during good Behavior" and shall receive a salary that shall not be diminished during their terms of office. Article I, Section 8 further affirms the power of Congress to create lower courts.

The Virginia Plan

These provisions were surprisingly similar to those that Edmund Randolph first introduced in the Virginia Plan on May 29, which proposed the creation of a judicial branch. Under the Articles of Confederation, there was no federal system of courts, although Congress could resolve disputes between states over territories, and it had also created a federal Court of Appeals in Cases of Capture (see Jameson 1889). The Virginia Plan had provided for legislative rather than executive appointment of judges. The other primary difference is that it provided that judicial salaries could neither be *increased* nor decreased (Farrand 1937, I, 21).

The Establishment of Lower Federal Tribunals

Although a number of resolutions were adopted affirming one or another of these clauses, the first significant discussion at the Convention took place on June 5. John Rutledge of South Carolina wanted to expunge the provision relative to inferior judicial tribunals in the belief that state courts would be sufficient for this purpose as long as there was a right of appeal to the national tribunal to ensure "national rights & uniformity of Judgmts" (I, 124). He feared that creating lower federal tribunals would be "an unnecessary encroachment" on state jurisdiction that would create "unnecessary obstacles" to state acceptance of the new system (II, 124). Connecticut's Roger Sherman seconded Rutledge's proposal. Virginia's James Madison was adamantly opposed. He argued that "unless inferior tribunals were dispersed throughout the Republic with final jurisdiction in *many* cases, appeals would be multiplied to a most oppressive degree" (I, 124). Madison feared that it would be difficult to remedy problems "obtained under the biased directions of a dependent Judge, or the local prejudices of an undirected jury" (I, 124). He further observed that "A Government without a proper Executive & Judiciary would be the mere trunk of a body without arms or legs to act or move" (I, 124). Pennsylvania's James Wilson, a lawyer and future U.S. Supreme Court justice, was particularly concerned that federal courts would handle cases of admiralty that transcended state boundaries. Similarly, John Dickinson of Delaware said that a national judiciary would be a logical complement to a national legislature. The Convention voted 5-4-2 against Rutledge's motion.

The Convention then considered a proposal, which Wilson and Madison introduced and Dickinson supported, that provided "that the National Legislature be empowered to institute inferior tribunals." The apparent attempt of this resolution was to give more explicit authority not only to appoint judges but also to institute inferior courts. South Carolina's Pierce Butler argued that "The people will not bear such innovations." He counseled that "We must follow the example of Solon [an eminent ancient lawgiver] who gave the Athenians not the best Govt. he could devise; but the best they wd. receive" (I, 125). Focusing on an equally practical consideration, Rufus King of Massachusetts said that it would be less expensive to establish such lower federal courts than to provide for the expense of the appeals that they would save. The Convention then approved the motion by a vote of 8-2-1.

The Convention returned to this issue on July 18. This time South Carolina's Pierce Butler led the attack on such courts believing that state tribunals could do the work. Maryland's Luther Martin agreed, believing that lower federal courts would create "jealousies & oppositions in the State tribunals" (II, 45–46). Nathaniel Gorham of Massachusetts pointed to the existence of courts for the trial of piracies and maritime matters and argued that "Inferior tribunals are essential to render the authority of the Natl. Legislature effectual" (II, 46). Virginia's Edmund Randolph did not think state courts could be trusted to carry out national policies. Although Sherman was now willing to approve of such courts, he wanted the government to make use of state courts wherever possible, and Virginia's George Mason argued that there would be occasions, some not then foreseeable, when such courts would be necessary. The Convention unanimously agreed.

Judicial Salaries

Most Convention debates on the judicial branch centered on its mode of appointment, but on July 18 the delegates did discuss judicial salaries. On that date, Gouverneur Morris suggested striking out the provision whereby increases in judicial salaries were forbidden. Surprisingly, Benjamin Franklin, another Pennsylvania delegate who had proposed at the Convention that the president should serve without pay, agreed. He observed: "Money may not only become plentier [as in a time of inflation], but the business of the department may increase as the Country becomes more populous" (II, 45). Madison was not convinced. He feared that judges would agitate Congress, and be unduly compliant, when they wanted pay in-

creases. In what seems a quaint proposal, Madison suggested that judicial salaries might be kept constant by "taking for a standard wheat or some other thing of permanent value." Moreover, the government could accommodate increases in workloads by appointing new judges (II, 45). Morris observed that "the value of money may not only alter but the State of Society may alter. In this event the same quantity of wheat, the same value would not be the same compensation. The Amount of salaries must always be regulated by the manners & the style of living in a Country" (II, 45). Morris must have been persuasive; his measure carried by a vote of 6-2-2, with Virginia and North Carolina in dissent.

On August 27, after the discussion of judicial removal discussed below, Madison, seconded by Maryland's James McHenry, reintroduced the idea of limiting increases in judicial salaries during their terms of office. Morris continued his opposition, but Mason strongly supported Madison's motion. He argued that salaries could be altered for new individuals entering office, without thereby seeming to grasp the inequalities that this might create over time in a system where judges served "during good behavior." General Pinckney of South Carolina pointed to this problem, and contended that large salaries would be necessary to attract individuals with talent. Morris said that judges would evade restrictions on pay raises by resigning and then getting reappointed. This time, the Convention defeated Madison's motion by a vote of 6-2-1. The Convention rejected a similar motion, offered by Randolph and Madison, that would have limited any pay raises for three years from the adoption of the last one.

A Threat to Judicial Independence

On August 27, the Convention considered a proposal by Delaware's John Dickinson, seconded by Elbridge Gerry of Massachusetts, to amend the provision giving judges tenure during good behavior so as to provide that presidents could remove them on the application of the House and Senate. Gouverneur Morris said it was contradictory "to say that the Judges should hold their offices during good behavior, and yet be removeable without a trial" (II, 428). Sherman saw no problem, but Rutledge thought that it would make it difficult for the Supreme Court to judge conflicts between the national government and the states. Responding to Sherman's argument that the English constitution contained a similar mechanism, Wilson argued that the two houses of Parliament were less likely to concur than the two houses of Congress. Randolph feared that the proposal would weaken judicial independence, although Dickinson did not think it likely that two branches of Congress "constructed on such different principles, would improperly unite for the purpose of displacing a Judge" (II, 429). The Convention rejected Dickinson's motion by a 7-1 vote with three states being absent.

Analysis

The Convention provided for the congressional creation of, but did not mandate, the establishment of lower federal courts. Since the Judiciary Act of 1789, largely formulated by Connecticut's Oliver Ellsworth, such lower federal courts have existed. Today, the federal court system is divided into three basic tiers. These consist of U.S. District Courts that serve as trial courts; U.S. Courts of Appeal, acting as intermediate courts of appeal; and the U.S. Supreme Court, which accepts cases both from lower federal courts and from state supreme courts. The U.S. Supreme Court is the only one of these courts that the Constitution specifically mentioned by name.

The Convention ensured the independence of federal judges by giving them tenure "during good behavior," by preventing their removal short of impeachment for specifically designated offenses, and by protecting their salaries against cuts. Madison's hope to prevent increases, as well as decreases, in such salaries was idealistically motivated by the desire for still greater judicial impartiality, but, in contrast to most of his other proposals, was not very realistic. The judicial system would certainly be much different, and probably filled with far less capable individuals, if judges serving for life had to give up any prospect of future pay raises.

See Also Appointments and Confirmations; Ellsworth, Oliver; Judicial Jurisdiction

FOR FURTHER READING

Farrand, Max, ed. 1937. *The Records of the Federal Convention*. 4 vols. New Haven, CT: Yale University Press.

Holt, Wythe. 1992. "Judiciary Act of 1789." In Kermit L. Hall, ed. *The Oxford Companion to the Supreme Court of the United States*. New York: Oxford, 472–474.

Jameson, J. Franklin, ed. 1889. "The Predecessor of the Supreme Court." *Essays in the Constitutional History of the United States in the Formative Period 1775–1789*. Boston: Houghton Mifflin, 1–45.

Steamer, Robert J. 1962. "The Legal and Political Genesis of the Supreme Court." *Political Science Quarterly* 77 (December): 546–569.

JUDICIAL REVIEW

One of the powers that sets U.S. courts apart from their predecessors in Great Britain is that whereas English citizens consider the British Parliament to be supreme, or sovereign, U.S. courts exercise the power of judicial review. This power enables judges to invalidate legislative or executive acts that the courts believe to be unconstitutional when such laws or acts are presented in the form of cases or controversies that arise before the courts. Chief Justice John Marshall established judicial review of congressional legislation in *Marbury v. Madison* (1803), but the Court had previously exercised its power to invalidate state legislation that it considered to be unconstitutional.

Constitutional Foundations

The supremacy clause in Article VI states that "the Constitution, and the Laws of the United

States which shall be made in Pursuance thereof; and all Treaties made, or which shall be made, under the Authority of the United States, shall be the supreme Law of the Land," but it does not specifically invest courts with the responsibility for invalidating laws contrary to the Constitution. The supremacy clause does arguably provide more solid textual support for invalidation of unconstitutional state legislation by further providing that "the Judges in every State shall be bound thereby [to the U.S. Constitution], any Thing in the Constitution or Laws of any State to the contrary notwithstanding." Article III, while not specifically vesting courts with the power of judicial review, does vest them with jurisdiction in a variety of controversies arising under the Constitution and laws of the United States; similarly, public officials at both state and national levels take oaths to support the Constitution.

Because the Constitution does not specifically vest federal courts with the power to invalidate congressional legislation, scholars have long debated whether the authors of that document intended for courts to exercise this power. Historian Charles Beard professed to show that a majority of those who wrote the Constitution favored judicial review, but he had to rely on private letters, on subsequent votes on the Judiciary Act in the first Congress, and on other expressions of opinion not made during the Convention itself (Beard 1962). The Convention, does, however, provide some insight into the Framers' views.

Discussions of Early Proposals

The Virginia Plan, which Edmund Randolph introduced at the Convention on May 29, did not specifically vest courts with the power of judicial review. The Virginia Plan did include a provision, however, whereby "a convenient number of the National Judiciary" would be allied with the executive to compose a Council of Revision. The council would have the power to examine any act of Congress before it went into operation and invalidate such law until Congress overrode this veto by an unspecified majority. Similarly, although Congress had power "to negative all laws

passed by the several States, contravening in the opinion of the National Legislature the articles of Union," the council could again reverse this judgment, subject again to potential override (Farrand 1937, I, 21).

The first recorded mention of judicial review at the Constitutional Convention came on June 3 during discussion of the proposed Council of Revision. Elbridge Gerry of Massachusetts expressed doubt over whether members of the judiciary should be part of this council. He observed that

> they will have a sufficient check agst. encroachments on their own department by their exposition of the laws, which involved a power of deciding on their Constitutionality. In some States the Judges had [actually] set aside laws as being agst. the Constitution. This was done too with general approbation. It was quite foreign from the nature of ye. office to make them judges of the policy of public measures. (I, 97–98)

Gerry's words are remarkable in that they not only indicate familiarity with judicial review at the state level and anticipate its exercise under the new government (although, as his words against "encroachments" suggest, he may have expected this review to be exercised simply to protect incursions against the judicial branch). In addition, Gerry distinguishes between exercising power to void laws on the basis that they are unconstitutional from exercising power to strike them down on the basis that they contravene public policy.

Gerry proposed vesting the veto in the president, subject to legislative override, and Rufus King, also of Masssachusetts, seconded the motion. King did not comment directly on judicial review. He did, however, note "that the Judges ought to be able to expound the law as it should come before them, free from the bias of having participated in its formation" (I, 98).

The Convention delegates then began discussing whether the veto should be absolute or whether it should be subject to legislative override. During the course of this discussion, Gunning Bedford of Delaware, although not mentioning the judiciary by name, observed that he "was opposed to every check on the Legislative, even the Council of Revision first proposed" (I, 100). Following this observation with the comment that "He thought it would be sufficient to mark out in the Constitution the boundaries to the Legislative Authority, which would give all the requisite security to the rights of the other departments," he added that "The Representatives of the People were the best judges of what was for their interest, and ought to be under no external controul whatever" (I, 100–101). The Convention subsequently voted to vest the veto power in the president subject to override by a two-thirds vote of both houses of Congress.

The New Jersey Plan, which William Paterson introduced to the Convention on June 15, did not include a Council of Revision although it did include the provision that developed into the supremacy clause. A plan that New York's Alexander Hamilton presented to the Convention on June 18 proposed that "All laws of the particular States contrary to the Constitution or laws of the United States" would be "utterly void," but the specific method he proposed for invalidating them consisted of allowing the national government to appoint state governors and give them the power to negative such laws (I, 293).

Discussions in July

On July 17, the day after the Convention settled on the Great Compromise whereby it allocated representation in the two houses of Congress between the large and small states, Roger Sherman of Connecticut indicated that he thought a congressional negative of state laws would be unnecessary since "the Courts of the States would not consider as valid any law contravening the Authority of the Union, and which the legislature would wish to be negatived" (II, 27). Virginia's James Madison argued for the superiority of the congressional negative on the ground that it was better to stop bad legislation in its tracks than to attempt to deal with it after it had inflicted its injuries. He expressed lack of faith in state tribunals, but, in the process, he expressed admiration for some exercises of judicial review, at least over state legislation:

In all the States these are more or less dependt. on the Legislatures. In Georgia they are appointed annually by the Legislature. In R. Island the judges who refused to execute an unconstitutional law were displaced, and others substituted, by the Legislature who would be willing instruments of the wicked & arbitrary plans of their masters. A power of negativing the improper laws of the States is at once the most mild & certain means of preserving the harmony of the system. (II, 27–28)

In opposing the congressional negative of state laws, Pennsylvania's Gouverneur Morris indicated that he expected courts under the new system to exercise judicial review. He thus observed: "The proposal of it would disgust all the States. A law that ought to be negatived will be set aside by the Judiciary department, and if that security should fail, may be repealed by a nationl. law (II, 28).

In apparent reiteration of his earlier view that courts would be able to invalidate unconstitutional legislation, Sherman observed that the negative of state laws operated upon the false assumption "that a law of a State contrary to the articles of the Union, would if not negatived, be valid & operative" (II, 28).

On July 21, Pennsylvania's James Wilson reintroduced the idea of associating the national judiciary with the executive in vetoing laws. In so doing, he indicated that he believed judges would exercise judicial review, but that he wanted them to have even greater power:

The Judiciary ought to have an opportunity of remonstrating agst projected encroachments on the people as well as on themselves. It had been said that the Judges, as expositors of the Laws would have an opportunity of defending their constitutional rights. There was weight in this observation; but this power of the Judges did not go far enough. Laws may be unjust, may be unwise, may be dangerous, may be destructive, and yet not be so unconstitutional as to justify the Judges in refusing to give them effect. Let them have a share of the Revisionary power, and they will have an opportunity of taking notice of these characters of a law, and of counteracting, by the weight of their opinions the improper views of the Legislature. (II, 73)

Nathaniel Gorham of Massachusetts did not dispute the judges' role in assessing legislation for its constitutionality, but thought that judges "are not to be presumed to possess any peculiar knowledge of the mere policy of public measures" (II, 73). By contrast, Connecticut's Oliver Ellsworth approved of Wilson's proposal believing that judges "will possess a systematic and accurate knowledge of the Laws, which the Executive can not be expected always to possess" as well as better knowledge of the law of nations (II, 74).

Madison saw the alliance of the executive and the judiciary as a way of counteracting "a powerful tendency in the Legislature to absorb all power into its vortex" (II, 74). Virginia's George Mason favored the provision as giving "a confidence to the Executive" (II, 74). Gerry objected that this was improperly mixing powers, and Caleb Strong, also of Massachusetts, feared that "The Judges in exercising the function of expositors might be influenced by the part they had taken, in framing the laws" (II, 75).

Maryland's Luther Martin disfavored Wilson's proposal as "a dangerous innovation" (II, 76), but, as in earlier debates, he clearly anticipated judicial review. He observed:

A knowledge of mankind, and of Legislative affairs cannot be presumed to belong in a higher degree to the Judges than to the Legislature. And as to the Constitutionality of laws, that point will come before the Judges in their proper official character. In this character they have a negative on the laws. Join them with the Executive in the Revision and they will have a double negative. (II, 76)

After Madison again defended the proposal, Mason praised it for helping to discourage "demagogues" from getting unjust laws adopted and attempted to answer Martin, in part by reiterating the view that judges would exercise judicial review, but that such review would be limited to examining the constitutionality of legislation:

It had been said (by Mr. L. Martin) that if the Judges were joined in this check on the laws, they would have a double negative, since in their expository capacity of Judges they would have one negative. He would reply that in this capacity they could impede in one case only, the operation of laws. They could declare an unconstitutional law void. But with regard to every law however unjust, oppressive or pernicious, which did not come to them plainly under this description, they would be under the necessity as Judges to give it a free course. He wished the further use to be made of the Judges, of giving aid in preventing every improper law. (II, 78)

Most subsequent discussion of the mechanism centered on separation of powers, but Gorham reiterated two additional themes:

the 1st. is that the Judges ought to carry into the exposition of the laws no prepossessions with regard to them. 2d. that as the Judges will outnumber the Executive, the revisionary check would be thrown entirely out of the Executive hands, and instead of enabling him to defend himself, would enable the Judges to sacrifice him. (II, 79)

John Rutledge of South Carolina added that "the Judges ought never to give their opinion on a law till it comes before them" (II, 80), and Wilson's motion narrowly lost on a 4-3-2 vote.

On July 23, the delegates at the Convention were discussing whether it was appropriate to submit the Constitution to special conventions rather than to state legislatures for approval. In defending the former mechanism, Madison said that the difference between a system founded on the people (whom he considered conventions to embody) and one founded on the legislature was the distinction "between a *league or treaty,* and a *Constitution*" (II, 93). He further commended ratification by conventions as establishing a foundation for judicial review: "A law violating a treaty ratified by a preexisting law, might be respected by the Judges as a law, though an unwise or perfidious one. A law violating a constitution established by the people themselves, would be considered by the Judges as null & void" (II, 93).

Madison further argued that whereas the breach of an article by a party to a treaty could be regarded as dissolving other parties from their obligation, "In the case of a union of people under one Constitution, the nature of the pact has always been understood to exclude such an interpretation" (II, 93).

Discussions in August

On August 15, Madison resurrected a different version of his Council of Revision by proposing a motion, which Wilson seconded, providing that all laws should be submitted to "the Executive and Supreme Judiciary Departments," and that when one objected, it should take two-thirds of the Congress to override it and when both objected, it should take three-fourths of each House to enable the law (II, 298). Charles Pinckney of South Carolina objected that this would unduly involve judges in legislative business and in party disputes. John Mercer of Maryland approved of Madison's motion, but he did so on the apparent basis that such a provision would obviate the need for judicial review. He observed: "He disapproved of the Doctrine that the Judges as expositors of the Constitution should have authority to declare a law null. He thought laws ought to be cautiously made, and then to be uncontroulable" (II, 298).

After the Convention rejected Madison's motion, Gouverneur Morris expressed his regrets. Delaware's John Dickinson appeared to equivocate on the need for judicial review. Professing to have been "strongly impressed with the remark of Mr. Mercer as to the power of the Judges to set aside the law," he said: "He thought no such power ought to exist. He was at the same time at a loss what expedient to substitute. The Justiciary of Aragon he observed became by degrees the lawgiver" (II, 299).

In supporting an absolute executive veto, Gouverneur Morris observed:

> He could not agree that the Judiciary which was part of the Executive, should be bound to say that a direct violation of the Constitution was law. A controul over the legislature might have

its inconveniences. But view the danger on the other side. The most virtuous citizens will often as members of a legislative body concur in measures which afterwards in their private capacity they will be ashamed of. Encroachments of the popular branch of the Government ought to be guarded agst. (II, 299)

Sherman, who had earlier expressed support for judicial review, apparently distinguished the invalidation of measures that were unconstitutional from the practice of "Judges meddling in politics and parties," which he opposed (II, 300).

When the Convention was discussing a prohibition on ex post facto laws on August 22, North Carolina's Hugh Williamson supported such a provision. Whereas Daniel Carroll and James Wilson questioned the efficacy of such a prohibition, North Carolina's Hugh Williamson observed that a similar prohibition had proved beneficial in his home state. He observed that such a provision was good because "the Judges can take hold of it" (II, 376). This certainly appears to anticipate a power of judicial review.

Madison was probably contemplating a distinction between judicial review and judicial meddling similar to that which Roger Sherman had earlier introduced when on August 27 Madison questioned whether courts should have jurisdiction over all cases arising under the Constitution. He observed that he thought jurisdiction should be "limited to cases of a Judiciary Nature," and argued that "The right of expounding the Constitution in cases not of this nature ought not to be given to that Department" (II, 430). Although he did not succeed in striking the provision of the Constitution, he observed that it "was generally supposed that the jurisdiction given was constructively limited to cases of a Judiciary nature" (II, 430).

Analysis

The delegates at the Convention were clearly familiar with the concept of judicial review. Those who expressed themselves on the subject at the Convention overwhelmingly, but not unanimously, supported judicial review. Elbridge Gerry, Rufus King, Roger Sherman, James Madison, James Wilson, Luther Martin, George Mason, and Gouverneur Morris (all among the Convention's leading lights) expected and/or favored the exercise of some type of judicial review, while Nathaniel Gorham, Oliver Ellsworth, Caleb Strong, and John Rutledge all passed up apparent opportunities to deny that judges would or should have this power. Two lesser lights at the Convention (Gunning Bedford and John Mercer) opposed it, and John Dickinson seemed conflicted on the matter.

The issue is complicated by the fact that some might have distinguished between judicial invalidation of national laws and judicial invalidation of state laws. Some, like Gerry, might have viewed judicial review primarily as a means for the judiciary to defend itself (and not necessarily the Constitution as a whole) against encroachments. No delegate extensively discussed whether he thought the judiciary should be generally deferential to legislation or fairly active in scrutinizing it. A number of delegates did indicate that the exercise of judicial review would not necessarily serve as the basis for invalidating unwise legislation–a task ultimately left chiefly up to the presidential veto– but only legislation that was unconstitutional. Early in U.S. constitutional history, Chief Justice John Marshall generally foreswore judicial review based on general natural law principles in preference to review based on specific texts (see Wilmarth 2003).

See Also Beard, Charles; Council of Revision; Judicial Organization and Protections; Oaths of Office; Supremacy Clause

FOR FURTHER READING

Beard, Charles A. 1962. *The Supreme Court and the Constitution.* Introduction by Alan F. Westin. Englewood Cliffs, NJ: Prentice-Hall.
Burger, Warren. 1996. "The Judiciary: The Origins of Judicial Review." *National Forum* 76 (Fall): 37–38.
Farrand, Max, ed. 1937. *The Records of the Federal Convention.* 4 vols. New Haven, CT: Yale University Press.
Kramer, Larry D. 2004. *The People Themselves: Popular Constitutionalism and Judicial Review.* New York: Oxford University Press.
Wilmarth, Arthur E., Jr. 2003. "Symposium: Judicial Review before John Marshall: Elusive Foundation: John Marshall, James Wilson, and the Problem of Reconciling Popular Sovereignty and Natural Law Jurisprudence in the New Federal Republic." *George Washington Law Review* 72 (December): 113–193.

JURY, TRIAL BY

Trial by jury has deep roots in English history. Jurymen were designed to limit the power of oppressive judges and to ensure that individuals with knowledge of the local situation were involved. Article III, Section 3 accordingly provides that "The Trial of all Crimes, except in Cases of Impeachment, shall be by Jury; and such Trial shall be held in the State where the said Crimes shall have been committed; but when not committed within any State, the Trial shall be at such Place or Places as the Congress may by Law have directed." Significantly, this has been identified as "the only procedural right included in the original U.S. Constitution" (Levine 2002, 454).

The first part of this provision emerged from, and is almost identical to, a provision that the Committee of Detail submitted in its report to the Convention on August 6 in filling out the provisions related to the national judiciary (Farrand 1937, II, 187). The second part was added on August 28 so as to make it clear that a jury trial would also apply to offenses that were not committed within individual states (II, 438).

On August 28, North Carolina's Hugh Williamson suggested that the Convention should also make provision for jury trials in civil cases. Nathaniel Gorham responded that it would not be possible "to discriminate equity cases from those in which juries are proper" (II, 587) and suggested that "the Representatives of the people may be safely trusted in this matter" (II, 587). Elbridge Gerry, who like Gorham was from Massachusetts, expressed the view that juries were necessary to guard against "corrupt Judges." Virginia's

George Mason recognized the force of Williamson's suggestion and did not think jury cases could be specified. Nonetheless, he favored setting down "A general principle . . . on this and other points" and wanted this to be done in "a Bill of Rights," which he thought "would give quiet to the people" (II, 587). Gerry seconded this motion, but Connecticut's Roger Sherman observed that state declarations of rights would remain in effect and that the legislatures could be trusted in other cases. The Convention then rejected the idea of having a committee prepare a bill of rights and did not revisit the issue of jury trials in civil cases.

On September 15, Charles Pinckney of South Carolina and Gerry attempted to insert a provision that "a trial by jury shall be preserved as usual in civil cases," but Gorham observed that "The constitution of Juries is different in different states and the trial itself is usual in different cases in different States," and it was affirmed by King (II, 628). Charles Cotesworth Pinckney of South Carolina further commented that "such a clause in the Constitution would be pregnant with embarrassments" (II, 628), and the Convention unanimously rejected the idea.

Rufus King's notes indicate that Elbridge Gerry, who had favored the right of juries in civil cases, likened the judiciary on September 15 to a "Star Chamber" (an English court noted for its injustice) in explaining his reasons for opposing the Constitution (II, 635). Mason also offered the failure to secure such a right as a reason for his opposition to the document.

Antifederalist opponents of the Constitution subsequently repeated this criticism. Eventually, the Sixth Amendment reaffirmed the right of jury trials, drawn not only from the state but also from the district, in criminal cases. The Seventh Amendment further secured this right in civil cases.

See Also Bill of Rights; Common Law; Great Britain

FOR FURTHER READING

Farrand, Max, ed. 1937. *The Records of the Federal Convention.* 4 vols. New Haven, CT: Yale University Press.

Levine, James P. 2002. "Jury." In Kermit L. Hall, ed. *The Oxford Companion to American Law.* New York: Oxford University Press, 458–463.

JUSTICE

The first purpose of the Constitution that is stated in the Preamble is that of establishing justice. Jane Mansbridge has argued that this goal, which is mentioned in the Pledge of Allegiance to the flag, has been second only to that of liberty in the United States (1998, 361). Justice is usually equated with fairness and the rule of law. It is also associated with the idea of a "public good" that is greater than individual interests.

In the Declaration of Independence, Thomas Jefferson had accused the king of applying unjust laws and of making war against the people of the United States. A major impetus to the Constitutional Convention was the belief that states were not treating all classes of citizens fairly. There is, as yet, no concordance to the Records of the Constitutional Convention, and the index to these volumes does not contain specific references to justice. However, delegates to the Convention did express concerns about state emissions of paper money that inflated currency values and thus favored debtors over creditors. One of the prohibitions within the Constitution forbade further issues of such money at the state level. Yet another provision was that states had to extend to all citizens the same "privileges and immunities" that they extended to their own. Yet another prohibited states from abridging contracts. A number of other provisions anticipated the type of prohibitions on government—for example, the prohibition of ex post facto laws—that would later find their way into the Bill of Rights.

More generally, the Constitution was so devised as to prevent groups of citizens, even when in a majority, from uniting around what James Madison described in *Federalist* No. 10 as "some common impulse of passion, or of interest, adverse to the rights of other citizens, or to the permanent and aggregate interests of the community" (Hamilton, Madison, and Jay 1961, 78). In *Federalist* No. 10, of course, Madison focused on the manner in which a large nation, embracing a multiplicity of interests, was likely to moderate factions, as was a system of representation. Ralph Ketcham has observed that the phrase "public good" appears nine separate times in *Federalist* No. 10 alone (1993, 59). Similarly, in *Federalist* No. 51, Madison argued that separated powers would combine with the extended republic in promoting justice. In that essay, Madison observed that "Justice is the end of government. It is the end of civil society. It ever has been and ever will be pursued until it be obtained, or until liberty be lost in the pursuit" (324).

In *Federalist* No. 17, Alexander Hamilton pointed to another use of justice when he observed that citizens would continue to be attached to their states because of their control over "the ordinary administration of criminal and civil justice" (120). Hamilton further observed:

This of all others, is the most powerful, most universal, and most attractive source of popular obedience and attachment. It is this which, being the immediate and visible guardian of life and property, having its benefits and its terrors in constant activity before the public eye, regulating all those personal interests and familiar concerns to which the sensibility of individuals is more immediately awake, contributes more than any other circumstances to impressing upon the minds of the people affection, esteem, and reverence towards the government. (120)

In this essay, Hamilton stressed the role that states would have in guarding against improper assumptions of power by the national government. In later essays, Hamilton also put great emphasis on the need for an independent and impartial judiciary to interpret and enforce the Constitution. This desire helps account for the fact that members of the judiciary are appointed by the president and confirmed by the Senate rather than being elected, that they serve "during good behavior," and that their salaries cannot be lowered during their term of office.

It is possible to view bicameralism as yet another protection against injustice. By passing legislation through two sets of filters rather than one, this mechanism should at the very least guarantee that legislation receives more than casual attention (see Brams and Taylor 1995, 698–700). The president's veto provides yet another check against unjust or ill-considered measures.

The Antifederalist agitation for a bill of rights was predicated on fear that the new government might assume unjust powers. Significantly, a number of these amendments specifically deal with justice related to persons accused of, or on trial for, crimes. Most notable is the Fifth Amendment provision, traced back to the Magna Carta of 1215, prohibiting the government from depriving an individual of "life, liberty, or property without due process of law." This provision was later imposed on the states in the Fourteenth Amendment (ratified in 1868).

See Also Bill of Rights; Congress, Bicameralism; Constitutionalism; Contracts Clause; Declaration of Independence; *Federalist, The;* Judicial Organization and Protections; Magna Carta; Money, State Coining and Emissions of; Parties, Factions, and Interests; Preamble; Presidential Veto; Privileges and Immunities Clause; Separation of Powers

FOR FURTHER READING

Brams, Steven J., and Alan D. Taylor. 1995. "Fair Division and Politics." *PS: Political Science and Politics* 28 (December): 697–703.

Hamilton, Alexander, James Madison, and John Jay. 1961. *The Federalist Papers.* Ed. Clinton Rossiter. New York: New American Library.

Ketcham, Ralph. 1993. *Framed for Posterity: The Enduring Philosophy of the Constitution.* Lawrence: University Press of Kansas.

Mansbridge, Jane. 1998. "Justice." In Richard Wightman Fox and James T. Kloppenberg, eds. *A Companion to American Thought.* Malden, MA: Blackwell.

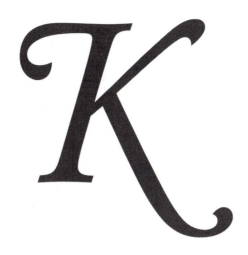

KENTUCKY

At the time of the Constitutional Convention in 1787, the area of present-day Kentucky was part of the state of Virginia, but delegates already anticipated that it would soon become an independent state. Virginia delegates were among those who had successfully opposed a treaty that John Jay had negotiated under the Articles of Confederation with Spain, which the delegates believed unfairly compromised rights to navigation on the Mississippi River. Such navigation was essential to the development of commerce in this area, and its termination threatened to dislodge Western states from their union with those in the East.

On June 25, Oliver Ellsworth of Connecticut cited Virginia's difficulty in governing Kentucky as an example of the inability of such a government to extend its sway over a large land area (Farrand 1937, I, 406). On July 23, Nathaniel Gorham of Massachusetts cited Kentucky, along with Vermont, Maine and Franklin (Tennessee), as areas that would soon be added as states (II, 94). On August 30, John Rutledge of South Carolina said that there was no reason to fear either that Virginia would fail to permit Kentucky to become a separate state or that North Carolina would forbid Tennessee from doing the same (II, 462).

In the report that Maryland's Luther Martin filed with the state legislature explaining his opposition to the new Constitution, he indicated his fears that Maryland could be called upon "to as-

sist, with her wealth and her blood, in subduing the inhabitants of Franklin [Tennessee], Kentucky, Vermont, and the provinces of Maine and Sagadahoc [also part of today's Maine], and in compelling them to continue in subjection to the States which respectively claim jurisdiction over them" (III, 226). Fortunately, this prophecy did not come to pass. Kentucky was admitted as the fifteenth state (Vermont had been admitted the previous year) in 1792.

Curiously, the Congress under the Articles of Confederation had previously adopted an enabling act providing for Kentucky's admission as a separate state, to which Virginia had consented. The Congress under the Articles had deferred action when it found that the new Constitution had been ratified by the requisite number of states. There is continuing discussion as to whether Congress deferred action because it thought it specifically lacked the power to admit states into the Union or whether it simply thought that it would be more prudent to defer this decision to the incoming Congress (Kesavan 2002, 71–73).

See Also Jay-Gardoqui Negotiations; States, Admission and Creation; Tennessee; Vermont; Virginia

FOR FURTHER READING

Farrand, Max, ed. 1937. *The Records of the Federal Convention.* 4 vols. New Haven, CT: Yale University Press.

Kesavan, Vasan. 2002. "When Did the Articles of Confederation Cease to Be Law?" *Notre Dame Law Review* 78 (December): 35–82.

Onuf, Peter S. 1982. "From Colony to Territory: Changing Concepts of Statehood in Revolutionary America." *Political Science Quarterly* 97 (Autumn): 447–459.

——. 1986. "Liberty, Development, and Union: Visions of the West in the 1780s." *William and Mary Quarterly*, 3rd ser. 53 (1986): 179–213.

Paine, Thomas. 1780. *Public Good: Being an Examination into the Claim of Virginia to the Vacant Western Territory, and of the Right of the United States to the Same, to Which Is Added, Proposing for Laying off a New State, to be applied as a Fund for Carrying on the War, or Redeeming the National Debt.* Albany, NY: Charles R. and George Webster. Reprinted 1976, Berea, KY: Kentucky Imprints.

Turner, Frederick Jackson. 1896. "Western State-Making in the Revolutionary Era II." *American Historical Review* 2 (January): 251–269.

——. 1895. "Western State-Making in the Revolutionary Era I." *American Historical Review* 1 (October): 70–86.

Rufus King, delegate from Massachusetts
(Pixel That)

KING, RUFUS (1755–1827)

Rufus King was born in present-day Scarboro, Maine (then Massachusetts) on March 24, 1755, to the family of a merchant. Educated at Harvard, he served briefly in the Revolutionary War before studying law under Theophilus Parsons, chief of the Massachusetts Supreme Court, and being admitted to the Massachusetts bar. Although he was an able attorney, he spent most of his life in public office. King represented Massachusetts in the Congress under the Articles of Confederation where he was influential in excluding slavery from the area northwest of the Ohio River.

Rufus King was present at the Convention when it began work on May 25, he was there for the signing on September 17, and he was active in between. He served on a record six committees. These included the following: the Committee on Original Apportionment of Congress (July 6); the Committee to Reconsider Representation in the House, which he chaired (July 9); the Committee on State Debts and Militia (August 18); the Committee on Slave Trade and Navigation (August 22); the Committee on Postponed Matters (August 31); and the Committee of Style and Arrangement (September 8).

Rules and Records

King made an important contribution to Convention deliberations on May 28 when he suggested that the rules proposed by Virginia's George Wythe and the committee Wythe chaired be so modified that delegates could not call for roll-call votes during the proceedings. King observed that "as the acts of the Convention were not to bind the Constituents it was unnecessary to exhibit this evidence of the votes." Perhaps more importantly, he feared that such a record might make it more difficult for delegates to change their votes as they changed their minds during Convention deliberations (Farrand 1937, I, 10). On the final day of the Convention, King made the last recorded motion when he proposed that the journals of the Convention should either be destroyed or entrusted to the president. Otherwise, he feared that "a bad use would be made of them by those who would wish to prevent the adoption of the Constitution" (II, 648).

Congress

Apportionment

On May 30, King observed that he did not think that the House should be apportioned according to state contributions. He was concerned first that monies might be so collected by the government as to make it difficult to know how much states had contributed and second that such funds would vary too much to make them a good standard (I, 36). On June 11, he further observed that, if the national government were to rely on taxes on imports, this would work particular hardship on such nonimporting states as Connecticut and New Jersey (I, 197). On June 11, King also introduced a motion that representation in the new Congress should be "according to some equitable ratio of representation" rather than as under the Articles of Confederation (I, 196).

King further elaborated on his views on June 30. Expressing willingness to accept a plan proposed by Pennsylvania's James Wilson under which each state would have at least one senator but would otherwise be represented according to population, King thought that it was more important to see that men were represented than states: "if we were convinced that every *man* in America was secured in all his rights, we should be ready to sacrifice this substantial good to the phantom of *State* sovereignty" (I, 489). King indicated that he thought that granting states equal suffrage in the Senate was to found government "in a vicious principle of representation" that was likely to shorten its life (II, 490).

On July 6, King opposed setting the number of representatives at one for every 40,000 voters on the basis that increases in population would one day result in a House with too many members. He was also concerned that recent legislation allowed states northwest of the Ohio River to enter when they had populations equal to that of Delaware, giving new states greater representation than that to which they would otherwise be entitled (I, 541). On July 14, King seconded a motion by Elbridge Gerry to limit future representation of the Western states to no more than that currently possessed by those in the East (II, 3).

King joined the Southern delegates in agreeing that their slaves should be counted as three-fifths of a person in apportioning state representation in the House of Representatives (see, however, the section on Slavery below). He thought that this would be a fair trade for "preferential distinctions in Commerce & other advantages" that the Northern states could expect from Union (I, 562). He observed that 11 of the 13 states had agreed to the three-fifths formula for apportioning taxes and that representation and taxation should go together (I, 562).

King attempted to incorporate compromises between the East (North) and South in the report of the committee that proposed that the House be composed of 65 members. Indeed, King said that he believed the chief fault line at the Convention was not between the large and small states but between those of the East and those of the South. He explained the work of his committee:

> For this reason he had been ready to yield something in the proportion of representatives for the security of the Southern. No principle would justify giving them a majority. They were brought as near an equality as was possible. He was not averse to giving them a still greater security, but did not see how it could be done. (I, 566).

When Morris objected on July 11 to fixing the standard of representation and favored allowing future Congresses to make adjustments as they chose, King said that he believed that "there was great force" in Morris's objections but that "he would however accede to the proposition for the sake of doing something" (I, 582). He expressed further reservations later in the day, observing that he thought that his committee had probably given the Southern states more than they would be entitled to under the three-fifths clause (I, 586). The next day, King noted that there was nothing that could keep the Southern states in the Union if they did not want to stay, and he expressed the view that Congress should be able to vary the three-fifths clause if in the future it found that "the foregoing Rule of Taxation is not in a just proportion to the relative Wealth and population of the several States" (I, 597). King was among those who resisted a last-minute attempt at the Convention (September 15) to readjust representation in the House by granting North Carolina and Rhode Island each an additional seat (II, 623). However, King joined Maryland's Daniel Carroll in seconding a motion, supported in a rare speech by George Washington and subsequently adopted, changing the minimum formula of representation to one representative for every 30,000 persons rather than one for every 40,000 (II, 644).

On June 13, King expressed his opposition to Elbridge Gerry's view, which ultimately prevailed at the Convention, that money bills should have to originate in the House of Representatives (I, 234). However, on July 14, King seconded a motion by Gerry to limit future representation of the Western states to no more than then possessed by those in the East (II, 3).

King correctly observed that it would be difficult to allow for state legislative selection of members of the U.S. Senate unless this body were either to be "very numerous, or *the idea of proportion among the States was to be disregarded*" (I, 51). King reasoned that unless there were a minimum of 80 to 100 senators, the smallest state (Delaware) would not be entitled to a single one.

On June 21, King indicated that he favored popular election of members of the House of Representatives. He feared that if such selection were left to state legislatures, they "wd. constantly choose men subservient to their own views as contrasted to the general interest" (I, 359). The following day, King opposed allowing states to pay members of Congress for the same reason (I, 372).

On the very eve of a compromise on representation in Congress, King continued to oppose equal state representation in the Senate. He thought that the government being formed would be "a General and National Government" that would operate directly on individuals rather than on state governments (II, 6). He did not believe that granting states equality was consistent with "just principles." Indeed, "he preferred the doing of nothing, to an allowance of an equal vote to all the States. It would be better he thought to submit to a little more confusion & convulsion, than to submit to such an evil" (II, 7). He did not follow up on the point or make it clear in which cases the third branch would operate, but he suggested during this speech that it might be possible to construct a Congress of three houses (II, 7). After the Great Compromise was effected, King was among those who favored allowing senators to vote individually rather than by states (II, 94).

Qualifications and Limitations

When the Convention debated a resolution on June 22 preventing members of Congress from accepting appointments to other offices during this service or for one year after, King fretted that the delegates "were refining too much." Not only did he think such a provision would "discourage merit," but he also feared that it would provide the president with an excuse for bad appointments (I, 376). King repeated his argument the following day, further pointing to examples that appeared to show that "the idea of preventing intrigue and solicitation of offices was chimerical" (I, 387).

On July 26, King opposed a proposal that would have required that members of Congress own property. He believed that this "would exclude the monied interest, whose aids may be essential in particular emergencies to the public safety" (II, 123).

Powers

King favored granting Congress power over elections. He observed that many delegates still seemed to support the idea of "erecting the Genl. Govt. on the authority of the State Legislatures" even though this had proven "fatal to the federal establishment" (II, 241).

King did not think that Congress should be able to move to another site without adopting a law for this purpose (II, 261). He favored providing that the national government would assume existing state debts, appealing not only to "considerations of justice and policy" but also as a way of garnering support for the new Constitution; otherwise, he feared opposition to the new Constitution from state creditors (II, 328). He thought that if Congress did assume state debts, states should in turn give up their "unlocated lands" (II, 328).

King wanted to grant the sole power to punish treason to the national government (II, 348). He seemed to think that states could, however, punish similar offenses as "high misdemeanors" (II, 348). Moreover, he did not think delegates could draw a clear line between treason against an individual state and against the states collectively (II, 349).

A committee on which King served proposed granting Congress power to organize, arm, and discipline the militia while allowing states to appoint and train it. King attempted to defend this report by distinguishing among the terms "organizing," "arming," and "disciplining" (II, 385). King favored allowing Congress to appoint the national treasurer by a joint ballot rather than allowing this officer to be appointed and confirmed like other officers recognized in the Constitution (II, 614). Late in the Convention (September 14), King opposed a motion by James Madison allowing Congress to create corporations. King feared that "the States will be prejudiced and divided into parties by it," citing conflicts that had erupted in Philadelphia and New York City over the establishment of a national bank under the Articles of Confederation (II, 616).

On September 15, King opposed a motion to grant Congress, rather than the president, the power to pardon treason. King argued that this revision would be inconsistent with the idea of separation of powers. He further observed that "a Legislative body is utterly unfit for the purpose. They are governed too much by the passions of the moment" (II, 626). Consistent with amendments that have been proposed to this power, however, King suggested that it might be appropriate to require Senate concurrence in such pardons (II, 627).

Other Matters Related to Congress

On August 7, King indicated that he did not think that it was necessary to establish in the Constitution a fixed meeting time each year for Congress. He did not think that Congress would need to meet each year. In his view, the objects of Congress would be chiefly focused on "commerce & revenue," and, once these were settled, there would not be much to do. He further observed that "A great vice in our system was that of legislating too much" (II, 198). On September 7, King reiterated his view that the Senate should not have to sit constantly. Consistent with his view that Congress could legislate too much, he expressed concern about the multiplication of offices "which must increase the expense as well as influence of the Government" (II, 539).

King favored a motion setting a bare majority of the first Congress as necessary for a quorum but allowing future Congresses to increase them or not as Congress grew. He feared that "the future increase of members would render a majority of the whole extremely cumbersome," but he apparently thought such adjustments would be subject to a presidential veto (II, 253). King disfavored requiring majorities of two-thirds of the Senate to approve treaties; he believed that requiring the president and the Senate jointly to approve treaties would provide sufficient protection (II, 540).

Presidency

On June 4, King was one of three delegates (the others were James Wilson and Alexander Hamilton) who expressly favored an absolute executive veto (I, 108; Ernst 1968, 96). He subsequently supported a proposal for a conditional executive veto rather than associating the presidency with members of the judiciary in a Council of Revision (I, 98). On June 6, he observed that the virtue of executive unity was as applicable to the revisionary power as others to be wielded by the executive (I, 139).

On July 19, King indicated that he did not like the idea of making the president ineligible for re-election. King reasoned that "he who has proved himself to be most fit for an Office, ought not to be excluded by the constitution from holding it" (II, 55).

King believed that the people could choose a president, but he thought that "an appointment by electors chosen by the people for this purpose, would be liable to fewest objections" (II, 56). He opposed a plan whereby electors would be chosen by lot, observing that "We ought to be governed by reason, not by chance" (II, 106). He later argued that the Electoral College helped balance the influence of the large and the small states (II, 514), and he introduced the motion preventing members of Congress from serving in the capacity of electors (II, 521). He favored allowing Congress as a whole to select the president when no candidate received a majority rather than leaving this choice to the Senate alone (II, 522).

When the delegates voted on July 19 against a seven-year presidential term, King expressed concern that they might "shorten the term too much" (II, 59). On July 24, King followed motions by Luther Martin for a presidential term of 11 years and a motion by Elbridge Gerry for a term of 15 years by proposing that the president serve for twenty years, but King's comment, that "This is the medium life of princes," suggests that he was being ironic (II, 102).

King feared the impeachment mechanism as undermining executive independence. He thought that such a mechanism was only proper in the case of officials who served "during good behavior" rather than for limited terms and thought it particularly inappropriate for the president to be tried by members of Congress (II, 67–68). When the Convention did establish an impeachment mechanism for members of the executive branch, King joined Madison in opposing a provision that would suspend the executive until the charges were tried (II, 612).

Judiciary

On June 4, King opposed associating members of the judiciary with the presidency in a Council of Revision. He observed that "the Judges ought to be able to expound the law as it should come before them, free from the bias of having participated in its formation" (I, 98).

When fellow delegates were debating whether Congress should be able to establish federal courts below that of the Supreme Court or whether they should simply take appeals from existing state courts, King added a touch of realism by observing that it would be less costly to establish inferior federal tribunals than to multiply appeals (I, 125).

Federalism

King's views of federalism were often tied to his comments, described above, relative to how states should be represented in the new system. King delivered an important speech on June 19 in which he discussed the nature of the government being contemplated. He objected to the term "sovereignty" being applied to the states:

> The States were not "sovereigns" in the sense contended for by some. They did not possess the peculiar features of sovereignty. They could not make war, nor peace, nor alliances, nor treaties. Considering them as political Beings, they were dumb, for they could not speak to any foreign Sovereign whatever. They were deaf, for they could not hear any propositions from such Sovereign. They had not even the organs or faculties of defense or offense, for they could not of themselves raise troops, or equip vessels, for war. (I, 323)

Similarly, the Union of states comprised not only "the idea of a confederation" but "also of consolidation" (I, 323). He continued: "If the States therefore retained some portion of their sovereignty, they had certainly divested themselves of essential portions of it. If they formed a confederacy in some respects—they formed a Nation in others" (I, 324). Although King said that he did not favor annihilating the states, he said that he "thought that much of their power ought to be taken from them" (I, 324).

In this same speech, King made an impassioned plea for continuing with the Virginia Plan rather than with simply patching up the Articles of Confederation as William Paterson had proposed in the New Jersey Plan. Notes that King prepared for his speech indicate that he argued that even though Congress had not authorized such a plan, the Virginia Plan was authorized by "The public Expectations, & the public Danger" (I, 332). He further argued that the Virginia Plan was "no crude and undigested plan, the Child of narrow and unextensive views, brought forward und[er] the auspices of Cowardice & Irresolution" but "a measure of Decision," the "foundation of Freedom & of national Glory." It was, he said, "no idle Experiment, no romantic Speculation," but a measure that "forces itself upon wise men" (I, 332).

Because King put greater emphasis on the rights of individuals than the rights of states, he did not favor equal representation of the states in one or both houses of Congress. On June 30, however, King indicated that he did not think that "a full answer had been given to those who apprehended a dangerous encroachment" on state jurisdiction (I, 492–493). He believed that the Constitution could be so devised as to provide for such security, as the English had provided for the security of Scotland when the two nations united. King expressed special concern (I, 493) over the intemperate language of Delaware's Gunning Bedford, who had previously suggested that the small states might seek an alliance with foreign powers, but Yates's notes indicate that King may in part have prompted this response when King had indicated that if states were granted equal suffrage in the Senate, then "our business here is at an end" (I, 499; Ernst, 103). King's contrast of "our common Country" with "some foreign land" indicates that he had a keen sense of national patriotism (I, 493).

On August 28, King introduced a motion for the provision that the Convention eventually incorporated into Article I, Section 10 of the Con-

stitution, prohibiting states from interfering with private contracts (II, 439); initially defeated, the proposal reemerged from the Committee of Style of which King was a member (Ernst, 112). That same day, he opposed prohibiting congressional taxation of exports (II, 442). When Gerry objected that the federal power over property used for forts could undermine the states, King moved to insert the words "by the consent of the Legislature of the State" after "purchases" (II, 510).

Slavery

After the Convention fixed the rule for representation in the House according to the rule previously adopted for taxation, King wanted to know how this would affect slave representation, and he came out swinging against the institution of slavery. He said that "The admission of slaves was a more grating circumstance to his mind" (II, 220). Observing that the delegates had tied the hands of the legislature in regard both to slave importation and the taxation of exports, he questioned, "Is this reasonable?" (II, 220). Believing that the two great objects of Union were internal and external defense, he believed these agreements injured both:

> Shall all the States then be bound to defend each; & shall each be at liberty to introduce a weakness which will render defence more difficult? Shall one part of the U.S. be bound to defend another part, and that other part be at liberty not only to increase its own danger, but to withhold the compensation for the burden? If slaves are to be imported shall not the exports produced by their labor, supply a revenue the better to enable the Genl. Govt. to defend their Masters? (II, 220)

A unique mix of moralistic and practical concerns, King ended this speech by observing that "either slaves should not be represented, or exports should be taxable" (II, 220). King later observed that the Northern and Middle states would not think it fair if slaves were the only imports exempted from federal duties (II, 373). King served on the committee that proposed allowing states to import slaves until 1808 in exchange for securing the power to tax them, and he believed the two parts of the compromise were linked together (II, 416).

Ratification

On June 5, King observed that, according to the Articles of Confederation, state legislatures were competent to ratify the new Constitution. He believed, however, that it would be more expeditious for conventions within the states to do so since such conventions would meet in a single body at a time when most state legislatures were bicameral and because state legislators, slated "to lose power, will be most likely to raise objections" (I, 123). King repeated this view on July 23, indicating as an additional advantage of popular ratification that it would "get rid of the scruples which some members of the States Legislatures might derive from their oaths to support & maintain the existing Constitutions" (II, 92). King proposed the motion that limited the application of the new Constitution only to the states that ratified it (II, 475). As the Convention progressed, King became even more persuaded of the desirability of ratifying the Constitution by state conventions. He thus remarked on August 31 that

> striking out "convenient" as the requisite mode was equivalent to giving up the business altogether. Conventions alone, which will avoid all the obstacles from the complicated formation of the Legislatures, will succeed, and if not positively required by the plan, its enemies will oppose that mode. (II, 476)

Observing that the constitution of Massachusetts, which he represented, contained a provision making its constitution unalterable until 1790, he observed that "this was no difficulty with him. The State must have contemplated a recurrence to first principles before they sent deputies to this Convention" (II, 477). King thought it would be respectful to Congress to submit the Constitution to it without requiring that it approve or disap-

prove of it, and he suggested that the approval of nine states would be adequate for the new Constitution to go into effect (II, 561). To require congressional approval or to allow states to decide on the appropriate number required to ratify would throw everything into confusion and risk losing everything (II, 563).

Life after the Convention

After the Convention, King represented Massachusetts at the ratifying convention, where he was an effective advocate for the new Constitution. In one speech, he made a particularly powerful appeal for the new document. Pointing to the failure of the Articles of Confederation to get states to pay their quotas, he said that it was essential that the government be able to operate directly on individuals:

> It has been objected to the proposed constitution, that the power is too great, and by this constitution is to be sacred. But if the want of power is the defect in the old confederation, there is fitness and propriety in adopting what is here proposed. . . . It is an objection in some gentlemen's minds, that Congress should possess the power of the purse and the sword. But, sir, I would ask, whether any government can exist, or give security to the people, which is not possessed of this power. . . . To conclude, sir, if we mean to support an efficient federal government, which under the old confederation can never be the case, the proposed constitution is, in my opinion, the only one that can be substituted. (Quoted in Ernst 1968, 115–116)

Despite his efforts at the Constitutional Convention and in the state's ratifying convention, his marriage in 1786 to Mary Alsop of New York (the only daughter of a merchant, she was 16 when they were married), with whom he would have seven children, changed his residency, and after Massachusetts ruled that he was ineligible to represent that state in the U.S. Senate, the people of New York elected him to their legislature, which selected him as one of its first two senators.

King became a strong Federalist and joined Alexander Hamilton in authoring essays in support of the Jay Treaty. King served from 1796 to 1803 under three U.S. presidents as a minister to Great Britain, a post that he resumed from 1825 to 1826 but had to give up because of declining health. He served again as a U.S. senator from New York from 1813 to 1825, in which capacity he opposed the Missouri Compromise, and he was twice defeated as a candidate for vice president (both times running with Charles Cotesworth Pinckney) and once defeated as a candidate for president on the Federalist ticket. He died in Jamaica, New York, on April 29, 1827.

See Also Committees at the Constitutional Convention; Massachusetts

FOR FURTHER READING

Ernst, Robert. 1968. *Rufus King: American Federalist.* Chapel Hill: University of North Carolina Press.

Farrand, Max, ed. 1937. *The Records of the Federal Convention.* 4 vols. New Haven, CT: Yale University Press.

Siry, Steven E. 1999. "King, Rufus." In John A. Garraty and Mark C. Carnes, eds. *American National Biography.* New York: Oxford University Press, 12: 711–712.

KINGSHIP

See MONARCHY

KNOWLEDGE OF THE CONSTITUTIONAL CONVENTION

Although scores of books deal with the U.S. Constitution and the Convention that gave it birth, from time to time studies reveal that citizens lack basic knowledge of both. Studies have shown that they are confused about the distinction between the Constitution and the Declaration of Independence and which documents contain which words, about which of the American Founders attended the Convention (many incorrectly include John Adams, Patrick Henry, and/or Thomas Jefferson), about what principles are specifically stated within the Constitution and which have to be implied from the text, and about other matters. In exhaustive analysis, Michael Kammen has demonstrated that such errors have often extended even to writings by members of the academic community (Kammen 1987, 4, 24). Such errors were almost guaranteed in the early years of American history before publication of the records of the Convention, but they have persisted thereafter. As documentary evidence has expanded that should give greater insights into the Constitution, the chronological distance between the Convention and modern times has increased, making once-familiar terms, and the ideologies behind them, seem illusive.

Clearly, it would be better if accurate knowledge of the American Founding and of the specific words of the Constitution were more widespread (indeed, this is one of the purposes of these volumes), and there are a number of historical sites and educational organizations devoted to this task. Nonetheless, the Framers undoubtedly anticipated that every citizen would not be well versed in the document they were creating. They created a system in which individuals would have incentives to protect their own rights, and, largely as a result of the ratification debates, they further provided a bill of rights that would guide citizens as to their own rights that they could protect through the judicial system. Commenting on the surveys that appear to show confusion over the Constitution, and especially over its relation to the Declaration of Independence, Robert A. Goldwin has observed that "Americans may not have the text of the Constitution in their heads, but they have the meaning of it in their hearts and in their bones" (Goldwin 1990, 45).

See Also Bill of Rights; Commemorations of the Constitutional Convention; Declaration of Independence

FOR FURTHER READING

Goldwin, Robert A. 1990. *Why Blacks, Women, and Jews Are Not Mentioned in the Constitution, and Other Unorthodox Views*. Washington, DC: AEI Press.

Kammen, Michael. 1987. *A Machine That Would Go of Itself: The Constitution in American Culture*. New York: Alfred A. Knopf.

LAND DISPUTES

Article III, Section 2 of the U.S. Constitution vests jurisdiction in the federal courts to deal with matters involving "controversies between two or more states." It further provides that the U.S. Supreme Court shall have original jurisdiction in such cases and prohibits states from entering into interstate compacts without congressional consent (Caldwell 1920, 55).

Not having a federal judicial system to handle such matters, Article IX of the Articles of Confederation had provided for a complex plan to settle disputes between states over boundaries. Such disputes had previously been the responsibility of the English Privy Council (Caldwell, 38). Under the provision in the Articles of Confederation, states petitioned Congress, which then appointed, by joint consent of the states, commissioners or judges to hear the case. Alternatively, Congress chose three persons from each state, and states alternately struck names until they arrived at a panel of 13, from which seven to nine names were to be chosen by lot, at least five of which could compose a panel. These judges were then to decide the matter, and this judgment was to be treated as a binding act of Congress. Although six disputes arose among the states over boundary questions (one involving the controversy among New York, Massachusetts, and New Hampshire over what was eventually to become the state of Vermont) under the Articles of Confederation

(Caldwell, 53–54), the formal procedure was used only once under the Articles in 1782. This occurred when five commissioners peacefully settled a dispute between Connecticut and Pennsylvania over immigrants from Connecticut, acting under the authority of the Susquehannah Company, who had settled in the Wyoming Valley near Wilkes-Barre, in favor of Pennsylvania (Taylor 1969).

The Committee of Detail incorporated the procedure that had been used under the Articles of Confederation in the draft of the Constitution that it submitted to the Convention on August 6. The Convention discussed this provision on August 24. John Rutledge of South Carolina argued that such a mechanism was unnecessary because the federal judiciary would resolve such matters, and William Johnson of Connecticut seconded his provision to strike it. Roger Sherman of Connecticut and Jonathan Dayton of New Jersey agreed that the provision was no longer necessary. North Carolina's Hugh Williamson wanted to postpone the provision whereas Nathaniel Gorham of Massachusetts thought that the mechanism would be preferable to judicial resolution of such issues. After the motion to delay was rejected, Pennsylvania's James Wilson (who had been among those who had represented Pennsylvania in its dispute with Connecticut under the Articles of Confederation) expressed his support for striking the mechanism, and the Convention agreed by a vote of 8-2. On August 27, the Convention further voted to extend judicial jurisdiction to cases involving "Citizens of the same State claiming lands under grants of different States" (II, 431–432).

See Also Articles of Confederation; Committee of Detail; Judicial Jurisdiction; Vermont; Wilson, James

FOR FURTHER READING

Caldwell, Robert G. 1920. "The Settlement of Inter-State Disputes." *American Journal of International Law* 14 (Jan.-Apr.): 38–69.

Taylor, Robert J. 1969. "Trial at Trenton." *William and Mary Quarterly*, 3rd ser. 26 (October): 521–547.

LANGDON, JOHN (1741–1819)

Born near Portsmouth, New Hampshire, in 1741, John Langdon served as an apprentice to a merchant and soon became a merchant and shipbuilder reputed to be the wealthiest man in New Hampshire. An ardent Patriot, Langdon helped seize gunpowder from the British in December of 1774 and was soon thereafter elected to the legislature, where he served from 1776 to 1781 as the speaker. The previous year he had served in the Continental Congress where he helped build the first ship for the U.S. Navy. Langdon personally advanced money to finance troops to face the armies of General John Burgoyne and participated in a number of battles as well, but he also advanced his fortune as a Continental agent for New Hampshire.

Langdon was president of New Hampshire from 1784 to 1786 and fronted the money to pay for Nicholas Gilman and him (the state's representatives to Congress) to attend the Constitutional Convention. Because the trip awaited his own financing, however, he and Gilman did not arrive at the Constitutional Convention until July 23. They thus arrived a week after the Convention's critical decision regarding representation in Congress.

Positions Taken at the Convention

On July 26, Langdon supported a motion by Pennsylvania's James Wilson to strike a provision that would have prevented individuals with unsettled accounts from serving in Congress. Langdon supported Wilson's very practical arguments that this would give too much power to auditors, who might delay settling accounts in order to exclude individuals from office (Farrand 1937, II, 125). Later that day, Langdon supported a motion by Virginia's George Mason preventing the seat of the national government from being moved to a city that was serving as a state capital. However, he expressed concern that a state might evade this requirement by moving its capital to the national capital after public buildings were constructed in the latter (II, 127).

On August 14, Langdon opposed having states pay the salaries of members of Congress. Not only did he foresee difficulty in establishing the amount of such payment, but he felt it would be unjust to "distant States" with greater expenditures for their "members' travel costs" (II, 290–291).

John Langdon, delegate from New Hampshire
(Pixel That)

When the Convention was discussing whether to grant Congress power to "emit bills," that is, whether to print paper money, as it had done under the Articles of Confederation, Delaware's George Read said that the words "would be as alarming as the mark of the Beast in Revelations" (II, 310). Langdon added that he would "rather reject the whole plan than retain the three words [and emit bills]" (II, 310).

When Elbridge Gerry of Massachusetts objected to a provision allowing Congress to send troops into a state when the legislature could not request the same, Langdon supported the provision. He observed that "the apprehension of the national force, will have a salutary effect in preventing insurrections" (II, 317). Similarly, Langdon opposed Gerry's attempt to limit the size of standing armies in peacetime. On this occasion, Langdon said that he "saw no room for Mr. Gerry's distrust of the Representatives of the people" (II, 330). Similarly supporting a motion by Virginia's George Mason entrusting Congress with the power to regulate the militia and the states to appoint their officers, Langdon said that "He saw no more reason to be afraid of the Genl. Govt than of the State Govts. He was more apprehensive of the confusion of the different authorities on this subject, than of either" (II, 331). On a later day, Langdon indicated that he did not share the concerns of other delegates as to which powers were exercised by the states and which were to be exercised by the national governments:

The General & State Govts. were not enemies to each other, but different institutions for the good of the people of America. As one of the people he could say, the National Govt. is mine, the State Govt is mine—In transferring power from one to the other—I only take out of my left hand what it cannot so well use, and put it into my right hand where it can be better used. (II, 386)

In later supporting allowing two-thirds majorities in Congress to negative state laws, Langdon said that "he considered it as resolvable into the question whether the extent of the National Constitution was to be judged of by the Genl or the State Governments" (II, 391).

Again opposing a motion by Elbridge Gerry that would apportion direct taxes on the states until the first meeting of Congress on the basis of the number of representatives that they had in the first branch, Langdon said that his opposition stemmed from his belief that this would be unreasonably hard on New Hampshire (II, 350). Acknowledging that he was at a disadvantage since he was not present when the representation for New Hampshire was apportioned, Langdon indicated on August 21 that if it had been given extra representatives to which it was not entitled, then "he did not wish for them" (II, 358). By contrast on September 15, Langdon indicated that he thought that both Rhode Island and New Hampshire were entitled to an extra representative in the U.S. House (II, 622).

Langdon expressed concern on August 21 that states were to this point left free to tax exports. He thought that this would work to the disadvantage of New Hampshire and other nonexporting states and thought that was unacceptable. Also pointing to fears that Northern interests would attempt to oppress those from the South, he proposed as a remedy that two-thirds or three-fourths majorities should be required for such commercial regulations (II, 359). He also favored prohibiting states from taxing exports of other states that left their harbors (II, 361).

By contrast, Langdon thought that Congress should be entrusted with the power to prohibit slave importation: "He cd. not with a good conscience leave it with the States who could then go on with the traffic" (II, 373). However, when Connecticut's Roger Sherman objected that allowing the taxation of slave imports classified them as property, Langdon joined Rufus King of Massachusetts in indicating that he thought this was a necessary part of the compromise (II, 416).

Langdon wanted to leave the status of debts against the U.S. just where they were under the Articles (II, 413). He further favored leaving Congress the option of admitting new states into the Union with fewer privileges than the original states (II, 454). Langdon was concerned that if Vermont did not join the Union and remained exempt from taxes, this could hurt New Hampshire (II, 456). Langdon expressed concern over the clause preventing ships from one state from paying duties in another, believing that there may be cases when the general government needed to adopt such regulations to deal with smuggling (II, 481). Langdon feared that a provision allowing states to lay duties for the costs of inspection could be abused (II, 589). Similarly, he thought that states should have nothing to do with regulating tonnage since this was an aspect of trade committed to Congress (II, 625).

When the delegates were still considering allowing Congress to select the president, Langdon proposed that they should do this by joint ballot rather than by individual houses, even though he did not believe this would help his home state. Langdon said that he feared that a negative vote by the Senate "would hurt the feelings of the man elected by the votes of the other branch" (II, 402).

In part because he arrived late, Langdon appeared to have a penchant for addressing relatively minor details of the Constitution, many dealing with commercial matters, rather than for tackling larger questions. He appeared less concerned than some delegates over the respective relations between the national government and the states in general, but continued to concern himself with some of the particulars of this relationship.

Life after the Convention

Langdon returned to Congress after the Convention, served again as his state's president, and worked for ratification of the Constitution, which he initially thought would be ratified more quickly than proved to be the case (see Mayo 1970, 206–212). He served as one of New Hampshire's first two senators and had the honor, as Senate pro tempore, to count the votes that elected George Washington as president. Initially a supporter of Hamilton's fiscal programs, Langdon found himself drawn, in part by his Anglophobia, to the Democratic-Republican Party of Thomas Jefferson. He subsequently returned to New Hampshire to serve in the state legislature and for a number of terms as governor where he helped get the state capital moved to Concord and stopped slave importation through Ports-

mouth. In 1805 fellow delegate Nicholas Gilman supported him in a successful race for governor over Gilman's older brother. Langdon turned down the opportunity to run as vice president to James Madison in 1812 but was active in the American and New Hampshire Bible Societies. He died in Portsmouth in 1819.

See Also Gilman, Nicholas; New Hampshire

FOR FURTHER READING

Farrand, Max, ed. 1937. *The Records of the Federal Convention*. 4 vols. New Haven, CT: Yale University Press.

Mayo, Lawrence Shaw. 1970. *John Langdon of New Hampshire*. Port Washington, NY: Kennikat Press.

Van Atta, John R. 1999. "Langdon, John." In John A. Garraty and Mark C. Carnes, eds. *American National Biography*. New York: Oxford University Press, 13: 138–139.

LANSING, JOHN (1754–1829)

John Lansing was born in Albany in 1754, the descendant of Dutch immigrants. He is believed to have been the wealthiest man in the state, with vast landholdings and numerous slaves. He read law under Robert Yates, with whom he would attend the Constitutional Convention, and with James Duane. A military secretary to General Philip Schuyler during the Revolution, Lansing had served six terms in the New York legislature prior to being elected to serve at the Convention. At the time he attended the Convention, he was allied with New York governor George Clinton and was serving as the mayor of Albany.

None of New York's three delegates to the Constitutional Convention especially liked the direction that it took. Along with Robert Yates, John Lansing was one of two members who left before the Convention ended and did not therefore sign the document. Although Alexander Hamilton, the state's third delegate, did so, he was convinced that the new government was not strong enough. Lansing did not speak frequently

John Lansing, delegate from New York
(Library of Congress)

at the Convention. His central contribution to debates at the Convention was to support the New Jersey Plan, which he believed was more consistent with the purpose of the Convention and more likely to be accepted by the states than the more visionary Virginia Plan, which Lansing believed imperiled state sovereignty.

Positions Taken at the Convention

Convention records indicate that Lansing was seated on Saturday, June 2 (Farrand 1937, I, 76). His first recorded action occurred nearly two weeks later after William Paterson presented the New Jersey Plan when Lansing and some unnamed "gentlemen" argued for postponing a meeting of the Committee of the Whole so that supporters would have more time to examine and defend the new plan (I, 242). On this occasion he observed that "the two systems [that of the New Jersey and Virginia Plans] are fairly contrasted. The one [the New Jersey Plan] now offered is on the basis of amending the federal government, and the other [the Virginia Plan] to be reported as

a national government, on propositions which exclude the propriety of amendment" (I, 246).

The following day, June 16, Lansing developed his ideas in greater detail. Interestingly, he led off in defense of the New Jersey Plan, with Paterson following. Lansing portrayed the New Jersey Plan as sustaining "the sovereignty of the respective States" whereas the Virginia Plan, with its provision for a congressional negative on state laws, destroyed it (I, 249). Although Lansing had concerns about the perceived derogation of state sovereignty, he focused not so much on the undesirability of the Virginia Plan in and of itself but on the "want of power in the Convention to discuss & propose it" and "the improbability of its being adopted" (I, 249). Arguing that the Convention was exceeding its power by even considering the Virginia Plan, Lansing said that his own state "would never have concurred in sending deputies to the convention, if she had supposed the deliberations were to turn on a consolidation of the States, and a National Government" (I, 249). As to ratification, Lansing did not think the states were likely to ratify proposals that exceeded the Convention's mandate and pointed to previous difficulties under the Articles of Confederation in extending congressional powers. He believed it even less likely that the states would approve a plan of government like that advocated in the Virginia Plan:

> The States will never feel a sufficient confidence in a general Government to give it a negative on their laws. The Scheme is itself totally novel. There is [no] parallel to it to be found. The authority of Congress is familiar to the people, and an augmentation of the powers of Congress will be readily approved by them. (I, 250)

Lansing further elaborated his views on June 20, when he restated his opinion that the Convention had no authority to adopt the Virginia Plan and that the people would not follow the Convention in ratifying it. As to the first point, he observed that, whether elected by state legislatures or by the people, the delegates were there not to represent people as individuals but "as forming a sovereign State" (I, 336). Although some believed that necessity could warrant exceeding Convention instructions, Lansing and other delegates did not agree on such a necessity (I, 336). Pennsylvania's James Wilson had argued that since the Convention was only making recommendations, it should recommend what it would, but Lansing feared that such recommendations, if rejected by the people, "will be a source of great dissentions" (I, 336). For his part, he did not believe that it was likely that states that currently possessed sovereignty were likely to part with it.

Lansing went on to answer a number of other arguments that delegates had raised. He did not believe that equal representation in Congress was equivalent to the system of rotten boroughs in England. He believed any configuration of Congress would result in the representation of state prejudices. If, as Alexander Hamilton had asserted, there was no commonality of interests among the large states and interests were relatively uniform, then it could not matter if small states retained their equality. Lansing did not believe that Congress would have sufficient "leisure" to oversee the laws of individual states and void those that Congress thought to be inappropriate. He further argued that Congress was not competent to do so and likened such oversight to that which the British had exercised in America prior to independence. A government like that proposed by the Virginia Plan would require greater influence on the part of the national government than the states would give. As long as the states existed, they could be expected to protect themselves. Their reluctance would be expanded by the novelty of the new system and by their inability to predict its consequences: "The system was too novel & complex. No man could foresee what its operation will be either with respect to the Genl. Govt. or the State Govts. One or other it has been surmised must absorb the whole" (I, 338). In Yates's notes of the speech, which provide a useful supplement to Madison's, Lansing was recorded as asking, "Fond as many are of a general government, do any of you believe it can pervade the whole continent so effectively as to secure the peace, harmony and happiness of the whole?" (I, 345).

Although the Convention voted to proceed with its discussion of the Virginia Plan, Lansing remained unconvinced. On June 28, he introduced a motion to restore representation in the first branch of Congress to that which existed under the Articles of Confederation, under which states were equally represented (I, 445).

Life after the Convention

Lansing and Yates subsequently left the Convention on July 10 and returned to New York to oppose it, authoring an open letter to Governor Clinton expressing their opposition (III, 246–247). Along with Melancton Smith, Lansing was one of the primary opponents of ratification of the Constitution at the New York ratifying convention. He introduced numerous amendments and unsuccessfully attempted to condition New York's ratification on their adoption. Lansing served for 11 years on the New York Supreme Court and then served from 1801 to 1814 as chancellor of the state, where he was widely respected for his integrity but as a result of which he became a defendant in a case where he was sued by John Van Ness Yates. After retiring from the bench at the mandatory age of 60, Lansing resumed his legal practice. In 1824 New Yorkers chose him as a presidential elector for Georgia's William Crawford, and in 1826 he published an account of some of his cases. After leaving a hotel room in New York City, he mysteriously disappeared after going to post a letter in December 1829.

See Also Hamilton, Alexander; New York; Yates, Robert

FOR FURTHER READING

Bradford, M. M. 1994. *Founding Fathers: Brief Lives of the Framers of the United States Constitution.* Lawrence: University Press of Kansas.

Farrand, Max, ed. 1937. *The Records of the Federal Convention.* 4 vols. New Haven, CT: Yale University Press.

Hanyan, Craig. 1999. "Lansing, John." In John A. Garraty and Mark C. Carnes, eds. *American National Biography.* New York: Oxford University Press, 13: 180–181.

LAW, RULE OF

See CONSTITUTIONALISM

LEGALITY OF THE CONVENTION

Although with the long passage of years the issue is largely of theoretical interest, there is continuing debate about the legality of the Constitutional Convention and the method that the delegates specified for constitutional ratification. Working from the controversial view (for critique, see Vile 1993, 75–96) that a deliberate majority of "We the People" did and can in the future exercise popular sovereignty apart from established constitutional forms, Akhil Reed Amar has argued that the work of the Constitutional Convention was completely legal (1988). By contrast, Bruce Ackerman and Neal Katyal (1995) and Richard Kay (1987) have argued that the American founding was "unconventional," and even illegal. They work from a number of widely recognized facts.

First, Article XII of the Articles of Confederation specified that it could not be amended except by the unanimous consent of the state legislatures, but the Convention not only met with delegates from only 12 states present (and at times with less) but also specified in Article VII that the new Constitution would go into effect when nine states ratified it. Second, although the congressional call for the Convention specified that it was designed to "correct and enlarge" the Articles, influenced by Edmund Randolph's early introduction of the Virginia Plan, the delegates to the Convention instead began contemplating, and eventually proposed, a drastically new system. Third, the Convention designated that states would ratify the Constitution not, as specified in the Articles of Confederation, through existing legislatures, but through special conventions called for this purpose (see Ackerman and Katyal; Kay). Bruce Ackerman cites these facts to support his contention that America is a "dualist democracy" in which periods of ordinary politics are from time to time interrupted by "constitutional moments" during which laws are evaded and rules are bent in order to meet ongoing crises. Ackerman identifies the Constitutional Convention as the first of three such constitutional moments, the post–Civil War era constituting a second, and the New Deal a third.

Ackerman and Kay are hardly the first to point to anomalies in the writing and adoption of the Constitution, but in light of the times, it might be more accurate to argue that the adoption of the Constitution was "extra-legal" rather than simply "illegal." Historian Jack Rakove (who actually prefers the term "super-legal") has observed that the writing of the Constitution needs to be understood not simply as a single event that happened in 1787 but as an occasion that was part of a larger tapestry of events constituting a revolutionary era. The period from 1776 to 1787 witnessed massive experimentation with constitutions. Members of Congress had written the Articles of Confederation at a time when they were concerned with other pressing business, including waging a war against Great Britain. Although all of the state legislatures had eventually ratified the Constitution, many of the state constitutions of the period had no higher sanction than that of the legislatures that had both written and adopted them. As Rakove notes, most had been "promulgated, not ratified" (Rakove 1999, 1942). The mechanism that required unanimous ratification of amendments of the Articles of Confederation had proven to be overly wooden and unworkable.

However unconventional it may have been, Rakove describes the writing and ratification of the U.S. Constitution as "definitely expedient" but "no less deeply principled" (1945). He observes that the idea of writing a Constitution in convention and ratifying it through popular, rather than mere legislative, approval—a mechanism first successfully utilized by Massachusetts in 1780—represented "a superior grasp of the nature of constitutionalism itself" (1945). He notes that what the Framers did was certainly not "illegal" in the sense that they could have been prosecuted for it. As he observes, "the worst crime of which they [the Founding Fathers] could have been accused, had the proposed Constitution come to naught, was of committing a profound error in political judgment and wasting the opportunity they had worked so hard to create" (1939).

Congress approved calling the Constitutional Convention and, although it did not specifically approve the Constitution, it later passed the work of the Convention on to the states for approval in conventions. Many members of the Convention were also present or former members of the confederal Congress. When Federalists presented the new Constitution to the nation, they were able to point to the fact that both George Washington and Benjamin Franklin had attended the Convention and supported the document.

Given the mechanisms for reflecting popular choice that were available in the eighteenth century, the Constitution had far greater legitimacy than the Articles of Confederation that preceded it. Significantly, those who classify the actions of the Framers as illegal generally have not done so as a way of suggesting that such proceedings were therefore illegitimate but as a way of suggesting that there have been, and might still be, times when strict adherence to existing legal forms should be modified.

See Also Articles of Confederation; Constitutional Convention Mechanism; Constitutional Moments; Ratification, Convention Debates, and Constitutional Provision; State Constitutions

FOR FURTHER READING

Ackerman, Bruce, and Neal Katyal. 1995. "Our Unconventional Founding." *University of Chicago Law Review* 62 (Spring): 475–573.

Amar, Akhil Reed. 1988. "Philadelphia Revisited: Amending the Constitution outside Article V." *University of Chicago Law Review* 55 (Fall): 1043–1104.

Kay, Richard S. 1987. "The Illegality of the Constitution." *Constitutional Commentary* 4 (Winter): 57–80.

Rakove, Jack N. 1999. "The Super-Legality of the Constitution, or, a Federalist Critique of Bruce Ackerman's Neo-Federalism." *Yale Law Journal* 108 (June): 1931–1958.

Vile, John R. 1993. *Contemporary Questions Surrounding the Constitutional Amending Process.* Westport, CT: Praeger.

LEGISLATIVE BRANCH OF GOVERNMENT

See Entries beginning with CONGRESS

LEGITIMACY OF THE CONVENTION

See LEGALITY OF THE CONVENTION

LETTER OF TRANSMITTAL

Notes in the handwriting of Virginia's Edmund Randolph from the Committee of Detail, which met from July 26 to August 6, indicate that the committee was considering an address to the people to accompany the Constitution. Randolph anticipated that such an address would have eight parts. They would, respectively, "state the general objects of confederation," show how the Articles of Confederation had fallen short of such goals, list the powers of the new government, show how these could not be vested in the existing Congress, show how a partial confederation would not be adequate, establish the need for a national government, explain the principles of this government, and conclude (Farrand 1937, II, 149–150).

On September 10, South Carolina's Charles Pinckney proposed that the Committee of Style and Arrangement should prepare such an address (II, 564), indicating that it had not as yet been done. The committee reported, and the Convention adopted, an accompanying letter on September 12 (II, 585). William Jackson, the Convention secretary, wrote a letter to John Quincy Adams on October 21, 1818, indicating that Jared Ingersoll had reported that Benjamin Franklin, Gouverneur Morris, and he were assigned the responsibility of drafting the letter (IV, 83), but this hearsay recollection is suspect not only because of its date but because Ingersoll was not a member of the committee. By contrast, historian Ralph Ketcham reports that Madison authored the letter (1971, 230).

In any event, Maryland's Daniel Carroll apparently wanted something longer (this is presumably reflected in the distinction that the notes reflect between a "letter" and an "address"). On September 15, just two days before the delegates signed the Constitution, he proposed establishing a special committee for this purpose. South Carolina's John Rutledge objected that this would lead to delay and that it would be improper to address the people "before it was known whether Congress would approve and support the plan" (II, 623). Sherman concurred with Rutledge and the Convention rejected Carroll's motion by a vote of 6-4-1 (II, 623).

When the Convention sent the Constitution to Congress, it thus accompanied it with a resolution and with the cover letter. George Washington signed the letter as president of the Convention. It essentially described and attempted to justify what the Convention had done. The letter has an introductory sentence followed by four paragraphs.

The first cited the need that "friends of our country" had seen of vesting "the power of making war, peace, and treaties, that of levying money and regulating commerce, and the correspondent executive and judicial authorities" "fully and effectively . . . in the general government of the Union" but indicating that such a delegation could not properly be given to a single body of men (Farber 1995, 649). This paragraph thus justified an increase in the powers of a national government of separated powers.

The second major paragraph referred to the impracticality of securing "all rights of independent sovereignty to each" state while providing for "the interest and safety of all." It further noted the difficulty of precisely drawing the line "between those rights which must be surrendered, and those which may be reserved" (Farber, 649).

The third major paragraph pointed to "the greatest interest of every true American" in "the consolidation of our Union." Recognition of this interest was said to have led states to concede minor points. The Constitution was thus portrayed as "the result of a spirit of amity, and of that mutual deference and concession which the peculiarity of our political situation rendered indispensable" (Farber, 649).

The fourth major paragraph noted that "the full and entire approbation of every state is not perhaps to be expected" but urged each state to consider that "had her interest been alone consulted the consequences might have been particularly disagreeable or injurious to others." It further expressed the hope that the new Constitution would "promote the lasting welfare of that country so dear to us all, and secure her freedom and happiness" (Farber, 649–650).

Professor Daniel Farber has cited the letter of transmittal, which was unanimously adopted by the Convention, as evidence that those who framed the Constitution understood that they were significantly expanding national powers over state powers. He argues that the letter thus contradicts key elements of the "New Federalism," with its emphasis on state sovereignty, as enunciated in recent U.S. Supreme Court decisions.

See Also Federalism; Resolution Accompanying the Constitution

FOR FURTHER READING

Farber, Daniel A. 1995. "The Constitution's Forgotten Cover Letter: An Essay on the New Federalism and the Original Understanding." *Michigan Law Review* 94 (December): 615–650.

Farrand, Max, ed. 1937. *The Records of the Federal Convention.* 4 vols. New Haven, CT: Yale University Press.

Ketcham, Ralph. 1971. *James Madison: A Biography.* New York: Macmillan.

LIBERALISM

One of the central strands of thought that is believed to have influenced both the American Revolution and the Constitutional Convention of 1787 is that of classical liberalism. Not to be confused with modern "liberalism," which is largely a theory about the need for governmental activism (as in Franklin D. Roosevelt's New Deal and Lyndon B. Johnson's Great Society programs) in the pursuit of interests that conservatives more typically leave to market mechanisms, classical liberalism actually served as the fount of many of the ideas shared by both modern liberals and conservatives.

Scholars generally trace classical liberalism to the thinking of the English philosophers Thomas Hobbes (1588–1679) and John Locke (1632–1704), especially the latter. Both attempted to understand government by positing what men would be like if they were in a "state of nature," that is, a state without any government. Hobbes hypothesized that, in such circumstances, all men would be in a relatively equally vulnerable position. The result was that the life of man would be "solitary, poor, nasty, brutish, and short" and men would be in a continual state of war. Although Locke presented a somewhat less gruesome picture of the state of nature, he posited that such a stateless state would have three weaknesses. First, the law of nature, or rules of ethical conduct, would not be "established, settled, [and] known" (Locke 1982, 75). Second, there would be no entity, no "known and indifferent judge," to settle disputes that arose between individuals in such a state of nature (76). Third, there would be no power that could enforce such impartial judgments, even if they could be made (76).

Locke believed that, in such circumstances, individuals would join a mutual pact, or social compact, to secure common rights. In a philosophy echoed by Thomas Jefferson in the Declaration of Independence, Locke further argued that if governments did not secure such rights, individuals had the right to "appeal to heaven" and revolt to establish new governments that did so. Locke opposed hereditary privilege and especially the idea of the divine right of kings. He posited that government was not based on the will of God but on popular consent.

Liberalism put great emphasis on securing property. It emphasized the origins of property in the idea that property became personal when it was mixed with the fruits of human labor. Scholars often associated liberalism with the idea of the unlimited acquisition of property. They often also associated it with the related idea that the individual pursuit of private gain will inevitably lead to social good. Adam Smith was among the philosophers who applied this philosophy to the idea of economics. Proponents of liberalism often advocated the expansion of commerce and industry as a means of national greatness.

Scholars sometimes contrast the philosophy of liberalism with republicanism. This philosophy, with roots in classical and Renaissance thinking, stressed the idea of citizen participation in government and the need for citizen "virtue," usually defined as dedication to the commonwealth. In contrast to advocates of liberalism, advocates of republicanism often emphasized the need for small face-to-face societies where individuals would be tied more closely to their governments. Advocates of republicanism tended to favor agrarianism as a means to promote citizen independence and patriotism.

In addition to liberalism and republicanism, other strands of thought—for example, Protestantism (Dienstag [1996] argues that Lockean liberalism was in part based on Protestant work values) and the philosophy of Scottish Enlightenment thinkers—as well as experiences with British institutions and familiarity with the history of other governments, ancient and modern, influenced the thoughts of the Founding Fathers. Although early scholars of republicanism often presented this philosophy as an alternative to liberalism, in more recent times, scholars often view the two movements together, not so much as opposites but as different strains of thought among individuals who were highly devoted to liberty and opposed to hereditary privilege.

See Also Declaration of Independence; Locke, John; Protestantism; Puritanism; Republicanism; Scottish Enlightenment

FOR FURTHER READING

Dienstag, Joshua Foa. 1996. "Serving God and Mammon: The Lockean Sympathy in Early American Political Thought." *American Political Science Review* 90 (September): 497–511.

Hartz, Louis. 1955. *The Liberal Tradition in America: An*

Interpretation of American Political Thought since the Revolution. New York: Harcourt, Brace and World.

Kloppenberg, James T. 1987. "The Virtues of Liberalism: Christianity, Republicanism, and Ethics in Early American Political Discourse." *Journal of American History* 74 (June): 9–33.

Locke, John. 1982. *Second Treatise of Government.* Ed. Richard Cox. Arlington Heights, IL: Harlan Davidson.

Matson, Cathy. 2001. "Liberalism and Republicanism." In Mary K. Cayton and Peter W. Williams, eds. *Encyclopedia of American Cultural and Intellectual History.* Vol. 1 of 2. New York: Charles Scribner's Sons, 169–175.

Pangle, Thomas L. 1988. *The Spirit of Modern Republicanism: The Moral Vision of the American Founders and the Philosophy of Locke.* Chicago: University of Chicago Press.

LIBERTY

One of the goals announced in the Preamble to the Constitution is that of securing "the blessings of liberty." One of the nation's most enduring symbols, the Liberty Bell (located in a special building outside Independence Hall where the Declaration of Independence and Constitution were drafted), bears words from Leviticus 25:10: "Proclaim liberty thro' all the land to all the inhabitants thereof." Similarly, the Pledge of Allegiance to the U.S. flag refers to the nation as providing "liberty and justice for all."

Initial Mention of Liberty

Significantly, Edmund Randolph's first resolution in the Virginia Plan, which he introduced on May 29, called for revising the Articles so as to protect "common defence, security of liberty and general welfare" (Farrand 1937, I, 20; also see I, 30). The current wording of this phrase emerged from the Committee of Style, which Gouverneur Morris of Pennsylvania chaired near the end of the Convention (II, 590).

Meaning of Liberty

The American Founders used the word "liberty" chiefly to designate the idea of self-government (Salvemini 1968, 112). They frequently contrasted it to "license" or "licentiousness" (Shain 1999; also see Snyder 1983, 390). They further associated liberty with the idea of personal rights, democratic government, and the rule of law. Framers, in turn, sometimes divided liberties into personal liberties, or the rights of man, and civil liberties, or political liberties that one would secure within society (Salvemini, 113). The Declaration of Independence focused on the rights of mankind in referring to the rights of "life, liberty, and the pursuit of happiness." The Fifth and Fourteenth Amendments subsequently focused on civil liberties by providing for the protection of "life, liberty, and property" against deprivation without "due process of law."

Discussions of Liberty at the Convention

Pennsylvania's James Wilson addressed the issue of liberty on June 8 during discussion of the congressional negative that the Virginia Plan had proposed over state laws. He was attempting to answer concerns by Connecticut's Roger Sherman about the scope of this power. In the process, Wilson developed a complex analogy that illuminated the distinction between natural liberty and civil liberty in the context of federalism. Wilson thus observed:

> There is no instance in which the laws say that the individuals shd. be bound in one case, & at liberty to judge whether he will obey or disobey in another. The cases are parallel. Abuses of the power over the individual person may happen as well as over the individual States. Federal liberty is to States, what civil liberty, is to private individuals. And States are not more unwilling to purchase it, by the necessary concession of their political sovereignty, than the savage is to purchase Civil liberty by the surrender of the personal sovereignty, which he enjoys in a State of nature. (I, 166).

Wilson thus concluded that "a definition of the cases in which the Negative should be exercised, is impracticable" (I, 166).

Delegates could use "liberty" to refer to the freedom of individuals or to the power of the states. Referring to the latter, Robert Yates thus observed on June 9 that "every sovereign state according to a confederation must have an equal vote, or there is an end to liberty" (I, 183).

As indicated above, Wilson had tried to convince Sherman of the need for a veto of state legislation. Wilson does not appear to have succeeded. In any event, Sherman indicated his own concern over liberty in a speech he delivered on June 26 at a time when the Convention was discussing a possible nine-year term for senators. Believing that either a four- or six-year term would be preferable, he opined:

> Govt. is instituted for those who live under it. It ought therefore to be so constituted as not to be dangerous to their liberties. The more permanency it has the worst if it be a bad Govt. Frequent elections are necessary to preserve the good behavior of rulers. They also tend to give permanency to the Government, by preserving that good behavior, because it ensures their re-election. (I, 423)

One of the most fascinating discussions at the Constitutional Convention regarding liberty took place the day after Independence Day. The discussion is important precisely because it appeared to pit the goals of securing liberty and property. Objecting to the proposal whereby states would have one member of Congress for every 40,000 inhabitants in what would become the House of Representatives, Morris argued that the value of liberty, which he saw embodied in this formula of representation, was in conflict with that of property. He was especially concerned about threats to property that might be posed by the admission of Western states. Morris thus observed:

> He thought property ought to be taken into the estimate as well as the number of inhabitants. Life and liberty were generally said to be of more value, than property. An accurate view of the

matter would nevertheless prove that property was the main object of Society. The savage State was more favorable to liberty than the Civilized; and sufficiently so to life. It was preferred by all men who had not acquired a taste for property; it was only renounced for the sake of property which could only be secured by the restraints of regular Government. (I, 533)

Although John Rutledge of South Carolina joined Morris in arguing that "Property was certainly the principal object of Society," Virginia's George Mason observed that the Committee that had proposed the compromise had thought, as he did, that new states "ought to be subject to no unfavorable discriminations" (I, 534) and, in this case, at least, the idea of liberty prevailed over that of property. On August 7, Delaware's George Read further supported an absolute executive veto on the basis that this would lead to "the preservation of liberty, & to the public welfare" (II, 200).

The liberty that the delegates to the Convention sought on behalf of the majority remained contradicted by the institution of slavery, which the new Constitution never mentioned but continued to permit. The contradiction was not new. During the American Revolution, England's Samuel Johnson had asked, "How is it that we have the loudest yelps for liberty among the drivers of negroes?" (quoted in Burns 1982, 25). James MacGregor Burns observed that "American whites somehow were able collectively to love liberty, recognize the evils of slavery, and tolerate slavery, all at the same time" (Burns, 25).

Antifederalist Uses of Liberty

The commitment to liberty undoubtedly united Federalists and Antifederalists more than it divided them, but, after the Convention proposed the Constitution, Antifederalists continued to fear that a new government might imperil liberty, and they continued to be more likely to associate liberty with states' rights than the Federalists. Defending itself against the disapprobation that its failure to send delegates to the Convention had generated, Rhode Island attributed this omission to "the love of true Constitutional liberty, and the fear we have of making innovations on the Rights and Liberties of the Citizens at large" (Jensen 1976, 225). Similarly, Antifederalist Rawlins Lowndes of South Carolina opposed ratification of the Constitution in his state by melodramatically proclaiming that he wished the epitaph on his tomb would read: "Here lies the man that opposed the Constitution, because it was ruinous to the liberty of America" (quoted in Weir 1989, 222).

These expressions of concern for liberty chiefly focused on the absence of a bill of rights within the new Constitution. The pressure for such a bill was one of the Antifederalists' most important contributions to American constitutionalism.

See Also Bill of Rights; Declaration of Independence; Slavery; Three-fifths Clause

FOR FURTHER READING

Burns, James MacGregor. 1982. *The Vineyard of Liberty.* New York: Alfred A. Knopf.

Farrand, Max, ed. 1937. *The Records of the Federal Convention.* 4 vols. New Haven, CT: Yale University Press.

Fleming, Thomas. 1997. *Liberty! The American Revolution.* New York: Viking.

Jensen, Merrill. 1976. *The Documentary History of the Ratification of the Constitution.* Vol. 1 of *Constitutional Documents and Records, 1776–1787.* Madison: State Historical Society of Wisconsin.

Salvemini, Gaetano. 1968. "The Concepts of Democracy and Liberty in the Eighteenth Century." In Conyers Read, ed. *The Constitution Reconsidered.* New York: Harper and Row Publishers, 105–119.

Shain, Barry Alan. 1999. *Liberty and License: The American Founding and the Western Conception of Freedom.* Ed. Gary L. Gregg II. Wilmington, DE: ISI Books.

Snyder, K. Alan. 1983. "Foundations of Liberty: The Christian Republicanism of Timothy Dwight and Jedediah Mores." *New England Quarterly* 56 (September): 382–397.

Weir, Robert M. 1989. "South Carolina: Slavery and the Structure of the Union." In Michael Allen Gillespie and Michael Lienesch, eds. *Ratifying the Constitution.* Lawrence: University Press of Kansas.

LIBERTY BELL

The Liberty Bell is one of America's most revered symbols. Rung in celebration of both the adoption of the Declaration of Independence and the ratification of the U.S. Constitution, the bell was catapulted to the forefront of America's imagination when abolitionist editors used it as a frontispiece to an edition of *Liberty,* which the New York Anti-Slavery Society published in 1837. William Lloyd Garrison's publication *The Liberator* subsequently published a poem in 1839 that appears first to have designated the bell as the Liberty Bell.

Although the bell is dated 1753, the most accepted view is that it was designed to commemorate the fiftieth anniversary of the Charter of Privileges, which William Penn had issued to Pennsylvania in 1701. This explanation accounts for the fact that the bell was inscribed with the words from the Bible book of Leviticus 25:10 saying, "Proclaim Liberty throughout the land unto all the inhabitants thereof," since this verse came

America's most famous bell is the bronze Liberty Bell, which rang out the news of the Declaration of Independence, approved on July 4, 1776. The bell is now situated in its own building outside Independence Hall. (Bettmann/Corbis)

from a passage describing the year of Jubilee, every fiftieth year, during which slaves were freed and debts forgiven. The bell was also engraved with the words, "By Order of the Assembly of the Province of Pensylvania for the State House in Philada," indicating that the name of the state had not yet become standardized.

The Pennsylvania Assembly ordered the bell from the Whitechapel Foundry in England, and it arrived on September 2, 1752, and was hung in the steeple of the Pennsylvania State House, the building where both the Declaration of Independence and the Constitution would be written, on March 10, 1753. It was immediately cracked by a stroke of its clapper, perhaps because it was too brittle or because it had been improperly cast.

In any event, the Assembly commissioned John Pass and John Stow, two Philadelphia foundry workers, to recast the bell. In so doing, they added additional copper (copper and tin are the bell's central ingredients). The new bell was installed on March 29, 1753, but the tone was displeasing. Pass and Stow recast it once again, and it was rehung in early June 1753.

Continued complaints about the sound led the city to commission the purchase of yet another replacement bell from England, but its sound was not better, and it was placed in the cupola on the roof of the State House, where it was attached to the clock to sound the hours. Pass and Stow's bell was rung so frequently that nearby residents signed a petition of complaint in 1772.

Prior to the British occupation of Philadelphia in October 1777, the bell was removed and hidden beneath the floorboards of the Zion Reformed Church of Allentown, Pennsylvania, so that the British could not melt it down for cannonballs. Installed back at the State House, it continued to be rung on historic occasions. Historians are uncertain when the crack first appeared in the bell, but it appears to have become unringable in 1846, when it cracked commemorating the birthday of George Washington.

The bell weighs approximately 2,080 pounds and is 12 feet in circumference at the base and 7.5 feet at the crown. It is 3 feet tall and has a 3-foot, 2-inch clapper that weighs 44.5 pounds. The visible fracture is 2 feet, 4 inches long, and its yoke is made of American (sometimes called slippery) elm.

The bell was taken down from the steeple in 1852 and has traveled to the World Industrial and Cotton Exposition in New Orleans (1885), the Chicago World's Fair (1893), the Cotton State and Atlantic Exposition in Atlanta (1895), the International and West Indian Exposition in Charleston (1902), the commemoration in Boston of the Battle of Bunker Hill (1903), the Louisiana Purchase Exposition in St. Louis (1904), and the Panama-Pacific Exposition in San Francisco (1915).

In 1976 the bell was moved from the "Declaration Chamber" of Independence Hall to a pavilion across the street. On October 9, 2003, the National Park Service opened a new Liberty Bell Center between Independence Hall and the Constitution Center. On June 6, 2004, a Normandy Liberty Bell, designed to replicate the original as much as possible, was cast to commemorate the sixtieth anniversary of the Allied invasion of Normandy.

See Also Declaration of Independence; National Constitution Center; Pennsylvania State House; Philadelphia

FOR FURTHER READING

Fischer, David H. 2005. *Liberty and Freedom.* New York: Oxford University Press.

"Liberty Bell Facts." http://www.ushistory.org/liberty bell/facts.html.

"Liberty Bell Timeline." http://www.ushistory.org/libertybell/timeline.html.

LIBRARY PRIVILEGES

Inspired by Benjamin Franklin, Philadelphia was the home of the nation's first lending library. Many delegates undoubtedly arrived in Philadelphia after having already consulted volumes related to government; Thomas Jefferson is known to have sent James Madison almost 200 volumes on the subject of government from France.

On July 7, George Washington received a letter written by W. Rawle, the secretary of the Philadelphia Library Company, the previous day. It indicated that the library, which is recorded as having some 8,000 volumes on the eve of the American Revolution (Colbourn 1965, 14), had voted to "furnish the gentlemen who compose the Convention now sitting with such books as they may desire during their continuance at Philadelphia, taking receipts for same" (Farrand 1937, I, 549). William Jackson, the Convention secretary, returned a note of thanks.

Subsequent notes by the library committee indicate that Luther Martin of Maryland failed to return Sir William Jones's *Asiatic Poems* and Rufus King of Massachusetts failed to return John Groce's *Voyage to the East Indies* (2 volumes) or John Andrews's *Letters to a Young Gentleman on His Setting out for France: Containing a Survey of Paris.* Both offered to make restitution for the problem, which they attributed to their servants (Hutson 1987, 154). An analyst has observed that of the three works, only that of Andrews was remotely related to political theory (*Bicentennial Daybook,* July 7).

See Also Franklin, Benjamin; Philadelphia

FOR FURTHER READING

Bicentennial Daybook, July. Bicentennial of the Constitution of the United States. Research Project Working Files, 1983–1987. Archives Library of Independence National Historic Park, Philadelphia, Pennsylvania.

Colbourn, H. Trevor. 1965. *The Lamp of Experience: Whig History and the Intellectual Origins of the American Revolution.* Chapel Hill: University of North Carolina Press.

Farrand, Max, ed. 1937. *The Records of the Federal Convention.* 4 vols. New Haven, CT: Yale University Press.

Hutson, James H., ed. 1987. *Supplement to Max Farrand's* The Records of the Federal Convention of 1787. New Haven, CT: Yale University Press.

LIVINGSTON, WILLIAM (1723–1790)

In 1723, William Livingston was born in Albany, New York to one of the state's most wealthy and powerful families. As a boy, he spent a year with a Moravian missionary family living with the Mohawk Indians. He subsequently graduated from Yale where he mastered a number of languages and developed a love for writing. He returned to New York where he studied under two different lawyers before joining the bar, where he developed a highly successful practice (Klein 1958). In addition to serving as a member of New York's colonial legislature, Livingston wrote in a variety of media, but was particularly critical of what he believed was the desire of the Episcopal Church to establish itself over its rivals.

His wealth allowed Livingston to decide to retire at the age of 49. He then moved to Elizabethtown, New Jersey, and built a house that he named "Liberty Hall." Shortly thereafter, he and

William Livingston, delegate from New Jersey
(Pixel That)

his family befriended Alexander Hamilton who had come from the West Indies.

Duty called Livingston out of retirement in New Jersey. He was elected to the Continental Congress, served as a militia commander, and then was continually elected governor from 1776 to 1790, when he died in Elizabethtown. Livingston apparently divided his duties as a delegate to the Constitutional Convention with his responsibilities as state governor and rarely participated in Convention debates. He was seated on June 5 and signed the Constitution on September 17. As the putative author and introducer of the New Jersey Plan, William Paterson appears to have taken a much more active role in the Convention than the state's governor.

Livingston served as chairman of the Committee on State Debts and Militia which the Convention appointed on August 18 and was a member of the Committee on Slave Trade and Navigation which the delegates created on August 22 (interestingly, when in New York, Livingston had freed his own two slaves and joined an antislavery society). Delegates also appointed Livingston to the Committee on Sumptuary Legislation which was formed on September 13 but appears never to have met.

Because the only records of Livingston's participation come from the motions that came out of the committees that he chaired, our most extensive knowledge of Livingston's role at the Constitutional Convention is found in a letter that Virginia's James Madison wrote on February 12, 1831, in answer to a query about Livingston's role. Madison observed that Livingston had not taken "an active part in its debates" but that he had served on some committees, "where it may be presumed he had an agency and a due influence" (Farrand 1937, III, 496). Madison specifically cited the respect Livingston gained as a result of "the celebrity of his name" (III, 496).

As to whether Livingston "had a leaning to the federal party [that is, to the group at the Convention favoring increased national powers] and principles," Madison was uncertain. He observed that, given Livingston's silence, he could only surmise what he might have thought from how the state of New Jersey cast its votes:

The votes of N. Jersey corresponded generally with the Plan offered by Mr. Paterson; but the main object of that being to secure to the smaller States an equality with the larger in the structure of the Govt, in opposition to the outline previously introduced, which had reversed the object, it is difficult to say what was the degree of power to which there might be an abstract leaning. (III, 496)

Madison further observed that "with those . . . who did not enter with debate, and whose votes could not be distinguished from those of their State colleagues, their opinions could only be known among themselves, or to their particular friends" (III, 496). Madison ended by noting that "my acquaintance with Gov Livingston was limited to an exchange of the common civilities, and these to the period of the Convention" (III, 496). It would appear to be the nation's loss that this highly articulate governor did not participate more actively in Convention debates.

Livingston was the father of Brockholst Livingston, who was later appointed to the U.S. Supreme Court. He also fathered Sarah Van Brugh Livingston, who married John Jay, the Court's first chief justice.

See Also New Jersey; New York

FOR FURTHER READING

Bradford, M. M. 1994. *Founding Fathers: Brief Lives of the Framers of the United States Constitution*. Lawrence: University Press of Kansas.

Farrand, Max, ed. 1937. *The Records of the Federal Convention*. 4 vols. New Haven, CT: Yale University Press.

Klein, Milton M. 1993. *The American Whig: William Livingston of New York*. Rev. ed. New York: Garland Publishing.

——. 1958. "The Rise of the New York Bar: The Legal Career of William Livingston." *William and Mary Quarterly*, 3rd ser. 15 (July): 334–358.

LOCKE, JOHN (1632–1704)

The English political philosopher John Locke is often credited with being a major influence on the U.S. Revolution, and on subsequent American political ideals, especially those associated with classical liberalism (Hartz 1955), a viewpoint that is sometimes compared with, and sometimes contrasted to, republicanism and the influence of Protestant Christianity. Locke, the author of *Two Treatises on Government*, had posited that individuals would find a state of nature unsuitable to the protection of their lives, liberties and property. They would accordingly leave such a stateless state to form a civil society through consent—what Locke referred to as a social contract—where they could secure these objectives. If governments failed to secure the purposes for which they were founded, individuals had the right to overthrow such governments and form new ones that would achieve these objectives. Thomas Jefferson repeated these themes in the Declaration of Independence (see Becker 1970).

Although he championed individual liberty, Locke did not go into much detail in delineating the governmental structures that would be necessary to secure such freedoms. Alpheus Mason observed that "Locke's constitutionalism boiled down to political limitations on government—those imposed at elections, plus the hope that rulers and ruled alike would be guided by considerations of justice and common sense." Mason further observed: "The idea of a constitution limiting and superintending the operations of the supreme legislative authority forms no serious part of Locke's system" (Mason 1965, 6). Philosophers like the Baron de Montesquieu devoted more attention to such structures and were thus more likely to be cited during the Constitutional Convention when delegates were concerned with constructing a new and improved government through reason rather than with overthrowing the existing one and its leaders through force.

The only recorded mention of Locke at the Constitutional Convention occurred on June 27 in a speech by Maryland's Luther Martin in which he was defending a continuation of the equal rep-

John Locke (1632–1704), British philosopher. Engraving by Freeman from a painting by Sir G. Kneller. (Bettmann/Corbis)

resentation in Congress that states had under the Articles of Confederation. Martin attempted to use Locke's idea of a state of nature not, as Locke himself had done, to describe the relationship between individuals, but to describe the relationship among the existing states. By his analysis, the government under the Articles of Confederation was intended "merely to preserve the State Governts: not to govern individuals" (Farrand 1937, I, 437). He argued "that to resort to the Citizens at large for their sanction to a new Governt. will be throwing them back into a State of Nature: that the dissolution of the State Govts. is involved in the nature of the process: that the people have no right to do this without the consent of those to whom they have delegated their power for State purposes" (II, 437). He further contended that "the States like individuals were in a State of nature equally sovereign & free" (II, 437). Accordingly, "the States being equal cannot treat or confederate so as to give up an equality of votes without giving up their liberty" (II, 438).

See Also Declaration of Independence; Liberalism;

Liberty; Protestantism; Republicanism; Social Contract

FOR FURTHER READING

Becker, Carl. 1970. *The Declaration of Independence: A Study in the History of Political Ideas.* New York: Vintage Books.

Farrand, Max, ed. 1937. *The Records of the Federal Convention.* 4 vols. New Haven, CT: Yale University Press.

Hartz, Louis. 1955. *The Liberal Tradition in America: An Interpretation of American Political Thought since the Revolution.* New York: Harcourt, Brace and World.

Mason, Alpheus T. 1965. *Free Government in the Making: Readings in American Political Thought.* New York: Oxford University Press.

LODGING OF THE DELEGATES

Philadelphia had the advantage of being the most populous city in North America, and, as the center of Pennsylvania government and the site of the Continental Congresses, it was used to providing lodging for out-of-town guests. Out-of-state delegates are known to have stayed in a number of different inns and private residences during their stay at the Convention. The inns included Mary House's Boarding House on 5th and Market Streets, the Indian Queen Tavern which she owned on nearby 4th and Chestnut/Market Street, Mrs. Dailey's Boarding House on 3rd and Market Streets, and Mrs. Marshall's Boarding House on Carter's Alley and Smith's Alley.

Five delegates are known to have stayed at Mary House's Boarding House (Lloyd, Garot, and Edwards). They included James Madison, Edmund Randolph, and James McClurg of Virginia, and George Read and John Dickinson (who shared a room) from Delaware. George Washington had planned to stay there before being importuned by Robert Morris to lodge at his home. Delaware's George Read observed in a letter to John Dickinson that "Mrs. House's, where I am, is very crowded, and the room I am presently in so

small as not to admit of a second bed" (Farrand 1937, III, 25).

Virginia's George Mason, Georgia's William Pierce, and Delaware's Richard Bassett stayed at the nearby Indian Queen. It was apparently named, like inns in six other states, after Pocahontas, the Indian princess from Virginia who was credited with having saved the life of John Smith and who had married John Rolfe (Carr 1990, 25). A contemporary, Manasseh Cutler, described the inn as being "kept in an elegant style" and as consisting "of a large pile of buildings, with many spacious halls, and numerous small apartments, appropriated for lodging rooms" (III, 58). On July 13, he reported meeting Nathaniel Gorham of Massachusetts, James Madison of Virginia, George Mason and his son from Virginia, Alexander Martin and Hugh Williamson of North Carolina, John Rutledge and one of the Pinckneys of South Carolina and Alexander Hamilton of New York there (III, 58).

Lloyd, Garot, and Edwards report that Alexander Hamilton of New York and Gouverneur Morris of Pennsylvania stayed at Mrs. Dailey's Boarding House and were joined by Elbridge Gerry of Massachusetts after his wife and newborn son left the private house they had rented in Philadelphia to go to New York. They further report that Hamilton considered Dailey to be an "astute businesswoman" and that women owned a fifth of all taverns, many of which were on 2nd Street, a block east of Mrs. Dailey's, and even more of those associated with boardinghouses. Widows were granted preferential treatment for licenses for such establishments.

Connecticut's Roger Sherman and Oliver Ellsworth stayed at Mrs. Marshall's Boarding House, which was also close to the City Tavern (also known as the Merchants' Coffee House) where the signers of the Constitution had a farewell dinner (III, 81; Staib 1999). Thomas Procter (1739–1806) had constructed the inn in 1771 on land purchased from Samuel Powel, a former Philadelphia mayor who had purchased the tavern in 1784. John Adams described it as "the most genteel one in America" (Peterson). In addition to fine food and wine, the tavern was the site of dramas and music (Lloyd, Garot, and Edwards). The original tavern burned in 1834 and was razed again in 1854; the current tavern was rebuilt in 1975 and opened in 1976. The restaurant concession was closed to the public in 1992 but reopened on July 4, 1994 (Staib, 5).

With the possible exception of Gouverneur Morris, who had recently moved to the city and apparently stayed at Mrs. Dailey's Boarding House, members of Pennsylvania's own delegation, all eight of whom lived in Philadelphia, were able to stay in their own homes. Benjamin Franklin, who lived on Market Street, relished his role as a host (George Washington called upon him the first day he came to town). Robert Morris, then a wealthy merchant and land speculator who later went bankrupt and was sent to a debtor's prison, insisted that Washington, who had planned to stay at the home of Mary House, stayed instead at his elegant house on 6th and Market Streets, which later served as the president's house when the nation's capital moved there from 1790 to 1800. James Wilson invited South Carolina's John Rutledge to spend the first three weeks with him.

See Also Philadelphia

FOR FURTHER READING

Carr, William G. 1990. *The Oldest Delegate: Franklin in the Constitutional Convention.* Newark: University of Delaware Press.

Commanger, Henry Steele. 1961. *The Great Constitution: A Book for Young Americans.* Indianapolis, IN: Bobbs-Merrill.

Farrand, Max, ed. 1937. *The Records of the Federal Convention.* 4 vols. New Haven, CT: Yale University Press.

Lloyd, Gordon, Colleen Garot, and Angela Edwards. "Map of Historic Philadelphia in the Late 18th Century." http://teachingamericanhistory.org/convention/map/.

Peterson, Charles E. "Thomas Proctor and the City Tavern." http://www.ushistory.org/carpentershall/history/procter.htm.

Staib, Walter. 1999. *City Tavern Cookbook: 200 Years of Classic Recipes from America's First Gourmet Restaurant.* Philadelphia, PA: Running Press.

MADISON, JAMES, JR.
(1751–1836)

Often dubbed the "Father" of the U.S. Constitution, Virginia's James Madison was certainly one of the most intellectual and influential delegates at the Constitutional Convention. Born in 1751 at Port Conway, Virginia, the son of planter James Madison and Eleanor Conway Madison, Madison attended boarding school before going to the

James Madison, Jr., delegate from Virginia, often designated as the "Father" of the Constitution (Pixel That)

University of New Jersey (today's Princeton) where he studied theology and law, without directly pursuing either occupation. Madison, barely 100 pounds and 5 feet, 4 inches tall, graduated early and worked himself into a virtual state of exhaustion, staying an extra six months at Princeton to do further study under President John Witherspoon before returning home.

Returning to Virginia, Madison was elected to the Orange County Committee of Safety in 1774 and to the state's constitutional convention in 1776. In addition to managing his family's plantation in Orange, Virginia (known as Montpelier, the spacious house, which was long owned by the Dupont family and is being restored to its eighteenth-century appearance, is now open to the public as is a small museum in downtown Orange, Virginia, about 35 miles away from Charlottesville), Madison spent most of his life as a career politician. He served from 1778 to 1779 as a member of the Governor's Council of Virginia, from 1780 to 1783 as a member of the Congress under the Articles of Confederation, from 1784 to 1786 as a member of the Virginia legislature, and from 1787 to 1788 as a member of Congress. In Congress Madison had been instrumental in Virginia's accession of the Old Northwest, and in Virginia he had helped enact the Statute for Religious Freedom.

As an elected official, Madison became increasingly convinced of the inadequacy of the Articles of Confederation and of injustices at the state level. Not informed by Governor Patrick Henry of his appointment to the Mount Vernon Conference in time to attend, Madison was one of the prime movers at the Annapolis Convention. He followed up this service with work to get the Virginia legislature to issue a call for the Constitutional Convention. In addition to the important role that he played in the Convention debates, Madison took the most comprehensive notes of the Convention's proceedings. Without his notes, the simple record of ayes and nays that the official secretary, William Jackson, took would be relatively worthless. Madison, however, provided that his notes would not be published until after his death, and he lived a long time.

The Virginia Plan

Prior to attending the Convention, Madison had asked his friend Thomas Jefferson to send him books on government from Europe, where Jefferson was serving as an ambassador to France. Madison in turn reviewed these books, focusing on the history of previous republics, and writing an essay titled "The Vices of the Political System." In this essay, he analyzed the situation under the Articles of Confederation and possible remedies. He envisioned a stronger national government over a large landmass as a means of increasing the number of factions, or interest groups, and therefore moderating their influence so as to protect individual rights.

Although Governor Edmund Randolph presented the Virginia Plan to the Convention on May 29, the ideas of this plan correspond so closely to ideas that Madison expressed in letters he had written just before the Convention that scholars generally attribute chief authorship to him. The sheer audacity of the plan, which was used to set the initial agenda of the Convention, is perhaps its most intriguing feature. Instead of simply adding to the powers of Congress, the plan proposed a whole new system. The plan proposed a new government divided into three branches rather than one. It proposed dividing Congress into two houses, the first to be elected directly by the people and apportioned according to population and the second to be chosen by members of the first branch from among nominees proposed by the states. Given Madison's belief that the Senate should be a relatively small body to check excesses of the House, it is not altogether clear whether, as the Virginia Plan promised, this would have allowed for proportional state representation in this body or whether (as seems more likely) it would simply have given each state the opportunity to nominate individuals for such posts.

Rather than enumerating the powers of Congress, as had the Articles of Confederation, Madison proposed to invest Congress with the power "to legislate in all cases to which the separate States are incompetent, or in which the harmony of the United States may be interrupted by the exercise of individual Legislation" (Farrand 1937, I, 21). In another prized provision, Madison hoped to give Congress power "to negative all laws passed by the several States, contravening in the opinion of the National Legislature the articles of Union" (I, 21). As late as August 27, Madison was still arguing for the efficacy of a congressional veto of state laws (II, 440). In a provision about which he would shortly after express doubts (see I, 54), the Virginia Plan also provided that the national government could use force against states that failed to perform their duties.

The Virginia Plan initially called for the legislature to select a national executive for a single term. In combination with members of the judiciary, the Virginia Plan called for vesting the executive with the power to examine and veto all laws of the states or of Congress, with Congress having the power to override such a veto by an unspecified supermajority. Congress would appoint members of the national judiciary who would serve during good behavior and try impeachments of national officers. The Virginia Plan further provided for the admission of new states, for guaranteeing them a republican form of government, and for an amending provision. The new plan was to go into effect when ratified by state conventions.

A day after Hamilton's long speech of June 18 proposing a plan of government that called for stronger powers than either the Virginia or New

Jersey Plan, Madison delivered a lengthy speech of his own designed to urge the Convention to continue with its consideration of the Virginia Plan. He began by arguing that the government under the Articles of Confederation was not completely federal and that the Virginia Plan was not therefore proposing a complete alternative. Madison argued that the New Jersey Plan could not adequately preserve the Union against threats from abroad or guard against threats to national authority at home. He also argued that the government proposed under the New Jersey Plan would be inadequate in preventing "trespasses of the States on each other" (I, 317), securing internal tranquillity within the states (I, 318), obtaining good legislation and administration within the states (I, 318), and securing the Union against foreign influences (I, 319). Madison urged the smaller states to reconsider their attachment to the New Jersey Plan. The timing may or may not have been significant, but it was Madison's speech, rather than the more extreme and more noticed speech by Hamilton, that directly preceded the Convention's decision to continue with consideration of the Virginia rather than the New Jersey Plan.

Long after others had given in to demands by the smaller states, Madison continued to insist on the injustice of equal state representation in one or both houses of Congress; Madison believed that he was fighting for a basic principle and not just for the interest of his own state (then the most populous of the 13). In a long speech on June 28, in which Madison ransacked the history of previous republics for illustrations and support, he argued that the matter involved "fundamental principles" (I, 446). Madison's tone was not as belligerent as that of many other delegates, and so the timing may have been merely coincidental, but shortly after this speech Benjamin Franklin, in an apparent attempt to promote concord, proposed that the Convention should open each session with prayer (I, 451). The next day, Madison continued to implore his fellow delegates against incorporating a principle of representation that was "confessedly unjust, which cd. never be admitted, & if admitted must infuse mortality into a Constitution which we wished to last forever" (I, 464). On the day after, Madison

somewhat prophetically attempted to convince delegates that the real principle of division was not that between the large states and the small ones but between the Northern and Southern interests (I, 476). Madison reiterated this theme on June 30 (I, 485–486) and on July 13 (I, 601).

On June 30, Madison said he was willing to accept an idea, which Pennsylvania's James Wilson proposed, whereby states would have a minimum of one senator for every 100,000 people with representation otherwise according to population. He felt he could only agree to such a plan, however, if the delegates granted senators independence from the states. Otherwise he feared that the Senate would be "only another edition of Congs." (I, 490), that is, the woefully weak Congress under the Articles of Confederation. On July 9, Madison floated another plan whereby states would be represented according to free population in the House of Representatives and according to the sum of both free persons and slaves in the Senate (I, 562). On July 14, Madison expressed willingness to accept a proposal by South Carolina's Charles Pinckney whereby existing states would have one to five delegates in the Senate (II, 5).

On July 14, Madison seemed to offer another proposal. He suggested:

> In all cases where the Genl. Governt. is to act on the people, let the people be represented and the votes be proportional. In all cases where the Governt. is to act on the States as such, in like manner as Congs. now acts on them, let the States be represented & the votes be equal. This was the true ground of compromise if there was any ground at all. (II, 8–9)

Madison almost immediately, however, appeared to take back this concession by denying that there was "a single instance in which the Genl. Govt. was not to operate on the people individually" (II, 9). Madison continued with a list of evils that would flow from equal state suffrage in the Senate:

1. the minority could negative the will of the majority of the people.

2. they could extort measures by making them a condition of their assent to other necessary measures.

3. they could obtrude measures on the majority by virtue of the peculiar power which would be vested in the Senate.

4. the evil instead of being cured by time, would increase with every new State that should be admitted, as they must all be admitted on the principle of equality.

5. the perpetuity it would give to the [preponderance of the] Northn. agst. the Soutn. Scale was a serious consideration. (II, 9)

Madison may have had the stronger arguments (contemporary critics still complain about the unrepresentative nature of the U.S. Senate), but the Convention defeated his proposal with the acceptance of the Great Compromise on July 16.

On the day after that, Madison suffered yet another devastating defeat. He had continued to argue that his proposed congressional negative of state laws was "essential to the efficacy & security of the Genl. Govt." and that "nothing short of a negative" could control "the propensity of the States to pursue their particular interests in opposition to the general interest" (II, 27). Gouverneur Morris of Pennsylvania responded that such a negative "would disgust all the States" (II, 28), and the Convention defeated this proposal by a vote of 7-3.

Federalism

One of the enigmas of James Madison is attempting to ascertain and reconcile his positions on issues related to federalism at the Constitutional Convention with those that he later took as a leader of the Democratic-Republican Party and as an author of the Virginia Resolutions of 1798. Madison's primary concern at the Constitutional Convention was that of state encroachments on the national government. In comparing the Virginia and New Jersey Plans on June 21, Madison thus observed that he thought that "there was 1. less danger of encroachment from the Genl. Govt. than from the State Govts. 2. that the mis-

chief from encroachments would be less fatal if made by the former, than if made by the latter" (I, 356).

He attempted to illustrate his points by reference to past confederacies. He went so far as to suppose that the national government should exercise indefinite power and that the states should be "reduced to corporations dependent on the Genl. Legislature" (I, 357). He hypothesized that, even in such an extreme case, he did not believe that the national government would have an incentive to "take from the States [any] branch of their power as far as its operation was beneficial, and its continuance desirable to the people" (I, 357).

In addition to favoring a broad grant to Congress to legislate over matters over which individual states were incompetent, Madison advocated granting Congress power "to grant charters of incorporation where the interest of the U.S. might require & the legislative provisions of individual State may be incompetent" (II, 615). He also wanted to grant Congress the power "to establish an University, in which no preferences or distinctions should be allowed on account of religion" (II, 616).

As a politician Madison would later question some broad exercises of federal power. Near the end of the Convention, however, he indicated that "He was more & more convinced that the regulation of Commerce was in its nature indivisible and ought to be wholly under one authority" (II, 625).

Congress

On May 30, Madison said that his belief in proportional representation stemmed from his conviction that "whatever reason might have existed for the equality of suffrage when the Union was a federal one among sovereign States, it must cease when a national Governt. should be put into the place" (I, 37). A day later, he said that the popular election of at least one branch of Congress was "essential to every plan of free government" (I, 49). Although he favored "the policy of refining the popular appointments by successive filtrations" (I, 50), he believed that the legislature should be kept close to the people. As he put it, "the great fabric to be raised would be more stable and durable if it should rest on the solid foundation of the people themselves, than if it would stand merely on the pillars of the Legislatures" (I, 50). When the Convention settled on an initial House of Representatives consisting of 65 members, Madison suggested that this number should be doubled (I, 568).

On July 26, Madison cautioned against excluding individuals from Congress who were in debt, although he was willing to consider excluding those who did not account for public money (II, 122). Similarly, he worked against a provision requiring that members have "landed" property. He observed that "every class of Citizens should have an opportunity of making their rights be felt & understood in the public Councils"; this included members of "the landed[,] the commercial & the manufacturing" interests (II, 124).

Madison, however, opposed a proposal to consolidate individuals in districts across state lines for the selection of senators, believing that this would disadvantage members of the smaller states (I, 52). That same day, Madison professed to have brought "a strong bias in favor of enumeration and definition of the powers necessary to be exercised by the national Legislature." However, he also said that he had increasing doubts about the practicality of such enumeration and that "he should shrink from nothing which should be found essential to such a form of Govt. as would provide for the safety, liberty and happiness of the Community" (I, 53).

When Delaware's John Dickinson proposed on June 7 that state legislators should select members of the Senate, Madison objected that this would either require a deviation "from the doctrine of proportional representation" or require a number of senators too large for it to perform its moderating function. Applying his theory of factions, Madison observed:

The more the representatives of the people therefore were multiplied, the more they partook of the infirmaties of their constituents, the more liable they became to be divided among them-

selves either from their own indiscretions or the artifices of the opposite factions, and of course the less capable of fulfilling their trust. (I, 152)

Madison reiterated his support for an absolute congressional veto of state acts on June 8. He viewed this veto as an alternative to the use of national force against states, which he had earlier labeled as impractical. Citing an astronomical analogy, Madison said that "the prerogative of the General Govt. is the great pervading principle that must controul the certrifugal tendency of the States; which, without it, will continually fly out of their proper orbits and destroy the order & harmony of the political system" (I, 165). Later that same day, Madison did suggest that there might be "some emanation of the power from the Natl. Govt. into each State so far as to give temporary assent" (I, 168); he also proposed that the Convention might vest this power in the Senate rather than in the entire Congress. As late as August 23, Madison was still trying to revive the idea of a congressional veto over state laws (II, 390).

The original Virginia Plan did not specify the length of congressional terms. On June 12, Madison seconded a motion to set terms of members of the House of Representatives at three years. He hoped this term would prevent "instability" and would give legislators, many of whom he estimated would spend a year preparing for and traveling to and from the seat of government, adequate time to learn their duties (I, 214; also see I, 361). He answered Gerry's argument that the people preferred annual elections by saying that the delegates should exercise their best judgments and hope that public opinion would follow (I, 215). Madison initially favored a seven-year term for U.S. senators (I, 218), although he later did not express opposition to a term of nine years (I, 423).

Madison argued that congressional pay, for members of both the House and the Senate, should be fixed and paid by the national government in order to prevent undue dependency on the states. Madison feared that allowing the states to pay senators would "make the Senate like Congress, the mere Agents & Advocates of State interests & views, instead of being the impartial umpires & Guardians of justice and general Good" (I,

428). On a number of occasions, Madison expressed the hope that such pay might be stabilized by settling on an exchange rate based on the average price of wheat or some other common commodity (II, 216; also see I, 373). Madison, the author of the putative Twenty-seventh Amendment ratified in 1991, thought that it would be "indecent" for members of Congress to set their own salaries (I, 374), and he opposed allowing members to accept offices that had been created or augmented while they were in office–the basis of the current emoluments clause (I, 380, 386). He unsuccessfully proposed that the Constitution might restrict Congress by "fixing at least two extremes not to be exceeded by the Natl. Legislre. in the payment of themselves" (II, 291).

Madison was among those who consistently favored the origination of money bills from either house of Congress. He argued that the Senate would also be a representative institution and that it would be composed of more capable men (I, 233). He further believed that, however senators were restricted, they would exercise similar powers in amending money bills (I, 234). When the restriction of money bills was tied into the Great Compromise on congressional representation, Madison continued to insist that he "could not regard the exclusive privilege of originating money bills as any concession on the side of the small States" (I, 527). Again on August 13, Madison argued that at the very least the Senate should have power to *reduce* sums appropriated by the House (II, 276).

Madison thought that congressional meeting times could be fixed by law rather than needing to be fixed within the Constitution (II, 198). If such a time were to be fixed, he thought that May would be more appropriate than December, when travel would be more difficult (II, 199).

Madison apparently favored confining the right to vote to freeholders (II, 208). He feared that those without such property might be too dependent upon their patrons.

Madison opposed long residency requirements for members of Congress, fearing that they might leave new Western states without adequate representation (II, 217). He had the foresight to realize that if states were guaranteed one representative

for every 40,000 persons, rather than making this a minimum, there would eventually be an "excessive" number of House members (II, 221). Madison opposed a 14-year residency requirement for members of the Senate on the basis that "it will give a tincture of illiberality to the Constitution: because it will put it out of the power of the Natl Legislature even by special acts of naturalization to confer the full rank of Citizens on meritorious strangers & because it will discourage the most desirable class of people from emigrating to the U.S." (II, 236). Madison repeated this argument in arguing for minimal residency requirements for members of the Senate (II, 268), arguing with special vehemence against an argument by Connecticut's Roger Sherman that the national government was under no obligation to honor pledges made by the states (II, 270–271).

Madison favored allowing Congress to regulate elections (II, 240), but he opposed allowing Congress to set voting qualifications. He feared that by such means "A Republic may be converted into an aristocracy or oligarchy" (II, 250). Similarly, he thought that it should require a two-thirds vote for Congress to expel one of its own members (II, 254).

Madison thought it was essential to find a centrally located place for the nation's new capital (probably favoring a spot in or near Virginia). He argued:

> As the powers & objects of the new Govt. would be far greater, more private individuals wd. have business calling them to the seat of it, and it was more necessary that the Govt should be in that position from which it could contemplate with the most equal eye, and sympathize most equally with, every part of the nation. (II, 261)

Madison thought that the power of taxing exports was appropriate, but that the United States should do this collectively rather than individually (II, 306); he favored requiring consent of two-thirds of the states to such embargoes rather than prohibiting them completely (II, 363). He believed that the time might come when the national government might also need to enact complete embargoes (II, 361). He opposed prohibiting the emission of bills on the credit of the U.S. but apparently favored prohibiting making them legal tender (II, 309). He supported allowing Congress to define felonies on the high seas so as to promote "uniformity" and "stability" in the law (II, 316).

Similarly, Madison was the delegate who proposed granting Congress the power to "declare" rather than to "make" war (II, 318). He argued that Congress should have the power to regulate the militia, believing that such a power "did not seem in its nature to be divisible between two distinct authorities" (II, 332; also see II, 386–387). He was apparently willing for states to appoint lower officers (II, 388). Madison saw provisions for an effective militia as a way to guard against the danger of large standing armies (II, 388), and he was willing to include language in the Constitution designed to indicate concern over standing armies (II, 617).

Madison argued against a narrow definition of treason. He believed that Congress should have "more latitude" and that "it was inconvenient to bar a discretion which experience might enlighten, and which might be applied to good purposes as well as be abused" (II, 345). He apparently favored limiting the definition of treason to acts committed against the U.S. rather than leaving open the possibility of double punishment from state and national authorities (II, 346). Madison did not favor requiring supermajorities in Congress to regulate navigation, believing that existing constitutional checks would be adequate to protect the states (II, 451–452).

The Executive

When, on June 1, the Convention first debated whether the presidency should be singular or plural, Madison suggested that it might first be wise "to fix the extent of the Executive authority" (I, 66). He proposed that it should have power to carry out congressional laws, to appoint officers not otherwise provided for, and to exercise other powers that Congress delegated to it. Notes taken by New York's Alexander Hamilton suggest that Madison argued that allowing for a plural execu-

tive would prevent "contention" and be closer to "republican genius" (I, 72). Notes by Georgia's William Pierce from the same day suggest that Madison may simply have been advocating that a single executive should be aided by a Council of Revision (I, 74).

Madison advocated separation of the legislative and executive branches. To this end, he thought it essential that the legislature should not select the presidency. He gave at least tepid support to a proposal by fellow Virginian and friend James McClurg for appointing the presidency "during good behavior" (II, 34–35), but he seemed more concerned about the principle of separation of powers. Madison was especially wary of the "tendency in our governments to throw all power into the Legislative vortex" (II, 35).

On July 19, Madison repeated his concern that legislative and executive powers should be exercised independently. Agreeing with James Wilson that the people were "the fittest" to make such a decision, he feared that they might not have knowledge of candidates outside their own states and that conflict would occur because suffrage was more "diffusive" in the North, which had fewer slaves. This led Madison to advocate some form of electors, independent of Congress (II, 57).

On June 2, Madison went on record as opposing a proposal that would allow states to petition for removal of the presidency. He disfavored this mechanism in part because it put states of differing populations in similar situations and in part because he did not think it wise to mix state and national institutions (I, 86). He opposed, however, an absolute executive veto, partly on the basis that he thought it contradicted the national temper (I, 100). At one point, Madison favored three-fourths rather than two-thirds congressional majorities to override presidential vetoes. He believed this was necessary both "to defend the Executive Rights" and "to prevent popular or factious injustice" (II, 587).

Similarly, in discussions of an impeachment mechanism, Madison favored some provision "for defending the Community agst the Incapacity, negligence or perfidy of the chief Magistrate" (II, 65). He thought such a mechanism was particularly necessary in the case of an institution, like the presidency, that would be vested in a single individual. Madison objected to impeachments on the grounds of "maladministration," believing the term to be too vague and "equivalent to a tenure during the pleasure of the Senate" (II, 550). Similarly, Madison opposed suspending the president from office during impeachment trials, believing that such a suspension "will put him in the power of one branch only" (II, 612).

Madison reaffirmed the need to combine the executive with a Council of Revision. He felt that combining the executive with the executive would help both to "support" and "control" the former (I, 138). He further argued that allying the executive and members of the judiciary would be much different than allying the presidency and the legislative branch, as he thought the British had done (II, 77). Losing out on his plan for a Council of Revision, near the end of the Convention, Madison supported Mason's idea for a Council of State (II, 542).

Madison feared that legislative selection of the president would lead the latter to be unduly dependent on the former. On July 25, Madison reviewed the various mechanisms that had been proposed for presidential selection, and said that he liked popular election the best. He feared, however, that direct election would overly advantage the large states and those in the North, where suffrage was more widespread. Fellow delegates agreed with his critique, rather than his preference for popular selection, and voted to allow Congress to choose the president. When presidential selection was still to be left to Congress, Madison argued that the two houses should vote jointly rather than giving each house a veto over the other (II, 403). Madison, however, favored a system that made "eventual resort to any part of the Legislature improbable" (II, 513).

Slavery

Madison recognized that the problem of race was a problem of a minority being kept in subjection by the majority. Thus, on June 6, he said that "We have seen the mere distinction of colour made in the most enlightened period of time, a ground of the most oppressive dominion ever exercised by man over man" (I, 135). He made no apparent effort to eliminate slavery at the Convention, however, suggesting at one point that states should be represented by the population of free persons in one house and by the number of such persons and slaves in the other. He did strongly oppose the motion extending the right of states to import slaves from 1800 to 1808, noting that "twenty years [from the adoption of the Constitution to 1808] will produce all the mischief that can be apprehended from the liberty to import slaves. So long a term will be more dishonorable to the National character than to say nothing about it in the Constituton" (II, 415). In discussing slave duties, Madison further observed that he "thought it wrong to admit in the Constitution the idea that there could be property in men" (II, 417).

The Judiciary

On June 5, Madison argued against granting Congress, or any other numerous body, the power to select judges, although he suggested that the Senate might appropriately exercise such a function (I, 120; also see I, 232). Madison suggested that federal courts should be dispersed throughout the nation as a way of keeping down the number of appeals and of avoiding verdicts by "the biased directions of a dependent Judge, or the local prejudices of an undirected jury" (I, 124). Madison offered a rather novel proposal for judicial appointments (a kind of legislative veto), by suggesting that the president might appoint judges subject to confirmation of one-third of the Senate (II, 42), or disapproval by two-thirds (II, 44). Madison argued that, with such a check, the executive was the more appropriate appointing authority. By his arguments, the executive would be better able to select fit individuals, and would (after adoption of the Great Compromise giving states equal representation in the Senate) be more likely to represent a majority than a minority of the people (II, 80–81). Madison eventually modified his proposal, in accord with the present Constitution, so that a majority of the Senate could reject such nominees.

As in the case of members of Congress, he favored tying increases in judicial salaries to the price of a commodity like wheat (II, 45). Madison proposed that judicial jurisdiction should extend "to all cases arising under the Natl. laws; And to such other questions as may involve the Natl. peace & harmony" (II, 46). He thought, however, that the courts should be limited "to cases of a Judiciary Nature," explaining that "the right of expounding the Constitution in cases not of this nature ought not to be given to that Department" (II, 430).

Extended Republic

At a time when many Antifederalists held the view, which Charles Louis de Secondat Baron de Montesquieu espoused, that republican government would be impossible in a government the size of that which the Constitution was creating, Madison is probably best known for his view that an extended democratic republic was not only feasible but that it could actually serve as a guard against faction. Madison expressed this view on June 6 when he cited "the security of private rights, and the steady dispensation of Justice," as among the key objects of government (I, 134). Here, as in *Federalist* No. 10, Madison connected oppression with small states. The remedy followed accordingly:

> The only remedy is to enlarge the sphere, & thereby divide the community into so great a number of interests & parties, that in the 1st place a majority will not be likely at the same moment to have a common interest separate from that of the whole or of the minority; and in the 2d. place, that in case they shd. have such an interest, they may not be apt to unite in the pursuit of it. (I, 136).

Amending Process

The Virginia Plan had rather vaguely called for the necessity of an amending provision. Madison gave a clearer idea of what he favored on September 10 when he proposed that

the Legislature of the U-S–whenever two thirds of both Houses shall deem necessary, or on the application of two thirds of the Legislatures of the several States, shall propose amendments to this Constitution, which shall be valid to all intents and purposes as part thereof, when the same shall have been ratified by three fourths at least of the Legislatures of the several States, or by Conventions in three fourths thereof, as one or the other mode of ratification may be proposed by the Legislature of the U.S. (II, 559)

When this provision was amended to allow for states to require Congress to call a convention to propose amendments, Madison indicated that he "did not see why Congress would not be as much bound to propose amendments applied for by two thirds of the States as to call a Convention on the like application." He continued by observing that "He saw no objection however against providing for a Convention for the purpose of amendments, except only that difficulties might arise as to the form, the quorum &c which in Constitutional regulations ought to be as much as possible avoided" (II, 629–630).

Ratification

Madison thought the proposal for ratifying the Constitution through state conventions was essential. He feared that if state legislatures ratified, the parties would be able to make a breach of the Constitution by one party a way of absolving the allegiance of all. He wanted the Constitution to be "ratified in the most unexceptionable form, and by the supreme authority of the people themselves" (I, 123). On July 23, Madison argued that "the difference between a system founded on the Legislatures only, and one founded on the people, to be the true difference between a league or treaty, and a *Constitution*" (II, 93). Madison proposed at one point that the Constitution might be ratified by seven or more states with at least 33 seats (the majority of 66) in the House of Representatives (II, 475). He continued to insist on popular ratification: "The people were in fact, the fountain of all power, and by resorting to them, all difficulties were got over. They could alter constitutions as they pleased. It was a principle in the Bills of rights, that first principles might be resorted to" (II, 476).

Committee Work

Madison served on four committees at the Constitutional Convention. He was on the committee, appointed on July 9, that reconsidered the original apportionment of the U.S. House of Representatives and increased that number from 56 to 65. He was a member of the committee created on August 22 that devised a compromise regarding the slave trade and navigation. Committee assignments would appear to indicate that he rose in the estimation of his colleagues as the Convention proceeded. He was thus appointed both to the Committee on Postponed Matters, which the delegates created on August 31, and to the Committee of Style and Arrangement, which delegates appointed on September 8. He did not, however, chair any of the committees on which he served.

Life after the Convention

After the Convention Madison distinguished himself, along with Alexander Hamilton and John Jay, as a leading Federalist by serving as one of three authors of *The Federalist Papers*. Madison's essays on republican government (No. 10) and on separation of powers (No. 51) are regarded as classics and are often taken as embodiments of the central underlying philosophy of the Constitution. Elected to the Virginia ratifying convention, Madison successfully applied cool reason to beat back the powerful rhetoric of Patrick Henry opposing the new Constitution.

The biggest threat to the new Constitution seemed to come from those who argued for a second convention, which Madison feared might undo the work of the first. To avoid this contingency, and in possible response to letters that he was receiving from his friend, Thomas Jefferson, Madison agreed to support a bill of rights once the new Constitution was adopted. He was defeated by machinations of Governor Patrick Henry from getting a spot in the U.S. Senate. Narrowly defeating future president James Monroe, Madison was elected to the House of Representatives (he served there until 1797) where he took the lead in the formulation of the Bill of Rights. Madison generally worded these rights so as to protect rights of citizens without undermining the authority of the new national government. Madison did not succeed in getting an amendment that would restrict state powers over civil liberties—a development that would wait until Supreme Court interpretations (largely in the twentieth century) of the Fourteenth Amendment.

Although they worked together on *The Federalist Papers*, Madison became increasingly suspicious of Alexander Hamilton and his program for the new government. Madison accordingly secretly authored the Virginia Resolution of 1798, which opposed the Alien and Sedition Acts of the Adams administration (Jefferson wrote the corresponding Kentucky Resolution) and, somewhat contrary to the positions Madison had taken at the Constitutional Convention, appeared to advocate the right of states to interpose themselves against federal legislation. Madison served again in the Virginia state legislature from 1799 to 1800. A strong friend of Thomas Jefferson, whose Democratic-Republican Party he supported, Madison was selected as a Jeffersonian elector in 1800. Madison served as Jefferson's secretary of state from 1801 to 1809, a period during which the U.S. purchased the Louisiana Territory and in which Jefferson declared a highly unpopular embargo that unsuccessfully attempted to bring Great Britain to heel. Madison's buxom wife, Dolley Todd Madison, a former widow whom he had married in 1794 when he was 43, was a popular host during this time and into Madison's presidency. Madison was elected president in 1808 (defeating Charles Cotesworth Pinckney who had also attended the Constitutional Convention as a delegate from South Carolina) and served for two terms, the second of which witnessed the War of 1812 and the burning of the nation's capital. He sought to preserve Jefferson's memory after Jefferson's death and served for a time as rector of the University of Virginia, which Jefferson had founded.

James Madison the Campaigner

Today, James Madison is known as the "Father" of the Constitution and of the Bill of Rights, as well as the nation's fourth president. However, as a politician in a democracy Madison learned that he was not always accorded deference simply because he came from a respected family and was well educated. After serving a term in the Virginia legislature at the outbreak of the Revolutionary War, Madison lost his bid for reelection from his native Orange County. He later attributed his defeat to his failure to supply free alcohol at his campaign rallies. Madison apparently refused to supply alcohol on the basis that it was "inconsistent with the purity of moral and republican principles," but voters in his district apparently saw his actions as a token of his "pride or parsimony" (quoted in Sheldon 2001, 32, from an autobiographical account). Madison may have been particularly exasperated by the fact that the winner was a local tavern keeper named Charles Porter.

Fortunately, others in Virginia had recognized Madison's talents, and the legislature elected him to the Governor's Council of State, where he probably wielded greater power than had he simply been a legislator. A Madison biographer has speculated that he likely "made certain that in all his other election campaigns a full barrel of mellow cider was available for the thirsty electorate" (Rutland 1987, 11–12). He further notes that "He never lost another election over the next forty years" (12).

Indeed, eleven years after Porter defeated him, Madison bested Porter in Orange County in a race for a seat at the Virginia ratifying convention where Madison proved to be among the most influential proponents of the Constitution. Garrett Ward Sheldon observes that Madison's friends declared "that 'the sinners of Orange [County]' have 'turned from their wicked ways'" (Sheldon, 75). He further observes that Madison had the support of John Leland, a Baptist preacher who had been impressed by Madison's defense of religious minorities and who is believed to have helped persuade Madison of the desirability of adding a bill of rights.

FOR FURTHER READING

Rutland, Robert Allen. 1987. *James Madison: The Founding Father.* New York: Macmillan Publishing Company.

Sheldon, Garrett Ward. 2001. *The Political Philosophy of James Madison.* Baltimore, MD: Johns Hopkins University Press.

Called out of retirement from his farm in 1820, Madison cochaired Virginia's state constitutional convention. He died on June 28, 1836, at Montpelier, the last surviving member of the Convention that he so influenced. His papers of the Convention were published in 1840 and remain the best single source of information about its proceedings.

Madison had become increasingly concerned in his old age about the controversies over slavery that were racking the country, and he tried to distinguish his own careful appeals to fellow states in the Virginia Resolutions from the theory of concurrent majorities that John C. Calhoun of South Carolina and others were espousing that would allow a single state to nullify a federal law (Ford 1994, 51–55). Appealing as it were from beyond the grave, his "Advice to My Country" was first published in the *National Intelligencer* in 1850. Sounding a nationalistic note similar to that which he had consistently advocated at the Convention but not always consistently followed thereafter, Madison implored his countrymen to cherish the Union:

The advice nearest to my heart and deepest in my convictions is that the Union of the States be cherished and perpetuated. Let the open enemy to it be regarded as a Pandora with her box opened; and the disguised one, as the Serpent creeping with his deadly wiles into Paradise. (Meyers 1973, 576)

See Also Annapolis Convention; Bill of Rights; Council of Revision; Federalist and Democratic-Republican Parties; *Federalist, The;* Hume, David; Jefferson, Thomas; Madison's Notes of the Convention; Negative on State Laws; Vices of the Political System of the United States; Virginia; Virginia Plan

FOR FURTHER READING

Banning, Lance. 1995. *The Sacred Fire of Liberty: James Madison and the Founding of the American Republic.* Ithaca, NY: Cornell University Press.

———. 1983. "James Madison and the Nationalists, 1780–1783." *William and Mary Quarterly,* 3rd ser. 40 (April): 227–255.

Conniff, James. 1975. "On the Obsolescence of the General Will: Rousseau, Madison, and the Evolution of Republican Political Thought." *Western Political Quarterly* 28 (March): 32–58.

Farrand, Max, ed. 1937. *The Records of the Federal Convention.* 4 vols. New Haven, CT: Yale University Press.

Ford, Lacy K., Jr. 1994. "Inventing the Concurrent Majority: Madison, Calhoun, and the Problem of Majoritarianism in American Political Thought." *Journal of Southern History* 60 (February): 19–58.

Hobson, Charles F. 1979. "The Negative on State Laws: James Madison, the Constitution, and the Crisis of Republican Government." *William and Mary Quarterly,* 3rd ser. 36 (April): 214–235.

Kernell, Samuel, ed. 2003. *James Madison: The Theory and Practice of Republican Government.* Palo Alto, CA: Stanford University Press.

Koch, Adrienne. 1950. *Jefferson and Madison: The Great Collaboration.* New York: Oxford University Press.

Matthews, Richard K. 1995. *If Men Were Angels: James Madison and the Heartless Empire of Reason.* Lawrence: University Press of Kansas.

Meyers, Marvin, ed. 1973. *The Mind of the Founder: Sources of the Political Thought of James Madison.* Indianapolis, IN: Bobbs-Merrill.

Miller, William L. 1992. *The Business of May Next: James Madison and the Founding.* Charlottesville: University Press of Virginia.

Rakove, Jack N. 1990. *James Madison and the Creation of the American Republic.* Glenview, IL: Scott, Foresman.

Read, James H. 1995. "'Our Complicated System': James Madison on Power and Liberty." *Political Theory* 23 (August): 452–474.

Rutland, Robert A. 1987. *James Madison: The Founding Father.* New York: Macmillan.

Rutland, Robert A., ed. 1994. *James Madison and the American Nation, 1751–1836.* New York: Charles Scribner's Sons.

Sheldon, Garrett Ward. 2001. *The Political Philosophy of James Madison.* Baltimore, MD: Johns Hopkins University Press.

Siemers, David J. 2002. *Ratifying the Republic: Antifederalists and Federalists in Constitutional Time.* Palo Alto, CA: Stanford University Press.

Spencer, Mark G. 2002. "Hume and Madison on Faction." *William and Mary Quarterly,* 3rd ser. 59 (October): 869–896.

Zuchert, Michael P. 2003. "The Political Science of James Madison." In Bryan-Paul Frost and Jeffrey Sikkenga, eds. *History of American Political Thought.* Lanham, MD: Lexington Books, 149–166.

Zvesper, John. 1984. "The Madisonian Systems." *Western Political Quarterly* 37 (June): 236–256.

MADISON'S NOTES OF THE CONVENTION

The most complete and accurate source of information about the Constitutional Convention is found in notes taken by James Madison of Virginia. Madison, who went on to serve as a member of the first Congress, as secretary of state under Thomas Jefferson, as a cofounder, with Jefferson, of the Democratic-Republican Party, and as fourth president, was the last member of the Constitutional Convention to die (in 1836). Congress purchased his papers from Dolley Madison for $30,000, and they were first published in 1840, at which time H. D. Gilpin edited them.

Madison was present for every meeting of the Convention. At a time when he was anticipating that his notes would later be published, Madison explained how he had collected materials for his book:

I chose a seat in front of the presiding member, with the other members, on my right and left hand. In this favorable position of hearing all that passed, I noted in terms legible and in abbreviations and marks intelligible to myself what was read from the Chair or spoken by the members; and losing not a moment unnecessarily between the adjournment and reassembling of the Convention, I was enabled to write out my daily notes during the session or within a few finishing days after its close. (Cited in Benton 1986, I, 3–4)

Madison went on to describe his techniques:

In the labor and correctness of this I was not a little aided by practice, and by a familiarity with the style and the train of observation and reasoning which characterized the principal speakers. It happened, also, that I was not absent a single day, nor more than a casual fraction of an hour in any day, so that I could not have lost a single speech, unless a very short one.

It may be proper to remark, that, with a very few exceptions, the speeches were neither furnished, nor revised, nor sanctioned, by the speakers, but written out from my notes, aided by the freshness of my recollections. (Benton, 4)

Madison, whose hyperbolic words need to be understood in the context of his reputation for hypochondria, confided in the Virginia governor that "the confinement to which his attendance in Convention subjected him, almost killed him; but that having undertaken the task, he was determined to accomplish it" (quoted in Farrand 1907, 52).

Historian Max Farrand collected Madison's notes, and other materials from the Convention, in a four-volume set published, and republished, by Yale University Press. James H. Hutson subsequently substituted a fourth updated volume for the original one. Farrand's and Hutson's works continue to be the primary reference work for Convention debates, although, because of their completeness, Madison's own notes are often cited by themselves.

In his article on the subject, Farrand demonstrated that Gilpin "took considerable liberties with the text" (1907, 53). He further noted that Madison added to his own notes largely to bring

them in conformity with the journal of the official secretary, William Jackson (which largely recorded motions and votes, although not always accurately, rather than the specific debates at the Convention) and with other accounts of the Convention. In some cases, Madison's original, which is now available in Farrand's four-volume work, appears to be more accurate than his amended version. Despite what must have been a considerable temptation, there is little evidence suggesting that Madison altered his notes in order to present his own views in a better light than they might have otherwise seemed, although at least one scholar believes that Madison may have downplayed the role that disputes over navigation on the Mississippi River may have played in the debates (Merritt 1991, 146–149). Although consistently referring to himself as "Mr. Madison," from time to time he inserts an editorial comment, as when he noted early in debates that one of his motions for proportional representation in Congress had been "generally relished" and "would have been agreed to" had Delaware's George Read not offered a motion to postpone (Farrand 1937, I, 36; for observation on the comment see Miller 1992, 67). As impressive as Madison's job was, readers of his notes should be aware that they were never intended to be a verbatim transcript of the Convention proceedings. Moreover, while scholars and politicians often cite his notes in attempts to explain or understand what provisions of the Constitution mean, Madison himself preferred delaying publication of his notes "till the Constitution should be well settled by practice, and till a knowledge of the controversial part of the proceedings of its framers can be turned to no improper account" (quoted in Rakove 1990, 174).

See Also Farrand, Max; Jackson, William; Madison, James, Jr.; Records of the Constitutional Convention

FOR FURTHER READING

Benton, Wilbourne E., ed. 1986. *1787: Drafting the U.S. Constitution.* 2 vols. College Station: Texas A and M University Press.

Farrand, Max. 1907. "The Records of the Federal Convention." *American Historical Review* 13 (October): 44–65.

Farrand, Max, ed. 1937. *The Records of the Federal Convention.* 4 vols. New Haven, CT: Yale University Press.

Hutson, James H., ed. 1987. *Supplement to Max Farrand's* The Records of the Federal Convention of 1787. New Haven, CT: Yale University Press.

Madison, James. 1977. *The Papers of James Madison*, vol. 10: *27 May 1787–3 March 1788.* Ed. Robert A. Rutland, Charles F. Hobson, William M. M. Rachal, and Fredrika J. Teute. Chicago: University of Chicago Press.

Merritt, Eli. 1991. "Sectional Conflict and Secret Compromise: The Mississippi River Question and the United States Constitution." *American Journal of Legal History* 33 (April): 117–171.

Miller, William Lee. 1992. *The Business of May Next: James Madison and the Founding.* Charlottesville: University Press of Virginia.

Rakove, Jack N. 1990. *James Madison and the Creation of the American Republic.* Glenville, IL: Scott, Foresman.

———. 2004. "Thinking Like a Constitution." *Journal of the Early Republic* 24 (Spring): 1–20.

Facsimile of the Magna Carta, signed by King John of England at Runnymede, laying the basis for political and personal liberty. Barons' coats of arms and royal seals surround the document. (Bettmann/Corbis)

MAGNA CARTA

The delegates to the Constitutional Convention do not appear to have explicitly referred to the Magna Carta during the Convention proceedings. However, many historians of the U.S. Constitution trace the roots of the U.S. Constitution, as well as the Bill of Rights, back to this great charter of English liberties, which an English nobleman extracted from King John I at Runnymede on June 12, 1215. After John attempted to renounce it, it was reissued by his successor Edward I in 1225 and was confirmed by kings and Parliaments 32 times by 1628 (Siegan 2003, 45).

The great English jurist Sir Edward Coke, and other defenders of English liberty, often read subsequent recognitions of English liberties back into the document. They portrayed the Magna Carta not only as the fountain of all important principles but also as the embodiment of common law principles that they believed had grown out of an earlier more virtuous Saxon system (Colbourn 1965, 36). Similarly, the English Whig Algernon

Sidney, who was martyred under Charles II, referred to the Magna Carta as a reflection of "the native and original rights of our nation" (Colbourn, 37). The document also reinforced the liberal idea that government was based on a social contract.

A copy of this historic document was purchased by billionaire businessman (later independent presidential candidate) Ross Perot and displayed in Philadelphia during the bicentennial of the U.S. Constitution. It set the groundwork for both the idea of representative government that developed into the English Parliament (a bicameral body that served as something of a model for the U.S. Congress) and the idea of individual rights. Although the English constitution is generally considered to be "unwritten," the Magna Carta is one of a number of written documents upon which English practices are based. The idea of getting an agreement in writing is certainly a prelude to the idea of charters and constitutions that took root in the New World setting.

The Magna Carta is arranged in 63 articles. Among the most important is Article 39, which forbade a freeman being "taken or imprisoned, or disseised [stripped of property], or outlawed, or banished, or any ways destroyed . . . unless by the lawful judgment of his peers, or by the law of the land" (McClellan 2000, 68). In addition to serving as a general guarantee of procedural fairness, this provision is often tied to the due process provisions of the Fifth and Fourteenth Amendments.

Like the U.S. Constitution, the Magna Carta is highly regarded not only for its substantive provisions but also as a symbol of individual rights and of opposition to arbitrary government.

See Also Common Law; Great Britain

FOR FURTHER READING

The American Constitution: The Road from Runnymede. 1981. 58-minute film. http://www.insight.media.com.

Colbourn, H. Trevor. 1965. *The Lamp of Experience: Whig History and the Intellectual Origins of the American Revolution.* Chapel Hill: University of North Carolina Press.

McClellan, James. 2000. *Liberty, Order, and Justice: An Introduction to the Constitutional Principles of American Government.* Indianapolis, IN: Liberty Fund.

Pocock, J. G. A. 1985. "The Influence of British Political Thought on the American Constitution: Magna Carta in Context." In Robert S. Peck and Ralph S. Pollock, eds. *The Blessings of Liberty: Bicentennial Lectures at the National Archives.* Chicago: American Bar Association.

Siegan, Bernard H. 2003. "Protecting Economic Liberties." *Chapman Law Review* 6 (Spring): 43–121.

Walker, David M. 1980. *The Oxford Companion to Law.* Oxford, UK: Clarendon Press.

MAINE

At the time of the Constitutional Convention, the present-day state of Maine was part of Massachusetts, lying on its frontier with Canada, but delegates were already contemplating that it would one day be on its own. On June 29, Nathaniel Gorham of Massachusetts observed that his state had been formed from Plymouth, Massachusetts and Maine and used this as an example of the advantages that a small area, or state, could gain from association with a larger one (Farrand 1937, I, 462). This same day, Robert Yates's notes indicate that Gorham also said that "Massachusetts cannot long remain a large state. The province of Maine must soon become independent of her" (I, 470). Gorham observed again on July 6 that "In the province of Mayne a Convention is at this time deliberating on a separation from Masts." He further said that he wished "to see all the States made small by proper divisions, instead of their becoming formidable as was apprehended, to the Small States" (I, 540).

On July 23, Gorham cited Maine, along with Kentucky, Vermont, and Franklin (present-day Tennessee), as likely new states (II, 94). On August 30, Maryland's Luther Martin cited "the unreasonableness of forcing & guaranteeing the people of Virginia beyond the Mountains, the Western people, of N. Carolina. & of Georgia, & the people of Maine, to continue under the States now governing them without the consent of those States to their separation" (II, 463). Martin later repeated this argument in his negative report on the Constitution which he delivered to the Maryland legislature on November 29, 1787 (III, 224).

Unlike Kentucky, North Carolina, and Vermont, which continued to gain in population and joined the Union relatively quickly, Maine was not admitted into the Union until 1820. It was accepted as part of the Missouri Compromise, which Congress designed to preserve the equality of slave and free states in the U.S. Senate by allowing Missouri to enter as a slave state and Maine as a free one (Wiltse 1961, 65).

See Also Kentucky; States, Admission and Creation; Tennessee; Vermont

FOR FURTHER READING

Farrand, Max, ed. 1937. *The Records of the Federal Convention.* 4 vols. New Haven, CT: Yale University Press.

Wiltse, Charles M. 1961. *The New Nation, 1800–1845.* New York: Hill and Wang.

MARSHALL, JOHN (1755–1835)

Probably no single individual has had more influence on the interpretation and success of the U.S. Constitution than John Marshall. Born in Fauquier County, Virginia, in 1755, Marshall's most formative experience was probably his service from 1775 to 1779 in the Continental Army, where he developed nationalist sympathies. He subsequently attended a series of lectures by George Wythe at the College of William and Mary (the law school is now called the Marshall-Wythe School of Law) and began the practice of law, and engaged in local politics, in 1780.

Although he did not attend the Constitutional Convention of 1787, Marshall was selected as a delegate to the Virginia ratifying convention, held in Richmond in June 1788. Marshall had worked within the state legislature to issue the call for the ratifying convention, which would meet in Richmond, to discuss the proposed Constitution. At the Convention, Marshall joined forces with men such as James Madison, Edmund Pendleton, and Edmund Randolph in favor of the new Constitution in opposition to such men as Patrick Henry, George Mason, and future president James Monroe.

Marshall delivered three primary speeches on behalf of the Constitution at the ratifying convention. In the first, he attempted to answer Patrick Henry's arguments that the Philadelphia delegates had abandoned democratic principles. In point of fact, he argued that the existing government under the Articles of Confederation had failed to provide "a strict observance of justice and public faith, and a steady adherence to virtue," which Marshall associated with democracy and "good government" (Baker 1974, 129). Marshall argued that the new Constitution provided for "necessary" power, while ensuring that such power was "guarded" (Baker, 130). In a second major speech, Marshall argued that states would maintain adequate control over their militias in the new system. His third speech was the most prophetic of the future role that he would himself play. Answering Antifederalist objections to the establishment of the federal judiciary, Marshall argued that such a judiciary would be necessary to safeguard the new Constitution and the liberties of the people. He observed that if Congress attempted to exercise powers that the Constitution did not give, the courts would strike the law down:

> If they were to make a law not warranted by any of the power enumerated, it would be considered by the Judges as an infringement of the Constitution which they are to guard. They would not consider such a law as coming under their jurisdiction. They would declare it void. (Smith 1996, 137)

Today, this power is recognized as the power of judicial review.

Marshall lived in Richmond and was well liked. His constituents elected him to the ratifying convention apparently not because they agreed with his sentiments but because they trusted his judgment and character. As a man who was somewhat less stuffy than some of the Founding Fathers, one

Portrait of John Marshall, by Saint Memin, ca. 1808 (Library of Congress)

biographer observed that "Marshall's greatest contribution may well have been to balance Henry's affability in Richmond's public houses" (Smith, 133). Having served as a kind of unofficial lobbyist for their interests, Marshall appears to have had special influence with those in the western part of the state (today's Kentucky) who were otherwise disinclined to support the new government.

With his belief in the necessity for a strong national government, Marshall naturally gravitated toward the Federalist Party. In 1798, Marshall served as part of the XYZ mission to France, where, with Charles Cotesworth Pinckney and Elbridge Gerry, he refused to offer a bribe. He subsequently served briefly in the U.S. House of Representatives, and then as secretary of state to President John Adams. Adams subsequently nominated Marshall as chief justice of the U.S. Supreme Court, where he served from 1801 to 1835, often coming into conflict with the Democratic-Republican administration of Thomas Jefferson and his successors. Most observers credit Marshall with helping to make the judicial branch a coequal branch of government. Prior to his tenure, justices generally wrote separate opinions. Marshall instead convinced the majority to craft an opinion for the Court, which he often authored.

There are few areas of the law that Marshall did not influence. In the case of *Marbury v. Madison*, 1 Cranch (5 U.S.) 137 (1803), Marshall helped establish the judiciary's power to void federal laws that it considered to be unconstitutional. In cases like *Cohens v. Virginia*, 6 Wheat. (19 U.S.) 264 (1821), Marshall upheld the supremacy of congressional laws over conflicting state laws. In *McCulloch v. Maryland*, 17 U.S. 316 (1819), Marshall upheld Congress's power to establish a national bank as an implied power rightfully exercised under the necessary and proper clause. *Dartmouth College v. Woodward*, 4 Wheat. (17 U.S.) 518 (1819), was one of a number of cases in which Marshall used the contract clause to protect vested property rights. Similarly, in *Gibbons v. Ogden*, 9 Wheat. (22 U.S.) 1 (1824), Marshall read congressional powers under the commerce clause broadly, and invalidated a monopoly grant by New York to steamboats on its waters as being in conflict with a federal pilotage license.

Although Marshall had not attended the Constitutional Convention, he interpreted the document with the certainty of those who had done so. In *Marbury v. Madison*, he argued from the singularity of the Convention to the foundational nature of the document it created:

> The exercise of this original right is a very great exertion; nor can it, nor ought it, to be frequently repeated. The principles therefore, so established, are deemed fundamental. And as the authority from which they proceed is supreme, and can seldom act, they are designed to be permanent.

Herbert Johnson is among those who have credited Marshall and other early justices with "putting flesh and muscle upon the skeletal federal Constitution they had been given by the 1787 Philadelphia convention" (2003, 495).

See Also Judicial Review; Ratification in the States; Virginia; Wythe, George

FOR FURTHER READING

Baker, Leonard. 1974. *John Marshall: A Life in Law.* New York: Macmillan Publishing Co.

Johnson, Herbert A. 2003. "Marshall, John." In John R. Vile, ed. *Great American Judges: An Encyclopedia.* Vol. 1 of 2. Santa Barbara, CA: ABC-CLIO, 487–496.

Smith, Jean Edward. 1996. *John Marshall: Definer of a Nation.* New York: Henry Holt and Company.

MARTIN, ALEXANDER
(1740–1807)

Alexander Martin was born in 1740 into the family of a Presbyterian minister in Hunterdon County, New Jersey, who had immigrated there from Ireland. Martin earned both a bachelor's and a master's degree from the College of New Jersey (today's Princeton) and moved, as did most

Alexander Martin, delegate from Maryland
(Pixel That)

of his siblings, to North Carolina where he was both a merchant and an attorney. He was a justice of the peace and briefly served as a judge. On one occasion, a crowd of Westerners associated with the Regulator Movement beat him. He later served in the North Carolina legislature and helped defend Charleston against British attacks. Subjected to a court martial for cowardice at the battle of Germantown, Martin was not convicted but resigned. He was elected to the North Carolina legislature and served from 1782 to 1785 as state governor.

Martin was present when the Convention opened on May 25, and he appears to have stayed until late August. However, he did not serve on any Convention committees, and his public participation appears to have been limited to seconding three motions. On June 23 he seconded a motion by James Madison of Virginia to prohibit members of the House of Representatives from being eligible for offices during their service and for one year afterward that were established, or

the emoluments of which were increased, during their service (Farrand 1937, I, 386). On July 10, Martin joined South Carolina's General Pinckney in proposing that North Carolina be granted six U.S. representatives instead of the five that were proposed (I, 568). Again, on July 26, Martin seconded a motion, this one by Virginia's George Mason, that would limit the nation's new capital from being located in the same city as the capital of any state until such time as the necessary building could be constructed (II, 127). Significantly, in each case, Martin seconded a motion of a fellow Southerner.

Fellow delegate Hugh Williamson, the intellectual leader of the North Carolina delegation, wrote a letter dated July 8, 1787, to future Supreme Court Justice James Iredell explaining Martin's reticence to participate in the proceedings. He observed: "I am inclined to think that the great exertions of political wisdom in our late Governor [Martin], while he sat at the helm of our State, have so exhausted his fund, that time must be required to enable him again to exert his abilities to the advantage of the nation" (III, 55).

On August 20, Martin wrote to the North Carolina governor to tell him that he would be leaving the Convention in early September. In this letter he observed that "the Deputation from the State of North Carolina have generally been unanimous on all great questions, and I flatter myself will continue so until the Objects of their mission be finished" (III, 72–73).

Martin supported ratification of the Constitution in North Carolina but was not elected to the state's ratifying convention. He served as the state's first governor under the Constitution, a position he occupied for three subsequent terms. The state legislature chose him as a U.S. senator in 1792. Although generally aligned in the Senate with the Democratic-Republican Party, he supported the Alien and Sedition Acts in 1798. He went on to serve as a trustee of the University of North Carolina and as speaker of the North Carolina Senate. He died in 1807. A lifelong bachelor, Martin acknowledged paternity of Alexander Strong Martin.

See Also North Carolina

FOR FURTHER READING

Bradford, M. M. 1981. *Founding Fathers: Brief Lives of the Framers of the United States Constitution.* 2nd ed. Lawrence: University Press of Kansas.

Craige, Burton. 1987. *The Federal Convention of 1787: North Carolina in the Great Crisis.* Richmond, VA: Expert Graphics.

Farrand, Max, ed. 1937. *The Records of the Federal Convention.* 4 vols. New Haven, CT: Yale University Press.

MARTIN, LUTHER (1744–1826)

Born near New Brunswick, New Jersey, in 1744 to a farmer, Martin attended the College of New Jersey (now Princeton University) before settling in Maryland as a schoolteacher. He later studied for the bar, to which he was admitted after an examination by George Wythe and John Randolph of Virginia. Partly because of his enthusiasm for the Patriot cause, Martin was elevated as attorney general of Maryland and served in this post consecutively for 27 years and later again for a brief time. Known for excessive drinking, Martin was better known for his rhetoric—one scholar says his arguments were characterized by "their orotundity, antiquarian scholarship, otiose circumambient development, and irresistible conclusion" (Bradford 1994, 112).

Martin attended the Convention in part because members of the state legislature feared leaving lest the state adopt a paper money scheme. Martin was seated at the Constitutional Convention on June 9. He left on September 4, before the Convention was completed, but after it was clear that it had departed too much from his sentiments for him to consent to it.

Martin's first recorded position at the Convention was a motion to strike the requirement that state officials pledge to uphold the new Constitution. He observed that if such an oath were contrary to the pledge they had taken to support their state constitutions, the oath would be "improper," whereas if it coincided with this pledge, such prior oaths would be "sufficient" (Farrand 1937I, 203).

Luther Martin, delegate from Maryland
(Pixel That)

Federalism and Representation

On June 19, Luther introduced the view, based on social contract theory, that the U.S. Revolution had "placed the 13 States in a state of nature towards each other." He believed that the states had therefore entered the Articles of Confederation on the basis of equality, and he said that he could never agree to a plan that did not provide for equal state representation in Congress (Farrand 1937, I, 324). Even after the Convention had rejected the New Jersey Plan for the Virginia Plan, Martin indicated that he opposed a number of the latter plan's provisions. He thus observed that he would support the state governments over the national government, and that he could see no reason to divide Congress into two houses (I, 340). Martin believed that the American people had entrusted "the security of their lives, liberties & property" to the state governments (I, 341). The people had accordingly formed the federal government for limited purposes and continued to be on guard against it:

The federal Govt. they formed, to defend the whole agst. foreign nations, in case of war, and to defend the lesser States agst the ambition of the larger: they are afraid of granting powers unnecessarily, lest they should defeat the original end of the Union; lest the powers should prove dangerous to the sovereignties of the particular States which the Union was meant to support; and expose the lesser to being swallowed up by the larger. (II, 341)

Martin elaborated on his view of the relation between the nation and the states in a speech of more than three hours that he delivered on June 27. Madison's summary indicates that Martin delivered the speech with his usual exuberance, and that Madison was only able to record its central points:

The General Govt. was meant merely to preserve the State Governts: not to govern individuals: that its powers ought to be kept within narrow limits; that if too little power was given to it, more might be added; but that if too much, it could never be resumed: that individuals as such have little to do but with their own States; that the Genl. Govt. has no more to apprehend from the States composing [the Union] while it pursues proper measures, that a Govt. over individuals has to apprehend from its subject: that to resort to the Citizens at large for their sanction to a new Governt. will be throwing them back into a State of Nature: that the dissolution of the State Govts. is involved in the nature of the process: that the people have no right to do this without the consent of those to whom they have delegated their power for State purposes. (I, 437)

Luther continued to argue that states remained in the state of nature, and hence of equality, relative to one another. Clearly unable to get everything, Madison observed that Luther had "read passages from Locke, Vattel, Lord Summers–Priestley" (I, 437) in support of his argument from the state of nature. Martin accused the three largest states of seeking to enslave the 10 smaller ones. He opposed the veto that Madison had proposed over state laws and suggested that it would

be better to carve up the large states than to join small ones together (I, 438). Madison observed that Martin was "too much exhausted" to finish his speech. In his notes of the speech, New York's Robert Yates recorded that Martin said that he would not accept a government organized on the principles of the Virginia Plan "for all the slaves of Carolina or the horses and oxen of Massachusetts." He further recorded that Martin charged that the "feeling" that the large states professed on behalf of justice "are only the feelings of ambition and the lust of power" (I, 441).

When he resumed his speech on the following day, Martin continued to argue that the general government had been formed on behalf of the states rather than for the people, and he continued to fear that small states would be enslaved if they were not represented equally. He said that "it will be in vain to propose any plan offensive to the rulers of the States, whose influence over the people will certainly prevent their adopting it" (I, 445). He also stated that he would rather see the formation of partial confederacies between the large states and the small ones than give sanction to the plan being considered (I, 445). This is one of the few occasions on which Yates's notes were more complete than Madison's, perhaps reflecting the latter's exasperation with Martin's arguments. In addition to the arguments above, Yates observed that Martin expressed a clear preference for government by the states on the basis that the general government "is too remote for their good. The people want it nearer home" (I, 454). Toward the end of his speech, Yates cited Martin as saying that "we are already confederated, and no power on earth can dissolve it but by the consent of *all* the contracting powers—and four states, on this floor, have already declared their opposition to annihilate it" (I, 455).

When Elbridge Gerry later argued against the idea of state sovereignty, Martin "remarked that the language of the States being, Sovereign & independent, was once familiar & understood; though it seemed now so strange & obscure" (I, 468). He further quoted passages from the Articles of Confederation to prove his point. When on June 30, New Jersey's Jonathan Dayton objected that the plan of government being proposed was "an amphibious monster," Martin, in apparent agreement, said that he could "never confederate if it could not be done on just principles" (I, 490). On July 2, he reiterated that "no modifications whatever could reconcile the Smaller States to the least diminution of their equal Sovereignty" (I, 511). However, Martin was appointed that day to the Committee of Compromise on Representation in Congress, and this seems to have served to moderate his views. Thus, on July 14, Martin said that although he liked neither the idea of a bicameral Congress nor the idea of unequal representation in the lower house, he "was willing . . . to make trial of the plan, rather than do nothing" (II, 4). He quickly established an even more forceful defense of his new position, however, in declaring that "He had rather there should be two Confederacies, than one founded on any other principle than an equality of votes in the 2d branch at least" (II, 4). Martin later carried his state in singular opposition to allowing members of the Senate to vote "per capita" as "departing from the idea of the *States* being represented in the 2d. branch" (II, 95). Similarly, on August 14, Martin argued that "as the Senate is to represent the States, the members of it ought to be paid by the States" (II, 292).

On June 21, Martin seconded a motion by South Carolina's Charles Pinckney to allow for election of members of the House of Representatives in the manner that states chose rather than requiring that this be done by popular election (I, 358). On June 23, Martin seconded a motion offered by James Madison that restricted members of Congress from accepting offices during their tenure or for one year after for offices established or the emoluments of which were increased during their terms (I, 386).

When during a discussion of whether to restrict officeholding to individuals with debts or unsettled accounts, fellow Maryland delegate Daniel Carroll proposed striking out the prohibition on those with unsettled accounts. Martin replied that this would leave it in the interest of such candidates "to keep their accounts unsettled as long as possible" (II, 125).

On August 17, Martin expressed opposition to allowing the national government to subdue re-

bellion within the state without the consent of the legislature as giving Congress "a dangerous & unnecessary power" (II, 317). The next day, Martin proposed restricting the number of troops in peacetime to a limited, but yet to be specified, number (II, 330). Although Martin favored limiting direct taxes, he favored a mechanism, similar to that under the Articles of Confederation, whereby Congress would requisition the states and that only in cases where states failed to comply would it then "devise and pass acts directing the mode, and authorizing the collection of the same" (II, 359).

Martin opposed congressional superintendence over state militia. He argued both that states would never concede this power and that, if they did so, "the militia would be less attended to by the Genl. than by the State Governments" (II, 387). Martin and Carroll also introduced a motion preventing Congress from using its power over commerce to favor ports of some states over those of others (II, 417). On August 29, Martin introduced a motion to require two-thirds majorities of Congress to enact commercial regulations (II, 449).

When the Convention was debating a provision on August 29 whereby new states could not be admitted into the Union without the consent of those already present, Martin said that this would "alarm" the landlocked states. He feared that the provision could be used to deny independence to Vermont, trying to establish a separate identity from Massachusetts, or Frankland (meaning Franklin), the current state of Tennessee, which was attempting to secure its independence from North Carolina (II, 455). He reiterated this argument the following day and used it as a launching pad to reiterate the value of state sovereignty. Directing his argument toward the nationalistic James Wilson, Martin observed that "In the beginning, when the rights of the small States were in question, they were phantoms, ideal beings. Now when the Great States were to be affected, political Societies were of a sacred nature" (II, 464). Somewhat injudiciously, Martin matched a threat by Gouverneur Morris that large states would leave the Union if they were split without their consent with a threat that small states would leave if the Constitution forced them to guarantee existing large state boundaries (II, 464). Martin unsuccessfully offered a motion providing for the admission of new states within their existing territories, but Morris's motion, providing for both state and national consent, succeeded in passing instead.

Presidency

On July 19, at a time when the Convention was still anticipating that Congress would choose the president, Martin moved to reinstate a provision making a president ineligible for reelection (II, 52, 58). He reintroduced this opposition on July 24 (II, 101) and followed by proposing that the president serve for an 11-year term (II, 102). On August 27, Martin introduced a motion requiring that the president should not be able to issue reprieves or pardons until after individuals have been convicted, but he withdrew the motion after Pennsylvania's James Wilson indicated that it might sometimes be necessary to issue pardons beforehand, as in cases where this was necessary to get the names of accomplices (II, 426).

Judiciary

On June 20, Martin expressed his view that extending the national judiciary into the states would prove to be "ineffectual, and would be viewed with a jealousy inconsistent with its usefulness" (I, 341). Arguing on July 17 against the congressional negative of state laws, Martin indicated that he thought the new government could depend on state courts since they "would not consider as valid any law contravening the Authority of the Union, and which the legislature would wish to be negatived" (II, 27).

Martin appears to have been partly responsible for the introduction of the supremacy clause in the New Jersey Plan, but the version he introduced was apparently designed to see that state judges would still enforce state constitutions and bills of rights (albeit not state laws) in cases where they conflicted with the national constitution (see Clarkson and Jett 1970, 114–115; Farrand II, 29). Seeking to rely on state rather than on federal courts, Martin argued that lower federal tribunals "will create jealousies & oppositions in the State tribunals, with the jurisdiction of which they will interfere" (II, 45–46).

Martin favored vesting the Senate, rather than the president, with the power to appoint federal judges. He argued that thus "Being taken from all the States it wd. be best informed of characters & most capable of making a fit choice" (II, 41).

Martin strongly opposed associating judges with the executive in a Council of Revision. In the process of expressing his opposition, however, he indicated not only that he doubted that judges had superior understanding to other public officials but also that he anticipated that judges would, in their judicial capacity, be exercising the power to declare laws to be unconstitutional:

A knowledge of mankind, and of Legislative affairs cannot be presumed to belong in a higher degree to the Judges than to the Legislature. And as to the Constitutionality of laws, that point will come before the Judges in their proper official character. In this character they have a negative on the laws. Join them with the Executive in the Revision and they will have a double negative. (II, 76)

Luther further observed that judges would lose the confidence of the public "if they are employed in the task of remonstrating agst. popular measures of the Legislature," and he wondered how many judges would serve on such a council (II, 77).

On August 20, Martin proposed that individuals convicted of treason could be convicted not only on the testimony of two witnesses but also "on confession in open court" (II, 349–350). Interestingly, Martin later defended Aaron Burr against prosecution for treason during the Jefferson administration. On August 30, Martin failed to get a motion adopted that would have the U.S. Supreme Court decide on all claims respecting the governing of U.S. territory or property (II, 466); delegates thought that the Constitution already offered protection in regard to such matters.

Slavery

On August 21, Martin proposed allowing the taxation of slaves. He made three arguments. Two were practical, and one was based on morality. He observed that the three-fifths clause would give states an incentive to import slaves and that "slaves weakened one part of the Union which the other parts were bound to protect" (II, 364). He also observed, however, that "it was inconsistent with the principles of the revolution and dishonorable to the American character to have such a feature in the Constitution" (II, 364). Perhaps with a view to how earlier service on the committee to adjust state representation had moderated his views, the next day the Convention placed Martin on the committee to adjust the issue of slave trade and navigation.

Bill of Rights

In presenting his reasons for opposing the Constitution to the Maryland legislature, Martin said that he had opposed suspension of the writ of habeas corpus and the presence of standing armies, but Madison's notes do not record any of his comments on the subject (such notes would not, of course, reflect Martin's individual votes within his state delegation on such issues). Martin offered a rather novel, albeit not unconvincing, explanation as to why he had not supported a committee to propose such a bill:

A very few days before I left the Convention, I shewed to an honorable member sitting by me a proposition, which I then had in my hand, couched in the following words; "Resolved that a committee be appointed to prepare and report a bill of rights, to be prefixed to the proposed Constitution," and I then would instantly have moved for the appointment of a committee for that purpose, if he would have agreed to second the motion, to do which he hesitated, not as I understand from any objection to the measure, but from a conviction in his own mind that the motion would be in vain. (Quoted by Clarkson and Jett 1970, 133 citing the *Maryland Journal,* March 21, 1788, 391)

Martin had apparently left the Convention by September 12 (Clarkson and Jett 1970, 133–134), when the states voted 10 to 0 against George Mason's proposal for a committee to draft a bill of rights (II, 588).

Interestingly, Martin suggested to the Maryland legislature that he had disfavored the provision prohibiting religious oaths:

there were some members so unfashionable as to think, that a belief of the existence of a Deity, and of a state of future rewards and punishments would be some security for the good conduct of our rulers, and that, in a Christian country, it would be at least decent to hold out some distinction between the professors of Christianity and downright infidelity or paganism. (III, 227)

As he presented his view to the state legislature, Martin's critique does not seem to recognize that an oath specifying adherence to Christianity would also have excluded adherents of Judaism (presumably lumped in with proponents of "infidelity or paganism") from national public office.

Ratification

Martin opposed allowing state conventions to ratify the Constitution (I, 341). He reiterated this opposition on August 31:

He argued the danger of commotions from a resort to the people & to first principles in which the Governments might be on one side & the people on the other. He was apprehensive of no such consequences however in Maryland, whether the Legislature or the people should be appealed to.

Both of them would be generally against the Constitution. (II, 476).

Martin followed these observations by proposing, along with Daniel Carroll, who together with Martin carried Maryland as the only state favoring this mechanism, that all the states should have to ratify the Constitution before it went into effect (II, 477). He soon thereafter observed that he did not believe the states would ratify the Constitution "unless hurried into it by surprise" (II, 478).

Life after the Convention

Shortly after arriving back in Maryland, Martin delivered his extensive criticism of the Constitutional Convention and its work in what the Maryland legislature later printed as *The Genuine Information*. This was in turn reprinted in 1838, along with notes by Robert Yates, as the *Secret Proceedings and Debates of the Convention*. Martin almost always interpreted the Convention proceedings with a jaundiced eye as a conspiracy by those who favored the powers of the large states and of the national government. He was especially critical of the Convention's secrecy and concerned about what he considered the undue erosion of state power. Still, his analysis is quite useful in confirming a number of particulars that scholars know about the Convention from other sources and in filling in some details that would not otherwise be known.

After the Convention, Martin established himself as one of the greatest attorneys of his day, arguing such cases as *Fletcher v. Peck* (1810), involving the sale by Georgia of its western lands; defending his friend Samuel Chase in an impeachment trial sanctioned by Thomas Jefferson and conducted in 1804 by the House of Representatives; defending Aaron Burr in a trial for treason (also pursued by Jefferson) in Richmond, Virginia in 1807; and serving as one of the attorneys unsuccessfully arguing that Maryland could tax the national bank in *McCulloch v. Maryland* (1819). Ironically, Jefferson (whom he often opposed) described the man who was such a defender of states' rights at the Constitutional Convention as a "Federalist bulldog."

Stricken by a stroke in 1819, the Maryland bar passed a resolution assessing each member of the bar $5 for his support. Aaron Burr subsequently took Martin into his house where he died in 1826, the same year that witnessed the deaths of Thomas Jefferson and John Adams.

See Also Antifederalists; Maryland

FOR FURTHER READING

Bradford, M. M. 1994. *Founding Fathers: Brief Lives of the Framers of the United States Constitution.* 2nd ed. Lawrence: University Press of Kansas.

Clarkson, Paul S., and R. Samuel Jett. 1970. *Luther Martin of Maryland.* Baltimore, MD: Johns Hopkins Press.

Farrand, Max, ed. 1937. *The Records of the Federal Convention.* 4 vols. New Haven, CT: Yale University Press.

Reynolds, William L., II. 1987. "Luther Martin, Maryland and the Constitution." *Maryland Law Review* 47 (Fall): 291–321.

Secret Proceedings and Debates of the Convention Assembled at Philadelphia, in the Year 1787, for the Purpose of Forming the Constitution of the United States of America. 1838. Cincinnati, OH: Alston Mygatt.

Vile, John R., ed. 2001. *Great American Lawyers.* 2 vols. Santa Barbara: ABC-CLIO.

MARYLAND

Maryland was formed when King Charles I granted a charter in 1633 to Cecilius Calvert, better known as Lord Baltimore. Baltimore was particularly interested in establishing religious toleration, especially for Roman Catholics. Although Maryland shared Virginia's dependence on tobacco and slavery, the state proved to be more diverse. Its interests also differed because of smaller size.

Maryland had waged its initial war for independence against the proprietor of the colony rather than the king of England and was initially somewhat reluctant to join the larger revolution against the Crown. The state had created a conservative constitution with property qualifications both for members of the electorate and for officeholders. The conservative Senate often checked the more popular Assembly and had blocked attempts by the Assembly to issue paper money.

Maryland and the Articles of Confederation

Maryland was the last state to approve the Articles of Confederation, waiting until 1781 when

The Maryland State House where the Annapolis Convention took place in 1786. Engraving by John Vallace based on a painting by Charles Willson Peale. (MPI/Getty Images)

Virginia and other states gave up their claim to the Northwest Territories. Even after joining the confederation, Maryland continued to be concerned that it could be called upon to defend the interests of states with large Western land claims without having opportunity to profit from them. Maryland wanted its citizens to be able to participate in the development of the West on an equal level with other citizens, and it shared many commercial interests with Virginia.

Maryland and Virginia were the two states that met at Mount Vernon to discuss navigation on the Potomac River and other concerns and issued a call for a larger convention of states that took place at the state capital in Annapolis. Ironically, although Maryland served as the site of this meeting, it did not send delegates.

Representation at the Convention

Five delegates represented Maryland at the Constitutional Convention. They were Daniel Carroll, Luther Martin, James McHenry, John Francis Mercer and Daniel of St. Thomas Jenifer. A number of men of greater reputation stayed behind in the state legislature, largely to forestall calls for the issuance of paper money. Of Maryland's delegates who went to Philadelphia, Martin participated most actively in the Convention, which he and John Mercer ultimately decided not to sign. Maryland was on the border of the Southern and Middle states, sharing the institution of slavery with states to the South. A landlocked state with larger populations than other states its size, it was considered one of the smaller states.

Ratification

After returning from the Convention in Philadelphia, Luther Martin published a speech that he gave to the state legislature called "The Genuine Information," which was highly critical of the new government. In what Federalists must have regarded as an act of Providence, the bombastic, if not always organized, orator had laryngitis and was unable to participate in debates at the ratifying convention. Martin favored small states and feared that the new Constitution would serve as an obstacle to further state division. He further feared that the large states would seek to dominate the small within the new government.

By contrast, the majority of people in Maryland appear to have believed that the Connecticut Compromise effectively provided for the state's interest while a strengthened national government held out the prospect of increased commerce and of guaranteeing Maryland citizens the rights to purchase and develop Western lands. Most believed that Maryland would be better protected within such a strengthened government than if it were left outside it. The Maryland ratifying convention began meeting on April 21, 1788, and approved the Constitution on April 28 by a vote of 63 to 11, the seventh state to do so.

The primary opponents were Samuel Chase (who would later serve as a U.S. Supreme Court justice) and William Paca. The support of the latter was secured when Federalists allowed him to present a list of proposed amendments to a special committee at the ratifying convention. Maryland's vote undoubtedly had a positive effect on the ratification in nearby Virginia, where the issue was more closely contested. Although the option was discussed, Maryland did not follow the precedent set by Massachusetts and followed by a number of subsequent states of proposing a number of recommendatory amendments to accompany its ratification.

See Also Carroll, Daniel; Martin, Luther; McHenry, James; Mercer, John; Jenifer, Daniel, of St. Thomas

FOR FURTHER READING

Crowl, Philip A. 1947. "Anti-Federalism in Maryland, 1787–1788." *William and Mary Quarterly,* 3rd ser. 4 (October): 446–469.

Onuf, Peter S. 1989. "Maryland: The Small Republic in the New Nation." In Michael Allen Gillespie and Michael Lienesch, eds. *Ratifying the Constitution.* Lawrence: University Press of Kansas.

Stiverson, Gergory. 1988. "Necessity, the Mother of Union: Maryland and the Constitution, 1785–1789." In Patrick T. Conley and John P. Kaminski, eds. *The Constitution and the States: The Role of the Original Thirteen in the Framing and Adoption of the Federal Constitution.* Madison, WI: Madison House.

MASON, GEORGE (1725–1792)

A Virginia planter, George Mason was born in 1725 to George Mason III and Ann Thomas Mason, a fourth-generation Virginian who amassed a plantation of over 5,000 acres and 300 slaves. George's father died in 1735. George, who was educated by private tutors, was strongly influenced both by his mother and by an uncle, John Mercer of Marborough, an attorney with an impressive library. Although he was a planter rather than an attorney, Mason was chosen as a justice of the Fairfax County Count in 1749, was soon after elected a vestryman, and married Ann Eilbeck, from across the Potomac in Maryland. The couple worked on Gunston Hall, an impressive plantation in Virginia that is now open to the public, from 1744 to 1758. Ann died in 1773, leaving her husband with nine children; he married Sarah Brent in 1780.

Mason served in the Virginia House of Burgesses from 1758 to 1761. However, Mason appeared to accept public office more from a sense of public duty than from a feeling of personal enjoyment. Gout frequently served as a rationale for dodging such service and seems to have endowed Mason with a somewhat dyspeptic personality. Mason participated little in public affairs in the 1760s and early 1770s, but he did help draft the Fairfax Resolves in July of 1774. He was subsequently elected to the Virginia convention where he was the chief author of the Virginia Declaration of Rights. In 1777 he was appointed to a commission charged with rewriting the laws of Virginia. In 1785 he participated in the Mount Vernon Conference which served as one of the stepping-stones to the Constitutional Convention (Bradford 1994, 148–156), but the governor apparently did not notify him in time of his selection to the Annapolis Convention for him to attend. Mason's trip of approximately 120 miles to

George Mason, delegate from Virginia
(Pixel That)

Philadelphia to attend the Constitutional Convention was the longest that he made during his life.

Mason's Failure to Sign the Constitution

George Mason was one of only three delegates who attended the Constitutional Convention from start to finish and yet still refused to sign the document. The facts that Mason attended the entire session and that he began on a hopeful note indicate that he probably did not anticipate being one of three dissenters. Thus, writing to his son on June 1, Mason observed:

> I have the pleasure to find in the convention, many men of fine republican principles. America has certainly, upon this occasion, drawn forth her first characters; there are upon this Convention many gentlemen of the most respectable abilities, and so far as I can discover, of the purest intentions. (Farrand 1937, III, 32)

Given such a hopeful start and a dramatic declaration more than a month into Convention deliberations that "he would bury his bones in this city rather than expose his Country to the Consequences of a dissolution of the Convention without any thing being done" (I, 533), it seems almost tragic that Mason did not sign the Constitution. As late as August 10, Mason had indicated that "He thought the Constitution as now moulded was founded on sound principles, and was disposed to put into it extensive powers" (II, 252). Twenty-one days later, however, he declared "that he would sooner chop off his right hand than put it to the Constitution as it now stands" (II, 479), and he indicted that if the document were not amended, he would favor calling yet another convention.

Although he began the Convention with hope, he left fearing that the Constitution created there would embody aristocracy and/or lead to anarchy. He was also concerned about the omission of a bill of rights and subsequently went on to oppose the Convention in his home state, beginning a rift with his longtime neighbor and friend, George Washington. The fact that Mason remained at the Convention rather than leaving early, however, undoubtedly contributed to changes that made the document more palatable to Antifederalists than it would otherwise have been.

Convention Rules

Mason was present for the first day of Convention proceedings on May 25. On the next day of Convention business, May 28, Mason went on record, seconding a motion by Rufus King of Massachusetts, as opposing recording Convention votes under individual names. He had two reasons—first, he feared that this would make it more difficult for delegates to change their mind, and second, he feared that a record of such votes might later "furnish handles to the adversaries of the Result of the Meeting" (I, 10). The latter argument clearly reveals that Mason hoped to be able to support the Convention's work.

The Necessity for a New Government

As a Virginian, it is likely that Mason knew about, and may have had a part in shaping, the Virginia Plan, which Edmund Randolph introduced on May 29 and which scholars generally attribute to James Madison. On May 30, Mason indicated that he believed the Articles of Confederation to be deficient in being unable to act against "delinquent States." Like Madison, he believed the solution was to grant a new government power to act directly upon individuals (I, 34). On July 18, Mason supported the congressional guarantee of republican government in the states by observing that "If the Genl Govt. should have no right to suppress rebellions agst. particular States, it will be in a bad situation indeed. As Rebellions agst. itself originate in & agst. individual States, it must remain a passive Spectator of its own subversion" (II, 47).

On June 20, Mason compared the Virginia and New Jersey Plans and came down strongly in favor of the former. Indicating that both plans called for increasing the power of Congress, Mason did not think it likely that the people would entrust such powers to a unicameral body. He believed the people were attached both to the principle of republicanism and to bicameralism (I, 339). He further observed that the New Jersey Plan might require military coercion, whereas the Virginia Plan would give Congress power to act on individual citizens. Mason's voice may have had a particular effect, as he favored the Virginia Plan as a way of preserving, rather than of abolishing, state government: "He never would agree to abolish the State Govts. or render them absolutely insignificant. They were as necessary as the Genl. Govt. and he would be equally careful to preserve them. He was aware of the difficulty of drawing the line between them, but hoped it was not insurmountable" (I, 340).

Congress

Mason favored the election of members of the House of Representatives by the people—even to the extent of discounting slaves in the apportionment of state representation (I, 581). As one who would later express reservations about the Senate, it is telling that Mason referred on May 31 to the House as "the grand depository of the democratic principle of the Govt.," as "our House of Commons" (I, 48). Admitting that "we had been too democratic," he seemed more concerned that "we sd. incautiously run into the opposite extreme" (I, 49). He portrayed the House as a body that would represent "the rights of every class of people" (I, 49). Noting that the posterity of the rich would someday be scattered among the lower classes, he argued that "every selfish motive therefore, every family attachment, ought to recommend such a system of policy as would provide no less carefully for the rights—and happiness of the lowest than of the highest orders of Citizens" (I, 49). Mason repeated this view on June 21 (I, 359). On July 10, he indicated that he favored a House of more than 65 members both so that its members would have "all the necessary information relative to various local interests" and so that they would "possess the necessary confidence of the people" (I, 569).

Mason favored biennial elections for the House of Representatives, but the reason he gave for biennial as opposed to annual elections was quite practical. He believed that annual elections would advantage the Middle states, which would be more likely to be able to get and keep their representatives in a centrally located capital (I, 362). Mason favored a minimum age of 25 for members of the House, arguing that individuals of 21 years who were old enough to vote were not yet mature enough to make laws (I, 375). Mason was among the delegates who favored disqualifying members of Congress for other offices for a year after they left Congress. Indeed, he referred to this mechanism, designed to prevent corruption, as "a corner stone in the fabric" (I, 376). Mason thought that Madison's emoluments clause—limiting ineligibility only to offices created during a legislator's tenure—was "but a partial remedy for the evil" (I, 387). Mason also believed that the Constitution should specify that Congress must meet at least once a year, and he anticipated that it would have "inquisitorial" as well as lawmaking powers (II, 199).

Although he conceived of Congress, especially the House, as a mirror of the people, Mason was concerned about demagoguery. He accordingly proposed on July 26 that members of Congress should have to own a certain amount of landed property. He was particularly concerned that individuals with "unsettled accounts" would use their congressional offices to advance their own personal interests (II, 121). Similarly, Mason did not believe that the House should have a veto on treaties (II, 197).

Mason, who favored a six-year term, appears to have believed that the Senate would represent a different class of people than the House of Representatives. He accordingly favored property qualification for senators (I, 428). Although Mason favored a large House, he opposed a motion providing for three senators from each state both as too expensive and as creating a body that was too numerous (II, 94). Mason believed that under the new system, "the Senate did not represent the *people,* but the *States* in their political character" (II, 273). It was thus appropriate that "the purses-trings should be in the hands of the Representatives of the people" (II, 274). Mason seemed consistent in his fear of the Senate, reinforcing his view that it should not have the power to originate money bills by observing in an almost paranoid tone that it "could already sell the whole Country by means of Treaties" (II, 297).

Mason was a member of the five-person committee appointed on July 2 to bridge the gap between the large states and the small states on representation in Congress. On July 5, Mason expressed his willingness to accept the Great Compromise providing for states to be represented by population in the U.S. House of Representatives and equally in the U.S. Senate. On the next day, he indicated that "He was a friend to proportional representation in both branches; but supposed that some points must be yielded for the sake of accommodation" (I, 544). Mason favored that part of the Connecticut Compromise limiting the origination of money bills to the House of Representatives. His reasoning showed a continuing suspicion of the Senate. He argued that, should senators "have the power of giving away the peoples money, they might soon forget the Source from whence they received it. We might soon have an aristocracy" (I, 544; also see II, 233). On August 9, Mason said that he would withdraw his support for the Connecticut Compromise unless it continued to exclude the Senate from the origination of money bills (II, 234).

Some members of the Convention were willing to allow the House of Representatives to decide how and when to apportion itself, but Mason thought it was essential to provide a fixed rule. His observations indicate that he was among those who feared that individuals would generally be unwilling to part with power: "From the nature of man we may be sure, that those who have power in their hands will not give it up while they can retain it. On the Contrary we know they will always when they can rather increase it" (I, 578).

Like many other Southerners, Mason anticipated that the South would grow more quickly than other parts of the nation, and he feared that, without mandatory reapportionment, the North would hold on to its power. Reminding fellow delegates of opposition in some Eastern states to admitting Western states on an equality with those in the East (a principle that Mason, and most other Southern delegates who spoke at the Convention on the subject, thought to be essential), Mason tied the interests of the South and West together (I, 578–579). Indeed, on July 11, Mason announced that he could not vote for the Constitution unless it provided for continuing adjustments to representation in the House (I, 578).

Mason favored a seven-year (rather than a three-year) residency for members of the House of Representatives. He observed that he "was for opening a wide door for emigrants; but did not chuse to let foreigners and adventurers make laws for us & govern us" (II, 216). Similarly, Mason favored a residency requirement for members of the Senate, especially in light of its relatively few members (II, 218). Were it not for the contributions that foreigners had made during the Revolution, Mason indicated that he would have favored a qualification of native birth for members of the Senate (II, 235; also see II, 271).

Mason thought that it was essential that it take at least a majority of Congress to constitute a quorum. He was especially concerned that states at the periphery of the nation might find that their interests were ignored if members of the central states could vote for measures by less than such a majority (II, 251–252). In such a case, the nation might be "governed by a Juncto" (II, 252). Mason favored a provision requiring a two-thirds vote of Congress to expel a member (II, 254), and he thought it essential for Congress to publish its proceedings (II, 260). Mason unsuccessfully pushed for a requirement, favored mostly by fellow Southerners, prohibiting Congress from enacting navigation acts prior to 1808 without the consent of two-thirds majorities (II, 631). Mason was a member of the Committee on Commercial Discrimination which was appointed on August 25 and which proposed that Congress should not have power to favor one port over another.

Because he did not believe it was possible to foresee all contingencies, Mason was willing to allow the Congress to have the power to emit, or issue, paper money (II, 309). He did not believe the nation could have won the Revolutionary War without such power. Mason objected to providing that Congress "shall" pay the debts as being too strong and possibly impossible to honor (II, 412–413). He served on the Committee on State Debts and Militia which the Convention appointed on August 18 and which recommended that Congress would have the power to assume state debts without being obligated to do so. Mason opposed the contracts clause on the basis that its wording was too restrictive (II, 440).

Mason was among those who favored allowing Congress, rather than the president, to appoint the secretary of the Treasury: "if [the money belonged to the] people, the legislature representing the people ought to appoint the keepers of it" (II, 315). Mason also supported the provision entrusting Congress with the power to "declare" rather than to "make" war (II, 319).

Mason feared large standing peace-time armies. Believing that the states "will never concur in any one system, if the disciplining of the Militia be left in their hands," he favored granting this power to Congress (II, 326), while allowing the states to appoint officers for the militia (II, 330). He did not think it would be prudent to prevent the government from ever diverting funds from

public creditors to other purposes, but thought that it might be wise to put a limit on the time for which individual taxes were levied" (II, 327). Mason twice pushed unsuccessfully for the congressional power to enact sumptuary laws, believing that "No Government can be maintained unless the manners be made consonant to it" (II, 344; also see II, 606).

Mason favored strict construction of congressional powers. When James Wilson observed that Congress would have the power to create "mercantile monopolies" as part of its power to regulate commerce, Mason not only expressed opposition to such monopolies but also indicated that he did not think Congress would have the power to create them (II, 616).

Nation's Capital

Consistent with his fear of aristocratic tendencies, Mason was quite concerned that members of Congress might develop interests separate from those of their constituents. He accordingly moved that the nation's capital should not be located in the capital of an existing state. He believed this would result in disputes over jurisdiction between the two governments and lend "a provincial tincture to ye Natl. deliberations" (II, 127). Perhaps Mason also hoped that a new capital might be located, as it eventually was, on the Potomac River, near his home.

Executive Powers

Like many other proponents of the Virginia Plan, Mason initially favored a seven-year executive term, with the executive being ineligible so as not to lead to possible intrigue with the legislative branch (I, 68). He expressed similar concerns about providing a way of making the president accountable without making him overly dependent on the legislature—"a violation of the fundamental principle of good Government" (I, 86).

Although he professed on June 1 to favor the proposal by Pennsylvania's James Wilson for direct election of the president, he thought it was impractical (I, 69). On July 17, Mason argued that "it would be as unnatural to refer the choice of a proper character for chief Magistrate to the people, as it would, to refer a trail of colours to a blind man" (II, 31). Mason did not denigrate the capacities of the common people, however, but rather their knowledge of individuals who would seek the presidential office. As he explained, "The extent of the Country renders it impossible that the people can have the requisite capacity to judge of the respective pretensions of the Candidates" (II, 31). Mason also shared Elbridge Gerry's fear that popular election "would throw the appointment into the hands of the Cincinnati, a Society for the members of which he had a great respect; but which he never wished to have a preponderating influence in the Govt." (II, 119).

At a time when Congress was slated to elect the president for six-year terms, Mason supported a resolution that would allow the president to serve only six of every 12 years (II, 112). He believed this would prevent executive/legislative intrigue when sitting presidents were seeking reappointment. He also thought it was essential that "the great officers of State, and particularly the Executive should at fixed periods return to that mass from which they were at first taken, in order that they may feel & respect those right & interests [of the people]" (II, 119–120). He later supported a single seven-year term (II, 120).

Perhaps with a view to the colonial experience under Britain's King George III, Mason was suspicious of executive power. On June 4, he expressed concern over the possibility that the Convention would create an "elective" monarchy (I, 101). Opposing an absolute executive veto of congressional legislation, he observed that it would be better "to enable the Executive to suspend offensive laws, till they shall be coolly revised, and the objections to them overruled by a greater majority than was required in the first instance" (I, 102). On July 17, Mason opposed a motion for presidents to serve "during good behavior." He argued that this "was a softer name only for an Executive for life" and "that the next would be an easy step to hereditary Monarchy" (II, 35). Mason favored a mechanism for impeachment as an assurance that no one, including the president, would be above

the law (II, 65). He appears to have been responsible for substituting the words "other high crimes & misdemeanors" for "maladministration" (II, 550). Mason added the words "giving them aid and comfort" to the definition of treason (II, 349), and he also favored allowing Congress to override presidential vetoes by two-thirds rather than by three-fourths majorities (II, 586).

Mason, who had apparently missed the vote settling on a single executive (see I, 101), was particularly hesitant to give broad powers to a single individual. He later advocated an "Executive in three persons" [although this may be merely coincidental, the formula sounds much like those used to describe the Christian view of the Trinity] (I, 111), with one representing each of the three major regions–North, Middle, and South–of the nation (I, 113). Acknowledging that a single executive was known for "the secrecy, the dispatch, the vigor and energy which the government will derive from it," he attributed such praise to "monarchical writers" and suggested that advocates of republican government relied instead on "the love, the affection, the attachment of the citizens to their laws, to their freedom, and to their country" (I, 112).

Fellow delegate James Madison had favored a Council of Revision blending the executive and the judiciary. Mason appears to have favored this council as opposed to one combining the president and members of his cabinet. One reason that Mason advanced for a plural presidency was to give it greater weight in such a body (I, 111–112). He emphasized the need to keep the power of the purse and the power of the sword in separate hands (I, 139–140). He thought that allying members of the judiciary with the executive would "give a confidence to the Executive, which he would not otherwise have, and without which the Revisionary power would be of little avail" (II, 74). He further thought that combining the executive and judicial powers would "discourage demagogues" from attempting to pass unjust legislation (II, 78). He saw nothing inappropriate about allowing judges to review the justice, as well as the constitutionality, of legislation (II, 78).

When the Convention devised the Electoral College, Mason observed that it had helped remove "the danger of cabal and corruption." However, he feared an early version of the plan on the basis that 19 out of twenty times, it would leave presidential selection in the Senate, which he considered "an improper body for the purpose" (II, 500; also see II, 512). On September 5, Mason observed that "He would prefer the Government of Prussia to one which will put all power into the hands of seven or eight men, and fix an Aristocracy worse than absolute monarchy" (II, 515). Mason seems to have been one of the delegates who helped persuade fellow delegates to move the power of selection from the Senate to the House of Representatives (II, 527).

Mason was not pleased with the institution of the vice presidency. He indicated that he thought that it was "an encroachment on the rights of the Senate; and that it mixed too much the Legislative & Executive, which as well as the Judiciary departments, ought to be kept as separate as possible" (II, 537). He suggested establishing a Privy Council as a substitute. Like the plural presidency he had suggested earlier, the council would have representatives from each of the three major sections of the United States (two from each). One reason he favored such a council was his belief that it "would prevent the constant sitting of the Senate which he thought dangerous, as well as keep the departments separate & distinct" (II, 537; also see II, 541–542).

Judiciary

In discussing the presidential nomination of judges, Mason argued that the mode of judicial selection should depend in part on the impeachment mechanism. He did not think it would be appropriate for the president to select judges if they in turn would sit in judgment on his impeachment. He also feared that executives would favor individuals from their own state (II, 42). Mason continued to oppose executive appointments of judges (presumably favoring appointment by Congress) even after this power was tempered by a power of confirmation in the Senate (II, 83). His opposition may have stemmed from his continuing concerns about the aristocratic nature of this body.

Mason anticipated, and apparently favored, the exercise of judicial review—the power of courts to declare laws to be unconstitutional. Indeed, he was willing to give the judges even greater powers. In defending a Council of Revision, which would ally the judges with the executive, he observed:

They could declare an unconstitutional law void. But with regard to every law however unjust oppressive or pernicious, which did not come plainly under this description, they would be under the necessity as Judges to give it a free course. He wished the further use to be made of the Judges, of giving aid in preventing every improper law. Their aid will be the more valuable as they are in the habit and practice of considering laws in their true principles, and in all their consequences. (II, 78)

Mason was on record as believing that it would be necessary to have a system of lower federal courts, rather than simply relying on state courts that were in place (II, 46). Mason may have changed his mind on this point, or he may have opposed the subsequent delineation of federal judicial jurisdiction. In either event, at the end of the Convention he charged that "the Judiciary of the United States is so constructed and extended, as to absorb and destroy the judiciaries of the several states; thereby rendering law as tedious, intricate and expensive, and justice as unattainable, by a great part of the community, as in England, and enabling the rich to oppress and ruin the poor" (II, 638).

States' Rights

Although he thought the national government under the Articles of Confederation was deficient, Mason favored states' rights. On June 7, he spoke out in favor of state legislative selection of senators. He observed that

whatever power may be necessary for the Natl. Govt. a certain portion must necessarily be left in the States. It is impossible for one power to pervade the extreme parts of the U.S. so as to carry equal justice to them. The State Legislatures also ought to have some means of defending themselves agst encroachment of the Natl. Govt. (I, 155)

Similarly, on August 20, in supporting a provision allowing punishment for treason against individual states, Mason observed that "the United States will have a qualified sovereignty only. The individual States will retain a part of the Sovereignty" (II, 347). Mason derisively referred on August 21 to those who favored "reducing the States to mere corporations," and opposed congressional taxation of exports on the basis that it might allow a majority of states to oppress the minority (II, 362–363). Mason had reservations about granting Congress power to void state legislation. Thus, on August 23, he questioned: "Are all laws whatever to be brought up? Is no road nor bridge to be established without the Sanction of the General Legislature? Is this to sit constantly in order to receive & revise State Laws?" (II, 390).

Although he was outvoted on both issues, Mason thought that states should have the right to declare embargoes and to level export taxes (II, 440–441). Mason's support for two-thirds majorities in Congress to regulate commerce stemmed from his fear, undoubtedly stimulated by the Jay-Gardoqui negotiations over rights to navigate the Mississippi River, that Congress could work against certain regional interests:

If the Govt. is to be lasting, it must be founded in the confidence & affections of the people, and must be so constructed as to obtain these. The *Majority* will be governed by their interests. The Southern States are the *minority* in both Houses. Is it to be expected that they will deliver themselves bound hand & foot to the Eastern States, and enable them to exclaim, in the words of Cromwell on a certain occasion—"the lord hath delivered them into our hands." (II, 451)

On June 12, however, Mason supported Madison's motion that members of Congress be paid out of the national treasury. He observed that otherwise different states would provide for different salaries, and some might be so parsimonious

as to leave the office open not to those "who were most fit to be chosen, but who were most willing to serve" (I, 216).

Mason opposed limiting voting to freeholders on the basis that some states had already gone farther than that. He thought that "A power to alter the qualifications would be a dangerous power in the hands of the Legislature" (II, 202). Although he favored property qualifications for running for certain offices, Mason argued that "every person of full age and who can give evidence of a common Interest with the community shd. be an Elector" (II, 207).

The Need to Provide for Future Constitutional Amendments

When some members questioned the need for a constitutional amending process, Mason observed both that such a process was needed and that it would be wise to provide a means of amending the Constitution in cases when the legislature did not assent:

The plan now to be formed will certainly be defective, as the Confederation has been found on trial to be. Amendments therefore will be necessary, and it will be better to provide for them in an easy, regular and Constitutional way than to trust to chance and violence. It would be improper to require the consent of the Natl. Legislature, because they may abuse their power, and refuse their consent on that very account. (I, 203)

Two days before the Constitution was signed, Mason was influential in providing for the still-unused mechanism whereby two-thirds of the states can petition Congress to call a Constitutional Convention. This proposal stemmed from Mason's fear that Congress might otherwise fail to propose such amendments on its own:

As the proposing of amendments is in both the modes to depend, in the first immediately, and in the second, ultimately, on Congress, no amendments of the proper kind would ever be obtained by the people, if the Government should become oppressive, as he verily believed would be the case. (II, 629)

Slavery

Mason owned many slaves, but he had a strong moralistic streak. It was perhaps most evident in a speech of August 22. Although Mason's speech reflected racist assumptions of the superiority of white settlers over blacks, no one at the Convention but Gouverneur Morris offered a more extensive criticism of slavery:

> Slavery discourages arts & manufactures. The poor despise labor when performed by slaves. They prevent the immigration of Whites, who really enrich & strengthen a Country. They produce the most pernicious effect on manners. Every master of slaves is born a petty tyrant. They bring the judgment of heaven on a Country. As nations can not be rewarded or punished in the next world they must be in this. By an inevitable chain of causes & effects providence punishes national sins, by national calamities. (II, 370)

Tragically, although he influenced the decision to allow minimal taxation of them (II, 417), Mason did not succeed in efforts to ban the continuing importation of slaves. Although it favored the interests of the Southern states, Mason also opposed the three-fifths compromise as "unjust" (I, 581).

Bill of Rights

Mason, the primary author of the Virginia Declaration of Rights, is probably best known at the Constitutional Convention for his support of a bill of rights. There is some irony in this since, as observed above, Mason was often fearful of constitutional provisions, like the ex post facto clause and a ban on standing armies in peacetime, that seemed too restrictive. Moreover, Mason actually offered his proposal for a bill of rights *in opposition to* a provision suggested by North Carolina's Hugh

Williamson and Elbridge Gerry of Massachusetts to provide for trial by jury in civil cases. Mason appears to have favored an earlier kind of bill of rights announcing general principles phrased as "oughts" that would not necessarily be enforceable, as are current provisions, in courts of law. In supporting Nathaniel Gorham's (MA) statement responding to Williamson and Gerry's proposal for trial by jury that "It is not possible to discriminate equity cases from those in which juries are proper" (II, 587), Mason thus observed that

> a general principle laid down on this and some other points would be sufficient. He wished the plan had been prefaced with a Bill of Rights, & would second a Motion if made for the purpose—It would give great quiet to the people; and with the aid of the State declarations, a bill might be prepared in a few hours. (II, 588)

When Connecticut's Roger Sherman observed that the new Constitution would not repeal state bills, Mason argued that "the Laws of the U.S. are to be paramount to State Bills of Rights" (II, 588). Absent a showing of areas where the new Constitution would restrict rights beyond those that the states were already offering, this response does not appear altogether responsive to Sherman's observation.

Mason cast further light on what his proposed bill of rights might have looked like on September 14. Noting that he did not believe it would be possible absolutely to prohibit standing armies in time of peace, he nonetheless moved to add words before the section giving Congress power to organize, arm, and discipline the militia: "And that the liberties of the people may be better secured against the danger of standing armies in time of peace" (II, 617). Similarly, he renewed his plea to strike the clause prohibiting ex post facto laws on the basis that it "was not sufficiently clear that the prohibition meant by this phrase was limited to cases of a criminal nature—and no Legislature ever did or can altogether avoid them in Civil cases" (II, 617). This suggests again that Mason preferred a bill of rights with fairly general declarations that the people could cherish rather than with precisely worded provisions that courts could enforce.

Still, Mason later praised the Bill of Rights that James Madison introduced in Congress. Mason observed that "I have received much Satisfaction from the Amendments to the federal Constitution, which have lately passed the House of Representatives" (quoted in Senese 1989, 80). Perhaps he never saw anything as quite perfect, since, after observing that he hoped the Senate would adopt the rights, he added "With two or three further Amendments . . . I cou'd cheerfully put my Hand & Heart to the new Government" (80).

Ratification of the Constitution

Even before he seems to have decided to oppose the document, Mason thought that it was essential for the people to ratify the document through conventions rather than by existing state legislatures. He thought that legislators did not have sufficient authority to do so, and he feared that if legislatures were allowed to ratify, then they would also claim the power to dissolve (II, 88). Mason believed the new Constitution should go into effect when ratified by nine or more states (II, 477).

In expressing his reservations about signing the Constitution, Mason advocated yet another convention. Without such a further meeting, he could not sign:

Mason . . . followed Mr. Randolph in animadversions on the dangerous power and structure of the Government, concluding that it would either end in monarchy, or a tyrannical aristocracy; which, he was in doubt, but one or other, he was sure. This Constitution had been formed without the knowledge or idea of the people. A second Convention will know more of the sense of the people, and be able to provide a system more consonant to it. It was improper to say to the people, take this or nothing. As the Constitution now stands, he could neither give it his support or vote in Virginia; and he could not sign here what he could not support there. With the expe-

dient of another Convention as proposed, he could sign. (II, 632)

Mason expressed his objections to the new Constitution to his colleagues and later circulated his observations in pamphlet form. His objections included many familiar themes and some new ones. These consisted of the Constitution's lack of a declaration of rights; its failure to secure the protection of the common law; concern that the House of Representatives was not large enough to provide adequate representation; fear of the Senate's power to alter money bills; apprehension of the powers vested in the Senate; fear that the federal judiciary would swallow that of the states; concern about the failure to have a constitutional council; concern over the office of the vice presidency; concern over the president's unrestricted power to grant pardons for treason; fear that declaring treaties to be the supreme law of the land gave too much power to the Senate; apprehension that Congress would abuse its power to enact navigation acts without supermajorities; fear of monopolies in trade and commerce; concern over the absence of provisions providing for freedom of the press, trials in civil cases, and opposing standing armies in peacetime; concern over stripping states from taxing exports; opposition to the ex post facto clause; fear that the new government had created an aristocracy that could lead to tyranny; and displeasure over the failure to prohibit slave importation (II, 637–640).

Mason, who had been chosen from a neighboring county, and Patrick Henry were the leading opponents of the new Constitution at the Virginia ratifying convention. Mason warmed somewhat to the Constitution after the adoption of the Bill of Rights. Although he never healed the rift with his neighbor, George Washington, or accepted any public offices under the new government, he frequently entertained members of the new government as they passed through his neighborhood, and he established himself back in good graces with James Madison and Thomas Jefferson (Leibiger 1993, 467).

See Also Bill of Rights; Common Law;

Republicanism; Signing of the Constitution; Virginia; Virginia Declaration of Rights

FOR FURTHER READING

Bradford, M. M. 1994. *Founding Fathers: Brief Lives of the Framers of the United States Constitution.* 2nd ed. Lawrence: University Press of Kansas.

Conley, Patrick T., and John P. Kaminski, eds. 1992. *The Bill of Rights and the States: The Colonial and Revolutionary Origins of American Liberties.* Madison, WI: Madison House.

Farrand, Max, ed. 1937. *The Records of the Federal Convention.* 4 vols. New Haven, CT: Yale University Press.

Ganter, Herbert Lawrence. 1937. "The Machiavellianism of George Mason." *William and Mary College Quarterly Historical Magazine,* 3rd ser. 17 (April): 239–264. [Stresses the tie between Mason and classical republican thought.]

Leibiger, Stuart. 1993. "James Madison and Amendments to the Constitution, 1787–1789: 'Parchment Barriers.'" *Journal of Southern History* 59 (August): 441–468.

Lynch, Jack. 2004. "Mirroring the Mind of Mason." *Colonial Williamsburg* 26 (Spring): 52–55.

Rutland, Robert A. 1981. "George Mason: The Revolutionist as Conservative." In Robert A. Rossum and Gary L. McDowell, eds. *The American Founding: Politics, Statesmanship, and the Constitution.* Port Washington, NY: Kennikat Press.

Senese, Donald J., ed. 1989. *George Mason and the Legacy of Constitutional Liberty: An Examination of the Influence of George Mason on the American Bill of Rights.* Fairfax County, VA: Fairfax County Historical Commission.

MASONS

The Masons, or Freemasons, are a nondenominational fraternal organization. They promote brotherhood and morality and are committed to belief in the existence of God, but they do not otherwise dictate an individual's religious beliefs (Eidsmoe 1987, 45). Historian Gordon Wood has described freemasonry as "a surrogate religion for an Enlightenment suspicious of traditional Chris-

Washington as a Freemason. Strobridge & Gerlach Lithographers, ca. 1866. (Library of Congress)

tianity" (1992, 223). He observes that "it offered ritual, mystery, and congregativeness without the enthusiasm and sectarian bigotry of organized religion." He further observes that freemasonry was both "enlightened" and "republican" (223). Masons are featured in the movie *National Treasure,* an action-packed account tying them and the Knights Templar to a fictional treasure, the clues to which are found in invisible ink on the back of the Declaration of Independence.

Because Masonic membership is more private than public, there is no way to know with complete certainty how many of the delegates to the Constitutional Convention were Masons, but a number are known to have been so. Most prominent were George Washington and Benjamin Franklin, with the latter (one of the Convention's quintessential "joiners") having been initiated at the age of 25.

Roger Sherman of Connecticut and John Langdon of New Hampshire may have been Masons, but the evidence for either is not conclusive.

Other delegates who are known to have been members include Rufus King of Massachusetts; David Brearly, Jonathan Dayton, and William Paterson of New Jersey; Jacob Broom and Gunning Bedford of Delaware; Daniel Carroll of Maryland; and John Blair of Virginia. The Masons inducted James McHenry of Maryland in 1806.

Masons played prominent roles in the laying of the cornerstone of the U.S. Capitol on September 18, 1793 and appear to have influenced the iconography of the Great Seal of the United States. The Rising Sun Chair on which Washington sat during the Constitutional Convention may also have embodied Masonic symbolism. In the 1820s and 1830s an Anti-Mason Party was formed. It was concerned, as earlier opponents of the Society of the Cincinnati had been, about the secret nature of the organization and its feared aristocratic influence. The Anti-Mason Party was the first to invent the national nominating mechanism for presidential candidates.

The Masons have printed colorful books detailing the lives of all the signers of the Declaration of Independence and the U.S. Constitution.

See Also Delegates, Collective Profile; Rising Sun Chair; Society of the Cincinnati

FOR FURTHER READING

Eidsmoe, John. 1987. *Christianity and the Constitution: The Faith of the Founding Fathers*. Grand Rapids, MI: Baker Book House.

Hieronimus, Robert. 1989. *America's Secret Destiny: Spiritual Vision and the Founding of a Nation*. Rochester, VT: Destiny Books. [This volume has a lot of speculation about Founding Fathers and secret societies that is difficult to verify, but its treatment of the Masons, 17–18 and 23ff., is useful.]

The Sesquicentennial of the Constitution of the United States of America and Inauguration of George Washington First President 1787–1939: A Masonic Tribute. N.p., n.d.

Walker, Wendell K. 1976. "Foreword." The Masonic Book Club Edition of *The Signers of the Constitution of the United States*. Bloomington, IL: Masonic Book Club.

Wood, Gordon S. 1992. *The Radicalism of the American Revolution*. New York: Alfred A. Knopf.

MASSACHUSETTS

The current state of Massachusetts began as a royal colony. The Crown appointed its governor, who was advised by a Council of 28, which served as the upper house of the bicameral legislature. Massachusetts, the site of the Boston Tea Party, the Boston Massacre, and the initial battles of Lexington and Concord, was one of the colonies in which conflict developed relatively early with English authorities. It provided such key leaders in the movement for revolution as James Otis and John and Samuel Adams.

As this conflict developed, members of the lower house and delegates from county conventions formed a series of three provincial congresses that governed the state. The state legislature, known as the General Court, constituted itself into a constitutional convention, but in a move that set the standard for the adoption of future state constitutions in the United States, the voters overwhelmingly rejected the document, believing that a special constitutional convention called for this purpose should have this responsibility. The General Court then called a convention that met in Cambridge in September 1779. It appointed a committee of 30 to draft a document. This committee in turn appointed a three-man committee composed of Governor James Bowdoin and John and Samuel Adams. John Adams did most of the work. The convention then submitted the document to the towns who were supposed to approve by a two-thirds vote. After considerable confusion, due largely to reservations that individual towns tried to make, the General Court decided that the required popular majorities had ratified the constitution.

The constitution of Massachusetts is the oldest such document in continuing existence, and it contained a number of features that found their way into the Constitution of the U.S. As in the latter, the constitution divided the legislative branch into two houses, designated as a House of Representatives and a Senate. Male property owners selected members of both branches annually. The governor was also elected annually but was otherwise relatively strong. In addition to serving as commander-in-chief of the militia, the governor

Engraving of Harvard Yard at Harvard University, Cambridge, Massachusetts, ca. 1780 (Kean Collection/Getty Images)

had power to issue pardons with the council's consent and could veto acts of the legislature subject to override by a two-thirds majority in both houses. Nine senators sat as a council that advised the governor and that consented to his appointment of members of the judicial branch. The legislature chose most other officers. The constitution contained a declaration of rights consisting of 30 articles. The constitution specifically acknowledged the principle of separation of powers and proclaimed its intention, in a phrase borrowed from England's political philosopher, James Harrington (1611–1677), to have a "government of laws and not of men" (Kaminski and Saladino 1997, xxvii; also see *We the People* 1995, 49–50).

Massachusetts Politics

Massachusetts had a relatively large debt left over from the Revolutionary War, and the state's attempt to collect this debt at a time when specie was scarce was the primary catalyst for Shays's Rebellion, which alarmed so many opinion leaders in the former colonies. Although Massachusetts crushed the rebellion, it resulted in the subsequent replacement of conservative governor James Bowdoin by the more democratically inclined John Hancock. The rebellion highlighted continuing tensions between Boston and areas on the coast, where sentiments for rebellion against Britain had been strong, and the central region of the state, which had previously inclined toward the Tories rather than the Patriots. A student of the subject credits Shays's Rebellion both with releasing "leveling tendencies" that alarmed even the old revolutionaries and with discrediting the conservatives who had suffered at the polls (Gillespie 1989, 144).

Massachusetts and the Articles of Confederation

Massachusetts had agreed to join the Articles of Confederation in July 1778, after having unsuccessfully pushed for adoption of a number of amendments. On a number of occasions, including participation in a meeting of New England states in Hartford, Connecticut in November 1780 (not to be confused with a later meeting that discussed possible disunion during the War of 1812), the state had supported increased congressional powers. Massachusetts had favored a proposal made in February 1781 that would have enabled Congress to enact a tariff, and it supported proposals for an impost in 1783. Not only had Massachusetts supported a proposal granting Congress the power to close down trade with countries that did not have a treaty with the United States, but state merchants had even agreed to impose a boycott on their own against those nations that were discriminating against trade from the U.S.

Representation and Mentions at the Convention

Elbridge Gerry, Nathaniel Gorham, Rufus King, and Caleb Strong ably represented Massachusetts at the Constitutional Convention. Gorham and King signed on the state's behalf. Strong left in late August because of an illness in the family. Gerry refused to sign and subsequently led Antifederalist opposition to the document in the state. A fifth delegate, Francis Dana, was prevented from attending the Convention because of sickness. The state was clearly in the Northern (Eastern) tier of states and, with the port of Boston, had a clear interest in mercantile concerns. Delegates referenced Shays's Rebellion a number of times during Convention deliberations.

When he introduced the Virginia Plan, Edmund Randolph cited one of the problems of the Articles as its inability to deal with quarrels between states or rebellions within them (Farrand 1937, I, 19). Virginia's James Madison twice mentioned Massachusetts in a speech of June 19. He first observed that the state had raised troops to put down Shays's Rebellion under the Articles (I, 316) and then noted that Shays's Rebellion had "admonished all the States of the danger to which they were exposed" (I, 318). Oliver Ellsworth of Connecticut cited Massachusetts as illustrating the principle that large states found it difficult to govern, noting that "Masts can not keep the peace one hundred miles from her capitol and is now forming an army for its support" (I, 406). Similarly, Gorham conceded on June 29 that Massachusetts was expecting Maine to form its own government (I, 462).

By contrast, Gouverneur Morris of Pennsylvania used Massachusetts and New York as examples of how the people in populous states found it difficult to rig elections (II, 30). Gorham cited the practice in Massachusetts as support for having the executive appoint judges with the advice and consent of the second branch (II, 41). He favorably cited the role that members of the clergy had played in forming and establishing the state's constitution (II, 90). He also referred to the state's negative experience with electing officials by joint ballot of the legislature (II, 196), and in allowing a single member to call for roll-call votes within the legislature (II, 255).

Ratification

When Governor Hancock transmitted the Constitution to the state legislature, it voted 120 to 32 to call a ratifying convention. This convention subsequently met from January 9 to February 7 of 1788, and it approved the Constitution by a vote of 187 to 168. Massachusetts was the sixth state to ratify the Constitution; the vote demonstrated that the contest in this state had been the closest to date.

There is general agreement that the key to ratification in Massachusetts was the role of Samuel Adams and John Hancock. Both played prominent roles in the Revolution, during which Hancock had placed his bold signature on the Declaration of Independence. Elbridge Gerry's opposition to the Constitution also played a part. In early December of 1787, Samuel Adams had indicated his initial concerns:

> I confess, as I enter the Building, I stumble at the Threshold. I meet with a National Government, instead of a Federal Union of Sovereign States. I am not able to conceive why the Wisdom of the Convention led them to give the Preference of the former before the latter. (Quoted in Gillespie 1989, 145)

Similarly, Hancock either was, or professed to be, ill during the opening days of the Convention, leaving doubt as to where he stood and leading opponents to believe that he was testing the political waters.

Although Federalists succeeded in electing more notable delegates than the Antifederalists, many accounts of the state's ratification attribute the support of Adams and Hancock to concerns about their own popularity. Some further claim that Federalists held out the prospect that Hancock, who prided himself on public adulation, might become the first president should Virginia not join the Union or should George Washington decline this position. Scholar Michael Gillespie has largely discounted these claims. He has shown that both Adams and Hancock were principled republicans who consistently worked toward the idea of approving a Constitution that they thought was necessary. At the same time, they supported a series of recommendatory amendments that would accompany this ratification (proposals that, with others, eventually resulted in the Bill of Rights) but not serve as a condition for it. Initially opposed by the Federalists, who were pursuing a more strident all-or-nothing approach, the strategy advanced by Adams and Hancock ultimately proved the key to ratifying the Constitution not only in Massachusetts but also in the rest of the country.

The better-educated and more articulate Federalists won most of the arguments at the Convention but sometimes alienated those to whom they were directed. In the end, delegates from the East voted overwhelmingly for the Constitution; those representing the central section from whence Shays's Rebellion had arisen and where there was still strong sentiment on behalf of paper money, voted against it; and Westerners opposed the Constitution, but by a smaller majority than would have been expected from the initial balloting for delegates. Hancock and Adams continued their leadership under the new Constitution. Adams succeeded Hancock as governor, and Elbridge Gerry, who had refused to sign the Constitution, was eventually elected to serve as vice president under James Madison.

See Also Adams, John; Gerry, Elbridge; Gorham, Nathaniel; King, Rufus; Massachusetts Constitution of 1780; Shays's Rebellion; Strong, Caleb

FOR FURTHER READING

Farrand, Max, ed. 1937. *The Records of the Federal Convention.* 4 vols. New Haven, CT: Yale University Press.

Gillespie, Michael Allen. 1989. "Massachusetts: Creating Consensus." In Michael Allen Gillespie and Michael Lienesch, eds. *Ratifying the Constitution.* Lawrence: University Press of Kansas.

Harding, Samuel B. 1896. *The Contest over the Ratification of the Federal Constitution in the State of Massachusetts.* New York: Longmans, Green, and Co.

Kaminski, John P., and Gaspare J. Saladino, eds. 1997. *Ratification of the Constitution by the States: Massachusetts.* Vol. 4 of *The Documentary History of the Ratification of the Constitution.* Madison: State Historical Society of Wisconsin.

Walker, Joseph B. 1888. *Birth of the Federal Constitution: A History of the New Hampshire Convention for the Investigation, Discussion, and Decision of the Federal Constitution and of the Old North Meeting-House of Concord, in Which It Was Ratified by the Ninth State, and Thus Rendered Operative . . . on . . . the 21st of June, 1788.* Boston: Cupples and Hurd, Publishers.

We the People: The Citizen and the Constitution. 1995. Calabasas, CA: Center for Civil Education.

MASSACHUSETTS BODY OF LIBERTIES

One of the precursors to the Massachusetts Constitution of 1780, the U.S. Constitution, and the Bill of Rights is the Massachusetts Body of Liberties of 1641. Written by onetime attorney Nathaniel Ward (1578?–1652), who would later return to England, the manuscript had 95 subdivisions. They combined principles from the Old Testament and from British common law (Frohnen 2002, 15).

The document contains many provisions that foreshadow those in later documents. The very first section, similar to modern due process clauses, protects persons against punishments except "by vertue or equitie of some expresse law of the Country warranting the same, established by a generall Court and sufficiently published" (Frohnen, 15). Section 42 contains a provision against double jeopardy.

Perhaps influenced by biblical injunctions regarding the treatment of strangers, the Body of Liberties is notable for providing security for foreign residents of Massachusetts as well as for citizens. Section 26 permits an individual to receive help from another in court, "Provided he give him noe fee, or reward for his paines" (Frohnen). Section 45 limits the use of torture to exact confessions in criminal cases. Section 80 prohibits a man from beating his wife, "unlesse it be in his owne defence upon her assault" (20). The document limited servitude to periods of seven years, after which masters were obligated not to send servants "away emptie" (21).

Old Testament prohibitions are most evident in Sections 92–94, which listed capital offenses. These include punishment for the following: idolatry, witchcraft, blasphemy, various forms of murder, bestiality, homosexual relations, adultery, kidnapping, false witness, and insurrection and rebellion (21).

See Also Bill of Rights; Common Law; Massachusetts Constitution of 1780; Puritanism

FOR FURTHER READING

Frohnen, Bruce, ed. 2002. *The American Republic: Primary Sources.* Indianapolis, IN: Liberty Fund.

MASSACHUSETTS CONSTITUTION OF 1780

One writer has ranked the Massachusetts Constitution of 1780 with the Declaration of Independence, the U.S. Constitution, the Bill of Rights, and *The Federalist,* as "one of the five most important documents of the revolutionary era" (Peters 1978, 13). The document was an exemplary expression of the doctrine that legitimate government was based on a social compact. Some of its most important underlying principles, as well as its specific constitutional mechanisms, were later incorporated into the U.S. Constitution.

Significantly, Massachusetts rejected a constitution that its legislature had penned in 1778. It did so in the belief, later reflected in the drafting and ratification of the U.S. Constitution, both that a body specifically designated for this task should

formulate such a constitution and that the people should subsequently ratify such a document. The Massachusetts constitutional convention convened in the fall of 1779 and the early months of 1780. Male voters 21 years and older subsequently ratified it.

Although 251 delegates were present during the opening sessions, other sessions had fewer members, and much of the convention's work was done in committees. Three men, convention president James Bowdoin and cousins John and Samuel Adams, did the first draft. John Adams was by far the most influential of the delegates. Largely at his insistence, the constitution referred to Massachusetts as a "commonwealth."

Although it has been frequently amended, this constitution, and the basic structure of government that it established, remain. It is thus the longest continuous written constitutional government in existence in the world today. The document is divided into chapters, sections, and articles for easy reference. It has three main divisions—a preamble that delineates the origin and purposes of government; a declaration of rights (partly modeled on those of Virginia and Pennsylvania), which contains many provisions that prefigure those in the U.S. Bill of Rights; and the frame, or organization, of government. This frame, like Articles I through III of the U.S. Constitution, respectively outlines the structures and powers of the legislative, executive, and judicial branches, which are designed to check and balance one another.

As in the case of the future U.S. Congress, the Massachusetts Constitution divided the legislature, known as the General Court, into two houses, called the Senate and House of Representatives. Each had a veto on the other. The executive consisted of a governor with the power of a veto. Two-thirds of both houses of the legislature could override his veto. The governor had a fixed salary, served as commander-in-chief of the state's militia and had the power to pardon. He also had the power to appoint judges who, while holding their offices during good behavior, could be removed by an address by the governor to a joint session of the legislature.

The Massachusetts Constitution drew on British documents for formulating provisions designed to protect civil liberties. Although it provided religious freedom for all those who did not "disturb the public peace or obstruct others in their religious worship," it also provided for the legislature to support "the institution of the public worship of God and for the support and maintenance of public Protestant teachers of piety, religion and morality in all cases where such provision shall not be made voluntarily" (Article III). Reflecting the important role that the institution had played in the state, the constitution also provided for the perpetuation of Harvard College and for encouraging "literature" and education.

See Also Adams, John; Constitutional Convention Mechanism; Massachusetts

FOR FURTHER READING

Bullock, Alexander H. 1881. *The Centennial of the Massachusetts Constitution.* Worcester, MA: Press of Charles Hamilton.

Constitution of Massachusetts. National Humanities Institute. http://www.nhinet.org/ccs/docs/ma-1780.htm.

Peters, Ronald M., Jr. 1978. *The Massachusetts Constitution of 1780: A Social Compact.* Amherst: University of Massachusetts Press.

Taylor, Robert J. 1980. "Construction of the Massachusetts Constitution." *Proceedings of the American Antiquarian Society* 90 (October): 317–340.

MAYFLOWER COMPACT

Like the English Magna Carta, the Mayflower Compact is often cited as one of the predecessors to the U.S. Constitution. Originally named the "Plymouth Combination," it apparently received its current name after 1793 (Lutz 1980, 106). The Compact is arguably the first constitution to be written in the New World. The Compact was written aboard the *Mayflower* in 1620 after Pilgrims from Holland (refugees from religious persecution in England) and other travelers arrived near Cape Cod. Far north of land that had been granted them by the Virginia Company and with no charter from the English king, this intrepid group of settlers decided to agree to be governed collectively before settling in the new land. William Bradford, the Pilgrim leader, was especially concerned that, without such an agreement, some settlers accompanying the Pilgrims were planning to "use their owne libertie" and to ignore the rules of the Pilgrims (Foner and Garraty 1991, 708).

Beginning with the words, "In ye name of God, Amen," the one-paragraph agreement did not outline specific institutions of government. It did, however, pledge the parties to "covenant & combine our selves together into a civill body politick, for our better ordering & preservation & furtherance of ye ends aforesaid" (Long 1926, 4). The colonists further pledged "to enacte, constitute, and frame such just and equall lawes, ordinances, acts, constitutions & offices, from time to time, as shall be thought most meete & convenient for ye generall good of ye Colonie, unto which we promise all due submission and obedience" (Long, 4). The 41 adult males who were present on ship signed the document on November 11, 1620. The best-known signatories were William Bradford and Myles Standish (Frohnen 2002, 11).

The Mayflower Compact appears to have remained in effect until 1686. Like the later Constitution, this document was an attempt to base government on the rule of law, agreed to by popular consent.

See Also Constitutionalism; Magna Carta; Protestantism

FOR FURTHER READING

Anastaplo, George. 2000/2001. "Constitutionalism, the Rule of Rules, Explorations." *Brandeis Law Journal* 39 (Fall): 17–217.

Foner, Eric, and John A. Garraty, eds. 1991. *The Reader's Companion to American History.* Boston: Houghton Mifflin Company.

Frohnen, Bruce. 2002. *The American Republic: Primary Sources.* Indianapolis, IN: Liberty Fund.

Kendall, Willmoore, and George W. Carey. *The Basic

Pilgrims aboard the Mayflower *sign the Mayflower Compact in 1620, a document that set an important precedent for the constitutions that would later be written in America. (Library of Congress)*

Symbols of the American Political Tradition. Baton Rouge: Louisiana State University Press.

Long, Breckinridge. 1926. *Genesis of the Constitution of the United States of America.* New York: Macmillan.

Lutz, Donald S. 1980. "From Covenant to Constitution in American Political Thought." *Publius* 10 (Fall): 1–34.

Sargent, Mark L. 1988. "The Conservative Covenant: The Rise of the Mayflower Compact in American Myth." *The New England Quarterly* 61 (June): 233–251.

MCCLURG, JAMES (1746–1823)

Born in Elizabeth City County, Virginia, to the family of a physician, James McClurg entered the same occupation. After receiving his undergradu-

ate education at the College of William and Mary, McClurg went to the University of Edinburgh, where he wrote a respected thesis and received his medical degree. McClurg served for a time during the American Revolution as a surgeon for the militia and was appointed as a professor of anatomy and medicine at William and Mary, where he may or may not have taught. McClurg was serving as a member of Virginia's Council of State when he was recruited to attend the Constitutional Convention after Patrick Henry and Richard Henry Lee had declined their appointments.

McClurg was present on the opening day of business on May 25, but he left sometime toward the end of July or early August and did not return. A man of relatively little governmental influence compared to other convention delegates and one whose silence within his delegation was matched only by that of George Washington and John

James McClurg, delegate from Virginia
(Library of Congress)

Blair, McClurg must have felt especially daunted by his better-known Virginia colleagues. Writing to James Madison after he had left the Convention in August of 1787, McClurg observed:

> If I thought that my return could contribute in the smallest degree to its Improvement, nothing should keep me away. But as I know that the talents, knowledge, & well-establish'd character, of our present delegates, have justly inspired this country with the most entire confidence in their determination; & that my vote could only *operate* to produce a division, & so destroy the vote of the State, I think that my attendance now would certainly be useless, perhaps injurious. (Hutson 1987, 205)

It is interesting to speculate as to how McClurg thought his presence might have split the Virginia delegation. His scanty comments certainly offer little with which to work. He does not appear to have openly spoken until July 17, at which time he proposed substituting service by the president during "good behavior" rather than for a term of seven years. His motives may, however, have been mixed as his resolution directly followed a Convention decision to make the president, whom the Convention was still expecting Congress to select, re-eligible for election. In this context, it is likely that McClurg was in fact (perhaps at the instigation of Madison) attempting to point to the difficulty that such dependency on the legislature might bring—better to be chosen for life than to remain subject to the legislature (Farrand 1937, II, 33). Referring specifically to the president's re-eligibility, McClurg said that the president "was put into a situation that would keep him dependent for ever on the Legislature; and he conceived the independence of the Executive to be equally essential with that of the Judiciary department" (II, 33). Further responding to objections that his proposal would lead to monarchy, McClurg said that he

> was not so much afraid of the shadow of monarchy as to be unwilling to approach it; nor so wedded to Republican Govt. as not to be sensible of the tyrannies that had been & may be exercised under that form. It was an essential object with him to make the Executive independent of the Legislature; and the only mode left for effecting it, after the vote destroying his ineligibility a second time, was to appoint him during good behavior. (II, 36)

The next day, McClurg seconded a motion by fellow Virginian James Madison, who had helped recruit him for the Convention, providing that Congress should guarantee states against both domestic and foreign violence (II, 48). He did not take part in resulting debates as to whether states needed such help or whether states needed congressional guarantees against domestic violence.

Madison recorded that McClurg, like him, favored a single executive (I, 97) and a congressional veto of state laws (I, 168). Perhaps more bravely, McClurg had asked on July 20 whether consideration should be given "to determine on the means by which the Executive is to carry the laws into effect, and to resist combinations agst. them." He asked, "Is he to have a military force for the purpose, or to have the command of the Militia, the only existing force that can be applied to that use?" (II, 69). Although Pennsylvania's James Wilson agreed that delegates should address this issue, it is not clear that anyone did so. If McClurg were in fact pointing to a specific issue, it is possible, but by no means certain, that McClurg considered that the question he had posed would, if he were present, have further divided the Virginia delegation.

George Washington appointed McClurg, a man of considerable financial means, as one of the original directors of the U.S. Bank, but passed him up in favor of Edmund Randolph for secretary of state. After his service at the Convention, McClurg served again on the Virginia Council of State and three times as mayor of Richmond, but fellow citizens continued to regard him chiefly for his expertise as a medical doctor. He died in Richmond, Virginia, in 1823.

See Also Madison, James, Jr.; Virginia

FOR FURTHER READING

Bradford, M. M. 1994. *Founding Fathers: Brief Lives of the Framers of the United States Constitution.* Lawrence: University Press of Kansas.

Farrand, Max, ed. 1937. *The Records of the Federal Convention.* 4 vols. New Haven, CT: Yale University Press.

Hutson, James H., ed. 1987. *Supplement to Max Farrand's* The Records of the Federal Convention of 1787. New Haven, CT: Yale University Press.

"The Medical Men of Virginia." *William and Mary College Quarterly Historical Magazine* 19 (January): 145–172.

MCHENRY, JAMES (1753–1816)

James McHenry was born to a merchant family at Ballymena, Ireland, in 1753. His parents, who later followed and set up a store in Baltimore, Maryland, sent him to America in 1771 in hopes that it would improve his health. McHenry appears to have attended the Newark Academy in

James McHenry, delegate from Maryland
(U.S. Army Center of Military History)

Delaware and to have studied medicine under Benjamin Rush. McHenry eagerly volunteered for the Continental Army in 1774 and served as a surgeon for a Pennsylvania battalion. Captured and paroled, he was freed from this restriction and rejoined the army, serving as a surgeon at Valley Forge and subsequently serving as a secretary to George Washington, Alexander Hamilton, and the Marquis de Lafayette. McHenry served from 1781 to 1786 as a member of the Maryland Senate and from 1783 to 1785 as a delegate to the Continental Congress. He married Margaret Caldwell in 1784, and they had four children.

McHenry took his seat as a Maryland delegate to the Constitutional Convention on May 28, but upon hearing news that his younger brother was ill, he left the Convention on June 1 (Farrand 1937, I, 75). He is next recorded as taking notes of conversations with fellow delegates from Maryland on August 7, the day after fellow delegate John Mercer was seated (II, 176). Fortunately, McHenry's notes give us insight into his view of a number of issues that the Convention had discussed, and may be combined with what he said throughout the remainder of the Convention.

Notes of August 7

These notes indicate that McHenry was strongly opposed to the provision (proposed as part of the Connecticut Compromise) that limited the origination of money bills to the House of Representatives. Whereas debates on the floor of the Convention tended to center on whether this provision would be of any value—with proponents saying that it was a major concession and opponents claiming that it was simply inconsequential—McHenry, and fellow delegate Daniel Carroll, apparently believed that the provision could actually prove dangerous. He observed

> that lodging in the house of representatives the sole right of raising and appropriating money, upon which the Senate had only a negative, gave to that branch an inordinate power in the constitution, which must end in its destruction. That without equal powers they were not an equal check upon each other. (II, 211)

McHenry's notes indicate that he and Carroll also opposed the provision that navigation acts should require a two-thirds vote of Congress, although his explanation appears to point in the other direction—with concern being expressed that trade might otherwise be controlled by four states (II, 211). McHenry and Carroll were greatly concerned over the congressional power to levy taxes and to regulate interstate commerce: "We almost shuddered at the fate of the commerce of Maryland should we be unable to make any change in this extraordinary power" (II, 211).

McHenry feared that the possibility that the new Constitution might be ratified by nine states was contrary to the commission that Maryland had given to him and other commissioners as well as to the unanimity requirement for constitutional amendments under the Articles of Confederation. He observed: "If we relinquished any of the rights or powers of our government to the U.S. of America, we could not otherwise agree to

that relinquishment than in the mode our constitution prescribed for making changes or alterations in it" (II, 212).

According to McHenry's account, as he and Carroll talked, Daniel of St. Thomas Jenifer entered the room. Although Jenifer agreed that the delegates from Maryland should act "in unison," according to McHenry, he "seemed to have vague ideas of the mischiefs of the system as it stood in the report." McHenry then volunteered his view that the plan being contemplated was too expensive:

> An army and navy was to be raised and supported, expensive courts of judicature to be maintained, and a princely president to be provided—That it was plain that the revenue for these purposes was to be chiefly drawn from commerce. That Maryland in this case would have this resource taken from her, without the expences of her own government being lessened.—That what would be raised from her commerce and by indirect taxation would far exceed the proportion she would be called upon to pay under the present confederation. (II, 212)

John Mercer, who later left without signing the Constitution, then joined the conversation and indicated that he was convinced that the delegates needed to construct a better system than the one proposed (II, 212). It would thus appear that McHenry and the rest of the Maryland delegation were leaning against the new Constitution, although it may be significant that Luther Martin, who would be the state's most prominent critic of the Constitution, was not reported to be in attendance.

Other Comments at the Convention

Consistent with his earlier notes, on August 13, McHenry is recorded as condemning the provision for the origination of money bills as "an extraordinary subterfuge, to get rid of the apparent force of the Constitution" (II, 280). On August 21, McHenry seconded a motion by Luther Martin relating to direct taxation. The two wanted to have the states collect such taxes and resort to other means only in cases when states did not meet these requisitions on their own (II, 359).

McHenry took a position that seemed to implicate the doctrine of implied powers when on August 21 he suggested that Congress would have the right to declare embargoes under its power to declare war (II, 362). On August 22, McHenry joined Elbridge Gerry in supporting a ban on congressional adoption of bills of attainder or ex post facto laws (II, 375).

On August 25, McHenry and General Pinckney proposed a complicated resolution that would have prohibited Congress from collecting duties or imposts within the states unless the state legislatures should first fail to do so. They also introduced the provision that all duties, imposts, and excises should be uniform throughout the United States (II, 418).

On August 27, McHenry joined Madison in supporting a provision that would prohibit any judicial increases during a judge's term of office (II, 429).

On August 31, McHenry told the Convention, as he had told his fellow delegates privately, that they were under oath to support the mode of ratification that was specified under the Articles of Confederation rather than the method that fellow delegates were proposing (II, 476). In discussing the provision preventing vessels entering one state from having to pay duties in another, McHenry offered the view that this restriction would "not shreen a vessel from being obliged to take an officer on board as a security for due entry &c" (II, 481).

In notes that he took on September 4, McHenry indicated that it did not appear that the Constitution granted Congress power to erect lighthouses or clear harbors for purposes of navigation. He further indicated that he thought this was a power that should be shared by the states collectively rather than by a single state. He further asked, "Is it proper to declare all the navigable waters or rivers and within the U.S. common high way?" (II, 504). Records indicate that McHenry waited until September 15 to introduce a motion prohibiting the government from restraining states from laying duties for the purpose of erecting lighthouses or clearing harbors (II, 625).

On September 8, McHenry moved that the president should be given power to convene either house of Congress (II, 553).

Signing the Constitution

We know more about McHenry's thoughts on the basis of his own notes than from the notes of others, and the occasion of the signing of the Constitution on September 17 proved to be no exception. Although Madison did not record that he said anything, McHenry wrote that "being opposed to many parts of the system I made a remark why I signed it and mean to support it" (II, 649). He does not say whether he made this remark publicly or privately, but he continues, not with a single remark but with three arguments. The first appears to summarize the more frequently cited speech that Benjamin Franklin made on the same occasion but indicates that McHenry's own objections appear to have been even stronger. McHenry thus observed: "I distrust my own judgment, especially as it is opposite to the opinions of a majority of gentlemen whose abilities and patriotism are of the first cast; and as I have had already frequent occasions to be convinced that I have not always judged right" (II, 649).

McHenry's second argument was that if future alterations were needed, the Constitution had an amending process to accommodate them. Finally, he thought the existing situation called for some expedient:

> Comparing the inconveniences and the evils which we labor under and may experience from the present confederation, and the little good we can expect from it—with the possible evils and probable benefits and advantages promised us by the new system, I am clear that I ought to give it all the support in my power. (II, 650)

Life after the Convention

McHenry served in the Maryland ratifying convention and was elected back to the Maryland legislature. He served under Presidents George Washington and John Adams as secretary of the Treasury, but was eventually fired by Adams who believed that McHenry, whose inefficiencies as an administrator others had noticed, was also taking too much direction from Alexander Hamilton, who was undermining the Adams administration. McHenry retired at the age of 46. McHenry was a Mason and he served in retirement as president of the Baltimore Bible Society. The Baltimore fort, whose defense against the British during the War of 1812 is recorded in the "Star Spangled Banner," is named after McHenry. He died in Maryland in 1816.

See Also Maryland

FOR FURTHER READING

Farrand, Max, ed. 1937. *The Records of the Federal Convention.* 4 vols. New Haven, CT: Yale University Press.
Whitney, David C. 1974. *Founders of Freedom in America: Lives of the Men Who Signed the Constitution of the United States and So Helped to Establish the United States of America.* Chicago: J. J. Ferguson Publishing.

MEETING TIMES

The Constitutional Convention began meeting on May 25, 1787. It met regularly from Mondays through Saturdays until September 17, 1787. In the opening weeks, the Convention met as a Committee of the Whole. The Convention took a break for July 4 and for the Committee of Detail to meet and do its work between Friday, July 27 and Monday, August 6. The Convention generally met between the hours of 10 A.M. and 3 or 4 P.M. On August 18, the Convention attempted to move the proceedings along by meeting until 4 P.M. each day, but this was altered back to 3 P.M. on August 14 (Farrand 1937, I, 2 n.1). The Convention did not break for a noon meal, and members of committees that the delegates appointed at various times during the Convention had to do their work before and after hours.

See Also Calendar; Committee of Detail; Committee of the Whole

FOR FURTHER READING

Bowen, Catherine Drinker. 1966. *Miracle at Philadelphia: The Story of the Constitutional Convention, May to September 1787.* Boston: Little, Brown, and Company.
Farrand, Max, ed. 1937. *The Records of the Federal Convention.* 4 vols. New Haven, CT: Yale University Press.

MERCER, JOHN (1759–1821)

John Mercer was born in Stafford County, Virginia in 1759 to Colonel John Mercer (a lawyer) and his wife, Ann Roy Mercer. The Mercers were a landholding family. Mercer was first educated at home and then at the College of William and Mary before studying law under Thomas Jefferson, who was then governor, but whose trust he never appears to have earned. Mercer served in a

John Francis Mercer, delegate from Maryland
(Hulton Archive/Getty Images)

number of positions during the Revolutionary War and participated in the battle of Yorktown. After serving in the Virginia House of Delegates and the Continental Congress, where he strongly opposed the expansion of federal powers, Mercer married Sophia Sprigg in 1785, and they had three children. He moved to her estate in Maryland, where the legislature selected him as a delegate to the Constitutional Convention. A man of resources who later lost money in Western land speculation, Mercer was nonetheless concerned about the dangers of aristocracy.

Mercer was not seated at the Constitutional Convention until August 6, and he appears to have left after August 17, but he was an active participant during his attendance. Notes that fellow delegate James McHenry took on August 7 give the first glimpse into Mercer's thoughts. According to McHenry, Mercer indicated that he would go along with attempts by his fellow delegates to change the proposals, but

> he would wish it to be understood however, that he did not like the system, that it was weak—That he would produce a better one since the Convention has undertaken to go radically to work, that perhaps he would not be supported by any one, but if he was not, he would go with the stream. (Farrand 1937, II, 212)

Mercer somewhat clarified these words when, on August 8, during a discussion of the provision for electing members of the House of Representatives, he was recorded as expressing "his dislike of the whole plan, and his opinion that it never could succeed" (II, 215).

Congress

Mercer's first specific criticism, which he raised on August 8, centered on the direct election of members of the House. He said that he "did not object so much to an election by the people at large" as long as they had "some guidance." According to Madison's notes, Mercer "hinted" that state legislatures should first nominate the candidates (II, 216).

On August 8 Mercer joined Virginia's James Madison in criticizing a proposal requiring that members of the House of Representatives reside for seven years in the state that elected them. He observed that this requirement would be greater than that under the existing Articles of Confederation and said that "It would interweave local prejudices & State distinctions in the very Constitution which is meant to cure them" (II, 217). He further pointed to disputes that had arisen in Maryland as to the meaning of "residence" (II, 217), and feared that the substitution of the term "inhabitant" might exclude individuals who returned from a state after an absence but were clearly conversant with its affairs (II, 218). On August 13, Mercer seconded a motion that Pennsylvania's Gouverneur Morris advanced to limit the application of the residency requirement to any individuals who were citizens at the time the Constitution was adopted (II, 270). He went on to characterize a disability on existing citizens as "a breach of faith" (II, 272).

Like fellow delegate James McHenry, Mercer believed that the provision allowing the House of Representatives to originate money bills was both weighty and dangerous. Indeed, he thought that it would give the House of Representatives such an advantage "that it rendered the equality of votes in the Senate ideal & of no consequence" (II, 224).

On August 10, Mercer indicated that he thought a congressional quorum should not require a majority. He feared that setting the quorum too high would enable some members to "secede" and thus prevent business from being done. He favored allowing Congress to set its own quorum, as the British Parliament did (II, 251). He subsequently seconded a motion, offered by Gouverneur Morris, that set an initial quorum at half of the membership (33 of 65 in the House and 14 of 28 in the Senate) but allowed Congress to decide whether this number needed to be raised as membership grew (II, 252; II, 253).

When, on August 11, Madison offered a motion allowing the Senate to keep certain of its proceedings secret, Mercer objected that this implied that it would conduct something other than legislative business, which he did not believe would be appropriate (II, 259). That same day, Mercer said it was necessary to specify where the first

Congress would meet because he did not think the two houses would be able to come to an agreement on this point (II, 262).

On August 16, Mercer strongly opposed the idea of granting Congress the power to tax exports. He argued that "Such taxes were impolitic, as encouraging the raising of articles not meant for exportation" (II, 307). He further observed that, under the Articles, the states had the right to tax both imports and exports and that they should only be expected to sacrifice one of these powers. As to arguments that the South was most in need of naval protection, Mercer somewhat defensively argued: "Were it not for promoting the carrying trade of the Northn States, the Southn States could let their trade go into foreign bottoms, where it would not need our protection" (II, 308). He ended by commenting that by taxing its own tobacco, Virginia had given an advantage to that grown in Maryland.

Although generally wary of increased national powers, Mercer seconded a motion by Elbridge Gerry of Massachusetts granting Congress power over "post-roads" as well as post offices (II, 308). Professing himself to be "a friend of paper money," Mercer did not believe it was consistent with the current temper of the people. Consistent with his own view of its propriety, however, he did not want to prohibit Congress from issuing it altogether. In observations consistent with his view of influence that is explained in a section below, Mercer observed:

> It was impolitic also to excite the opposition of all those who were friends of paper money. The people of property would be sure to be on the side of the plan, and it was impolitic to purchase their further attachment with the loss of the opposite class of Citizens. (II, 309)

Mercer's Fear of Aristocracy and Support of Executive Authority

One of Mercer's most notable speeches occurred on August 14 during discussion of whether members of Congress should be eligible during their terms for other offices. Proponents of this restriction believed that it would lead to an aristocracy. Although he was concerned about aristocracy, Mercer apparently believed that the president needed to be able to make appointments from Congress (he appears to have been contemplating something like the present-day parliamentary system where members of the cabinet are drawn from parliament) in order to resist aristocratic tendencies.

Mercer began his speech by observing that "it is a first principle of political science, that whenever the rights of property are secured, an aristocracy will grow out of it" (II, 284). He believed this was true even in "elective governments" since "the rulers being few can & will draw emoluments for themselves from the many" (II, 284). He believed that state governments had already become aristocratic and that "public measures are calculated for the benefit of the governors, not of the people" (II, 284). He further believed that the people were dissatisfied with this system. What was the solution? Much as Alexander Hamilton of New York had argued elsewhere at the Convention, Mercer believed that governments depended on "force or influence" (II, 284). However, he thought that the Convention had not entrusted the executive with sufficient amounts of either. Mercer seems to have envisioned a mixed government like that in England, where the executive would weigh in against aristocrats on the side of the people. To this end, he suggested that the president needed to be buttressed by a council, consisting of member of Congress:

> The Legislature must & will be composed of wealth & abilities, and the people will be governed by a Junto. The Executive ought to have a Council, being members of both Houses. Without such an influence, the war will be between the aristocracy & the people. He wished it to be between the Aristocracy & the Executive. Nothing else can protect the people agst. those speculating Legislatures which are now plundering them throughout the U. States. (II, 284–285)

This appears to be the incubus of an alternate plan that Mercer had told McHenry he had in view.

Mercer further elaborated on his views later in the day when the Convention was discussing whether congressional disabilities should be extended to state appointments. Mercer feared that if congressmen were so ineligible, the most influential men would stay home "& prefer appointments within their respective States" (II, 289). Mercer recognized that a parchment would have limited influence over the lives of men:

It is a great mistake to suppose that the paper we are to propose will govern the U. States? It is the men whom it will bring into the Govent. and interest in maintaining it that is to govern them. The paper will only mark out the mode & the form—Men are the substance and must do the business. All Govt. must be by force or influence. (II, 289)

Absent granting the government substantial force, Mercer thought that it was imperative to grant it influence.

Mercer's concern for influence appears to have been reflected in his opposition to allowing the Senate to ratify treaties. He argued on August 15 that this power belonged, as in Britain, to the executive. However, he further observed that "Treaties would not be final so as to alter the laws of the land, till ratified by legislative authority" (II, 297).

Mercer's attempt to bolster executive powers was also reflected in his approval of the idea of a Council of Revision granting the executive and members of the judiciary power, subject to override by congressional supermajorities, to invalidate laws. In expressing this view, however, Mercer opposed the idea that members of the judiciary should have the power to invalidate laws because they believed them to be unconstitutional, the power that is today known as judicial review:

It is an axiom that the Judiciary ought to be separate from the Legislative: but equally so that it ought to be independent of that department. The true policy of the axiom is that legislative usurpation and oppression may be obviated. He disapproved of the Doctrine that the Judges as expositors of the Constitution should have authority to declare a law void. He thought laws ought to be made well and cautiously made, and then to be uncontroulable. (II, 298)

On August 17, Mercer seconded a motion allowing the National Treasurer to be appointed by the president like other officers rather than being appointed by Congress (II, 315).

Mercer's last recorded act at the Convention was on August 17, a month before the document was signed. On this occasion, he seconded a motion by fellow delegate Luther Martin opposing striking a provision that would require a state legislature to request help before Congress could introduce troops into a state to suppress rebellion there (II, 317). Mercer was clearly concerned about preserving state sovereignty.

Life after the Convention

It is not surprising to find that Mercer opposed adoption of the Convention and worked against it at the Maryland state ratifying convention. Although he did not succeed in blocking Maryland's ratification, his insistence on accompanying ratification with proposed amendments appears to have influenced subsequent deliberations in neighboring Virginia. Antifederalists subsequently elected him to the Maryland state legislature and to the U.S. House of Representatives where he aligned with the Democratic-Republicans in opposition to Alexander Hamilton's fiscal policies. Mercer was twice elected as governor, in which capacity he helped to eliminate property qualifications for voting. He died seeking medical attention in Philadelphia in 1821.

See Also Maryland

FOR FURTHER READING

Bradford, M. M. 1994. *Founding Fathers: Brief Lives of the Framers of the United States Constitution.* Lawrence: University Press of Kansas.
Farrand, Max, ed. 1937. *The Records of the Federal Convention.* 4 vols. New Haven, CT: Yale University Press.

MESSENGER

See WEAVER, NICHOLAS

MIFFLIN, THOMAS
(1744–1800)

Thomas Mifflin was born in Philadelphia, Pennsylvania, in 1744. A member of a merchant Quaker family (the denomination later expelled him because of his military activity), he attended the College of Philadelphia (today's University of Pennsylvania), traveled abroad for a year, and served as a clerk before becoming a merchant. He was chosen to serve in the Pennsylvania colonial legislature and joined the Patriot side. Elected to serve in the Continental Congress, Mifflin became an aide-de-camp to George Washington, who appointed him as quartermaster-general of the Continental Army, a position in which Mifflin does not appear to have been very effective. With his political connections, Congress promoted Mifflin to the rank of major general, in which capacity he was linked to General Thomas Conway in the "Conway Cabal," in what was alleged to have been an attempt to displace Washington from his position as commander-in-chief of the colonial forces.

Retaining popularity within his home state where he portrayed himself as a man of the common people (he later supported the Democratic-Republican Party), Mifflin represented Pennsylvania in Congress under the Articles of Confederation. He served for about a year as its president.

Thomas Mifflin was seated at the Constitutional Convention on May 28. Because of his previous military service, fellow delegates addressed him as "general." He is believed to have attended almost every session of the Convention, and he signed the document, but he is not recorded as giving a single speech. In light of accusations that would later be raised against Mifflin, it may be ironic, but it is otherwise difficult to draw much from his only recorded action, that of seconding a

Thomas Mifflin, delegate from Pennsylvania
(Pixel That)

motion on August 14 by Charles Pinckney proposing that members of Congress who accepted offices would have to resign their seats (Farrand 1937, II, 284).

As he aged, Mifflin's reputation for patriotism and for public speaking was replaced by suspicions that he was too free with, and too little accountable for, public money and that he was unable to control an alcohol problem—perhaps it was fortunate that he did not combine such a problem with oratorical bombast. After the Convention ended, Mifflin succeeded Benjamin Franklin as president of the state and went on to head the convention that wrote a new state constitution. He served for nine years as Pennsylvania's governor, was then elected to the state legislature, and died almost penniless in Lancaster in 1800.

Despite the offices that he held after serving at the Convention, it would appear that Mifflin's service in Philadelphia came at a time when his powers were already ebbing. Clearly capable of great things, he evidenced little such greatness at the Convention. Not only did Mifflin not speak there, but he is not reported as having served on any committees. Fortunately, he was a member of a brilliant delegation that was well able to represent the interests of both the state and the nation without his contributions.

See Also Pennsylvania

FOR FURTHER READING

Farrand, Max, ed. 1937. *The Records of the Federal Convention*. 4 vols. New Haven, CT: Yale University Press.

Whitney, David C. 1974. *Founders of Freedom in America: Lives of the Men Who Signed the Constitution of the United States and So Helped to Establish the United States of America.* Chicago: J. J. Ferguson Publishing.

MILITARY, CONGRESSIONAL GOVERNANCE OF

In Article I, Section 8, Clause 14, of the Constitution, the Convention vested Congress with the power "to make Rules for the Government and Regulation of the land and naval Forces." Delegates added this provision relatively late in the Convention on August 18 with no recorded debate on the subject (Farrand 1937, II, 323). As James Madison's notes indicate (II, 330), they took it almost directly from language in the Articles of Confederation.

At the suggestion of Luther Martin of Maryland and Elbridge Gerry of Massachusetts, the Convention then discussed whether the Convention should limit the number of standing troops in times of peace. After the Convention voted against such a limitation, Virginia's George Mason further proposed vesting Congress with the power "to make laws for the regulation and discipline of the Militia of the several States reserving to the States the appointment of the Officers" (II, 330). This formed the basis of Article I, Section 8, Clause 16.

In a much-debated provision, the Second Amendment later reaffirmed the importance of "a well regulated Militia" to "the security of a free state" and affirmed "the right of the people to keep and bear Arms." The Fifth Amendment further exempted members of the militia, "When in

---

U.S.S. CONSTITUTION

It is significant that one of the enduring symbols of the new nation was named the U.S.S. *Constitution*. One of six frigates authorized in 1794, the ship was designed by Joshua Humphreys and Josiah Fox and built by Colonel George Claghorn between 1794 and 1797 at the Edmond Hartt's Shipyard in Boston. The ship was christened and launched in 1797, fitted for sea in 1798, and saw action in the war against the Barbary pirates and in the War of 1812 when it defeated the HMS *Guerrière* and the HMS *JAVA*. It is often called *Old Ironsides* because cannonballs were said to have bounced off the heavy oak walls of the ship during battle.

After false reports that the navy intended to reduce the ship, which like other ships was being surveyed to ascertain repair costs, to salvage, Oliver Wendell Holmes, Sr. (father of a future Supreme Court justice), wrote a poem that mobilized popular sentiment on its behalf about 1830, and the navy has periodically refurbished it. It continues to be part of the U.S. Navy. It now sits in Boston Harbor, where tourists can visit it. It sails out into the harbor at least once each year. Just as the ship is named after the Constitution, so too, the nation is often likened to a "ship" of state.

Much like medieval artifacts attributed to saints or sacred objects, objects purportedly made from the ship, presumably the result of materials removed during reconstructions, are often sold as constitutional relics.

FOR FURTHER READING

"USS Constitution: History Timeline." www.uss constitution.navy.mil/Shiphistoryx.htm.

Defeat of the HMS Guerrière *by the USS* Constitution *on August 19, 1812 (National Archives)*

actual service in time of War or public danger," from the requirement of indictment by grand juries.

See Also Armies, Standing; Armies and Navies, Raising and Supporting; Militia, Congressional Power to Organize and Govern; Republicanism

FOR FURTHER READING

Farrand, Max, ed. 1937. *The Records of the Federal Convention.* 4 vols. New Haven, CT: Yale University Press.

Fields, William S., and David T. Hardy. 1992. "The Militia and the Constitution: A Legal History." *Military Law Review* 136 (Spring): 1–42.

MILITIA, CONGRESSIONAL POWER TO CALL

Article I, Section 8, Clause 15 vests Congress with the power "to provide for calling forth the Militia to execute the Laws of the Union, suppress Insurrections and repel Invasions." The subsequent provision allows Congress to govern the militia, albeit while reserving to the states the power to appoint its officers.

The Virginia Plan, which Edmund Randolph presented to the Convention on May 29, provided that Congress would have the power "to call forth the force of the Union agst. any member of the Union failing to fulfill its duty under the articles thereof" (Farrand 1937, I, 21). Although James Madison is believed to have been the primary author of the Virginia Plan, he expressed reservations about this provision just two days into its debate. When it was brought up for consideration on May 31, he "observed that the more he reflected on the use of force, the more he doubted the practicability, the justice and the efficacy of it when applied to people collectively and not individually." He continued:

A Union of the States [containing such an ingredient] seemed to provide for its own destruction. The use of force agst. a State, would look more like a declaration of war, than an infliction of punishment, and would probably be considered by the party attacked as a dissolution of all previous compacts by which it might be bound. He hoped that such a system would be framed as might render this recourse unnecessary. (I, 54)

The Convention accepted Madison's proposal to postpone this provision. Notes by James McHenry of Maryland on this motion are not altogether clear. McHenry observed that Elbridge Gerry of Massachusetts "thought this clause 'ought to be expressed so as the people might not understand it to prevent their being alarmed.'" Although he had previously recorded the motion as being postponed, he also observed that "This idea [was] rejected on account of its *artifice,* and because the system without such a declaration gave the government the means to secure itself" (I, 61).

Whatever Madison's reservations may have been, a similar provision reemerged in the New Jersey Plan, which William Paterson introduced on June 15. In Section 6, which contains the genesis of the supremacy clause, Paterson specified that

if any State, or any body of men in any State shall oppose or prevent ye. carrying into execution such acts or treaties, the federal Executive shall be authorized to call forth ye power of the Confederated States, or so much thereof as may be necessary to enforce and compel an obedience to such Acts, or an Observance of such Treaties. (I, 245)

It is possible that the New Jersey Plan actually favored direct action on individual states as being more consistent with the continuation of a federal (or confederal) system than a system, like the Virginia Plan seemed increasingly to be becoming, that would allow the national government to act directly on individuals.

In any event, by the time that the Committee of Detail issued its report on August 6, the provision related to the congressional power to call forth the militia had undergone considerable reorientation. Rather than vesting Congress with power to call the militia to *punish* other states, the provision had been reoriented into a provision vesting Congress with power to call the militia to *protect* the states. Specifically, the committee proposed vesting Congress with power "to call forth the aid of the militia, in order to execute the laws of the Union, enforce treaties, suppress insurrections, and repel invasions" (II, 182). However, the Convention devoted considerably more attention to dividing the powers of regulating the militia and appointing its members between the national government and the states than to the specific functions it would perform when called into national service.

When the Convention addressed this provision on August 23, the delegates accepted the wording of the Committee of Detail regarding the purposes of the militia, with only one minor revision. This was to accept Gouverneur Morris's motion to strike the provision to "enforce treaties" as superfluous (II, 390). The delegates incorporated this provision into the current Constitution without any further alterations.

The new language dealing with congressional powers to call out the militia sounded as though it was primarily providing for a shield to protect states against domestic insurrections or foreign invasion rather than for a sword that might be employed against them when they defied federal laws. However, the latter possibility remained to be worked out in practice.

See Also Militia, Congressional Power to Organize and Govern; Supremacy Clause

FOR FURTHER READING

Edling, Max M. 2003. *A Revolution in Favor of Government.* New York: Oxford University Press.

Farrand, Max, ed. 1937. *The Records of the Federal Convention.* 4 vols. New Haven, CT: Yale University Press.

Higginbotham, Don. 1998. "The Federalized Militia Debate: A Neglected Aspect of Second Amendment Scholarship." *William and Mary Quarterly,* 3rd ser. 55 (January): 39–58.

MILITIA, CONGRESSIONAL POWER TO ORGANIZE AND GOVERN

Article I, Section 8, Clause 16 of the Constitution vests Congress with the power "To provide for organizing, arming, and disciplining, the Militia, and for governing such Part of them as may be employed in the Service of the United States." Using language that anticipates that which the Tenth Amendment later employed, the provision continues by "reserving to the States respectively, the Appointment of the Officers, and the Authority of training the Militia according to the discipline prescribed by Congress."

Mason Initiates Debate on August 18

This provision grew out of debates at the Constitutional Convention on August 18. Relatively early in the day's proceedings, Virginia's George Mason observed that the general government needed to have power over the militia. This need for congressional power would actually derive from federal reliance on the states:

> He hoped there would be no standing army in times of peace, unless it might be for a few garrisons. The Militia ought therefore to be the more effectively prepared for the public defence. Thirteen States will never concur in any one system, if the disciplining of the Militia be left in their hands. If they will not give up the power over the whole, they probably will over a part as select militia. (Farrand 1937, II, 326)

Apparently unsuccessful in getting this matter sent to the Committee of Detail, later in the day Mason proposed granting Congress the power "to make laws for the regulation and discipline of the Militia of the several States reserving to the States the appointment of the Officers" (II, 330). Connecticut's Roger Sherman seconded the motion. Mason justified the addition of this provision on the need for uniformity. General Charles C. Pinckney of South Carolina affirmed that the lack of such uniformity had presented problems during the Revolutionary War, and he indicated that, without such a requirement, "States would never keep up a proper discipline of their militia" (II, 330).

Connecticut's Oliver Ellsworth feared that Mason's motion went too far. Although agreeing that the militia needed to have the same arms and be regulated by the U.S. when employed in its service, he feared that, if too much power were taken from the states, their "consequence would pine away to nothing after such a sacrifice of power" (II, 331). He also observed the difficulty that Congress would have of tailoring legislation "to the local genius of the people" (II, 331).

Gravely observing that the Convention was now dealing with "a most important matter, that of the sword," Delaware's John Dickinson offered a proposal whereby the national government would govern only one-fourth of the militia at a time, until, by rotation, it had trained the whole. Pierce Butler of South Carolina thought that Congress needed to govern the whole. This led Mason to withdraw his original proposal for one that would vest the national government with the regulating and disciplining of only one-tenth of the state militia each year but continue to reserve to the states the right of appointing officers. General Pinckney instead renewed Mason's original motion, continuing to see the need for uniformity and arguing that there was no reason to distrust national authority in this area. In seconding him, New Hampshire's John Langdon said that he was more fearful of confusion flowing from different rules than from the power of either state or national government.

Virginia's James Madison argued that the power to regulate the militia was not easily "divisible between two distinct authorities." He thought that the general government could be as easily trusted with the use of military force as with the public monies. Madison argued that "the States would not be separately impressed with the general situation, nor have the due confidence in the concurrent exertions of each other" (II, 332). Ellsworth believed that the idea of a select militia was impractical and that state habits were too different to impose national authority. Charles Pinckney favored congressional control and expressed skepticism over the ability of militia to substitute for regular troops; he attributed the near state of "anarchy" in Massachusetts (see Shays's Rebellion) to reliance on militia troops.

Roger Sherman said that states needed militia to defend themselves and to enforce their own laws and that, as in the case of taxation, they needed to maintain a concurrent power in this area. Elbridge Gerry of Massachusetts was almost apoplectic over the prospect of forcing the states to give up their militia—he described this as "as black a mark as was set on Cain" (II, 332)—and believed that the states would share his lack of confidence in the new national government. For his part, Mason was willing to exempt that part of the militia that the states needed for their own use.

Delaware's George Read shifted attention to a somewhat different issue. He expressed concern over leaving the appointment of the officers of the militia to the states and insisted that, at the least, the Convention should require that state executives make such decisions (II, 333). The Convention then voted to commit these matters to the 11-man Committee on State Debts and Militia, which William Livingston of New Jersey headed.

Debate over Report of August 21

This committee reported back to the Convention on August 21, with a provision that contains all the elements, and most of the language, of the current provision (II, 352). It provided that Congress would have power

to make laws for organizing, arming & disciplining the Militia, and for governing such parts of them as may be employed in the service of the U.S. reserving to the States respectively, the appointment of the officers, and authority of training the militia according to the discipline prescribed. (II, 384–385)

The Convention began discussion of this provision on August 23.

Sherman moved to strike the last phrase on the basis that states would have the authority to appoint and train militia even without such an express provision. Ellsworth thought the phrase might be needed but wanted clarification of the term "discipline" (II, 385). Rufus King of Massachusetts said that the committee had intended for the term "organizing" to refer to "proportioning the officers and men," the term "arming" to "specifying the kind size and caliber of arms," and the term "disciplining" to "prescribing the manual exercise evolutions &c." (II, 385). Sherman then withdrew his motion.

Gerry feared that the provision left the states with little more than the power of "drill-sergeants." He further raised the specter of congressional "Despotism" (II, 385). Madison elicited further explanation from King over the intended meaning of terms.

Dayton offered a motion to postpone in favor of a differently worded motion; it failed by a vote of 8-3. Ellsworth and Sherman then offered a motion "To establish an uniformity of arms, exercise & organization for the Militia, and to provide for the Government of them when called into the service of the U. States" (II, 386). Their stated purpose was "to refer the plan for the Militia to the General Govtr. but leave the execution of it to the State Govts." (II, 386). Likening the power of the nation and the states to that of the right and left hands, Langdon professed bewilderment over the distrust that delegates were expressing toward the proposed government. Gerry questioned whether national liberty could be safely reposed in the national government. Dayton questioned whether the proposal might lead to too much uniformity. General Pinckney preferred the committee's language, and Madison reiterated that the discipline of the militia was a national concern. Luther Martin did not think the states would ever part with this power, and he thought that they would be more likely to attend to it than the national government. Randolph did not think it likely that the militia would commit suicide. He feared that state legislators "courted popularity too much to enforce a proper discipline" and thought that leaving the states with the right to appoint officers would provide adequate security for their interests. The Convention thus rejected Ellsworth's motion by a vote of 10 to 1. It then voted 9-2 to agree to the first part of the motion, which the committee had offered.

Madison subsequently proposed altering the part of the resolution relating to appointments so that states could only appoint those "under the rank of General officers" (II, 388). Sherman thought this would be "absolutely inadmissible" (II, 388). Similarly, Gerry "warned the Convention agst pushing the experiment too far," even predicting that insisting on federal powers that were too extensive could lead to civil war. By contrast, Madison argued that the greatest danger was that of "disunion of the States," and that if liberty were to be protected by guarding against standing armies, then the Convention needed effectually to provide for the militia" (II, 388). The Convention rejected Madison's motion by an 8-3 vote. It then unanimously accepted the reservation of state appointment of officers, and voted 7-4 to allow states to train militia under discipline prescribed by Congress. Finally, it unanimously voted to accept the entire clause.

Analysis

Like the later mention of the need for a well-regulated militia that Congress incorporated into the Second Amendment, debates over the governance of state militia seem relatively quaint, if not antiquated, at a time like today when the national government largely relies on troops recruited from throughout the nation. The Convention debates make it clear that many delegates were suspicious of the newly created government and were unwilling to concede full authority to it over even the most basic needs of national defense. Compromises allowing states to apply national rules of dis-

cipline and to appoint officers cooled, but may not completely have assuaged such worries.

See Also Militia, Congressional Power to Call

FOR FURTHER READING

Cress, Lawrence Delbert. 1981. "Republican Liberty and National Security: American Military Policy as an Ideological Problem, 1783 to 1798." *William and Mary Quarterly*, 3rd ser. 38 (January): 73–96.

Farrand, Max, ed. 1937. *The Records of the Federal Convention.* 4 vols. New Haven, CT: Yale University Press.

Fields, William S., and David T. Hardy. 1992. "The Militia and the Constitution: A Legal History." *Military Law Review* 136 (Spring): 1–42.

Higginbotham, Don. 1998. "The Federalized Militia Debate: A Neglected Aspect of Second Amendment Scholarship." *William and Mary Quarterly*, 3rd ser. 55 (January): 39–58.

MISSISSIPPI RIVER

Not all histories of the Constitutional Convention treat navigation on the Mississippi River. However, negotiations over this subject influenced the calling and deliberations of the Convention in a number of significant ways.

Background Prior to the Convention

John Jay, secretary of foreign affairs, had been negotiating for the U.S. with Spain since 1779. In 1781, when the former colonies were especially in need of financial help, the Congress under the Articles of Confederation had expressed willingness to negotiate with Spain over navigation on the Mississippi River, the lower reaches of which Spain controlled (Merritt 1991, 123).

Once Americans won the war, however, Congress provided Jay with specific instructions forbidding him from conceding this right, which was of special interest to immigrants to the West, to Spain. Often otherwise separated from Easterners

February 1779: An expedition on the Mississippi during the War of Independence (MPI/Getty Images)

by mountain ranges, Westerners frequently depended on access to the Mississippi River to carry out their trade. Moreover, if Easterners failed to secure these rights, Westerners might be tempted to break away and ally with Spain to gain this objective. Despite congressional instructions to Jay, Spain, which was fairly skeptical about the strength of the government under the Articles of Confederation, closed American access to the Mississippi in 1784.

In May of 1786, Jay informed Congress that he had reached an impasse in his negotiations with Spain and requested a committee to give him advice. On August 3, Jay spoke to Congress. He indicated that, contrary to his instructions, he had discussed with Spain giving up U.S. trade on the Mississippi for a period of 25 to 30 years in exchange for certain trading and fishing advantages for the Northeastern states off the coast of Newfoundland. Southerners, who were, however, bound by congressional rules of secrecy on the subject, widely denounced the plan in Congress. Still, states voted 7-5 (with all Southern states in dissent) to allow for a reversal of Jay's earlier instructions on the subject.

This vote presented a real problem for advocates of the Constitution. America's weak bargaining position with the Spanish seemed to confirm the weakness of the existing government under the Articles of Confederation relative to foreign affairs and the need for a stronger national government. Simultaneously, however, if word were to get out about Jay's willingness to bargain away Western rights, many people would be even more fearful of investing greater powers in the new government that was to be considered. Especially since the end of the Revolution, population had been growing rapidly in the American West, which, in addition to the Northwest Territories, then encompassed the present-day states of Kentucky and Tennessee, which were at the time respectively parts of Virginia and North Carolina.

Virginia's James Madison, who was among the strongest congressional opponents of Jay's willingness to bargain over the Mississippi, apparently also thought that this issue needed to be "managed" at the Convention. His tone on the subject at the Convention was consistently moderate, and there is some evidence that his notes may purposely have downplayed the role that debates on the subject played in the debates (Merritt, 146–149).

Issues Influenced

Concerns generated by the issue of navigation on the Mississippi River nevertheless appear to have had a major influence on general discussions about the configuration of the new government and its need for checks and balances as well as on specific provisions. This issue appears to have been the primary impetus for the insistence, especially by Southern states (who had been stunned by the 7-5 vote of the states to rescind Jay's earlier instructions on negotiation over the Mississippi), for a two-thirds majority of the Senate for ratification of treaties.

Although Southerners did not succeed in getting a similar supermajority for the adoption of all navigation acts (a desire also stimulated by fears generated by Jay's negotiations), delegates from the Deep South used this as a bargaining chip to get recognition of the continuing importation of slaves over the next twenty years. Indeed, on August 22, South Carolina's John Rutledge indicated that issues of slavery and commerce "may form a bargain among the Northern and Southern states" (Farrand 1937, II, 449).

Specific Discussions at the Convention

On July 11, in arguing that Western states should, when admitted, be treated as equals, Virginia's George Mason predicted that they might in time "be both more numerous & more wealthy than their Atlantic brethren" (I, 579). Striking a hopeful note, he further expressed the view that Spanish attempts to curtail navigation on the Missis-

sippi were doomed to failure. Mason thus observed that "the extent & fertility of their soil, made this [the greater population and wealth of the West] probable; and though Spain might for a time deprive them of the natural outlet for their productions, yet she will, because she must, finally yield to their demands" (I, 579). James Madison reiterated this theme on the same day, observing that the Mississippi would actually be a source of secure revenue for the new government: "Whenever the Mississippi should be opened to them, which would of necessity be ye. case as soon as their population would subject them to any considerable share of the public burdin, imposts on their trade could be collected with less expense & greater certainty, than on that of the Atlantic states" (I, 585).

The Mississippi as a Possible Cause for War

Aware of the controversy that the Jay negotiations had generated in Congress, Gouverneur Morris of Pennsylvania, an opponent of granting equal rights to the Western states, saw the Mississippi River as a likely cause of war, pitting section against section. Thus on July 5, Morris expressed the opinion that Westerners "will be little scrupulous of involving the Community in wars the burdens & operations of which would fall chiefly on the maritime States" (I, 533). On July 10, when debating representation in Congress, Morris said that although Southern states might furnish the money for wars, "The Northn. States are to spill their blood" (I, 567). On July 13, he repeated this concern:

> In this struggle between the two ends of the Union, what part ought the Middle States in point of policy to take: to join their Eastern brethren according to his ideas. If the Southn. States get the power into their hands, and be joined as they will be with the interior Country they will inevitably bring on a war with Spain for the Mississippi. This language is already held. The interior Country having no property nor interest exposed on the sea, will be little affected by such a war. He wished to know what security the

Northn. & middle States will have against this danger. (I, 604)

On August 28, however, Morris, whom one scholar describes as having "frequently oscillated between the Northern and Southern viewpoints" (Merritt, 161), supported a provision providing that any taxes on exports would go into the national treasury. He observed that the regulation was "necessary to prevent the Atlantic States from endeavouring to tax the Western States—& promote their interest by opposing the navigation of the Mississippi which would drive the Western people into the arms of G. Britain" (II, 442). Moreover, on September 8, Morris referred to Fisheries and the Mississippi as "the two great objects of the Union" (II, 548). He argued against requiring two-thirds consent of the Senate to treaties of peace on the ground that Congress would be unwilling to make war on behalf of national objects for fear that they could not easily enough bring such war to an end.

This Convention nonetheless retained this provision. The arguments for it are probably best explained, not by notes taken during the Convention itself but by a letter that North Carolina's Hugh Williamson wrote to James Madison on June 2, 1788. Williamson, who was attempting, like Madison, to get his state to ratify the Constitution, observed that men from the West, and especially Kentucky, were falsely claiming that members of the Convention had attempted to give up the rights of Westerners to navigate the Mississippi. Williamson recollected the Convention debates:

> Your recollection must certainly enable you to say that there is *a Proviso in the new Sistm* which was inserted for the express purpose of preventing a majority of the Senate or the States which is considered as the same thing from giving up the Mississippi. It is provided that two-thirds of the Members present in the Senate shall be required to concur in making Treaties and if the Southern states attend to their Duty this will imply ⅔ of the States in the Union together with the president, a security rather better than the present 9 States. (Quoted in Merritt, 162)

Williamson further added that

> when a member, Mr. Wilson objected to this Proviso, saying that in all govts. the Majority should govern it was replied that the Navigation of the Mississippi after what had already happened in Congress was not to be risked in the Hands of a mere Majority and the Objection was withdrawn. (Quoted in Merritt, 162)

The Louisiana Purchase

During the presidency of Thomas Jefferson in 1803, negotiations for navigation rights on the Mississippi with France, which had subsequently acquired rights from Spain, led to American acquisition of the entire Louisiana Territory. This almost doubled the size of the United States and furthered the dream of many of the Founders, most notably James Madison, for an extended republic that might mitigate the dangers of faction, which Madison believed were so injurious to liberty. Had the Convention not provided for the interests of Westerners both in being able to form their own states and in protecting them against transient majorities, these states might have formed their own confederation or alliance with Spain or France, and the course of American history would have been quite different.

See Also Jay, John; Jay-Gardoqui Negotiations; Kentucky; Northwest Ordinance of 1787; States, Admission and Creation

FOR FURTHER READING

Farrand, Max, ed. 1937. *The Records of the Federal Convention.* 4 vols. New Haven, CT: Yale University Press.

Foner, Eric, and John A. Garraty, eds. 1991. *The Reader's Companion to American History.* Boston: Houghton Mifflin.

McClendon, R. Earl. 1931. "Origin of the Two-Thirds Rule in Senate Action upon Treaties." *American Historical Review* 36 (July): 768–772.

Merritt, Eli. 1991. "Sectional Conflict and Secret Compromise: The Mississippi River Question and the United States Constitution." *American Journal of Legal History* 35 (April): 117–171.

MIXED GOVERNMENT

Historians and political scientists probably most frequently identify the government created by the U.S. Constitution as a "democratic" or a "republican" government, but there is reason to exercise caution in classifying the document by any simple label. The delegates to the Constitutional Convention, who often referred to classical history, were knowledgeable about Rome through many sources, including the historian Polybius who described its government as a "mixed" government. One student of classical influences on the Framers has argued that "Mixed government theory set the terms of the founders' political discourse" (Richard 1994, 123).

The idea of a mixed government is to blend various elements together into a system that would be more just and stable than a form based simply on rule by one (monarchy), rule by the few (aristocracy), or rule by the many (democracy). Mixed constitutions were thus thought to guard against "corruption" (Farber and Sherry 1990, 7). Similarly, schemes of mixed government sometimes attempt to provide for the representation of different classes—for example, patricians and plebeians, the rich and the poor—within government. In his long-winded speech to the Convention on June 18, New York's Alexander Hamilton (who favored the government of Britain, which was often described as mixed) probably came close to arguing for a system of mixed government when he argued that society was naturally divided "into two political divisions—the *few* and the *many*, who have distinct interests" (Farrand 1937, I, 308). Hamilton went on to argue that, without checks, demagogues would prevail among the people. He proposed that a "monarch" provide one check on the people and a separate "aristocracy" another (I, 309).

The most democratic element of the U.S. government is the U.S. Congress, and especially the U.S. House of Representatives, whose members are elected by the people to two-year terms. Although the U.S. Senate is not, like the British House of Lords, composed of noblemen, its smaller size and the longer terms of its members (who were initially selected by state legislatures rather than directly by the people) were designed so that this body would act as a brake on the passions of the larger and more democratic House. Judges, who are not elected but appointed by the president with the advice and consent of the Senate "during good behavior," constitute a type of aristocracy of legal training, if not of birth. Although there are no guarantees that the president will be well-born, the Framers attempted to preserve the "energy" of this office by vesting this office in a single individual.

The idea of mixed government is not widely employed today. However, it is closely related to the more familiar ideas of separation of powers and checks and balances.

See Also Checks and Balances; Classical Allusions and Influences; Corruption; Forms of Government; Polybius; Separation of Powers

FOR FURTHER READING

Eidelberg, Paul. 1968. *The Philosophy of the American Constitution: A Reinterpretation of the Intentions of the Founding Fathers.* New York: The Free Press.

Farber, Daniel A., and Suzanna Sherry. 1990. *A History of the American Constitution.* Saint Paul, MN: West Publishing.

Farrand, Max, ed. 1937. *The Records of the Federal Convention.* 4 vols. New Haven, CT: Yale University Press.

Richard, Carl J. 1994. *The Founders and the Classics: Greece, Rome, and the American Enlightenment.* Cambridge, MA: Harvard University Press.

MONARCHY

A monarchy is a government in which a single individual, often designated a king or queen, has sole or primary power. Monarchs typically succeed one another by the principle of hereditary succession through which a king or queen passed the office to his or her children. Ancient philosophers sometimes distinguished kings, who worked on behalf of the common good, from tyrants, or dictators, who attempted simply to enrich themselves.

Portrait of George I, king of England
(Library of Congress)

Consistent with such a distinction, the American colonies initially took a somewhat benign view of the English king by limiting their dispute with England to the claims of the British Parliament to sovereignty in the New World, especially over taxes. King George III did not, however, offer the colonists the relief they were seeking. Moreover, after Thomas Paine published *Common Sense* attacking the institution of monarchy and hereditary succession, the American revolutionaries proclaimed in the Declaration of Independence that the king, in conjunction with this Parliament, was attempting to subject the colonies to an absolute despotism, or tyranny.

Uses of the Term at the Convention

On June 1, Charles Pinckney of South Carolina expressed his fears that extending too many powers to the president could convert him into "a Monarchy, of the worst kind, to wit an elective one" (Farrand 1937, I, 65). On that same day, Pennsylvania's James Wilson observed that "he did not consider the Prerogatives of the British Monarch as a proper guide in defining the Executive powers" (I, 65).

In arguing on June 2 for the rather novel view that the president should not be paid, Benjamin Franklin indicated that he feared monarchy, in part because he thought there was a natural predisposition in its favor:

But there is a natural inclination in mankind to Kingly Government. It sometimes relieves them from Aristocratic domination. They had rather have one tyrant than five hundred. It gives more of the appearance of equality among Citizens, and that they like. I am apprehensive therefore, perhaps too apprehensive, that the Government of these States, may in future times, end in a Monarchy. But this Catastrophe I think may be long delayed, if in our proposed system we do not sow the seeds of contention, faction & tumult, by making our posts of honor, places of profit. (II, 83)

In reflecting later in the day on executive removal, Delaware's John Dickinson said that he personally considered "a limited Monarchy . . . as *one* of the best Governments in the world" (I, 87). He went on to observe: "A limited monarchy however was out of the question. The spirit of the times—the state of our affairs, forbade the experiment, if it were desirable" (I, 87). He added: "A House of Nobles was essential to such a Govt. Could these be created by a breath, or by a stroke of the pen? No. They were the growth of ages, and could only arise under a complication of circumstances none of which existed in this Country" (I, 87).

On June 4, Virginia's George Mason opposed an absolute executive veto and favored a Council of Revision. He expressed fears that "We are not indeed constituting a British Government, but a more dangerous monarchy, an elective one" (I, 101). He was convinced that the people would not approve: "He hoped that nothing like a monarchy would ever be attempted in this Country. A hatred to its oppressions had carried the people through the late Revolution" (I, 101–102). Similarly, on June 12, Elbridge Gerry of Massachusetts

Potential Kings? Prince Henry of Prussia and the Bishop of Osnaburg

The biographer of Friederich von Steuben (1730–1794), the Prussian-born officer who had aided the American cause during the Revolution, reported in an 1859 book that von Steuben had once responded to a query about the willingness of Prince Henry of Prussia, the brother of Frederick the Great, to be president by saying: "As far as I know the prince he would never think of crossing the ocean to be your master. I wrote to him a good while ago what kind of fellows you are; he would not have the patience to stay three days among you" (quoted in Krauel 1911, 44).

Scholars long speculated as to whether von Steuben and others might in fact have approached Prince Henry about such a prospect. Scholars have found evidence that now suggests that in 1786, the year before the Constitutional Convention, Nathaniel Gorham, then president of the Congress and a future delegate to the Constitutional Convention from Massachusetts, with the knowledge of Rufus King from the same state, may also have corresponded with Prince Henry about the possibility that he might serve in America, should it choose a system of government similar to that of England (Krauel, 46). Prince Henry's response was quite cautious, suggesting both that it was unlikely that Americans would abandon a republican form of government and that, should they do so, they might want to look for a prince among their French allies (Krauel, 47–48).

Although Alexander Hamilton of New York indicated in a speech of June 18 that he favored an executive who was chosen during good behavior, he did not propose a hereditary monarch (Farrand 1937, I, 292), and delegates clearly considered the temperament of the American people to be "republican." Nonetheless, one of the relatively few negative press accounts to be published about the Constitutional Convention found its way into Connecticut's *Fairfield Gazette* on July 25, when it published part of a letter purportedly written on June 19 by a loyalist in Philadelphia. It advanced the idea that the Bishop of Osnaburg, the second son of England's George III, should be enthroned as king in America. It further asserted that the delegates

at the Convention agreed with this assessment and that "the means only of accomplishing so great an event, appears principally to occupy their counsels" (quoted in Alexander 1990, 129).

In what has been called "the only direct statement attributed to delegates in the period before the Convention was made public" (Alexander, 131), the editor of the Pennsylvania *Herald* reported on August 18 that

> we are well informed, that many letters have been written to the members of the federal convention from different quarters, respecting the reports idly circulating, that it is intended to establish a monarchical government, to send for the Bishop of Osnaburgh, &c. &c.–to which it has been uniformly answered, 'tho' we cannot, affirmatively, tell you what we are doing; we can, negatively, tell you what we are not doing–we never once thought of a king. (Alexander, 131)

This statement was widely reprinted, and appeared to calm public nerves, that the Convention might be considering abandoning republicanism for monarchy. Delegate Alexander Martin of North Carolina sent a letter to the state governor on August 20, 1787 repeating the substance of the Pennsylvania *Herald* denial (III, 73). The popular fear of a European monarch and attempts to quiet it may explain, in part, the citizenship requirement for the presidency (Nelson 1987).

FOR FURTHER READING

Alexander, John K. 1990. *The Selling of the Constitutional Convention: A History of News Coverage*. Madison, WI: Madison House.

Farrand, Max, ed. 1937. *The Records of the Federal Convention*. 4 vols. New Haven, CT: Yale University Press.

Krauel, Richard. 1911. "Prince Henry of Prussia and the Regency of the United States, 1786." *American Historical Review* 17 (October): 44–51.

Nelson, Michael. 1987. "Constitutional Qualifications for the President." *Presidential Studies Quarterly* 17 (Spring): 383–399.

observed both that "the genius of the people" was opposed to monarchy and that "having no hereditary distinctions among us, we were destitute [he meant destitute] of the essential materials for such an innovation" (I, 215).

The individual at the Convention who came closest to advocating a monarchy was New York's Alexander Hamilton. During a lengthy speech on June 18, he proposed a chief executive who would serve during good behavior. In replying to criticisms that he was thereby advocating "an *elective Monarch*," Hamilton replied "that *Monarch* is an indefinite term" (I, 290), and that selections of executives for life did not necessarily lead to tumults. Not surprisingly, his highly praised speech appears to have had no tangible influence on his fellow delegates. On June 26, Elbridge Gerry of Massachusetts hazarded the view that less than one in one thousand citizens favored any "approach toward Monarchy" (I, 425).

Quieting Public Fears outside the Convention

Although Gerry may have exaggerated, it would appear that his general perception of public sentiment on the subject was accurate. Indeed, public fears that the Convention might consider a monarchy were sufficient for the delegates unofficially to release a statement to the *Pennsylvania Herald* on August 18. Consistent with the rules of secrecy that the Convention had adopted, the statement indicated that "'tho' we cannot, affirmatively, tell you what we are doing; we can, negatively, tell you what we are not doing—we never once thought of a king" (Van Doren 1948, 145).

The Founders' Solution

Given the Founders' concerns over abuses of monarchy, it is surprising that they created a chief executive with as much power as they did, but they ultimately came to see such an office as essential to a strong government in which each of the three branches could balance one another. Almost as wary of aristocracy, or rule by the few, as

of monarchy, members of the Convention also recognized the dangers of what they regarded as excessive democracy, in which legislators with short terms almost completely dominated the government. Members of the Convention often designated the system of government that that created to balance these excesses as "free" or "republican" government. It is based on a number of counterbalancing structures, on allowing the popular will to be expressed through representatives rather than directly, and on the hope that a government encompassing a large land area would serve to multiply the number of interests, or factions, so that no single one would dominate.

See Also Aristocracy; Declaration of Independence; Democracy; Forms of Government; Paine, Thomas; Republicanism

FOR FURTHER READING

Farrand, Max, ed. 1937. *The Records of the Federal Convention.* 4 vols. New Haven, CT: Yale University Press.
Van Doren, Carl. 1948. *The Great Rehearsal: The Story of the Making and Ratifying of the Constitution of the United States.* New York: Viking.

MONEY, CONGRESSIONAL COINING

Article I, Section 8 of the Constitution grants Congress power "to coin Money, regulate the value thereof, and of foreign Coin, and fix the Standard of Weights and Measures." Under the Articles of Confederation, Congress had "the sole and exclusive right and power of regulating the alloy and value of coin struck by their own authority, or by that of the respective states," but the power of coining money and regulating its value required a vote by nine or more states. Moreover, the Articles did not prohibit the states from coining their own money, and they often issued such money in an inflationary manner that undercut the interests of creditors. Rhode Island, the only state not to send delegates to the Convention, was a particular object of scorn.

Like most of the enumerated powers of Congress, the power over money appears to have originated in the report of the Committee of Detail, which reported to the Convention on August 6. It actually proposed a series of three congressional powers including the power "To coin money; To regulate the value of foreign coin; [and] To fix the standards of weights and measures" (Farrand 1937, II, 182).

All of these provisions may have been taken from the Pinckney Plan (see II, 136), which appears to have been forwarded to the committee along with other documents. The reference to foreign coin appears odd, but was included at a time when specie was scarce and when foreign coins were often used as means of exchange.

The Committee of Detail also proposed that states be prohibited from coining money (II, 187). This provision eventually found its way into Article I, Section 10. It prohibited states from emitting bills of credit or making "any Thing but gold or silver Coin a Tender in Payment of Debts."

There is no recorded discussion of the power to coin money when the Convention approved it on August 16. Modifications by the Committee of Style and Arrangement were minimal.

See Also Committee of Detail; Money, State Coining and Emissions of

FOR FURTHER READING

Farrand, Max, ed. 1937. *The Records of the Federal Convention*. 4 vols. New Haven, CT: Yale University Press.

Schweitzer, Mary M. 1989. "State-Issued Currency and the Ratification of the U.S. Constitution." *Journal of Economic History* 49 (June): 311–322.

MONEY, STATE COINING AND EMISSIONS OF

One of the injustices that many of the Framers had perceived under the Articles of Confederation was that caused by state issues, or emissions, of paper money. Some states had used the power to issue such money in a responsible way that facilitated the payment of taxes and that combated deflation (see Schweitzer 1989, 313–315). Others, most notably Rhode Island, had used this power to inflate currency in a manner that was perceived to further the interests of debtors over creditors, both in and out of state, who were required by state law to accept such inflated currency in payment of debts. Tight state fiscal policies provided some of the impetus for Shays's Rebellion in Massachusetts, which had served as a major catalyst to the Constitutional Convention.

On August 6, the five-member Committee of Detail, chaired by John Rutledge of South Carolina, recommended vesting Congress with power "to coin money" and "to emit bills on the credit of the United States" (Farrand 1937, II, 182). In line with this, it proposed absolutely prohibiting states from coining money and (less absolutely) prohibiting states from emitting bills of credit without congressional consent (II, 187). When the Convention first discussed this proposal on August 28, Pennsylvania's James Wilson, who had served on the committee, and Connecticut's Roger Sherman proposed to add to the first provision "Nor emit bills of credit, nor make any thing but gold & silver coin a tender in payment of debts" (II, 439), thus making the prohibition against coining money absolute. Perhaps with Shays's Rebellion in mind, Nathaniel Gorham of Massachusetts, who had also served on the Committee of Detail, feared that such an absolute prohibition "would rouse the most desperate opposition from its partisans," but Sherman argued that the Convention was presented with "a favorable crisis for crushing paper money" (II, 439). He observed that "If the consent of the Legislature could authorize emissions of it, the friends of paper money would make every exertion to get into the Legislature in order to license it" (II, 439). Perhaps influenced by its governor, Edmund Randolph, who had served on the Committee of Detail, only Virginia voted against the motion (Maryland was divided on the issue) to restrict state emissions of paper money, and the Convention voted unanimously to accept the rest of the motion (II, 439).

In *Federalist* No. 44, James Madison observed: "The extension of the prohibition to bills of credit must give pleasure to every citizen in proportion to his love of justice and his knowledge of the true springs of public prosperity" (Hamilton, Madison, and Jay 1961, 251). He continued at considerable length, tying emissions of paper money to perceived state injustices under the Articles of Confederation. Significantly, he used language typical in religious discourse of the period relating to the payment of sins:

> The loss which America has sustained since the peace, from the pestilent effects of paper money on the necessary confidence between man and man, on the necessary confidence in the public councils, on the industry and morals of the people, and on the character of republican government, constitutes an enormous debt against the States chargeable with this unadvised measure, which must long remain unsatisfied; or rather an accumulation of guilt, which can be expiated no otherwise than by a voluntary sacrifice on the altar of justice of the power which has been the instrument of it. (281–282)

The prohibition against state issues of paper money elicited little comment during the debate over ratification of the Constitution by Federalists and Antifederalists (Schweitzer, 320). Significantly, the constitutional provision preventing future state emissions of money did not require that they retire existing currency. Mary Schweitzer has observed that Pennsylvania continued to receive such currency in the 1790s. Moreover, the need for such state issues of currency apparently declined with the increased circulation of bank notes (321).

See Also Committee of Detail; Congress, Collective Powers; Justice; Rhode Island; Shays's Rebellion; States, Limits on

FOR FURTHER READING

Farrand, Max, ed. 1937. *The Records of the Federal Convention.* 4 vols. New Haven, CT: Yale University Press.
Hamilton, Alexander, James Madison, and John Jay. 1961. *The Federalist Papers.* Ed. Clinton Rossiter. New York: New American Library.
Holton, Woody. 2004. "'From the Labours of Others': The War Bonds Controversy and the Origins of the Constitution in New England." *William and Mary Quarterly,* 3rd ser. 61 (April): 271–307.
Schweitzer, Mary M. 1989. "State-Issued Currency and the Ratification of the U.S. Constitution." *Journal of Economic History* 49 (June): 311–322.

MONROE, JAMES (1758–1831)

The last of the early presidents to wear knee britches, James Monroe did not participate in the Constitutional Convention of 1787, although he did attend the Virginia ratifying convention. Born in Westmoreland County, Virginia, in 1758, Monroe studied briefly at the College of William and Mary before enlisting on the Patriot side in the Revolutionary War. During the war, he established a friendship with the Marquis de Lafayette, spent the winter at Valley Forge, crossed the

James Monroe, based on a portrait by Stuart Gilbert (published 1904) (Library of Congress)

Delaware with Washington in the famous raid on the Hessians at Trenton, and was wounded.

After studying law under Thomas Jefferson, Monroe married and established a law practice first in Fredericksburg and then in Charlottesville. His "cabin castle," Ash Lawn, or the Highlands, which is within a few short miles of Jefferson's Monticello, is still a tourist attraction.

Newly settled in Fredericksburg at the time of the Constitutional Convention, Monroe had already served a term in the Virginia legislature and another in the Continental Congress. The Virginia legislature had not nominated him as a delegate to the Constitutional Convention. Although he appears to have felt slighted, there is some evidence that leaders might have been trying to spare him and his new wife the financial costs implicit in such service (Ammon 1971, 67). In retrospect, he would appear to have been a much more effective delegate than John Blair, James McClurg, or George Wythe (who left the Convention early because of his wife's illness). Had he stayed and opposed the document, however, it is possible that Virginia would not have been able to cast its vote on behalf of the new document since Randolph and Mason were both opposed and only Blair, Madison, and Washington were left to sign.

Monroe was a moderate Antifederalist. After the Convention, he drafted, but never published, a pamphlet critiquing the new document but also criticizing the government under the Articles of Confederation. As befitted a citizen of a large state who believed in republican principles, he was especially critical of states' equal representation in the U.S. Senate. He also opposed the ability of the new national government to levy direct taxes, wanted further limits on the power to make treaties, and joined other Antifederalists in criticizing the omission of a bill of rights (Ammon, 69).

Selected as a delegate to the state ratifying convention by neighboring Spotsylvania County after his own King George County (influenced by George Washington) elected a Federalist, Monroe's position at the Convention was closer to that of the more moderate George Mason, who was more insistent in getting a bill of rights ratified, than to the more bombastic Patrick Henry, who was less persuaded that the document could be rescued by such tinkering. Monroe spoke four times at the Convention. In the first speech he advocated amending the Constitution prior to ratifying it; he specifically wanted amendments limiting Congress's power to enact direct taxes and requiring a quorum before the Senate could ratify treaties. He further expressed the latter concern in a second speech in which he argued that the new Constitution threatened the interests of the West. In a third speech, Monroe criticized the Electoral College mechanism for selecting the president, preferring direct election. His fourth speech reiterated his belief that it was better to amend the Constitution prior to its adoption rather than afterwards. Monroe subsequently served on a committee at the Virginia ratifying convention that recommended amendments to the document (Ammon, 71–73).

James Madison defeated Monroe in a contest for a seat in the first U.S. House of Representatives, but their friendship was not severed, and Monroe would soon become active in the Democratic-Republican Party which Jefferson and Madison founded. Monroe went on to serve as a minister to France under George Washington; as a Virginia governor; as a minister to France under Thomas Jefferson, where he and Robert Livingston helped negotiate the Louisiana Purchase; as secretary of state under James Madison; and as a two-term president from 1817 to 1825. His first term ushered in an "Era of Good Feeling," and he won reelection by 231 votes to 1. During his second term, he promulgated the Monroe Doctrine (in which Secretary of State John Quincy Adams had a strong hand), indicating that the United States would not look favorably on further European colonization in the Western Hemisphere. Monroe presided over the Virginia constitutional convention in 1829. He died at the New York home of his daughter on July 4, 1831, five years to the day after the deaths of John Adams and Thomas Jefferson.

See Also Jefferson, Thomas; Madison, James, Jr.; Mason, George; Ratification in the States; Virginia

FOR FURTHER READING

Ammon, Harry. 1971. *James Monroe: The Quest for National Identity.* New York: McGraw-Hill Book Company.

Nelson, Mike, ed. 1996. *The Presidency.* London: Salamander Books Ltd.

O'Brien, Steven G. 1991. *American Political Leaders: From Colonial Times to the Present.* Santa Barbara, CA: ABC-CLIO.

MONTESQUIEU, CHARLES LOUIS DE SECONDAT DE (1686–1755)

The most-quoted European political writer during the American Founding era was France's Baron de Montesquieu, the author of the magisterial book *The Spirit of the Laws.* Indeed, approximately 60 percent of all references to Enlightenment thinkers that have been documented in American political writings during the late eighteenth century can be traced to him, with the number of references increasing during the 1780s when the U.S. Constitution was formulated (Lutz 1984, 192).

Charles Louis de Secondat de Montesquieu, 18th-century French philosopher and author of The Spirit of the Laws *(Library of Congress)*

Delegates referred to Montesquieu a number of times during the Convention debates. On June 1, Pennsylvania's James Wilson favorably cited Montesquieu's commendation of a confederated republic (Farrand 1937, I, 71). Montesquieu provides one of the authorities for Alexander Hamilton's speech to the Convention on June 18 (I, 308). On June 23, Pierce Butler of South Carolina observed that "the great Montesquieu says, it is unwise to entrust persons with power, which by being abused operates to the advantage of those entrusted with it" (I, 391). On June 30, Virginia's James Madison cited Montesquieu as authority for the view that the Lycian confederacy vested members with votes "proportioned to their importance" (I, 485), and on July 17 he cited Montesquieu as opposing undue dependence of the executive on the legislative body (II, 34). Maryland's James McHenry drew a similar conclusion on September 6 (II, 530). On July 11, Virginia's Edmund Randolph cited Montesquieu as saying that suffrage is "a fundamental article in Republican Govts" (I, 580). Other delegates reflected sentiments that Montesquieu had advocated (McDonald 1985, 233).

Montesquieu's greatest contribution to the theory of the Constitution appears to have been his emphasis on separation of powers, an idea Montesquieu appears to have adopted in part from Polybius's emphasis on mixed governments. The Convention translated the idea of separation of powers into the division of the new government in legislative, executive, and judicial branches. Montesquieu, however, had also advocated the view that republican government, such as the Framers favored, was only practical in small nations. Partly by utilizing arguments of David Hume, James Madison argued against this position, not only at the Constitutional Convention but also in his famous *Federalist* essay No. 10. Antifederalists who relied on this aspect of Montesquieu's thought thus cited him during the ratification debates almost as frequently as did the Federalists (Lutz, 195).

See Also Antifederalists; European Influences on

Delegates to the Convention; Federalists; Hume, David; Madison, James, Jr.; Polybius; Separation of Powers

FOR FURTHER READING

Carrithers, David W., Michael A. Mosher, and Paul A. Rahe, eds. 2001. *Montesquieu's Science of Politics: Essays on* The Spirit of the Laws. Lanham, MD: Rowman and Littlefield Publishers.

Farrand, Max, ed. 1937. *The Records of the Federal Convention.* 4 vols. New Haven, CT: Yale University Press.

Lutz, Donald S. 1984. "The Relative Influence of European Writers on Late Eighteenth-Century American Political Thought." *American Political Science Review* 189, no. 78 (March): 197.

McDonald, Forrest. 1985. *Novus Ordo Seclorum: The Intellectual Origins of the Constitution.* Lawrence: University Press of Kansas.

Montesquieu, Baron de. 1949. *The Spirit of the Laws.* Trans. Thomas Nugent. New York: Hafner Press.

Gouverneur Morris, delegate from Pennsylvania
(Pixel That)

MORRIS, GOUVERNEUR (1752–1816)

Gouverneur Morris was one of the most vocal and influential members of the Constitutional Convention. A committed nationalist, he is perhaps best known as the member of the Committee of Style and Arrangement who gave the final polish to the Constitution. In this capacity, he authored its Preamble, which substituted the words "We the People" for a list of states and eloquently described the goals of the new document.

Morris was born on the family estate at Morrisania, New York, the current site of the Bronx. Morris's father died when his son was only ten. Initially educated by tutors, Morris attended King's College (today's Columbia University), studied law under William Smith, and was admitted to the New York bar by age 20. Morris served as a member of New York's provincial congress from 1775 to 1777, during which time he also served at the New York constitutional convention.

As a delegate from New York to the Continental Congress, Morris signed the Articles of Confederation. He also inspected the dismal situation that George Washington and his men faced at Valley Forge and served as an associate to Robert Morris (not related), the superintendent of finance. At the end of his term, he remained in Philadelphia.

Morris was 35 years old when he served as one of Pennsylvania's delegates to the Constitutional Convention. He was notable for his florid speech and a wooden leg that had resulted from the loss of a leg in a carriage accident in 1780. He had also largely lost the use of an arm from a burn in another accident, but standing over six feet tall, his physical disabilities did nothing to detract from his reputation as a lady's man, a reputation he kept until he married Anne Carey Randolph of Virginia in 1809 and by whom he subsequently fathered a son. Morris missed the month of June attending to business in New York but still managed to be recorded as speaking the most and playing an important part in the rest of the Convention's proceedings.

Morris's Early Comments at the Convention

On May 30, the day after Edmund Randolph presented the Virginia Plan and the Convention met as a Committee of the Whole, Morris seconded the resolutions constituting the Virginia Plan as well as a substitute motion that Randolph introduced proposing that a merely "federal" union "will not accomplish the objects proposed by the articles of confederation" (Farrand 1937, I, 30). That same day, Morris explained that a federal government was "a mere compact resting on the good faith of the parties" whereas a national government had "a *compleat* and compulsive operation" (I, 34).

Morris seconded Madison's proposal that an "equitable ratio of representation" should be established in Congress (I, 36). When delegates from Delaware indicated that they might not be able to continue if the Convention considered changing the states' equal representation in Congress, Morris observed that this change in representation was "so fundamental an article in a national Govt. that it could not be dispensed with" (I, 37). Maryland's James McHenry reported that Morris believed the Convention would either accept "a supreme government now" or a "despot" in twenty years (I, 43). Morris left the Convention on May 31 to deal with his estate at Morrisania and to take care of business for Robert Morris, and he did not return until July 2.

Morris on Congress

The Senate

Morris did not allow his absence to keep him from withholding his opinions about the Convention's seeming impasse over representation in the Senate shortly after he returned. Although he opposed its report, Morris initially favored the appointment of a committee to resolve this issue. He also favored a radically more aristocratic Senate than most of the other delegates were contemplating. Like them, Morris conceived of the Senate's primary role as that of checking the excesses of the House of Representatives. To do this, he

thought its members would require "*abilities* and *virtue*" (I, 512). Members of the Senate should have a personal interest in checking the democratic excesses of the House. They should have "great personal property" and "an aristocratic spirit" and they should be independent (I, 512). Morris believed that this required that they have life tenure. Because he envisioned a Senate that would represent wealth, Morris did not favor paying its members. Moreover, he favored executive appointment, rather than state or congressional selection.

Morris professed not to care how senators were apportioned: "The members being independt. & for life, may be taken as well from one place as from another" (I, 513). Morris feared that existing proposals were too dependent upon the states. The only security against encroachments of the House would be "a select & sagacious body of men, instituted to watch agst. them on all sides" (I, 514).

Morris proposed that the members of the Senate should vote "per capita," that is, by casting individual votes instead of voting as states (II, 94). He initially favored giving each state three senators (II, 94). Morris expressed doubts as to whether the Senate should have any role in the making of treaties (II, 392). When the Convention established that a two-thirds majority of the Senate would be required to approve treaties, however, Morris did not favor exempting treaties of peace (II, 548).

Congressional Representation

When the Committee of Eleven proposed on July 5 that representation should be apportioned according to population in the House and equally in the Senate, Morris objected that this plan was too state-centered. Morris professed to be attending the Convention as "a Representative of America," indeed, as "a Representative of the whole human race" (I, 529). Morris thought it best not to worry about public sentiment but to recommend what is "reasonable & right" in the hope that "all who have reasonable minds and sound intentions will embrace it (I, 529).

In somewhat intemperate language that seemed to respond to earlier threats by Delaware's Gunning Bedford that small states might seek foreign allies, Morris anticipated that if the large states formed a government on their own, factions would form within the smaller states to join them, and "If persuasion does not unite it, the sword will" (I, 530). Repeating that "State attachments, and State importance have been the bane of this Country," Morris said that "we cannot annihilate, but we may perhaps take the teeth out of the serpent" (I, 530).

Like Virginia's James Madison, Morris saw little value in the "concession" by the small states prohibiting money bills from originating in the Senate. Openly espousing the Senate's aristocratic function, Morris feared that such a restriction "will take away the responsibility of the 2d branch, the great security for good behavior" (I, 545). Morris was still advocating this opinion on August 8 (II, 224); and, on the following day, he accused George Mason of trying to scare the smaller states into continuing support for this provision, lest they lose their right to equal state representation (II, 234). Morris may have undercut this argument for the need for both houses to be able to originate money bills when he argued on August 13 that the Senate veto on money bills would give it just as much power as if it had the power to originate such measures (II, 276).

Morris said on July 7 that he favored "supporting the dignity and splendor of the American Empire" (I, 552). He feared that a Senate overrepresenting the small states would be an obstacle to these objectives and thought that the small states were pressing an unfair advantage:

> The small States aware of the necessity of preventing anarchy, and taking advantage of the moment, extorted from the large ones an equality of votes. Standing now on that ground, they demand under the new system greater rights as men, than their fellow Citizens of the large States. The proper answer to them is that this same necessity of which they formerly took advantage does not now exist, and that the large States are at liberty now to consider what is right, rather than what might be expedient. (I, 552)

Representation in the House of Representatives

Morris objected that the scheme of representation in the House of Representatives did not include property, which he considered to be "the main object of Society" (I, 533). In a position that evoked strong opposition from many Southern delegates, Morris further argued that "the rule of representatives ought to be so fixed as to secure to the Atlantic States a prevalence in the National Councils" (I, 533). Morris opposed requiring Congress to reapportion itself on a regular basis, repeating that he feared "the danger of throwing such a preponderancy into the Western Scale" (I, 571). He later argued: "The Busy haunts of men not the remote wilderness, was the proper School of political Talents. If the Western people get the power into their hands they will ruin the Atlantic interest. The Back members are always most adverse to the best measures" (I, 583).

Morris did not think it possible to stop Western migration, but he disfavored throwing "the power into their hands" (II, 454). He proposed that the admission of new states should require approval by two-thirds of Congress, but he substituted a motion, to which the Convention agreed, that no new states should be formed within existing states without their consent (II, 455). He apparently attempted to protect New York's interest in what happened in Vermont (II, 463).

Consistent with his view that the legislature should have considerable discretion, Morris did not think the Constitution needed to specify the frequency of congressional meetings (II, 198). He did, however, favor establishing a quorum for Congress at 33 for the House and 14 for the Senate (a majority plus one). He feared that if the number were set lower, members might absent themselves in order to prevent such a quorum from being able to conduct business (II, 252). Morris thought that the Constitution could entrust the power of expelling members to such a majority (II, 254). He also believed that members of Congress should be allowed to accept other offices, so long as they had to vacate their seats in order to take them (II, 286). He was especially concerned about the possibility that the Constitution could be so worded as to prevent the appointment of the individual most qualified to conduct a war simply because he was a congressman (II, 289). Morris believed that the national government should pay the salaries of members of Congress. In light of his prior comments on representation of the Western states, one might question his newly professed concern about putting an "unequal burden" on such states, as well as the realism of his belief that "there could be no reason to fear that they would overpay themselves" (II, 290).

On July 6, the Convention appointed Morris to the committee to come up with a plan of apportionment for the House. He chaired the Committee of Five, which suggested an initial allocation of 56 members, allocated according to what they believed would be one representative for every 40,000 inhabitants, albeit not altogether disregarding wealth, apparently a reference to slaves (I, 560; also see I, 567). Morris further served on the Committee of Eleven, which reconsidered this number and arrived at the new number of 65. He was concerned that these proposals raised conflicts between the North and South. It is not altogether clear that he poured oil on this water when he observed that while Southern states might supply more of the money for future wars, the Northern states would spill more of their blood (I, 567).

Slave Representation

Morris initially opposed the three-fifths clause for representation of slaves. He thought that counting slaves as partial persons conflicted with the Convention's earlier agreement to consider them as wealth (I, 582). Morris also observed that the people of Pennsylvania would "revolt at the idea of being put on a footing with slaves. They would reject any plan that was to have such an effect" (I, 583).

On July 11, Morris observed that "he could never agree to give such encouragement to the slave trade as would be given by allowing them a representation for their Negroes, and he did not believe those States would ever confederate on terms that would deprive them of that trade" (I, 588). The next day, proposing to leave future allo-

cations of representation to Congress, Morris observed that he did not think that either side could accept the existing compromise: "it is in vain for the Eastern States to insist on what the Southn States will never agree to. It is equally vain for the latter to require what the other States can never admit; and he verily believed the people of Pena. will never agree to a representation of Negroes" (I, 593).

Morris continued to oppose the three-fifths compromise on July 13:

> If Negroes were to be viewed as inhabitants, and the revision was to proceed on the principle of numbers of inhabts. they ought to be added in their entire number, and not in the proportion of 3/5. If as property, the word wealth was right, and striking it out would produce the very inconsistency which it was meant to get rid of. (I, 604)

Harkening back to his expressed concern over the admission of Western states, Morris argued that the main distinction in the nation was between the "maritime" and the "interior & landed interest" (I, 604). In a speech that seems to anticipate Abraham Lincoln's idea that the Union could not survive half slave and half free (without Lincoln's emphasis on the necessity of Union), Morris argued that if North and South were so radically different, perhaps they should consider separating: "If it be real, instead of attempting to blend incompatible things, let us at once take a friendly leave of each other. There can be no end of demands for security if every particular interest is to be entitled to it" (I, 604).

Harkening back to a dispute in the Continental Congress, Morris further feared that the Southern states would join with new states in the West to war against Spain for the control of the Mississippi River (I, 604).

Morris returned to the theme of slavery on August 8 by suggesting that the term "free" be inserted before a provision designed to allocate one representative for every 40,000 inhabitants. Morris gave perhaps the Convention's strongest speech against slavery. As on other occasions, his candor appears to have overtaken his sensitivity to the interest of fellow delegates:

He never would concur in upholding domestic slavery. It was a nefarious institution—It was the cure of heaven on the States where it prevailed. Compare the free regions of the Middle States, where a rich & noble cultivation marks the prosperity & happiness of the people, with the misery & poverty which overspread the barren wastes of VA. Maryd. & the other States having slaves. (II, 221)

Morris further observed:

The admission of slaves into the Representation when fairly explained comes to this: that the inhabitant of Georgia and S.C. who goes to the Coast of Africa, and in defiance of the most sacred laws of humanity tears away his fellow creatures from their dearest connections & dam(n)s them to the most cruel bondages, shall have more votes in a Govt. instituted for the protection of the rights of mankind, than the Citizen of Pa or N. Jersey who views with a laudable horror, so nefarious a practice. (II, 222)

Morris proclaimed that "he would sooner submit himself to a tax for paying for all the Negroes in the U. States. than saddle posterity with such a Constitution" (II, 223), but he does not appear to have offered a concrete proposal to this effect. Although he later withdrew the motion, Morris proposed listing the two Carolinas and Georgia in the Constitution as the states with permission to continue to import slaves so that it would "be known also that this part of the Constitution was a compliance with those States" (II, 415).

Other Congressional Issues

Morris thought that it would be wiser to establish requirements for electors than for members of Congress. He was particularly concerned about a proposal that would bar individuals with unsettled accounts from accepting offices. He asked, "What will be done with those patriotic Citizens who have lent money, or services or property to their Country, without having been yet able to obtain a liquidation of their claims? Are they to be ex-

cluded?" (II, 121). Interestingly, he observed that delegates should not only heed the ancient precept not to "be righteous overmuch" but also guard against "being wise over much" (II, 122). Morris did not believe it was necessary to prohibit citizens from voting for nonresidents for Congress since they would rarely elect them (II, 217). He favored restricting the vote to freeholders (II, 201; also see II, 217). He supported a motion raising the required residency for members of the House of Representatives from three years to seven (II, 216). Similarly, he moved to increase the required number of years of citizenship for senators from four to 14 years (II, 235). However, Morris proposed that the citizenship requirement should not affect anyone who was currently a citizen (II, 270), although he did not think it necessary to make a similar exception for those then under the age of 25 (II, 271).

In responding to an emotional appeal by Pennsylvania's James Wilson, an immigrant, for liberality toward immigrants, Morris said that it was important for the delegates to "be governed as much by our reason, and as little by our feelings as possible" (II, 237). Ironically, he followed with a highly emotional example of the practice, which he attributed to American Indians, of sharing their wives with guests! Perhaps unintentionally, Morris further called into question his own earlier characterization of himself as a citizen of the world:

As to those philosophical gentlemen, those Citizens of the World, as they called themselves, He owned he did not wish to see any of them in our public Councils. He would not trust them. The men who can shake off their attachments to their own Country can never love any other. These attachments are the wholesome prejudices which uphold all Governments. (II, 238)

National Powers

The day after the Convention finally settled on the Connecticut Compromise, Morris moved to reconsider the whole issue of representation (II, 25). The delegates appear to have politely ignored him. After Connecticut's Roger Sherman proposed that Congress should be prevented from interfering in the internal police affairs of the states, Morris was unsympathetic. In his view, "The internal police, as it would be called & understood by the States ought to be infringed in many cases, as in the case of paper money & other tricks by which Citizens of other States may be affected" (II, 26). In a similar vein, Morris favored direct taxation by the national government instead of a system of "quotas & requisitions, which are subversive of the idea of Govt." (II, 26). Morris opposed Madison's plan for a negative on state laws, however, "as likely to be terrible to the States, and not necessary, if sufficient Legislative authority should be given to the Genl. Government" (II, 27).

Morris might have reflected the view of more timid delegates when, on July 18, he indicated that he would have reservations about the guarantee clause if it were to be interpreted so as to provide that Congress would have to guarantee the existing government of Rhode Island. Known for its legislative measures favoring debtors by inflating currency, it was the sole state that did not send delegates to the Convention (II, 47).

On August 9, Morris supported congressional oversight of congressional elections, fearing that, otherwise, "the States might make false returns and then make no provisions for new elections" (II, 241). Morris opposed the restriction, introduced by Southern delegates, prohibiting Congress from taxing exports. He believed that such taxes would constitute "a necessary source of revenue" and indicated that he favored them over direct taxes which might push the people "into Revolts" (II, 307). He later favored a provision specifying that taxes on exports would have to go to the benefit of the entire nation. He feared that otherwise the Atlantic states might force the Western states into the arms of Great Britain by taxing navigation on the Mississippi River (II, 442).

Morris favored granting Congress power to "emit bills on the credit of the U. States"; he reasoned that "If the United States had credit such bills would be unnecessary; if they had not unjust & useless" (II, 309). He wanted wide powers to restrict counterfeiting (II, 315) and thought that Congress should have power to put down insurrections within states, even without a request from the states. He complained that "We are acting a very strange part. We first form a strong man to protect us, and at the same time wish to tie his hands behind him. The legislature may surely be trusted with such a power to preserve the public tranquility" (II, 317). Morris feared that the prohibition of export taxes might be interpreted to prohibit general embargoes that might be needed in time of war (II, 360). Morris opposed national sumptuary laws (as proposed by Virginia's George Mason) on the grounds that they "tended to create a landed Nobility, by fixing in the great-landholders and their posterity their present possessions" (II, 344). Morris favored allowing Congress to make regulations to provide for uniform bankruptcy laws (II, 489). He opposed a statement in the Constitution disfavoring standing armies for fear that it would set "a dishonorable mark of distinction on the military class of Citizens" (II, 617).

Morris was far less attached to state governments than many other delegates. However, he opposed a provision prohibiting states from interfering with private contracts as going too far. Believing that judges could guard against abuses, he observed that "within the State itself a majority must rule, whatever may be the mischief done among themselves" (II, 439). In an ultimate irony, Morris introduced the provision specifying that states could not be deprived of their equal representation in the Senate without their consent (II, 631).

The Presidency

Morris thought the executive branch was quite important: "Make him too weak: The Legislature will usurp his powers: Make him too strong. He will usurp on the Legislature" (II, 105). During the ten-day adjournment of the Convention beginning on July 26 to allow the Committee of Detail to do its work, Morris vacationed at Valley Forge with George Washington, whom he idolized, and whose august presence Morris anticipated would be the first to occupy the presidency.

When the Convention considered a provision for congressional appointment of the presidency, Morris objected. He favored popular election, believing that the people "will never fail to prefer some man of distinguished character, or service; some man, if he might so speak, of continental reputation." By contrast, he believed that legislative selection was likely to be "the work of intrigue, of cabal, and of faction," to "the election of a pope by a conclave of cardinals" (II, 29). He further believed that legislative selection would lead to undue dependency of the presidency on that body.

After the Convention initially settled on July 17 on the selection of the presidency by Congress, Morris seconded a motion by Virginia's James McClurg to strike the provision for a seven-year term and to substitute an appointment "during good behavior" in its place (II, 33). He apparently believed that such tenure would obviate the problem of legislative intrigue that he had previously identified. He denied that this was likely to lead to monarchy, professing that the chief obstacle to such government was "to establish such a Repub. Govt. as wd. make the people happy and prevent a desire of change" (II, 36). Morris also believed that it was wise to prevent frequent rotation in the presidency as "a change of men is ever followed by a change of measures," and this would contribute to governmental instability (II, 112). Moreover, a president who anticipated that he would not be reelected to the presidency would try to keep the door open to the legislature (II, 113).

Of all the modes of selecting the president, Morris argued that legislative appointment was the worst. His fear was that it would make the president the "mere creature" of Congress (II, 103). Somewhat prophetically, he observed that legislatures typically split into two parties and that such parties would seek to influence presidential selection (II, 104).

Morris appears to have been one of the originators of the idea that the president should be chosen by electors chosen by the states (II, 404). This institution was largely formulated by the Committee on Postponed Matters, which the Convention established on August 31, and of which Morris was a member. Although he did not serve as the committee's chairman, Morris emerged as a primary defender of this proposal on the floor of the Convention (II, 500; also see II, 512). When Elbridge Gerry objected that the newly created vice president should not preside over the Senate because of the "close intimacy" that would exist between the president and him, Morris bluntly responded that "the vice president then will be the first heir apparent that ever loved his father" (II, 537).

When the Convention reconsidered presidential re-eligibility for office on July 29, Morris observed that "It has been a maxim in political Science that Republican Government is not adapted to a large extent of Country, because the energy of the Executive Magistracy can not reach the extreme parts of it" (II, 52). Noting the wide extent of the United States, Morris portrayed the executive branch as the branch that would have to check Congress. His description sounds a bit like the later arguments that Andrew Jackson and Woodrow Wilson would make on behalf of the presidency:

It is necessary that the Executive Magistrate should be the guardian of the people, even of the lower classes, agst. Legislative tyranny, against the Great & the wealthy who in the course of things will necessarily compose—the Legislative body. . . . The Executive therefore ought to be so constituted as to be the great protector of the Mass of the people. (II, 52)

In this same speech, Morris further argued that the president should be vested with the power of making key appointments. Morris opposed the restriction on presidential re-eligibility on the basis that if the "love of fame," which he considered to be "the great spring to noble & illustrious actions," was closed, the executive would be tempted "to make the most of the Short space of time allotted him, to accumulate wealth and provide for his friends" (II, 53).

Morris favored popular election as the check on the executive rather than legislative impeachment:

If he is to be the Guardian of the people let him be appointed by the people. If he is to be a check on the Legislature let him not be impeachable. Let him be of short duration, that he may with propriety be re-eligible. (II, 53)

When the Convention insisted that presidents should be impeachable, Morris pushed to have offenses "enumerated & defined" (II, 65). Indeed, he admitted to having changed his mind on the subject, now arguing for such impeachment by observing that "This Magistrate is not the King but the prime-Minister. The people are the King" (II, 69). An objection by Morris resulted in a motion by George Mason substituting the words "other high crimes & misdemeanors" for the word "maladministration" (II, 550). Morris further supported the view that the Senate would be a more appropriate body to try presidential impeachments than would the smaller Supreme Court (II, 551). Curiously (such a measure would appear to undermine independence and give the initiative to those initiating impeachment charges), he also supported a proposal that would have suspended an individual from office until that person could be tried (II, 612).

On August 7, Morris seconded a proposal by Delaware's George Read designed to give the president an absolute veto of congressional legislation (II, 200), and Morris supported this measure again on August 15 (II, 299). He observed: "The most virtuous citizens will often as members of a legislative body concur in measures which afterwards in their private capacity they will be ashamed of. Encroachments of the popular branch of the Government ought to be guarded against" (II, 299). He voted late in the Convention in favor of a provision that it take three-fourths rather than two-thirds of Congress to override a presidential veto, observing that "the excess rather than the deficiency of laws was to be dreaded" (II, 585). When Mason opined that the larger majority might serve as an obstacle to the repeal of bad laws, Morris argued that legal instability was a greater danger (II, 586).

The Judiciary

Just as he had feared the intrigues that congressional selection of the president might generate, so too, Morris feared the intrigues that would be generated if judges were required to sit on impeachment trials (II, 42). Morris seconded the proposal, eventually incorporated into the Constitution, by Nathaniel Gorham of Massachusetts that the president should appoint judges with the advice and consent of the Senate (II, 44), although he later indicated that he favored vesting absolute appointment power in the president (II, 82). Morris strongly opposed senatorial appointment of judges. He believed that it would be "too numerous for the purpose; as subject to cabal; and as devoid of responsibility" (II, 389). By contrast, Morris defended the system of presidential appointment and senatorial confirmation: "as the President was to nominate, there would be responsibility, and as the Senate was to concur, there would be security" (II, 539).

Morris was the individual who first explained that it would be unfair to appoint judges for life and prevent them from receiving any pay increases during their tenure (II, 44). He observed that if new judges received more than those on the bench, the latter might simply resign and seek reappointment (II, 430). Similarly, he thought it was inconsistent to say that judges served during good behavior and allow the president to remove them on the application of Congress (II, 428). Morris thought that it was essential to have a system of lower federal courts (II, 46), and he was willing to allow judges to participate in a Council of Revision, assessing the validity of laws before they went into effect (II, 75; also see II, 78). On August 20, Morris renewed the call for a Council of State to consist of the chief justice of the U.S. Supreme Court and of various secretaries of executive departments (II, 342–344), which appears to be something of a precursor to the present cabinet. Explaining the action of the Committee on Postponed Matters in not proposing such a council, however, Morris observed that the committee had "judged that the Presidt. by persuading his Council—to concur in his wrong measures, would acquire their protection for them" (II, 542).

Location of the Capital

When Virginia's George Mason argued for the establishment of the nation's capital in a city other than one already housing a state government,

Morris said that he did not "dislike the idea" but indicated that he feared that establishing such a requirement in the Constitution would lead to opposition in Philadelphia and New York City, both of which hoped to be such a site (II, 127). Later in the Convention, Morris said that it exhibited improper "distrust" to believe that the government would never leave New York (II, 261). In a position that stretched, if it did not break, the idea of enumerated powers, Morris argued that the power of the national government over the seat of government would give it power, without further enumeration, to establish a national university (II, 616).

Amending Clause

When the delegates discussed the provision requiring Congress to call a convention for proposing amendments upon the request of Congress, Morris unsuccessfully suggested that "the Legislature should be left at liberty to call a Convention, whenever they please" (II, 468). Somewhat ironically, Morris introduced the provision specifying that states could not be deprived of their equal representation in the Senate without their consent (II, 631). The delegates subsequently entrenched this provision against constitutional amendment.

Ratification of the Constitution

Morris favored ratification of the Constitution by the people acting in conventions. He did not believe that existing state legislatures had adequate authority to ratify (II, 92). When this plan was initially rejected, Morris proposed that "the reference of the plan be made to one general Convention, chosen & authorized by the people to consider, amend, & establish the same" (II, 93). This motion died for lack of a second. Morris later proposed that a smaller number of states should be required to ratify the new Constitution if these states were contiguous than if they were not (II, 468). On August 31, he proposed striking out the requirement for ratification by conventions in favor of allowing states to ratify the docu-

ment in a manner of their own choosing (II, 475), but he appears to have changed his mind by day's end: "his object was to impress in stronger terms the necessity of calling Conventions in order to prevent enemies to the plan, from giving it the go by" (II, 478). His strategy may have been tactical, but he responded to George Mason's call for a second convention by saying that he favored the idea of yet another Convention in the hope that it "will have the firmness to provide a vigorous Government, which we are afraid to do" (II, 479).

Morris attempted to word the resolution approving the Constitution so that delegates would simply sign "in witness" to the fact that the states had been unanimous in approving the document rather than as testifying to their own support for it, but this wording was insufficient to persuade Elbridge Gerry of Massachusetts and George Mason and Edmund Randolph of Virginia to sign. On the day that the delegates signed the Constitution, Morris indicated that he had objections but that, like Benjamin Franklin, he considered the plan adopted to be the best possible that could be attained and that "he should take it with all its faults" (II, 645). He said that he was yielding his concerns to the will of the majority and observed: "The moment this plan goes forth all other considerations will be laid aside—and the great question will be, shall there be a national Government or not? and this must take place or a general anarchy will be the alternative" (II, 645). In 1802, Morris observed that "I not only took it as a man does his wife, for better, for worse, but what few men do with their wives, I took it knowing all its bad qualities" (quoted in Brookhiser 2003, 92).

Life after the Convention

Morris did not participate in the ratification debates and in fact declined an invitation by Alexander Hamilton to contribute to writing of *The Federalist Papers.* The year after the Constitution was signed, Morris went to Europe as an agent for Robert Morris. When Washington became president, he appointed Morris as his agent in Great Britain, and he then served from 1792 to

1794 as the American ambassador to France. Morris served as a Federalist senator from the state of New York from 1800 to 1803 and was later chairman of the Erie Canal Commission. Ironically, the great proponent of national unity was one of the leading proponents of the Hartford Convention, which considered Northern disunion during the War of 1812. Morris died shortly thereafter at Morrisania in 1816.

See Also Authorship of the Constitution; Committee of Style and Arrangement; Pennsylvania

FOR FURTHER READING

Brookhiser, Richard. 2003. *Gentleman Revolutionary: Gouverneur Morris–The Rake Who Wrote the Constitution.* New York: The Free Press.

Farrand, Max, ed. 1937. *The Records of the Federal Convention.* 4 vols. New Haven, CT: Yale University Press.

Whitney, David D. 1974. *Founders of Freedom in America: Lives of the Men Who Signed the Constitution of the United States and So Helped to Establish the United States of America.* Chicago: J. J. Ferguson Publishing.

MORRIS, ROBERT (1734–1806)

Born in 1734 in Liverpool, England, to an ironmonger who later became a Maryland tobacco agent, Morris came to the United States in 1747 and earned a fortune as a Philadelphia merchant that made him one of the richest men in America. He married Mary White of Maryland in 1769, and they had seven children. A loyal Patriot, Morris served as a Pennsylvania representative to the Continental Congress where he signed both the Declaration of Independence and the Articles of Confederation. His greatest service to the nation occurred from 1781 to 1783, when he served as the superintendent of finance, often using his personal credit to obtain supplies for the Continental Army. He also founded the Bank of North America during his term. After resigning as superintendent, Morris resumed his work as a merchant

Robert Morris, delegate from Pennsylvania
(Pixel That)

and helped outfit the *Empress of China,* the first ship to go to and from China from the U.S. Long a strong nationalist, in 1786 Morris served as a delegate to the Annapolis Convention.

On the Convention's opening day of business, Morris nominated George Washington as the president and subsequently escorted him to the presiding chair. Morris also had Washington as a house guest and accompanied him on a number of trips during this period. Madison observed on May 28 that Gouverneur Morris (no relation), Robert Morris, and other Pennsylvania delegates thought "that the large States should unite in firmly refusing to the small States an equal vote, as unreasonable, and as enabling the small States to negative every good system of Government, which must in the nature of things, be founded on a violation of that equality" (Farrand 1937, I, 11).

Morris did not, however, take an active part in Convention deliberations. Perhaps he considered that his own abilities were in the area of finance rather than oratory. On June 25, Morris wrote to his son describing members of the Convention as "gentlemen of great abilities . . . many of whom were in the first Congress, and several that were concerned in forming the Articles of Confederation now about to be altered and amended" (III, 49). On June 7, he seconded a motion by James Wilson proposing that the people should elect members of the U.S. Senate as well as the House of Representatives (I, 151). Similarly, on June 25, he seconded a motion proposing that senators serve "during good behavior" (I, 409). On August 13, James Wilson observed that Morris, Fitzsimons, and he were all foreign-born (II, 269).

Morris signed the Constitution on September 17. The following January he wrote a friend with the following observations:

> This paper has been the subject of infinite investigation, disputation, and declamation. While some have boasted it as a work from Heaven, others have given it a less righteous origin. I have many reasons to believe that it is a work of plain, honest men, and such, I think, it will appear. Faulty it must be, for what is perfect? But if adopted, experience will, I believe, show that its faults are just the reverse of what they are supposed to be. (III, 243)

After he signed the Constitution, Pennsylvania selected Morris as one of its first two senators. He served on a record number of committees and was influential in the negotiations that led to the eventual placement of the nation's capital in the District of Columbia. Heavily engaged in Western land speculation, Morris subsequently went bankrupt and was confined for a time in debtor's prison. He died in 1806 in the city he had adopted.

See Also Banking; Pennsylvania

FOR FURTHER READING

Farrand, Max, ed. 1937. *The Records of the Federal Convention.* 4 vols. New Haven, CT: Yale University Press.

Whitney, David C. 1974. *Founders of Freedom in America: Lives of the Men Who Signed the Constitution of the United States and So Helped to Establish the United States of America.* Chicago: J. J. Ferguson Publishing.

MOTIVES OF THE FOUNDING FATHERS

A key to understanding interpretations of those who write about the Constitutional Convention of 1787 is to focus on the motives and influences that they attribute to the delegates who attended the meeting and to those who later voted to ratify the document. Explanations of such motives have varied widely from one historian to another and from one historical period to another.

Views of the Federalists and Antifederalists

Federalist supporters of the Constitution, like most of the delegates themselves, argued that they had made a statesmanlike effort to remedy the problems under the Articles of Confederation. One tactic that the Federalists used in getting the Constitution adopted was to point to the illustrious members of the Convention, and especially to Benjamin Franklin and George Washington, whose patriotism could not be gainsaid. They hoped the general public would attribute the same public spirit to other delegates that most were willing to attribute to its two most illustrious members. Some Antifederalists attributed monarchical or aristocratic motives to the delegates during the ratification debates, but they appear to have acquiesced relatively quickly to the document once it was adopted (Siemers 2002, xiv).

Interpretations in Early American History

Early Americans often disputed its meaning (and particularly how it intended for power to be divided between the national government and the states) and were sometimes confused about particular facts of its history (Kammen 1987)—key elements of which were not known until after publication of the Convention's journal in 1819 and of James Madison's notes in 1840. However, most early Americans appear to have honored the Constitution and those who wrote it. William Gladstone and James Bryce added encomiums from Britain while American nationalist historians George Bancroft (Kraus 1934) and John Fiske (Sanders 1930) further added to the luster of the early Framers (Wright 1961, 171). To such historians, the Constitution was the consummation of the ideals that had been proclaimed in the Declaration of Independence.

The Progressive Reaction

Progressive historians in the first decade or two of the twentieth century, led by Charles Beard and J. Allen Smith at a time when the U.S. Supreme Court was using the Constitution to advance conservative ideas of laissez-faire individualism, began to question the consensus. They tended to emphasize the disjunction between the high ideals of the Declaration of Independence and the gritty compromises of the Constitutional Convention, and they sometimes portrayed the Constitution as a counterrevolutionary document. Beard, who later took a more positive view of the Convention, initially charged that the Framers had been influenced by individual economic concerns. Merrill Jensen in turn accused the Framers, and their subsequent interpreters, of having exaggerated the crisis of the day (1966), leading to further attention to Antifederalism, the historiography of which is reviewed in Cornell (1990). Crowe (1966) has, in turn, analyzed the historiography of the Progressive Era.

Reactions to Beard

A variety of scholars have attacked Beard and have attempted both to demonstrate that initial analyses were mistaken or incomplete and to show that Federalist supporters and Antifederalist opponents of the Constitution often shared similar financial interests (Brown 1956; McDonald 1958). Still, the Beardian thesis continues to show new life, as subsequent interpreters have tried to refine his thesis (see, for example, McGuire 2003).

A number of fine narratives of the Constitutional Convention, including those by Max Farrand, Carl Van Doren, Catherine Drinker Bowen, Clinton Rossiter, and Christopher and James Collier, have, in turn, redirected attention to the flesh and blood people who attended the Convention and the work that they did in seeking compromise and accommodation. Bernstein (1987, 1613–16) has a good review of this and related literature. Onuf (1989), Hutson (1984), and Scheiber (1987) offer other good reviews of the literature on the Constitution at or about the time of the constitutional bicentennial.

Martin Diamond has stressed the role of the Framers in seeking to establish a democratic republic. He has argued that the Framers were more divided by what powers to entrust to the national government than by their divisions into large and small states (1981). John Roche is perhaps best known for reviving the idea that the Founders were consummate politicians attempting to get a job done—what he calls "a reform caucus in action" (1961). Other scholars have followed with attention to the shifting alignments at the Convention (see, for example, Jillson 1981). In a theme that several other scholars have pursued, Douglass Adair has added an important dimension to the debate by emphasizing the degree to which the Founding Fathers were motivated by their quest for fame (1974). A recent volume has reemphasized the way that foreign concerns motivated the Framers (Hendrickson 2003).

Modern Emphases on Ideological Influences

Recent scholars have put greater emphasis on the ideological origins not only of the American Revolution but also of the Constitutional Convention. Louis Hartz emphasized the Lockean liberal roots of the individuals who waged the revolution against England and wrote the Constitution (1955). Bernard Bailyn (1967), Lance Banning (1974), and Gordon Wood (1969) have in turn emphasized the "Whig" or "republican" connections, which, however, some, like Wood, believe gradually gave way to more liberal influences (also see Shalhope 1982). Still others have emphasized Christian or "Scottish Enlightenment" roots or have attempted to synthesize the views (Kloppenberg 1987).

Because the Constitution is not simply a historical document but also a governing instrument, disputes about the Constitution and its formulation continue to be tied to questions about constitutional interpretation. Most notable has been the controversy, especially pronounced in the Reagan administration and the time period following, about the "original intent" of the Framers and ratifyers (Rakove 1990), at a time when scholars continue to document the varied history of the latter (see Jensen 1976 and successive volumes). Bruce Ackerman has directed similar attention to the Convention in attempts to prove that its work represented one of three important "constitutional moments" in American history, in which constitutional forms were not always followed (Ackerman and Katyal 1995). Akhil Reed Amar has, in turn, tried to use the example of the Convention to prove that it is possible to amend the Constitution outside the forms prescribed by the formal constitutional amending process (1988).

Lessons and Directions for the Future

Given the degree to which this period of history has already been studied, although scholarship continues apace, future understandings of the Constitutional Convention are less likely to be influenced by new discoveries in the field than by reinterpretations of existing data; such reinterpretations are sometimes in turn stimulated by a desire to influence modern constitutional understandings and interpretations. The history of writing about the Convention suggests that paradigms will vary from one period to another, but that a broad middle ground is likely to remain between those who take the view that the Founders could do no wrong and those who argue that they were crass partisans seeking their own advantage. Arguably, some of the progressive attacks on the motives of the Framers, while they have not always held up to scrutiny, have helped subsequent

writers recognize that they were not disembodied spirits but "explicable and human figures" (Wright 1961, 178).

See Also Beard, Charles; Constitutional Moments; Declaration of Independence; Fame; Farrand, Max; Legality of the Convention; Liberalism; Protestantism; Republicanism; Scottish Enlightenment

FOR FURTHER READING

Ackerman, Bruce, and Neal Katyal. 1995. "Our Unconventional Founding." *University of Chicago Law Review* 62 (Spring): 475–573.

Adair, Douglass. 1974. "Fame and the Founding Fathers." *Fame and the Founding Fathers: Essays.* Ed. Trevor Colburn. New York: Norton.

Amar, Akhil Reed. 1988. "Philadelphia Revisited: Amending the Constitution outside Article V." *University of Chicago Law Review* 55 (Fall): 1043–1104.

Bailyn, Bernard. 1967. *The Ideological Origins of the American Revolution.* Cambridge, MA: Belknap Press of Harvard University Press.

Banning, Lance. 1974. "Republican Ideology and the Triumph of the Constitution, 1789 to 1793." *William and Mary Quarterly,* 3rd ser. 31 (April): 167–188.

Bernstein, Richard B. 1987. "Charting the Bicentennial." *Columbia Law Review* 87 (December): 1565–1624.

Brown, Robert E. 1956. *Charles Beard and the Constitution: A Critical Analysis of "An Economic Interpretation of the Constitution."* Princeton, NJ: Princeton University Press.

Cornell, Saul A. 1990. "Symposium: Roads Not Taken: Undercurrents of Republican Thinking in Modern Constitutional Theory: The Changing Historical Fortunes of the Anti-Federalists." *Northwestern University Law Review* 85 (Fall): 39–73.

Crowe, Charles. 1966. "The Emergence of Progressive History." *Journal of the History of Ideas* 27 (Jan.-March): 109–124.

Diamond, Martin. 1981. *The Founding of the Democratic Republic.* Itasca, IL: F. F. Peacock Publishers.

Hartz, Louis. 1955. *The Liberal Tradition in America: An Interpretation of American Political Thought since the Revolution.* New York: Harcourt, Brace and World.

Hendrickson, David D. 2003. *Peace Pact: The Lost World of the American Founding.* Lawrence: University Press of Kansas.

Hoffer, Peter C. 2002. "Vox Pop: Consensus and Celebration." *Common-Place* 2, no. 4 (July) http://www.common-place.org.

Hutson, James H. 1984. "The Creation of the Constitution: Scholarship at a Standstill." *Reviews in American History* 12 (December): 463–477.

Jensen, Merrill. 1966. *The Articles of Confederation.* Madison: University of Wisconsin Press.

——, ed. 1976. *Constitutional Documents and Records, 1776–1787.* Vol. 1: *The Documentary History of the Ratification of the Constitution.* Madison: State Historical Society of Wisconsin.

Jillson, Calvin C. 1981. "Constitution-Making: Alignment and Realignment in the Federal Convention of 1787." *American Political Science Review* 74 (September): 598–612.

Kammen, Michael. 1987. *A Machine That Would Go of Itself: The Constitution in American Culture.* New York: Alfred A. Knopf.

Kloppenberg, James T. 1987. "The Virtues of Liberalism: Christianity, Republicanism, and Ethics in Early American Political Discourse." *Journal of American History* 74 (June): 9–33.

Kraus, Michael. 1934. "George Bancroft 1834–1934." *New England Quarterly* 7 (December): 662–686.

McDonald, Forrest. 1958. *We the People: The Economic Origins of the Constitution, 1781–1789.* New York: Harper and Row Publishers.

McGuire, Robert A. 2003. *To Form a More Perfect Union: A New Economic Interpretation of the United States Constitution.* New York: Oxford University Press.

Onuf, Peter S. 1989. "Reflections on the Founding: Constitutional Historiography in Bicentennial Perspective." *William and Mary Quarterly,* 3rd ser. 46 (April): 341–375.

Rakove, Jack N. 1990. *Interpreting the Constitution: The Debate over Original Intent.* Boston: Northeastern University Press.

Roche, John P. 1961. "The Founding Fathers: A Reform Caucus in Action." *American Political Science Review* 55 (December): 799–816.

Sanders, J. J. 1930. "John Fiske." *Mississippi Valley Historical Review* 17 (September): 264–277.

Scheiber, Harry N. 1987. "Introduction: The Bicentennial and the Rediscovery of Constitutional History." *Journal of American History* 74 (December): 665–674.

Shalhope, Robert E. 1982. "Republicanism and Early American Historiography." *William and Mary Quarterly,* 3rd ser. 39 (April): 334–356.

Siemers, David J. 2002. *Ratifying the Republic: Antifederalists and Federalists in Constitutional Time.* Palo Alto, CA: Stanford University Press.

Wood, Gordon S. 1969. *The Creation of the American Republic, 1776–1787.* Chapel Hill: University of North Carolina Press.

Wright, Esmond. 1961. *Fabric of Freedom, 1763–1800.* New York: Hill and Wang.

MOUNT VERNON CONFERENCE

Just as the Annapolis Convention preceded the U.S. Constitutional Convention, so too, the Mount Vernon Conference of 1785 preceded the Annapolis Convention. The Mount Vernon Conference consisted of a smaller convocation of delegates from Virginia and Maryland who met at George Washington's home at Mount Vernon, Virginia in March 1785.

Virginia and Maryland shared a border along the Potomac and Pocomoke Rivers and the Chesapeake Bay, and the Articles of Confederation failed to plug the gaps in regulating these common waterways, which the common supervisory authority of the British government had filled prior to the American Revolution. Apparently, the Virginia Constitution of 1776 actually recognized the rights of Maryland to the Virginia side of the river, and Madison discovered in 1784 that foreign vessels were loading and unloading cargo on the Potomac free of customs or duties (Morris 1985, 38). Virginia and Maryland had appointed commissioners to discuss such problems as early as 1777, but their meeting apparently accomplished nothing of significance (McLaughlin 1905, 179).

Although Virginia's instructions to its delegates were less than complete, Virginia and Maryland respectively reappointed delegates to deal with these problems in June of 1784 and in January of 1785. Unfortunately, Virginia governor Patrick Henry failed to notify delegates Alexander Henderson, James Madison, George Mason, and Edmund Randolph of their appointments. As a consequence, when the three Maryland delegates,

Engraving of George Washington's Mount Vernon estate (Library of Congress)

Samuel Chase, Daniel of St. Thomas Jenifer, and Thomas Stone, arrived in Alexandria, Virginia the week of March 21, 1785, they found that city native Henderson and the other delegates knew nothing about their own commissions. Henderson notified George Mason, who lived nearby, and who was unwilling for further delay. George Washington, who was engaged with other investors in constructing a series of locks designed to bypass the Great Fall of the Potomac about 15 miles north of modern-day Washington, D.C., so as to open navigation on the Potomac to the Shenandoah and Ohio Valleys (Achenbach 2004), invited all five delegates to his house on the Potomac at Mount Vernon. They convened on March 25, 1785.

By their commissions, which they had not seen, neither state was to act without the presence of three delegates, but the two commissioned Virginia delegates in attendance did not know this (Washington had no official role) and proceeded in good faith with their negotiations. The results were fruitful. The commission prepared a report for the two state legislatures on March 18, 1785. The report contained 13 proposals known as the Mount Vernon Compact. These declared the Potomac River to be "a Common High Way, for the purpose of Navigation and Commerce to the Citizens of Virginia and Maryland and of the United States" (Rutland 1970, 818). They provided for mutual fishing rights for splitting the costs of constructing "Light Houses, Beacons, Buoys, or other necessary Signals" (Rutland, 819); dealt with piracy and mutual defense; outlined judicial jurisdiction for problems that arose; and made provision for commissioners to work out further problems. The Mount Vernon delegates further sent a letter to the president of the Pennsylvania Executive Council proposing that duty-free commerce be extended through the waters of Pennsylvania.

Both Maryland and Virginia ratified this agreement. Maryland attempted to include Delaware. Although John Tyler (father of a future U.S. president) was the official sponsor, James Madison was the floor manager chiefly responsible for securing the approval of the Virginia state legislature (Morris, 40). Although he failed to convince the state to submit the agreement to Congress for approval as the Articles of Confederation required, Madison did use this agreement to arrange for the Virginia General Assembly to issue a call for a convention in Annapolis, to which he would be a delegate,

> to take into consideration the trade of the United States; to examine the relative situations of the trade of the United States; to consider how far a uniform system in their commercial regulations may be necessary to their common interest and their permanent harmony; and to report to the several States, such an act relatively to this great object, as, when unanimously ratified by them, will enable the United States in Congress, effectually to provide for the same. (Solberg 1958, 54)

Bungled as some aspects of the Annapolis Convention were, wise leadership helped ensure that the meeting not only signaled some of the problems under the Articles of Confederation but also pointed to a conference or convention as the way of addressing them.

George Washington, George Mason, Daniel of St. Thomas Jenifer as well as James Madison and Edmund Randolph (who never received their commissions to the Mount Vernon Conference) attended the Constitutional Convention. At the Convention, Gouverneur Morris of Pennsylvania made an apparent reference to the results of the Mount Vernon Conference when defending the initial provision that would have required three-fourths, rather than two-thirds, majorities in Congress to override the president. He observed that the "Inspection laws of Virginia & Maryland to which all are now so much attached were unpopular at first" (Farrand 1937, II, 586), thereby indicating that their wisdom had been subsequently recognized.

See Also Annapolis Convention; Jenifer, Daniel, of St. Thomas; Maryland; Mason, George; Randolph, Edmund; Virginia; Washington, George

FOR FURTHER READING

Achenbach, Joel. 2004. *The Grand Idea: George Washington's Potomac and the Race to the West.* New York: Simon and Schuster.

Farrand, Max, ed. 1937. *The Records of the Federal Convention.* 4 vols. New Haven, CT: Yale University Press.

McLaughlin, Andrew C. 1905. *The Confederation and the Constitution, 1783–1789.* New York: Harper and Brothers.

Morris, Richard B. 1985. "The Mount Vernon Conference: First Step toward Philadelphia." *this Constitution,* no. 6 (Spring 1985): 38–40.

Rutland, Robert A., ed. 1970. *The Papers of George Mason, 1725–1792.* Vol. 2: *1779–1786.* Chapel Hill: University of North Carolina Press.

Solberg, Winton U., ed. 1958. *The Federal Convention and the Formation of the Union of the American States.* Indianapolis, IN: Bobbs-Merrill.

MUSIC

Philadelphia, the city that hosted the Constitutional Convention, was an urbane city that boasted of musical performances of works not only by European composers but also by individuals who had made their home in the New World. These would have included Alexander Reinagle, who had emigrated from England to New York in 1786 and moved to Philadelphia soon after. He is known to have given a concert of piano sonatas in Philadelphia in June 1787 and to have tutored Nellie Custis (Washington's adopted daughter) and the children of other Founding Fathers (Boasberg 1986, 1-C). Songs commemorating the Revolutionary War and General Washington were especially popular during the time leading up to the Constitutional Convention.

Musical compositions later served the purpose of urging the ratification or commemorating the ratification of the new Constitution. In 1787 the Federalist Francis Hopkinson published a song entitled "The New Roof: A New Song for Federal Mechanics," or "The Raising," in which the writing of the Constitution was likened to the construction of a new roof for the nation. The opening stanza began:

Come muster, my lads, your mechanical tools,
Your saws and your axes, your hammers and rules;
Bring your mallets and planes, your level and line,
And plenty of pins of American pine;
For our roof we will raise, and our song still shall be,
A government firm, and our citizens free.
   (Howard and Bowen, 7)

Successive stanzas continued the building theme.

In March 1788 a poem was composed about the just-completed ratification of the Constitution by Massachusetts to be sung to the tune of "Yankee Doodle Dandy." It recounted various highlights of the Massachusetts ratifying convention. Celebrations were held in a number of cities after ratification of the Constitution. Philadelphia held an especially notable celebration on July 4, 1788. It included a "Federal March" composed by Alexander Reinagle.

Musical compositions and performances continued into the inauguration of President Washington, many of them focusing on Washington's exploits as well as the glory of the new nation. Among the songs of the period was one called "The Grand Constitution: or The Palladium of Columbia: A New Federal Song." One stanza read:

With gratitude let us acknowledge the worth
Of what the Convention has called into birth,
And the Continent wisely confirm what is done
By Franklin's sage, and by brave Washington
   (Howard and Bowen, 16)

In a similar vein, "A New Federal Song," published in August 1788, provided that

No more shall Anarchy bear sway,
Nor petty states pursue their way,
But all united firm as one,
Shall seek the gen'ral good alone.
Great Washington shall rule the land,
While Franklin's council aids his hand. (18)

A publication produced for the sesquicentennial of the Constitution recounted the musical legacy connected to the ratification of the new Constitution. It also suggested numerous musical selections that could be used to commemorate the formation and ratification of the Constitution, to recall Washington's inauguration, and for constitutional celebrations (Howard and Bowen, 20–21).

See Also Commemorations of the Constitutional Convention

FOR FURTHER READING

Boasberg, Leonard W. 1986. "An Opportunity to Hear Music Washington Heard." *Philadelphia Inquirer,* January 16, 1-C, 4-C.

Howard, John Tasker, and Eleanor S. Bowen, eds., n.d. *Music Associated with the Period of the Formation of the Constitution and the Inauguration of George Washington.* Washington, DC: United States Sesquicentennial Commission.

Lawrence, Vera Brodsky. 1975. *Music for Patriots, Politicians, and Presidents: Harmonies and Discords of the First Hundred Years.* New York: Macmillan Publishing Co.

Rigal, Laura. 1996. "'Raising the Roof': Authors, Spectators and Artisans in the Grand Federal Procession of 1788." *Theatre Journal* 48, no. 3: 253–277.